AIR FORCES
OF THE WORLD

This 1990 edition is published by Crescent Books
Distributed by Crown Publishers, Inc.

Copyright © Brian Trodd Publishing House Limited 1990

ISBN 0-517-69205-8

h g f e d c b a

Printed in Spain

AIR FORCES
OF THE WORLD

CHRISTOPHER CHANT

CRESCENT BOOKS
New York

On the deck of USS *Constellation*, an F/A-18 Hornet is prepared for catapult launch.

CONTENTS

Aeritalia F-104S Starfighter

(Italy)

Type: interceptor fighter and multi-role attack aeroplane

Accommodation: pilot on a Martin-Baker IQ7A zero/zero ejector seat

Armament (fixed): one 20-mm General Electric M61A1 Vulcan rotary-barrel cannon with 725 rounds (an optional package instead of the Sparrow/Aspide missile-guidance package)

Armament (disposable): this is carried on nine hardpoints (three under the fuselage, two under each wing and one at each wingtip, with the centreline unit rated at 2,000 lb/907 kg and the two lateral units each at 250 lb/113 kg, the inner two underwing units each rated at 1,000 lb/454 kg and the outer two underwing units each at 500 lb/227 kg, and the wingtip units each rated at 1,000 lb/454 kg) up to a maximum weight of 3400 kg (7,495 lb); for the interception role the standard armament is two AIM-7 Sparrow or two Aspide 1/1A AAMs under the wings plus two AIM-9 Sidewinder AAMs at the wingtips; for the attack role the weapons include launchers for 2·75- and 5-in (70- and 127-mm) or 81- and 122-mm (3·2- and 4·8-in) rockets, 250-, 500-, 750- and 1,000-lb (113-, 227-, 340- and 454-kg) bombs, cluster bombs, incendiary bombs and other weapons

Electronics and operational equipment: communication and navigation equipment, plus Fiar R21G/H multi-role interception, ground-mapping and terrain-avoidance radar, Litton LN-3-2A INS, weapon-delivery system, optical sight and air-data computer

Powerplant and fuel system: one 8119-kg (17,900-lb) afterburning thrust Fiat-built General Electric J79-GE-19 turbojet, and a total internal fuel capacity of 3390 litres (746 Imp gal) plus provision for two 740-litre (163-Imp gal) and two 645-litre (142-Imp gal) drop tanks; no provision for inflight refuelling

Performance: maximum speed 2330 km/h (1,450 mph) or Mach 2·2 at 11000 m (36,090 ft), and 1,465 km/h (910 mph) or Mach 1·2 at sea level; cruising speed 980 km/h (609 mph) at 11,000 m (36,090 ft); service ceiling 17,680 m (58,005 ft); radius 1245 km (774 miles) with maximum fuel; ferry range 2920 km (1,815 miles) with maximum internal and external fuel

Weights: empty 6760 kg (14,903 lb); normal take-off 9840 kg (21,693 lb); maximum take-off 14,060 kg (30,996 lb)

Dimensions: span 6·68 m (21 ft 11 in) without tiptanks; length 16·69 m (54 ft 9 in); height 4·11 m (13 ft 6 in); wing area 18·22 m² (196·1 sq ft)

There is little external difference between the F-104S and the F-104G, but the Italian version has updated electronics suiting it for use of the Sparrow and Aspide AAMs.

Variants

F-104S: Italian development of the basic F-104 concept but derived more specifically from the F-104G multi-role fighter with an air-to-air specialization through the use of the AIM-7 Sparrow medium-range AAM and a fire-control system optimized for the air-to-air rather than air-to-surface role; production totalled 245 aircraft (205 for Italy and 40 for Turkey), flying from December 1968. In 1976 production ended

F-104S ASA: mid-life updated variant of the basic F-104S with the ASA (Aggiornamento Sistemi d'Arma, or updated weapon system) improvement to the interdiction and offensive/defensive air-to-air capabilities without any modification of the airframe/powerplant combination; the ASA programme was designed to maintain the operational viability of the F-104S series (at least 140 aircraft being modified) up to 1995, and was centred on the retrofit of Fiar R21G/M1 Setter radar (giving a useful look-down/shoot-down capability) combined with a new fire-control computer/missile guidance system matched to the advanced Selenia Aspide 1A AAM, enhanced IFF, state-of-the-art ECM and a new navigation system linked to the autopilot and nav/attack computer; the revised electronics free enough space to include a 20-mm General Electric M61A1 six-barrel rotary cannon (or, more often in the basic F-104S, the missile-guidance package)

Aeritalia G91 R/1

(Italy)

Type: tactical close support and reconnaissance aircraft

Accommodation: pilot on a Martin-Baker Mk 4 ejector seat

Armament (fixed): four 0·5-in (12·7-mm) Colt-Browning M3 machine-guns with 300 rounds per gun

Armament (disposable): this is carried on four hardpoints (two under each wing, with each unit rated at 250 kg/551 lb) up to a maximum weight of 680 kg (1,500 lb); typical weapons are 2·75-in (70-mm) or 81-mm (3·2-in) rockets, 250- and 500-lb (113- and 227-kg) bombs, machine-gun pods each containing one 0·5-in (12·7-mm) machine-gun and 150 rounds, and AS.30 ASMs

Electronics and operational equipment: communication and navigation equipment, plus Bendix DRA-12A Doppler navigation and a SFOM optical sight

Powerplant and fuel system: one 2268-kg (5,000-lb) thrust Fiat-built Rolls-Royce (Bristol Siddeley) Orpheus Mk 803 non-afterburning turbojet, and a total internal fuel capacity of 1600 litres (352 Imp gal) plus provision for two 520-litre (114-Imp gal) drop tanks; no provision for inflight refuelling

Performance: maximum speed 1085 km/h (674 mph) at 1500 m (4,920 ft); cruising speed 650 km/h (403 mph); initial climb rate 1830 m (6,005 ft) per minute; service ceiling 13,100 m (42,980 ft); combat radius typically 320 km (199 miles); ferry range 1850 km (1,150 miles)

Weights: empty 3100 kg (6,835 lb); normal take-off 5440 kg (11,995 lb); maximum take-off 5500 kg (12,125 lb)

Dimensions: span 8·56 m (28 ft 1 in); length 10·30 m (33 ft 9·25 in); height 4·00 m (13 ft 1·25 in); wing area 16·42 m² (176·74 sq ft)

Variants

G91R/1: initial service version resulting from a 1954 NATO requirement for a light attack fighter for European service; the prototype first flew in August 1956, and proved fully able to meet the requirements of the specification, but in the event only West Germany and Italy adopted the type, which is now obsolescent and being phased out of front-line service

G91R/1A: updated G91R/1 introduced in 1959 with the improved navigation package of the G91R/3

G91R/1B: strengthened version of the G91R/1A with reinforced structure and landing gear, and incorporating a number of equipment changes dictated by operational experience

G91R/3: version of the G91R/3 built in West Germany, and incorporating more capable navigational equipment (including Doppler radar and a position-and-homing indicator) plus a revised gun armament of two DEFA 552 30-mm cannon with 120 rounds per gun

G91R/4: version of the G91R/3 with the armament of the G91R/1 and detail equipment modifications

G91T/1: Italian-built operational trainer version of the G91R series, with a gun armament of two 0·5-in (12·7-mm) machine-guns and provision for external stores on two underwing hardpoints

G91T/2: West German-built operational trainer version of the G91R very similar to the G91T/1

Aeritalia G91Y

(Italy)

Type: tactical close support and reconnaissance aircraft

Accommodation: pilot on a Martin-Baker zero/zero ejector seat

Armament (fixed): two 30-mm DEFA 552 cannon with 125 rounds per gun

Armament (disposable): this is carried on four hardpoints (two under each wing, with each unit rated at 500 kg/1,102 lb) up to a maximum weight of 1814 kg (4,000 lb); typical weapons are the AIM-9 Sidewinder AAM, AS.30 ASM, 50- or 70-mm (2- or 2·75-in) rocket pods, 5-in (127-mm) rocket pods, 81-mm (3·2-in) rocket pods, and 250-, 500-, 750- and 1,000-lb (113-, 227-, 340- and 454-kg) bombs of various types

Electronics and operational equipment: communication and navigation equipment, plus a Smiths HUD, a Ferranti ISIS-B gyro sight and Bendix DRA-12A Doppler navigation

Powerplant and fuel system: two 4,080-lb (1850-kg) afterburning thrust General Electric J85-GE-13A turbojets, and a total internal fuel capacity of 3200 litres (704 Imp gal) plus provision for two drop tanks; no provision for inflight refuelling

Performance: maximum speed 1040 km/h (646 mph) or Mach 0·95 at 9145 m (30,000 ft) and 1140 km/h (708 mph) or Mach 0·93 at sea level; cruising speed 800 km/h (497 mph) at 10,670 m (35,000 ft); initial climb rate 5180 m (17,000 ft) per minute; service ceiling 12,500 m (41,010 ft); combat radius 385 km (240 miles) on a lo-lo-lo mission with a 1320-kg (2,910-lb) warload; ferry range 3500 km (2,175 miles)

Weights: empty 3682 kg (8,117 lb); normal take-off 7800 kg (17,196 lb); maximum take-off 8700 kg (19,180 lb)

Dimensions: span 9·01 m (29 ft 6·5 in); length 11·67 m (38 ft 3·5 in); height 4·43 m (14 ft 6·5 in); wing area 18·13 m² (195·15 sq ft)

Variant

G91Y: sole production version of the much improved twin-engined version of the G91 family, with the two engines offering some 63% more power (for an increase in empty weight of only 18%) as well as the tactical advantages of twin-engined reliability and of greater payload and/or greater range; the type was based on the airframe developed for the G91T series, and apart from more modern avionics the G91Y offered such advantages as a pressurized and air-conditioned cockpit and a zero/zero ejector seat; the first G91Y flew in December 1966, and production totalled 77 aircraft

Top right: The G91Y is essentially a twin-engined development of the G91R with much enhanced payload/range performance.

Above right: Though still in service, the G91R/1 is a type whose electronics and armament make it obsolescent by modern standards, and the G91R series is thus in process of replacement by the considerably more capable AMX.

Aeritalia G222

(Italy)

Type: general-purpose and tactical transport aeroplane

Accommodation: flightcrew of three or four plus 53 troops, or 40 paratroops or 9000 kg (19,841 lb) of freight in the hold

Armament (fixed): none

Armament (disposable): none

Electronics and operational equipment: communication and navigation equipment

Powerplant and fuel system: two 3,400-shp (2535-kW) Fiat-built General Electric T64-GE-P4D turboprops, and a total internal fuel capacity of 12,000 litres (2,638 Imp gal); no provision for drop tanks or inflight refuelling

Performance: maximum speed 540 km/h (336 mph) at 4575 m (15,000 ft); cruising speed 439 km/h (273 mph) at 6000 m (19,685 ft); initial climb rate 520 m (1,705 ft) per minute; service ceiling 7620 m (25,000 ft); range 1370 km (851 miles) with maximum payload or 4635 km (2,880 miles) with maximum fuel

Weights: empty 15,700 kg (34,612 lb); normal take-off 26,500 kg (58,422 lb); maximum take-off 28,000 kg (61,728 lb)

Dimensions: span 28·70 m (94 ft 2 in); length 22·70 m (74 ft 5·5 in); height 9·80 m (32 ft 1·75 in); wing area 82·00 m² (882·67 sq ft)

Variants

G222: though originating in a NATO requirement for a V/STOL tactical transport aircraft, the design was recast in the late 1960s as a trim twin-engined transport of conventional though attractive type geared to the requirements of the Italian air force; the prototype was first flown in July 1970, and production for the Italian air force amounted to 50 aircraft in several versions; production of the type was completed in 1988, and though the manufacturer is continuing to study AEW, inflight-refuelling tanker, drone launch/control and anti-submarine warfare versions it is unlikely that this will materialize; the AEW variant would have GEC APY-922 radar

G222RM: Radio Misure navaid calibration version

G222T: version produced for Libya with European avionics and 4,860-shp (3624-kW) Rolls-Royce Tyne RTy·20 Mk 801 turboprops in place of the US engines used in other models, the greater power offering higher payload or, alternatively, better performance in hot-and-high conditions with the standard payload; the type has a maximum take-off weight of 29,000 kg (63,933 lb); the G222T first flew in May 1980

G222VS: Versione Speciale developed for the Italian air force in the Sigint and Elint roles; specialist equipment carried by this model includes signal-processing and data-recording gear

Right: Seen in the form of the first production example for the Italian air force, the AMX is a highly capable attack platform within the limits of its electronics, which restrict the type to daylight and modest adverse-weather conditions.

Left: Despite its small size, the G222 is of typical airlifter configuration with a high-set wing, wide-diameter fuselage, externally located main landing gear units, and an upswept tail unit above a rear ramp/door.

Aeritalia/Aermacchi/EMBRAER (AMX International) AMX

(Italy & Brazil)

Type: interdiction, close air support and reconnaissance aeroplane with a secondary counter-air capability

Accommodation: pilot on a Martin-Baker IT10LY zero/zero ejector seat

Armament (fixed): one 20-mm M61A1 Vulcan six-barrel rotary cannon with 350 rounds or (Brazilian aircraft) two 30-mm DEFA 554 cannon with 125 rounds per gun

Armament (disposable): this is carried on seven hardpoints (one under the fuselage, two under each wing and one at each wingtip, with the double unit under the fuselage rated at 907 kg/2,000 lb, the inner two underwing units each rated at 907 kg/2,000 lb and the outer two underwing units each at 454 kg/1,000 lb, and the wingtips units each rated an unrevealed weight) up to a maximum weight of 3800 kg (7,377 lb) of AAMs, ASMs, anti-ship missiles, free-fall, retarded and special-purpose bombs and rocket pods

Electronics and operational equipment: communication and navigation equipment, plus Fiar Pointer ranging radar, HUD, HDD, stores management and delivery system, INS, GEC/Aeritalia air-data and central computers, comprehensive ECM (including the Elettronica ELT-555 jammer) used in conjunction with an Elettronica RWR, and LRMTS optionally replaceable by any one of three Aeroelectronica sensor pallets carried instead of a centreline IR/optronic reconnaissance pod

Powerplant and fuel system: one 5000-kg (11,023-lb) thrust Alfa Romeo Avio/Fiat/Piaggio-built Rolls-Royce Spey Mk 807 non-afterburning turbofan, and a total internal fuel capacity of 3555 litres (782 Imp gal), plus provision for two 1000-litre (220-Imp gal) and two 500-litre (110-Imp gal) drop tanks; provision for inflight refuelling

Performance: maximum speed 1163 km/h (723 mph) or Mach 0·95 at sea level with maximum payload; cruising speed 950 km/h (590 mph); initial climb rate 3840 m (12,600 ft) per minute; service ceiling 13,000 m (42,650 ft); radius 520 km (323 miles) on a hi-lo-hi mission with a 2722-kg (6,000-lb) warload or 370 km (230 miles) on a lo-lo-lo mission with a 2722-kg (6,000-lb) warload; ferry range 3150 km (1,957 miles)

Weights: empty 6700 kg (14,771 lb); normal take-off 10,750 kg (23,699 lb); maximum take-off 12,500 kg (27,557 lb)

Dimensions: span 10·00 or 8·874 m (32 ft 9·75 in or 29 ft 1·4 in) with or without wingtip AAMs; length 13·575 m (44 ft 6·4 in); height 4·576 m (15 ft 0·25 in); wing area 21·00 m² (226·04 sq ft)

Variants

AMX: originated in Italy as the M.B.340 but now a joint Italo-Brazilian project (the work split being 70% and 30% respectively for anticipated production of 238 and 79 aircraft), the AMX was designed as a lightweight attack fighter with STOL performance from semi-prepared strips; keynotes of the design are basic simplicity and low cost (resulting in transonic rather than supersonic performance) with utmost versatility of weapon capability, though great attention has been paid to 'stretch' potential, especially in the avionics (the planned anti-ship single-seater will have Fiar/SMA P2801 Grifo multi-mode radar and an armament of Kormoran and/or Sea Killer Mk 2 missiles in Italian aircraft, or SMA/Tecnasa radar and unspecified anti-ship missiles in Brazilian aircraft); in the reconnaissance role the type can carry any one of three centreline-mounted pods, one carrying three cameras for tactical reconnaissance, the second carrying a side-looking camera of long focal length for operational reconnaissance, and the third carrying high-altitude mapping equipment; the first prototype flew in May 1984, and the type began to enter Italian service in April 1989; the Brazilian aircraft have the service designation **A-1**

AMX(T): two-seat version for the operational conversion role, with specialist EW and anti-ship variants to be developed; within the total AMX requirement mentioned above there are 51 two-seaters for Italy and 14 for Brazil

Aermacchi M.B.326L

(Italy)
Type: basic and advanced flying and weapon trainer with a secondary light attack capability
Accommodation: pupil and instructor in tandem on Martin-Baker Mk 6A ejector seats
Armament (fixed): none
Armament (disposable): this is carried on six hardpoints (three under each wing, with the inner four units each rated at 454 kg/1,000 lb and the outer two units each at 340 kg/750 lb) up to a maximum weight of 1814 kg (4,000 lb); typical weapons are 2·75- and 5-in (70- and 127-mm) rocket pods, 68- and 81-mm (2·68- and 3·2-in) rocket pods, pods for one 0·5-in (12·7-mm) M3 machine-gun, or 7·62-mm (0·3-in) Minigun or one 30-mm Aden cannon, bombs of various types, and AS.12 ASMs
Electronics and operational equipment: communication and navigation equipment, plus Doppler navigation, SFOM Type 83 or Ferranti LFS 5/102A gyro sight and provision for a weapon-delivery computer and laser rangefinder
Powerplant and fuel system: one 1814-kg (4,000-lb) thrust Piaggio-built Rolls-Royce Viper Mk 632-43 non-afterburning turbojet, and a total internal fuel capacity of 1660 litres (366 Imp gal) plus provision for two 340-litre (75-Imp gal) drop tanks; no provision for inflight refuelling
Performance: maximum speed 890 km/h (553 mph) at 1525 m (5,000 ft) clean, or 685 km/h (426 mph) at 9145 m (30,000 ft) with external stores; initial climb rate 1980 m (6,500 ft) per minute; service ceiling 14,325 m (47,000 ft); combat radius 268 km (167 miles) on a lo-lo-lo mission with a 1280-kg (2,822-lb) warload; ferry range 2130 km (1,323 miles)
Weights: empty 2964 kg (6,534 lb); normal take-off 4211 kg (9,285 lb); maximum take-off 5897 kg (13,000 lb)
Dimensions: span 10·85 m (35 ft 7 in) over fixed tiptanks; length 10·673 m (35 ft 0·25 in); height 3·72 m (12 ft 2 in); wing area 19·35 m² (208·29 sq ft)

Variants
M.B.326: initial version of this highly successful two-seat trainer and light attack aircraft series; the design was started in 1954, and the first prototype flew in December 1957 on the power of a 1,750-lb (794-kg) thrust Bristol Viper 8 turbojet; the type was adopted by the Italian air force from 1962 with the 2,500-lb (1134-kg) thrust Viper 11, and has no provision for armament
M.B.326B: armed trainer for Tunisia derived from the proposed M.B.326A with the Viper 11 and six underwing hardpoints for a total of 907 kg (2,000 lb) of disposable stores

M.B.326E: hybrid type for Italy with the fuselage and powerplant of the M.B.326 combined with the wings and armament provision of the M.B.325GB
M.B.326F: armed flying and weapons trainer for Ghana, basically similar to the M.B.326B
M.B.326GB: upgraded version based on the M.B.326G unarmed trainer with the 3,410-lb (1547-kg) thrust Viper 20 Mk 540 turbojet and the ability to carry 1814 kg (4,000 lb) of disposable stores under the wings; the **M.B.326GC** is generally similar and has been built under licence in Brazil as the **EMBRAER EMB-326**, which is usually operated in single-seat configuration by the Brazilian air force as the **AT-26 Xavante** weapons trainer and light attack aeroplane; EMBRAER has recently begun a programme under which several AT-26s are being adapted to **RT-26 Xavante** reconnaissance configuration with a nose-mounted inflight-refuelling probe and specialized reconnaissance sensors
M.B.326H: armed two-seat trainer for Australia with the Viper 11 engine, built under licence in Australia as the **Commonwealth Aircraft CA-30**
M.B.326K: much improved single-seat operational training and light attack model based on the airframe of the M.B.326GB but fitted with the 4,000-lb (1814-kg) thrust Viper 20 Mk 540 engine (in the prototype, which first flew in August 1970) or Viper Mk 632-43 (in production aircraft); the volume of the erstwhile rear cockpit is used for avionics, fuel and inbuilt armament (two 30-mm DEFA 553 cannon with 125 rounds per gun), and the type can be provided with a limited air-to-air capability by the carriage of two Matra 550 Magic AAMs; a wide assortment of underwing armament can be lifted, typical weapons being older-generation ASMs (AS.11 and AS.12), free-fall bombs, gun pods etc; the type was built in South Africa with the Viper Mk 540 engine as the **Atlas Aircraft Corporation Impala Mk 2**
M.B.326L: armed two-seater based on the M.B.326K with a second cockpit instead of the inbuilt cannon armament
M.B.326M: Viper 11-engined unarmed two-seater for South Africa; the type was also built in that country as the armed **Atlas Aircraft Corporation Impala Mk 1**

Right: The M.B.339 retains much of the M.B.326 (notably the unswept flying surfaces and Viper turbojet) with a new forward fuselage featuring upward-staggered seats.

Below: A classic of its time, the M.B.326 (here an M.B.326H) is now thought limited because of its vertically unstaggered seats.

Aermacchi M.B.339A

(Italy)
Type: basic and advanced flying and weapon trainer with a secondary attack capability
Accommodation: pupil and instructor in tandem on Martin-Baker IT10F zero/zero ejector seats
Armament (fixed): none
Armament (disposable): this is carried on six hardpoints (three under each wing, with the inner four units each rated at 454 kg/1,000 lb and the outer two units at 340 kg/750 lb) up to a maximum weight of 1815 kg (4,001 lb); typical weapons are the Matra 550 Magic or AIM-9 Sidewinder AAMs, 2·75- and 5-in (70- and 127-mm) rocket pods, 50-, 68- and 81-mm (2-, 2·68- and 3·2-in) rocket pods, a variety of 250-, 500-, 750- and 1,000-lb (113-, 227-, 340- and 454-kg) bombs, cluster bombs, incendiary bombs, and gun pods containing one 30-mm DEFA 553 cannon with 150 rounds, or one 7·62-mm (0·3-in) Minigun with 1,500 rounds or one 0·5-in (12·7-mm) M3 machine-gun with 350 rounds
Electronics and operational equipment: communication and navigation equipment, plus an Elettronica ECM pod, or reconnaissance pod with four Vinten cameras, RWR, and Aeritalia, Saab or Thomson-CSF reflector sight
Powerplant and fuel system: one 1814-kg (4,000-lb) thrust Piaggio-built Rolls-Royce Viper Mk 632-43 non-afterburning turbojet, and a total internal fuel capacity of 1413 litres (311 Imp gal) plus provision for two 325-litre (71·5-Imp gal) drop tanks; no provision for inflight refuelling
Performance: maximum speed 817 km/h (508 mph) at 9145 m (30,000 ft) and 898 km/h (558 mph) at sea level; initial climb rate 2010 m (6,595 ft) per minute; service ceiling 14,630 m (48,000 ft); radius 270 km (168 miles) on a lo-lo-lo mission with a 1360-kg (2,998-lb) warload; ferry range 2110 km (1,310 miles)
Weights: empty 3135 kg (6,911 lb); normal take-off 4400 kg (9,700 lb); maximum take-off 5895 kg (12,996 lb)
Dimensions: span 10·858 m (35 ft 7·5 in) over fixed tiptanks; length 10·972 m (36 ft 10 in); height 3·994 m (13 ft 1·25 in); wing area 19·30 m² (207·75 sq ft)

Variants
M.B.339A: first flown in prototype form in August

Aermacchi M.B.339K

1976, the M.B.339A is a much improved conceptual development of the M.B.326 with more advanced aerodynamics and structure for better performance and handling using the same basic engine as the M.B.326 series; apart from its better handling characteristics, the chief operational advantage of the M.B.339A is the considerably better seating arrangement, which raises the instructor above the level of the front-seat pupil for good forward vision; a slightly modified version is the **M.B.339PAN** for the Italian air force aerobatic team, with smoke-generating equipment but no tiptanks

M.B.339B: version of the M.B.339A designed for the dual training and light attack roles with the Viper Mk 680 turbojet, larger tiptanks and greater weapons capability

M.B.339C: first flown in December 1985, this variant was designed for the introduction of pilots to modern mission-management systems, and as such is the combat-capable two-seat mission training version of the series (offering capability for the close-support and maritime attack roles) carrying a digital nav/attack system compatible with the latest weapons; the first production example flew in November 1988, and is fitted with GEC AD-660 Doppler navigation and AD-620K integrated tactical navigation system linked with a Litton LR80 inertial platform, two Kaiser Sabre HUDs, Aeritalia HDDs, a Logic stores-management system, a Fiar P-0702 laser ranger, and an Elettronica ELT/156 RWR, as well as provision for items such as the ELT/555 jammer pod and Tracor ALE-40 chaff/flare dispenser; the weapon options are similar to those of the Veltro 2 (which is offered with avionics improvements of the M.B.339C) plus provision for AGM-65 Maverick ASMs and the Marte Mk II system for Sea Killer Mk 2 anti-ship missiles; the type is powered by the 4,450-lb (2019-kg) thrust Piaggio-built Viper Mk 680-43 turbojet, and the capacity of the tip tanks is increased to 510 litres (112 Imp gal) each for a total fuel capacity of 1773 litres (390 Imp gal)

M.B.339D: in 1988 Aermacchi revealed that it is studying a version of the M.B.339 with twin Pratt & Whitney Canada JT15D turbofans mounted over the wings

(Italy)

Type: operational trainer and light attack aeroplane

Accommodation: pilot on a Martin-Baker IT10F zero/zero ejector seat

Armament (fixed): two 30-mm DEFA 553 cannon with 125 rounds per gun

Armament (disposable): this is carried on six hardpoints (three under each wing, with the inner four units each rated at 454 kg/1,000 lb and the outer two units at 340 kg/750 lb) up to a maximum weight of 1935 kg (4,265 lb); typical weapons are two Matra 550 Magic or AIM-9 Sidewinder AAMs, 2·75- and 5-in (70- and 127-mm) rocket pods, 50-, 68- and 81-mm (2-, 2·68- and 3·2-in) rocket pods, 250-, 500-, 750- and 1,000-lb (113-, 227-, 340- and 454-kg) bombs of various types, and gun pods containing one 30-mm DEFA 553 cannon with 150 rounds, or one 7·62-mm (0·3-in) Minigun with 1,500 rounds or one 0·5-in (12·7-mm) M3 machine-gun with 350 rounds

Electronics and operational equipment: communication and navigation equipment, plus a Saab RGS2 gyro sight and an assortment of customer options such as a HUD, RWR, Elettronica ELT-555 warning and deception jamming pod, and laser rangefinder

Powerplant and fuel system: one 2020-kg (4,453-lb) thrust Piaggio-built Rolls-Royce Viper Mk 680-43 non-afterburning turbojet, and a total internal fuel capacity of 2050 litres (451 Imp gal)

Below: The M.B.339K is the single-seat attack derivative of the M.B.339, and is seen here with 'iron' bombs, a jammer pod and an AAM.

including the fixed tiptanks, plus provision for two 325-litre (71·5-Imp gal) drop tanks; no provision for inflight refuelling

Performance: maximum speed 900 km/h (559 mph) at sea level; initial climb rate 2400 m (7,875 ft) per minute; service ceiling 14,000 m (45,930 ft); radius 648 km (403 miles) on a hi-lo-hi mission with a 1088-kg (2,400-lb) warload, or 376 km (234 miles) on a lo-lo-lo mission with the same warload

Weights: empty 3245 kg (7,154 lb); normal take-off 5050 kg (11,133 lb); maximum take-off 6350 kg (13,999 lb)

Dimensions: span 11·22 m (36 ft 9·75 in) over tiptanks; length 10·85 m (35 ft 7 in); height 3·994 m (13 ft 1·25 in); wing area 19·30 m² (207·75 sq ft)

Variant

M.B.339K: originally called the Veltro 2 (greyhound 2), this is the single-seat light attack aircraft derivative of the M.B.339C analogous to the M.B.326K; the rear cockpit is again used for fuel, avionics (including an INS), a HUD is fitted, and two 30-mm DEFA 553 cannon are installed in the lower fuselage

Aero L-29 Delfin 'Maya'

(Czechoslovakia)
Type: basic and advanced flying and weapon trainer
Accommodation: pupil and instructor in tandem on ejector seats
Armament (fixed): none
Armament (disposable): this is carried on two hardpoints (one under each wing each rated at 100 kg/220 lb) up to a maximum weight of 200 kg (440 lb); typical weapons are pods each with one 7·62-mm (0·3-in) machine-gun, 100-kg (220-lb) bombs and 55-mm (2·17-mm) rocket pods
Electronics and operational equipment: communication and navigation equipment, and an optical sight
Powerplant and fuel system: one 890-kg (1,960-lb) thrust Motorlet M701 non-afterburning turbojet, and a total internal fuel capacity of 1050 litres (231 Imp gal) plus provision for two 150-litre (33-Imp gal) drop tanks; no provision for inflight refuelling
Performance: maximum speed 655 km/h (407 mph) at 5000 m (16,405 ft); initial climb rate 840 m (2,755 ft) per minute; service ceiling 11,000 m (36,090 ft); range 640 km (397 miles) on internal fuel and 895 km (555 miles) with external fuel
Weights: empty 2280 kg (5,027 lb); normal take-off 3280 kg (7,231 lb); maximum take-off 3540 kg (7,804 lb)
Dimensions: span 10·29 m (33 ft 9 in); length 10·81 m (35 ft 5·5 in); height 3·13 m (10 ft 3 in); wing area 19·78 m² (212·88 sq ft)

Variants

L-29 Delfin: designed to meet Warsaw Pact requirements for a simple yet capable basic and advanced jet trainer, the aircraft designated **'Maya'** by NATO first flew in April 1959 with a Rolls-Royce (Bristol) Viper turbojet, and was subsequently built in very large numbers for the Warsaw Pact countries and for export with a Czech engine; among the type's advantages are great strength, viceless handling characteristics, and the ability to operate from semi-prepared, sandy and even waterlogged airstrips; the **L-29A Delfin Akrobat** was a single-seat aerobatic model produced in very small numbers; the L-29R attack version failed to enter production

Aero L-39ZA Albatros

(Czechoslovakia)
Type: light attack and reconnaissance aeroplane
Accommodation: pilot and optional co-pilot on VS-1-BRI zero/150-km/h (91-mph) ejector seats
Armament (fixed): one 23-mm GSh-23L twin-barrel cannon with 150/180 rounds in a ventral pack
Armament (disposable): this is carried on four hardpoints (two under each wing, with the two inner units each rated at 500 kg/1,102 lb and the outer two units each at 250 kg/551 lb) up to a maximum weight of 1290 kg (2,844 lb); typical weapons are AA-2 'Atoll' and AA-8 'Aphid' AAMs, S-130 130-mm (5·12-in) rockets, UV-16-57 pods each carrying 16 55-mm (2·17-in) rockets, and 100-, 250- and 500-kg (220-, 551- and 1,102-lb) bombs
Electronics and operational equipment: communication and navigation equipment, plus an ASP-3-NMU-39 gyro sight and provision for a five-camera reconnaissance pod
Powerplant and fuel system: one 1720-kg (3,792-lb) thrust Walter Titan (licensed Ivchyenko AI-25-TL) non-afterburning turbofan, and a total internal fuel capacity of 1055 litres (232 Imp gal) excluding 200 litres (44 Imp gal) in two non-jettisonable wingtip tanks, plus provision for two 350-litre (77-Imp gal) drop tanks; no provision for inflight refuelling
Performance: maximum speed 750 km/h (466 mph) clean at 5000 m (16,405 ft) or 610 km/h (379 mph) with external stores at sea level; initial climb rate 1260 m (4,135 ft) per minute clean or 960 m (3,160 ft) per minute with stores; service ceiling 11,000 m (36,090 ft); range 780 km (485 miles) with typical warload; ferry range 1600 km (994 miles)
Weights: empty 3565 kg (7,859 lb); normal take-off 4635 kg (10,218 lb); maximum take-off 5600 kg (12,346 lb)
Dimensions: span 9·46 m (31 ft 0·5 in); length 12·13 m (39 ft 9·5 in); height 4·77 m (15 ft 7·75 in); wing area 18·80 m² (202·36 sq ft)

Variants

L-39C Albatros: designed as successor to the L-29 in much the same way as the Aermacchi M.B.339 was developed from the basis of the M.B.326, the L-39 was the initial production version of this important tandem-seat basic and advanced trainer, and first flew in prototype form during November 1968; apart from a host of aerodynamic and other changes (including modular construction for ease of replacement, and features for simple maintenance access), for economy combined with performance the L-39 introduced turbofan power in the form of a version of the AI-25-TL rated at 1720-kg (3,792-lb) non-afterburning thrust; the type's unswept wing limits flight performance, but this is of little significance in a design intended for the flying and weapons training roles rather than for attack in the sense accepted for genuine dual-role trainer/light attack aircraft of Western design; the type has one hardpoint under each wing for light stores, and its empty and maximum take-off weights are 3455 and 4700 kg (7,617 and 10,362 lb) respectively, producing slightly better performance than that of the heavier armed models
L-39V Albatros: target-tug version of the L-39 with single-seat accommodation
L-39ZA Albatros: L-39ZO development for ground attack and reconnaissance with appropriately modified avionics, a ventral cannon pack, reinforced landing gear and a strengthened wing with four hardpoints
L-39ZO Albatros: weapon training version of the L-39 first flown in August 1975 with four hardpoints under the reinforced wings
L-39MS Albatros: uprated variant introduced in 1987 after a first flight in 1986 with a 2200-kg (4,850-lb) turbofan for better performance (including climb rate improved by 20%) though not increased weapons load; the type also has an improved airframe and revised avionics, the latter including CRT cockpit displays

Right: The L-39 bears the same relationship to the L-29 as does the M.B.339 to the M.B.326 with staggered seating but unswept flying surfaces. Both Czechoslovak aircraft are turbofan-powered, however, and are thus more economical in operation than the Italian aircraft.

Below: An overhead view of the L-29 reveals the type's unsophisticated flying surfaces including straight wings and a T-tail.

Aérospatiale CM.170-1 Magister

(France)
Type: basic flying and weapon trainer with a secondary light attack capability
Accommodation: pupil and instructor in tandem
Armament (fixed): two 7·62-mm (0·3-in) machine-guns with 200 rounds per gun
Armament (disposable): this is carried on two hardpoints (one under each wing rated at 70 kg/154 lb) up to a maximum weight of 140 kg (309 lb); standard weapons are pods for 18 37-mm (1·46-in) or six 68-mm (2·68-in) rockets, eight 81-mm (3·2-in) rockets, two 50-kg (110-lb) bombs or two AS.11 ASMs
Electronics and operational equipment: communication and navigation equipment, plus a gyro sight
Powerplant: two 400-kg (882-lb) thrust Turboméca Marboré IIA non-afterburning turbojets, and a total internal fuel capacity of 980 litres (216 Imp gal); no provision for drop tanks or inflight refuelling
Performance: maximum speed 715 km/h (414 mph) at 9145 m (30,000 ft) and 650 km/h (403 mph) at sea level; initial climb rate 1020 m (3,345 ft) per minute; service ceiling 11,000 m (36,090 ft); range 925 km (575 miles)
Weights: empty 2150 kg (4,750 lb); normal take-off 3100 kg (6,834 lb); maximum take-off 3200 kg (7,055 lb)
Dimensions: span 12·15 m (39 ft 10 in) over tip-tanks; length 10·06 m (33 ft 0 in); height 2·80 m (9 ft 2 in); wing area 17·30 m² (186·22 sq ft)

Variants

CM.170-1 Magister: designed as the world's first jet trainer by Fouga (later Potez and later still Aérospatiale), the CM.170 flew in prototype form during July 1952 on the power of two 400-kg (882-lb) thrust Turboméca Marboré II turbojets, and entered service with a number of detail improvements; the type was built to the extent of 761 aircraft in France, Finland, West Germany and Israel
CM.170-2 Super Magister: uprated version with two 480-kg (1,058-lb) thrust Marboré VI turbojets for a maximum take-of weight of 3260 kg (7,187 lb) and a maximum speed of 725 km/h (451 mph) at 9000 m (29,530 ft); production amounted to 137 aircraft

CM.175 Zephyr: designation of 32 navalized aircraft for the French navy, basically to CM.170-1 standard but fitted with arrester hooks
Israel Aircraft Industries Improved Fouga: enhanced model available from IAI as rebuilt aircraft or as an updating kit for local modification; in this programme the airframe is strengthened, the avionics are brought up to modern standards, Marboré VI engines are fitted, the inbuilt armament is standardized as two 0·3-in (7·62-mm) Browning machine-guns with 180 rounds per gun, and four underwing hardpoints are fitted for the carriage of rocket-launcher pods, Minigun pods, free-fall bombs, reconnaissance pods etc; the type has a maximum take-off weight of 3400 kg (7,496 lb)
Israel Aircraft Industries AMIT Fouga: serving with the Israeli air force as the *Tzukit* (thrush), this is the Advanced Multi-mission Improved Trainer version of the Magister incorporating all the Improved Fouga modifications plus extra avionics to improve reliability and operational capability

Aérospatiale Epsilon

(France)
Type: primary and basic trainer with a secondary light attack capability
Accommodation: pupil and instructor in tandem
Armament (fixed): none
Armament (disposable): this is carried on four hardpoints (two under each wing, with the inner two units each rated at 160 kg/352 lb and the outer two units at 80 kg/176 lb) up to a maximum weight of 300 kg (662 lb) of light bombs, rocket launchers and gun pods
Electronics and operational equipment: communication and navigation equipment, plus a gyro sight
Powerplant: one 300-hp (224-kW) Avco Lycoming AEIO-540-L1B5D piston engine, and a total internal fuel capacity of 210 litres (46·2 Imp gal); no provision for drop tanks (except on export model with underwing hardpoints) or inflight refuelling
Performance: maximum speed 378 km/h (236 mph) at sea level; cruising speed 358 km/h (222 mph) at 1830 m (6,000 ft); initial climb rate 564 m (1,850 ft) per minute; service ceiling 7000 m (23,000 ft); range 1250 km (777 miles); endurance 3 hours 45 minutes
Weights: empty 932 kg (4,750 lb); maximum take-off 1250 kg (2,756 lb)
Dimensions: span 7·92 m (25 ft 11·8 in); length 7·59 m (24 ft 10·8 in); height 2·66 m (8 ft 8·7 in); wing area 9·00 m² (96·88 sq ft)

Variants

Epsilon: this light trainer was schemed by SOCATA, a subsidiary of Aérospatiale, in two forms as the TB 30A and TB 30B with 260- and 300-hp (194- and 224-kW) engines respectively; the TB 30B won a development contract in 1979 and the first prototype flew in December of the same year; the second prototype was used to refine the design with rounded tips on a wing of greater span, a redesigned rear fuselage and a revised empennage, and this model formed the basis of the Epsilon production model; deliveries of the unarmed initial variant began in July 1983 for the French air force, and of the armed model in 1986 to the Togolese air force
Omega: first flown as the TB 30C in November 1985, this is the turboprop-powered version for much superior performance; the type has the 268-kW (360-shp) Turboméca TM-319 turboprop in a fuselage shortened to 7·81 m (25 ft 7·5 in), and at empty and maximum weights of 1012 and 1400 kg (2,231 and 3,086 lb) respectively, this version has a performance that includes a maximum speed of 414 km/h (257 mph), and initial climb rate of 640 m (2,100 ft) per minute, a service ceiling of 9145 m (30,000 ft); the internal fuel capacity of 270 litres (59·4 Imp gal) maintains range at 1250 km (777 miles)

Above left: Seen in inverted flight, the Epsilon is a simple flying trainer designed for good flying characteristics in combination with great economy of purchase and operation.

Left: The Magister was the world's first purpose-designed jet trainer to enter widespread service, and is still used by several countries.

Aérospatiale SA 315B Lama

(France)
Type: utility light helicopter
Accommodation: pilot and two passengers at the front of the cockpit, and four passengers, or two litters and one attendant, or 1135 kg (2,502 lb) of freight in the rear of the cabin or carried as a slung load
Armament (fixed): none
Armament (disposable): none
Electronics and operational equipment: communication and navigation equipment
Powerplant and fuel system: one 649-kW (870-shp) Turboméca Artouste IIIB turboshaft derated to 405 kW (543 shp), and a total internal fuel capacity of 575 litres (126·5 Imp gal); no provision for drop tanks or inflight refuelling
Performance: cruising speed 192 km/h (119 mph); initial climb rate 330 m (1,080 ft) per minute; service ceiling 5400 m (17,715 ft); hovering ceiling in ground effect 5050 m (16,565 ft) and out of ground effect 4600 m (15,090 ft); range 515 km (320 miles)
Weights: empty 1021 kg (2,251 lb); normal take-off 1950 kg (4,299 lb); maximum take-off 2300 kg (5,070 lb)
Dimensions: main rotor diameter 11·02 m (36 ft 1·75 in); length overall, rotors turning 12·91 m (42 ft 4·25 in) and fuselage 10·23 m (33 ft 6·75 in); height 3·09 m (10 ft 1·25 in); main rotor disc area 95·38 m² (1,026·7 sq ft)

Variant
SA 315B Lama: developed to meet an Indian requirement of the late 1960s for a general-purpose helicopter with good hot-and-high performance, the SA 315B first flew in March 1969 and is in essence the airframe of the Alouette II combined with the dynamic system of the Alouette III; the type began to enter service in 1970, and has since been built under licence in India as the **Hindustan Aeronautics Ltd Cheetah** and in Brazil as the **Helibras HB 315B Gaviao**

Aérospatiale SA 318C Alouette II Astazou

(France)
Type: utility light helicopter
Accommodation: pilot and passenger at the front of the cockpit, and up to three passengers, or two litters and one attendant, or freight in the rear of the cabin
Armament (fixed): none
Armament (disposable): provision for a wide variety of stores to customer requirement, typical fits being a magazine- or belt-fed 20-mm cannon or 7·62-mm (0·3-in) machine-gun, rocket pods or two AS.11 ASMs
Electronics and operational equipment: communication and navigation equipment
Powerplant and fuel system: one 395-kW (530-shp) Turboméca Astazou IIA turboshaft derated to 268 kW (360 shp), and a total internal fuel capacity of 580 litres (128 Imp gal); no provision for drop tanks or inflight refuelling
Performance: maximum speed 205 km/h (127 mph) at sea level; cruising speed 180 km/h (112 mph) at sea level; initial climb rate 400 m (1,312 ft) per minute; service ceiling 3300 m (10,825 ft); range 100 km (61 miles) with a 600-kg (1,323-lb) payload; ferry range 720 km (447 miles)
Weights: empty 890 kg (1,961 lb); maximum take-off 1650 kg (3,630 lb)
Dimensions: main rotor diameter 10·20 m (33 ft 5·6 in); length, fuselage 9·75 m (31 ft 11·75 in) with tail rotor turning; height 2·75 m (9 ft 0·25 in); main rotor disc area 81·71 m² (879·58 sq ft)

Variants
SE 313B Alouette II: the Alouette (lark) was the world's first turboshaft-powered helicopter to enter production (by Sud-Aviation, later Aérospatiale) after the turboshaft powerplant had been pioneered by the SE 3130 Alouette II which first flew in March 1955 on the power of a 268-kW (360-shp) Turboméca Artouste I; the Alouette II was powered by a 395-kW (530-shp) Artouste IIC6 turboshaft derated to 269 kW (360 shp), and served with some 22 air arms; production amounted to 923 helicopters for civil and military operators; apart from what was for the time good performance, the Alouette II was notable for its ability to carry a 600-kg (1,323-lb) slung load; the type is now obsolescent except in the communications role, but still in comparatively widespread service
SA 318C Alouette II Astazou: first flown in January 1961, this is a much improved version of the SE 313B with the more fuel-efficient Astazou IIA turboshaft, which also offers greater reliability than the Artouste as it is down-rated from 395 kW (530 shp) to 268 kW (360 shp) in this application; production lasted into 1975, some 350 aircraft being built; of the Alouette II series some 963 went to military operators, and many of these are still in service as utility helicopters

Right: The Alouette II was one of the world's first turboshaft-powered helicopters, and is seen here in the form of an Alouette II Astazou.

Below: Aérospatiale Helicopters Lama.

Aérospatiale SA 319B Alouette III Astazou

(France)
Type: utility light helicopter
Accommodation: pilot and two passengers at the front of the cockpit, and four passengers, or two litters and two attendants, or 750 kg (1,653 lb) of freight in the cabin rear or carried as a slung load
Armament (fixed): none
Armament (disposable): provision for a wide variety of stores to customer requirement, typical fits being a magazine- or belt-fed 20-mm cannon (MG151/20 with 480 rounds or M621 with 350 rounds) or 7·62-mm (0·3-in) machine-gun (AA52 with 1,000 rounds), four 68-mm (2·68-in) rocket pods, or four AS.11 or AS.12 ASMs, or two Mk 46 torpedoes
Electronics and operational equipment: communication and navigation equipment, plus (land warfare) one APX-Bézu 260 gyro-stabilized missile sight or (naval warfare) Omera-Segid Héracles ORB 31 search radar and optional Crouzet MAD equipment
Powerplant and fuel system: one 649-kW (870-shp) Turboméca Astazou XAV turboshaft derated to 447 kW (600 shp), and a total internal fuel capacity of 575 litres (126 Imp gal); no provision for drop tanks or inflight refuelling
Performance: maximum speed 220 km/h (136 mph) at sea level; cruising speed 197 km/h (122 mph) at sea level; initial climb rate 270 m (885 ft) per minute; hovering ceiling in ground effect 3100 m (10,170 ft); range 605 km (375 miles) with six passengers
Weights: empty 1108 kg (2,442 lb); maximum take-off 2250 kg (4,960 lb)
Dimensions: main rotor diameter 11·02 m (36 ft 1·75 in); length overall, rotors turning 12·84 m (42 ft 1·5 in) and fuselage 10·03 m (32 ft 10·75 in) with tail rotor turning; height 3·00 m (9 ft 10 in) to rotor head; main rotor disc area 95·38 m² (1,026·68 sq ft)

Variants
SA 316A Alouette III: developed under the designation SE 3160, the Alouette III was a basic upgrading and updating of the Alouette II, featuring greater power (in the form of the 649-kW/870-shp Turboméca Artouste IIIB turboshaft derated to 425 kW/570 shp and matched to an upgraded transmission system), a fully-covered pod-and-boom fuselage, a large cabin and other improvements to offer higher payload and performance together with the reliability and altitude performance as the Alouette II; the prototype first flew in February 1959, and production followed in 1961
SA 316B Alouette III: improved 1968 model with a strengthened transmission and improved landing gear, a combination allowing a further increase in payload; the type was built under licence in Switzerland by FFA, and is still built in India as the **Hindustan Aeronautics Ltd Chetak**, which the Indian company has developed into role-optimized land and naval subvariants; the land version is designed for the anti-tank role with four ASMs and a stabilized roof sight, while the naval version of the Chetak is intended for the shipborne anti-submarine role and is armed with two Mk 44/46 anti-submarine torpedoes (only one torpedo is carried if the optional podded MAD kit is fitted), a harpoon down-haul system, and folding rotor blades
SA 316C Alouette III: limited-production version powered by the Artouste IIID turboshaft
SA 319B Alouette III Astazou: just as the SA 318C was developed as an Astazou-powered SE 313B, the SA 319B was produced and first flown in 1967 as a more economical and reliable machine than the SA 316B; total production of the Alouette III amounted to 1,453, the greater portion of them for military service in a number of roles
Atlas Aircraft Corporation Alpha XH-1: South African gunship development (largely for experimental purposes) combining the dynamic system of the Alouette III with a new fuselage and an advanced weapon system; the crew of two is seated in tandem in upward staggered separate cockpits, and the gun armament comprises a GA1 20-mm cannon (with 1,000 rounds) in a servo-actuated mounting under the fuselage; it is unlikely that this prototype will be developed into a production model, though such a model was initially mooted with stub wings for the carriage of rocket pods and/or anti-tank missiles for addi-

Aérospatiale SA 321G Super Frelon

tional capability in the battlefield role; primary data for the Alpha XH-1 include empty and maximum take-off weights of 1400 and 2200 kg (3,086 and 4,850 lb) respectively, a maximum speed of 185 km/h (115 mph), an initial climb rate of 245 m (804 ft) per minute and a combat radius of 275 km (171 miles)

ICA-Brasov IAR-316B Alouette III: basic type licence-built in Romania; a much developed version of the type is the **IAR-317 Airfox**, locally evolved on the basis of the Alouette III/Artouste IIIB combination as a light attack helicopter with a tandem two-seat in a forward fuselage terminating in a solid nose for a fuselage length of 9·80 m (32 ft 1·75 in); the prototype first flew in April 1984 and the type has been developed with two fixed 7·62-mm (0·3-in) machine-guns (perhaps to be replaced by 20-mm cannon), and six hardpoints under a transverse load-carrying beam for the carriage of 750 kg (1,653 lb) of external stores such as four pods for 55-mm (2·17-in) unguided rockets, four twin machine-gun pods, four 50- or 100-kg (110- or 220-lb) bombs, or six AT-3 'Sagger' anti-tank missiles, or a mix of such weapons together with IR-homing AAMs at a maximum take-off weight of 2200 kg (4,850 lb); the type has a maximum speed of 200 km/h (124 mph) at sea level, a service ceiling of 6300 m (20,670 ft) and a standard range of 545 km (338 miles) that can be boosted to 870 km (540 miles) with two external tanks; there are suggestions that the Airfox did not proceed past the advanced development level

(France)

Type: anti-submarine heavy helicopter

Accommodation: flightdeck crew of two, plus a mission crew of three and up to 27 passengers or 5000 kg (11,023 lb) of freight in the cabin

Armament (fixed): none

Armament (disposable): this is carried on the sides of the fuselage outside the cabin, and can comprise four L4 or Mk 46 torpedoes, or two AM.39 Exocet anti-ship missiles, or eight 250-kg (551-lb) mines, or Mk 49, Mk 52 and Mk 54 depth charges

Electronics and operational equipment: communication and navigation equipment (the latter including a self-contained Doppler system), plus Thomson-CSF Sylphe search radar in the outrigger floats and Crouzet DHAX 3 dunking sonar (anti-submarine role) or Omera-Segid Héracles ORB 31-D or ORB 32-WAS target-acquisition and designation radar (anti-ship role)

Powerplant and fuel system: three 1200-kW (1,609-shp) Turboméca Turmo IIIC7 turboshafts, and a total internal fuel capacity of 3975 litres (874 Imp gal), plus provision for four 550-litre (110-Imp gal) auxiliary tanks (two internal and two external); no provision for drop tanks or inflight refuelling

Performance: maximum speed 248 km/h (154 mph) at sea level; initial climb rate 300 m (985 ft) per minute; service ceiling 3100 m (10,170 ft); range 1020 km (633 miles) with a 3500-kg (7,716-lb) slung load

Weights: empty 6863 kg (15,130 lb); maximum take-off 13,000 kg (28,660 lb)

Dimensions: main rotor diameter 18·90 m (62 ft 0 in); length overall, rotors turning 23·03 m (75 ft 6·7 in) and fuselage 19·40 m (63 ft 7·75 in); height 6·76 m (22 ft 2·1 in); main rotor disc area 280·55 m² (3,019·93 sq ft)

Variants

SA 321G Super Frelon: developed as the production version of the SA 3210 Super Frelon (itself a development of the SA 3200 Frelon, or hornet)

designed with the aid of Sikorsky in the USA, the SA 321G first flew in November 1965 and provides the French navy with a powerful amphibious anti-submarine helicopter for the clearing of the approaches to the base at Brest used by French nuclear submarines

SA 321H Super Frelon: simplified land-based transport helicopter produced as the SA 321K/L series with three Turmo IIIE turboshafts, and a payload of 30 troops, or 15 litters, or a load of 4000 or 5000 kg (8,818 or 11,023 lb) carried internally or externally

SA 321J Super Frelon: float-equipped transport version sold to China with 1155-kW (1,549-shp) Turmo IIIC 6 turboshafts and a maximum weight of 13000 kg (28,660 lb)

SA 321K Super Frelon: non-amphibious transport and assault version developed for Israel on the basis of the SA 321J commercial model; delivered from 1967 with 1100-kW (1,475-shp) Turmo IIIE 3 engines, the helicopters have since been re-engined with 1,895-shp (1413-kW) General Electric T58-GE-16 turboshafts

SA 321L Super Frelon: modified version of the SA 321K without floats or radar, and powered by 1170-kW (1,569-shp) Turmo IIIE 6 turboshafts

SA 321M Super Frelon: version for Libya without radar but with floats and 1170-kW (1,569-shp) Turmo IIIE 6 turboshafts

Changhe Aircraft Manufacturing Corporation Zhi-8: Chinese development of the SA 321J that first flew in December 1985 with three 1120-kW (1,502-shp) Wozhou-6 turboshafts, a six-blade main rotor, a five-blade tail rotor, clamshell rear doors, a maximum take-off weight of 13,000 kg (28,660 lb), a maximum speed of 300 km/h (186 mph) and a range of 800 km (497 miles)

Far left: The Alouette III was a simple evolution of the Alouette II with greater power, a larger cabin and an enclosed boom.

Below: An SA 321G Super Frelon in flight.

Aérospatiale SA 330L Puma

(France)
Type: utility and transport medium helicopter
Accommodation: flightcrew of one, two or three, and up to 20 troops, or six litters and six seated casualties, or 3000 kg (6,614 lb) of freight in the cabin, or a slung load of 3200 kg (7,055 lb)
Armament (fixed): none
Armament (disposable): generally none
Electronics and operational equipment: communication and navigation equipment
Powerplant and fuel system: two 1175-kW (1,575-shp) Turboméca Turmo IVC turboshafts, and a total internal fuel capacity of 1544 litres (340 Imp gal), plus provision for 2600 litres (572 Imp gal) of ferry fuel in four internal and two external tanks; no provision for drop tanks or inflight refuelling
Performance: cruising speed 258 km/h (160 mph); cruising speed 160 km/h (99 mph); initial climb rate 366 m (1,200 ft) per minute; service ceiling 4800 m (15,750 ft); range 550 km (341 miles)
Weights: empty 3615 kg (7,970 lb); maximum take-off 7500 kg (16,534 lb)
Dimensions: main rotor diameter 15·00 m (49 ft 2·5 in); length overall, rotors turning 18·15 m (59 ft 6·6 in) and fuselage 14·06 m (46 ft 1·5 in); height 5·14 m (16 ft 10·5 in); main rotor disc area 176·71 m² (1,902·20 sq ft)

Variants

SA 330B Puma: designed from the early 1960s in response to a French army requirement for an all-weather day/night tactical transport helicopter, the Puma first flew in prototype form during April 1965, and the SA 330B initial production version (powered by two 990-kW/1,328-shp Turmo IIIC4 turboshafts for a maximum take-off weight of 6400 kg/14,109 lb with a 3000-kg/6,614-lb payload) began to enter service in March 1969, proving highly successful in its intended role and paving the way for substantial export orders
SA 330C Puma: export version of the SA 330B with 1045-kW (1,402-shp) Turmo IVC turboshafts
SA 330E Puma: version of the SA 330B for the UK, which designates the type **Puma HC.Mk 1**
SA 330H Puma: uprated version of the SA 330C with 1175-kW (1,576-shp) Turmo IVC turboshafts for a maximum take-off weight of 7000 kg (15,432 lb)
SA 330L Puma: improved export model with Turmo IVC turboshafts, inlet de-icing and rotor blades of composite rather than steel/light alloy structure
Atlas Aircraft Corporation Beta: using technology and features pioneered on the Alpha XH-1 (evolved from the Aérospatiale Alouette), the XTP-1 prototype was evolved in similar fashion from the Aérospatiale Puma as a radical South African development of the Puma as a dedicated gunship and anti-tank helicopter; under development since 1981 and first flown as the XTP-1 in 1987, the type has the Rattler cannon system (with a 20-mm GA1 Cobra gun in a servo-operated chin turret fed from a magazine in the hold and operated in conjunction with a helmet sight worn by the co-pilot/gunner in the forward cockpit) and a variety of disposable loads on the six hardpoints under the two new stub wings (produced as a single unit passing through the erstwhile passenger cabin); it is likely that the wing armament will comprise rocket pods and/or anti-tank missiles on the four underwing hardpoints, and a pair of AAMs on the tip rails; the Beta uses the dynamic system of the Puma married to a slimmer fuselage with separate stepped cockpits for the co-pilot/gunner (forward) and pilot (aft), and fixed tailwheel landing gear
ICA-Brasov IAR-330L Puma: version built under licence in Romania

Below: The Ethiopian air force's sole SA 330 Puma helicopter is used for VIP transport.

Below right: The AS 332M-1 is the version of the AS 332 Super Puma optimized for hot-and-high operations with Makila 1A1 turboshafts.

Aérospatiale AS 332B-1 Super Puma

(France)

Type: transport and utility medium helicopter

Accommodation: flightcrew of one, two or three, and up to 21 troops, or six litters and seven seated casualties or 4000 kg (8,818 lb) of freight in the cabin, or a slung load of 4500 kg (9,921 lb)

Armament (fixed): none

Armament (disposable): generally none

Electronics and operational equipment: communication and navigation equipment, the latter including a Decca or Nadir self-contained navigation system

Powerplant and fuel system: two 1400-kW (1,877-shp) Turboméca Makila IA1 turboshafts, and a total internal fuel capacity of 1560 litres (343 Imp gal), plus provision for 2600 litres (572 Imp gal) of ferry fuel in four internal and two external tanks; no provision for drop tanks or inflight refuelling

Performance: cruising speed 262 km/h (163 mph) at sea level; initial climb rate 426 m (1,397 ft) per minute; service ceiling 4100 m (13,450 ft); hovering ceiling in ground effect 2700 m (8,860 ft) and out of ground effect 1600 m (5,250 ft); range 618 km (384 miles) on standard fuel

Weights: empty 4290 kg (9,458 lb); maximum take-off 9000 kg (19,841 lb) with an internal load or 9350 kg (20,613 lb) with a slung load

Dimensions: main rotor diameter 15·60 m (51 ft 2·2 in); length overall, rotors turning 18·70 m (61 ft 4·2 in) and fuselage 14·76 m (48 ft 5 in); height 4·92 m (16 ft 1·75 in); main rotor disc area 191·13 m² (2,057·43 sq ft)

Variants

AS 332B Super Puma: the Super Puma was designed from 1974 as a successor to the basic SA 330 Puma with two 1327-kW (1,789-shp) Makila IA turboshafts for greater payload (two crew plus 21 rather than 18 troops) and improved performance, and with features to reduce cabin noise, maintenance requirements and operational vulnerability; the AS 331 prototype was first flown in September 1977 to test the revised dynamic system (new powerplant and upgraded transmission), and the first AS 332 production helicopter flew in September 1978; deliveries began in November 1981, and the Super Puma has proved attractive for its low-maintenance and damage-resistant composite rotor blades and other tactically desirable features; the current variant is the **AS 332B-1 Super Puma** with upgraded engines for better performance under hot-and-high conditions

AS 332F Super Puma: naval version with a folding tail, a deck landing-assistance device, enhanced anti-corrosion protection and nose-mounted radar; the variant is suitable for the SAR role with Bendix RDR 1400 or RCA Primus 40/50 radar, the anti-submarine role with Alcatel HS 12 dunking sonar and two Mk 46 torpedoes, or the anti-ship role with Omera-Segid Héracles ORB 3214 radar and an anti-ship missile armament of two AM.39 Exocets, or six AS.15TTs, or one Exocet and three AS.15TTs; use of the AS.15TT requires the installation of Thomson-CSF Agrion-15 radar in place of the ORB 3214; the current variant is the AS 332F-1 Super Puma with Makila IA1 turboshafts and provision for two AM.39 Exocet anti-ship missiles

AS 332M Super Puma: upgraded version of the AS 332B with the cabin lengthened by 0·76 m (2·5 ft) to make possible the carriage of 25 troops at a maximum take-off weight of 9350 kg (20,613 lb) with a fuel capacity of 2060 litres (453 Imp gal) for a range of 842 km (523 miles) on standard tankage; there is also a further upgraded **AS 332M-1 Super Puma** designed for hot-and-high operations with Makila IA1 turboshafts for unimpaired performance with 25 fully equipped troops

AS 332 Super Puma Mk II: under this designation Aérospatiale has developed a much improved Super Puma variant with upgraded electronics and systems, a higher-rated power train and an advanced rotor with lengthened blades terminating in parabolic tips; the first such helicopter flew in February 1987 and displayed improved performance and manoeuvrability, as well as superior hot-and-high capability; the type is due to enter service in 1993, and it is likely that the type will be offered in the current military and naval versions; after trials with an SA 330B, the French are scheduled to bring into service during 1995 a battlefield surveillance derivative of the SA 332 Mk II with Orchidée pulse-Doppler radar to provide 360° coverage out to a range of 150 km (93 miles) from a height of 3000 m (9,845 ft); the radar antenna is located ventrally under the rear of the payload hold on a hinged arm that allows it to be swung 90° to the rear under the boom when not in use; the radar is linked to its Mistrigri ground station by an Agatha data-link

IPTN NAS-332 Super Puma: type built under licence in Indonesia; similar helicopters have also been assembled in Singapore and Spain by SAMCo (17 AS 332Ms) and CASA (12 AS 332Bs) from kits of French-supplied components

Aérospatiale SA 341 F Gazelle

(France)
Type: utility light helicopter

Accommodation: flightcrew of one or two, and up to three passengers or freight in the cabin rear, or a slung load of 700 kg (1,540 lb)

Armament (fixed): provision for one 20-mm M621 cannon attached to the starboard side of the fuselage

Armament (disposable): this is carried on two hardpoints, one at each end of the tubular weapons beam that can be installed transversely through the fuselage, and can comprise two machine-gun pods each with a single 7·62-mm (0·3-in) AA52 or MAG machine-gun, or two AS.12 or four AS.11 ASMs, or four TOW anti-tank missiles, or two 81-mm (3·2-in) rocket pods

Electronics and operational equipment: communication and navigation equipment, plus (AS.11/12 installation) APX-Bézu 334 or (TOW installation) XM26 gyro-stabilized sight

Powerplant and fuel system: one 440-kW (590-shp) Turboméca Astazou IIIC turboshaft, and a total internal fuel capacity of 445 litres (98 Imp gal), plus provision for 290 litres (64 Imp gal) of ferry fuel in two internal tanks; no provision for drop tanks or inflight refuelling

Performance: maximum speed 264 km/h (164 mph) at sea level; cruising speed 233 km/h (144 mph) at sea level; initial climb rate 540 m (1,770 ft) per minute; service ceiling 5000 m (16,405 ft); range 360 km (223 miles) with a 500-kg (1,102-lb) payload; ferry range 670 km (416 miles)

Weights: empty 920 kg (2,028 lb); maximum take-off 1800 kg (3,968 lb)

Dimensions: main rotor diameter 10·50 m (34 ft 5·5 in); length overall, rotors turning 11·97 m (39 ft 3·3 in) and fuselage 9·53 m (31 ft 3·2 in); height 3·18 m (10 ft 5·25 in); main rotor disc area 86·59 m² (932·08 sq ft)

Variants
SA 341B Gazelle: this important light helicopter originated in a French army requirement of the early 1960s for a light observation helicopter (successor to the Alouette II series) characterized by good manoeuvrability and considerable speed; the type was developed initially as the SA 340 with a conventional tail rotor (first flown in April 1967), though this was replaced in later prototypes with a shrouded rotor built into the fin; the initial production model was the SA 341B with an Astazou IIIA turboshaft, and this model was adopted for British army service as the **Gazelle AH.Mk 1** with the Astazou IIIN turboshaft; several British helicopters have been retrofitted with a Nightsun searchlight and Doppler navigation, and a programme is in hand to provide the helicopters with a Ferranti AWARE-3 RWR

SA 341C Gazelle: naval version of the SA 341B for the Royal Navy, which accepted the type as the **Gazelle HT.Mk 2**

SA 341D Gazelle: trainer version of the SA 341B for the RAF, which accepted the type as the **Gazelle HT.Mk 3**

SA 341E Gazelle: communications version for the RAF, which accepted the type as the **Gazelle HCC.Mk 4**

SA 341F Gazelle: initial version for the French army with the Astazou IIIC turboshaft; the **SA 341F/Canon** is an interim escort and gunship version with a 20-mm M621 cannon on the starboard side of the cabin; there is also a reconnaissance version with a simplified version of the Athos magnifying sight used on the HOT-armed SA 342M variant

SA 341H Gazelle: export version of the SA 341B/F type with the Astazou IIIB turboshaft, and built under licence in Yugoslavia as the **SOKO SA 341H Partizan** liaison and reconnaissance helicopter; in the armed reconnaissance role the Yugoslav variant carries an armament of four AT-2 'Swatter' wire-guided anti-tank missiles and two examples of the air-to-air version of the SA-7 'Grail' shoulder-launched SAM

SA 342K Gazelle: the SA 342 designation is used for the uprated model powered by the Astazou XIV turboshaft for greater performance and payload, especially under hot-and-high conditions; the SA 342K series has the 649-kW (870-shp) Astazou XIVH with momentum-separation shrouds over the inlet

SA 342L-1 Gazelle: military version of the uprated SA 342J civil helicopter with the 640-kW (858-shp) Astazou XIVM turboshaft, an improved tail rotor and a number of detail modifications allowing the type to operate at a maximum take-off weight of 2000 kg (4,409 lb) with a wide assortment of military loads; the variant is built under licence in Yugoslavia as the **SOKO SA 342 HERA** special-purpose and **SA 342 GAMA** gunship models

SA 342M Gazelle: dedicated anti-tank version of the SA 342L-1 for the French army, and powered by the 640-kW (858-shp) Astazou XIVM turboshaft for a maximum take-off weight of 1900 kg (4,188 lb); the type is fitted with Crouzet Nadir navigation system, Decca Doppler and the SFIM APX-Bézu M397 Athos gyro-stabilized sight for the guidance of four or six HOT anti-tank missiles in two twin or triple installations, though the type can also be armed with two 7·62-mm (0·3-in) machine-gun pods or one M621 20-mm cannon (in the latter guise being designated **SA 342M/Canon**); deliveries began in June 1980, and other modifications are an autopilot, an exhaust deflector for reduced vulnerability to ground-launched IR-homing missiles and, in a retrofit programme for all armed Gazelles, a SFIM Viviane night/adverse-weather thermal sight and Matra Mistral AAMs for self-defence

Despite its lightweight structure, the Gazelle has high performance and is a useful multi-role type seen here in the form of a French army SA 341F used for training and as an air observation post.

Aérospatiale AS 355M-2 Ecureuil 2

(France)

Type: utility light helicopter

Accommodation: pilot and five passengers or 900 kg (1,984 lb) of freight in the cabin, or a slung load of 750 kg (1,653 lb)

Armament (fixed): none

Armament (disposable): see Variants (below)

Electronics and operational equipment: communication and navigation equipment, and (when required by the weapon fit) missile sights and/or other equipment

Powerplant and fuel system: two 420-shp (313-kW) Allison 250-C20F turboshafts, and a total internal fuel capacity of 730 litres (160 Imp gal); no provision for drop tanks or inflight refuelling

Performance: maximum speed 224 km/h (139 mph) at sea level; initial climb rate 390 m (1,280 ft) per minute; service ceiling 3400 m (11,155 ft); hovering ceiling in ground effect 1800 m (5,905 ft) and out of ground effect 1350 m (4,430 ft); range 703 km (437 miles)

Weights: empty 1360 kg (2,998 lb); normal take-off 2540 kg (5,600 lb); maximum take-off 2600 kg (5,732 lb)

Dimensions: main rotor diameter 10·69 m (35 ft 0·75 in); length overall, rotors turning 12·94 m (42 ft 5·4 in) and fuselage 10·93 m (35 ft 10·5 in) with tail rotor turning; height 3·34 m (10 ft 11·5 in); main rotor disc area 89·75 m² (966·12 sq ft)

Variants

AS 350L-1 Ecureuil: designed in the early 1970s as a fuel-economical successor to the Alouette II on the civil market, and first flown in June 1974, the AS 35OB Ecureuil (squirrel) is one of the manufacturer's most successful light helicopters and has also sold moderately well on the military market, largely as a communications machine; the type is built in Brazil as the **Helibras HB 350 Esquilo**; though the older AS 350B and AS 350B-1 versions are in limited military service and communication/liaison helicopters with the 478- or 510-kW (641- or 684-shp) Turboméca Arriel IB or Arriel ID turboshafts respectively, the AS 350L-1 is the oldest dedicated military version of the Ecureuil series and, fitted with the 478-kW (684-shp) Arriel ID turboshaft, was designed for the export market and fitted with outrigger pylons in a removable through-cabin beam for the carriage of light weapons, a TOW anti-tank missile installation also being available (Denmark's AS 350L-1s being fitted with the Heli Tow system); other modifications are a strengthened floor, upgraded landing gear and sliding rather than hingedG doors; the type has a maximum take-off weight of 2450 kg (5,401 lb)

AS 350L-2 Ecureuil: introduced in 1989, this is a simple development of the AS 350L-1 with the 515-kW (691-shp) Arriel ID1 turboshaft for a slight improvement in performance with a higher maximum take-off weight

AS 355F-1 Ecureuil 2: the AS 355 is the twin-engined ersion of the AS 350, and first flew in September 1979; the French air force operates 10 examples of the AS 355F-1 version with Allison 250-C20F turboshafts for surveillance around major air bases

AS 355M Ecureuil 2: twin-engined equivalent of the AS 350L-1 with a strengthened airframe, reinforced landing gear and improved instrumentation; the variant possesses the same armament provisions as the AS 350 and can be subjected to comparable modifications for improved operational reliability; the current version used by France has an armament of Matra Mistral light AAMs, TOW anti-tank missiles, pintle-mounted machine-guns, and podded machine-guns or a 20-mm M621 cannon; the AS 355M is currently powered by two 420-shp (313-kW) Allison 250-C20F turboshafts for maximum take-off weights of 2540 or 2600 kg (5,600 or 5,732 lb) with or without a slung load, but are to be retrofitted with 380-kW (509-shp) Turboméca TM319 turboshafts for considerably improved performance at higher weights

AS 355M-2 Ecureuil 2: basically similar variant of the AS 355M for the export market

AS 355N Ecureuil 2: version of the AS 355F-1 for the French air force with two 340-kW (456-shp) Turboméca TM319 turboshafts

The designation AS 350 covers the single-engined Ecureuil series here epitomized by an AS 350L with a transverse beam for rocket or machine-gun pods.

Aérospatiale SA 365F Dauphin 2

(France)
Type: naval utility light helicopter
Accommodation: flightcrew of two, and 10 passengers or 1700 kg (3,748 lb) of freight in the cabin, or 1600 kg (3,527 lb) as a slung load
Armament (fixed): none
Armament (disposable): up to four AS.15TT light anti-ship missiles
Electronics and operational equipment: communication and navigation equipment, plus Omera-Segid Héracles ORB 32 or (AS.15TT version) Thomson-CSF Agrion-15 search radar
Powerplant and fuel system: two 529-kW (710-shp) Turboméca Arriel IM turboshafts, and a total internal fuel capacity of 1140 litres (250·75 Imp gal); no provision for drop tanks or inflight refueling
Performance: maximum speed 296 km/h (184 mph) at optimum altitude; cruising speed 282 km/h (175 mph) at sea level; initial climb rate 1900 m (6,234 ft) per minute; hovering ceiling in ground effect 2150 m (7,055 ft) and out of ground effect 1200 m (3,935 ft); service ceiling 4575 m (15,010 ft); range 898 km (558 miles)
Weights: empty 2017 kg (4,447 lb); maximum take-off 4100 kg (9,039 lb)
Dimensions: main rotor diameter 11·93 m (39 ft 1·7 in); length overall, rotors turning 13·74 m (45 ft 0·9 in) and fuselage 10·98 m (36 ft 0 in); height 3·51 m (11 ft 6·2 in); main rotor disc area 111·78 m² (1,203·25 sq ft)

Variants

SA 365F Dauphin 2: developed in the late 1960s and early 1970s as successor to the Alouette III series, the SA 360 Dauphin first flew in June 1972 is a trim helicopter with a 783-kW (1,050-shp) Turboméca Astazou XVIIIA turboshaft, a shrouded tail rotor and accommodation for a crew of two plus up to 12 passengers, or four litters and a medical attendant, or 2·5 m 3 (88·2 cu ft) of freight; only limited sales were made to the military, largely in the communications role, and though an

SA 361H anti-tank/assault transport was developed as a private venture, Aérospatiale soon appreciated that both military and civil applications would be better served by a twin-engine powerplant; the initial twin-engine version was the SA 365C Dauphin 2, flown in prototype form during January 1975 with two Turboméca Arriel turboshafts and produced later in the decade with 492-kW (660-shp) Arriel IA turboshafts or, in the improved SA 365N Dauphin 2 version, with 529-kW (710-shp) Arriel IC turboshafts; the SA 365N introduced a large degree of composite construction as well as retractable landing gear; the SA 365F Dauphin 2 is the versatile naval development of the SA 365N intended primarily for the anti-ship role with Agrion-15 search radar, optional MAD with a towed 'bird', an armament of two or four AS.15TT short-range anti-ship missiles, and the avionics for mid-course targeting update of ship-launched Otomat long-range anti-ship missiles; the type is also available in SAR configuration with Omera-Segid ORB 32 search radar (or in the unarmed Irish version Bendix RDR-L500 search radar and a Crouzet ONS-200A long-range navigation system), a rescue winch, an automatic navigation system and a hover/transition coupler; the manufacturer is also proposing a more advanced antisubmarine capability in a derivative with Alcatel HS 12 dunking sonar, Crouzet DHAX 3 MAD and an armament of two lightweight homing torpedoes

SA 365F-1 Dauphin 2: uprated version of the SA 365F-1 with two 592-kW (794-shp) Arriel IM1 turboshafts

SA 365K Panther: version of the Panther battlefield helicopter with two 592-kW (794-shp) Arriel IM1 turboshafts, and evolved after the SA 365M; it is likely that improved versions will be developed for service after 1992 with more advanced systems for greater capability in the day and night roles

SA 365M Panther: first flown in February 1984,

the Panther is a dedicated military version of the SA 365N Dauphin 2 series with two 681-kW (913-shp) Turboméca TM333-1M turboshafts for a maximum take-off weight of 4100 kg (9,039 lb), greater use of composite materials, and a fuselage 12·07 m (39 ft 7 in) long fitted with armoured seats, cable cutters, a strengthened cabin floor and landing gear, sliding rather than hinged doors, crash-resistant fuel tanks and IR-reducing exhausts; the type can carry eight or 10 troops in the assault role, or two quadruple launch units for HOT anti-tank missiles in the offensive role; the HOT missiles are targeted with the aid of a Viviane day/night unit for an SFIM gyro-stabilized platform holding a TRT Hector IR camera and SAT deviation-measuring equipment; other elements of the advanced avionics suite are Lacroix chaff dispenser and a Sherloc RWR; alternative armament fits on the weapons beam are launchers for Matra Mistral light AAMs, 20-mm cannon pods or two pods each containing 22 68-mm (2·68-in) unguided rockets

SA 366G-1 Dauphin 2: development of the SA 365N for the US Coast Guard's short-range recovery role with two 618-shp (461-kW) Avco Lycoming LTS101-750A-1 turboshafts and much US-made equipment for a maximum take-off weight of 4050 kg (8,929 lb); the type has a crew of three, and can detect people in the water with the aid of FLIR equipment before hauling them to safety with a rescue winch; the SA 366G prototype first flew in July 1980, and the improved SA 366G-1 was accepted for the USCG with the designation **HH-65A Dolphin**

Harbin Aircraft Manufacturing Corporation Zhi-9 Haitun: SA 365N built under licence in China; the later **Zhi-9A** is equivalent to the French SA 365N1 variant with payload increased from 1863 kg (4,107 lb) to 2038 kg (4,493 lb) at only a slight reduction in flight performance; China has also developed an anti-tank version of this Haitun (dolphin) with a primary armament of Red Arrow 8 anti-tank missiles

Agusta A 109A Mk II

(Italy)
Type: general-purpose light helicopter
Accommodation: flightcrew of two, and six passengers or 1180 kg (2,601 lb) of freight in the cabin, or 907 kg (2,000 lb) of freight as a slung load
Armament (fixed): none
Armament (disposable): this is carried on four hardpoints (two under the pylon projecting from each side of the fuselage) up to a maximum weight of 344 kg (758 lb); the armament fit can be extremely varied, but the normal load is one or two pintle-mounted 7·62-mm (0·3-in) machineguns plus a mix of 81- or 122-mm (3·2- or 4·8-in) rocket pods and machine-gun pods, or eight antitank missiles
Electronics and operational equipment: communication and navigation equipment, plus a wide assortment of operational items to customer specification
Powerplant and fuel system: two 420-shp (313-kW) Allison 250-C20B turboshafts each derated to 346 shp (258 kW), and a total internal fuel capacity of 560 litres (123 Imp gal) plus provision for 170 litres (37·4 Imp gal) in an auxiliary fuselage tank; no provision for drop tanks or inflight refuelling
Performance: maximum speed 285 km/h (177 mph) at optimum altitude; cruising speed 233 km/h (145 mph); initial climb rate 640 m (2,100 ft) per minute; service ceiling 5485 m (18,000 ft); hovering ceiling out of ground effect 1490 m (4,890 ft); range 593 km (368 miles)
Weights: empty 1560 kg (3,439 lb); maximum take-off 2600 kg (5,732 lb)
Dimensions: main rotor diameter 11·00 m (36 ft 1 in); length overall, rotors turning 13·05 m (42 ft 9·8 in) and fuselage 10·706 m (35 ft 1·5 in); height 3·30 m (10 ft 10 in); main rotor disc area 95·03 m² (1,022·96 sq ft)

Variants
A 109A: though a conventional helicopter in design and construction, the A 109A is notable for the elegance of its low-drag design (complete with retractable landing gear) which is largely responsible for high performance on modest power; the type was aimed at the civil and military markets, and first flew in August 1971; greater sales success has been achieved in the civil market
A 109A Mk II: improved model of the A 109A with differences of only a minor nature
A 109K: dedicated military variant of the A 109A Mk II with a lengthened nose, fixed landing gear, and a powerplant of two 539-kW (723-shp) Turboméca Arriel IK turboshafts driving a main rotor that uses a new composite hub designed for high resistance to sand dust abrasion; the type has the improved hot-and-high performance that the company hopes will make the type attractive to Middle Eastern buyers; the A 109K has a maximum take-off weight of 2850 kg (6,283 lb) and a hovering ceiling, out of ground effect, of 3350 m (10,990 ft)
A 109EOA: Italian army observation version of the A 109K with Allison 250-C20R turboshafts and specialized equipment

Left: The SA 365F Dauphin 2 with Agrion-15 radar and AS.15TT anti-ship missiles.

Above right: The A 109A with TOW missiles.

Right: The A 129 Mangusta anti-tank helicopter.

Agusta A 129 Mangusta

(Italy)
Type: anti-tank, attack and scout light helicopter
Accommodation: co-pilot/gunner and pilot in tandem
Armament (fixed): none
Armament (disposable): this is carried on four hardpoints (two under each stub wing, with each unit rated at 300 kg/661 lb) up to a maximum weight of 1200 kg (2,646 lb); the primary armament is up to eight BGM-71 TOW anti-tank missiles carried in two two-, three- or four-round pods on the outer hardpoints, leaving the inner hardpoints for the carriage of two 0·5-in (12·7-mm) M3 machine-gun pods or two pods each with seven 2·75-in (70-mm) or 81-mm (3·2-in) rockets; seven- and 19-round launchers for 2·75-in (70-mm) and 81-mm (3·2-in) rockets can also be carried under the outer hardpoints
Electronics and operational equipment: communication and navigation equipment, plus a nose-mounted Saab/Emerson HeliTOW sight with laser rangefinder and FLIR, and a defensive package comprising an Elettronica/E-Systems RWR, Perkin-Elmer radar- and laser-warning receivers, ITT radar jammer, Sanders IR jammer and a powerplant IR diffuser
Powerplant and fuel system: two 825-shp (615-kW) Piaggio-built Rolls-Royce Gem 2 Mk 1004D turboshafts, and a total internal fuel capacity of unrevealed quantity plus provision for self-ferry two drop tanks; no provision for drop tanks or inflight refuelling
Performance: maximum speed 315 km/h (196 mph) at 2000 m (6,560 mph); initial climb rate 655 m (2,150 ft) per minute; hovering ceiling in ground effect 3750 m (12,305 ft) and out of ground effect 3015 m (9,890 ft); endurance 3 hours
Weights: empty 2529 kg (5,575 lb); maximum take-off 4100 kg (9,038 lb)
Dimensions: main rotor diameter 11·90 m (39 ft 0·5 in); length overall, rotors turning 14·29 m (46 ft 10·6 in) and fuselage 12·275 m (40 ft 3·25 in); height 3·315 m (10 ft 10·5 in); main rotor disc area 111·22 m² (1,197·20 sq ft)

Variants
A 129 Mangusta: first tandem-seat anti-tank helicopter developed in Europe, the Mangusta (mongoose) offers good performance, powerful anti-tank armament and associated sights, and a small fuselage profile featuring vertically staggered tandem seating for the gunner (front cockpit) and pilot (rear cockpit); the type first flew in September 1983, and entered service in 1988; the type offers full day and night offensive capability, and the Integrated Multiplex System monitors the helicopter and all its systems via two computers, so leaving the crew to devote their attentions to the mission; the manufacturer has proposed a navalized version (able to undertake the anti-ship or close-support roles, the former with an armament of two Sea Killer Mk 2 or four Sea Skua missiles supported by appropriate search/designation radar, and the latter with an armament of AGM-65 Maverick ASMs in addition to the A 129's standard TOW and rocket fit) and a battle-field version (able to carry eight troops, an undernose machine-gun turret and side-looking airborne radar); the standard A 129 has provision for the retrofit of a mast-mounted sight system
A 129 Tonal: proposed co-production Mk 2 anti-tank/anti-helicopter/armed scout version to be developed and produced with Westland in the UK, Fokker in the Netherlands and CASA in Spain; the type will have advanced avionics and weapons, and a powerplant comprising either a single Rolls-Royce/Turboméca RTM322 or two Rolls-Royce Gem 2 Mk 1004 turboshafts

AIDC (Aero Industry Development Centre) AT-TC-3 Tse Tchan

(Taiwan)

Type: advanced flying and weapon trainer with a secondary light attack capability

Accommodation: pupil and instructor in tandem on zero/zero ejector seats

Armament (fixed): provision for two 0·5-in (12·7-mm) Browning M3 heavy machine-guns in a ventral pack

Armament (disposable): this is carried in a lower-fuselage weapons bay (machine-gun pack or reconnaissance equipment) and on seven hardpoints (one under the fuselage rated at 907 kg/2,000 lb, two under each wing with the inner units each rated at 635 kg/1,400 lb and the outer units at 272 kg/600 lb, and two at the wingtips each rated at 91 kg/200 lb) up to a maximum weight of 2720 kg (5,996 lb); typical stores are two wingtip-mounted AIM-9J Sidewinder AAMs, ASMs, and an assortment of cannon pods, rocket pods and bombs of the free-fall and cluster varieties

Electronics and operational equipment: communication and navigation equipment, plus a gunsight and optional reconnaissance equipment in the lower-fuselage bay

Powerplant and fuel system: two 3,500-lb (1588-kg) thrust Garrett TFE731-2-2L non-afterburning turbofans, and a total internal fuel capacity of 1630 litres (358·5 Imp gal) plus provision for two 568-litre (125-Imp gal) drop tanks; no provision for inflight refuelling

Performance: maximum speed 904 km/h (562 mph) or Mach 0·85 at 11,000 m (36,090 ft) and 898 km/h (558 mph) or Mach 0·73 at sea level; cruising speed 882 km/h (548 mph) at 11,000 m (36,090 ft); initial climb rate 3080 m (10,105 ft) per minute; service ceiling 14,650 m (48,065 ft); range 2280 km (1,417 miles) on internal fuel; endurance 3 hours 12 minutes on internal fuel

Weights: empty 3855 kg (8,500 lb); normal take-off 5215 kg (11,497 lb); maximum take-off 7940 kg (17,505 lb)

Dimensions: span 10·46 m (34 ft 3·75 in); length including probe 12·90 m (42 ft 4 in); height 4·36 m (14 ft 3·75 in); wing area 21·93 m² (236·05 sq ft)

Variants

AT-TC-3 Tse Tchan: developed from 1975, this first flew in September 1980 and the type began to enter service in 1984; keynotes of the design are simplicity and ease of maintenance in the airframe and powerplant, advanced avionics, and compact dimensions for great manoeuvrability

AIDC (Aero Industry Development Centre) T-CH-1

(Taiwan)

Type: basic flying and weapon trainer with a secondary ground-attack capability

Accommodation: pupil and instructor seated in tandem

Armament (fixed): none

Armament (disposable): this is carried on two hardpoints (one under each wing) up to an unrevealed maximum weight, and can comprise machine-gun pods, rocket launchers or light bombs

Electronics and operational equipment: communication and navigation equipment, plus a gunsight

Powerplant and fuel system: one 1,450-shp (1081-kW) Avco Lycoming T53-L-701 turboprop, and a total internal fuel capacity of 963 litres (254 US gal); no provision for drop tanks or inflight refuelling

Performance: maximum speed 590 km/h (367 mph) at 4670 m (15,000 ft); initial climb rate 1035 m (3,395 ft) per minute; service ceiling 9750 m (31,990 ft); range 2000 km (1,243 miles) with maximum fuel

Weights: empty 2600 kg (5,732 lb); normal take-off 3400 kg (7,496 lb); maximum take-off 5060 kg (11,155 lb)

Dimensions: span 12·19 m (40 ft 0 in); length 10·26 m (33 ft 8 in); height 3·66 m (12 ft 0 in); wing area 25·18 m² (271·0 sq ft)

Variant

T-CH-1: though claimed an an indigenous Taiwanese aircraft from the start of the design process in 1970, the T-CH-1 that first flew in November 1973 is little more than the North American T-28 Trojan piston-engined trainer revised for a turboprop powerplant; the provision of light armament capability suits the type to the weapon training and light attack/counter-insurgency roles, and the aeroplane began to enter service in late 1976 after evaluation of the unarmed T-CH-1A and armed T-CH-1B prototypes had confirmed the advantages of the latter

Opposite, left: A Polish An-2 biplane on floats, one of many possible configurations.

Opposite, above right: The An-12BP is still a standard airlifter with many countries.

Below: AIDC AT-3 tandem two-seat trainer

AIDC (Aero Industry Development Centre) Ching-kuo

(Taiwan)

Type: lightweight air-defence fighter with a secondary anti-ship capability

Accommodation: pilot on a zero/zero ejector seat

Armament (fixed): one 20-mm M61A1 Vulcan rotary-barrel cannon with an unrevealed number of rounds

Armament (disposable): this is carried on an unrevealed number of hardpoints up to an unrevealed maximum weight; typical stores are four Sky Sword 1/2 AAMs, or three Hsiung Feng II anti-ship missiles and two Sky Sword 1/2 AAMs, and an assortment of cannon pods, rocket pods, bombs and ASMs

Electronics and operational equipment: communication and navigation equipment, plus Golden Dragon 53 multi-mode radar, an Electro-Optical Industries of Israel HUD, Litton LN-39 INS, and other items

Powerplant and fuel system: two 8,500-lb (3856-kg) afterburning thrust Garrett TFE1042 turbofans, and a total internal fuel capacity of unrevealed quantity plus provision for drop tanks; no provision for inflight refuelling

Performance: maximum speed Mach 1·2+ at high altitude

Weights: not revealed

Dimensions: not revealed

Variant

Ching-kuo: developed as the Indigenous Defence Fighter but now named after the late President Chiang Ching-kuo (the son of Generalissimo Chiang Kai-shek), this lightweight air-defence fighter was developed in Taiwan to reduce the country's susceptibility to politically motivated import problems such as that which prevented the island republic's purchase of the Northrop F-20 Tigershark; first appearing late in 1988 and flying in June 1989, the type is of of the relaxed-stability type with a Lear Astronics fly-by-wire flight-control system and is due to enter service in the early 1990; later models will have engines uprated to about 12,000-lb (5443-kg) afterburning thrust, resulting in a maximum speed of between Mach 1·6 and Mach 1·8; the main sensor is the Green Dragon 53 radar, a local adaptation of the General Electric APG-67(V) with feature of the Westinghouse APG-66 to create an air- and sea-search radar with a range of 150 km (93·2 miles) and look-down/shoot-down capability

Antonov An-2 'Colt'

(USSR)

Type: short-range utility STOL transport aeroplane

Accommodation: flightcrew of two, and 12 passengers or 1300 kg (2,866 lb) of freight in the cabin

Armament (fixed): none

Armament (disposable): none

Electronics and operational equipment: communication and navigation equipment

Powerplant and fuel system: one 746-kW (1,000-hp) Shvetsov ASh-62R or PZL Kalisz ASz-62IR piston engine, and a total internal fuel capacity of 1200 litres (264 Imp gal); no provision for drop tanks or inflight-refuelling

Performance: maximum speed 258 km/h (160 mph) at 1750 m (5,740 ft); cruising speed 190 km/h (118 mph); initial climb rate 210 m (690 ft) per minute; service ceiling 4400 m (14,435 ft); range 900 km (559 miles) with a 500-kg (1,102-lb) payload

Weights: empty 3450 kg (7,606 lb); maximum take-off 5500 kg (12,125 lb)

Dimensions: span 18·18 m (59 ft 8·5 in); length 12·74 m (41 ft 9·5 in); height 6·10 m (20 ft 0 in); wing area 71·60 m² (770·72 sq ft)

Variants

An-2 'Colt': though apparently an anachronism is these days of advanced-technology aircraft, the An-2 biplane has technically obsolete features such as a piston engine and fixed landing gear but is still a very worthy type in the STOL utility transport role for which it was designed, especially in those less-advanced areas of the world where the communist creed predominates; the type first flew in prototype form in August 1947, and more than 5,000 examples had been produced in the USSR by 1960, when continued production was switched to Poland's WSK-PZL Mielec, which produced another 10,000 by the end of 1984 as production began finally to tail off; the type has been produced in a number of subvariants over the years, the more notable types optimized for the aerial survey, air ambulance, general-purpose transport and parachuting roles

Shijiazhuang Y-5: An-2 built in China since 1957 to the extent of 1,500 or more aircraft; the Chinese are also developing a turboprop-powered model analogous to the Soviet An-3 development

Antonov An-12BP 'Cub-A'

(USSR)

Type: medium-range tactical transport aeroplane

Accommodation: flightcrew of five plus a rear gunner, and 100 paratroops or 20000 kg (44,092 lb) of freight in the hold

Armament (fixed): two 23-mm NR-23 cannon in the rear turret

Armament (disposable): none

Electronics and operational equipment: communication and navigation equipment, and as a retrofit flare/decoy launchers

Powerplant and fuel system: four 2985-kW (4,004-shp) Ivchyenko AI-20K turboprops, and a total internal fuel capacity of 18100 litres (3,981 Imp gal); no provision for drop tanks or inflight refuelling

Performance: maximum speed 775 km/h (482 mph) at high altitude; cruising speed 670 km/h (416 mph); initial climb rate 600 m (1,970 ft) per minute; service ceiling 10,200 m (33,465 ft); range 3600 km (2,237 miles) with maximum payload or 5700 km (3,542 miles) with maximum fuel

Weights: empty 28,000 kg (61,729 lb); normal take-off 51,100 kg (121,473 lb); maximum take-off 61,000 kg (134,482 lb)

Dimensions: span 38·00 m (124 ft 8·1 in); length 33·10 m (108 ft 7·1 in); height 10·53 m (34 ft 6·6 in); wing area 121·70 m² (1,310·0 sq ft)

Variants

An-12BP 'Cub': designed in the mid-1950s on the basis of the An-10 airliner, the An-12 was first

flown in prototype form during 1958, and production amounted to some 900 aircraft all featuring the high wing and upswept tail designed to provide an unobstructed and easily loaded hold in a fuselage supported for rough-field operations on main landing gear units retracting into fuselage blister fairings; the primary roles of the type in air force service are tactical transport and airborne movement

An-12 'Cub-A': Elint variant with revised interior and small exterior modifications such as blade antennae in the area of the flight deck and small pressurized compartment

An-12 'Cub-B': Elint derivative of the standard aircraft for service with the Soviet naval air arm; these aircraft (perhaps 10 in all) sport four blister fairings under the forward and centre fuselage, and also feature a number of blade antennae; the specific role of the type is the collection of radiation intelligence about Western warships, the hold being provided with receivers, analyzers, recording and (probably) data-link equipment for realtime communication of findings to ship and shore bases

An-12 'Cub-C': ECM variant of the standard aircraft with a solid ogival tailcone in place of the tail turret; the type carries several tonnes of electronic equipment including palletized jammers (operating in at least five and possibly 10 wavebands) and chaff dispensers

An-12 'Cub-D': Elint and ECM variant of the standard aircraft with two large blister fairings extending side-by-side from the nose to the main landing gear fairings; the type also possesses active jammers and decoy systems

An-12 'Cub-?': type fitted with a palletized command system in the hold, providing Soviet forces with excellent battlefield command capabilities in areas where conventional radio equipment cannot function adequately because of terrain limitations

Shaanxi Transport Aircraft Factory Y-8: version of the An-12BP produced in China largely for tactical transport, though roles comparable to those of the Soviet aircraft are almost certainly planned as production steps up; the prototype flew in 1974, and full-scale production was launched in 1980 after flight trials had confirmed the viability of the type with its slightly modified design (a more pointed nose increasing overall length by about 0·91 m/3 ft) and the 3170-kW (4,252-shp) Shanghai Wojiang-6 turboprops developed from the Soviet Ivchyenko AI-20K units; the type has also been developed for maritime patrol with the nose of the Harbin H-6 (Tu-16 'Badger'), Litton Canada APS-504 search radar and an INS of Western origins

Antonov An-14 'Clod'

(USSR)

Type: short-range STOL utility transport aeroplane

Accommodation: pilot and one passenger on the flightdeck, and seven passengers or 1590 kg (3,505 lb) of freight in the cabin

Armament (fixed): none

Armament (disposable): none

Electronics and operational equipment: communication and navigation equipment

Powerplant and fuel system: two 225-kW (302-hp) Ivchyenko AI-14RF piston engines, and a total internal fuel capacity of 383 litres (84 Imp gal); no provision for drop tanks or inflight refuelling

Performance: maximum speed 220 km/h (137 mph) at 1000 m (3,280 ft); cruising speed 180 km/h (112 mph) at 2000 m (6,560 ft); initial climb rate 305 m (1,000 ft) per minute; service ceiling 5200 m (17,060 ft); range 650 km (404 miles) with maximum payload; ferry range 800 km (497 miles)

Weights: empty 2600 kg (5,732 lb); maximum take-off 3630 kg (8,003 lb)

Dimensions: span 22·00 m (72 ft 3 in); length 11·44 m (37 ft 6·5 in); height 4·63 m (15 ft 2·5 in); wing area 39·72 m² (427·56 sq ft)

Variant

An-14 'Clod': designed in the mid-1950s, the An-14 first flew in prototype form during March 1958; production was undertaken between 1965 and 1975, some 300 aircraft being produced

Right: The An-22 is a mainstay of the USSR's long-range heavy airlift capability.

Below: The An-14 is a simple utility transport.

Opposite: The An-24V serves both civil and military transport needs in the USSR.

Antonov An-22 'Cock'

(USSR)

Type: long-range strategic freight transport aeroplane

Accommodation: flightcrew of five or six, and 29 passengers plus 80,000 kg (176,367 lb) of freight in the hold

Armament (fixed): none

Armament (disposable): none

Electronics and operational equipment: communication and navigation equipment

Powerplant and fuel system: four 11,185-kW (15,000-shp) Kuznetsov NK-12MA turboprops, and a total internal fuel capacity of 53,875 litres (11,850 Imp gal); no provision for drop tanks or inflight refuelling

Performance: maximum speed 740 km/h (460 mph) at optimum altitude; cruising speed 520 km/h (323 mph); service ceiling 7500 m (24,605 ft); range 5000 km (3,107 miles) with maximum payload, or 10,950 km (6,804 miles) with a 45000-kg (99,206-lb) payload and maximum fuel

Weights: empty 114,000 kg (251,323 lb); maximum take-off 250,000 kg (551,146 lb)

Dimensions: span 64·40 m (211 ft 4 in); length 57·90 m (189 ft 11·5 in); height 12·53 m (41 ft 1·5 in); wing area 345·00 m² (3,713·67 sq ft)

Variant

An-22 'Cock': developed primarily for resources-exploitation tasks in Siberia, the An-22 was in its time the world's largest aircraft; the type first flew in February 1965, and is characterized by its large unobstructed hold with access via a rear ramp, and by its multi-wheel landing gear to provide good soft-field performance in association with the 'blown' double-slotted flaps in the slipstream of the propellers of the four great turboprop engines; production ended in 1974 after some 100 aircraft had been made, Aeroflot and the Soviet air force transport force each receiving about equal numbers

Antonov An-24RT 'Coke'

(USSR)

Type: short-range utility freight transport aeroplane

Accommodation: flightcrew of five, and 5700 kg (12,566 lb) of freight in the hold

Armament (fixed): none

Armament (disposable): none

Electronics and operational equipment: communication and navigation equipment

Powerplant and fuel system: two 1900-kW (2,548-shp) Ivchyenko AI-24A turboprops plus one 900-kg (1,984-lb) thrust Tumanskii RU-19-300 auxiliary turbojet in the starboard nacelle, and a total internal fuel capacity of 5550 litres (1,220 Imp gal); no provision for drop tanks or inflight refuelling

Performance: cruising speed 450 km/h (280 mph) at 6000 m (19,685 ft); initial climb rate 205 m (675 ft) per minute; service ceiling 9000 m (29,530 ft); range 640 km (397 miles) with maximum payload; ferry range 3000 km (1,864 miles)

Weights: empty 14,725 kg (32,32,463 lb); maximum take-off 21,800 kg (48,060 lb)

Dimensions: span 29·20 m (95 ft 9·5 in); length 23·53 m (77 ft 2·5 in); height 8·32 m (27 ft 3·5 in); wing area 74·98 m² (807·10 sq ft)

Variants

An-24V Series I 'Coke': first flown in December 1959 as the precursor of an important twin-turboprop transport family to supplant the Ilyushin Il-14 series, the An-24V Series I has accommodation for 28 to 40 passengers and entered service in October 1962 with 1900-kW (2,548-shp) Ivchyenko AI-24 turboprops

An-24V Series II 'Coke': improved version with accommodation for 52 passengers and introduced in 1967 with water-injected AI-24A turboprops plus a TG-16 gas turbine APU in the starboard nacelle for independent starting

An-24RV 'Coke': development of the An-24V Series II with a 900-kg (1,984-lb) thrust Tumanskii RU-16-300 auxiliary turbojet (instead of the APU and designed to provide extra take-off thrust as well as APU capability) and two 2103-kW (2,820-shp) AI-24T turboprops

An-24T 'Coke': dedicated freighter version of the An-24V Series II with a freight door in the underside of the rear fuselage, and a freight-handling sstem in the cabin for a total payload of 4610 kg (10,163 lb)

An-24RT 'Coke': freighter version of the An-24RV with the same provisions as the An-24T

Xian Aircraft Company Y-7: An-24 derivative built in China with a wider fuselage, wing span increased to 29·20 m (95 ft 9·5 in), different avionics and 2080-kW (2,790-shp) Harbin Wojiang-5A-21 (Ivchyenko AI-24A) turboprops; the type has a flightcrew of five and accommodation for 48 passengers or 4700 kg (10,362 lb) of freight carried at a maximum speed of 478 km/h (297 mph) at 4000 m (13,125 ft) over a range of 910 km (565 miles); improved versions are the **Y7-100** with accommodation for a flightcrew of three and 52 passengers or 5500 kg (12,125 lb) plus winglets for reduced fuel burn and improved performance, the **Y7-200** with further fuel-burn reductions, and the reduced-weight **Y7-300**

Xian Aircraft Company Y-8: Chinese tactical transport version of the Y-7 with a rear ramp; this variant was scheduled to fly in 1989, and amongst the revealed data are a payload of 38 troops or 39 paratroops or 24 litters, and a maximum take-off weight of 24,000 kg (52,910 lb) with a 5000-kg (11,023-lb) payload; the powerplant comprises two Wojiang-5A turboprops plus a turbojet booster, the wings are fitted with winglets, weather radar is installed in the nose, and modern avionics are standard

Antonov An-26B 'Curl'

(USSR)

Type: short-range utility and tactical transport aeroplane

Accommodation: flightcrew of five, and 40 troops, or 24 litters and one attendant, or 5500 kg (12,125 lb) of freight in the cabin

Armament (fixed): none

Armament (disposable): none

Electronics and operational equipment: communication and navigation equipment

Powerplant and fuel system: two 2100-kW (2,817-shp) Ivchyenko AI-24VT turboprops plus one 800-kg (1,765-lb) thrust Tumanskii RU-19A-300 auxiliary turbojet in the starboard nacelle, and a total internal fuel weight of 5500 kg (12,125 lb); no provision for drop tanks or inflight refuelling

Performance: cruising speed 440 km/h (273 mph) at 6000 m (19,685 ft); initial climb rate 480 m (1,575 ft) per minute; service ceiling 7500 m (24,605 ft); range 1100 km (684 miles) with maximum payload; ferry range 2550 km (1,584 miles)

Weights: empty 15,020 kg (33,113 lb); maximum take-off 24,000 kg (52,911 lb)

Dimensions: span 29·20 m (95 ft 9·5 in); length 23·80 m (78 ft 1 in); height 8·575 m (28 ft 1·5 in); wing area 74·98 m² (807·10 sq ft)

Variants

An-26 'Curl': first seen by the West in 1969, the An-26 is clearly a freighter derivative of the An-24 series though radically redesigned around the rear fuselage to permit the incorporation a full-width door/ramp in its underside; the type also introduced a pressurized hold; the rear ramp can be swung under the fuselage to provide clear access to the hold from the beds of trucks, and to permit simple airdropping of embarked loads; other features are a 2000-kg (4,409-lb) capacity winch on a track running along the length of the hold, a floor-mounted conveyor belt, and tip-up seats for a maximum of 40 paratroops; the type can also be outfitted for the carriage of 24 litters

An-26B 'Curl': improved version of 1981 with revised handling arrangements so that two men can deal with three pallets weighing 5500 kg (12,125 lb)

An-30 'Clank': this 1974 derivative is the dedicated aerial survey member of the An-24/An-26 family based generally on the fuselage of the An-24 with the flying surfaces and powerplant of the An-26; the main modification is a revised forward fuselage with a raised flightdeck leaving the extensively glazed nose for the navigator; there are five camera ports (two of them oblique), and the fuselage has a darkroom and film storage facilities

Xian Aircraft Company Y-8: first flown early in 1989, this is a Chinese development of the An-26 retaining as much commonality as possible with

Antonov An-32/AI-20M 'Cline'

the Y-7 derivative of the An-24 including the wing (but fitted with drag-reducing winglets), front fuselage and Wojiang-5A turboprops; the type has an auxiliary turbojet for good field performance in hot-and-high conditions, and in addition to a crew of five can carry 38 troops, or 39 paratroops, or 24 litters plus one attendant, or 5500 kg (12,125 lb) of internal freight supplemented by 2000 kg (4,409 lb) more freight carried on fuselage attachment points; the type has empty and maximum take-off weights of 15,400 and 24,230 kg (33,951 and 53,417 lb) respectively, and its dimensions include a span of 29·20 m (95 ft 9·5 in) and a length of 23·98 m (78 ft 8 in); performance data include a cruising speed of 445 km/h (276 mph) at 6000 m (19,685 ft) and a range of 1038 km (645 miles) with maximum payload

Below: The An-26 freighter version of the An-24 also serves in civil and military roles.

(USSR)
Type: short/medium-range transport aeroplane
Accommodation: flightcrew of five, and 39 troops, or 30 paratroops, or 24 litters and one attendant, or 6000 kg (13,228 lb) of freight in the hold
Armament (fixed): none
Armament (disposable): none
Electronics and operational equipment: communication and navigation equipment
Powerplant and fuel system: two 3860-kW (5,177-shp) Ivchyenko AI-20M turboprops, and a total internal fuel weight of 5500 kg (12,125 lb); no provision for drop tanks or inflight refuelling
Performance: cruising speed 510 km/h (317 mph) at 8000 m (26,245 ft); service ceiling 9500 m (31,170 ft); range 800 km (497 miles) with maximum payload; ferry range 2200 km (1,367 miles) with maximum fuel
Weights: empty 16,000 kg (35,273 lb); maximum take-off 27,000 kg (59,524 lb)
Dimensions: span 29·20 m (95 ft 9·5 in); length 23·80 m (78 ft 1 in); height 8·75 m (28 ft 8·5 in); wing area 74·98 m² (807·10 sq ft)

Variants

An-32/AI-20M 'Cline': first flown in 1977, the An-32 is another derivative of the An-24 and An-26 series, but in this instance optimized for maximum performance under hot-and-high conditions; to this end the wings and Ivchyenko-designed powerplant are extensively modified, the former having automatic leading-edge slats and triple-slotted trailing-edge flaps, and the latter being the AI-20M turboprop with 3·9-m (12·8-ft) diameter propellers for use in moderate-temperature areas
An-32/AI-20DM: version with 3865-kW (5,184-shp) AI-20DM and 4·7-m (15·4-ft) diameter propellers for better performance in high-temperature areas; to provide adequate tip clearance the engines are raised to positions above the wings; the type can operate from airfields as high as 4500 m (14,765 ft), and is operated by the Indian air force under the name **Sutlej**

Above: An Antonov An-32/AI-20DM version of the Indian Air Force

Antonov An-74 'Coaler-B'

(USSR)

Type: short/medium-range STOL utility transport aeroplane

Accommodation: flightcrew of four, and 32 passengers, or 24 litters and one attendant, or 10,000 kg (22,046 lb) of freight (reduced to 3500 kg/7,717 lb for STOL operations) in the hold

Armament (fixed): none

Armament (disposable): none

Electronics and operational equipment: communication and navigation equipment

Powerplant and fuel system: two 6500-kg (14,330-lb) thrust Lotarev D-36 non-afterburning turbofans, and a total internal fuel capacity of unrevealed quantity; no provision for drop tanks or inflight refuelling

Performance: maximum speed 705 km/h (438 mph) at optimum altitude; cruising speed 550 km/h (342 mph) at 10,000 m (32,810 ft); service ceiling 10,000 m (332,810 ft); range 1150 km (715 miles) with maximum payload or 4200 km (2,610 miles) with a 1500-kg (3,307-lb) payload

Weights: empty not revealed; maximum take-off 34,500 kg (76,058 lb)

Dimensions: span 31·89 m (104 ft 7·5 in); length 28·07 m (92 ft 1·25 in); height 8·75 m (28 ft 8·5 in); wing area not revealed

Variants

An-72 'Coaler-A': designed as the STOL counterpart to the An-24 and An-28, this first flew in 1977; the concept used to provide STOL performance is upper-surface blowing with the two turbofans exhausting over the upper surface of the wings and flaps; to keep the tailplane out of this disturbed airflow a T-tail is fitted on a rear fuselage derived conceptually from that of the An-26; the An-72 is believed to have been the pre-production variant with wings of 25·83 m (84 ft

A fascinating type using upper-surface blowing to secure STOL field performance, the An-72 paved the way for the definitive An-74 with greater span and length.

9 in) span and outer panels of constant taper, and a fuselage length of 26·576 m (87 ft 2·25 in)

An-74 'Coaler-B': production was slow to get under way, but by the mid-1980s the type was beginning to get into useful service as a STOL tactical transport with the Soviet air arms; the full-production model is the An-74 with its fuselage stretched by just under 1·50 m (4 ft 11 in) and fitted with nose radar, provision for greater maximum payload, alternative wheel/ski landing gear making arctic operations feasible, and a revised wing of 6·06 m (19 ft 10·6 in) greater span; the type also features extensive de-icing capability and advanced all-weather avionics

An-74 'Coaler-C': intended for civil as well as military operations, this derivative of the 'Coaler-B' has a flightdeck crew of two, less advanced navigation instrumentation, conventional landing gear, and accommodation for 68 persons in austere removable seating along the cabin sides, centre and even the inside of the ramp; with a maximum take-off weight of 33,000 kg (72,751 lb), this model has ranges of 860 km (534 miles) with maximum payload or 5000 km (3,106 miles) with maximum fuel

An-72A 'Coaler-D': upgraded version of the 'Coaler-C' with D-36 turbofans each delivering 1000 kg (2,205 lb) more thrust

An-74 'Madcap': introduced in 1987, this AEW aeroplane is based on the An-74 STOL transport; the large radome is mounted on top of an extensively modified and swept-forward vertical tail, and Western analysts are probably correct in assessing the relationship of the An-74 to the Ilyushin Il-76 'Mainstay' as basically identical to that of the Grumman E-2 Hawkeye to the Boeing E-3 Sentry, though it remains to be seen if the 'Madcap' will also have a naval role on the USSR's new generation of conventional aircraft-carriers

Antonov An-124 'Condor'

Antonov An-225 Mriya

(USSR)
Type: long-range strategic heavy transport aeroplane
Accommodation: flightcrew of six (with a full relief crew accommodated behind the flight-deck), up to 88 passengers in a cabin above the hold and aft of the wing, and 150,000 kg (330,693 lb) of freight in the hold
Armament (fixed): none
Armament (disposable): none
Electronics and operational equipment: communication and navigation equipment including radar, all-weather avionics and triple INSs
Powerplant and fuel system: four 23,425-kg (51,642-lb) thrust Lotarev D-18T non-afterburning turbofans, and a total internal fuel capacity of unrevealed quantity; no provision for drop tanks or inflight refuelling
Performance: maximum cruising speed 865 km/h (537 mph) at 12,000 m (39,370 ft); cruising speed 800 km/h (497 mph); range with maximum payload 4500 km (2,796 miles) or with maximum fuel 16,500 km (10,253 miles)
Weights: empty not revealed; maximum take-off 405,000 kg (892,872 lb)

Dimensions: span 73·30 m (240 ft 5·8 in); length 69·50 m (228 ft 0·2 in); height 22·00 m (72 ft 2·1 in); wing area 628·0 m² (6,759·6 sq ft)

Variant
An-124 'Condor': designed in the 1970s as successor to the same bureau's An-22 in the strategic airlift role, the An-124 is sized to be able to lift a whole SS-20 missile system in a single load; the type entered service in 1986 and is a truly prodigious machine of typical transport configuration with a hold 36·0 m (118·1 ft) long, 6·4 m (21 ft) wide and 4·4 m (14·4 ft) high; the hold ceiling has two longitudinal travelling gantries each rated at 10,000 kg (22,046 lb) and fitted with two 5000-kg (11,023-lb) capacity transverse moving winches; like the comparable Lockheed C-5 Galaxy, the An-124 is designed for through loading with a rear ramp and an upward-hinged nose

Below: The An-124 exceeds the An-22 in payload, and also offers higher performance and the economy of turbofan power.

Bottom: The An-225 is the world's largest aeroplane, and a truly prodigious lifter.

(USSR)
Type: long-range strategic heavy transport aeroplane
Accommodation: flightcrew of six, and 250,000 kg (551,150 lb) of freight in the hold
Armament (fixed): none
Armament (disposable): none
Electronics and operational equipment: communication and navigation equipment including weather radar, all-weather avionics and triple INS
Powerplant and fuel system: six 23,425-kg (51,642-lb) thrust Lotarev D-18T non-afterburning turbofans, and a total internal fuel capacity of unrevealed quantity; no provision for drop tanks or inflight refuelling
Performance: maximum cruising speed 850 km/h (528 mph) at optimum altitude; normal cruising speed 700 km/h (435 mph); range 4500 km (2,796 miles) with maximum payload
Weights: empty not revealed; maximum take-off 600,000 kg (1,322,760 lb)
Dimensions: span 86·0 m (282 ft 1·8 in); length 84·0 m (275 ft 7 in); height not revealed; wing area not revealed

Variant
An-225 Mriya: the world's largest aeroplane, the Mriya (dream) is a truly prodigious heavy-lift type designed to carry massive loads in the fuselage hold, or outsize loads (including the Soviet space shuttle) weighing up to 70,000 kg (154,321 lb) in a 'piggy-back' location above the fuselage; this latter consideration led to the design of the tailplane with its widely separated endplate vertical surfaces; the outer wing panels appear to be the wings of the An-124 complete with podded engines, and these are attached to a centre section (complete with two more engines) that is part of the new fuselage, which has a hold approximately 43 m (141 ft 1 in) long, 6·4 m (21 ft 0 in) wide and 4·4 m (14 ft 5·25 in) high; the landing gear comprises two 14-wheel main gear units and two twin-wheel nose units, the multi-wheel arrangement being designed to spread the load and so prevent damage to standard runways; the type first flew in December 1988, one of its key capabilities being the ability to operate from 1000-m (1,095-yard) runways; there is little doubt that the An-225 was designed for the civil, space and resources-exploitation freight roles, but it clearly possesses a secondary importance for military strategic freighting

ASTA (Aerospace Technologies of Australia) Nomad N22 Mission Master

(Australia)
Type: short-range STOL utility transport aeroplane
Accommodation: flightcrew of one or two, and 14 passengers or 3,600 lb (1633 kg) of freight in the cabin
Armament (fixed): none
Armament (disposable): this is carried on four hardpoints (two under each wing, each rated at 500 lb/227 kg) up to a maximum weight of 2,000 lb (907 kg); typical weapons are light bombs, rocket pods and machine-gun pods
Electronics and operational equipment: communication and navigation equipment
Powerplant and fuel system: two 400-shp (298-kW) Allison 250-B17B turboprops, and a total internal fuel capacity of 224 Imp gal (1018 litres) plus provision for 74 Imp gal (336 litres) of ferry fuel in optional tiptanks; no provision for inflight refuelling
Performance: maximum speed 193 mph (309 km/h) at sea level; cruising speed 161 mph (259 km/h) at sea level; initial climb rate 1,460 ft (445 m) per minute; service ceiling 22,000 ft (6705 m); range 688 miles (1074 km) with standard fuel and 907 miles (1460 km) with ferry tanks
Weights: empty 4,741 lb (2150 kg); maximum take-off 8,950 lb (4060 kg)
Dimensions: span 54 ft 0 in (16·46 m); length 41 ft 2·4 in (12·56 m); height 18 ft 1·5 in (5·52 m); wing area 324·0 sq ft (30·10 m²)

Variants

Nomad N22 and N24: this is the basic STOL model developed by GAF (Government Aircraft Factories) as a commercial model but also been bought by some air arms; the type is available as the N22 with accommodation for 12/13 passengers or an equivalent freight load, and as the N24 with the fuselage stretched by 3·75 ft (1·14 m) to carry 17 passengers or an equivalent freight load; GAF was later absorbed into ASTA, which thus has responsibility for support of the Nomad series

Nomad N22 Mission Master: utility military transport derived from the N22 series
Nomad N22 Search Master B: coastal patrol model based on the Mission Master but fitted with Bendix RDR-1400 search radar to scan 60° to each side of the flightpath
Nomad N22 Search Master L: improved version of the Search Master B with Litton APS-504 radar with its larger antenna in a 'guppy' radome under the nose for 360° search coverage; in a typical sortie the Search Master L can search an area 325% greater than the Search Master B; the type is available in two variants, the **Search Master I** with APS-504(V)2 radar, and the **Search Master II** with upgraded APS-504(V)5 radar plus a FLIR sensor under the belly

Below: The Nomad N22 Search Master L is a modest but effective short-range maritime patroller with search radar in an undernose 'guppy' radome.

Beechcraft C-12A Huron

(USA)

Type: short/medium-range utility light transport aeroplane

Accommodation: flightcrew of one or two, and 13 passengers or freight in the cabin

Armament (fixed): none

Armament (disposable): none

Electronics and operational equipment: communication and navigation equipment

Powerplant and fuel system: two 750-shp (559-kW) Pratt & Whitney Canada PT6A-38 turboprops, and a total internal fuel capacity of 386 US gal (1461 litres) plus provision for 158 US gal (598 litres) of ferry fuel; no provision for drop tanks or inflight refuelling

Performance: maximum speed 303 mph (488 km/h) at 15,000 ft (4570 m); cruising speed 272 mph (438 km/h) at 30,000 ft (9145 m); service ceiling 29,200 ft (8900 m); range 1,825 miles (2937 km)

Weights: empty 7,800 lb (3538 kg); maximum take-off 12,500 lb (5670 kg)

Dimensions: span 54 ft 6 in (16·61 m); length 43 ft 9 in (13·34 m); height 15 ft 0 in (4·57 m); wing area 303·00 sq ft (28·15 m²)

Variants

C-12A Huron: this was the first version of the Super King Air A200 light transport to be ordered by the US forces; the Model 200 first flew in October 1972 as a much improved King Air 100 with a T-tail, greater span and fuel capacity, more powerful engines and a higher cabin pressurization differential, all combining to increase range and cruising altitude; the C-12A is a utility transport for the US Air Force (30 aircraft) and US Army (60 aircraft), the examples operated by the latter having been retrofitted with 850-shp (634-kW)

Pratt & Whitney Canada PT6A-41 turboprops

UC-12B: version of the Model A200C for the US Navy and Marine Corps (66 aircraft) with PT6A-41s, high-flotation landing gear and a cargo door

C-12C Huron: US Army version (14 aircraft) delivered with PT6A-41 turbopropsv

C-12D Huron: upgraded C-12C for the US Army (50 aircraft) with a cargo door and tip tanks, the latter increasing span to 55 ft 6 in (16·92 m)

RC-12D Huron: special-mission version of the C-12D designed for battlefield Sigint in the South Korean and European theatres with the advanced USD-9(V)2 Improved Guardrail V Sigint and direction-finding equipment including signal-processing gear, an ARW-83(V)5 secure data-link, ALQ-136 and ALQ-162 defensive ECM pods at the wingtips increasing span to 57 ft 10 in (17·63 m) and antennae above/below the wings; the type also features the ALQ-156 missile detection system and is powered by PT6A-41 turboprops

UC-12D Huron: version of the C-12D for the US Air Force and Air National Guard

C-12E Huron: US Air Force C-12A utility aircraft retrofitted with PT6A-42 turboprops

C-12F Huron: operational support version of the Model B200C for the US Air Force, powered by PT6A-42 turboprops and able to carry a 2,500-lb (1134-kg) payload over a range of 2,400 miles (3862 km) at maximum and cruising speeds of 336 and 330 mph (541 and 531 km/h) respectively

UC-12F: US Navy equivalent of the C-12F

RC-12H Huron: variant similar to the RC-12D but with the Guardrail Common Sensor and a maximum take-off weight of 15,000 lb (6804 kg); six aircraft were delivered in 1985

C-12J Huron: Air National Guard military version of the Model 1900 Airliner, a stretched develop-

ment of the Super King Air 200 for the carriage of up to 19 passengers or 5,300 lb (2404 kg) of freight at a maximum cruising speed of 295 mph (475 km/h) at 8,000 ft (2440 m) on two 820-kW (1,100-shp) PT6A-65B turboprops; the type spans 54 ft 5·75 in (16·61 m) and is 57 ft 10 in (17·63 m) long, and at a maximum weight of 16,600 lb (7530 kg) has a range of 915 miles; Model 1900 Airliners are also operated by Egypt and Taiwan

RU-21J Huron: despite its designation this was the first model for the US services, the type being accepted by the US Army in 1974 for the battle-field Elint role in the 'Cefly Lancer' programme; the aircraft have a maximum take-off weight of 15,000 lb (6804 kg) and carry a mass of electronic equipment similar to (but not as advanced as) that of the RC-12D

RC-12K Huron: classified electronic warfare derivative of the C-12D delivered from the spring of 1988 with PT6A-67 turboprops, a maximum take-off weight of 16,000 lb (7257 kg) and the Guardrail Common Sensor electronic suite

RU-12K Huron: updated version of the RU-12D with more efficient PT6A-42 turboprops

UC-12M: US Navy equivalent of the C-12F with more advanced equipment standards

Maritime Patrol B200T: coastal patrol aircraft based on the Super King Air B200 with high-flotation landing gear and optional tip tanks; there is a choice of two search radars (each with its antenna in a ventral radome for 360° coverage), FLIR, low-light-level TV, advanced navigation systems and other modern systems; the type has a patrol range of 2,060 miles (3315 km)

Super King Air 200T: special high-altitude photographic and weather reconnaisaance type for France with Wild RC-10 cameras, Doppler navigation and optional tip tanks

Beechcraft T-34C-1

(USA)

Type: flying and weapon trainer with a secondary FAC and COIN capability

Accommodation: pupil and instructor in tandem

Armament (fixed): none

Armament (disposable): this is carried on four hardpoints (two under each wing, with the inner units each rated at 600 lb/272 kg and the outer units at 300 lb/136 kg) up to a maximum weight of 1,200 lb (544 kg); weapons that can be carried include 250-lb (113-kg) bombs, incendiary bombs, pods for 7·62-mm (0·3-in) Miniguns and 2·75-in (69·85-mm) rocket pods

Electronics and operational equipment: communication and navigation equipment, plus a Chicago Aerial CA-513 reflector sight

Below left: The C-12A is the military counterpart of the Super King Air A200.

Below: T-34C flying and weapon trainers of the Peruvian naval air arm.

Powerplant and fuel system: one 715-shp (533-kW) Pratt & Whitney Canada PT6A-25 turboprop flat-rated to 550 shp (410 kW), and a total internal fuel capacity of 129 US gal (488 litres); no provision for drop tanks or inflight refuelling

Performance: maximum speed 221 mph (355 km/h) at 17,000 ft (5180 m); initial climb rate 880 ft (268 m) per minute; range 115 miles (185 km) on a FAC mission with 2 hours 36 minutes over the target or 345 miles (555 km) on an attack mission with four stores

Weights: empty 2,630 lb (1193 kg); normal take-off 4,300 lb (1950 kg); maximum take-off 5,500 lb (2495 kg)

Dimensions: span 33 ft 4 in (10·16 m); length 28 ft 8·5 in (8·75 m); height 9 ft 11 in (3·02 m); wing area 179·9 sq ft (16·71 m²)

Variants

T-34A: trainer developed from the Model 35 Bonanza as the Beech Model 45 in response to a USAF requirement; the type first flew in December 1948 and was adopted as the USAF's primary

trainer in 1953; the type is powered by a 225-hp (168-kW) Continental O-470-13 piston engine, has a maximum take-off weight of 2,950 lb (1315 kg) and possesses a maximum speed of 189 mph (304 km/h)

T-34B Mentor: US Navy equivalent of the T-34A with the 225-hp (168-kW) O-470-4 engine

T-34C: much improved turbine-engined derivative produced in the period between 1977 and 1988 in response to a US Navy requirement for an updated model with considerably improved performance but greater reliability and fuel economy provided by a 715-shp (533-kW) PT6A-25 turboprop flat-rated to 400 shp (298 kW); the YT-34C prototype first flew in September 1973 and production has amounted to 353 aircraft; the export version is designated **Turbine Mentor 34C**

T-34C-1: privately developed weapon training, FAC and light attack version; this has four underwing hardpoints for a wide diversity of armament, and useful sales were made to a number of countries mainly in Africa and South America

Beechcraft U-21A Ute

(USA)

Type: short/medium-range utility light transport aeroplane

Accommodation: flightcrew of two, and 10 troops, or six staff, or three litters and three seated casualties plus an attendant, or 3,000 lb (1361 kg) of freight in the cabin

Armament (fixed): none

Armament (disposable): none

Electronics and operational equipment: communication and navigation equipment

Powerplant and fuel system: two 550-shp (410-kW) Pratt & Whitney Canada PT6A-20 turboprops, and a total internal fuel capacity of 384 US gal (1454 litres)

Performance: maximum speed 249 mph (401 km/h) at 11,000 ft (3355 m); maximum cruising speed 245 mph (394 km/h) at 10,000 ft (3050 m); initial climb rate 2,000 ft (609 m) per minute; service ceiling 25,500 ft (7770 m); range 1,167 miles (1878 km) with maximum payload and reserves or 1,676 miles (2697 km) with maximum fuel and reserves

Weights: empty 5,464 lb (2478 kg); maximum take-off 9,650 lb (4377 kg)

Dimensions: span 45 ft 10·5 in (13·98 m); length 35 ft 6 in (10·82 m); height 14 ft 2·5 in (4·33 m); wing area 279·7 sq ft (25·98 m²)

Variants

VC-6A: VIP transport version of the civil King Air A90 for the USAF with PT6A-20 turboprops

VC-6B: improved VIP transport version of the King Air C90 with more capable pressurization; the basic type was also developed as the civil/military King Air E90 series with 680-shp (507-kW) PT6A-28 turboprops flat-rated at 550 shp (410 kW)

T-44A: advanced trainer for the US Navy based on the King Air E90 but with features of the King Air C90, and with 750-shp (559-kW) PT6A-34B turboprops flat-rated at 550 shp (410 kW)

U-21A Ute: unpressurized military utility transport developed on the basis of the fuselage of the Queen Air 65-80 combined with the wings, tail surfaces and landing gear of the King Air 65-90 series of pressurized civil light transports

EU/RU-21: highly classified series serving mainly with the US Army Security Agency for specialized Elint with advanced electronic sensors, sophisticated navigation and communication equipment, and many other modifications; known variants within this important series are the **EU-21A** electronic reconnaissance, **RU-21A** electronic reconnaissance/interception (with the ALQ-38 'Left Jab') direction-finding system), **RU-21D** revised electronic reconnaissance/interception aircraft with the same powerplant as the U-21A, the **RU-21B** and **RU-21C** electronic reconnaissance/interception aircraft with 620-shp (462-kW) PT6A-29 turboprops, and the **RU-21E** and **RU-21H** upgraded and modernized electronic reconnaissance/interception aircraft with T74-CP-700 turboprops

U-21F: USAF version of the civil King Air A100 with 680-shp (507-kW) PT6A-28 turboprops and full cabin pressurization for a crew of two and up to 13 passengers

U-21G: updated version of the U-21A, of which at least 17 have been converted to the new standard

Right: U-21A Ute of the US Army.

Opposite, top: UH-1D of the German army.

Opposite, bottom: UH-1B tactical helicopter.

Bell Model 204 (UH-1B/E Iroquois)

(USA)

Type: tactical and utility light helicopter

Accommodation: pilot and eight troops, or three litters, two seated casualties and one attendant, or 3,000 lb (1361 kg) of freight in the cabin

Armament (fixed): generally none, but two flexible 7·62-mm (0·3-in) M60 machine-guns can be installed in the cabin doors, or four fixed 7·62-mm (0·3-in) M60 machine-guns on the fuselage sides

Armament (disposable): generally none, but two packs each with 24 2·75-in (70-mm) rockets can be fixed to the fuselage sides

Electronics and operational equipment: communication and navigation equipment

Powerplant and fuel system: one 1,100-shp (820-kW) Avco Lycoming T53-L-1 turboshaft, and a total internal fuel capacity of 220 US gal (183 litres); no provision for drop tanks or inflight refuelling

Performance: maximum speed 138 mph (222 km/h) at sea level; initial climb rate 2,350 ft (716 m) per minute; service ceiling 16,700 ft (5090 m); range 212 miles (341 km)

Weights: empty 4,750 lb (2155 kg); maximum take-off 8,500 lb (3856 kg)

Dimensions: main rotor diameter 44 ft 0 in (13·41 m); length, fuselage 42 ft 7 in (12·98 m); height 14 ft 7 in (4·44 m); main rotor disc area 1,520·53 sq ft (141·26 m²)

Variants

UH-1A Iroquois: generally known as the **'Huey'** rather than by its official name, this was the initial production version of the **Model 204** utility helicopter developed as the US Army's first turbine-engined aircraft under the designation XH-40; the first prototype flew in October 1956; the production version was initially designated HU-1A and began to enter service in June 1959, initial helicopters being powered by a 770-shp (574-kW) T53-L-1A turboshaft and having accommodation for a crew of two plus six passengers or two litters, and later helicopters having the 960-shp (716-kW) T53-L-5 turboshaft for improved performance with the same load; the type could be armed with two 7·62-mm (0·3-in) flexible machine-guns and two pods each with 16 2·75-in (70-mm) rockets; production amounted to 182 helicopters, of which 14 were converted to **TH-1A** dual-control trainers

UH-1B Iroquois: updated version with the 960-shp (716-kW) T53-L-5 or later with the 1,100-shp (820-kW) T53-L-11 turboshaft driving a main rotor blade with wider-chord blades and with increased accommodation for eight troops or three litters; the type was fitted with the same armament installations as the UH-1A, and total

production was 1,014

UH-1C Iroquois: 1965 model based closely on the UH-1B but having greater fuel capacity and a 'door-hinge' main rotor with wider-chord blades for improved speed and greater manoeuvrability; production amounted to 767 helicopters

UH-1E: version of the UH-1B for the US Marine Corps with a rotor brake, special avionics, wider-chord main rotor blades, increased fuel capacity and a rescue winch; production amounted to 192 helicopters

UH-1F: utility version of the UH-1B for the USAF with the 1,100-shp (820-kW) General Electric T58-GE-3 turboshaft driving a 48-ft (14·63-m) diameter main rotor for a payload of 10 passengers or 4,000 lb (1814 kg) of freight in the missile site-support role; production amounted to 120 helicopters excluding 26 **TH-1F** dual-control trainers

HH-1K: search-and-rescue variant of the UH-1E for the US Navy, but fitted with the 1,400-shp (1044-kW) T53-L-13 turboshaft; production amounted to 27 helicopters

UH-1L: utility version of the UH-1E for the US Navy, but fitted with a T53-L-13 derated to 1,100 shp (820 shp); production amounted to eight helicopters, and there was also a **TH-1L** dual-control trainer of which 90 examples were delivered

UH-1P Iroquois: psychological warfare version of the UH-1F

Model 204B: developed as a civil machine with the 1,100-shp (820-kW) Avco Lycoming T5311A turboshaft and a 48-ft (14·63-m) diameter main rotor, this version could carry 10 passengers and useful export sales were made to several overseas air arms

Agusta (Bell) AB.204B: built between 1961 and 1974 for a number of armed forces, this is the Italian licence-built version of the Bell Model 204B utility helicopter; the type can be fitted with a number of light armament installations, and is found with main rotors of 44-ft (13·41-m) or 48-ft (14·63-m) diameter; the type is also found with the Avco Lycoming T53, General Electric T58 or Rolls-Royce Gnome H.1200 turboshaft

Agusta (Bell) AB.204AS: dedicated naval version developed in Italy, and able to handle anti-submarine and/or light anti-ship tasks from comparatively small naval platforms

Fuji (Bell) HU-1B: developed as the Fuji (Bell) Model 204B-2 in its civil form, this is the Japanese licence-built version of the Model 204B for military use with the 820-kW (1,100-shp) Kawasaki T53-K-11A turboshaft plus a tractor rather than pusher tail rotor; later helicopters have the 1044-kW (1,400-shp) T53-K-13B turboshaft

36

Bell Model 205 (UH-1H Iroquois)

Type: tactical and utility light helicopter

Accommodation: pilot and 14 troops, or six litters and one attendant, or 3,880 lb (1759 kg) of freight in the cabin

Armament (fixed): none

Armament (disposable): none

Electronics and operational equipment: communication and navigation equipment

Powerplant and fuel system: one 1,400-shp (1044-kW) Avco Lycoming T53-L-13 turboshaft, and a total internal fuel capacity of 223 US gal (844 litres) plus provision for 300 US gal (1136 litres) of ferry fuel in two internal tanks; no provision for drop tanks or inflight refuelling

Performance: maximum speed 127 mph (204 km/h) at 5,700 ft (1735 m); initial climb rate 1,600 ft (488 m) per minute; service ceiling 12,600 ft (3840 m); hovering ceiling in ground effect 13,600 ft (3840 m) and out of ground effect 4,000 ft (1220 m); range 320 miles (515 km)

Weights: empty 5,210 lb (2363 kg); normal take-off 9,039 lb (4100 kg); maximum take-off 9,500 lb (4309 kg)

Dimensions: main rotor diameter 48 ft 0 in (14·63 m); length overall, rotors turning 57 ft 9·7 in (17·62 m) and fuselage 31 ft 10·75 in (12·77 m); height 14 ft 6 in (4·42 m); main rotor disc area 1,809·56 sq ft (168·11 m²)

Variants

UH-1D Iroquois: developed with the company designation **Model 205** as a version of the Model 204 series with a stretched fuselage for greater payload, this variant first flew in August 1961 and was powered by the 1,100-shp (820-kW) T53-L-11 turboshaft for a payload of one pilot plus 12 troops, or six litters and an attendant, or 4,000 lb (1814 kg) of freight; the type also introduced greater fuel capacity and provision for auxiliary fuel; production amounted to 2,015 excluding licensed construction in West Germany by

Dornier

UH-1H Iroquois: uprated version of the UH-1D with the 1,400-shp (1044-kW) T53-L-13 turboshaft; production amounted to 5,435 helicopters, and the type was also built under licence in Taiwan by AIDC; in the early 1980s a few UH-1Hs were converted into **EH-1H** battlefield ECM helicopters with the ALQ-151 'Quick Fix IA/B' communications interception, direction-finding and jamming equipment (GLR-9 intercept receiver combined with either the TLQ-27A or more powerful TLQ-17A jammer in the IA and IB systems respectively), the APR-39(V)2 Special Electronic Mission Aircraft (SEMA) RWR receiver, the M130 chaff/flare dispenser, and the ALQ-144 IR jammer; another battlefield development of the UH-1H is the **UH-1H SOTAS** targeting helicopter fitted with a General Dynamics radar (with moving target indication facility) and a ventral antenna; some 220 surviving UH-1Hs were also converted into **UH-1V** casevac helicopters during the 1980s; some 2,700 of the US Army's initial inventory are to be maintained in service into the next century with updated features such as composite main rotor blades (glassfibre and Nomex with polyure-

thane leading edges protected over their outer sections by a stainless steel capping) and the Aerospace APR-39 RWR, Sanders ALQ-144 IR jammer and M130 chaff/flare dispenser systems

HH-1H: on-base rescue variant for the USAF with special equipment for rescue of aircrew from crashed aircraft; production amounted to 30 helicopters

CH-118: variant of the UH-1H for the Canadian Armed Forces, and originally designated CUH-1H

Model 205A-1: civil version of the basic type with a 1,400-shp (1044-kW) Avco Lycoming T5313B turboshaft derated to 1,250 shp (932 kW) and able to carry a slung load of 5,000 lb (2268 kg); many have been sold to export military customers

Agusta (Bell) AB.205: Italian licence-built version of the UH-1D/H type differing only in small details from the US pattern; from 1969 the company produced the **AB.205A-1** with detail improvements

Fuji (Bell) HU-1H: Japanese licence-built version of the UH-1H with a 1044-kW (1,400-shp) Kawasaki T53-K-13B turboshaft and a tractor rather than pusher tail rotor

Bell Model 206 (OH-58C Kiowa)

(USA)

Type: observation and scout light helicopter

Accommodation: pilot and three passengers or freight in the cabin

Armament (fixed): one M27 armament kit centred on a 7·62-mm (0·3-in) GAU-2B/A Minigun on the port side of the fuselage

Armament (disposable): none

Electronics and operational equipment: communication and navigation equipment

Powerplant and fuel system: one 420-shp (313-kW) Allison T63-A-720 turboshaft, and a total internal fuel capacity of 73 US gal (276 litres); no provision for drop tanks or inflight refuelling

Performance: maximum speed 138 mph (222 km/h) at sea level; initial climb rate 1,780 ft (543 m) per minute; service ceiling 18,900 ft (5760 m); range 305 miles (491 km) on an armed scout mission

Weights: empty 1,585 lb (719 kg); maximum take-off 3,200 lb (1451 kg)

Dimensions: main rotor diameter 35 ft 4 in (10·77 m); length overall, rotors turning 40 ft 11·7 in (10·67 m) and fuselage 32 ft 7 in (9·93 m); height 9 ft 6·5 in (2·91 m); main rotor disc area 980·52 sq ft (91·09 m²)

Variants

OH-58A Kiowa: developed during the early 1960s as the **Model 206** in response to a US Army requirement for a light observation helicopter, the OH-4 prototype first flew in December 1962, but failed to find initial selection against the Hughes OH-6; however, in 1967 the LOH competition was reopened because of difficulties with the production programme and cost of the Hughes helicopter, and the improved Model 206A this time prevailed, entering production as the OH-58A with the 317-shp (237-kW) Allison T63-A-700 turboshaft; some 2,200 examples were produced up to 1974, this variant having empty and maximum take-off weights of 1,464 and 3,000 lb (664 and 1361 kg) respectively

OH-58B: 12 OH-58 helicopters for Austria

OH-58C Kiowa: improved development of the OH-58A with flat-plate canopy for reduced glint, an uprated powerplant for better performance under hot-and-high conditions, and IR reduction package to reduce the chances of destruction by IR-homing missiles

OH-58D Aeroscout: developed as the **Model 406**, this is a radically upgraded Kiowa produced in the early 1980s as part of the Army Helicopter Improvement Program; some 477 OH-58As (originally 580) are to be converted to the new AHIP standard, which includes the 650-shp (485-kW) Allison 250-C30R turboshaft for a maximum speed of 147 mph (237 km/h) and a range of 345 miles (556 km) with 105 US gal (398 litres) of fuel and a maximum take-off weight of 4,500 lb (2041 kg); more importantly, the OH-58D introduces a cockpit control and display subsystem and a mast-mounted sight above the 35-ft (10·67-m) main rotor, which has four composite-construction blades; this sight includes a TV camera and FLIR unit for observation under battlefield conditions as the helicopter hovers behind cover; the type can also designate targets for laser-homing missiles, and has an air-to-air capability through the carriage of Stinger lightweight missiles used in conjunction with the Thomson-CSF/Hamilton Standard VH-100 ATAS (Air-To-Air Stinger) wide-angle HUD; in 1987 the US Army began to operate the type in interim armed form as the **Armed OH-58D**, though full-production examples are now designated **AH-58D Warrior** with the ALQ-144 IR jammer and the mast-mounted sight, the latter used with all four weapon types carried by the helicopter, namely the AGM-114A Hellfire air-to-surface/anti-tank missile, the AIM-92A Stinger light AAM, the Hydra 70 2·75-in (70-mm) unguided rocket (carried in pods with varying numbers of launch tubes) and a 0·5-in (12·7-mm) machine-gun pod; the Warrior can carry four Hellfires, or four Stingers, or two rocket pods, or two machine-gun pods, or a combination of these weapons

Model 406 Combat Scout: export version of the OH-58D with a roof-mounted HeliTOW sight rather than the mast-mounted sight for use with BGM-71 TOW anti-tank missiles, a quick-change weapons system (including two NC621 pods each with a single GIAT M621 20-mm cannon, or unguided rocket pods, or machine-gun pods) and simplified systems; empty weight is reduced from the OH-58's 2,825 lb (1281 kg) to 2,283 lb (1035 kg), and as the export model is cleared to the same maximum take-off weight as the OH-58D this allows the carriage of more fuel and/or weapons; the type is being supplied to Saudi Arabia with the US military designation **MH-558D**

CH-136: helicopter similar to the OH-58A for the Canadian Armed Forces, and originally designated COH-58A

Commonwealth Aircraft Corporation Model 206B-1: OH-58A built under licence in Australia

Bell Model 206L-1 LongRanger II

(USA)
Type: utility light helicopter
Accommodation: flightcrew of two, and five passengers, and two litters and two seated casualties and/or attendants, or freight in the cabin rear
Armament (fixed): none
Armament (disposable): none
Electronics and operational equipment: communication and navigation equipment
Powerplant and fuel system: one 500-shp (373-kW) Allison 250-C28B turboshaft, and a total internal fuel capacity of 98 US gal (371 litres); no provision for drop tanks or inflight refuelling
Performance: cruising speed 134 mph (215 km/h) at 5,000 ft (1525 m); initial climb rate 1,520 ft (463 m) per minute; service ceiling 19,500 ft (5945 m); range 385 miles (620 km)
Weights: empty 2,155 lb (978 kg); maximum take-off 4,150 lb (1882 kg)
Dimensions: main rotor diameter 37 ft 0 in (11·28 m); length, fuselage 33 ft 3 in (10·13 m); height 10 ft 0 in (3·05 m) to rotor head; main rotor disc area 1,075·21 sq ft (99·87 m²)

Variants

Model 206A JetRanger: civil and very successful helicopter derived from Bell's unsuccessful Model 206 entry in the US Army's LOH competition of 1962, with many examples going to overseas air arms; the type is powered by the 317-shp (237-kW) Allison 250-C18A turboshaft driving a 33·33-ft (10·16-m) diameter main rotor; the type was adopted as a primary training helicopter by the US Navy with the designation **TH-57A SeaRanger**
Model 206B JetRanger II: simple improvement of the Model 206A with the 400-shp (298-kW) Allison 250-C20 turboshaft; the type was adopted by the US Navy as the **TH-57B SeaRanger** primary trainer
Model 206B JetRanger III: further upgraded model with the 420-shp (313-kW) Allison 250-C20B turboshaft for better performance under 'hot-and-high' conditions; the type was adopted by the US Navy as the **TH-57C SeaRanger** instrument trainer
Model 206L LongRanger: stretched version of the JetRanger II with a 37-ft (11·28-m) diameter main rotor and 420-shp (313-kW) Allison 250-C20B turboshaft
Model 206L-1 LongRanger II: upgraded version of the Model 206L LongRanger
Model 206L-3 LongRanger III: further upgraded version with the 650-shp (485-kW) Allison 250-C30P flat-rated at 557 shp (415 kW) for better performance especially under hot-and-high conditions
Model 206L TexasRanger: Bell-developed armed version of the series with the 500-shp (373-kW) Allison 250-C28B turboshaft and provision for advanced sights plus an assortment of disposable ordnance including up to four TOW anti-tank missiles
Model 400A Combat Twin: company proposal for a twin-engine derivative of the JetRanger/LongRanger series; the prototype flew in October 1983 with two Allison 250 turboshafts, though

Left: An AB.206A utility helicopter of the Italian army is seen on Alpine duty.

Above right: In its TH-57A form the Model 206A JetRanger is the US Navy's standard helicopter for the training of pilots.

the 6,000-lb (2722-kg) production version will have twin 900-shp (671-kW) Pratt & Whitney PW209T turboshafts (driving a four-blade main rotor and two-blade tail rotor) and provision on two fuselage hardpoints for TOW anti-tank missiles, Stinger lightweight AAMs, machine-gun/cannon pods, or rocket pods; the production centre is Bell's Canadian subsidiary, which is also developing the **Model 440** version with a largely composite structure

Agusta (Bell) AB.206: under this overall designation Bell's Italian licensee has produced JetRanger and LongRanger helicopters basically similar to the US originals; one development separate from the US mainstream has been the **AB.206A-1** military model with several armament options, and the anti-submarine **HKP 6** derivative for Sweden with longer landing gear legs to permit the carriage of torpedoes or depth charges under the fuselage

Bell Model 209 (AH-1G HueyCobra)

(USA)

Type: battlefield close-support and attack helicopter

Accommodation: co-pilot/weapons operator and pilot in tandem

Armament (fixed): one M28 chin turret able to accommodate two 7·62-mm (0·3-in) GAU-2B/A Miniguns with 4,000 rounds per gun, or two 40-mm M129 grenade-launchers each with 300 rounds, or one Minigun and one grenade-launcher

Armament (disposable): this is carried on four hardpoints (two under each stub wing) up to an unrevealed maximum weight; the weapons that can be carried include four M159 launchers each with 19 2·75-in (70-mm) rockets, or four M157 launchers each with seven 2·75-in (70-mm) rockets, or two M18E1 7·62-mm (0·3-in) Minigun pods, or one M35 armament system with one 20-mm M61A1 Vulcan rotary-barrel cannon (on the port inner hardpoint) with 1,000 rounds; the weapon operator is primarily responsible for the turreted armament and the pilot for the disposable armament, though each officer can control the whole armament

Electronics and operational equipment: communication and navigation equipment, plus secure voice communications link, M73 rocket sight and M130 chaff dispenser

Powerplant and fuel system: one 1,400-shp (1044-kW) Avco Lycoming T53-L-13 turboshaft derated to 1,100 shp (820 kW), and a total internal fuel capacity of 268 US gal (1014 litres); no provision for drop tanks or inflight refuelling

Performance: maximum speed 172 mph (277 km/h) at sea level; initial climb rate 1,230 ft (375 m) per minute; service ceiling 11,400 ft (3475 m); range 357 miles (574 km)

Weights: empty 6,075 lb (2756 kg); normal take-off 9,407 lb (4266 kg); maximum take-off 9,500 lb (4309 kg)

Dimensions: main rotor disc diameter 44 ft 0 in (13·41 m); length overall, rotors turning 52 ft 11·4 in (16·14 m) and fuselage 44 ft 7 in (13·59 m); height 13 ft 6·25 in (4·12 m); main rotor disc area 1,520·53 sq ft (141·26 m²)

Variants

AH-1G HueyCobra: first flown in September 1965 as the Bell Model 209, this important attack helicopter was evolved in response to urgent requests from the US Army in Vietnam for a helicopter gunship able to escort troop-carrying helicopters and to provide fire support for the landed troops; the result was the dynamic system of the UH-1C mated to a new fuselage of remarkable slimness (38 in/0·97 m) tailored to the width of the tandem-seated crew and supporting stub wings for disposable armament; gun armament was located in a trim turret under the nose; the type was rushed into production as the AH-1G and proved highly successful in the close support and attack roles; total production amounted to 1,119 helicopters, and a few were converted as **TH-1G** trainers; the AH-1R HueyCobra was an uprated version of the AH-1G with the 1,800-shp (1342-kW) T53-L-703 turboshaft but without provision for TOW missiles, and is no longer in service

AH-1Q HueyCobra: developed in the early 1970s, this was an interim anti-tank helicopter converted from AH-1G standard with provision for eight TOW anti-tank missiles (four under each outer underwing hardpoint) controlled with the aid of an M65 sight system for the weapons officer in the front seat, who also had a Sperry-Univac helmet sight system

Bell Model 209 (AH-1S HueyCobra)

(USA)

Type: anti-tank and battlefield close support helicopter

Accommodation: co-pilot/weapons operator and pilot in tandem

Armament (fixed): one General Electric Universal Turret in the chin position and able to accommodate many weapons of 20- and 30-mm calibre (20-mm M197 three-barrel cannon and 750 rounds fitted in US aircraft)

Armament (disposable): this is carried on four hardpoints (two under each wing) up to an unrevealed maximum weight; the weapons carried include eight BGM-71 TOW anti-tank missiles (two quadruple launchers) on the outer hardpoints and two LAU-68 or LAU-6 pods for seven or 19 2·75-in (70-mm) rockets on the inner hardpoints

Electronics and operational equipment: communication and navigation equipment, plus a Hughes M65 TOW sight for the weapons officer, Kaiser HUD for the pilot, Teledyne digital fire-control system, Baldwin M138 underwing stores-management system, Hughes laser rangefinder, Rockwell laser tracker, Hughes LAAT (Laser-Augmented Airborne TOW) sight, APR-39 RWR, ALQ-136 radar jammer, Sanders ALQ-144 IR jammer, M130 chaff dispenser, secure voice communications link, weapon operator's and pilot's helmet sight system and (as a retrofit) Hughes FACTS (FLIR-Augmented Cobra TOW Sight)

Powerplant and fuel system: one 1,800-shp (1342-kW) Avco Lycoming T53-L-703 turboshaft, and a total internal fuel capacity of 259 US gal (980 litres); no provision for drop tanks or inflight refuelling

Performance: maximum speed 141 mph (227 km/h) at optimum height with TOW missiles; initial climb rate 1,620 ft (494 m) per minute; service ceiling 12,200 ft (3720 m); hovering ceiling in ground effect 12,200 ft (3720 m); range 315 miles (507 km)

Weights: empty 6,598 lb (2993 kg); normal take-off 9,975 lb (4524 kg); maximum take-off 10,000 lb (4536 kg)

Below: AH-1S HueyCobra with 20-mm chin cannon and eight BGM-81 TOW anti-tank missiles.

Below right: Trials AH-1S with the four-blade rotor adopted for modern Bell helicopters.

Dimensions: main rotor diameter 44 ft 0 in (13·41 m); length overall, rotors turning 53 ft 1 in (16·18 m) and fuselage 44 ft 7 in (13·59 m); height 13 ft 6·25 in (4·12 m); main rotor disc area 1,520·53 sq ft (141·26 m²)

Variants

Modified AH-1S HueyCobra: mid-1970s reworking of 245 AH-1Gs and the 92 AH-1Qs to improved anti-tank configuration with the powerplant of the AH-1R, eight TOW anti-tank missiles, better defensive capabilities and improved fire-control subsystems

Production AH-1S HueyCobra: 100 new-build helicopters to the same basic AH-1S standard but fitted with flat-plate canopies for reduced glint, a better cockpit layout, better intrumentation for nap-of-the-earth operations and (from the 67th helicopter) composite-construction rotor blades; in service the type is designated **AH-1P HueyCobra**

Up-gun AH-1S HueyCobra: 98 new-build helicopters identical to the Production AH-1S apart from their provision with the Enhanced Cobra Armament System including a General Electric undernose turret (allowing installation of 20- or 30-mm aircraft cannon) and the M138 underwing stores subsystem; in service the type is designated **AH-1E HueyCobra**

Modernized AH-1S HueyCobra: definitive production version of the single-engine HueyCobra series, with all the features of the Production and Up-gun AH-1S models plus Doppler navigation, a laser rangefinder and tracker, a ballistic computer linked to a low-airspeed sensor, a pilot's head-up display, secure communications, an IR jammer and a flat-plate canopy; in service the type is designated **AH-1F HueyCobra**; in service helicopters are to be modernized with the C-Nite system for nocturnal and adverse-weather target detection, acquisition and engagement, and the Ait-To-Air Stinger system for carriage of AIM-92A Stinger lightweight AAMs

Fuji (Bell) AH-1S: Japanese licence-built version of the AH-1S with the Kawasaki TT53-K-703 turboshaft

Bell Model 209 (AH-1T Improved SeaCobra)

(USA)

Type: battlefield close air support, attack and anti-tank helicopter

Accommodation: co-pilot/weapons operator and pilot in tandem

Armament (fixed): one General Electric Universal Turret in the chin position and accommodating one 20-mm M197 three-barrel cannon and 750 rounds

Armament (disposable): this is carried on four hardpoints (two under each stub wing) up to an unrevealed maximum weight; typical weapons include four LAU-61, LAU-69 or LAU-69 pods each with 19 2·75-in (70-mm) rockets, two CBU-55B fuel/air explosive devices, two M118 grenade dispensers, two M18E1 7·62-mm (0·3-in) GAU-2B/A Minigun pods, or alternatively BGM-71 TOW or AGM-114 Hellfire anti-tank missiles

Electronics and operational equipment: communication and navigation equipment, plus a Hughes M65 TOW sight for the weapons officer, Kaiser HUD for the pilot, Teledyne digital fire-control system, Baldwin M138 underwing stores-management system, Hughes laser rangefinder, Rockwell laser tracker, Hughes LAAT (Laser-Augmented Airborne TOW) sight, ALQ-136 radar jammer, Sanders ALQ-144 IR jammer, M130 chaff dispenser, secure voice communications link, weapon operator's and pilot's helmet sight system and (as a retrofit) Hughes FACTS (FLIR-Augmented Cobra TOW Sight)

Powerplant and fuel system: one 2,050-shp (1529-kW) Pratt & Whitney Canada T400-WV-402 coupled turboshaft, and a total internal fuel capacity of 304·5 US gal (1153 litres) plus provision for two 100-US (378-litre), or two or four 77-US gal (291-litre), or two 100-US gal (378-litre) and two 77-US gal (291-litre) external tanks; no provision for inflight refuelling

Performance: maximum speed 172 mph (277 km/h) at sea level; initial climb rate 1,785 ft (544 m) per minute; service ceiling 7,400 ft (2255 m); range 260 miles (418 km)

Weights: empty 8,608 lb (3904 kg); maximum take-off 14,000 lb (6350 kg)

Dimensions: main rotor diameter 48 ft 0 in (14·63 m); length overall, rotors turning 58 ft 0 in (17·68 m) and fuselage 48 ft 2 in (14·68 m); height 14 ft 2 in (4·32 m); main rotor disc area 1,809·56 sq ft (168·11 m²)

Variants

AH-1J SeaCobra: first flown in October 1969, the AH-1J was produced for the US Marine Corps as a derivative of the AH-1G with a twin-engine powerplant, in this instance the 1,800-shp (1342-kW) Pratt & Whitney Canada T400-CP-400 coupled turboshaft flat-rated at 1,100 shp (820 kW); maximum take-off weight is 10,000 lb (4536 kg). Power is comparable with that of the identically dimensioned AH-1G but sea-level maximum speed is 207 mph (333 km/h); the maximum weapons load is 2,200 lb (998 kg)

AH-1T Improved SeaCobra: developed from the AH-1J but incorporating features of the Bell Model 309 KingCobra and Bell Model 214, the first AH-1T flew in May 1976 and is notable for its increased length (for additional fuel capacity) and upgraded transmission to handle the full 1,970 shp (1469 kW) of the T400-WV-402 coupled turboshaft powerplant; the type can carry TOW or Hellfire anti-tank missiles on the outboard underwing hardpoints; 21 of the 57 helicopters are to be upgraded to AH-1W standard

AH-1W SuperCobra: version that entered service in 1987 with considerably improved capabilities resulting from the installation of two General Electric T700-GE-401 turboshafts for a total of 3,250 shp (2424 kW) driving through a new combining gearbox; the type has new subsystems including a Kaiser HUD for the pilot and an avionics suite that includes the Aerospace APR-39(V)1 radar detector, APR-44(V)1 RWR, Goodyear ALE-39 chaff/flare dispenser and Sanders ALQ-144 IR jammer; in combination with the latest weaponry, this provides the US Marine Corps with a highly advanced high-performance close support and attack helicopter ideally suited to support of beach-head operations from forward airstrips or from assault ships lying just offshore; the primary armament comprises eight BGM-71 TOW or AGM-114 Hellfire anti-tank missiles, supported by a pair of AIM-9L Sidewinder AAMs and AGM-122 Sidearm anti-radar missiles for battlefield self-defence; the variant has empty and maximum take-off weights of 10,200 and 14,750 lb (4627 and 6691 kg) respectively, and its performance data include a maximum speed of 175 mph (272 mph) at sea level, a cruising speed of 173 mph (278 km/h), a single-engined climb rate of 800 ft (244 m) per minute, a service ceiling of 14,000 + ft (4270 + m), hovering ceiling in and out of ground effect of 14,750 and 3,000 ft (4495 and 914 m) respectively, and a range of 395 miles (635 km)

Bell Model 212 (UH-1N Iroquois)

(USA)

Type: general-purpose light/medium helicopter

Accommodation: pilot and 14 troops, or six litters and one attendant, or 4,000 lb (1814 kg) of freight in the cabin

Armament (fixed): none

Armament (disposable): none

Electronics and operational equipment: communication and navigation equipment

Powerplant and fuel system: one 1,800-shp (1342-kW) Pratt & Whitney Canada T400-CP-400 coupled turboshaft flat-rated to 1,290 shp (962 kW), and a total internal fuel capacity of 215 US gal (814 litres) plus provision for 180 US gal (681 litres) of ferry fuel; no provision for drop tanks or inflight refuelling

Performance: maximum speed 142 mph (230 km/h) at sea level; initial climb rate 1,320 ft (402 m) per minute; service ceiling 15,000 ft (4570 m); hovering ceiling in ground effect 11,000 ft (3355 m); range 248 miles (400 km)

Weights: empty 6,169 lb (2798 kg); normal take-off 10,500 lb (4762 kg); maximum take-off 11,200 lb (5080 kg)

Dimensions: main rotor diameter 48 ft 2·25 in (14·69 m) with tracking tips; length overall, rotors turning 57 ft 3·25 in (17·46 m) and fuselage 42 ft 4·75 in (12·92 m); height 14 ft 10·25 in (4·53 m); main rotor disc area 1,823·72 sq ft (169·42 m²)

Variants

UH-1N Iroquois: developed from 1968 at the instigation of Canada, whose forces needed a version of the highly successful UH-1 with a twin-engine powerplant for extra reliability and safety in remote areas, the **Model 212** first flew in 1969 as a combination of the UH-1H's airframe with the

Left: An AH-1T SeaCobra twin-engined attack helicopter of the US Marine Corps.

Below: UH-1N of the US Marine Corps.

Pratt & Whitney Canada PT6T Turbo Twin Pac coupled turboshaft powerplant offering good performance added to single-engine flight capability; the production model features the PT6T-3B (military designation T400-CP-400) and substantial sales were made to the US forces and to overseas air arms including those of Canada which designates the type **CH-135**

VN-1N Iroquois: VIP transport version of the UH-1N; production amounted to two new-build helicopters, though another six were produced by conversion of UH-1Ns

Model 212: civil model, which won useful orders from civil and third-world military operators

Model 412: upgraded version with a four-blade main rotor and greater fuel capacity to increase speed and range, and further developed as the

Model 412AH for the attack role with a Lucas undernose turret (fitted with a 0·5-in/12·7-mm Browning M3 heavy machine-gun) and helmet sights for the cockpit crew

Agusta (Bell) AB.212: Italian licence-built version of the Bell Model 212/UH-1N series, with only marginal differences from the American original, including a main rotor diameter of 14·63 m (48 ft 0 in), and empty weight of 2630 kg (5,798 lb), a sea level speed of 204 km/h (107 mph), an initial climb rate of 567 m (1,860 ft) per minute, a service ceiling of 5180 m (16,995 ft) and a range of 494 km (307 miles); the type has sold in southern Europe, North Africa and the Middle East

Agusta (Bell) AB.212ASV/ASW: advanced three/four-seat anti-surface vessel and anti-submarine warfare model developed by Italy for use from larger naval platforms and from shore bases; the airframe is strengthened in comparison with that of the AB.212, but the uprated 1,875-shp (1398-kW) Pratt & Whitney PT6T-6 Turbo Twin Pac coupled turboshaft is fitted so that the maximum 490-kg (1,080-lb) weapon load of two Sea Killer or Sea Skua anti-ship missiles or alternatively two Mk 44 or Mk 46 anti-submarine torpedoes can be used to full effect with the aid of an advanced avionics suite that includes APN-

208(V)2 Doppler navigation, SMA-built Ferranti Seaspray search radar, Bendix AQS-13B dunking sonar and/or sonobuoys, an ESM suite and TG-2 data-link for use with ship-launched Otomat anti-ship missiles; the type can carry a slung load of 2268 kg (5,000 lb), and has proved popular with southern European, Middle Eastern and South American navies for its compact dimensions and very useful avionics/weapon combination; Italian helicopters are being upgraded with the Marte Mk II system for air-launched Sea Killer Mk 2 anti-ship missiles, and the Sea Skua lightweight anti-ship missile in another weapon option; the variant has empty and maxium take-off weights of 3420 and 5070 kg (7,540 and 11,177 lb), and amongst its performance data are a maximum speed of 196 km/h (12 mph) at sea level, a cruising speed of 185 km/h (115 mph), an initial climb rate of 396 m (1,300 ft) per minute, and a range of 667 km (414 mph)

Agusta (Bell) AB.412: Italian licence-built version of the **Bell Model 412**, a development of the Model 212 with a four-blade main rotor; the type is intended primarily for civil applications, but can also be used in the utility military role

Agusta (Bell) AB.412 Grifone: dedicated military version of the AB.412, intended as a multi-role aircraft but with particular capabilities in the assault transport and hard-target attack roles, in the former carrying 15 troops and in the latter using missiles such as the TOW anti-tank type and the Sea Skua anti-ship type; the Grifone is powered by the Pratt & Whitney Canada PT6T-3B Turbo Twin Pac coupled turboshaft delivering 1,800 shp (1342 kW) with 1250 litres (275 Imp gal) of standard fuel supplemented by an optional 682 litres (150 Imp gal) of ferry fuel, and its weights are 2840 kg (6,261 lb) empty rising to a maximum of 5400 kg (11,905 lb) with a 2290-kg (5,049-lb) payload; the type has a maximum speed of 225 km/h (140 mph) at sea level, an initial climb rate of 438 m (1,435 ft) per minute, a service ceiling of 5180 m (16,995 ft) and a range of 480 km (298 miles)

Bell Model 214ST Super Transport

(USA)

Type: general-purpose medium helicopter

Accommodation: flightcrew of two, and 18 passengers or more than 7,700 lb (3493 kg) of freight in the cabin rear

Armament (fixed): none

Armament (disposable): none

Electronics and operational equipment: communication and navigation equipment

Powerplant and fuel system: two 1,625-shp (1212-kW) General Electric CT7-2A turboshafts, and a total internal fuel capacity of 435 US gal (1647 litres) plus provision for 175 US gal (662 litres) of ferry fuel; no provision for drop tanks or inflight refuelling

Performance: cruising speed 159 mph (256 km/h) at 4,000 ft (1220 m); initial climb rate 1,850 ft (564 m) per minute; service ceiling 7,000 ft (2135 m) on one engine; hovering ceiling in ground effect 6,400 ft (1950 m); range 500 miles (805 km); ferry range 635 miles (1022 km)

Weights: empty 9,445 lb (4284 kg); maximum take-off 17,500 lb (7938 kg)

Dimensions: main rotor diameter 52 ft 0 in (15·85 m); length overall, rotors turning 62 ft 2·25 in (18·95 m) and fuselage 50 ft 0 in (15·24 m); height 15 ft 10·5 in (4·84 m); main rotor disc area 2,123·71 sq ft (197·29 m²)

Variants

Model 214A Isfahan: resulting from a 1972 Iranian requirement for a high-performance medium-lift helicopter, this model was developed from the up-engined Model 214 Huey Plus development of of the UH-1H; the type is powered by the 2,930-shp (2185-kW) Avco Lycoming LTC4B-8D turboshaft and has a maximum take-off weight of 16,000 lb (7257 kg)

Model 214C: SAR version of the Model 214A for the Iranian air force

Model 214ST Super Transport: twin-engine utility version with excellent performance and payload, and attractive to many overseas air arms; the type is available in the maritime role with 360° search radar, an optional turret-mounted FLIR sensor, MAD, dunking sonar and/or sonobuoys and armament options including six BAe Sea Skua light anti-ship missiles under the fuselage

Above: The Model 214ST is a version of the Model 214A/C with a twin-engined powerplant for improved payload, performance and safety.

Opposite: The V-22 Osprey, seen here in VTO mode, should become the world's first fully operational convertiplane in the early 1990s.

Bell/Boeing MV-22A Osprey

(USA)

Type: multi-role tilt-rotor V/STOL assault and logistic transport aeroplane

Accommodation: flightcrew of two, and 24 troops or 20,000 lb (9072 kg) of freight in the cabin, or 15,000 lb (6804 kg) of freight as a slung load

Armament (fixed): possibly one 0·5-in (12·7-mm) multi-barrel machine-gun in the nose with an unrevealed number of rounds

Armament (disposable): none

Electronics and operational equipment: communication and navigation equipment, plus Texas Instruments APQ-168 multi-mode radar, Honeywell AAR-47 missile-warning system, ALQ-127 IR jammer, Tracor ALE-40 chaff/flare dispenser, and a number of other items and systems yet to be revealed

Powerplant and fuel system: two 6,160-shp (4593-kW) Allison T406-AD-400 (501-M80C) turboshafts, and a total internal fuel weight of 13,650 lb (6192 kg) plus provision for 15,950 lb (7235 kg) of ferry fuel in two optional tanks carried in the hold; provision for inflight refuelling

Performance: maximum speed 345 mph (555 km/h) at optimum altitude in aeroplane mode and 115 mph (185 km/h) at sea level in helicopter mode; cruising speed 317 mph (510 km/h); service ceiling 25,000 ft (7620 m); range 460 miles (740 km) with pilot and 24 troops

Weights: empty 30,850 lb (13,993 kg); normal take-off 47,500 lb (21,546 kg) for VTO and 55,000 lb (24,947 kg) for STO; maximum take-off 60,500 lb (27,443 kg) for STO

Dimensions: rotor/propeller diameter, each 38 ft 0 in (11·58 m); width overall 84 ft 6 in (25·76 m); span excluding nacelles 46 ft 0 in (14·02 m); length, fuselage 57 ft 4 in (17·47 m); height, rotors in take-off position 20 ft 2 in (6·15 m); rotor/propeller disc area, total 2,268·23 sq ft (210·72 m²)

Variants

MV-22A Osprey: under development as a V/STOL assault transport for the US Marine Corps, and under consideration for a host of other applications, this fascinating tilt-rotor hybrid rotary/fixed-wing aircraft offers an excellent combination of payload/range and VTOL capability, the concept having been validated by the success of the Bell XV-15 prototype, which first flew in May 1977; the type first flew in March 1989 and is planned to enter service in the early 1990s, and amongst the specified requirements for the type are a combat radius of 230 miles (370 km) with a load of 24 troops, a hovering ceiling out of ground effect of 3,000 ft (915 m) with an external load of 8,300 lb (3765 kg), and a ferry range of 2,420 miles (3895 km) made possible by the installation of two special tanks in the cabin for 16,000 lb (7258 kg) of fuel; the type is fitted with two external hooks able to carry 15,000 lb (6804 kg) between them or 10,000 lb (4536 kg) on either of the two hooks; the internal payload area is 24 ft (7·32 m) long, 6 ft (1·83 m) wide and 6 ft (1·83 m) high; plans called for the delivery of 552 aircraft from a time between December 1991 and April 1992, though the US Department of Defense's 1989 review of financial commitments in the face of the USA's enormous budget deficit includes amongst its provisional proposals that there be a halt to further development of the Osprey in all its variants, the operating shortfall for the US Marines being overcome by additional purchases of helicopters; later in 1989 the US Congress restored the Osprey programme to full status

CV-22A Osprey: US Air Force special operations variant with additional fuel and low-level flight capability; the specification includes the ability to carry 12 troops over a 600-mile (966-km) combat radius, and to hover out of ground effect at 4,000 ft (1220 m)

HV-22A Osprey: US Navy combat SAR, special warfare and logistic support variant; the specification includes a crew of five, the ability to rescue four men from a radius of 530 miles (853 km), and a 3,000-ft (914-m) hover ceiling out of ground effect

SV-22A Osprey: proposed US Navy anti-submarine version with role-dedicated electronics and weapons

Beriev Be-12 (M-12) 'Mail'

(USSR)
Type: maritime reconnaissance amphibian flying boat
Accommodation: flightcrew of three or four, and a mission crew of undetermined size in the fuselage
Armament (fixed): none
Armament (disposable): this is carried in a fuselage bay and on four hardpoints (one large and one small under each wing) up to a maximum weight of about 5000 kg (11,023 lb); weapons are believed to include torpedoes and/or depth charges (weapons bay) and bombs, missiles and rockets
Electronics and operational equipment: communication and navigation equipment, plus Doppler navigation, search radar with its antenna in the nose 'thimble', MAD equipment in the tail 'sting', sonobuoys in a fuselage bay, and onboard tactical analysis equipment
Powerplant and fuel system: two 3125-kW (4,191-shp) Ivchyenko AI-20D turboprops, and a total internal fuel capacity of unrevealed quantity; no provision for drop tanks or inflight refuelling
Performance: maximum speed 608 km/h (378 mph); cruising speed 320 km/h (199 mph); initial climb rate 911 m (2,990 ft) per minute; service ceiling 11,300 m (37,075 ft); range 4000 km (2,485 miles)
Weights: empty 21,700 kg (47,840 lb); maximum take-off 30,000 kg (66,139 lb)
Dimensions: span 29·71 m (97 ft 5·7 in); length 30·17 m (98 ft 11·8 in); height 7·00 m (21 ft 11·6 in); wing area 105·00 m² (1,130·25 sq ft)

Variant
Be-12 'Mail': one of the few amphibians still in service, the Be-12 (also known as the **M-12**) first flew in the late 1950s, and has proved itself admirably suited to the requirements of anti-submarine warfare and maritime reconnaissance in the particular conditions of the USSR

Beriev A-40 Albatross

(USSR)
Type: maritime reconnaissance and anti-submarine amphibian flying boat
Accommodation: flightcrew of unrevealed size, and a mission crew of unrevealed size in the fuselage
Armament (fixed): none
Armament (disposable): this is carried in a fuselage bay and on an unknown number of hardpoints up to an unrevealed maximum weight; the weapon load is believed to include torpedoes and/or depth charges (weapons bay) and bombs, missiles and rockets (hardpoints)
Electronics and operational equipment: communication and navigation equipment, plus Doppler navigation, search radar, MAD equipment in the tail 'sting', sonobuoys, and onboard tactical analysis equipment
Powerplant and fuel system: two 23,500-kg (51,808-lb) thrust Lotarev D-18T non-afterburning turbofans, and a total internal fuel capacity of unrevealed quantity; provision for inflight refuelling
Performance: cruising speed 750 km/h (466 mph); radius 2500 km (1,553 miles); endurance 10 hours
Weights: empty not revealed; maximum take-off 150,000 kg (330,679 lb)
Dimensions: span 50·00 m (164 ft 0·5 in); other data not revealed
Variant
A-40 Albatross: known to have started tests at Taganrog early in 1988, this advanced amphibian is thought to have been designed as successor to the Be-12, and the type is likely to enter service in 1992

Left: The M-12 provides the USSR with valuable ASW capability in hostile regions.

Above right: The B-52G bristles with the bulges and antennae of its upgraded offensive/defensive electronic systems.

Boeing B-52G Stratofortress

(USA)

Type: strategic heavy bomber and missile-carrying aeroplane

Accommodation: flight and mission crew of six (pilot, co-pilot, navigator, radar operator, ECM officer and gunner)

Armament (fixed): four 0·5-in (12·7-mm) Colt-Browning M3 machine-guns in a rear barbette remotely controlled by an ASG-15 radar fire-control system

Armament (disposable): see Variants (below) to a maximum weight of about 50,000 lb (22,680 kg)

Electronics and operational equipment: communication and navigation equipment, plus a constantly updated electronic suite including Phase VI ECM, ASQ-151 advanced-capability radar, the Electro-optical Viewing System (EVS) comprising two steerable chin turrets (that on the port side containing a Westinghouse AVQ-22 low-light-level TV and that on the starboard side a Hughes AAQ-6 FLIR sensor), ALR-20A panoramic receiver, Motorola ALQ-122 Smart Noise Operation Equipment (SNOE), Dalmo Victor ALR-46(V)4 RWR, Westinghouse ALQ-153 pulse-Doppler tail-warning receiver, ITT ALQ-172 'Pave Mint' jammer suite, Northrop ALQ-155(V) advanced ECM system, eight ALE-24 wing-mounted launchers with 1,125 chaff packages, 12 ALE-20 wing-mounted launchers with 192 flares, AFSATCOM satellite communication system, and Boeing-integrated Offensive Avionics System (OAS) comprising Teledyne Ryan Doppler navigation, Honeywell ASN-131 INS, Raytheon ASQ-38 analog bombing and navigation system with IBM digital data processing, Lear Siegler attitude and heading reference system, and TERCOM (TERrain COntour Matching) guidance system

Powerplant and fuel system: eight 13,750-lb (6237-kg) thrust Pratt & Whitney J57-P-43WB non-afterburning turbojets, and a total internal fuel capacity of 46,000 US gal (174,130 litres) plus provision for two 700-US gal (2650-litre) underwing tanks; no provision for drop tanks but provision for inflight refuelling

Performance: maximum speed 595 mph (957 km/h) or Mach 0·9 at high altitude and 420 mph (676 km/h) or Mach 0·55 at low level; cruising speed 509 mph (819 km/h) or Mach 0·77 at high altitude; service ceiling 55,000 ft (16,765 m); range 7,500 + miles (12,070 + km) with maximum internal fuel

Weights: empty not revealed; maximum take-off 488,000 + lb (221,357 + kg)

Dimensions: span 185 ft 0 in (56·39 m); length 160 ft 10·9 in (49·05 m); height 40 ft 8 in (12·40 m); wing area 4,000·00 sq ft (371·60 m²)

Variants

B-52G Stratofortress: designed as a high-speed high-altitude strategic bomber with genuine intercontinental range, the B-52 was the manned bomber mainstay of the US Strategic Air Command between the time it entered service in its initial B-52B production form during 1955 until it was complemented by the Rockwell B-1B in the later 1980s; since its introduction the type has undergone enormous development (mainly in terms of its avionics and a strengthened airframe for the low-level role adopted during 1962), and the definitive turbojet-powered model was the B-52G, which first flew in October 1952 with integral wing and fixed underwing tankage for greater range, improvements to the six-man crew's pressurized compartment, shorter vertical tail surfaces of broader chord, a remotely-controlled tail turret, and provision for Quail decoy missiles and Hound Dog stand-off nuclear missiles; some 167 of the 193 B-52Gs survive, 90 of them fitted for the stand-off nuclear role with a primary armament of 12 AGM-86B cruise missiles under the wings (six rounds on each of two hardpoints) or 20 AGM-69A SRAMs, and the other 77 for the maritime surveillance/support role with a primary armament of eight to 12 AGM-84 Harpoon anti-ship missiles and/or GBU-15(V) guided glide bombs; the type can also be used for minelaying with 12 Mk 52 mines, or eight Mk 55, Mk 56 or Mk 60 mines

B-52H Stratofortress: ultimate development of the B-52 series, this variant first flew in March 1961 as the designated carrier for the Douglas AGM-87 Skybolt stand-off nuclear missile, which was later cancelled; the B-52H was internally redesigned for the low-level role, though more obvious external changes were the use of eight 17,000-lb (7711-kg) thrust Pratt & Whitney TF33-P-3 turbofan engines (for a range of 10,000 miles/16,093 km with maximum fuel) and the adoption of an M61A1 20-mm rotary cannon in the tail position with the ASG-21 fire-control radar; other changes were much enhanced avionics (including provision for terrain-avoidance radar) and the latest electronic countermeasures equipment; 90 of the 102 B-52Hs remain in service with a primary armament of 20 AGM-69A SRAM stand-off nuclear missiles, coupled with ASQ-151 radar, the EVS and introduction of Phase VI ECM and the Offensive Avionics System; some aircraft are earmarked for conventional support of the Rapid-Deployment Task Force (US Readiness Command) with GP and cluster bombs, the GBU-15 EO-guided glide bombs, and the AGM-130 rocket-assisted glide bomb; as the Rockwell B-1B enters service the 95 surviving B-52Hs are being converted into cruise missile aircraft, carrying 12 missiles under the wings (as in the B-52G) with provision for another eight in a modified bomb bay fitted with the Common Strategic Rotary Launcher

Boeing KC-135A Stratotanker

(USA)

Type: inflight-refuelling tanker aeroplane with a secondary airlift capability

Accommodation: crew of five (three pilots, radar operator and boom operator), and 80 troops in the cabin or 83,000 lb (37,650 kg) of freight in the cabin and hold

Armament (fixed): none

Armament (disposable): none

Electronics and operational equipment: communication and navigation equipment

Powerplant anf fuel system: four 13,750-lb (6237-kg) thrust Pratt & Whitney J57-P-59W non-afterburning turbojets, and a total internal fuel capacity of 31,200 US gal (118,105 litres) for self-use or transfer; no provision for drop tanks but provision for inflight refuelling

Performance: maximum speed 585 mph (941 km/h) or Mach 0·86 at 30,000 ft (9145 m); cruising speed 532 mph (856 km/h) or Mach 0·8 at 35,000 ft (10,670 m); initial climb rate 1,290 ft (393 m) per minute; service ceiling about 50,000 ft (15,240 m); radius 3,450 miles (5552 km) to offload 24,000 lb (10,886 kg) of fuel, or 1150 miles (1850 km) to offload 120,000 lb (54,432 kg) of fuel

Weights: empty 106,306 lb (48,220 kg); normal take-off 301,600 lb (136,806 kg); maximum take-off 316,000 lb (143,338 kg)

Dimensions: span 130 ft 10 in (39·88 m); length 134 ft 6 in (40·99 m); height 41 ft 8 in (12·69 m); wing area 2,433·00 sq ft (226·03 m²)

Variants

KC-135A Stratotanker: baseline inflight-refuelling tanker for the US Air Force's Strategic Air Command, though the aircraft are frequently used in support of Tactical Air Command assets at home and overseas; the type was the initial production development of Boeing privately-funded Model 367-80 prototype that also paved the way for the great Model 707 airliner; fitted as standard with Boeing's patented Flying Boom inflight-refuelling system, the initial KC-135A flew in August 1956, and the first of 724 production aircraft was delivered a mere three months later; the type has spawned an enormous number of variants in the tanker and other roles, and conversions from standard KC-135As included the **JC-135A** and **JKC-135A** special-duties aircraft (eventually redesignated **NC-135A** and **NKC-135A** in keeping with other test and research aircraft) and the seven **VC-135A** staff transports, of which two retained tanker capability; the 56 **KC-135Q** aircraft are KC-135As converted to deal with the special JP-7 fuel used only by the Lockheed SR-71A 'Blackbird' strategic reconnaissance aircraft

C-135A Stratolifter: designation of the initial transport version of the series, which was not produced in quantity as the Lockheed C-130 Hercules and Lockheed C-141 StarLifter proved more capable and flexible because of their optimized military transport design; production amounted to 15 aircraft (as well as three **C-135A Interim** aircraft adapted from KC-135As) powered by the J57-P-59W turbojet, and these began to enter service in 1961 with provision for 89,000 lb (40,370 kg) of freight, or 126 passengers, or 44 litters plus 54 sitting wounded

KC-135B Stratotanker: designation of a limited-production development (17 aircraft) of the KC-135A with 18,000-lb (8165-kg) thrust Pratt & Whitney TF33-P-5 turbofans, additional fuel capacity, an inflight-refuelling receptacle above the flightdeck and provision for service as airborne command posts, in which role all 17 production aircraft began to serve as soon as they entered service

C-135B Stratolifter: version of the C-135A with TF33-P-5 turbofans and a slightly enlarged tail (a feature also of later KC-135As); the 30 aircraft were rarely used in the transport role, five becoming **VC-135B** staff transports and 11 being turned into **WC-135B** weather reconnaissance aircraft (of which three were reconverted as **C-135C** transports)

KC-135E Stratotanker: under this designation 151 KC-135As operated by the Air Force Reserve and Air National Guard (104 ANG and 24 AFR tankers plus 23 special missions aircraft) are being upgraded in a programme that saw the first relivery in July 1982 so that they can remain in useful service into the next century; a primary change is the reskinning of the undersurfaces of the wings (a programme being undertaken for all KC-135s), while other features are re-engining with Pratt & Whitney JT3D-3B turbofans (together with their engine mountings and nacelles) and retrofit of the tails removed from surplus Model 707s; at the same time new brakes and anti-skid units are being installed

C-135F: designation of 12 KC-135A aircraft for France, designed for support of the Dassault Mirage IV intermediate-range bomber force; the 11 survivors were re-engined between 1985 and 1988 with the General Electric/SNECMA CFM56 turbofan for greater operating economy and range, and are now designated **C-135FR**

KC-135R Stratotanker: this is the designation for a planned 630 KC-135As upgraded in a programme (scheduled to run from 1983 to 1995) along the lines of the KC-135E but to a far more extensive degree; the selected powerplant is the 22,000-lb (9979-kg) thrust CFM International F108-CF-100 turbofan, the military version of the CFM56-2B-1 civil engine, and other features of the programme are strengthened landing gear with anti-skid units, an improved autopilot, an updated cockpit, an enlarged tailplane, a fuel capacity of 203,288 lb (92,210 kg) and an auxiliary power unit for self-start capability; the result is an aircraft able to transfer 150% more fuel than the KC-135A at a radius of 2,875 miles (4627 km), yet able to operate from considerably shorter runways; this last is of considerable importance, for the take-off run of a fully-laden KC-135A is so great that only the largest military (and in emergencies civil) airfields can be used, which has at times proved a tactical limitation to effective employment

Boeing EC-135A

(USA)

Type: operational and strategic communications relay aeroplane

Accommodation: flightcrew of three or four, and a variable mission crew in the cabin

Armament (fixed): none

Armament (disposable): none

Electronics and operational equipment: communication and navigation equipment, plus classified mission electronics

Powerplant and fuel system: four 13,750-lb (6237-kg) thrust Pratt & Whitney J57-P-59W non-afterburning turbojets, and a total internal fuel capacity of 23,855 US gal (90,299 litres); no provision for drop tanks or inflight refuelling

Performance: maximum speed 585 mph (941 km/h) or Mach 0·86 at 30,000 ft (9145 m); cruising speed 430 mph (853 km/h); initial climb rate 2,000 ft (610 m) per minute; service ceiling 50,000 ft (15,240 m); range not revealed

Weights: empty 98,466 lb (46,633 kg); maximum take-off 297,000 lb (134,717 kg)

Dimensions: span 130 ft 10 in (39·88 m); length 136 ft 3 in (41·43 m); height 41 ft 8 in (12·70 m); wing area 2,433·0 sq ft (226·03 m²)

Variants

EC-135A: confirmation of the C/KC-135's operating economics and performance in the late 1950s soon showed that the type was ideally suited to conversion in the airborne command post and communications relay roles with the cabin outfitted with a large quantity of advanced communications equipment; the availability of such aircraft would add enormously to the strategic flexibility of the US Air Force's Strategic Air Command by offering the possibility of a virtually indestructible command system operating in high orbits well clear of potentially destructible ground facilities; the EC-135A designation covers six communications relay and interim airborne command post aircraft thus converted from KC-135A tankers

EC-135B ARIA: four C-135Bs converted for the Advanced Range Instrumentation Aircraft role with a steerable antenna in a large nose fairing

EC-135C: 14 airborne command post aircraft for SAC's Post-Attack Command Control System

EC-135E: EC-135N aircraft converted from the ARIA role and used for test purposes with TF33 turbofans

EC-135G: four KC-135As converted as airborne control centres for ICBM launch purposes, but also able to double as communications relay aircraft

EC-135H: five airborne command post aircraft converted from one VC-135A and four KC-135As

EC-135J: four upgraded airborne command post aircraft converted from EC-135Cs

EC-135K: two Tactical Air Command airborne command post aircraft converted from KC-135As but upgraded with TF33 turbofans

EC-135L: eight radio relay aircraft converted from KC-135As

EC-135N: eight spacecraft-tracking aircraft converted from C-135As

EC-135P: three Pacific Air Forces airborne command post aircraft converted from KC-135As

Opposite: The KC-135R is the KC-135A re-engined with F108 turbofans and improved in a number of other significant ways.

Above: An EC-135H approaches a tanker to take on fuel via its upper-fuselage receptacle.

Boeing RC-135C

(USA)

Type: operational and strategic electronic reconnaissance aeroplane

Accommodation: flightcrew of three or four, and a variable mission crew in the cabin

Armament (fixed): none

Armament (disposable): none

Electronics and operational equipment: communication and navigation equipment, plus classified mission equipment in the cabin

Powerplant and fuel system: four 18,000-lb (8165-kg) thrust Pratt & Whitney TF33-P-9 non-afterburning turbofans, and a total internal fuel capacity of 23,855 US gal (90,299 litres) ; no provision for drop tanks or inflight refuelling

Performance: maximum speed 616 mph (991 km/h) or Mach 0·89 at 25,000 ft (7620 m); cruising speed 560 mph (901 km/h); service ceiling 40,600 ft (12,375 m); operational radius 2,675 miles (4305 km); ferry range 5,655 miles (9100 km)

Weights: empty 102,300 lb (46,403 kg); maximum take-off 275,500 lb (124,965 kg)

Dimensions: span 120 ft 10 in (39·88 m); length 128 ft 7·3 in (39·20 m); height 41 ft 8 in (12·70 m); wing area 2,433·0 sq ft (226·03 m²)

Variants

RC-135A: given the payload and range of the C/KC-135A series, it was natural that the type should be developed for the arcane science of Elint, and the first such machine was the RC-135A photo-mapping and electronic reconnaissance aircraft, based on the C-135A and using the same J57-P-59W engines

RC-135B: 10 electronic reconnaissance aircraft based on the C-135B but with Pratt & Whitney TF33-P-9 turbofans, and lacking any type of standardization in the electronic fit

RC-135C: RC-135B conversions with SLAR, an undernose radome and ventral camera installation, intended primarily for the Sigint role with the ASD-1 automatic reconnaissance system and the QRC-259 fast-sweep analyser

RC-135D: four electronic reconnaissance conversions from KC-135A (one) and C-135A (three) standard with SLAR, a thimble nose radome and other systems

RC-135E: one C-135B conversion similar to the RC-135C but with a wide glassfibre radome round the forward fuselage

RC-135M: at least six C/VC-135B conversions for electronic reconnaissance in the 'Rivet Card' and 'Rivet Quick' programmes and fitted with thimble noses, teardrop fairings on the fuselage sides forward of the tail and twin-lobe ventral antennae

RC-135S: several C-135B conversions with numerous blister fairings and a dipole aerial as part of the 'Rivet Ball' programme; one EC-135B has been converted into the sole **TC-135S** for telemetry intelligence training

RC-135T: one C-135B conversion for electronic surveillance in support of Strategic Air Command operations

RC-135U: two or three aircraft with SLAR and an undernose radome, plus Elint systems, and associated with the 'Combat Pink' and 'Combat Scent' programmes

RC-135V: seven or more conversions with SLAR, thimble noses and extensive antenna arrays under their fuselages for the Elint role

RC-135W: several variations on the RC-135V theme with SLAR and other Elint equipment

Boeing E-3A Sentry

(USA)

Type: airborne warning and control system (AWACS) aeroplane

Accommodation: flightcrew of four, and a mission crew of 16 in the cabin

Armament (fixed): none

Armament (disposable): none

Electronics and operational equipment: communication and navigation equipment, the former provided largely by Collins, Electronic Communications, E-Systems and Hughes, and the latter centred on Teledyne Ryan APN-213 Doppler navigation and two Delco ASN-119 INSs updated by Northrop ARN-120 Omega; the primary sensor is the Westinghouse APY-1 surveillance radar with its 24-ft (7·32-m) by 5-ft (1·52-m) antenna in a 30-ft (9·14-m) by 6-ft (1·83-m) rotodome turning at 0·25 rpm when the radar is not in use but at 25 rpm when the radar is in use; the radar antenna is backed by an AIL APX-103 IFF/TADIL-C system antenna, the complete system providing for the location and identification of all aircraft within a 230-mile (370-km) radius; radar and IFF/TADIL-C data are fed to an IBM 4 Pi CC-1 high-speed computer capable of 740,000 operations per second and with main and mass memories of 114,688 and 802,816 words respectively, the results being fed to nine Hazeltine multi-purpose and two auxiliary display consoles

Powerplant and fuel system: four 21,000-lb (9526-kg) thrust Pratt & Whitney TF33-P-100/100A non-afterburning turbofans, and a total internal

fuel capacity of 23,987 US gal (90,800 litres); no provision for drop tanks but provision for inflight refuelling

Performance: maximum speed 530 mph (853 km/h) or Mach 0·8 at high altitude; operating ceiling 29,000 ft (8850 m); radius 1,000 miles (1609 km) for a 6-hour patrol without refuelling; endurance 11 + hours without refuelling

Weights: empty 171,950 lb (77,996 kg); maximum take-off 325,000 lb (147,420 kg)

Dimensions: span 145 ft 9 in (44·42 m); length 152 ft 11 in (46·61 m); height 41 ft 9 in (12·73 m); wing area 3,050·00 sq ft (283·35 m²)

Variants

E-3A Sentry: one of the most expensive but important aircraft in the current military inventory, the Sentry is a highly capable Airborne Warning And Control System aeroplane designed for 3D surveillance of a massive volume of air and the direction of air operations within that volume; the E-3A is based on the airframe of the Model 707-300B airliner, and two EC-137D prototypes were delivered for operational evaluation of the Westinghouse APY-1 and Hughes APY-2 radars in competition as the Sentry's primary sensor; the Westinghouse radar was judged superior, and this type was selected for installation in the overfuselage radome of the 34 E-3A production aircraft, which began to enter service in March 1977; the last aircraft was delivered in 1984; the first 24 aircraft have only an overland capability and the designation **Core E-3A** (pulse-Doppler radar, CC-1 computer, nine situation display consoles, two auxiliary display units and 13 communication links), while the last 10 have the designation **Standard E-3A** with additional overwater sensor capability, faster-working CC-2 computer with a 665,360-word memory, secure voice communications facility, and Joint Tactical Information Distribution System; the same Standard E-3A type (though with improved APY-1 radar and provision for self-defence AAMs) was ordered for the multi-national NATO early warning force, and these 18 aircraft were delivered between January 1982 and April 1985; another five aircraft have been ordered by Saudi Arabia under the semi-official designation **E-3A/Saudi**, and these have slightly less capable electronics (no JTIDS, commercial communication links and reduced ECCM capability) and a powerplant comprising four 22,000-lb (9979-kg) thrust CFM56-A2-2 turbofans

E-3B Sentry: standard to which the Core E-3As have been raised with the CC-2 computer, JTIDS, improved ECM capability, 'Have Quick' communications system, and limited overwater sensor capability

E-3C Sentry: standard to which the Standard E-3As are being raised with five extra situation display consoles, additional UHF radio gear and the 'Have Quick-A' communications system; the type also has the capability to carry small underwing pylons, which could carry AIM-9 Sidewinder AAMs for a modest self-defence facility

E-3D Sentry: seven aircraft for the RAF, basically similar to the NATO aircraft but fitted with 22,000-lb (9979-kg) thrust CFM56A2-2 turbofans, ESM pods mounted at the wingtips and radar modified for over-water use; the aircraft are to enter service with the designation **Sentry AEW.Mk 1** from 1992, together with four similar French aircraft, have provision for inflight-refuelling using the flying boom or hose-and-drogue systems

E-6A: 15 aircraft planned for the US Navy based on the airframe of the E-3 but powered by four 22,000-lb (9979-kg) thrust CFM International F108 (CFM56-A2-2) turbofans and incorporating special electronics to provide a relay communications service between submerged missile-armed nuclear submarines and command post aircraft; this is the TACAMO (TAke Charge And Move Out) concept, and the E-6A is to replace Lockheed EC-130Q aircraft in the role with the ARC-182 VLF radio system transmitting through a 4·9-mile (7·9-km) trailing aerial; ALR-66(V) ESM equipment is fitted in the right wingtip; the E-6A has a flightcrew of four and a mission crew of six, with another eight seats available for relief crew; the aircraft has empty and maximum take-off weights of 172,793 and 342,000 lb (78,379 and 155,131 kg) respectively, at at a cruising speed of 525 mph (845 km/h) at 40,000 ft (12,190 m) possesses a range of 7,300 miles (11,748 km) on its 18,575 US gal (70,314 litres) of internal fuel; this translates into an endurance of 15 hours 25 minutes, rising to 28 hours 55 minutes with one inflight refuelling and to a maximum of 72 hours with additional inflight refuellings before the point of crew exhaustion is reached

Above left: The Sentry AEW.Mk 1 shows minor but important differences from the E-3 model.

Left: An RC-135U electronic reconnaissance platform of the 55th Strategic Reconaissance Wing based at Offutt AFB, Nebraska.

Boeing E-4B

(USA)

Type: advanced airborne command post (AABNCP) aeroplane

Accommodation: two alternating flightcrews of three or four, and about 50 command and communications staff in the cabin and hold

Armament (fixed): none

Armament (disposable): none

Electronics and operational equipment: communication and navigation equipment, the former being a highly advanced but classified communication, ESM and data-analysis system using items furnished mainly by Boeing, Burroughs, Collins, E-Systems, Electrospace Systems, RCA and Special Systems Group; the super-high-frequency satellite communications system is located with its antenna in the dorsal hump, and the Collins LF/VLF communication system has a 5-mile (8-km) trailing wire antenna; the main cabin is divided into six main stations (for the National Command Authority, conference room, briefing room, battle staff, communications and rest)

Powerplant and fuel system: four 52,500-lb (23,814-kg) thrust General Electric CF6-50E non-afterburning turbofans, and a total internal fuel weight of 331,565 lb (150,395 kg); no provision for drop tanks but provision for inflight refuelling

Performance: maximum speed 602 mph (969 km/h) or Mach 0·89 at 30,000 ft (9145 m); endurance 12 hours on internal fuel and 72 hours with inflight refuelling

Weights: empty not revealed; maximum take-off 800,000 lb (362,874 kg)

Dimensions: span 195 ft 8 in (59·64 m); length 231 ft 4 in (70·51 m); height 63 ft 5 in (19·33 m); wing area 5,500·00 sq ft (510·95 m²)

Variants

C-19A: little-used military designation for Model 747s owned and operated by airlines, but earmarked for military use in times of emergency as part of the Civil Reserve Air Fleet

VC-25A: under this designation the US Air Force is procuring two aircraft based on the Model 747-200 airliner and designed to replace the two VC-137Cs; as such they are being completely revised internally as presidential transports with national emergency airborne command post capability through installation of features such as secure communications; the variant is powered by four 56,750-lb (25,742-kg) thrust General Electric F103-GE-102 (CF6-80C2B1) non-afterburning turbofans with 53,611 US gal (202,940 litres) of fuel, and at a maximum take-off weight of 803,700 lb (364,552 kg) has a range of 6,910+ miles (11,120+ km)

E-4B: based on the airframe and powerplant of the Model 747-200B airliner, the E-4 was schemed in the early 1970s as replacement for the EC-135 series in the airborne national command post role, and the first three such aircraft entered service in 1974 and 1975 as E-4As with equipment stripped from EC-135s and updated by E-Systems; a fourth aircraft was built to a more advanced E-4B standard, and the three E-4As have since been upgraded to the more capable standard with an extremely wide-ranging assortment of voice, teletype and data communication links

Boeing Model 707-300C

(USA)

Type: long-range medium transport aeroplane
Accommodation: flightcrew of three or four, and 215 passengers or 141,100 lb (64,002 kg) of freight in the cabin and hold
Armament (fixed): none
Armament (disposable): none
Electronics and operational equipment: communication and navigation equipment
Powerplant and fuel system: four 19,000-lb (8618-kg) thrust Pratt & Whitney JT3D-7 non-afterburning turbofans, and a total internal fuel capacity of 23,855 US gal (90,299 litres); no provision for drop tanks or inflight refuelling
Performance: maximum speed 627 mph (1009 km/h) or Mach 0·95 at high altitude; cruising speed 605 mph (973 km/h) or Mach 0·87 at 25,000 ft (7620 m); initial climb rate 4,000 ft (1219 m) per minute; service ceiling 39,000 ft (11,885 m); range 4,300 miles (6920 km) with maximum payload; ferry range 7,475 miles (12,030 km)
Weights: empty 138,610 lb (62,872 kg); maximum take-off 333,600 lb (151,315 kg)
Dimensions: span 145 ft 9 in (44·42 m); length 152 ft 11 in (46·61 m); height 42 ft 5 in (12·93 m); wing area 3,050·00 sq ft (283·35 m²)

Variants

VC-137B: three Model 707-153s procured as VC-137A VIP transports with 13,500-lb (6123-kg) Pratt & Whitney JT3C-6 non-afterburning turbojets were thus redesignated after being re-engined with 18,000-lb (8165-kg) thrust Pratt & Whitney TF33-P-5 non-afterburning turbofans
VC-137C: two presidential-use VIP transports based on the civil Model 707-300B Intercontinental
KE-3A: convertible cargo/inflight-refuelling aeroplane adapted from ex-airline Model 707-300s for Saudi Arabia; these aircraft are powered by CFM56-A2-2 turbofans, and are provided with three hose-and-drogue units (one ventral and two underwing) for the transfer of 123,000 lb (55,792 kg) of fuel at a radius of 1,000 miles (1609 km) when the optional extra fuel tankage (for 5,000 US gal/18,927 litres) is fitted in the lower cargo hold; the cabin is fitted with facilities for interchangeable freighting, passenger, mixed freight and passenger, and VIP roles; similar aircraft for other countries are designated **KC-707**; in a separate programme two tanker versions of the Model 707 have been developed by Israel; the first was produced by IAI, and turns the transport into a single-point inflight-refuelling tanker with a flying boom under the rear fuselage; this is controlled with the aid of hydraulically actuated flying surfaces, the 'boomer' being equipped with a stereoscopic optronic system for precise control, and allows the transfer of fuel (boosted by cabin-located fuel drums containing 4,000 US gal/15,142 litres) at the rate of 1,000 US gal (3785 litres) per minute; the second variant was developed by the Bedek Aviation Division of IAI, and adds two underwing hose-and-drogue units

to the underfuselage boom, allowing the simultaneous refuelling of tactical aircraft fitted with two types of refuelling receptacle; each of the HDUs can supply fuel at the rate of 400 US gal (1514 litres) per minute, and in this variant the 23,855 US gal (90,300 litres) of standard fuel are supplemented by 4,500 US gal (17,034 litres) of additional fuel for empty and maximum take-off weights of 145,000 and 335,000 lb (65,772 and 151,956 kg) respectively
E-8A: Model 707-300 (C-18) variant planned and developed as the **EC-18C** but since redesignated E-8A as a battlefield surveillance and targeting aircraft with the JSTARS (Joint Surveillance and Target Attack Reconnaissance System) equipment in a combined US Air Force and US Army programme; the programme is being run by Boeing, with Grumman responsible for the mission equipment that includes Norden multi-mode SLAR (synthetic-aperture mode for surveillance of stationary targets and Doppler mode for the surveillance of slowly moving targets) and the JTIDS (Joint Tactical Information Distribution System); the first aeroplane flew in December 1988, and the requirement is for 21 aircraft for production from 1991
EC-18B: six aircraft converted from ex-American Airlines' Model 707-300 airliners as Advanced Range Instrumentation Aircraft with special electronics and a large steerable nose antenna, and intended mainly for missile and spacecraft tracking in parts of the world where the USA lacks ground-based tracking facilities
EC-18D: two aircraft converted from ex-American Airlines' Model 707-300s as cruise missile mission control aircraft in the US Air Force's programme to test remote tracking, command and control of RPVs and cruise missiles
Model 707-300: turbofan-engined civil model developed in Model 707-300B Intercontinental, Model 707-300C Convertible and Model 707-300C Freighter versions; several examples serve with air arms in a number of guises, including (in the case of Israel) electronic reconnaissance and intelligence-gathering; a few of the earlier Model 707-100 and Model 707-200 series aircraft (often re-engined with turbofans) also used by lesser air arms
Israel Aircraft Industries Model 707 Phalcon: airborne early warning conversion of the Model 707 transport in Israel with the Elta Phalcon solid-state surveillance radar with six conformal phased-array antennae (two on each side of the fuselage, one on the enlarged nose and one under the tail) to provide 360° coverage; the Phalcon system includes an advanced IFF capability, an ESM subsystem and a Comint subsystem

Above left: The E-4B is derived from the Model 747-20B airliner, but specially configured internally to serve as a high-endurance national command post with an extremely advanced suite of communications equipment (including a satellite communications subsystem) for the receipt of strategically vital information and the despatch of high-level orders.

Left: The first E-8A is seen on its initial take-off, at the beginning of the programme to prove the JSTARS (Joint Surveillance and Target Attack Reconnaissance System) suite.

Boeing Vertol CH-46D Sea Knight

(USA)
Type: assault transport medium helicopter
Accommodation: flightcrew of three, and 25 troops or 7,000 lb (3175 kg) of freight in the hold

Armament (fixed): none
Armament (disposable): none
Electronics and operational equipment: communication and navigation equipment

Powerplant and fuel system: two 1,400-shp (1044-kW) General Electric T58-GE-10 turboshafts, and a total internal fuel capacity of 350 US gal (1323 litres); no provision for drop tanks or inflight refuelling
Performance: maximum speed 166 mph (267 km/h) at sea level; cruising speed 165 mph (266 mph) at sea level; initial climb rate 1,715 ft (523 m) per minute; service ceiling 14,000 ft (5750 m); range 238 miles (383 km) with a 4,550-lb (2064-kg) payload
Weights: empty 13,067 lb (5927 kg); maximum take-off 23,000 lb (10,433 kg)
Dimensions: rotor diameter, each 51 ft 0 in (15·54 m); length overall, rotors turning 84 ft 4 in (25·70 m) and fuselage 44 ft 10 in (13·66 m); height 16 ft 8·5 in (5·09 m) to rear rotor head; rotor disc area, total 4,085·64 sq ft (379·56 m²)

Variants

CH-46A Sea Knight: this standard US Marine Corps assault transport helicopter was originated as the Model 107M military derivative of the Model 107-II commercial development of the underpowered and generally unsuccessful Model 107, which first flew in April 1958 and was evaluated as the YHC-1A for the US Army; the powerplant comprises two 1,250-shp (932-kW) General Electric T58-GE-8B turboshafts, and the type began to enter service in 1965 with a payload of 25 troops, or 15 litters and two attendants, or 4,000 lb (1814 kg) of freight carried over a range of 115 miles (185 km); production amounted to 164 helicopters
HH-46A Sea Knight: US Navy base rescue conversion of the CH-46A
CH-46D Sea Knight: much upgraded development of the CH-46A with 1,400-shp (1044-kW) T58-GE-10 turboshafts and cambered higher-lift rotor blades; the type can carry a slung load of 10,000 lb (4536 kg); production amounted to 266 helicopters
UH-46D Sea Knight: US Navy vertical replenishment (vertrep) equivalent of the CH-46D; production amounted to 10 helicopters, and two CH-46Ds were converted to this standard; the **HH-46D** is a base rescue conversion of the type
CH-46E Sea Knight: 300 CH-46A and CH-46D helicopters brought up to an improved operational standard with 1,870-shp (1394-kW) T58-GE-16 turboshafts, crash-attenuating crew seats, a crash-resistant fuel system and glassfibre rotor blades; the variant has empty and maximum take-off weights of 11,585 and 21,400 lb (5255 and 9707 kg) respectively, and has a range of 633 miles (1019 km) with a 2,400-lb (1088-kg) payload
CH-46F Sea Knight: improved version of the CH-46D with updated avionics and equipment; production amounted to 186 helicopters
CH-113 Labrador: utility helicopter derived from the CH-46A and in service with the Canadian air arm since 1963
CH-113B Voyageur: Canadian army equivalent of the CH-113
HKP-4: 21 Model 107-IIs (seven -II-5s and 14 -II-15s) for the Swedish navy and air force with Rolls-Royce Gnome H.1200 turboshafts

Left: A CH-46 Sea Knight in typical operating environment over a US Navy ship.

Right: A CH-47D Chinook shows off its triple-point external load capability with three rubber fuel cells.

Boeing Vertol CH-47D Chinook

(USA)
Type: transport medium/heavy helicopter
Accommodation: flightcrew of two or three, and between 33 and 55 troops depending on seating arrangement, or 24 litters and two attendants, or 18,000 lb (8164 kg) of freight in the hold, or a slung load of 28,000 lb (12,701 kg)
Armament (fixed): generally none, though there is provision for a machine-gun mounted on the rear ramp/door
Armament (disposable): none
Electronics and operational equipment: communication and navigation equipment
Powerplant and fuel system: two 4,500-shp (3356-kW) Avco Lycoming T55-L-712 turboshafts with an ordinary rating of 3,750 shp (2796 kW), and a total internal fuel capacity of 1,030 US gal (3899 litres); no provision for drop tanks or inflight refuelling
Performance: maximum speed 188 mph (302 km/h) at sea level; maximum climb rate 1,335 ft (407 m) per minute; service ceiling 22,100 ft (6735 m); hovering ceiling out of ground effect 17,700 ft (5395 m); radius 115 miles (185 km) with an 18,000-lb (8164-kg) load; ferry range 1,279 miles (2058 km)
Weights: empty 23,093 lb (10,475 kg); maximum take-off 54,000 lb (24,494 kg)
Dimensions: rotor diameter, each 60 ft 0 in (18·29 m); length overall, rotors turning 99 ft 0 in (30·18 m) and fuselage 51 ft 0 in (15·54 m); height 18 ft 7·8 in (5·68 m) to rear rotor head; rotor disc area, total 5,654·86 sq ft (525·34 m²)

Variants

CH-47A Chinook: initial production version of the Model 114/YHC-1B prototype, which first flew in September 1961 for service from late 1962; the type is in essence a scaled-up Model 107 with 2,200-shp (1641-kW) Avco Lycoming T55-L-5 turboshafts, later replaced by 2,650-shp (1976-kW) T55-L-7 turboshafts, driving larger-diameter rotors on a lengthened fuselage with quadricycle rather than tricycle landing gear but still fitted with a power-operated rear ramp/door for ease of loading/unloading; the extra power and size provides a typical payload of 44 troops or an external load of 16,000 lb (7257 kg); production amounted to 354 helicopters
CH-47B Chinook: upgraded model with 2,850-shp (2125-kW) T55-L-7C turboshafts, modified rotor blades and a number of detail improvements; service entry took place in 1967, and production amounted to 108 helicopters
CH-47C Chinook: much improved model with 3,750-shp (2796-kW) T55-L-11A turboshafts, strengthened transmission and a modest increase in internal fuel capacity; service entry took place in 1968, and production amounted to 270 helicopters; all surviving CH-47As and CH-47Bs were later upgraded to the same basic standard; from the late 1970s survivors have been fitted with glassfibre rotor blades
CH-47D Chinook: updated standard with 13 major improvements such as more powerful engines, further strengthened transmission, composite-construction rotor blades, crash-resistant features and more advanced avionics; the type has a three-point external attachment system to cater for heavy loads, and the first of a planned 472 older helicopters upgraded to this standard was redelivered in May 1982
CH-47D International Chinook: basic designation of military Chinooks for export; the original company designation for this variant, which is basically similar to the CH-47D, was **Model 414**
MH-47E Chinook: special forces version of the CH-47D under development in the later 1980s for service from 1991 with terrain-avoidance/following radar, the increased fuel capacity of the civil Chinook for an unrefuelled range of 1,450 miles (2333 km) with two auxiliary tanks, provision for inflight refuelling, and other advanced features for the clandestine insertion and extraction of covert forces at a maximum weight of 54,000 lb (24,494 kg) with a pair of T55-L-714 turboshafts rated to 4,000 shp (2983 kW) at up to 94°F (34·4°C) ; the type is to be fitted with a pair of 0·5-in (12·7-mm) machine-guns for the suppression of defensive fire, and also with an extensive suite of countermeasures (laser-warning receiver, RWR, radar jammer and chaff/flare launchers) and advanced sensors (FLIR, night-vision goggles etc) feeding into a modern cockpit with HDDs; the MH-47E is planned to have a 345-mile (555-km) unrefuelled radius with 36 troops in European conditions, declining to the same radius with 30 troops under hot-and-high conditions; the requirement eventually is for 51 such helicopters
CH-147: Canadian Armed Forces' version with T55-L-11C turboshafts and avionics optimized for Canadian conditions
Chinook HC.Mk 1: version for the UK and based on the CH-147 but with T55-L-11E turboshafts and a maximum external load capability of 28,000 lb (12700 kg); helicopter upgraded with glassfibre rotor blades and T55-L-512 turboshafts are redesignated **Chinook HC.Mk 1A**
Kawasaki (Boeing) CH-47J: CH-47D built under licence in Japan
Meridionali (Boeing) CH-47C: Italian licence-built CH-47C and differing little from the US standard; the type has been sold in southern Europe, North Africa and the Middle East; later helicopters are designated **CH-47C Plus** with T55-L-512E turboshafts

British Aerospace HS 748 Series 2B Military Transport

British Aerospace Buccaneer

HS 748 Series 2B (left column)

(UK)

Type: short/medium-range utility transport aeroplane

Accommodation: flightcrew of three, and 58 troops, or 48 paratroops, or 24 litters and nine attendants, or 12,975 lb (5885 kg) of freight in the cabin

Armament (fixed): none

Armament (disposable): none

Electronics and operational equipment: communication and navigation equipment

Powerplant and fuel system: two 2,280-shp (1800-kW) Rolls-Royce Dart RDa·7 Mk 536-2 turboprops, and a total internal fuel capacity of 1,440 Imp gal (6550 litres); no provision for drop tanks or inflight refuelling

Performance: cruising speed 280 mph (451 km/h) at optimum altitude; initial climb rate 1,420 ft (433 m) per minute; service ceiling 25,000 ft (7620 m); range 905 miles (1456 km) with maximum payload, or 1,475 miles (2374 km) with a 14,027-lb (6363-kg) payload

Weights: empty 25,730 lb (11,671 kg); maximum take-off 51,000 lb (23,133 kg)

Dimensions: span 102 ft 5·5 in (31·23 m); length 67 ft 0 in (20·42 m); height 24 ft 10 in (7·57 m); wing area 828·9 sq ft (77·00 m²)

Variants

Andover C.Mk 1: Avro (later HS) 780 derivative of the Avro (later HS) 748M military transport for the Royal Air Force in the STOL tactical transport (freighting, trooping and paratrooping) role; this requirement led to the strengthening of the floor in a fuselage lengthened to 77 ft 11 in (23·75 m) and fitted with an upswept tail to allow the fitting of a rear ramp/door for the straight-in loading and

unloading of lengthy items, the installation of 3,245-shp (2420-kW) Dart RDa·12 Mk 201C turboprops on a 98-ft (29·87-m) wing, the use of large-diameter low-pressure tyres, and the incorporation of a hydraulic system in the landing gear to align the ramp with the tailgates of trucks; the type entered service in July 1966, and seven were later modified as navaid calibration aircraft with the designations **Andover E.Mk 3** (four aircraft) and **Andover E.Mk 3A** (three aircraft)

Andover CC.Mk 2: passenger transport version of the HS 748 Series 2

HS 748M: military transport version of the HS 748 Series 1 civil transport, later known as the HS 757 and assembled by HAL in India from British components

HS 748 Series 2A Military Transport: development of the Series 2 civil transport with 2,280-shp (1,700-kW) Dart RDa·7 Mk 534-2 or Mk 532-2 turboprops, a strengthened floor and an upswept tail with ventral ramp; the variant has empty and maximum take-off weights of 25,998 and 45,095 lb (11,787 and 20,455 kg) respectively, the latter figure including an 11,512-lb (5221-kg) payload

HS 748 Series 2B Military Transport: improved version with uprated powerplant and a 4-ft (1·22-m) increase in span for better performance in hot-and-high conditions

HS 748 Coastguarder: version available for the maritime patrol, search-and-rescue and limited anti-ship/submarine roles with fuel capacity increased to 2,210 Imp gal (10047 litres) for greater operating range; the type has Litton APS-504(V)3 or MEL Marec 2 search radar, high-quality navigation systems, optional features (such as MAD, ECM, ESM etc) and weapons capability

British Aerospace Buccaneer (right column)

(UK)

Type: low-level attack and strike aeroplane

Accommodation: pilot and navigator in tandem on Martin-Baker Mk 4MS ejector seats

Armament (fixed): none

Armament (disposable): this is carried on the revolving door of the weapons bay (rated at 4,000 lb/1814 kg) and on four hardpoints (two under each wing, each unit rated at 3,000 lb/1361 kg) up to a maximum weight of 16,000 lb (7258 kg); a WE-177 free-fall nuclear weapon can be carried, but a more common load for the weapons bay is four Mk 10 1,000-lb (454-kg) bombs; the hardpoints can each carry one Mk 10 or Mk N1 1,000-lb (454-kg) bomb, or one triple ejector rack for three 1,000-lb (454-kg) bombs, or a multiple ejector rack for six 500-lb (227-kg) bombs, or two 500- or 540-lb (227- or 245-kg) bombs, or one pod for 18 68-mm (2·28-in) or 32 2-in (51-mm) rockets; alternatives are three AJ.168 Martel ASMs and a Martel data-link pod, or four Sea Eagle anti-ship missiles

Electronics and operational equipment: communication and navigation equipment, plus Fer-

ranti Blue Parrot attack and ground-avoidance radar, Decca Doppler navigation working with a twin-gyro platform and moving map display, HUD, Ferranti FIN1043 INS, Marconi Sky Guardian 200 (updated ARI.18228) RWR, Tracor ALE-40 chaff/flare dispenser, and provision (in the weapon bay) for a reconnaissance package comprising one F97 night and six F95 day cameras or IR linescan equipment; the type can also carry the ALQ-101(V)10 jammer pod and the 'Pave Strike' targeting pod

Powerplant and fuel system: two 11,100-lb (5035-kg) thrust Rolls-Royce Spey RB.168-1A Mk 101 non-afterburning turbofans, and a total internal fuel capacity of 1,560 Imp gal (7092 litres) plus provision for auxiliary fuel in the form of 425 Imp gal (1932 litres) in a tank on the revolving weapon-bay door, 440 Imp gal (2000 litres) in a weapon-bay tank and two 250- or 430-Imp gal (1136- or 1955-litre) drop tanks; provision for inflight refuelling, and for a Mk 20B or Mk 20C pod for buddy refuelling of other Buccaneers

Performance: maximum speed 645 mph (1038 km/h) or Mach 0·85 at 200 ft (61 m); initial climb rate 7,000 ft (2134 m) per minute; service ceiling 40,000 + ft (12,190 + m); radius 600 miles (966 km) on a hi-lo-hi mission with full warload or 1,150 miles (1850 km) with reduced warload

Weights: empty 29,980 lb (13,599 kg); normal take-off 56,000 lb (25,402 kg); maximum take-off 62,000 lb (28,123 kg)

Dimensions: span 44 ft 0 in (13·41 m); length 63 ft 5 in (19·33 m); height 16 ft 3 in (4·95 m); wing area 514·7 sq ft (47·82 m²)

Variants

Buccaneer S.Mk 2A: designed as the Blackburn B-103 (sometimes known as NA.39) low-level carrierborne attack aircraft, the Buccaneer first flew in April 1958 and entered service as the Buccaneer S.Mk 1 with 7,100-lb (3221-kg) thrust de Havilland Gyron Junior Mk 101 turbojets, but was soon developed into the considerably more capable S.Mk 2 type with Rolls-Royce Spey turbofans for service from 1965; with the rundown of the Royal Navy's carrier force the Buccaneers were reallocated to the Royal Air Force, the S.Mk 2 becoming the S.Mk 2A without provision for Martel ASMs; the type can now carry the powerful Sea Eagle anti-ship missile

Buccaneer S.Mk 2B: Buccaneers built for the RAF with a bulged bomb-bay door for the carriage of additional fuel, and provision for the TV-homing Martel ASM; the type can now carry the powerful Sea Eagle anti-ship missile; surviving Buccaneers have been upgraded with improved avionics such as revised Blue Parrot radar

Buccaneer S.Mk 50: derivative of the S.Mk 2 for South Africa, basically similar to the British aircraft apart from the retractable installation of a retractable 8,000-lb (3629-kg) thrust Bristol Siddeley BS.605 twin-chamber liquid-fuelled rocket engine to boost take-off performance under hot-and-high conditions

Below left: An HS 748 Series 2A of the Belgian air force shows off the type's lines.

Below: A Buccaneer S.Mk 2A of No.208 Squadron from RAF Honington (later Lossiemouth) carries four Sea Eagle underwing missiles.

British Aerospace Canberra B(I).Mk 8

(UK)
Type: light bomber and intruder

Accommodation: pilot and navigator/bomb-aimer

Armament (fixed): four 20-mm Aden Mk 4 cannon with 500 rounds per gun in a ventral pack which may be carried optionally in the rear of the bomb bay

Armament (disposable): this is carried in the bomb bay and two hardpoints (one under each wing rated at 1,000 lb/454 kg) up to a maximum weight of 8,000 lb (3620 kg); the bomb bay can carry six 1,000-lb (454-kg) bombs on two Avro triple carriers in the bomb bay (one triple carrier if the ventral gun pack is carried), or one 4,000-lb (1814-kg) and two 1,000-lb (454-kg) bombs, or eight 500-lb (227-kg) bombs; the underwing hardpoints can each accept one 1,000-lb (454-kg) or two 500-lb (227-kg) bombs, or one AS.30 ASM, or one 7·62-mm (0·3-in) machine-gun pod, or one pod for 37 2-in (51-mm) rockets

Powerplant and fuel system: two 7,500-lb (3402-kg) thrust Rolls-Royce Avon RA.7 Mk 109 non-afterburning turbojets, and a total internal fuel capacity of 2,277 Imp gal (10,351 litres), plus provision for two 250-Imp gal (1137-litre) tiptanks and one 300-Imp gal (1364-litre) in the forward part of the bomb bay, or one 650-Imp gal (2955-litre) ferry tank; no provision for drop tanks or inflight refuelling

Performance: maximum speed 541 mph (871 km/h) or Mach 0·82 at 40,000 ft (12,190 m) and 510 mph (821 km/h) or Mach 0·67 at sea level; initial climb rate 3,600 ft (1097 m) per minute; service ceiling 48,000 ft (14,630 m); range 805 miles (1295 km) with maximum warload

Weights: empty 27,950 lb (12,678 kg); normal take-off 43,000 lb (19,505 kg); maximum take-off 54,950 lb (24,925 kg)

Dimensions: span 63 ft 11·5 in (19·49 m) without tiptanks; length 65 ft 6 in (19·96 m); height 15 ft 7 in (4·75 m); wing area 960·00 sq ft (89·19 m²)

Variants

Canberra B.Mk 2: initial production version of the Canberra light bomber, first flown in May 1949; this version has a powerplant of two 6,500-lb (2948-kg) Rolls-Royce Avon RA.7 Mk 101 turbojets and an armament of six 1,000-lb (907-kg) bombs carried internally, and began to enter Royal Air Force service in 1951; export versions were the **Canberra B.Mk 20**, **Canberra B.Mk 52**, **Canberra B.Mk 62** and **Canberra B.Mk 82** for Australia, Ethiopia, Argentina and Venezuela respectively

Canberra T.Mk 4: baseline dual-control trainer version also produced as the **Canberra T.Mk 13**, **Canberra T.Mk 21**, **Canberra T.Mk 64** and **Canberra T.Mk 84** for New Zealand, Australia, Argentina and Venezuela respectively

Canberra B.Mk 6: definitive light bomber version powered by 7,500-lb (3402-kg) Avon Mk 109 turbojets and carrying eight 1,000-lb (454-kg) bombs (two of them under the wings, and replaceable by AS.30 ASMs, rocket pods etc)

Canberra PR.Mk 7: developed photographic reconnaissance model bearing the same relationship to the Canberra PR.Mk 3 as the B.Mk 6 to the B.Mk 2; the main export version was the **Canberra PR.Mk 57** for India, the **Canberra PR.Mk 83** being a version of the Canberra PR.Mk 3 for Venezuela

Canberra B(I).Mk 8: definitive nocturnal intruder version with a fighter-type pilot's cockpit offset to port and the navigator relocated to a glazed nose position; export versions were the **Canberra B(I).Mk 12**, **Canberra B(I).Mk 56**, **Canberra B(I).Mk 58**, **Canberra B(I).Mk 68** and **Canberra B(I).Mk 82** for New Zealand/South Africa, Peru (refurbished rather than new-build aircraft), India, Peru (new-build aircraft) and Venezuela respectively

Canberra PR.Mk 9: definitive photographic reconnaissance version with 10,500-lb (4763-kg) thrust Avon Mk 206 turbojets, a service ceiling of about 60,000 ft (18,290 m) and a range of 3,650+ miles (5875+ km) at a maximum take-off weight of some 56,250 lb (25,514 kg); this type is still in useful service, and has a span of 67 ft 10 in (20·68 m) and extended-chord inner wings for an area of 1,045·0 sq ft (97·08 m²); in the mid-1980s five aircraft were refurbished and upgraded for visual and electronic reconnaissance in British colours; recent improvements have seen the replacement of the original ARI.5800 'Orange Putter' RWR with the more modern ARI.18228 equipment (possibly those removed from Buccaneer S.Mk 2s retrofitted with the Sky Guardian 200 system)

Canberra T.Mk 17A: ECM trainer produced by converting Canberra B.Mk 2s with ARI.23363 or ARI.23379 radar jammer and GTE Dragonfly communications jammer in the nose, chaff dispensers in the bomb bay, and RWRs in the nose and tail

Canberra T.Mk 19: electronically silent target version produced as conversions of Canberra T.Mk 11 night-fighter trainers

Canberra T.Mk 22: conversion of Canberra PR.Mk 7s with Blue Parrot radar and other systems for the training of Fleet Air Arm crews

Left: A Canberra B(I).Mk 12 of the South African air force.

Right: Now out of service, the AV-8A was the USMC's version of the Harrier GR.Mk.3

British Aerospace Harrier GR.Mk 3

(UK)
Type: STOVL battlefield close support and reconnaissance aeroplane
Accommodation: pilot on a Martin-Baker Mk 9D zero/zero ejector seat
Armament (fixed): optional installation of two 30-mm Aden Mk 4 cannon with 150 rounds per gun in place of the underfuselage strakes
Armament (disposable): this is carried on five or seven hardpoints (one under the fuselage and two under each wing, with the underfuselage and inner underwing units each rated at 2,000 lb/907 kg and the outer underwing units each at 650 lb/295 kg, and the two optional outer-wing missile stations each at 220 lb/100 kg) up to a cleared maximum weight of 5,000 lb (2268 kg) though an 8,000-lb (3269-kg) warload has been demonstrated; typical weapons are 1,000-, 500- and 250-lb (454-, 227- and 113-kg) free-fall or retarded bombs, Paveway laser-guided bombs, Rockeye and BL755 cluster bombs, Matra 155 pods each with 16 68-mm (2·68-in) rockets, LAU-68 and LAU-69 pods each with seven or 19 2·75-in (70-mm) rockets, Mk 77 firebombs, and AIM-9 Sidewinder AAMs
Electronics and operational equipment: communication and navigation equipment, plus Ferranti FE451 inertial navigation and attack system, Smiths HUD, Marconi ARI.18223 RWR, Ferranti Type 106 LRMTS, and as possible wartime fits the Tracor ALE-40 chaff/flare dispenser and the Marconi Blue Eric AAA/SAM fire-control jammer
Powerplant and fuel system: one 21,500-lb (9752-kg) thrust Rolls-Royce Pegasus Mk 103 vectored-thrust non-afterburning turbofan, and a total internal fuel capacity of 630 Imp gal (2865 litres) plus provision for two 100-Imp gal (455-litre) drop tanks or two 330-Imp gal (1500-litre) ferry tanks; provision for inflight refuelling
Performance: maximum speed 737+ mph (1186+ km/h) or Mach 0·97+ at low altitude; initial climb rate 29,000 ft (8840 m) per minute; service ceiling 51,200 ft (15,605 m); radius 414 miles (667 km) on a hi-lo-hi mission after VTO with a 3,000-lb (1361-kg) warload; ferry range 3,445 miles (5560 km) with one inflight refuelling
Weights: empty 13,535 lb (6139 kg); maximum take-off 25,200 lb (11,431 kg)
Dimensions: span 25 ft 3 in (7·70 m) normal or 29 ft 8 in (9·04 m) with bolt-on ferry tips; length 46 ft 10 in (14·27 m); height 11 ft 11 in (3·63 m); wing area 201·1 sq ft (18·68 m²) without ferry tips

Variants

Harrier GR.Mk 3: designation of all current Harrier STOVL single-seat close-support aircraft, a few being built as such but most being produced by upgrading surviving Harrier GR.Mk 1A aircraft with an LRMTS in a chisel nose increasing length by 1 ft 3 in (0·38 m), with an RWR system, and with a Pegasus Mk 103 engine instead of the 20,500-lb (9299-kg) thrust Pegasus Mk 102; the type first flew as the Hawker Siddeley P.1127 in October 1960 and was developed as the Kestrel pre-production type before emerging as the Harrier for a first flight in August 1966 and service entry in April 1969
Harrier T.Mk 4: designation of Harrier T.Mk 2A trainers upgraded with Pegasus Mk 103 turbofans and with the operation equipment of the Harrier GR.Mk 3 other than the RWR
Harrier T.Mk 4A: type built with the Pegasus Mk 103 turbofan
Harrier T.Mk 4N: trainer for the Fleet Air Arm without the LRMTS
Harrier T.Mk 6: unspecified number of T.Mk 4s modified with FLIR sensors to assist in the conversion of Harrier pilots to the Harrier GR.Mk 7 used in the night attack role
Harrier T.Mk 60: trainer for the Indian navy with the electronics suite of the Sea Harrier FRS.Mk 51 apart from the Blue Fox radar
AV-8A Harrier: type for the US Marine Corps, this is basically similar to the Harrier GR.Mk 3 but lacking the LRMTS, RWR and INS; the variant has US equipment (including the Stencel S-III-S3 ejector seat) and provision for US weapons including AIM-9 Sidewinder AAMs, but is no longer in first-line service; the designation **AV-8S Matador** covers the basically identical version for Spain
TAV-8a Harrier: version of the Harrier T.Mk 4/4A for the US Marine Corps but without the LRMTS; the type is fitted, however, with UHF radio for use in the FAC role; the basically identical version for the Spanish amphibious forces is designated **TAV-8S Matador**
AV-8C: 47 AV-8A aircraft modified and life-extended by McDonnell Douglas with many of the systems improvements of the McDonnell Douglas AV-8B Harrier II, such as the lift-improvement devices, the ALE-39 chaff/flare dispenser system, onboard oxygen generation, secure voice communication equipment and an ALR-45 RWR with receivers in the wingtips and tail

British Aerospace Hawk T.Mk 1

(UK)

Type: basic and advanced flying and weapon trainer with a secondary air defence and attack capability

Accommodation: pupil and instructor in tandem on Martin-Baker Mk 10B zero/zero ejector seats

Armament (fixed): optional installation of one 30-mm Aden Mk 4 cannon and 120 rounds in an underfuselage pod

Armament (disposable): this is carried on a maximum of five hardpoints (one under the fuselage and one permanent plus one optional under each wing, with the underfuselage unit rated at 1,120 lb/508 kg and generally occupied by the cannon pod, and each underwing unit rated at 1,500 lb/680 kg) up to a cleared maximum weight of 5,660 lb (2567 kg) though a 6,800-lb (3084-kg) warload has been demonstrated; typical loads are five 1,000-lb (454-kg), or nine 500- or 250-lb (227- or 113-kg) free-fall or retarded bombs, or four pods for 18 68-mm (2·68-in) or 19 2·75-in (70-mm) or nine 80-mm (3·15-in) or four 5-in (127-mm) rockets, or nine 50-Imp gal (189-litre) napalm bombs, or two AIM-9 Sidewinder AAMs

Electronics and operational equipment: communication and navigation equipment, plus a Ferranti F195 sight and optional HUD, laser rangefinder and reconnaissance pod

Powerplant and fuel system: one 5,200-lb (2359-kg) thrust Rolls-Royce/Turboméca Adour Mk 151-01/02 non-afterburning turbofan, and a total internal fuel capacity of 375 Imp gal (1704 litres) plus provision for two 100-, 130- or 190-Imp gal (455-, 592- or 864-litre) drop tanks; no provision for inflight refuelling

Performance: maximum speed 645 mph (1038 km/h) or Mach 0·88 at 11,000 ft (3355 m); initial climb rate 9,300 ft (2835 m) per minute; service ceiling 50,000 ft (15,240 m); radius 345 miles (556 km) with a 5,600-lb (2540-kg) warload; ferry range 1,920 miles (3090 km)

Weights: empty 8,040 lb (3647 kg); normal take-off 12,284 lb (5572 kg) in the weapon training role; maximum take-off 18,890 lb (8569 kg)

Dimensions: span 30 ft 9·75 in (9·39 m); length 36 ft 7·75 in (11·17 m); height 13 ft 1·25 in (3·99 m); wing area 179·6 sq ft (16·69 m²)

Variants

Hawk T.Mk 1: designed as the Hawker Siddeley P.1182 to succeed the Hawker Siddeley (Folland) Gnat and Hawker Hunter flying and weapon trainers, the Hawk first flew in August 1974 and has matured into a highly capable multi-role trainer and light attack aircraft characterized by perfect handling for the carriage and delivery of a diverse weapons load

Hawk T.Mk 1A: 88 Hawk T.Mk 1s modified as secondary air-defence aircraft with four rather than two hardpoints and provision for AIM-9L Sidewinder AAMs and BL755 cluster bombs

Hawk Mk 50: export Hawks to basic T.Mk 1 standard but powered by the 5,340-lb (2463-kg) thrust Adour Mk 851 turbofan and cleared to a maximum take-off weight of 16,200 lb (7348 kg); the variant was bought by Finland (50 **Hawk Mk 51** aircraft with the Saab RGS2 sight), Kenya (12 **Hawk Mk 52** aircraft) and Indonesia (20 **Hawk Mk 53** aircraft)

Hawk Mk 60: uprated model with the 5,700-lb (2586-kg) thrust Adour Mk 861 turbofan in a fuselage stretched to give an overall length of 38·92 ft (11·86 m) and possessing empty and maximum take-off weights of 8,270 and 18,890 lb (3751 and 8569 kg) respectively; the result is much improved field performance, acceleration, climb rate and turn rate, as well as a 33% increase in payload and a 30% boost in range; the basic avionic fit of the type includes a Ferranti ISIS sight and SMS 2000 stores-management system; variants of this model have been bought by Zimbabwe (eight **Hawk Mk 60** aircraft), Dubai (nine **Hawk Mk 61** aircraft), Abu Dhabi (16 **Hawk Mk 63** aircraft), Kuwait (12 **Hawk Mk 64** aircraft), Saudi Arabia (30 **Hawk T.Mk 65** aircraft with braking parachutes and ground air-conditioning capability) and Switzerland (20 **Hawk T.Mk 66** aircraft)

Hawk Mk 100: also known as the **Enhanced Ground Attack Hawk**, this two-seat version was developed during the mid-1980s on the basis of the Hawk Mk 60 series with HOTAS (Hands On Throttle And Stick) controls and a MIL 1553B databus to allow full integration of modern weapons with new Singer Kearfott SKN 2416 INS, Smiths Industries HUD, HDD, weapon-aiming computer, SMS 2112 stores-management system, flare/chaff dispenser and RWR; the type can also carry a laser ranger and FLIR sensor as options; the maximum weapon load is 7,200 lb (3266 kg), lifted with the aid of a revised wing with wingtip missile rails for the carriage of two AIM-9 Sidewinder AAMs without detriment to the load of drop stores carried on the four underwing hardpoints; the type is powered by a 5,845-lb (2651-kg) thrust Adour Mk 871 turbofan in a fuselage that provides an overall length of 38 ft 4 in (17·39 m); the empty weight of this variant is 8,750 lb (3969 kg)

Below: The Hawk Mk 100 is based on the Mk 60 trainer but optimized for the ground-attack role with advanced electronics.

Opposite: Again based on the Mk 60 trainer, the Hawk Mk 200 is a single-seater developed for the multi-role and light attack roles.

British Aerospace Hawk 200

(UK)
Type: multi-role combat aeroplane
Accommodation: pilot on a Martin-Baker Mk 101 zero/zero ejector seat
Armament (fixed): one or two 25-mm Aden cannon and 100 rounds per gun in a lower-fuselage installation
Armament (disposable): this is carried on a maximum of five hardpoints (one under the fuselage rated at 1,120 lb/508 kg and two under each wing, with each unit rated at 2,000 lb/907 kg) up to a maximum weight of 7,700 lb (3493 kg); typical loads are five 1,000-lb (454-kg), or nine 500- or 250-lb (227- or 113-kg) free-fall or retarded bombs, or four pods for 18 68-mm (2·68-in) or 19 2·75-in (70-mm) or nine 80-mm (3·15-in) or four 5-in (127-mm) rockets, or nine 50-Imp gal (189-litre) napalm bombs, or two AIM-9 Sidewinder AAMs
Electronics and operational equipment: communication and navigation equipment, plus a Ferranti F195 sight and optional radar, HUD, laser rangefinder and reconnaissance pod to customer specification
Powerplant and fuel system: one 5,845-lb (2651-kg) thrust Rolls-Royce/Turboméca Adour Mk 871 non-afterburning turbofan, and a total internal fuel capacity of 375 Imp gal (1704 litres) plus provision for two 100-, 130- or 190-Imp gal (455-, 592- or 864-litre) drop tanks; no provision for inflight refuelling
Performance: maximum speed 645 mph (1038 km/h) at sea level; cruising speed 633 mph (1019 km/h) at sea level; initial climb rate 11,510 ft (5221 m) per minute; service ceiling 50,000 ft (15,240 m); radius 383 miles (617 km) on a hi-lo-hi mission with three Sea Eagle missiles and two 130-Imp gal (592-litre) drop tanks; ferry range 2,244 miles (3610 km) with three drop tanks
Weights: empty 9,100 lb (4128 kg); normal take-off 16,565 lb (7514 kg); maximum take-off 20,065 lb (9101 kg)
Dimensions: span 30 ft 9·75 in (9·39 m); length 36 ft 7·75 in (11·17 m); height 13 ft 1·25 in (3·99 m); wing area 179·6 sq ft (16·69 m²)

Variant

Hawk Mk 200: dedicated light attack single-seater first flown in May 1986 after development by BAe as a private venture based on the Hawk Mk 60 but fitted with the uprated thrust Adour Mk 871 turbofan, a new forward fuselage and advanced avionics such as a Smiths Industries HUD, Singer-Kearfott SKN 2416 INS and Ferranti LRMTS for highly accurate first-pass attacks with a wide assortment of disposable stores (including AIM-120 AMRAAM AAMs and Sea Eagle anti-ship missiles in aircraft fitted with nose radar rather than the LRMTS) on one underfuselage and four underwing hardpoints; the external fuel load is increased from the Hawk Mk 100's 380 Imp gal (1727·5 litres) to 510 Imp gal (2318·5 litres), which can be translated into an interdiction radius of 666 miles (1072 km) with a 3,000-lb (1361-kg) warload; the additional fuselage volume allows the fitting of (for example) single or twin 25-mm Aden 25 cannon. First flown in May 1986; planned production variants are the **Hawk Mk 200-60** using the nav/attack system of the Hawk Mk 60 for visual operations, and the **Hawk Mk 200-100** using the nav/attack system of the Hawk Mk 100 for all-weather operations in conjunction with Ferranti Blue Fox radar or, as ordered by Saudi Arabia, Westinghouse APG-66(H), and weapons such as Sea Eagle anti-ship and Sky Flash AAMs

British Aerospace Hunter FGA.Mk 9

(UK)
Type: ground-attack fighter and weapon trainer
Accommodation: pilot on a Martin-Baker Mk 3H ejector seat
Armament (fixed): four 30-mm Aden Mk 4 cannon with 135 rounds per gun in a detachable ventral pack
Armament (disposable): this is carried on four hardpoints (two under each wing, with the inner units each rated at 2,000 lb/907 kg and the outer units each at 1,000 lb/454 kg) up to a maximum weight of 6,000 lb (2268 kg); typical weapons are bombs up to a weight of 1,000 lb (454 kg), clusters of 3-in (76-mm) rockets, pods for rockets ranging in size from 2 to 2·75 in (51 to 70 mm), and napalm bombs
Electronics and operational equipment: communication and navigation equipment, plus ranging radar and an optical sight
Powerplant and fuel system: one 10,150-lb (4604-kg) thrust Rolls-Royce Avon RA.28 Mk 207 non-afterburning turbojet, and a total internal fuel capacity of 392 Imp gal (1782 litres) plus provision for four 100-, 230- or 330-Imp gal (455-, 1046- or 1500-litre) drop tanks; no provision for inflight refuelling
Performance: maximum speed 710 mph (1144 km/h) or Mach 0·93 at sea level and 620 mph (978 km/h) or Mach 0·94 at high altitude; initial climb rate 17,200 ft (5243 m) per minute; service ceiling 51,500 ft (15,700 m); radius 443 miles (713 km) on a hi-lo-hi mission with typical warload and two drop tanks; ferry range 1,840 miles (2965 km) with two 230-Imp gal (1046-litre) drop tanks
Weights: empty 14,400 lb (6532 kg); normal take-off 18,000 lb (8165 kg); maximum take-off 24,600 lb (11,158 kg)
Dimensions: span 33 ft 8 in (10·25 m); length 45 ft 10·5 in (13·98 m); height 13 ft 2 in (4·02 m); wing area 349·0 sq ft (32·42 m²)

Variants
Hunter F.Mk 6: the Hunter was developed as the Hawker P.1067 and first flew in prototype form during July 1951, entering service with the Royal Air Force as the Hunter F.Mk 1 in July 1954; the Hunter F.Mk 6 was the definitive fighter model and appeared in 1956 with the Avon Mk 200 series turbojet for more power and thus better performance than earlier models; variants of this basic theme are the **Hunter Mk 56** for India and **Hunter Mk 58** for Switzerland, the latter being particularly potent with their Saab weapon systems, AIM-9 Sidewinder AAMs and AGM-65 Maverick ASMs
Hunter T.Mk 7: side-by-side conversion trainer based on the Hunter F.Mk 4 fighter but with the Avon Mk 122 turbojet; export versions generally had the Avon Mk 200 series turbojet, and included the **Hunter T.Mk 66**, **Hunter T.Mk 72**, **Hunter T.Mk 75**, **Hunter T.Mk 77** and **Hunter T.Mk 79** for India, Chile, Singapore, Abu Dhabi and Qatar respectively
Hunter T.Mk 8: naval trainer version derived from the Hunter F.Mk 4 with specialized equipment and arrester hooks
Hunter FGA.Mk 9: dedicated fighter/ground-attack model introduced in 1959 with strengthened landing gear, a braking parachute and greater provision for external stores; export versions included the **Hunter FGA.Mk 57**, **Hunter FGA.Mk 70**, **Hunter FGA.Mk 71**, **Hunter FGA.Mk 74**, **Hunter FGA.Mk 76** and **Hunter FGA.Mk 78** for Kuwait, Lebanon, Chile, Singapore, Abu Dhabi and Qatar respectively
Hunter FR.Mk 10: tactical reconnaissance derivative of the Hunter FGA.Mk 9 with a fan of three cameras instead of the nose-mounted ranging radar; the **Hunter FR.Mk 74A** was the export version for Singapore
Hunter GA.Mk 11: version of the Hunter FGA.Mk 9 for the Fleet Air Arm, based on the Hunter F.Mk 4 and used for weapons training with the AST-4(V) missile simulation pod
Hunter PR.Mk 11: version for the Fleet Air Arm, based on the Hunter F.Mk 4 and used for photographic reconnaissance training

British Aerospace Nimrod

(UK)
Type: maritime patrol and anti-submarine aeroplane
Accommodation: flightcrew of three, and a mission crew of nine in the cabin, which can alternatively carry 45 troops in the Nimrod's secondary trooping capability
Armament (fixed): none
Armament (disposable): this is carried in a lower-fuselage weapons bay and on two hardpoints (one under each wing) up to a maximum weight of 13,500 lb (6123 kg); typical loads include nine Mk 46 or Stingray torpedoes, and the underwing hardpoints can carry AIM-9 Sidewinder AAMs, or AGM-84 Harpoon or Sea Eagle antiship missiles
Electronics and operational equipment: communication and navigation equipment, plus separate processing systems for tactical navigation, acoustic-processing and radar-processing functions; the tactical system is produced by Marconi with a 920 ATC central computer using data from the Ferranti INS, the Loral ARI.18240/1 (EW-1017) and/or Thomson-CSF ESM systems, the Emerson ASQ-10A MAD system, the acoustic system and the radar system; the Marconi AQS-901 acoustic processing and display system has twin 920 ATC computers and is compatible with many Western sonobuoys including advanced types such as the Australian Barra, the British Ultra X17255 command active multi-beam type, the Canadian Tandem, and the US SSQ-41 and SSQ-53; and the radar system is based on the EMI Searchwater long-range radar and a Ferranti FM1600D digital computer
Powerplant and fuel system: four 12,140-lb

Below: A Hunter FGA.Mk 9 is seen in the markings of No. 79 Squadron, a 'shadow' unit of No. 1 Tactical Weapons Unit at RAF Brawdy.

Right: This aeroplane reveals the initial MR.Mk 1 standard to which all current Nimrod maritime patrol aircraft were built.

MR.Mk 2

(5507-kg) thrust Rolls-Royce Spey RB.168-20 Mk 250 non-afterburning turbofans, and a total internal fuel capacity of 10,730 Imp gal (48,780 litres) plus provision for 1,890 Imp gal (8592 litres) of ferry fuel in six weapon-bay tanks; no provision for drop tanks but provision for inflight refuelling

Performance: maximum speed 575 mph (925 km/h) at optimum altitude; cruising speed 547 mph (880 km/h); patrol speed 230 mph (370 km/h) on two engines; service ceiling 42,000 ft (12,800 m); patrol endurance 12 hours; ferry range 5,755 miles (9265 km) on internal fuel

Weights: empty 86,000 lb (39,010 kg); normal take-off 177,500 lb (80,514 kg); maximum take-off 192,000 lb (87,091 kg)

Dimensions: span 114 ft 10 in (35·00 m) without wingtip ESM pods; length with probe 129 ft 1 in (39·34 m); height 29 ft 9·5 in (9·08 m); wing area 2·121·0 sq ft (197·00 m²)

Variants

Nimrod R.Mk 1: based on the Nimrod MR.Mk 1 maritime patrol and anti-submarine aircraft, itself based on the airframe of the de Havilland Comet 4C airliner and developed from 1964 by Avro and then Hawker Siddeley, the Nimrod R.Mk 1 was produced in small numbers (just three aircraft) for the dedicated Elint role; the three aircraft were handed over to the Royal Air Force in July 1971 for commissioning in May 1974 after an extensive fitting-out programme with Loral ARI.18240/1 (EW-1017) ESM in wingtip pods, and with other British and American Elint systems in the fuselage; little is known of the aircraft, but it is thought that they have excellent range through the installation of auxiliary fuel tanks in the volume reserved for weapons in the MR series; the overall length is 119 ft 9 in (36·50 m)

Nimrod MR.Mk 2: improved maritime patrol and anti-submarine aircraft produced by converting 31 of the 46 Nimrod MR.Mk 1 aircraft; the first mark had been delivered from 1969, but the pace of Soviet submarine development was such that by the mid-1970s the Nimrod MR.Mk 1s were beginning to show signs of obsolescence in their sensor and data-processing capabilities; this led to the Nimrod MR.Mk 2 upgrade programme, the much improved aircraft being redelivered from 1979 with a new tactical system, search radar (Searchwater in place of the original EMI ASV-21D), acoustic processing system, displays and consoles, inertial navigation and Loral ARI.18240/1 (EW-1017) wingtip ESM pods to complement the Thomson-CSF unit podded on top of the fin; further development in the 1980s added inflight-refuelling capability on 16 aircraft, plus the ability to carry AGM-84 Harpoon anti-ship missiles and up to four AIM-9 Sidewinder self-protection AAMs

Nimrod MR.Mk 3: in 1989 it was announced that in the first half of the 1990s the Nimrod MR.Mk 2 fleet will receive a mid-life update that will involve an almost completely new mission electronics suite; this will provide advanced capability against the latest submarines, and the system will probably be designed on a modular basis in such a way that it can be installed in the RAF's ultimate replacement for the Nimrod; the first Nimrod MR.Mk 3 is due to enter service in 1995

British Aerospace Sea Harrier FRS.Mk 1

(UK)

Type: carrierborne STOVL fighter, reconnaissance and strike aeroplane

Accommodation: pilot on a Martin-Baker Mk 10H zero/zero ejector seat

Armament (fixed): optional installation of two 30-mm Aden Mk 4* cannon with 150 rounds per gun in two pods carried in place of the underfuselage strakes

Armament (disposable): this is carried on five hardpoints (one under the fuselage and two under each wing, with the underfuselage unit rated at 2,000 lb/907 kg, the inner underwing units each at 2,000 lb/907 kg and the outer underwing units each at 650 lb/295 kg) to a cleared maximum weight of 5,000 lb (2268 kg) though an 8,000-lb (3629-kg) warload has been demonstrated; a WE-177 nuclear weapon can be carried, but typical weapons are 1,000-, 500- and 250-lb (454-, 227- and 113-kg) free-fall or retarded bombs, Paveway laser-guided bombs, Rockeye and BL755 cluster bombs, Matra 155 pods each with 16 68-mm (2·68-in) rockets, LAU-68 and LAU-69 pods with seven or 19 2·75-in (70-mm) rockets, RN launchers each with 19 2-in (51-mm)

rockets, Mk 77 fire bombs, AJ.168 Martel ASMs, Sea Eagle or AGM-84 Harpoon anti-ship missiles, and AIM-9 Sidewinder AAMs

Electronics and operational equipment: communication and navigation equipment, plus Ferranti Blue Fox pulse-Doppler multi-mode radar, Ferranti FE451 inertial navigation and attack system with a Decca twin-gyro reference system and Decca 72 Type Doppler navigation, Smiths HUD, Marconi ARI.18223 RWR, F.95 oblique camera, and (probably) Tracor ALE-40 chaff/flare dispenser

Powerplant and fuel system: one 21,500-lb (9752-kg) thrust Rolls-Royce Pegasus Mk 104 vectored-thrust non-afterburning turbofan, and a total internal fuel capacity of 630 Imp gal (2865 litres) plus provision for two 100-Imp gal (455-litre) drop tanks or two 190- or 330-Imp gal (684- or 1500-litre) ferry tanks; provision for inflight refuelling

Performance: maximum speed 690 mph (1110 km/h) or Mach 0·9 at sea level; initial climb rate about 50,000 ft (15,240 m) per minute; service ceiling 51,000 ft (15,545 m); radius 460 miles (740 km) on a hi-hi-hi mission with full AAM load,

or 288 miles (463 km) on a hi-lo-hi attack mission
Weights: empty 14,052 lb (6374 kg); maximum take-off 26,200 lb (11,884 kg)
Dimensions: span 25 ft 3 in (7·70 m); length 47 ft 7 in (14·50 m); height 12 ft 2 in (3·71 m); wing area 201·1 sq ft (18·68 m²)

Variants
Sea Harrier FRS.Mk 1: this carrierborne STOVL fighter, reconnaissance and strike derivative of the land-based Harrier proved itself a formidable weapon in the Falklands war of 1982 after development to give the Royal Navy's three 'Invincible' class light carriers a potent fixed-wing air strength; the programme began in 1975, and the type began to enter Fleet Air Arm service in 1981; compared with the Harrier, the Sea Harrier has a revised structure less susceptible to salt-water corrosion, naval equipment, and a totally new forward fuselage; this last seats the pilot higher under a bubble canopy for air-combat visibility, has a new nav/attack system and displays, and a Blue Fox multi-mode radar
Sea Harrier FRS.Mk 2: mid-life update version of the Sea Harrier FRS.Mk 1, designed to provide

the type with the ability to engage multiple beyond-visual-horizon targets (even those at low level) with four AIM-120 AMRAAM AAMs; to this end Ferranti Blue Vixen coherent pulse-Doppler track-while-scan radar replaces the original Blue Fox radar to improve acquisition and look-down capabilities; other improvements are a MIL 1553B digital databus (making it possible to carry Sea Eagle anti-ship and ALARM anti-radar missiles) and the installation of the Marconi Sky Guardian 200 RWR, the Joint Tactical Information and Distribution System for secure voice and data links, two additional underwing hardpoints, wingtip stations for two AIM-9 Sidewinder AAMs, wing improvements, a revised cockpit with HOTAS (Hands On Throttle And Stick) controls, larger drop tanks, 25-mm Aden 25 cannon in place of the elderly 30-mm weapons, and possibly the Plessey missile-approach warner; the Sea Harrier FRS.Mk 2 is some 14 in (0·356 m) longer than the FRS.Mk 1 as a result of a fuselage insert aft of the wing, and has slightly extended span
Sea Harrier FRS.Mk 51: designation of Sea Harrier FRS.Mk 1 aircraft for the Indian navy with revised systems and provision for Matra Magic rather than AIM-9 Sidewinder AAMs

Left: The latest Sea Harrier standard is the FRS.Mk 2 configuration seen here with Blue Vixen radar and AIM-120A AMRAAM air-to-air missiles.

Opposite, top: The Sea Harrier FRS.Mk 2 is designed for beyond-visual-range engagement of targets with its quartet of AIM-120A AMRAAMs carried under the fuselage and wings.

Opposite, bottom: A Sea Harrier FRS.Mk 1 of No. 800 Squadron on board the carrier USS *Dwight D. Eisenhower.*

British Aerospace Shackleton AEW.Mk 2

(UK)
Type: airborne early warning aeroplane

Accommodation: flightcrew of four, and a mission crew of six in the cabin

Armament (fixed): none

Armament (disposable): none

Electronics and operational equipment: communication and navigation equipment, plus APS-20F(1) surveillance radar, Orange Harvest broadband ESM equipment, APX-17 IFF and selective interrogator, and processing/display equipment

Powerplant and fuel system: four 2,455-hp (1831-kW) Rolls-Royce Griffon 57A piston engines, and a total internal fuel capacity of 4,248 Imp gal (19,285 litres); no provision for drop tanks or inflight refuelling

Performance: maximum speed 273 mph (439 km/h) at optimum altitude; initial climb rate 850 ft (259 m) per minute; service ceiling 23,000 ft (7010 m); range 3,050 miles (4908 km)

Weights: empty 57,000 lb (25,855 kg); maximum take-off 98,000 lb (44,452 kg)

Dimensions: span 120 ft 0 in (36·58 m); length 87 ft 4 in (26·62 m); height 16 ft 9 in (5·10 m); wing area 1,421·0 sq ft (132·0 m²)

Variant
Shackleton AEW.Mk 2: now the only variant of the Shackleton maritime patrol, anti-submarine and airborne early warning family in service (and retained in service only because of the cancellation of the Nimrod AEW.Mk 3 programme), the Shackleton AEW.Mk 2 is only one step removed from total obsolescence; the Shackleton MR series entered service in 1951, and the Shackleton AEW.Mk 2 was produced between 1971 and 1974 by conversion of surplus Shackleton MR.Mk 2s with World War II-vintage APS-20 radar stripped from Fairey Gannet AEW aircraft surplus to Fleet Air Arm requirements after the demise of its major carriers

British Aerospace Strikemaster Mk 88

(UK)
Type: light attack aeroplane

Accommodation: pilot and co-pilot on Martin-Baker Mk PB4 ejector seats

Armament (fixed): two 7·62-mm (0·3-in) FN MAG machine-guns with 550 rounds per gun

Armament (disposable): this is carried on four hardpoints (two under each wing and each rated

Above: The aged Shackleton AEW.Mk 2s of No. 8 Squadron are to be replaced by Sentry AEW.Mk 1s in the early 1990s.

Below: A Strikemaster Mk 81 of the South Yemeni air force.

Opposite: A VC10 K.Mk 2 tanker of No. 101 Squadron at RAF Brize Norton.

at 1,000 lb/454 kg) up to a maximum weight of 3,000 lb (1361 kg); typical weapons are 1,000-, 500- and 250-lb (454-, 227- and 113-kg) bombs, napalm bombs, Matra 155 pods each with 18 68-mm (2·68-in) rockets, LAU-68 pods each with seven 2·75-in (70-mm) rockets, banks of four 81-mm (3·2-in) SURA rockets, and pods for 7·62-mm (0·3-in) machine-guns or 20-mm cannon

Electronics and operational equipment: communication and navigation equipment, plus a SFOM optical sight or a GM2L reflector sight or a Ferranti LFS gyro sight

Powerplant and fuel system: one 3,140-lb (1424-kg) thrust Rolls-Royce Viper Mk 535 non-afterburning turbojet, and a total internal fuel capacity of 366 Imp gal (1664 litres) plus provision for two 48-Imp gal (218-litre) tiptanks as well as two 50- and two 75-Imp gal (two 227- and two 341-litre) drop tanks; no provision for inflight refuelling

Performance: maximum speed 480 mph (772 km/h) at 18,000 ft (5585 m); initial climb rate 5,250 ft (1600 m) per minute; service ceiling 40,000 ft (12,190 m); radius 145 miles (233 km) on a lo-lo-lo mission with maximum warload; ferry range 1,382 miles (2224 km)

Weights: empty 6,195 lb (2810 kg); normal take-off 10,600 lb (4808 kg); maximum take-off 11,500 lb (5215 kg)

Dimensions: span 36 ft 10 in (11·23 m) over tiptanks; length 33 ft 8·5 in (10·27 m); height 10 ft 11·5 in (3·34 m); wing area 213·7 sq ft (19·85 m²)

Variants
Jet Provost T.Mk 3: the Hunting Jet Provost first flew in prototype form in June 1954 and continues to serve the Royal Air Force well during the later 1980s; the Jet Provost T.Mk 3 was introduced in 1958 with the 1,750-lb (794-kg) thrust Viper 8 turbojet, ejector seats, a clear rather than framed canopy, and tip tanks; the installation of better navigational equipment resulted in the **Jet Provost T.Mk 3A**

Jet Provost T.Mk 4: improved version of 1960 with the 2,500-lb (1134-kg) thrust Viper 11

Jet Provost T.Mk 5: definitive trainer version with full pressurization, a slightly bulged canopy and the 2,500-lb (1134-kg) Viper Mk 201; the installation of better navigational equipment resulted in the **Jet Provost T.Mk 5A**

Jet Provost T.Mk 50: trainers for Sri Lanka and Sudan and strengthened trainer/light attack aircraft for Iraq and Venezuela

Strikemaster Mk 80: light attack variant derived from the Jet Provost with better ejector seats, provision for a wide assortment of armament, major structural strengthening (especially of the wings and landing gear), fuel relocated to integral and bag tanks in the wings and fixed tip tanks; the type first flew in October 1967 and has been used successfully in combat, where its great strength has proved a primary asset; variations within the type have been only small, and operators have included Saudi Arabia (**Strikemaster Mk 80** and improved **Strikemaster Mk 80A**), South Yemen (**Strikemaster Mk 81**), Oman (**Strikemaster Mk 82** and improved **Strikemaster Mk 82A**), Kuwait (**Strikemaster Mk 83**), Singapore (**Strikemaster Mk 84**), Kenya (**Strikemaster Mk 87**), New Zealand (**Strikemaster Mk 88**) and Ecuador (**Strikemaster Mk 89**)

Strikemaster Mk 90: final version, delivered in 1984 to Sudan with a number of modern features

British Aerospace VC10 C.Mk 1

(UK)
Type: long-range strategic transport aeroplane
Accommodation: flightcrew of four, and 150 passengers, or 78 litters plus attendants, or 61 seated casualties plus attendants, or 57,400 lb (26037 kg) of freight in the cabin
Armament (fixed): none
Armament (disposable): none
Electronics and operational equipment: communication and navigation equipment
Powerplant and fuel system: four 21,800-lb (9888-kg) thrust Rolls-Royce Conway RCo·43 Mk 301 non-afterburning turbofans, and a total internal fuel capacity of 19,365 Imp gal (88,032 litres); no provision for drop tanks but optional provision for inflight refuelling
Performance: cruising speed 425 mph (684 km/h) at 30,000 ft (9145 m); initial climb rate 2,300 ft (701 m) per minute; service ceiling 42,000 ft (12,800 m); range 3,900 miles (6276 km) with maximum payload
Weights: empty 146,000 lb (66,224 kg); maximum take-off 323,000 lb (146,510 kg)
Dimensions: span 146 ft 2 in (44·55 m); length 158 ft 8 in (48·38 m); height 39 ft 6 in (12·04 m); wing area 2,932·0 sq ft (272·38 m²)

Variants

VC10 C.Mk 1: original RAF version based closely on the fuselage of the VC10 civil airliner combined with other components (powerplant and fin fuel tank) of the Super VC10, and bought in small numbers for strategic and VIP transport
VC10 C.Mk 1(K): eight VC10 C.Mk 1s converted to the transport/tanker role with two wing-mounted Mk 32 hose-and-drogue units, a ventrally mounted closed-circuit TV system to monitor refuelling operations, and TACAN equipment; the other four VC10 C.Mk 1s will be converted to the same standard later
VC10 K.Mk 2: four ex-British Airways VC10s converted to an airframe, powerplant and avionics standard approximating that of the VC10 C.Mk 1 but finished as a three-point hose-and-drogue inflight-refuelling tanker with one Mk 17B hose-and-drogue unit in the lower rear fuselage with 81 ft (24·69 m) of hose and two Mk 32 HDUs, each with 50 ft (15·24 m) of hose, under the wings for 112,000 lb (50,802 kg) of transfer fuel; all VC10 tanker models are fitted as receivers for inflight refuelling; the VC10 K.Mk 2 has an overall length of 166 ft 1 in (50·62 m), an empty weight of 134,200 lb (60,875 kg) and a maximum take-off weight of 299,000 lb (135,622 kg) with 20,737 Imp gal (94,272 litres) of fuel; this variant has a forward cabin for 18 passengers and, in common with other VC10 tankers, has a Turboméca Artouste auxiliary power unit in the tailcone for self-start capability
VC10 K.Mk 3: five ex-East African Airways Super VC10s modified like the VC10 K.Mk 2s but with 190,400 lb (86,364 kg) of transfer fuel and an overall length of 171 ft 8 in (52·32 m) excluding the inflight-refuelling probe; the type has a maximum take-off weight of 322,000 lb (146,055 kg) with 22,609 Imp gal (102,782 litres) of fuel; this variant has a forward cabin for 17 passengers
VC10 K.Mk 4: five ex-British Airways Super VC10s converted to a tanker standard basically similar to that of the VC10 K.Mk 3 with a Mk 17B HDU in the lower fuselage and two Mk 32 HDUs under the wings, a ventral closed-circuit TV monitor system, TACAN equipment and an Artouste APU

British Aerospace Victor K.Mk 2

(UK)
Type: inflight-refuelling tanker aeroplane
Accommodation: flightcrew of four or five
Armament (fixed): none
Armament (disposable): none
Electronics and operational equipment: communication and navigation equipment, plus Marconi ARI.18288 RWR, and a refuelling system comprising one Mk 17B hose-and-drogue unit under the fuselage and two Mk 20B HDUs under the wings
Powerplant and fuel system: four 20,600-lb (9344-kg) thrust Rolls-Royce Conway Mk 201 non-afterburning turbofans, and a total internal fuel capacity of 15,875 Imp gal (72,168 litres) for self-use and transfer; no provision for drop tanks but provision for inflight refuelling
Performance: maximum transit speed 610 mph (982 km/h) at high altitude; service ceiling 52,500 ft (16,000 m); range 4,900 miles (7885 km) on internal fuel
Weights: empty 114,500 lb (51,936 kg); maximum take-off 238,000 lb (107,955 kg)
Dimensions: span 113 ft 0 in (33·44 m); length 114 ft 11 in (35·03 m); height 28 ft 1·5 in (8·57 m); wing area 2,200·0 sq ft (204·38 m²)

Variant

Victor K.Mk 2: now the only variant of the UK's three strategic V-bombers still in service, the Victor K.Mk 2 was produced urgently in the early 1970s by the conversion of the Victor B.Mk 2 bomber when the Vickers Valiant tanker fleet developed irremediable structural problems; no two conversions are identical, but a 'typical' Victor K.Mk 2 has some 100,000 lb (45,360 kg) of transfer fuel

Britten-Norman (Pilatus Britten-Norman) BN-2B Defender

(UK)

Type: utility and multi-role military aeroplane

Accommodation: pilot and nine passengers, or eight paratroops and one despatcher, or three litters and two attendants, or 2,250 lb (1021 kg) of freight in the cabin

Armament (fixed): none

Armament (disposable): this is carried on four optional hardpoints (two under each wing, with the inner units each rated at 700 lb/318 kg and the outer units each at 450 lb/204 kg) up to a maximum weight of 2,000 lb (907 kg); typical weapons are 500- or 250-lb (227- or 113-kg) bombs, banks of four 80-mm (3·15-in) SURA rockets, Matra 155 pods each with 18 68-mm (2·68-in) rockets, Matra 122 pods each with seven 68-mm (2·68-in) rockets, 7·62-mm (0·3-in) machine-gun pods, or AS.11 ASMs

Electronics and operational equipment: communication and navigation equipment

Powerplant and fuel system: two 300-hp (224-kW) Avco Lycoming IO-540-K1B5 piston engines, and a total internal fuel capacity of 114 Imp gal (518 litres) plus provision for two 24·5-Imp gal (111-litre) bolt-on ferry tanks and two 50-Imp gal (227-litre) drop tanks

Performance: maximum speed 174 mph (280 km/h) at sea level; cruising speed 159 mph (255 km/h) at 10,000 ft (3050 m); initial climb rate 1,300 ft (396 m) per minute; service ceiling 17,000 ft (5180 m); range 375 miles (603 km) with maximum payload; ferry range 1,723 miles (2772 km)

Weights: empty 4,020 lb (1824 kg); maximum take-off 6,600 lb (2993 kg)

Dimensions: span 49 ft 0 in (14·94 m) or 53 ft 0 in (16·15 m) with ferry tips; length 39 ft 5·75 in (12·02 m) with optional extended nose; height 13 ft 8·75 in (4·18 m); wing area 325·0 sq ft (30·19 m²) or 337·0 sq ft (31·31 m²) with bolt-on ferry tips

Variants

BN-2 Islander: initial civil model first flown in June 1965, and subsequently adopted by a number of air arms for the utility and tactical transport roles

BN-2A Islander: improved model also bought by some air arms

BN-2B Islander: definitive standard transport model with increased weights and other operational improvements

BN-2B Defender: capable multi-role military derivative capable of use in roles as different as long-range patrol to forward air control via logistical transport, trooping, casevac and paratrooping; the latest version of this military derivative is the **Defender 4000**, which has an improved airframe benefiting from structural developments evolved for the AEW Defender programme; though currently restricted to an 8,500-lb (3856-kg) maximum take-off weight, the type has a revised wing allowing growth to a maximum weight of 10,000 lb (4536 kg) with 50% more fuel than current Defenders, allowing the carriage of double the present payload

BN-2B Maritime Defender: maritime patrol version of the Defender with an enlarged nose for 120° scan Bendix RDR-1400 search radar, increasing length to 36 ft 3·75 in (11·07 m); a later version has 360° scan radar plus optional FLIR, MAD and an acoustic processing system plus associated sonobuoys; the latter model can also carry four Sea Skua anti-ship missiles or Sting Ray anti-submarine torpedoes

BN-2T Turbine Islander: turbine-engined model of the 1980s with two 400-shp (298-kW) Allison 250-B17C turboprops flat-rated at 320 shp (239 kW) for better performance with a 1,610-lb (730-kg) payload

BN-2T AEW Defender: proposed airborne early warning version with Thorn-EMI Skymaster pulse-Doppler surveillance radar (in a bulbous nose radome) for overland and overwater detection of targets at long range, IFF, air-to-ground data-link and advanced navigation system; with software modifications this same basic package is being offered in response to the British army's ASTOR (Airborne STand-Off Radar) requirement as an alternative to the CASTOR aircraft

BN-2T ELINT Defender: proposed Elint version with the Racal Kestrel electronic surveillance system installed in the cabin with sensors at various points of the airframe; the Kestrel system could also be fitted in the airframe of the standard piston-engined BN-2B

BN-2T Turbine Defender: combination of Defender capabilities with Turbine Islander performance and payload

BN-2T Turbine Defender/ASTOR: under this designation the British army is developing its Airborne STand-Off Radar system with the Ferranti ASTOR I radar (its radome in a platypus-type nose radome) for battlefield and rear-area surveillance; the definitive system may be switched to converted BAe Canberra airframes (using the ASTOR C derivative of the Thorn EMI Searchwater maritime surveillance radar) for improved performance over the battlefield, and thus less vulnerability to enemy countermeasures

BN-2A Mk III Trislander: stretched version with accommodation for 17 passengers and powered by three 260-hp (194-kW) Avco Lycoming O-540-E4C5 piston engines

BN-2A Mk III Trislander M: military version of the Trislander able to lift 17 troops over a range of 750 miles (1207 km) or 16 paratroops over a comparable range; the payload is 3,700 lb (1678 kg), and the type can be fitted with nose-mounted radar for the maritime patrol role

Canadair CL-41G-5 Tebuan

(Canada)
Type: advanced flying and weapon trainer, and light attack aeroplane
Accommodation: pilot and co-pilot side-by-side on Weber ejector seats
Armament (fixed): none
Armament (disposable): this is carried on six hardpoints (three under each wing) up to a maximum weight of 4,000 lb (1814 kg); typical weapons are 1,000-, 500- and 250-lb (454-, 227- and 113-kg) bombs, 7·62-mm (0·3-in) machine-gun pods and various types of rocket pod
Electronics and operational equipment: communication and navigation equipment, plus an optical sight
Powerplant and fuel system: one 2,950-lb (1338-kg) thrust General Electric J85-CAN-J4 non-afterburning turbojet, and a total internal fuel capacity of 250 Imp gal (1137 litres) plus provision for two 40-Imp gal (182-litre) drop tanks; no provision for inflight refuelling
Performance: maximum speed 470 mph (755 km/h) at 28,500 ft (8685 m); initial climb rate 4,250 ft (1295 m) per minute; service ceiling 42,200 ft (12,865 m); range 1,380 miles (2220 km) with drop tanks
Weights: empty 5,296 lb (2402 kg); normal take-off 10,000 lb (4536 kg); maximum take-off 11,288 lb (5120 kg)
Dimensions: span 36 ft 6 in (11·13 m); length 32 ft 0 in (9·75 in); height 9 ft 3 in (2·81 m); wing area 220·0 sq ft (20·44 m²)

Variants
CL-41A: this trim side-by-side two-seat pilot trainer was developed in Canada and first flew in January 1960 before entering service with the Canadian air arm as the **CT-114 Tutor** in 1963; the type was powered by one 2,850-lb (1293-kg) J85-CAN-40 turbojet, though surviving aircraft have received 2,950-lb (1338-kg) thrust engines in an updating programme launched in 1976 to extend service life, improve avionics and fit provision for external fuel; the type has a maximum take-off weight of 7,787 lb (3532 kg) and a maximum speed of 495 mph (797 km/h)
CL-41G-5 Tebuan: designation of the variant produced for Malaysia in the advanced training and light attack roles with strengthened airframe and landing gear, zero/zero ejector seats and six underwing hardpoints; the extra weight but only marginally more power means performance generally slightly inferior to that of the CL-41A

Opposite: Two BN-2B Defenders are the Belize Defence Force Air Wing's only aircraft.

Below: A Canadian CT-114 Tutor trainer.

Bottom: A CL-215 of the Greek air force.

Canadair CL-215

(Canada)
Type: multi-role amphibian flying boat
Accommodation: flightcrew of two, and 19 passengers or 6,260 lb (2839 kg) of freight in the cabin
Armament (fixed): none
Armament (disposable): none
Electronics and operational equipment: communication and navigation equipment
Powerplant and fuel system: two 2,100-hp (1566-kW) Pratt & Whitney R-2800-83AM2 piston engines, and a total internal fuel capacity of 1,300 Imp gal (5910 litres); no provision for drop tanks or inflight refuelling
Performance: cruising speed 181 mph (291 km/h) at 10,000 ft (3050 m); initial climb rate 1,000 ft (305 m) per minute; range 1,405 miles (2260 km) with a 3,500-lb (1587-kg) payload
Weights: empty 28,082 lb (12,738 kg); normal take-off 37,700 lb (17,100 kg) from water; maximum take-off 43,500 lb (19,731 kg) from land
Dimensions: span 93 ft 10 in (28·60 m); length 65 ft 0·25 in (19·82 m); height 29 ft 5·5 in (8·98 m) on land and 22 ft 7 in (6·88 m) on water; wing area 1,080·0 sq ft (100·33 m²)

Variants
CL-215: designed as a multi-role type of modest performance but great reliability and durability, the CL-215 amphibian first flew in October 1967 and has achieved a small but steady trickle of sales to civil and military operators, mainly in the SAR and fire-fighting roles, the latter with a maximum water payload of 12,000 lb (5443 kg); Spain and Thailand use the type for maritime patrol with RCA AVQ-21 or Bendix RDR-1400 radar in the nose
CL-215T: updated model featuring two 2,380-shp (1774-kW) Pratt & Whitney Canada PW123AF turboprops or identically rated hot-and-high versions of the same basic engine for improved overall performance, and under development in the late 1980s for the carriage of an additional 1500 kg (3,307 lb) of payload; the type first flew in December 1988, and though the type is generally similar to the basic CL-215 it differs in having maximum water and utility payloads of 13,500 and 10,560 lb (6123 and 4790 kg) respectively at land and water maximum take-off weights of 43,850 and 37,700 lb (19,890 and 17,100 kg) respectively, a maximum cruising speed of 240 mph (385 km/h) at 10,000 ft (3050 m), and a ferry range of 1,295 miles (2085 km) with a 1,950-lb (884-kg) payload

CASA (Construcciones Aeronauticas SA) C-101EB Aviojet

(Spain)

Type: basic and advanced flying and weapon trainer with a secondary light attack capability

Accommodation: pupil and instructor in tandem on Martin-Baker E10C zero/zero ejector seats

Armament (fixed): optional installation under the rear cockpit of two 0·5-in (12·7-mm) FN-Browning M3 machine-guns with 220 rounds per gun or one 30-mm DEFA 553 cannon with 130 rounds

Armament (disposable): this is carried on six hardpoints (three under each wing, with the two inner units each rated at 500 kg/1,102 lb, the two intermediate units each at 375 kg/827 lb and the two outer units each at 250 kg/551 lb) up to a maximum weight of 1500 kg (3,307 lb); typical loads are two 500-kg (1,102-lb) bombs, or four 375-kg (827-lb) bombs, or six 250-kg (551-lb) bombs, or four BLU-27 napalm bombs, or four LAU-10 pods each with four 5-in (127-mm) rockets, or six LAU-68 pods each with 19 2·75-in (70-mm) rockets, or six Matra 155 pods each with 18 68-mm (2·68-in) rockets, or two AIM-9 Sidewinder AAMs

Electronics and operational equipment: communication and navigation equipment, plus alternative packages (photo-reconnaissance, ECM or laser designation) in place of the lower-fuselage gun pack

Powerplant and fuel system: one 3,500-lb (1588-kg) thrust Garrett TFE731-2-2J non-afterburning turbofan, and a total internal fuel capacity of 2335 litres (514 Imp gal); no provision for drop tanks or inflight refuelling

Performance: maximum speed 690 km/h (429 mph) at sea level and 795 km/h (494 mph) or Mach 0·71 at 7620 m (25,000 ft); cruising speed 655 km/h (407 mph) at 9145 m (30,000 ft); initial climb rate 1152 m (3,780 ft) per minute; service ceiling 12,200 m (40,025 ft); radius 380 km (236 miles) on a lo-lo-lo interdiction sortie with 30-mm cannon pack and four 250-kg (551-lb) bombs; ferry range 3615 km (2,246 miles)

Weights: empty 3350 kg (7,385 lb); normal take-off 4850 kg (10,692 lb); maximum take-off 5600 kg (12,345 lb)

Dimensions: span 10·60 m (34 ft 9·3 in); length 12·25 m (40 ft 2·25 in); height 4·25 m (13 ft 11·25 in); wing area 20·00 m² (215·3 sq ft)

Variants

C-101EB Aviojet: designed in Spain with technical assistance from Northrop and MBB in the USA and West Germany respectively. the Aviojet is a neat tandem-seat advanced trainer that packs a useful light attack capability; the type features great strength, good handling characteristics, uncomplicated aerodynamics and structure and, for maximum fuel economy, a single high-bypass-ratio turbofan; an unusual feature is the provision in all versions of a lower-fuselage bay for the accommodation of armament, reconnaissance equipment, ECM equipment or a laser designator; the type first flew in June 1977 and was soon ordered for the Spanish air force, with which it entered service as the **E.25 Mirlo**; production was completed in 1985

C-101BB Aviojet: armed export version powered by the 3,700-lb (1678-kg) thrust TFE731-3-1J turbofan and sold to Honduras and Chile (**T-36 Halcon**), the latter producing the type under licence as well as importing a few knock-down kits

C-101CC Aviojet: improved light attack version also being produced by Chile, and powered by the 4,700-lb (2132-kg) thrust TFE731-5-1J turbofan for additional performance and an increase in weapons load to 2250 kg (4,460 lb) used with the Ferranti HUD and weapon-aiming computer system; the type has a maximum speed of 834 km/h (518 mph) at 4500 m (14,765 ft), a radius of 370 km (230 miles) on a lo-lo-lo close air support mission with a 50-minute armed loiter over the target, and a maximum take-off weight of 6300 kg (13,889 lb); Chile is qualifying its **A-36 Halcon** armed versions for the maritime attack role with a pair of BAe Sea Eagle missiles

C-101DD Aviojet: yet further enhanced model first flown in May 1985 with the TFE731-5-1J turbofan and the Ferranti FASTAC (Flexible Avionics Systems for Training And Combat) with the FD4503 HUD and weapon-aiming computer, and the FIN1100 attitude, heading and navigation system in a revised HOTAS (Hand On Throttle And Stick) cockpit

This Spanish air force C-101EB Aviojet carries a 30-mm cannon pack, two light bombs and four rocket-launcher pods.

CASA (Construcciones Aeronauticas SA) C-212 Series 200 Aviocar

(Spain)
Type: short-range STOL utility transport aero-plane

Accommodation: flightcrew of two, and 24 troops, or 23 paratroops, or 12 litters and four attendants, or 2770 kg (6,107 lb) of freight in the hold

Armament (fixed): none

Armament (disposable): none

Electronics and operational equipment: communication and navigation equipment

Powerplant and fuel system: two 900-shp (671-kW) Garrett TPE331-10R turboprops, and a total internal fuel capacity of 2040 litres (449 Imp gal); no provision for drop tanks or inflight refuelling

Performance: maximum speed 375 km/h (233 mph); cruising speed 365 km/h (227 mph) at 3050 m (10,000 ft); initial climb rate 474 m (1,555 ft) per minute; service ceiling 8535 m (28,000 ft); range 408 km (253 miles) with maximum payload or 1760 km (1,094 miles) with maximum fuel

Weights: empty 4115 kg (9,072 lb); maximum take-off 7450 kg (16,424 lb)

Dimensions: span 19·00 m (62 ft 4 in); length 15·16 m (49 ft 9 in); height 6·30 m (20 ft 8 in); wing area 40·00 m² (430·56 sq ft)

Uruguay operates one of its five C-212s in maritime patrol/SAR form with nose radar.

Variants

C-212A Aviocar: designed to replace the miscellany of military transports serving with the Spanish air arm in the 1960s, the Aviocar is a simple aircraft of modest performance, but requires little maintenance and has good STOL performance with a small but nonetheless useful 2000-kg (4,409-lb) load in an unobstructed hold 5·0 m (16 ft 5 in) long, 2·0 m (6 ft 7 in) wide and 1·7 m (5 ft 7 in) high accessed by a rear ramp/door; the type first flew in March 1971 and began to enter service in 1973 with 750-shp (560-kW) Garrett TPE331-5 turboprops, the freight capacity often being exchanged for accommodation for 15 paratroops and an instructor, or 12 litters and three seated casualties plus attendants, or 19 passengers; the type was also made in Indonesia as the **Nurtanio NC-212**, and the basically similar **C-212-5 Series 100** was also bought by some military operators

C-212AV Aviocar: VIP version of the C-212A

C-212B Aviocar: six pre-production C-212As converted into photo-survey aircraft with Wild RC-10 cameras and a darkroom in the hold

C-212C Aviocar: civil C-212A Series 100 aircraft in military service

C-212D Aviocar: last two of the eight pre-production aircraft after modification as navigation trainers; some production aircraft followed to the same standard

C-212 Series 200 Aviocar: introduced in 1979, this is a stretched version with more powerful engines, and the hold increased in length to 6·5 m (21·33 ft) for a payload of 2770 kg (6,107 lb) of freight, or 24 troops, or 23 paratroops, or 28 passengers; four aircraft optimized for the Elint role are in service with the United Arab Emirates, these machines having automatic signals interception, classification and localization capability; two similar aircraft in Portuguese service also possess a jamming capability

C-212 Series 300 Aviocar: standard version since 1987 with a span of 20·40 m (66 ft 11·15 in), a maximum take-off weight of 8000 kg (17,637 lb) with a 2820-kg (6,217-lb) payload, and provision for two 500-litre (110-Imp gal) underwing auxiliary tanks; in its standard utility transport version the Series 300 can carry a 2270-kg (5,004-lb) payload over 408 km (254 miles), and its other performance figures include a cruising speed of 345 km/h (214 mph), an initial climb rate of 455 m (1,493 ft) per minute, and a service ceiling of 8110 m (26,610 ft); the type is available in variants for electronic warfare, coastal patrol etc with customer-specified role equipment; the maritime model is offered with 270° scan APS-128 radar for the patrol role or 360° scan radar for the ASW role, plus optional equipment such as FLIR and SLAR, and two hardpoints for underwing armament such as Sea Skua (alternatively AS.15TT) anti-ship missiles or Sting Ray (alternatively Mk 46) anti-submarine torpedoes

CASA/IPTN (Airtech) CN-235M-100

(Spain/Indonesia)

Type: short-range utility transport aeroplane

Accommodation: flightcrew of two or three, and 48 troops, or 46 paratroops, or 24 litters plus four attendants, or 5000 kg (11,023 lb) of freight in the cabin

Armament (fixed): none

Armament (disposable): this is carried on six optional hardpoints (three under each wing) up to a maximum weight of 3500 kg (7,716 lb) of disposable stores including anti-ship missile and anti-submarine torpedoes

Electronics and operational equipment: communication and navigation equipment

Powerplant and fuel system: two 1,750-shp (1305-kW) General Electric CT7-7C turboprops, and a total internal fuel capacity of 5268 litres (1,159 Imp gal); no provision for drop tanks or inflight refuelling

Performance: cruising speed 452 km/h (280 mph) at 4575 m (15,000 ft); initial climb rate 579 m (1,900 ft) per minute; service ceiling 7620 m (25,000 ft); range 1240 km (770 miles) with maximum payload

Weights: empty 8600 kg (18,959 lb); normal take-off 14,400 kg (31,746 lb); maximum take-off 15,100 kg (33,289 lb)

Dimensions: span 25·81 m (84 ft 8 in); length 21·353 m (70 ft 0·75 in); height 8·18 m (26 ft 10 in); wing area 59·10 m² (636·1 sq ft)

Variants

CN-235M-10: first flown in November 1983, the CN-235 light utility transport was designed jointly by Spanish and Indonesian interests, and offers its operators a useful transport capability at modest

Cessna A-37B Dragonfly

cost and with limited maintenance requirements; the type is powered by two 1,700-shp (1268-kW) General Electric CT7-7 or slightly more powerful CT7-7A turboprops, and its purely military transport version is suffixed M in the designation; Indonesia is buying a maritime version with 360° scan radar in the lower fuselage and provision for weapons such as AM.39 Exocet anti-ship missiles and Mk 46 anti-submarine torpedoes

CN-235M-100: hot-and-high variant of the CN-235 with more power than the CN-235M-10

(USA)

Type: light attack aeroplane

Accommodation: pilot and co-pilot side-by-side on Weber ejector seats

Armament (fixed): one 7·62-mm (0·3-in) General Electric GAU-2B/A Minigun with 1,500 rounds in the nose

Armament (disposable): this is carried on eight hardpoints (four under each wing, with the innermost four units each rated at 870 lb/394 kg, the intermediate units each at 600 lb/272 kg, and the outermost units each at 500 lb/227 kg) up to a maximum weight of 5,000+ lb (2268+ kg); typical weapons are the 500- and 250-lb (227- and 113-kg) free-fall and retarded bombs, the 750-lb (340-kg) BLU-1 and BLU-32 500-lb (227-kg) napalm bombs, the 750-lb (340-kg) M118 demolition bomb, the SUU-11 7·62-mm (0·30-in) Minigun pod, the LAU-3 pod with 19 2·75-in (70-mm) rockets, the LAU-32 and LAU-59 pods each with seven 2·75-in (70-mm) rockets, and CBU-series bomblet dispensers

Electronics and operational equipment: communication and navigation equipment, plus a Chicago Aerial CA-503 sight

Powerplant and fuel system: two 2,850-lb (1293-kg) thrust General Electric J85-GE-17A non-afterburning turbojets, and a total internal fuel capacity of 507 US gal (1920 litres) plus provision for four 100-US gal (378-litre) drop tanks; provision for inflight refuelling

Performance: maximum speed 507 mph (816 km/h) at 16,000 ft (4875 m); cruising speed 489 mph (787 km/h) at 25,0000 ft (7620 m); initial climb rate 6,990 ft (2130 m) per minute; service ceiling 41,765 ft (12,730 m); range 460 miles (740 km) with a 4,100-lb (1860-kg) warload or 1,012 miles (1628 km) with maximum fuel

Weights: empty 6,211 lb (2817 kg); maximum take-off 14,000 lb (6350 kg)

Dimensions: span 35 ft 10·5 in (10·93 m) over tip-tanks; length excluding probe 28 ft 3·25 in (8·62 m); height 8 ft 10·5 in (2·70 m); wing area 183·9 sq ft (17·09 m²)

Variants

T-37B: this is the US Air Force's standard primary trainer, the production version of the Cessna Model 318 side-by-side two-seat design having flown in October 1952 as the T-37A on the power of two imported Turboméca Marboré turbojets; the type entered production in a licence-built version of the Marboré, the 920-lb (417-kg) thrust Teledyne CAE J69-T-9, and began to enter service in 1957; production amounted to 444, and all survivors were later upgraded to T-37B standard to complement some 552 new-build aircraft with 1,025-lb (465-kg) thrust J69-T-25 engines and additional fuel (in tip tanks) plus revised navigation and communication equipment; the USAF and Cessna are investigating the means to extend the

T-37B's life to fill the gap left by the cancellation of the Northrop T-46A; Cessna has offered an upgrade package (new canopy rails, reinforced wing main spars and a new forward wing spar carry-through structure, new rear-fuselage dorsal support fittings and new tailplane skins) to extend service life to 10,000 hours

T-37C: export version of the T-37B with provision for reconnaissance gear, 65-US gal (246-litre) optional tip tanks and/or light armament, the last carried on two underwing hardpoints and comprising two 250-lb (113-kg) bombs, two rocket pods or (extremely rarely) four AIM-9 Sidewinder AAMs for a maximum take-off weight of 8,000 lb (3629 kg); production amounted to 198 aircraft delivered to Brazil, Chile, Colombia, Greece, Pakistan, Peru, Portugal and Turkey

A-37A Dragonfly: initial light attack and counter-insurgency version of the T-37 trainer; the requirement for such an aeroplane was made clear by events in the late 1950s and early 1960s, and the YAT-37D prototype (converted from a T-37B) was flown in October 1963 at a maximum take-off weight of 14,000 lb (6350 kg), more than twice that of the standard T-37B; the need for such aircraft in the Vietnam War then led to the conversion of 39 T-37Bs as 'production' A-37As with 2,400-lb (1089-kg) thrust J85-GE-5 turbojets, beefed-up structure, increased internal fuel capacity and eight underwing hardpoints

A-37B Dragonfly: definitive production version of the A-37 type based on the A-37A but re-engineered for more powerful engines and greater underwing loads, and fitted with many operational and aereodynamic refinements, stronger landing gear with hydraulic rather than electrical actuation, flak curtains, an inflight-refuelling probe and night/adverse-weather avionics; production amounted to 577 aircraft

OA-37B Dragonfly: conversions of A-37Bs to forward air control aircraft

T-48A: provisional designation of the modernized T-37B proposed by Cessna with structural strengthening, new tail, upgraded avionics, pressurized cockpit and two 1,330-lb (603-kg) thrust Garrett F109-GA-100 turbofans; it now appears that the T-37 SLEP (Service-Life Extension Program) modifications will centre on new canopy rails, new rear-fuselage dorsal fin support mountings, new tailplane skins, reinforced front and rear wing spars, and a new carry-through structure for the forward spar

Opposite: The Spanish air force operates two CN-235s in the VIP role.

Below: The A-37A was the T-37 conversion that paved the way for the definitive A-37B.

Cessna O-2A

(USA)

Type: forward air control aeroplane

Accommodation: pilot and observer side-by-side on non-ejecting seats at the front of the cabin, and four passengers or light freight in the cabin rear

Armament (fixed): none

Armament (disposable): this is carried on four hardpoints (two under each wing) up to an unrevealed maximum weight, and can comprise SUU-11 7·62-mm (0·3-in) GAU-2B/A Minigun pods or LAU-series pods for 2·75-in (70-mm) rockets

Electronics and operational equipment: communication and navigation equipment

Powerplant and fuel system: two 210-hp (157-kW) Teledyne Continental IO-360-C/D piston engines, and a total internal fuel capacity of 92 US gal (348 litres) plus provision for two 28-US gal (108-litre) auxiliary tanks in the wings; no provision for drop tanks or inflight refuelling

Performance: maximum speed 199 mph (320 km/h) at sea level; cruising speed 144 mph (232 km/h) at 10,000 ft (3050 m); initial climb rate 1,180 ft (360 m) per minute; service ceiling 19,300 ft (5885 m); range 1,060 miles (1706 km)

Weights: empty 2,848 lb (1292 kg); maximum take-off 5,400 lb (2449 kg)

Dimensions: span 38 ft 2 in (11·63 m); length 29 ft 9 in (9·07 m); height 9 ft 4 in (2·84 m); wing area 202·5 sq ft (18·81 m²)

Variants

O-2A: designation of the 'off-the-shelf' FAC aeroplane procured by the US Air Force from 1966 on the basis of the Model 337 Super Skymaster civil aircraft; the type was fitted with revised avionics and provision four underwing hardpoint, and production amounted to 501 aircraft

O-2B: psychological warfare version of the O-2A with 600-watt amplifiers and directional speakers; 31 commercial Super Skymasters were converted for the task

Model 337: unusual push-pull twin-engine civil aircraft that was bought by several air arms in the light transport and utility roles; the type entered service in 1965 as the updated, retractable landing gear version of the Model 336 Skymaster, which first flew in February 1961

Brico O-2: 1983 version with a single 650-shp (485-kW) Allison 250-C30 turboshaft driving a shrouded pusher propeller for increased efficiency and reduced nose, and also leaving the nose clear for a FLIR sensor and a GAU-2B/A 7·62-mm (0·3-in) Minigun; the status of the project is not clear

Reims FTMA Milirole: introduced in May 1970, this is an upgraded military model produced by Cessna's French licensee in a number of subvariants, but all featuring STOL performance, four underwing hardpoints and a crew of two plus four passengers or two litters

Summit Sentry O2-337: introduced in 1980, this is a military version of the T337 pressurized civil aircraft powered by two 225-hp (186-kW) Continental TSIO-470 engines and fitted with four underwing hardpoints each rated at 350 lb (159 kg)

Chengdu Aircraft Corporation F-7M Airguard

(China)

Type: interceptor fighter with a secondary attack capability

Accommodation: pilot on a Chengdu zero/130-km/h (81-mph) ejector seat

Armament (fixed): two 30-mm Type 30-1 cannon with 60 rounds per gun

Armament (disposable): this is carried on four hardpoints (two under each wing, with each unit rated at 250 kg/551 lb) up to a maximum weight of 2000 kg (4,409 lb) of PL-2, PL-2A, PL-7 or Matra 550 Magic AAMs, rocket pods each containing 18 55-mm (2·17-in) or seven 90-mm (3·54-in) rockets, and free-fall weapons such as 50-, 100-, 250- and 500-kg (110-, 220-, 551- and 1,102-lb) bombs

Electronics and operational equipment: communication and navigation equipment, plus Type 226 ranging radar, Type 956 HUD and weapon-aiming computer system, and other items

Powerplant and fuel system: one 6100-kg (13,448-lb) afterburning thrust Chengdu Wopen-7B(BM) turbojet, and a maximum internal fuel capacity of 2385 litres (525 Imp gal) plus provision for one 800- or 500-litre (176- or 110-Imp gal) centreline drop tank and two 500-litre (110-Imp gal) underwing drop tanks; no provision for inflight refuelling

Performance: maximum speed 2180 km/h (1,355 mph) or Mach 2·05 at high altitude; initial climb rate 10,800 m (35,433 ft) per minute; service ceiling 18,200 m (59,710 ft); radius 600 km (373 miles) on a hi-lo-hi attack mission; ferry range 2230 km (1,386 miles)

Weights: empty 5275 kg (11,629 lb); normal take-off 7531 kg (16,603 lb); maximum take-off 8900 kg (19,621 lb)

Dimensions: span 7·154 m (23 ft 5·6 in); length without probe 13·945 m (45 ft 9 in); height 4·103 m (13 ft 5·5 in); wing area 23·00 m² (247·6 sq ft)

Variants

J-7 II: Chinese-built copy of the MiG-21 series, initially based on the MiG-21F 'Fishbed-C' day interceptor and produced in limited numbers as the **J-7 I** (or **F-7A** in its export form) during the 1960s but then suspended because of technical problems on the production line; the type re-entered production in the late 1970s to meet renewed Chinese demand, and this new-production J-7 II version (**F-7B** in its export version) has features of the 'Fishbed-E' and 'Fishbed-J' Soviet fighters as well as the basic airframe of the 'Fishbed-C'; greater performance is secured by the use of a Wopen-7B turbojet; heavier offensive punch is offered by the addition of a second 30-mm Type 30-1 cannon in the fuselage (each gun having 60 rounds of ammunition) and further capability is provided by two underwing hardpoints each able to carry one PL-2 AAM, a pod with 18 57-mm (2·24-in) rockets, or one 250- or 500-kg (551- or 1,102-lb) bomb; this model has empty and normal take-off weights of 5145 and 7372 kg (11,343 and 16,252 lb) respectively, an initial climb rate of 9000 m (29,525 ft) per minute, a service ceiling of 18,800 m (61,680 ft) and a range

of 1490 km (926 miles) with two AAMs and one 800-litre (176-Imp gal) drop tank

Shenyang Aircraft Corporation J-7 III: Chinese equivalent of the 'Fishbed-J' all-weather interceptor, known in its export form as the **F-7C**; the type has improved avionics including a Type 222 ranging radar in a fully-variable inlet centrebody, and an SM-3A optical sight; many F-7s have been fitted to carry the latest variants of the AIM-9 Sidewinder AAM used in conjunction with a retrofitted HUD

F-7M Airguard: much improved export model developed in the early 1980s for delivery from 1984 with an additional pair of underwing hardpoints (for the carriage of two PL-7 AAMs or two 480-litre/106-Imp gal drop tanks), relocated probes, a revised cockpit with new canopy and ejector seat, and a number of other Chinese developments such as the Type 226 ranging radar with improved ECCM (the GEC Sky Ranger is offered as an alternative); most important, however, is the inclusion of a mass of Western avionics such as the GEC Type 956 HUDWAS (HUD and weapon-aiming system), air data computer, radar altimeter and multi-mode radios; the type was under investigation for licensed manufacture in Pakistan as the **Sabre II**, possibly with a forward fuselage (complete with avionics etc) manufactured in the USA by Grumman, which was also investigating the feasibility of re-engining the type with a non-afterburning version of the General Electric F404 or Pratt & Whitney PW1120 turbofan; the Sabre II would have had a radar-fitted solid nose and lateral inlets, but Pakistan finally opted for a derivative of the F-7M, namely the **F-7P Skybolt** with a number of Western avionic features and the ability to carry both PL-5 and AIM-9 Sidewinder AAMs

Super-7: announced in 1988 as a collaborative venture between Chengdu, CATIC and Grumman, this is the latest version of the Sabre II concept with a 17,000-lb (7711-kg) thrust Turbo-Union RB199 or 18,000-lb (8165-kg) thrust General Electric F404 (in the form of a licence-built Volvo RM12) turbofan aspirated via lateral inlets so that a new nose can be fitted with the Westinghouse APG-66 radar; the type is to have much of the General Dynamics F-16's cockpit avionics (including the HUD) as well as the windscreen and canopy developed for the Northrop F-20 Tigershark; 500 kg (1,102 lb) more fuel will be accommodated in a larger dorsal fin on the upper surface of a fuselage lengthened to 15·0 m (49 ft 2,5 in), and other changes will include a wing of greater span (7·925 m/26 ft 0 in) and chord for increased wing area, leading-edge slats and combat flaps, two new inboard hardpoints each capable of carrying an AAM, an arrester hook, strengthened landing gear with larger wheels, and a new ejector seat

Guizhou Aviation Industry Group Company JJ-7: tandem-seat advanced and operational conversion trainer based on the J-7 fighter; the type resembles the Soviet MiG-21U 'Mongol-A' and first flew in July 1985; the type is generally similar to the J-7 apart from its revised fuselage, which increases overall length to 14·874 m (48 ft 9·5 in), empty and maximum take-off weights of 5330 and 8600 kg (11,750 and 18,960 lb) respectively, and slightly reduced performance in terms of climb rate, service ceiling and range; there is also an export **FT-7** variant based on the F-7 fighter

CNIAR (Centrul National al Industriei Aeronautice Romane) IAR-99 Soim

(Romania)
Type: advanced flying and weapon trainer with a secondary light attack capability
Accommodation: pupil and pilot in tandem on ejector seats
Armament (fixed): none
Armament (disposable): this is carried on four hardpoints (two under each wing) up to a maximum weight of 1000 kg (2,205 lb), and can include

Opposite, bottom: The USAF's 0-2As were used for psychological warfare and COIN.

Above: The F-7M Airguard is an advanced development of the J-7 and of the Mig-21.

cannon pods, launchers for S-55 55-mm (2·17-in) unguided rockets, light bombs and other stores
Electronics and operational equipment: communication and navigation equipment, and a gyro sight
Powerplant and fuel system: one 4,000-lb (1814-kg) thrust Rolls-Royce Viper Mk 632-41 non-afterburning turbojet, and a total internal fuel capacity of unrevealed quantity plus provision for at least two drop tanks; no provision for inflight refuelling
Performance: maximum speed 850 km/h (528 mph) at sea level; initial climb rate 2190 m (7,185 ft) per minute; service ceiling 12600 m

(41,340 ft); range not revealed
Weights: empty 3364 kg (7,416 lb); normal take-off 4600 kg (10,141 lb); maximum take-off 5641 kg (12,436 lb)
Dimensions: span 9·85 m (32 ft 3·8 in); length 10·88 m (35 ft 8·3 in); height not revealed; wing area 18·7 m² (201·29 sq ft)
Variant
IAR-99 Soim: first flown in December 1985, the Soim (hawk) is an indigenous Romanian replacement for the Aero L-29 Delfin, retaining a straight-wing design but with features to allow the type's use in roles varying from flight training via weapon training to light attack

Dassault-Breguet Alize

(France)
Type: carrierborne anti-submarine aeroplane
Accommodation: pilot and mission crew of two
Armament (fixed): none
Armament (disposable): this is carried in a lower-fuselage weapons bay and on eight hardpoints (four under each wing) up to an unrevealed maximum weight; the weapons bay can accommodate one 500-kg (1,102-lb) torpedo or three 160-kg (353-lb) depth charges, the two hardpoints under the inner wings can each carry one 160- or 175-kg (353- or 386-lb) depth charge, and the six hardpoints under the outer wings can take six 5-in (127-mm) rockets or two AS.12 ASMs
Electronics and operational equipment: communication and navigation equipment, plus Thomson-CSF Iguane (French aircraft) or Thomson-CSF DRAA-2B (Indian aircraft) search

radar, sonobuoys, and (French aircraft only) ECM equipment
Powerplant and fuel system: one 1,975-ehp (1473-kW) Rolls-Royce Dart RDa·7 Mk 21 turboprop, and a total internal fuel capacity of unrevealed quantity; no provision for drop tanks or inflight refuelling
Performance: maximum speed 520 km/h (323 mph) at 3000 m (9,845 ft); cruising speed 370 km/h (230 mph); initial climb rate 420 m (1,380 ft) per minute; service ceiling 6250 + m (20,505 + ft); range 2500 km (1,553 miles)
Weights: empty 5700 kg (12,566 lb); maximum

take-off 8200 kg (18,078 lb)
Dimensions: span 15·60 m (51 ft 2 in); length 13·86 m (45 ft 6 in); height 5·00 m (16 ft 4·75 in); wing area 36·00 m² (387·51 sq ft)

Variant
Alize: developed as the Breguet Br·1050, the Alize (tradewind) is a small carrierborne ASW aeroplane that first flew in October 1956; the type was based on an abortive attack aircraft with a turboprop in the nose for range and a turbojet in the rear fuselage for speed; removal of the turbojet made room for the DRAA 2A search radar and its retractable radome, so paving the way for the Alize; the type began to enter service in May 1959 and remains in French and Indian service, the French aircraft having been updated for continued utility in the most modern conditions

Dassault-Breguet Atlantique 2

(France)
Type: maritime reconnaissance and anti-submarine aeroplane
Accommodation: flightcrew of three, and a mission crew of nine in the cabin
Armament (fixed): none
Armament (disposable): this is carried in one lower-fuselage weapons bay and on four hardpoints (two under each wing, with the inner units each rated at 1000 kg/2,205 lb and the outer units each at 750 kg/1,653 lb) up to a maximum weight of 3500 kg (7,716 lb); the weapons bay has three carrying trusses, the two forward units being adaptable to carry one or two AM-39 Exocet anti-ship missiles, or each to take one L4 or four Mk 46 torpedoes, or three depth charges, or three 250-kg (551-lb) mines, or three air-sea rescue containers, and the rear unit being able to carry four depth charges, or three 250-kg (551-lb) mines or three air-sea rescue containers; the hardpoints can each carry one ASM
Electronics and operational equipment: communication and navigation equipment, plus Thomson-CSF Iguane search radar with its antenna in a retractable radome, SAT/TRT Tango FLIR in a trainable chin turret, Crouzet DHAX 3 MAD in the tail 'sting', Thomson-CSF DR 4000 (updated ARAR 13A) ESM equipment, 78 sonobuoys to provide data to the Thomson-CSF Sadang processor, ESD/Decca Doppler navigation, and two Sagem Uliss 53 INSs
Powerplant and fuel system: two 6,100-ehp (4549-kW) Rolls-Royce Tyne RTy.20 Mk 21 turboprops, and a total internal fuel capacity of 23,120 litres (5,085 Imp gal); no provision for drop tanks or inflight refuelling
Performance: maximum speed 648 km/h (402 mph) at optimum altitude and 592 km/h (368 mph) at sea level; cruising speed 315 km/h (195 mph) between sea level and 1525 m (5,000 ft); initial climb rate 610 m (2,000 ft) per minute; service ceiling 9145 m (30,000 ft); patrol endurance 5 hours at a radius of 1850 km (1,150 miles); range 9075 km (5,640 miles)
Weights: empty 25,700 kg (56,659 lb); normal take-off 45,000 kg (99,206 lb); maximum take-off 46,200 kg (101,852 lb)
Dimensions: span 37·42 m (122 ft 9·25 in) over tip pods; length 31·62 m (103 ft 9 in)); height 10·89 m (35 ft 8·75 in); wing area 120·34 m² (1,295·3 sq ft)

Variants

Atlantic 1: developed as the Breguet Br·1150 to meet a 1958 NATO requirement for a long-range maritime patrol and anti-submarine aircraft, the Atlantic was judged the best of 27 designs originating from seven NATO member countries; the type did not enter NATO-wide service, instead securing initial orders from France, West Germany, Italy and the Netherlands for 89 aircraft; the airframe was built by the five-country SEBCAT consortium, and the 5,665-ehp (4225-kW) Rolls-Royce Tyne Mk 21 turboprops by a four-nation consortium; the high aspect ratio of the wings combines with good fuel capacity and economical engines to provide moderate speed but great range, and the 'double-bubble' fuselage combines a capacious unpressurized weapons bay with a pressurized upper lobe for the flight crew of three, the mission crew of seven and, at the rear, two observers; the sensors (search radar, MAD, ARAR 13A ESM, sonobuoys etc) are mainly of Thomson-CSF manufacture, and are computer-integrated on the Plotac display and control panels in the tactical compartment; the type has a maximum take-off weight of 43,500 kg (95,900 lb), a span of 36·30 m (119 ft 1·1 in) and a range of 7970 km (4,950 miles) with 10% reserves; considerable updating has been achieved within the limitations of the 1950s-vintage electronics, and five of the West German navy's 15 survivors have been extensively converted as Sigint aircraft with an electronic intelligence suite installed by Vought and based on a Loral ESM suite with podded wingtip antennae; Italian and West German dedicated anti-submarine aircraft have also been upgraded to a limited extent in their operating countries
Atlantique 2: considerably updated version for the French navy (resulting in reversion to the French spelling of the name) developed under the designation Atlantic Nouvelle Génération; the same consortia have been revived for the construction of airframe and powerplant, and the airframe has been considerably developed to reduce the possibility of corrosion and fatigue problems; it is in the electronics that the greatest development has taken place, however, the whole suite being replaced by the latest French equipments (and expanded with the introduction of a FLIR sensor) as detailed in the specification; the first aircraft flew in May 1981 and deliveries of 42 aircraft to the Aeronavale began in 1989

Left: Seen here in landing configuration, the Alize is the French navy's only fixed-wing carrierborne ASW capability.

Below: Though it resembles the Atlantic 1 externally, the Atlantique 2 is markedly different in its mission electronics, notably the sensors, data-processing and tactical plotting systems.

Dassault-Breguet Mirage IIIE

(France)
Type: tactical fighter-bomber and strike aeroplane
Accommodation: pilot on a Martin-Baker RM4 ejector seat
Armament (fixed): two 30-mm DEFA 552A cannon with 125 rounds per gun
Armament (disposable): this is carried on five hardpoints (one under the fuselage rated at 1180 kg/2,600 lb and two under each wing, the inner two units each rated at 840 kg/1,852 lb and the outer two units each at 168 kg/370 lb) up to a maximum weight of 4000 kg (8,818 lb); the under-fuselage hardpoint can carry one 15-kiloton AN-52 tactical nuclear weapon, or one AS.30 ASM, or one Matra 530 AAM, or four 125- or 250-kg (276- or 551-lb) bombs, or four Durandal runway-cratering bombs, or one 400-kg (882-lb) free-fall or laser-guided bomb, or one ECM or reconnaissance pod; the inner underwing hardpoints can each carry four 125- or 250-kg (276- or 551-lb) bombs, or two 400-kg (882-lb) bombs, or

three Durandals, or one pod for six 100-mm (3·94-in) or 18 68-mm (2·68-in) rockets, or one CEM 1 multi-store pod, or one 30-mm cannon pod; and the outer underwing hardpoints can each carry one Matra 550 Magic AAM, or one pod with six 68-mm (2·68-in) rockets, or one ECM pod
Electronics and operational equipment: communication and navigation equipment, plus Thomson-CSF Cyrano II fire-control radar, one Thomson CSF 97 sight system, Marconi Doppler navigation, Thomson-CSF Type BF RWR and numerous ECM and reconnaissance options
Powerplant and fuel system: one 6200-kg (13,670-lb) afterburning thrust SNECMA Atar 9C turbojet, and a total internal fuel capacity of 3000 litres (660 Imp gal) plus provision for 3900 litres (858 Imp gal) of auxiliary fuel in 1700-, 1300-, 625- or 250-litre (374-, 286-, 137- or 55-Imp gal) drop tanks; no provision for inflight refuelling
Performance: maximum speed 2350 km/h (1,460 mph) or Mach 2·2 clean at 12,000 m

(39,370 ft) and 1390 km/h (863 mph) or Mach 1·13 at sea level; cruising speed 955 km/h (593 mph) or Mach 0·9 at 11,000 m (36,090 ft); climb to 11,000 m (36,090 ft) in 3 minutes; service ceiling 17,000 m (55,755 ft) without the optional 1500-kg (3,307-lb) thrust SEPR 844 rocket unit; radius 1200 km (745 miles) on a hi-hi-hi mission with maximum fuel and virtually no weapons; ferry range 4000 km (2,486 miles)
Weights: empty 7050 kg (15,542 lb); normal take-off 9600 kg (21,165 lb); maximum take-off 13,700 kg (30,203 lb)
Dimensions: span 8·22 m (26 ft 11·6 in); length 15·03 m (49 ft 3·7 in); height 4·50 m (14 ft 9 in); wing area 35·00 m² (376·7 sq ft)

Variants

Mirage IIIB: this operational conversion trainer of the Mirage III series was produced on the basis of the Mirage IIIA pre-production single-seater, which first flew in May 1958 with a 6000-kg (13,228-lb) thrust SNECMA Atar 9B afterburning

turbojet as a development of the Mirage III prototype of 1956 powered by the 4500-kg (9,921-lb) thrust Atar 101G turbojet; the Mirage IIIA carried Cyrano Ibis radar, and though the Mirage IIIB has provision for armament it lacks radar; the fuselage is 0·60 m (23·6 in) longer than that of the Mirage IIIA; basically similar subvariants are the **Mirage IIIBJ** for Israel, the **Mirage IIIBL** for Lebanon, the **Mirage IIIBS** for Switzerland and the **Mirage IIIBZ** for South Africa

Mirage IIIC: initial production single-seater of the Mirage III series, based on the Mirage IIIA and optimized for the all-weather interception and day ground-attack roles with the 6000-kg (13,228-lb) thrust Atar 9B afterburning turbojet plus optional rocket pack in place of the cannon; the first Mirage IIIC flew in October 1960 and the type was exported primarily to Israel and South Africa under the designations **Mirage IIICJ**(with different electronic equipment) and **Mirage IIICZ** respectively

Mirage IIID: two-seat operational conversion trainer development of the Mirage IIIO but with more advanced attack equipment; the type was built in Australia and France, the latter exporting several subvariants including the **Mirage IIIDP** for Pakistan and the uprated **Mirage IIID2Z** for South Africa with the Atar 9K-50 turbojet

Mirage IIIE: single-seat version optimized for the long-range intruder and fighter-bomber roles with the Atar 9C turbojet, a fuselage lengthened by 0·3 m (11·8 in), Doppler and TACAN navigation, Cyrano II radar and other tactical improvements; the type was widely exported in a number of subvariants such as the **Mirage IIIEE** for Spain, the **Mirage IIIEL** for Lebanon, the **Mirage IIIEP** for Pakistan and the **Mirage IIIEZ** for South Africa; the **Mirage IIIBE** is the two-seat trainer version of the variant; 18 of the Spanish aircraft are being updated in Spain by a consortium of CESELSA and CASA to a considerably more advanced standard with Emerson APQ-159(V)-XX multi-function air-to-air and air-to-surface radar, AYK-1 mission computer, MIL-1553B digital databus, RWR, HUD, two HDDs, INS, four new underwing hardpoints, inflight-refuelling probe and zero/zero ejector seat

Mirage IIIO: version of the Mirage IIIE licence-built in Australia by the Commonwealth Aircraft Corporation with different navigation equipment including twin Sperry gyro platforms

Mirage IIIR: reconnaissance version of the Mirage IIIE with five Omera 31 cameras instead of nose-mounted radar, increasing length to 15·50 m (50·85 ft); the type first flew in November 1961, and was also exported in its standard version (**Mirage IIIRP** for Pakistan and **Mirage IIIRS** for Switzerland) and as the uprated **Mirage IIIR2Z** for South Africa with the Atar 9K-50 turbojet

Mirage IIIRD: improved Mirage IIIR with Doppler navigation, automatic cameras, a SAT Cyclope IR reconnaissance package in a ventral fairing and two 1700-litre (374-Imp gal) underwing drop tanks

Mirage IIIS: much revised version of the Mirage IIIE for Switzerland with Hughes TARAN fire control for Hughes Falcon AAMs

Mirage 50M: current designation of the Mirage IIING (Nouvelle Génération) available in the later 1980s with fly-by-wire controls, canard foreplanes, 7200-kg (15,873-lb) afterburning thrust Atar 9K-50 turbojet and other items of advanced technology including an INS, digital mission computer, HUD and air-to-surface laser rangefinder; no orders have been placed for this variant, but several Latin American countries have undertaken modification programmes (in France or at home) to upgrade their Mirage IIIs and Mirage 5s at least partially to this standard; Brazil is modifying its Mirage IIIs with canard foreplanes, provision for the AIM-9 Sidewinder AAM in additional to the R530, improved gun electronics and a revised refuelling system with the local designation **F-103E**, and Venezuela has upgraded its Mirage IIIs with canards, Cyrano IV radar, a new nav/attack system and the Atar 9K-50 engine

Atlas Aircraft Corporation Cheetah DZ: South African Mirage IIIBZ, Mirage IIIDZ or Mirage IIIDZZ aircraft rebuilt to the same basic standard as the IAI Kfir-TC2 two-seat multi-role fighter with a slightly drooped nose carrying dual-role Elta EL/M-2001B radar and increasing length to 15.40 m (50 ft 6.3 in); the Cheetah DZ has two additional hardpoints (one under each inlet trunk) and a bolt-on inflight-refuelling probe

Atlas Aircraft Corporation Cheetah EZ: South African Mirage IIICZ, Mirage IIIEZ aircraft rebuilt to the same basic standard as the IAI Kfir-C2 single-seat multi-role fighter with its fixed canard surfaces, an integrated nav/attack system with a laser designator, a chaff/flare dispenser, under-fuselage strakes, dogtoothed leading edges, fixed canard foreplanes, INS etc; the type is therefore suitable for the air-to-air and air-to-surface roles, but uses the 7200-kg (15,873-lb) afterburning thrust Atar 9K-50 turbojet instead of the Israeli aeroplane's General Electric J79 turbojet and thus possesses slightly inferior performance; the Cheetah D is matched to South Africa's latest AAM, the highly capable Armscor Seeker; like the Cheetah DZ, the single-seater has a bolt-on inflight-refuelling probe, and probably possesses the same pair of additional hardpoints

This is the first of four Mirage IIIDBR combat-capable conversion trainers received by Brazil for use by the air-defence command.

Dassault-Breguet Mirage IVP

(France)
Type: penetration missile-carrying aeroplane
Accommodation: pilot and navigator in tandem on Martin-Baker BM4 ejector seats
Armament (fixed): none
Armament (disposable): one 100/150-kiloton ASMP missile
Electronics and operational equipment: communication and navigation equipment, plus Thomson-CSF Arcana pulse-Doppler radar, terrain-following radar, Marconi Doppler navigation, two Sagem Uliss INSs, Thomson-CSF Type BF RWR, and a new Electronique Serge Dassault suite of internal and external EW (ECM and ESM) equipment including Agacetta, Agiric and Agosol internal deception jammers, the Thomson-CSF Barem jamming pod and underwing Philips Elektronikindustrier BOZ-100 or Philips/Matra Phimat dispensers
Powerplant and fuel system: two 7000-kg (15,432-lb) afterburning thrust SNECMA Atar 9K-50 turbojets, and a total internal fuel capacity of 14,000 litres (3,080 Imp gal) plus provision for two 2500-litre (550-Imp gal) drop tanks; provision for inflight refuelling

Performance: maximum speed 2340 km/h (1,454 mph) or Mach 2·2 at 13,125 m (40,060 ft) or 1965 km/h (1,221 mph) or Mach 1·7 at 20,000 m (65,615 ft) for sustained flight; climb to 11,000 m (39,090 ft) in 4 minutes 15 seconds; service ceiling 20,000 m (65,615 ft); radius 1240 km (771 miles) without inflight refuelling; ferry range 4000 km (2,486 miles)
Weights: empty 14,500 kg (31,967 lb); normal take-off 31,600 kg (69,665 lb); maximum take-off 33,475 kg (73,779 lb)
Dimensions: span 11·85 m (38 ft 10·5 in); length 23·50 m (77 ft 1 in); height 5·40 m (17 ft 8·5 in); wing area 78·00 m² (839·6 sq ft)

Variants

Mirage IVA: first flown in June 1959 and immediately apparent in aerodynamic terms as a scaled-up Mirage III, the Mirage IVA began to enter service in 1964 as the bomber component of France's nuclear deterrent forces, each aeroplane being equipped with DR-AA 8A radar and provision for the carriage of one 60-kiloton AN-22 free-fall nuclear weapon on intermediate-range sorties, alternative loads being 16 450-kg (992-lb) conventional bombs or four AS.37 Martel ASMs;

the type has a maximum take-off weight of 33,475 kg (73,799 lb) on the power of two Atar 9K-50 afterburning turbojets
Mirage IVP: designation of 18 Mirage IVA aircraft converted in the mid- and late 1980s to carry the 150-kiloton ASMP short-range stand-off missile; in this role the Mirage IVP is optimized for low-level penetration with the aid of new Thomson-CSF Arcana pulse-Doppler radar, upgraded nav/attack and EW equipment, dual INSs, flare/chaff dispensers on the outboard underwing hardpoints, and provision for long-range drop tanks on the inboard underwing hardpoints
Mirage IVR: of the 62 Mirage IVA aircraft built, 12 were converted under this designation for the strategic reconnaissance role at high and low levels; the variant is fitted with special navaids, revised EW system and specific sensor systems including the CT52 pod designed to fit the underfuselage recess for the previous free-fall nuclear weapon, and carrying vertical, oblique and forward cameras (typically three low-level Omera 35s and three high-level Omera 36s) or a SAT Super Cyclope IR linescanner in place of the Omera 36 cameras

Below: This Mirage IVA is seen in original form with its AN-22 free-fall nuclear bomb semi-recessed under the fuselage.

Far right: The first Mirage 50 is seen in 'clean' configuration during a test flight.

Dassault-Breguet Mirage 5A

(France)
Type: clear-weather interceptor and ground-attack aeroplane
Accommodation: pilot on a Martin-Baker RM4 ejector seat
Armament (fixed): two 30-mm DEFA 552A cannon with 125 rounds per gun
Armament (disposable): this is carried on seven hardpoints (one under the fuselage rated at 1180 kg/2,600 lb and three under each wing, with the units of the inner tandem pairs each rated at 840 kg/1,852 lb and the outer two units each at 168 kg/370 lb) up to a maximum weight of 4000 kg (8,818 lb); the underfuselage hardpoint can carry one 15-kiloton AN-52 tactical nuclear weapon, or one AS.30 ASM, or one Matra 530 AAM, or four 125- or 250-kg (276- or 551-lb) bombs, or four Durandal runway-cratering bombs, or one 400-kg (882-lb) free-fall or laser-guided bomb, or one ECM or reconnaissance pod; the inner underwing hardpoints can each carry four 125- or 250-kg (276- or 551-lb) bombs, or two 400-kg (882-lb) bombs, or three Durandals, or one pod for six 100-mm (3·94-in) or 18 68-mm (2·68-in) rockets, or one CEM 1 multi-store pod, or one 30-mm cannon pod; the outer underwing hardpoints can each carry one Matra 550 Magic or AIM-9 Sidewinder AAM, or one pod with six 68-mm (2·68-in) rockets, or one ECM pod
Electronics and operational equipment: communication and navigation equipment, plus an INS, radar (depending on variant the Thomson-CSF Aida II with a Thomson-CSF LT102 or TAV34 laser rangefinder, or the Cyrano IVM-3 or the Agave), Thomson-CSF Type BF RWR, Alkan Type 5013 chaff/flare launcher, and numerous podded ECM and reconnaissance options
Powerplant and fuel system: one 6200-kg (13,670-lb) afterburning thrust SNECMA Atar 9C turbojet, and a total internal fuel capacity of 3470 litres (763 Imp gal) plus provision for 3900 litres (858 Imp gal) of auxiliary fuel in 1700-, 1300-, 625- or 250-litre (374-, 286-, 137- or 55-Imp gal) drop tanks; no provision for inflight refuelling
Performance: maximum sustained speed 1912 km/h (1,188 mph) or Mach 1·9 clean at 12,000 m (39,370 ft) and 926 km/h (575 mph) or Mach 0·76 with weapons at sea level; climb to 11,000 m (36,090 ft) in 3 minutes; service ceiling 17,000 m (55,755 ft); radius 650 km (404 miles) on a lo-lo-lo mission with 907-kg (2,000-lb) warload, or 1300 km (808 miles) on a hi-lo-hi mission with reduced warload; ferry range 4000 km (2,485 miles)
Weights: empty 6600 kg (14,550 lb); normal take-off 9600 kg (21,165 lb); maximum take-off 13,700 kg (30,203 lb)
Dimensions: span 8·22 m (26 ft 11·6 in); length 15·55 m (51 ft 0·2 in); height 4·50 m (14 ft 9 in); wing area 35·00 m² (376·7 sq ft)

Variants

Mirage 5A: this version of the Mirage IIIE resulted from an Israeli requirement for a less sophisticated and thus cheaper aircraft optimized for the ground-attack role in clear-weather conditions, eliminating search radar and other equipment to permit the carriage of more fuel and weapons; the first Mirage 5 was flown in May 1967, and though the original Israeli order was embargoed by the French government, the type soon scored useful sales in the Middle East, Africa and South America; the original aircraft entered service with the French air force under the designation **Mirage 5F**, and other useful European sales were made to Belgium; during the 1970s the advent of microminiaturization in electronics led to the development of much smaller and lighter avionics, and much of the all-weather capability deleted from the original Mirage 5 series was subsequently restored with optional radar such as the Thomson-CSF Agave, providing customers with electronic capabilities superior to those of the Mirage III plus the range and payload of the basic Mirage 5; Belgium is to upgrade its Mirage 5BA (and Mirage 5BD two-seaters) with rocket-powered Mk 10 zero/zero ejector seats (in place of the original Mk 4 cartridge-powered seats), an INS in place of the original Doppler system, and a more modern fire-control system; Peru has modernized its Mirage 5s with an INS and an inflight-refuelling probe
Mirage 5D: two-seat operational conversion trainer version of the Mirage 5
Mirage 5R: reconnaissance version of the Mirage 5 with a fan of five cameras in the nose
Mirage 5-50: final production standard with the uprated 7200-kg (15873-lb) afterburning thrust Atar 9K-50 turbojet, Thomson-CSF Agave or Cyrano IVM-3 search radar and advanced equipment such as a HUD for the accurate delivery of the type's considerable weapons load (more than 4000 kg/8,818 lb within a maximum take-off weight of 13,700 kg/30,200 lb); the type is also available in the same training and reconnaissance variants as the basic Mirage 5 series; Chile is upgrading its Mirage 5-50 fleet (Mirage 5-50C fighters and Mirage 5-50FC ground-attack fighters) to **Mirage 5-50CN Pantera** standard with canard foreplanes, a new nav/attack system, an RWR, automatic chaff/flare launchers and improvements to the armament, fuel and hydraulic systems

Dassault-Breguet Mirage 2000C

(France)

Type: interceptor and air-superiority fighter with a secondary attack capability

Accommodation: pilot on a Martin-Baker F10Q zero/zero ejector seat

Armament (fixed): two 30-mm DEFA 554 cannon with 125 rounds per gun

Armament (disposable): this is carried on nine hardpoints (five under the fuselage with the centreline unit rated at 1800 kg/3,968 lb and the tandem two under each wing root each rated at 400 kg/882 lb, and two under each wing with the inner two units each rated at 1800 kg/3,968 lb and the outer two units each at 300 kg/661 lb) up to a maximum weight of 6300 kg (13,889 lb); the centreline hardpoint can accept one Matra Super 530 AAM, or one AS.30L ASM, or one 1000-kg (2,205-lb) free-fall or laser-guided bomb, or four 250-kg (551-lb) bombs, or one 400-kg (882-lb) modular cluster bomb, or one Belouga cluster bomb, or 18 BAP 100 anti-runway or BAT 120 anti-vehicle bombs, or one Type 531 grenade-launcher; the four hardpoints of the two tandem sets can accommodate four 250-kg (551-lb) bombs, or three 250-kg (551-lb) laser guided bombs and one Thomson-CSF/Martin Marietta ATLIS II laser pod, or four Belouga cluster bombs, or four Type 531 grenade-launchers, or 12 BAP 100 or BAT 120 bombs, or two CC421 cannon pods each containing one 30-mm DEFA cannon; the inner underwing hardpoints can each take a Super 530 AAM, or one AM.39 Exocet anti-ship missile, or one AS.30L ASM, or one 1000-kg (2,205-lb) bombs, or four 250-kg (551-lb) bombs, or one 400-kg (882-lb) modular cluster bomb, or one Belouga cluster bomb, or one Type 531 grenade-launcher or a pod for six, 18 or 36 68-mm (2·68-in) rockets; the outer underwing hardpoints can each take one Matra 550 Magic AAM, or one 250-kg (551-lb) bomb, or one pod for 18 68-mm (2·68-in) rockets

Electronics and operational equipment: communication and navigation equipment, plus either Thomson-CSF RDM multi-role radar (first 50 French and most export aircraft) or Thomson-CSF/ESD RDI pulse-Doppler multi-mode radar, Thomson-CSF VE-130 HUD, Thomson-CSF VMC-180 HDDs, Sagem Uliss 52 INS feeding data to the ESD 2084 digital central computer, Thomson-CSF Serval-B RWR, Matra Spirale passive ECM, and an Electronique Serge Dassault/Thomson-CSF/Matra/Alkan/Lacroix ICMS 2000 integrated EW suite to complement and eventually supplant external ECM pods carried on the centreline and outer underwing hardpoints; a reconnaissance pod can also be carried on the centreline

Powerplant and fuel system: one 9000-kg (19,840-lb) afterburning thrust SNECMA M53-5 bleed turbojet (first 37 aircraft) or 9700-kg (21,384-lb) afterburning thrust SNECMA M53-P2 bleed turbojet, and a total internal fuel capacity of 4000 litres (880 Imp gal) plus provision for one 1300-litre (286-Imp gal) and two 1700-litre (374-Imp gal) drop tanks; provision for inflight refuelling

Performance: maximum speed 2350 + km/h (1,460 + mph) or Mach 2·2 + at 12,000 m (39,370 ft) and 1110 km/h (690 mph) or Mach 0·9 at sea level with warload; initial climb rate 17,060 m (55,970 ft) per minute; service ceiling 18,000 m (59,055 ft); range 1480 + km (920 + miles) with 1000-kg (2,205-lb) warload; ferry range 3335 km (2,073 miles)

Weights: empty 7500 kg (16,534 lb); normal take-off 10,860 kg (23,942 lb); maximum take-off 17,000 kg (37,478 lb)

Dimensions: span 9·13 m (29 ft 11·5 in); length 14·36 m (47 ft 1·25 in); height 5·20 m (17 ft 0·75 in); wing area 41·00 m² (441·3 sq ft)

Variants

Mirage 2000B: two-seat operational conversion trainer model based on the Mirage 2000C but with the fuselage lengthened by 0·20 m (7·9 in) to 14·55 m (47 ft 8·8 in) for the insertion of the second cockpit; export variants are, or course, those sold to countries which have also ordered single-seat variants, in the form of the **Mirage 2000BGM** for Greece, the **Mirage 2000BM** for Egypt, the **Mirage 2000DAD** for Abu Dhabi, the **Mirage 2000DP** for Peru and the **Mirage 2000TH** for India

Mirage 2000C: now lumped together with French combat-capable Mirage 2000Bs under the overall designation **Mirage 2000DA** (Defense Aérienne, or air defence), this is France's most important warplane of the later 1980s and early 1990s, and though bearing a visual similarity to the Mirage III series is a far more advanced aircraft with good radar (possessing an all-altitude search range of 100 km/62 miles), automatic leading-edge slats, relaxed stability and fly-by-wire controls for optimum performance once the pilot's inputs have been assessed in relation to aircraft conditions and translated into the appropriate commands; the Mirage 2000 first flew in March 1978, and the type is in production as France's main interceptor and air-superiority fighter with secondary reconnaissance, close support and interdiction capabilities; the first production aircraft began to enter service in 1983, and the initial 50 aircraft have the Thomson-CSF RDM non-coherent multi-mission radar, though later machines have the more capable RDI pulse-Doppler air interception radar;

variants of this basic model have been ordered for Abu Dhabi (**Mirage 2000EAD**), Egypt (**Mirage 2000EM**), Greece (**Mirage 2000EGM**), India (**Mirage 2000H** known locally as **Vajra**, or divine thunder) and Peru (**Mirage 2000P**); Dassault-Breguet is planning a modernized version of the Mirage 2000 for the export market with a new-technology cockpit designed to allow the pilot greater opportunity to assimilate the data offered by the type's advanced sensors and computers

Mirage 2000N: low-altitude penetration strike fighter based on the airframe of the Mirage 2000B strengthened to cope with the stresses of high-speed (Mach 0·9) low-altitude (60 m/200 ft) flight to deliver the 100/150-kiloton ASMP stand-off missile; the type first flew in September 1983, and amongst its features are the Thomson-CSF/ESD Antilope 5 terrain-following and ground-mapping radar, TRT AHV-12 radar altimeter, Thomson-CSF coloured HDDs, two Sagem Uliss 52 INSs, ECM such as the Matra Spirale chaff/flare dispenser and Thomson-CSF Remora jamming pod, and Omera vertical camera; the type entered service in February 1987, replacing Dassault-Breguet Mirage IIE and SEPECAT Jaguar A strike fighters

Mirage 2000N-1: variant of the Mirage 2000N capable of carrying France's latest conventional weapons for particular missions in the non-nuclear deep interdiction role; the type will probably carry the STAR radar-homing missile and its associated ASTAC sensor pod

Mirage 2000R: reconnaissance variant of the Mirage 2000DA with Dassault-Breguet COR-2 or AA-3-38 Harold camera pods; currently produced only for Abu Dhabi as the **Mirage 2000RAD** subvariant

Mirage 2000-3: multi-role export derivative of the Mirage 2000N-1 for the non-nuclear attack role; the main electronic feature of this model is the Thomson-CSF RDY multi-function radar that effectively combines the multi-role attributes of the RDM with the pulse-Doppler advantages of the RDI to offer capability in all-altitude interception and air combat, attacks on land and sea targets, and all-weather low-altitude navigation; other electronics are the ESD Antilope automatic terrain-following radar and two INSs; the type's primary attack weapons will be the AS.30L laser-homing ASM, ARMAT radar-homing missile, AM.39 Exocet anti-ship missile, and BAP 100 and Durandal runway-cratering bombs

Mirage 2000-5: air-defence counterpart to the Mirage 2000-3 for the export market, and carrying as its primary sensor and armament the Thomson-CSF RDI radar and MICA AAM

Dassault-Breguet Mirage F1C

(France)
Type: multi-role fighter and attack aeroplane
Accommodation: pilot on a Martin-Baker F1RM4 ejector seat
Armament (fixed): two 30-mm DEFA 553 cannon with 135 rounds per gun
Armament (disposable): this is carried on seven hardpoints (one under the fuselage rated at 200 kg/2,205 lb, two under each wing with the inner units each rated at 1270 kg/2,800 lb and the outer units each at 500 kg/1,102 lb, and two at the wingtips each rated at 125 kg/276 lb) up to a maximum weight of 4000 kg (8,818 lb); the under-fuselage hardpoint can carry one 1000-kg (2,205-lb) bomb, or four 125-, 250- or 400-kg (276-, 551- or 882-lb) bombs, or four Durandal runway-cratering bombs, or two Belouga cluster bombs, or one AS.30, AS.30L or AS.37 Martel ASM, or one CC421 pod carrying a 30-mm DEFA cannon; the underwing hardpoints can carry two Matra Super 530 AAMs, or two AS.30L ASMs or two 1000-kg (2,205-lb) bombs, or four 400-kg (882-lb) bombs, or 10 125- or 250-kg (276- or 551-lb) bombs, or four Durandal runway-cratering bombs, or two Belouga cluster bombs, or 12 BAP 100 anti-runway or BAT 120 anti-vehicle bombs, or two CEM 1 combined bomb dispensers and launchers for 18 68-mm (2·68-in) rockets, or four pods each for 18 or 38 68-mm (2·68-in) rockets, or two CC421 pods each carrying a 30-mm DEFA cannon; the two wingtip hardpoints can each carry one Matra 550 Magic AAM
Electronics and operational equipment: communication and navigation equipment, plus Thomson-CSF Cyrano IVM multi-mode radar, terrain-avoidance radar, Thomson-CSF VE-120C HUD, Doppler navigation, Sagem Uliss 47 INS supplying data to the EMD 182 digital central computer, Thomson-CSF Type BF RWR, and podded ECM such as the Thomson-CSF Caiman and Remora
Powerplant and fuel system: one 7200-kg (15,873-lb) afterburning thrust SNECMA Atar 9K-50 turbojet, and a total internal fuel capacity of 4300 litres (946 Imp gal) plus provision for one 2200- or 1700-litre (484- or 374-Imp gal) or three 1200-litre (264-Imp gal) drop tanks; no provision for inflight refuelling
Performance: maximum speed 2350 km/h (1,460 mph) or Mach 2·2 at 12,000 m (39,370 ft) and 1470 km/h (913 mph) or Mach 1·2 at sea level; initial climb rate 12,780 m (41,930 ft) per minute; service ceiling 20,000 m (65,615 ft); radius 425 km (265 miles) on a hi-lo-hi mission with 14 250-kg (551-lb) bombs; ferry range 3300 km (2,051 miles)
Weights: empty 7400 kg (16,314 lb); normal take-off 10,900 kg (24,030 lb); maximum take-off 16,200 kg (35,714 lb)
Dimensions: span 8·40 m or 9·32 m (27 ft 6·75 in or 30 ft 6·9 in) without or with wingtip AAMs; length 15·23 m (49 ft 11·75 in); height 4·50 m (14 ft 9 in); wing area 25·00 m² (269·1 sq ft)

Variants

Mirage F1A: bearing the same relationship to the Mirage F1C as the Mirage 5 to the Mirage IIIE, this is the clear-weather ground-attack version of the Mirage F1C designed for South African licensed production; the type has a secondary air-to-air capability, and is fitted with Thomson-CSF Aida II ranging radar instead of the same company's Cyrano IV search radar, and can carry the Matra Super 530 AAM; other additions are a SFIM inertial platform, a Thomson-CSF laser rangefinder and Doppler navigation; the type entered service in 1975, and has been sold to Ecuador (**Mirage F1-JA**) and Libya (**Mirage F1-AD**) in addition to South Africa (**Mirage F1-AZ**)
Mirage F1B: two-seat operational training version of the Mirage F1C with the fuselage lengthened by 0·30 m (11·8 in), the cannon deleted and the internal fuel capacity reduced; the type entered service in 1976 and has been widely exported; export variants are the **Mirage F1-JE** for Ecuador, **Mirage F1-BQ** for Iraq, **Mirage F1-BJ** for Jordan, **Mirage F1-BK** for Kuwait, **Mirage F-1BD** for Libya and **Mirage F1-BE** for Spain
Mirage F1C: initial production version of the important Mirage F1 family, which first flew in prototype form in December 1966; the type is designed primarily for the all-weather interception role with monopulse Cyrano IV radar and the Super 530 AAM, a combination that offers snap-up/snap-down capability at all operating altitudes; the type has been widely exported in Europe, Africa, the Middle East and South America with various versions of the Cyrano IVM radar such as the basic air-to-air Cyrano IVM-0, the Cyrano IVM-1 with moving target indication for limited air-to-surface capability, and the Cyrano IVM-2 with beam-sharpening for enhanced air-to-surface capability; specific export variants are the **Mirage F1-CG** for Greece, **Mirage F1-CJ** for Jordan, **Mirage F1-CK** for Kuwait, **Mirage F1-CH** for Morocco, **Mirage F1-CZ** for South Africa and **Mirage F1-CE** for Spain
Mirage F1C-200: French Mirage F1C modified for rapid overseas deployment with an inflight-refuelling probe that required a lengthening of the fuselage by 0·07 m (2·75 in)
Mirage F1CR-200: combat-capable reconnaissance version of the Mirage F1C for the French air force, first flown in November 1981 for service from July 1983 and retaining radar plus associated armament but fitted internally with the advanced SNAR navigation system (Cyrano IVM-R radar, Uliss 47 INS and ESD M 182 computer), Omera 33 vertical and Omera 40 panoramic cameras, Thomson-CSF Raphael SLAR located internally, and a SAT Super Cyclope WCM 2400 IR linescanner; under its fuselage the type can also carry a Dassault/Omera Harold reconnaissance pod, or a new SLAR pod, or a COR-2 or Nora optronic reconnaissance pod, or a Thomson-CSF ASTAC or Syrel Elint pod; SARA data-link equipment is standard, as is an inflight-refuelling probe; a retrofit programme is to add Matra Coreil conformal chaff/flare dispensers under each wing root to complement the current fit of one Phimat chaff dispenser (to be replaced by the Sycomor chaff/flare dispenser) and one Thomson-CSF Remora/Barem or Barracuda single- or twin-band jammer pod
Mirage F1CT: under this designation 55 Mirage F1Cs are to be modified from June 1991 for the tactical strike role with equipment modifications including revised avionics, TACAN and INS
Mirage F1D: two-seat combat-capable operational conversion trainer derivative of the Mirage F1E broadly similar to the Mirage F1B; the export variant is the **Mirage F1-DDA** for Qatar
Mirage F1E: designation of a subsequently abandoned all-weather version with advanced nav/attack systems and the SNECMA M53 bleed turbojet, and now applied to the improved Mirage F1C for export with upgraded electronics such as Cyrano IVM radar modified for terrain avoidance, air-to-surface ranging and look-down capability; the type also has a Sagem-Kearfott inertial platform, an EMD/Sagem digital central computer and an improved head-up display; the type entered service in 1976 and has achieved significant sales success in export variants such as the **Mirage F1-EQ** for Iraq in a number of sub-variants, **Mirage F1-EJ** for Jordan, **Mirage F1-ED** for Libya, **Mirage F1-EH** for Morocco, **Mirage F-1EDA** for Qatar and **Mirage F1-EE** for Spain

Opposite: A Mirage 2000C in the markings of the French air force's Escadre de Chasse 1/2.

Below: A Mirage F1CR-200 of the French air force's Escadre de Reconnaissance 2/33.

Dassault-Breguet Mystère-Falcon 20F

(France)
Type: medium-range light transport aeroplane
Accommodation: flightcrew of two and 14 passengers or freight in the cabin
Armament (fixed): none
Armament (disposable): none
Electronics and operational equipment: communication and navigation equipment
Powerplant and fuel system: two 4,500-lb (2041-kg) thrust General Electric CF700-2D-2 non-afterburning turbofans, and a total internal fuel capacity of 5180 litres (1,139 Imp gal); no provision for drop tanks or inflight refuelling
Performance: cruising speed 840 km/h (522 mph) or Mach 0·78 at 10,000 m (32,810 ft); service ceiling 12,800 m (41,995 ft); range 3300 km (2,050 miles) with eight passengers
Weights: empty 7530 kg (16,600 lb); maximum take-off 13,000 kg (28,660 lb)
Dimensions: span 16·30 m (53 ft 6 in); length 17·15 m (56 ft 3 in); height 5·32 m (17 ft 5 in); wing area 41·00 m² (441·33 sq ft)

Variants

Mystère-Falcon 20: sold in France as the Mystère and elsewhere as the Falcon, this trim twin-jet aircraft was conceived as a corporate transport and first flew in May 1963; the type is powered by two 4,125-lb (1871-kg) thrust General Electric CF700-2C non-afterburning turbofans, and has sold to air arms (as a VIP transport and for other roles) as well as to civil customers; Mystère-Falcon 20s of various types serve with the air forces of Canada, Morocco and Norway in the EW, Elint and Sigint roles with a variety of specialized equipment fits
Mystère-Falcon 20C: extended-range version of the Mystère-Falcon 20, using the same powerplant but featuring additional fuel
Mystère-Falcon 20D: uprated version with 4,250-lb (1928-kg) thrust CT700-2D turbofans
Mystère-Falcon 20E: further uprated version with 4,500-lb (2041-kg) thrust CF700-2D-2 turbofans
Mystère-Falcon 20F: current production version based on the Mystère-Falcon 20E but with better field performance resulting from improved high-lift devices; the **Falcon ST** is a systems trainer version with the Cyrano II radar of the Dassault-Breguet Mirage IIIE
Mystère-Falcon 20G: developed version with 5,440-lb (2468-kg) thrust Garrett AFT3-6-2C turbofans and 5770 litres (1269 Imp gal) of internal fuel, developed specifically to meet the requirements of the US Coast Guard for a medium-range surveillance aeroplane, 41 such aircraft being planned under the designation **HU-25A Guardian** with a maximum take-off weight of 15,200 kg (33,510 lb) for a range of 4170 km (2,590 miles); the type has accommodation for a flightcrew of two, plus a systems officer and two observers in the cabin, as well as provision for three passengers, and the mission electronics include Texas Instruments APS-127 search radar; the type can also be adapted as the **HU-25B** **'Aireye'** with an upgraded sensor suite that includes steerable TV with laser illumination, Texas Instruments RS-18C IR/UV linescanner in an underwing pod and Motorola APS-131 SLAR with its antenna in a pod on the starboard side of the fuselage; the **HU-25C** variant is fitted with a Texas Instruments FLIR and Westinghouse APG-66 radar for the interception of drug smugglers and other air intruders
Mystère-Falcon 200: hybrid derivative using the airframe of the Mystère-Falcon 20F with the powerplant of the Mystère-Falcon 20G; the type is in French service as the **Gardian 1** resources protection type with Thomson-CSF Varan pulse-compression radar, and a Crouzet Omega tactical navigation and plotting system; Dassault-Breguet also offers the upgraded **Gardian 2** with an enhanced version of the Gardian 1's electronic suite plus optional provision for roles such as target towing, target designation, anti-ship attack with improved ECM and ESM plus two AM.39 Exocet anti-ships missiles, and light attack with weapons such as the BLG66 Belouga cluster bomb, CEM 1 multi-store pod and 30-mm cannon pod; the Gardian 2 has a maximum speed of 860 km/h (534 mph) and a maximum take-off weight of 15,200 kg (33,510 lb) with a payload of 1640 kg (3,616 lb), and with 6000 litres (1,320 Imp gal) of fuel possesses a maximum range of 4490 km (2,790 miles)

Below: An Hu-25A of the USCG before delivery.

Opposite, bottom: A Super Etendard of the French navy is seen in strike configuration with the ASMP nuclear missile under the starboard wing, balanced to port by a tank.

Dassault-Breguet Super Etendard

(France)

Type: carrierborne attack and strike fighter
Accommodation: pilot on a Martin-Baker CM4A ejector seat
Armament (fixed): two 30-mm DEFA 553 cannon with 125 rounds per gun
Armament (disposable): this is carried on five hardpoints (one under the fuselage rated at 600 kg/1,323 lb, and two under each wing with the inner two units each rated at 1100 kg/2,425 lb and the outer two units each at 450 kg/992 lb) up to a maximum weight of 2100 kg (4,630 lb); typical weapons are one 15-kiloton AN-52 free-fall tactical nuclear weapon, one 100/150-kiloton ASMP missile, one AM.39 Exocet anti-ship missile, two Matra 550 Magic AAMs, six 400-kg (882-lb) bombs, eight 250-kg (551-lb) bombs, or four pods each with 18 68-mm (2·68-in) rockets
Electronics and operational equipment: communication and navigation equipment, plus Thomson-CSF/ESD Agave multi-role radar, Thomson-CSF VE-120 HUD, Sagem-Kearfott ETNA INS, Crouzet Type 66 computer and Type 97 navigation display/armament control system, and Thomson-CSF Type BF RWR; the centreline hardpoint can also carry a reconnaissance pod or a Thomson-CSF DB 3141 ECM pod, while underwing loads can include a Thomson-CSF Barem jammer pod and a Matra Sycomor or Philips/Matra Phimat chaff dispenser
Powerplant and fuel system: one 5000-kg (11,023-lb) thrust SNECMA Atar 8K-50 non-afterburning turbojet, and a total internal fuel capacity of 3270 litres (719 Imp gal) plus provision for one 600-litre (132-Imp gal) and two 1100-litre (242-Imp gal) drop tanks; the centreline 600-litre (132-Imp gal) tank can be replaced by a buddy refuelling pod; provision for inflight refuelling
Performance: maximum speed 1380 km/h (857 mph) or Mach 1·3 at 11,000 m (36,090 ft) and 1180 km/h (733 mph) or Mach 0·96 at sea level; initial climb rate 6000 m (19,685 ft) per minute; service ceiling 13,700 + m (44,950 + ft); radius 850 km (528 miles) on a hi-lo-hi mission with one AM.39 Exocet and two drop tanks
Weights: empty 6500 kg (14,330 lb); normal take-off 9450 kg (20,835 lb); maximum take-off 12,000 kg (26,455 lb)
Dimensions: span 9·60 m (31 ft 6 in); length 14·31 m (46 ft 11·2 in); height 3·86 m (12 ft 8 in); wing area 28·40 m² (305·7 sq ft)

Variants

Etendard IVM: now serving only in the training role, the Etendard (standard) was the French navy's basic attack fighter until the advent of the Super Etendard; the type first flew in July 1956 and, powered by a 4400-kg (9,700-lb) thrust SNECMA Atar 8B non-afterburning turbojet, can carry (in addition to its two inbuilt 30-mm cannon) some 1360 kg (3,000 lb) of stores on four underwing hardpoints; one of the type's principal limitations was the lack of search radar (the narrow nose holding only an Aida ranging radar) which limited the type to IR-homing missiles and free-fall ordnance
Etendard IVP: photo-reconnaissance version of the Etendard IVM without armament but carrying five Omera cameras (three in the nose and two in the ventral position previously occupied by cannon ammunition); the type can also carry Douglas-designed 'buddy' refuelling pods for the support of other Etendards
Super Etendard: upgraded Etendard variant,

though the design and structure have needed considerable development to secure true transonic performance; the type first flew in October 1974 and began to enter service in June 1978 with the advanced nav/attack system necessary for the accurate launch of the AM.39 Exocet anti-ship missile and other ordnance; 50 current aircraft are being retrofitted to a higher standard with provision for the ASMP nuclear stand-off missile, a Sagem INS, ESD Anémone radar, and a more modern cockpit
Super Etendard NG: improved version of the Super Etendard offered for land-based service in early 1990s; the main changes are to the avionics, which now include a Thomson-CSF Agave (or perhaps ESD Anémone) radar, Thomson-CSF VE-120 HUD and Sagem INS

Below: A French Super Etendard sports BAT 120 anti-vehicle bomb clusters, a chaff dispenser (starboard) and a radar jammer (port).

Dassault-Breguet/Dornier Alpha Jet

(France & West Germany)

Type: basic/advanced flying and weapon trainer (Alpha Jet E) or battlefield close air support and reconnaissance aeroplane (Alpha Jet A)

Accommodation: pupil and instructor in tandem on Martin-Baker AJRM4 zero/167-km/h (104-mph) ejector seats (French Alpha Jet E) or Martin-Baker Mk 10N zero/zero ejector seats (Belgian, Egyptian and Qatari Alpha Jet E), or pilot and co-pilot in tandem on Stencel S-III-S3AJ zero/zero ejector seats (Alpha Jet A)

Armament (fixed): optional installation of one 27-mm Mauser BK27 (Alpha Jet A) or 30-mm DEFA (Alpha Jet E) cannon with 150 rounds in a detachable underfuselage pod

Armament (disposable): this is carried on five hardpoints (one under the fuselage rated at 500 kg/1,102 lb and generally reserved for the optional cannon pod, and two under each wing with each unit rated at 500 kg/1,102 lb up to a maximum weight of 2500+ kg (5,511+ lb); some 75+ weapon combinations have been qualified for the Alpha Jet, and typical weapons are the Matra 550 Magic AAM, AGM-65 Maverick ASM, 400-kg (882-lb) Matra BLG laser-guided bomb, 125- and 250-kg (276- and 551-lb) free-fall and retarded bombs, 250- and 500-lb (113- and 227-kg) free-fall and retarded bombs, BL755 cluster bomb, 400-kg (882-lb) cluster bomb, Belouga cluster bomb, Durandal runway-cratering bomb, Matra 155 pod with 18 68-mm (2·68-in) rockets, LAU-3 and LAU-61 pod each with 19 2·75-in (70-mm) rockets, and CC421 pod with one 30-mm DEFA cannon

Electronics and operational equipment: communication and navigation equipment, plus Thomson-CSF 902 weapon-aiming system (Alpha Jet E) or Kaiser/VDO KM808 HUD, Teledyne Ryan APN-220 Doppler navigation and Elettronica ECM pods (Alpha Jet A)

Powerplant and fuel system: two 1350-kg (2,976-lb) thrust SNECMA/Turboméca Larzac 04-C6 non-afterburning turbofans, and a total internal fuel capacity of 1900 or 2040 litres (418 or 449 Imp gal) plus provision for two 310- or 450-litre (68- or 99-Imp gal) drop tanks on the outer underwing hardpoints and, in the Alpha Jet 2, two 450- or 625-litre (99- or 137·5-Imp gal) drop tanks on the inner underwing hardpoints; no provision for inflight refuelling

Performance: maximum speed 1005 km/h (624 mph) or Mach 0·85 at 10,000 m (32,810 ft) and 1000 km/h (621 mph) or Mach 0·82 at sea level; initial climb rate 3660 m (12,000 ft) per minute; service ceiling 14,630 m (48,000 ft); radius 390 km (242 miles) on a lo-lo-lo mission with cannon pod and external stores; ferry range 2940 km (1,827 miles)

Weights: empty 3345 kg (7,374 lb) as a trainer or 3515 kg (7,749 lb) as an attack aircraft; normal take-off 5000 kg (11,023 lb) as a trainer; maximum take-off 8000 kg (17,637 lb) as an attack aircraft

Dimensions: span 9·11 m (29 ft 10·75 in); length 11·75 m (38 ft 6·5 in) as a trainer or 13·23 m (43 ft 5 in) as an attack aircraft; height 4·19 m (13 ft 9 in); wing area 17·50 m² (188·4 sq ft)

Variants

Alpha Jet A: designed in the late 1960s and early 1970s as an advanced trainer and light attack type to replace aircraft such as the Aérospatiale Magister and Aeritalia G91, the Alpha Jet was a joint Franco-German programme that resulted in the first flight during October 1973 of the precursor of an important series; the Alpha Jet A is the West German light attack model, now designated the **Alpha Jet Close Support Version**, with a pointed nose and probe accommodating various air-data sensors; this model first flew in April 1978 and began to enter West German service in March 1979; an **Alpha Jet Alternative Close Support Version** with a less capable nav/attack system was sold to Cameroun and Egypt with the designation **Alpha Jet MS-2**; in 1987 West Germany

decided not to implement the major ICE (Improved Combat Efficiency) programme developed by Dornier to give the type greater battlefield capability; this programme would have featured a revised cockpit embodying a HUD for the front-seat pupil (video-relayed to the instructor in the rear seat), two CRT displays and a single control/display unit, two 1440-kg (3,175-lb) thrust Larzac 04-C20 turbofans, and the ability to carry weapons such as the AIM-132 ASRAAM, AGM-65 Maverick, AGM-88 HARM and various types of weapon dispensers; it was possible that a pulse-Doppler radar or FLIR might also have been fitted; in 1988 West Germany revealed a less ambitious upgrade for its Alpha Jet As with a jettisonable cannon pod, two AIM-9L Sidewinder AAMs, improved navigation and air data sensors, the addition of a stall warner and a number of systems improvements; in a separate programme the higher-thrust Larzac 04-C20 engine is to be retrofitted; the Alpha Jet A is accordingly to lose its combat role from 1995, thereafter becoming a trainer and flying hours substitution aircraft in wings equipped with the Panavia Tornado and McDonnell Douglas Phantom

Alpha Jet E: French advanced trainer model with a secondary light attack capability; the type has a rounded nose and began to enter French service in the summer of 1978, now being designated the **Alpha Jet Advanced Trainer/Light Attack Version**; since its French service debut the type has scored useful export sales as the **Alpha Jet B** (Belgium), **Alpha Jet C** (Ivory Coast, Qatar and Togo), **Alpha Jet MS-1** (Egypt) and **Alpha Jet N** (Nigeria)

Alpha Jet NGEA: this Nouvelle Génération pur l'Ecole et l'Appui (new generation for training and attack) is an improved close-support and limited air-combat version of the Alpha Jet E developed by Dassault-Breguet on the basis of the Alpha Jet MS-2 and now designated the **Alpha Jet 2** for the export market with an advanced nav/attack system comprising a Sagem Uliss 81 INS, Thomson-CSF VE-110C HUD, Thomson-CSF TMV-630 laser rangefinder, ESD Digibus multiplex digital databus and other improvements such as Larzac 04-C20 turbofans; the weapons can include two Matra 550 Magic dogfighting AAMs and free-fall ordnance or rocket pods on the four underwing hardpoints, in addition to the podded underfuselage cannon; the type first flew in April 1982 and though no such aircraft were built from scratch, Egypt's Alpha Jet MS-2s are being upgraded to this standard

Lancier: Dassault-Breguet version developed on the basis of the Alpha Jet NGEA as an improved type optimized for the close support and anti-ship roles with Larzac 04-C20 turbofans plus specialist avionics and weapons; the Lancier (lancer) has a longer nose for the considerably enhanced avionics fit (including air-to-air/air-to-surface Thomson-CSF/ESD Agave radar, FLIR in an undernose blister fairing, Thomson-CSF VE-130 wide-angle HUD behind the new single-piece windscreen, and a CP 2084 central computer); the type first flew in 1985 and exhaustive trials and weapon qualifications could result in sales during the 1990s; the type is being qualified with weapons such as the Matra 550 Magic AAM and the Aérospatiale AM.39 Exocet anti-ship missile, as well as laser-guided bombs and a podded 30-mm DEFA cannon

Alpha Jet Advanced Training System: announced by Dassault-Breguet in mid-1987, this **Alpha Jet 3** latest variant uses many of the features of the Lancier to take advantage of the latest developments in nav/attack systems through the adoption of a new cockpit with head-up and head-level displays, a video monitor in the rear cockpit, CRT displays and advanced control keyboards

The Alpha Jet 2 can lift a useful warload.

de Havilland Canada (Boeing of Canada/de Havilland Division) DHC-4A Caribou

(Canada)

Type: short-range STOL tactical transport aeroplane

Accommodation: flightcrew of two, and 32 troops, or 26 paratroops, or 22 litters, four seated casualties and four attendants, or 8,740 lb (3964 kg) of freight in the hold

Armament (fixed): none

Armament (disposable): none

Electronics and operational equipment: communication and navigation equipment

Powerplant and fuel system: two 1,450-hp (1081-kW) Pratt & Whitney R-2000-7M2 Twin Wasp piston engines, and a total internal fuel capacity of 690 Imp gal (3137 litres); no provision for drop tanks or inflight refuelling

Performance: maximum speed 216 mph (348 km/h) at 6,500 ft (1980 m); cruising speed 182 mph (293 km/h) at 7,500 ft (2285 m); initial climb rate 1,355 ft (413 m) per minute; service ceiling 24,800 ft (7560 m); range 242 miles (390 km) with maximum payload

Weights: empty 18,260 lb (8283 kg); normal take-off 28,500 lb (12,298 kg); maximum take-off 31,300 lb (14,198 kg)

Dimensions: span 95 ft 7·5 in (29·15 m); length 72 ft 7 in (22·12 m); height 31 ft 9 in (9·67 m); wing area 912·0 sq ft (84·7 m²)

Variants

DHC-4 Caribou: first flown in July 1958 after design by de Havilland Canada (now the de Havilland Division of Boeing Canada), this tactical transport continued the role specialization of earlier DHC aircraft, but offered considerably more payload without significant loss of STOL capability; the variant has a maximum take-off weight of 26,000 lb (11,793 kg)

DHC-4A Caribou: improved DHC-4 with a 2,500-lb (1134-kg) increase in maximum take-off weight, and the variant that amounted to all but 23 of the 307 Caribou transports built

The DHC-4A Caribou was used by the US Air Force during the Vietnam War with the designation C-7A, and proved an excellent light/medium tactical transport.

de Havilland Canada (Boeing of Canada/de Havilland Division) DHC-5D Buffalo

(Canada)

Type: short-range STOL tactical transport aeroplane

Accommodation: flightcrew of three, and 41 troops, or 35 paratroops, or 24 litters and six attendants, or 18,000 lb (8165 kg) of freight in the hold

Armament (fixed): none

Armament (disposable): none

Electronics and operational equipment: communication and navigation equipment

Powerplant and fuel system: two 3,133-shp (2336-kW) General Electric CT64-820-4 turboprops, and a total internal fuel capacity of 1,755 Imp gal (7978 litres); no provision for drop tanks or inflight refuelling

Performance: maximum speed 290 mph (467 km/h) at 10,000 ft (3050 m); cruising speed 261 mph (420 km/h) at 10,000 ft (3050 m); initial climb rate 1,820 ft (555 m) per minute; service ceiling 27,000 ft (8380 m); range 691 miles (1112 km) with maximum payload; ferry range 2,038 miles (3280 km)

Weights: empty 25,160 lb (11,412 kg); normal take-off 41,000 lb (18,597 kg) for STO; maximum take-off 49,200 lb (22,316 kg)

Dimensions: span 96 ft 0 in (29·26 m); length 79 ft 0 in (24·08 m); height 28 ft 8 in (8·73 m); wing area 945·0 sq ft (87·8 m²)

Variants

DHC-5A Buffalo: developed from the DHC-4 as a turboprop-powered tactical and utility transport in response to a US Army requirement, the Buffalo continued DHC's reputation for rugged STOL transports when the type first flew in April 1964; the DHC-4 had a payload of 11,200 lb (5080 kg), but only four trials aircraft for the US Army were built before the company switched production to the improved DHC-5A variant with CT64-810-1 turboprops and payload increased to 13,843 lb (6279 kg); the Canadian Armed Forces took 15 of the type, most being converted subsequently for the maritime patrol and SAR roles

DHC-5D Buffalo: main production version (the DHC-5B and DHC-5C having been proposals for Indian aircraft with CT64-P4C and Rolls-Royce Dart RDa·12 turboprops respectively) with greater power and payload; production totalled 123 aircraft, and was completed in February 1987 with the last two aircraft for Kenya

Ecuador operates two DHC-5D Buffalo transports under the aegis of TAME, the Ecuadorean air force's semi-civil airline and air transport command.

Dornier Do 228 Maritime Patrol Version A

EMBRAER (Empresa Brasileira de Aeronautica SA) EMB-111A/A Bandeirulha

(West Germany)
Type: short/medium-range maritime patrol aeroplane
Accommodation: flightcrew of two and a mission crew of three
Armament (fixed): none
Armament (disposable): none
Electronics and operational equipment: communication and navigation equipment, plus MEL Marec 2 or Super Marec search radar and an IR/UV linescanner
Powerplant and fuel system: two 715-shp (533-kW) Garrett TPE331-5-252D turboprops, and a total internal fuel capacity of 2390 litres (526 Imp gal); no provision for drop tanks or inflight refuelling
Performance: cruising speed 428 km/h (266 mph) at 3000 m (9,845 ft); cruising speed for maximum range 305 km/h (190 mph) and for maximum endurance 185 km/h (115 mph); initial climb rate 618 m (2,028 ft) per minute; service ceiling 9450 m (31,000 ft); range 1345 km (836 miles) with maximum payload; endurance 9 hours 45 minutes
Weights: empty 3935 kg (8,675 lb); maximum take-off 5980 kg (13,183 lb)
Dimensions: span 16·97 m (55 ft 8 in); length 15·04 m (49 ft 4·25 in); height 4·86 m (15 ft 11·5 in); wing area 32·00 m² (344·3 sq ft)

Variants

Do 228-101: first flown in March 1981, the **Do 228-100** is the shorter-fuselage version of Dornier's updated version of the Do 28 developed as the Do 29E with the TNT new-technology wing married to a pair of Garrett turboprops; a small number of these aircraft are used as utility transports by a number of air forces, but India has established a production line at the Kanpur facility of Hindustan Aeronautics Ltd for the licence-manufacture of the type (including the Do 228-101 with a reinforced fuselage) for civil and large-scale military employment; the Do 228-100/101 has a flightcrew of two and cabin accommodation for 15 passengers, or 21 troops, or 2127 kg (4,689 lb) of freight; the type is also available in two maritime patrol configurations, of which the **Do 228 Maritime Patrol Version A** is intended for fishery protection and anti-smuggling patrol with 360° scan MEL Marec 2 or in later aircraft Super Marec radar, while the **Do 228 Maritime Patrol Version B** is intended for anti-pollution patrol with Ericsson SLAR; the Indian coast guard uses the Do 228 Maritime Patrol Version A for the maritime surveillance role with Marec 2 radar, and the Indian navy operates the type in the maritime patrol role with anti-ship missiles carried on underwing pylons
Do 228-200: version identical with the Do 228-100 in all but its length and payload, which are increased to 16·55 m (54 ft 3 in) and decreased by 300 kg (661 lb) respectively, though a maximum passenger load of 19 is possible over decreased range; alternative loads are 25 troops or up to 2500 kg (5,511 lb) of freight; subvariants of the Do 228-200 are the **Do 228-201** with a strengthened fuselage, the **Do 228-202** with modified payload/range parameters, and the **Do 228-203F** freighter

Right: The Do 228–100 is ideally suited to quasi-military tasks such as resources surveillance and fisheries protection.

EMBRAER (Empresa Brasileira de Aeronautica SA) EMB-312 Tucano

(Brazil)
Type: medium-range maritime patrol aeroplane
Accommodation: flightcrew of two, and a mission crew of three in the cabin
Armament (fixed): none
Armament (disposable): this is carried on four hardpoints (two under each wing) for loads such as eight 5-in (127-mm) rockets or four launchers each carrying seven 2·75-in (70-mm) rockets
Electronics and operational equipment: communication and navigation equipment, plus Eaton AIL SPAR-1 (APS-128 Sea Patrol) search radar, Litton LN-33 INS, and ESM system
Powerplant and fuel system: two 750-shp (559-kW) Pratt & Whitney Canada PT6A-34 turboprops, and a total internal fuel capacity of 2586 litres (569 Imp gal); no provision for drop tanks or inflight refuelling
Performance: maximum speed 404 km/h (251 mph) at 3050 m (10,000 ft); cruising speed 347 km/h (216 mph) at 3050 m (10,000 ft); initial climb rate 402 m (1,319 ft) per minute; service ceiling 8230 m (27,000 ft); range 2075 km (1,290 miles) with maximum payload or 2725 km (1,695 miles) with maximum fuel
Weights: empty 3403 kg (7,502 lb); maximum take-off 7000 kg (15,432 lb)
Dimensions: span 15·96 m (52 ft 4·5 in) over tiptanks; length 14·83 m (48 ft 7·9 in); height 4·74 m (15 ft 6·5 in); wing area 29·00 m² (312·2 sq ft)

Left: Six EMB-110B aircraft are used for photo-survey by the Brazilian air force with the local designation R-95.

Variants

EMB-110 Bandeirante: baseline model of the series designed as a general-purpose transport in the 1960s with a payload of 15 passengers and a powerplant of two 680-shp (507-kW) Pratt & Whitney Canada PT6A-27 turboprops; the Bandeirante (pioneer) first flew in October 1968, and began to enter civil and military service in 1970
EMB-110A Bandeirante: navaid calibration version of the EMB-110
EMB-110B Bandeirante: photographic survey version with Doppler navigation and an electrically operated ventral door over the hatch for a battery of cameras
EMB-110C Bandeirante: improved transport version with accommodation for some 15 passengers or equivalent freight load
EMB-110K Bandeirante: improved transport with two 750-shp (559-kW) PT6A-34 turboprops and the fuselage stretched by 0·85 m (2·79 ft) to permit the carriage of a 1880-kg (4,125-lb) payload in the light freighting role; freight is loaded through an upward-opening door in the rear fuselage
EMB-110P1SAR Bandeirante: SAR version of the EMB-110P1 quick-change passenger/cargo transport
EMB-111A/A Bandeirulha: land-based maritime reconnaissance version of the EMB-110 series, visually identifiable from the transport series by its tip tanks and large nose radome for the search radar; later aircraft have MEL Super Searcher radar, a Thomson-CSF DR2000A Mk II/Dalia 1000A Mk II ESM system, and a Canadian Marconi CMA 771 Mk III navigation system as well as other electronic improvements

(Brazil)
Type: basic flying and weapon trainer
Accommodation: pupil and instructor in tandem on Martin-Baker BR8LC lightweight ejector seats
Armament (fixed): none
Armament (disposable): this is carried on four hardpoints (two under each wing, with each unit rated at 250 kg/551 lb) up to a maximum weight of 1000 kg (2,205 lb); typical weapons are 0·5-in (12·7-mm) machine-guns pods each with 350 rounds, 250-kg (551-lb) bombs, 250-lb (113-kg) bombs, and launchers for seven 2·75-in (70-mm) rockets
Electronics and operational equipment: communication and navigation equipment, and oprical sights
Powerplant and fuel system: one 750-shp (559-kW) Pratt & Whitney Canada PT6A-25C turboprop flat-rated to 585 shp (486 kW), and a total internal fuel capacity of 694 litres (153 Imp gal) plus provision for two 330-litre (73-Imp gal) ferry tanks; no provision for inflight refuelling
Performance: maximum speed 448 km/h (278 mph) at 3000 m (9,845 ft); cruising speed 411 km/h (255 mph) at 3000 m (9,845 ft); initial climb rate 680 m (2,231 ft) per minute; service ceiling 9150 m (30,000 ft); range 1844 km (1,145 miles) on internal fuel; ferry range 3350 km (2,069 miles)
Weights: empty 1810 kg (3,991 lb); normal take-off 2550 kg (5,622 lb); maximum take-off 3175 kg (7,000 lb)
Dimensions: span 11·14 m (36 ft 6·5 in); length 9·86 m (32 ft 4·25 in); height 3·40 m (11 ft 2 in); wing area 19·40 m² (208·82 sq ft)

Variant

EMB-312 Tucano: designed as a basic trainer with turboprop powerplant for a combination of performance, economy of operation and 'jet' handling, the Tucano (toucan) first flew in August 1980 and entered service in 1983 with the Brazilian air force designation **T-27**; the type is proving a successful contender in South American and world markets in the flying and weapon training roles; the Tucano was also adopted for the Royal Air Force in a version significantly modified to become the Shorts S.312 Tucano

Below: In the Brazilian air force the EMB-312 serves under the designation T-27.

ENAER (Empresa Nacional de Aeronautica de Chile) T-35 Pillan

European Helicopter Industries EH.101

(Chile)

Type: basic and intermediate flying and weapon trainer

Accommodation: pupil and instructor in tandem

Armament (fixed): none

Armament (disposable): this is carried on two hardpoints (one under each wing) up to a maximum weight of 500 kg (1,102 lb) of light stores such as two 250-kg (551-lb) bombs, or two 0·5-in (12·7-mm) machine-gun pods, or two pods for four or seven 2·75-in (70-mm) rockets

Electronics and operational equipment: communication and navigation equipment, and optical sights

Powerplant and fuel system: one 300-hp (224-kW) Avco Lycoming IO-540-K1K5 piston engine, and a total internal fuel capacity of 291·5 litres (64 Imp gal); no provision for drop tanks or inflight refuelling

Performance: maximum speed 311 km/h (193 mph) at sea level; cruising speed 266 km/h (166 mph) at 2700 m (8,860 ft); initial climb rate 465 m (1,525 ft); service ceiling 5840 m (19,160 ft); range 1362 km (846 miles)

Weights: empty 930 kg (2,057 lb); maximum take-off 1338 kg (2,950 lb)

Dimensions: span 8·84 m (29 ft 0 in); length 8·00 m (26 ft 3 in); height 2·64 m (8 ft 8 in); wing area 13·69 m² (147·34 sq ft)

Variants

T-35 Pillan: first flown during March 1981 in the USA after development by Piper from the PA-28 Dakota and PA-32 Saratoga series of lightplanes, the Pillan (devil) is a useful trainer and counter-insurgency aircraft intended for local manufacture by the developing Chilean aerospace industry; the type has been produced in several basically similar subvariants as the **T-35A** flying trainer for local use, the **T-35B** instrument trainer, also for Chile, the **T34C** flying trainer for Spain (which has the local designation **E.26 Tamiz**) and finally, the **T-34D** flying trainer for Panama

T-35S Pillan: single-seat version of the T-35 intended for aerobatic display purposes; the type was first flown in March 1988 with the standard piston engine, but a 420-shp (313-kW) Allison 250-B17 turboprop is planned for the production version

T-35T Aucan: developed as the Turbo-Pillan with a 420-shp (313-kW) Allison 250-B17D turboprop, the 1315-kg (2,800-kg) Aucan (blithe spirit) offers significantly improved performance (including a maximum speed of 367 km/h; 228 mph) and payload, especially in the armed role; the programme looked promising, but was discontinued in 1987 despite earlier plans to start production in 1988

(Italy & UK)

Type: multi-role helicopter

Crew: normally four for the anti-submarine role

Armament (fixed): none

Armament (disposable): this is carried on two hardpoints (one on each side of the fuselage) up to a maximum weight of 960 kg (2,116 lb); each hardpoint can accommodate two Sting Ray, A 244/S or Mk 46 anti-submarine torpedoes, or anti-ship missiles such as the AM.39 Exocet, AGM-84 Harpoon, Sea Eagle and Sea Skua

Electronics and operational equipment: communication and navigation equipment, plus

Below left: T-35 Pillan flying and weapon trainers of the Chilean air force.

Below: A pre-production EH.101 reveals the basic layout of this multi-role helicopter.

(Royal Navy anti-submarine version) Ferranti Blue Kestrel search radar, HELRAS dunking sonar and sonobuoys used in conjunction with the Marconi AQS-903 acoustic processing system, INS, Global Positioning System, Doppler navigation, Orange Reaper (Racal Kestrel) ESM system, and various countermeasures systems

Powerplant and fuel system: three 1725-kW (2,314-shp) Rolls-Royce/Turboméca RTM322-01 turboshafts, and a total internal fuel weight of 9,475 lb (4298 kg); no provision for drop tanks or inflight refuelling

Performance: cruising speed 184 mph (296 km/h) at optimum ltitude; cruising speed for maximum range 161 mph (259 km/h) and for maximum endurance 104 mph (167 km/h); service ceiling not revealed; ferry range 1,150 miles (1850 km); endurance 5 hours on station with maximum weapon load

Weights: empty 20,500 lb (9298 kg); maximum take-off 29,825 lb (13,529 kg)

Dimensions: main rotor diameter 61 ft 0 in (18·59 m); length overall, rotors turning 74 ft 10 in (22·81 m) and fuselage 74 ft 9·6 in (22·80 m); height 21 ft 10 in (6·65 m); main rotor disc area 2,922·5 sq ft (271·5 m²)

Variant

EH.101: designed as a collaborative venture between Westland and Agusta to replace the Sea King variants in service with the Italian and British navies, the EH.101 flew in the form of its first British and Italian prototypes during October and November 1987 respectively, all engined with General Electric CT7-6 turboshafts, to be replaced in the military and Italian naval variants by 1,714-shp (1278-kW) General Electric T700-GE-401A turboshafts; these and later prototypes

are being used to validate the concept of a weapon/sensor platform more capable and more powerful than the Sea King, yet possessing smaller overall dimensions; in British service the type will be called the **Merlin**; the type is also being developed in utility civil and military form with a payload of 13,435 lb (6094 kg) or 28 troops, and British plans call for use in production aircraft of the Rolls-Royce/Turboméca RTM322 turboshaft for greater power and thus greater performance in British helicopters, though the Italians have opted to fit their helicopters with the 2,000-shp (1491-kW) CT7-6A turboshaft, a growth version of the T700 (as used in the Sikorsky SH-60B Seahawk) developed by General Electric in collaboration with the Italian companies Alfa Romeo Avio and Fiat Aviazione; the use of two MIL 1553 databuses offers maximum flexibility in retrofitting additional equipment of the most modern types

Fairchild Metro III

(USA)
Type: light utility transport aeroplane
Accommodation: flightcrew of two or three, and 20 passengers or 4,880 lb (2214 kg) of freight in the cabin
Armament (fixed): none
Armament (disposable): none
Electronics and operational equipment: communication and navigation equipment
Powerplant and fuel system: two 1,000-shp (746-kW) Garrett TPE331-11U-611G turboprops, and a total internal fuel capacity of 648 US gal (2453 litres); no provision for drop tanks or inflight refuelling
Performance: maximum cruising speed 320 mph (515 km/h) at 12,500 ft (3810 m); cruising speed 295 mph (475 km/h) at 25,000 ft (7620 m); initial climb rate 2,350 ft (716 m) per minute; service ceiling 27,500 ft (8380 m); range 1,000 miles (1609 km) with maximum passenger payload or 2,558 miles (4117 km) with 1,078-lb (489-kg) payload
Weights: empty 8,737 lb (3963 kg); maximum take-off weight 14,500 lb (657 kg)
Dimensions: span 57 ft 10 in (17·37 m); length 59 ft 4·25 in (18·09 m); height 16 ft 8 in (5·08 m); wing area 309·0 sq ft (28·71 m²)

Variants

Metro III: this trim light transport was originally developed by Swearingen on the basis of the Beech Queen Air as a commuterliner (Metro) and executive transport (Merlin); the type first flew in August 1969, and the type has been successively developed over the following years; the current Metro III is used by several air forces including the US Air National Guard which calls its variant the **C-26A**; there is also a **Metro III(H)** with maximum take-off weight increased to 16,000 lb (7258 kg) and an **Expediter** all-cargo version capable of carrying a payload of 4,780 lb (2168 kg)
Metro III Special Missions Version: the manufacturer markets this model for a number of specialist military roles, notably the maritime patrol/surveillance and ASW mission with Litton APS-504(V) or Eaton AIL APS-128D search radar with its antenna in an underfuselage radome, a sonobuoy data-processing system, MAD in a long tailboom and options such as a FLIR, IR linescanner, low-light-level TV and Doppler navigation; the type has the same maximum take-off weight as the Metro III(H), and a maximum endurance of 10 hours; the Swedish air force is using one such aeroplane for the evaluation of an Ericsson AEW radar, which is of the SLAR type with its flat-plate antenna mounted longitudinally above the fuselage

Fairchild Republic A-10A Thunderbolt II

(USA)
Type: battlefield close air support and anti-tank aeroplane
Accommodation: pilot on a Douglas ACES II ejector seat
Armament (fixed): one 30-mm General Electric GAU-8/A Avenger rotary-barrel cannon with 1,174 rounds
Armament (disposable): this is carried on 11 hardpoints (three under the fuselage with the centreline unit rated at 5,000 lb/2268 kg and the two flanking units each at 3,500 lb/1587 kg, and four under each wing with each unit of the pairs [from inboard to outboard] rated at 3,500 lb/1587 kg, 2,500 lb/1134 kg, 1,000 lb/454 kg and 1,000 lb/454 kg respectively) up to a maximum weight of 16,000 lb (7258 kg) with reduced fuel or 14,340 lb (6505 kg) with maximum fuel; typical loads are six AGM-65 Maverick ASMs, eight or 16 AGM-114 Hellfire anti-tank missiles, Mk 82 and Mk 84 Paveway laser-guided bombs, GBU-15 2,000-lb (907-kg) EO-guided bombs, 28 500-lb (227-kg) free-fall or retarded bombs, six 2,000-lb (907-kg) free-fall or retarded bombs, eight BLU-1 or BLU-27 napalm bombs, 20 Rockeye II cluster bombs, 16 CBU-52 or CBU-71 bomb dispensers, and two SUU-23 20-mm cannon pods
Electronics and operational equipment: communication and navigation equipment, plus Kaiser HUD, Itek ALR-46(V) RWR, AAS-35 'Pave Penny' laser designator pod, ALQ-119 ECM pod, ALQ-37 chaff dispenser and, until cancelled in 1989, provision for the LANTIRN (Low-Altitude Navigation and Targeting Infra-Red for Night) pod system with FLIR and laser sensors for all-weather day/night terrain following and target acquisition/marking
Powerplant and fuel system: two 9,065-lb (4112-kg) thrust General Electric TF34-GE-100 non-afterburning turbofans, and a total internal fuel capacity of 1,605 US gal (6076 litres) plus provision for three 600-US gal (2271-litre) drop tanks; provision for inflight refuelling
Performance: maximum speed 439 mph (706 km/h) clean at sea level; cruising speed 387 mph (623 km/h) clean at 5,000 ft (1525 m); initial climb rate 6,000 ft (1830 m) per minute; service ceiling not revealed; radius 250 miles (402 km) with loiter time of 2 hours carrying 18 500-lb (227-kg) bombs and 750 30-mm rounds; ferry range 2,455 miles (3950 km)
Weights: empty 24,960 lb (11,321 kg); maximum take-off weight 50,000 lb (22,680 kg)
Dimensions: span 57 ft 6 in (17·53 m); length 53 ft 4 in (16·26 m); height 14 ft 8 in (4·47 m); wing area 506·0 sq ft (47·01 m²)

Variants

A-10A Thunderbolt II: first flown in May 1972 to enter service in late 1975, the A-10A is slow by modern standards of battlefield aircraft, but is prodigiously strong, highly manoeuvrable, well armoured and filled with the structural and system redundancies necessary for battlefield survival, and also possesses considerable endurance and an excellent weapons load; the type's primary failing is its restriction to clear-weather operations, though this limitation was to have been reduced with the adoption of the LANTIRN navigation and targeting pod system, the former with terrain-following radar and FLIR, and the latter with a large-aperture FLIR, an automatic tracker and a laser ranger and designator to provide the pilot's new wide-angle HUD with a thermal image of the land ahead and all necessary targeting information for the use of 'smart' weapons; current aircraft are being fitted with dual-rail adapters to allow the carriage of four AIM-9L Sidewinder AAMs
OA-10A Thunderbolt II: designation of the A-10As which were reconfigured for the FAC role from 1988 onwards

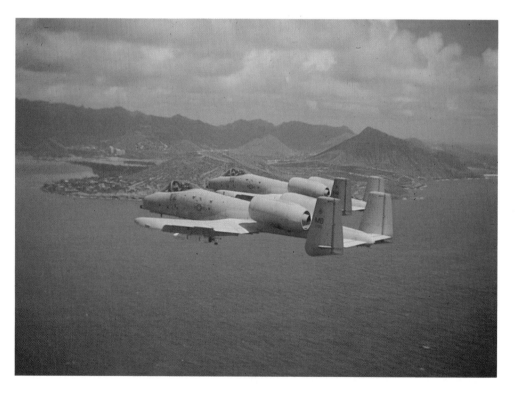

Left: The Swedish air force's experimental Metro III with over-fuselage AEW radar.

Above: A-10A Thunderbolt IIs of the 354th Tactical Fighter Wing based at Myrtle Beach AFB, South Carolina.

FAMA (Fabrica Argentina de Materiales Aeroespaciales) IA 58A Pucara

(Argentina)

Type: close air support and counter-insurgency aeroplane

Accommodation: pilot and co-pilot in tandem on Martin-Baker AP06A zero/zero ejector seats

Armament (fixed): two 20-mm Hispano-Suiza HS 804 cannon with 270 rounds per gun, and four 7·62-mm (0·3-in) FN M2-30 machine-guns with 900 rounds per gun

Armament (disposable): this is carried on three hardpoints (one under the fuselage rated at 1000 kg/2,205 lb, and one under each wing rated at 500 kg/1,102 lb) up to a maximum weight of 1620 kg (3,571 lb); typical loads are two Martin Pescador ASMs, or four 400-kg (882-lb) bombs, or 12 120-kg (265-lb) bombs, or varying numbers of 50- or 115-kg (110- or 254-lb) HE or fragmentation bombs, or six pods each with 19 2·75-in (70-mm) rockets

Electronics and operational equipment: communication and navigation equipment, plus a Matra sight and Bendix AWE-1 stores-management system

Powerplant and fuel system: two 730-kW (979-shp) Turboméca Astazou XVIG turboprops, and a total internal fuel capacity of 1280 litres (281 Imp gal) plus provision for one 1100-litre (242-Imp gal) and two 318-litre (70-Imp gal) drop tanks); no provision for inflight refuelling

Performance: maximum speed 500 km/h (311 mph) clean at 3000 m (9,845 ft); cruising speed 430 km/h (267 mph); initial climb rate 1080 m (3,545 ft) per minute; service ceiling 10,000 m (32,810 ft); radius 350 km (217 miles) on a hi-lo-hi mission with 1500-kg (3,307-lb) warload; ferry range 3040 km (1,889 miles)

Weights: empty 4020 kg (8,862 lb); maximum take-off 6800 kg (14,991 lb)

Dimensions: span 14·50 m (47 ft 6·9 in); length 14·253 m (46 ft 9 in); height 5·362 m (17 ft 7 in); wing area 30·3 m² (326·1 sq ft)

Variants

IA 58A Pucara: baseline model of this Argentine counter-insurgency and light attack aircraft, of which 108 were built by what was then known as the FMA (Fabrica Militar de Aviones); the Pucara (hill fort) first flew in August 1969, and began to enter service in 1974; some aircraft have been modified to single-seat layout with additional fuel capacity in place of the second seat

IA 58B Pucara Bravo: simple development of the basic model with two 30-mm DEFA 553 cannon with 140 rounds per gun in place of the IA 58A's two 20-mm cannon; this did not progress past the development stage

IA 58C Pucara Charlie: first flown in December 1985, this is the IA 58A modified to single-seat configuration with a nose-mounted armament of one 30-mm DEFA 554 cannon plus 270 rounds (as well as the standard two 20-mm cannon and four 7·62-mm/0·3-in machine-guns) and a Saab RSG-2 sight as well as upgraded avionics including a HUD and an RWR; other improvements include Astazou engines with reduced IR signature, and additional wingtip hardpoints for two R550 Magic AAMs (complementing the pair that can currently be carried on the underwing hardpoints as an alternative to the Martin Pescador ASMs or varied unguided ordnance); the payload/range balance is some 30% better than that of the IA-58A, but the programme was ended in 1988

IA 66 Pucara: first flown in 1980, this is an experimental/development model with two 1,000-shp (746-kW) Garrett TPE331 turboprops, and did not proceed past the development stage

The IA 58A Pucara is well suited to COIN operations, but is very vulnerable to advanced aircraft and AA weapons.

FAMA (Fabrica Argentina de Materiales Aeroespaciales) IA 63 Pampa

Fokker F.27 Maritime

(Argentina)

Type: basic/advanced flying and weapon trainer with a secondary light attack capability

Accommodation: pupil and instructor/pilot and co-pilot in tandem on Stencel S-III-S3IA63 lightweight ejector seats

Armament (fixed): none

Armament (disposable): this is carried on five hardpoints (one under the fuselage rated at 250 kg/551 lb and two under each wing with the inboard two units each rated at 400 kg/882 lb and the outboard two units each at 250 kg/551 lb) up to a maximum weight of 1550 kg (3,417 lb); typical weapons are a centreline pod for one 30-mm DEFA cannon, ASM-2 Martin Pescador ASMs, 400-kg (882-lb) bombs, 120-kg (265-lb) bombs, 50- or 115-kg (110- or 254-lb) HE or fragmentation bombs, and pods for 2·75-in (69·85-mm) rockets

Electronics and operational equipment: communication and navigation equipment, plus an optical sight

Powerplant and fuel system: one 3,500-lb (1588-kg) thrust Garrett TFE731-2-2N non-afterburning turbofan, and a total internal fuel capacity of 968 litres (213 Imp gal) plus provision for 415 litres (91 Imp gal) of auxiliary fuel in tanks in the outer wing panels; no provision for drop tanks or inflight refuelling

Performance: maximum speed 819 km/h (509 mph) or Mach 0·73 clean at 7000 m (22,965 ft); cruising speed 747 km/h (464 mph) at 4000 m (13,125 ft); initial climb rate 1813 m (5,950 ft) per minute; service ceiling 12,900 m (42,325 ft); radius 360 km (223 miles) on a hi-lo-hi mission with a 1000-kg (2,205-lb) warload; ferry range 2500 km (1,550 miles) with auxiliary fuel

Weights: empty 2821 kg (6,219 lb); normal take-off 3700 kg (8,377 lb); maximum take-off 4650 kg (10,251 lb) for training and 5000 kg (11,023 lb) for attack

Dimensions: span 9·686 m (31 ft 9·25 in); length 10·90 m (35 ft 9·25 in); height 4·29 m (14 ft 1 in); wing area 15·63 m² (168·2 sq ft)

Variant

IA 63 Pampa: designed with the assistance of Dornier in West Germany, the Pampa is a straight-wing two-seat trainer with light attack capability (the latter to be enhanced in later models), and the type first flew in October 1984; orders have been placed by the Argentine air force as well as the air forces of other South American nations

(Netherlands)

Type: medium-range maritime patrol aeroplane

Accommodation: flightcrew of two or three, and a mission crew of six in the cabin

Armament (fixed): none

Armament (disposable): none

Electronics and operational equipment: communication and navigation equipment, plus Litton APS-504(V)2 search radar, Litton LTN-72 INS and IDC air-data computer

Powerplant and fuel system: two 2,320-ehp (1730-kW) Rolls-Royce Dart RDa·7 Mk 536-7R turboprops, and a total internal fuel capacity of 7450 litres (1,639 Imp gal) plus provision for two 938-litre (206-Imp gal) non-jettisonable underwing tanks; no provision for drop tanks or inflight refuelling

Performance: cruising speed 465 km/h (289 mph) at 6100 m (20,015 ft); initial climb rate 442 m (1,450 ft) per minute; service ceiling 9000 m (29,530 ft); range 5000 km (3,107 miles)

Weights: empty 13,314 kg (29,352 lb); normal take-off 20,410 kg (45,000 lb); maximum take-off 21,320 kg (47,500 lb)

Dimensions: span 29·00 m (95 ft 2 in); length 23·56 m (77 ft 3·5 in); height 8·50 m (27 ft 11 in);

wing area 70·00 m² (753·5 sq ft)

Variants

F.27 Mk 400M Troopship: dedicated military transport version of the civil F.27 Friendship Mk 400 airliner; compared with the civil model the Mk 400M has a large cargo door, and (on each side) inflight-openable doors for the despatch of paratroops, of which 46 can be carried; alternative loads are 24 litters and nine attendants, or 6025 kg (13,283 lb) of freight; the type can also be fitted out as a photo-survey aircraft, and other marks of the Friendship series are used in military markings mainly for VIP transport; the basic F.27 was also proposed as the starting point for two EW machines, namely the **King Bird** airborne early warning and **Sentinel** Elint aircraft (**King Bird Mk 2** and **Sentinel Mk 2** on the basis of the new Fokker 50's airframe); the King Bird series would have AWG-9 or Thorn EMI Skymaster surveillance radar and an ESM system, while the Sentinel series would feature the Motorola APS-135(V) SLAR, cameras and an automatic Comint system

F50 Troopship Mk 2: the Fokker 50 is the fully modernized version of the F.27 airliner, and is also being offered in military variants with the designation Troopship Mk 2; the type is externally similar to the F.27, but has Pratt & Whitney Canada PW125B turboprops driving six- rather than four-blade propellers and a host of system improvements

F.27 Maritime: maritime patrol version of the standard Friendship airliner, and differing from this latter mainly in extra fuel capacity and the specialized role equipment suiting the type for coastal patrol, maritime reconnaissance, fishery protection, search-and-rescue, offshore resources protection etc with an endurance of 10 to 12 hours at patrol speeds between 277 and 333 km/h (172 and 207 mph) at an altitude of 460 m (1,510 ft)

F.27MPA Maritime Enforcer: basically the armed version of the F.27 Maritime designed for the anti-ship and anti-submarine roles with an avionics and armament system integrated by Marconi of the UK, and including a Litton APS-140(V) or digitally processed APS-504(V)5 search radar, the AQS-902 sonobuoy data-processing system, the TATTIX central tactical system and an ESM system; 3930 kg (8,664 lb) of weapons are carried on two underfuselage and six underwing hardpoints, typical loads managed by the Alkan stores management system being two or four torpedoes or two anti-ship missiles

F50 Maritime Mk 2: considerably developed version of the Maritime using many features of the 'F.27 Mk 2' airliner, namely the Fokker 50, with the mission-related equipment of the original Maritime

F50 Maritime Enforcer Mk 2: considerably developed version of the F.27MPA using many features of the 'F.27 Mk 2' airliner, namely the Fokker 50; the Maritime Enforcer Mk 2 has basically the same airframe as the F.27MPA but with aerodynamic refinements, flightdeck improvements and power provided by two 2,500-shp (1864-kW) Pratt & Whitney Canada PW125B turboprops driving six-blade propellers for greater economy of fuel (9322 litres/2,051 Imp gal), reduced exterior and interior noise levels, and lower vibration levels; the avionics have been considerably updated especially in terms of tactical co-ordination and ESM with the latter including the General Instruments ALR-606(V)2 system, and the weapons capability is increased to the extent that the Maritime Enforcer Mk 2 can carry up to eight torpedoes and/or depth bombs, or two or four AGM-84 Harpoon or AM.39 Exocet anti-ship missiles, or a mixed load of torpedoes and missiles; maximum take-off weight is 21545 kg (47,498 lb) and typical endurance 14 hours, and the aircraft can cruise at high or low level depending upon mission requirements (translating as a mission radius of 2200 km/1,367 miles with a weapon load of 1800 kg/3,968 lb); maximum range is 6800 km (4,225 miles)

Fuji T-1A

(Japan)

Type: intermediate flying and weapon trainer

Accommodation: pupil and instructor in tandem on ejector seats

Armament (fixed): one 0·5-in (12·7-mm) Browning M53-2 machine-gun with an unrevealed number of rounds

Armament (disposable): this is carried on two hardpoints (one under each wing) up to a maximum weight of 680 kg (1,500 lb); typical weapons are two 340-kg (750-lb) bombs or two pods each with 19 2·75-in (70-mm) rockets

Electronics and operational equipment: communication and navigation equipment, plus an optical sight

Powerplant and fuel system: one 4,000-lb (1814-kg) thrust Rolls-Royce (Bristol) Orpheus BOr·4 Mk 805 non-afterburning turbojet, and a total internal fuel capacity of unrevealed quantity plus provision for two drop tanks; no provision for inflight refuelling

Performance: maximum speed 925 km/h (575 mph) at optimum altitude; initial climb rate 1980 m (6,496 ft) per minute; service ceiling 14,400 m (47,250 ft); ferry range 1860 km (1,156 miles)

Weights: empty 2420 kg (5,335 lb); normal take-off 4150 kg (9,149 lb); maximum take-off 5000 kg (11,023 lb)

Dimensions: span 10·49 m (34 ft 5 in); length 12·12 m (39 ft 9·2 in); height 4·08 m (13 ft 4·6 in); wing area 22·22 m² (239·2 sq ft)

Variants

T-1A: in looks resembling the North American F-86 fighter of the 1950s, this trim intermediate flying and weapons trainer was developed in the 1950s as the T1F; it was Japan's first operational jet-powered aeroplane and flew in prototype form during January 1958

T-1B: version with the 1200-kg (2,646-lb) thrust Ishikawajima-Harima J3-IHI-3 turbojet and slightly lower performance

T-1C: T-1Bs converted with the 1400-kg (3,086-lb) thrust J3-IHI-7 turbojet

Opposite: The IA-63 Pampa is a useful trainer and light attack type whose performance is restrained by its straight flying surfaces.

Above left: A Thai navy F.27MPA Maritime Enforcer reveals part of the type's offensive capability with an underwing load that includes depth charges and Sting Ray anti-submarine torpedoes.

Above: The Fuji T-1A trainer.

General Dynamics F-16C Fighting Falcon

(USA)

Type: multi-role air combat and attack fighter

Accommodation: pilot on a Douglas ACES II ejector seat

Armament (fixed): one 20-mm General Electric M61A1 Vulcan rotary-barrel cannon with 515 rounds

Armament (disposable): this is carried on nine hardpoints (one under the fuselage rated at 2,200 lb/998 kg, three under each wing with the inner two units each rated at 4,500 lb/2041 kg, the intermediate two units each at 3,500 lb/1587 kg and the outer two units each at 700 lb/318 kg, and one at each wingtip rated at 425 lb/193 kg) up to a maximum weight of 20,450 lb (9276 kg) with reduced fuel and a limitation to 5-g manoeuvres or of 11,950 lb (5420 kg) for 9-g manoeuvre capability; typical among the many loads qualified for the F-16 are six AIM-9 Sidewinder AAMs, six AGM-65 Maverick ASMs, two AGM-88 HARM radar-homing missiles, four 2,000-lb (907-kg) free-fall or retarded bombs, 19 1,000-lb (454-kg) free-fall or retarded bombs, four GBU-series Paveway laser-guided bombs, and 13 CBU-series bomb dispensers; other weapons that can be carried include the 100/500-kiloton B61 and 1-megaton B43 nuclear weapons, 30-mm GPU-5/A cannon pod and LAU-series launchers for 2·75-in (70-mm) rockets

Electronics and operational equipment: communication and navigation equipment, plus Westinghouse APG-68 pulse-Doppler radar, GEC (Marconi) HUD, Kaiser HDDs, Dalmo Victor ALR-69 RWR, Litton LN-39 INS, Delco fire-control computer, two Tracor ALE-40 chaff/flare dispensers, and optional Martin Marietta AAS-35 'Pave Penny' laser tracker pod, Martin Marietta LANTIRN navigation and targeting system, Westinghouse ALQ-119 or ALQ-131 ECM pods, Raytheon ALQ-184 ECM pod and other electronic countermeasures

Powerplant and fuel system: one 27,600-lb (12,519-kg) afterburning thrust General Electric F110-GE-100 or 23,450-lb (10,637-kg) afterburning thrust Pratt & Whitney F100-P-220 turbofan, and a total internal fuel capacity of 1,047 US gal (3962 litres) plus provision for 300-, 370-, 450- and 600-US (1136-, 1400-, 1703- and 2271-litre) drop tanks; provision for inflight refuelling

Performance: maximum speed 1,320 + mph (2124 + km/h) or Mach 2·0 + at 40,000 ft (12,190 m) and 915 mph (1472 km/h) or Mach 1·2 at sea level;

initial climb rate 50,000 ft (15,240 m) per minute with AAM armament; service ceiling 50,000 + ft (15,240 + m); radius 340 miles (547 km) on a hi-lo-hi mission with six 1,000-lb (454-kg) bombs; ferry range 2,415 + miles (3887 + km)

Weights: empty 18,335 lb (8316 kg) with F100 engine or 19,100 lb (8663 kg) with F110 engine; normal take-off 21,585 lb (9791 kg); maximum take-off 42,300 lb (19,187 kg)

Dimensions: span 31 ft 0 in (9·45 m) over wingtip launchers; length 49 ft 4 in (15·03 m); height 16 ft 8·5 in (5·09 m); wing area 300·0 sq ft (27·87 m²)

Variants

A-16 Fighting Falcon: under this as-yet unofficial designation several derivatives of the Fighting Falcon are being studied as alternatives to the Vought A-7F in the close air support role with the added advantage of considerable capability in the increasingly important battlefield air interdiction role with low-level night and attack equipment

F-16A Fighting Falcon: the F-16 is one of the Western world's most important combat aircraft, a comparatively small and light air-combat fighter with potent secondary attack/strike capability; the need for such a fighter was first truly appreciated during the Vietnam War, in which high-performance but comparatively clumsy US fighters were often caught at a disadvantage by the nimbler Soviet and Chinese fighters flown by the North Vietnamese; in 1971 the USAF launched its LWF (Light-Weight Fighter) programme to produce experimental aircraft offering moderate performance but very high levels of manoeuvrability through the use of relaxed stability and a fly-by-wire flight-control system; the YF-16 prototype first flew in February 1974 and, with the competing Northrop YF-17, showed markedly superior agility than contemporary fighters; in 1975 the USAF decided to procure the F-16 as a first-line type, production deliveries beginning in 1978; the type has since proved itself an extremely potent short/medium-range combat aircraft; this original model has the 23,830-lb (10,809-kg) afterburning thrust Pratt & Whitney F100-P-100 turbofan or 25,000-lb (11,340-kg) afterburning thrust F100-P-200 version of the same engine, and is fitted with Westinghouse APG-66 radar; the variant has empty and maximum take-off weights of 17,780 and 35,400 lb (8065 and 16,057 kg) respectively

F-16(ADF) Fighting Falcon: 270 F-16A single- and F-16B two-seaters are being modified as air-defence fighters to replace Convair F-106As and McDonnell Douglas F-4s for the defence of the continental USA; the ADF modification is being undertaken in parallel with the OCU (Operational Capabilities Upgrade) and includes provision for the AIM-7 Sparrow AAM through the installation of a continuous-wave illuminator, revision of the APG-66 radar for use with the data-linked AIM-120A AMRAAM AAM, better avionics cooling to improve reliability, and the Global Positioning System

F-16A(R) Fighting Falcon: Dutch F-16A variant with internal revisions to allow the carriage of the Oude Delft Orpheus tactical reconnaissance pod under the fuselage; this pod contains a fan of three TA-8M cameras, one F-415G panoramic camera and an IR linescanner

F-16B Fighting Falcon: two-seat combat-capable operational conversion trainer derivative of the F-16A; this variant is also proposed as an 'Advanced Wild Weasel' type with the ALR-46 threat-warning system, ALQ-119 defensive jammer and offensive missiles such as the AGM-45 Shrike, AGM-78 Standard ARM and AGM-88 HARM

F-16C Fighting Falcon: F-16A development delivered from July 1984 within the context of the MSIP (Multi-national Staged Improvement Program), and using as its powerplant either the General Electric F110-GE-100 or Pratt & Whitney F100-P-220 afterburning turbofan; this variant has Westinghouse APG-68 radar (featuring a programmable digital processing system, increased search range, track-while-scan capability and high-resolution ground mapping), an enlarged tailplane, a revised cockpit with two multi-function coloured HDDs and a wide-angle HUD, wiring for the AIM-120 AMRAAM, and provision for items such as the LANTIRN (Low-Altitude Navigation and Targeting Infra-Red for Night) pod system, JTIDS (Joint Tactical Information Distribution System), GPS (Global Positioning System) and ASPJ (Airborne Self-Protection Jammer); the type also has improved capability for weapons such as the AGM-65 Maverick and General Electric 30-mm cannon pods; from 1988

The Fighting Falcon single-seat variants are F-16A (below) and F-16C (above right).

the Block 40 production standard features automatic terrain-following capability, a diffractive-optics HUD, a quadruplex digital flight-control system, larger computer cores, APG-68(V) radar with mode enhancements and better reliability, and full capability for LANTIRN and GPS as a means of producing an all-weather day/night version; the airframe has also been strengthened to improve the 9-g manoeuvring limit from 26,900 lb (12,202 kg) to 28,500 lb (12,928 kg) with an 8,000-hour airframe life, the landing gear has been strengthened to cater for higher take-off weight, and a more powerful leading-edge flap-drive system has been incorporated to improve aerial agility; from 1991 the standard will be further improved with the 29,000-lb (13,154-kg) afterburning thrust F100-P-229 or F110-GE-129 turbofan, radar and cockpit improvements, onboard oxygen generation, capability for the AGM-45 Shrike and AGM-88 HARM radar-homing missiles, new threat-warning and self-protection systems, and a number of reliability and maintenance enhancements; during the 1990s the type will be fitted with the Loral ALR-56M RWR, a miniaturized version of the ALR-56C used on the larger McDonnell Douglas F-15 Eagle air-superiority fighter; the Fighting Falcon has also been developed with private and service funding (notably as the F-16/101 with the 28,000-lb/12,701-kg General Electric F110 afterburning turbofan evolved as the F101DFE from the engine used in the Rockwell B-1B bomber, the F-16/AFTI with control-configured flying surfaces in the Advanced Fighter Technology Integration programme, and the F-16XL cranked-arrow wing version with very considerably enhanced range and weapon payload capabilities [twice the payload over nearly 50% greater range] offered to the USAF as a strike fighter with the designation F-16F), so there are still many ways in which the Fighting Falcon can yet be developed as an operational type; General Dynamics' latest thinking is centred on the restoration of the F-16A's agility without sacrifice of the F-16C's capabilities; in this **Agile Falcon** concept a larger wing would be used, increasing area by some 25% to reduce loading

F-16C Fighting Falcon (Israel): Israel is one of the main operators of the Fighting Falcon, and its F-16As have already seen much combat; to meet the particular requirements of the Israeli air force the F-16As were modified before delivery with about 25% of the avionics altered and the structure beefed up to allow a maximum take-off weight of 48,000 lb (21,773 kg); in service the aircraft have been extensively revised, the most noticeable feature being the enlarged dorsal fairing thought to accommodate additional electronic warfare equipment including the Loral ALQ-178 ECM system; Israel's F-16Cs are being produced with these modifications built into the standard F-16C, and provision is being made for retrofit of Israeli avionics (based on those of the defunct Israel Aircraft Industries Lavi) if this is thought desirable; another feature of the Israeli F-16s is provision for the Sharpshooter system, which is the LANTIRN targeting pod without the IR boresight correlator required for guidance of the EO-guided version of the AGM-65 Maverick ASM; the Sharpshooter is also used on Egyptian F-16s, which additionally have provision for the Pathfinder, essentially the LANTIRN's navigation pod without the terrain-following radar and thus reduced in weight by one-third

RF-16C Fighting Falcon: under this designation

General Dynamics is developing to USAF contract a tactical reconnaissance version of the F-16C to supplement and eventually to replace the McDonnell Douglas RF-4C Phantom II; development emphasis is placed on podded systems so that airframe changes can be minimized, and the primary reconnaissance sensor is the Control Data ATARS (Advanced Tactical Air Reconnaissance System) pod based on an EO sensor backed by an IR linescanner with secure digital data-link download to a ground station, plus an onboard digital recorder and a computer management system; the pod will also be carried by two US Navy aircraft, the Grumman F-14A Plus Tomcat and McDonnell Douglas F/A-18D Hornet

F-16D Fighting Falcon: two-seat combat-capable operational conversion trainer derivative of the F-16C

F-16N Fighting Falcon: version of the F-16C ordered by the US Navy as a dissimilar combat training aircraft, based on the F-16C but engined with the 27,600-lb (12,519-kg) afterburning thrust F110-GE-100 turbofan and fitted with the older APG-66 radar and naval avionics; the variant lacks the internal cannon of the other models

TF-16N Fighting Falcon: two-seat equivalent of the F-16N, but based on the F-16D model

F-16 Fighting Falcon (Japan): no full designation has yet been announced for the F-16 variant selected to meet Japan's FS-X tactical fighter requirement; based on the F-16C with features of the proposed Agile Falcon to restore to heavier Fighting Falcon variants the agility of the F-16A through the use of a 25% larger wing, this specifically Japanese model is temporarily designated **SX-3** and features a number of important modifications compared with the original type, including active phased-array radar (with its antenna group in a reprofiled radome and nose section), a new mission computer, a new INS, an integrated EW system, a reinforced windscreen, a larger wing of composite construction and with its leading edges made of radar-absorbent materials, a braking parachute, an uprated engine, a slightly lengthened fuselage, a fuselage structure of revised and modernized construction, oblique vertical canard foreplanes under the inlet for side-force manoeuvring capability, and provision for four semi-active radar homing medium-range AAMs or four anti-ship missiles

General Dynamics F-111F

Type: variable-geometry all-weather strike and attack aeroplane

Accommodation: pilot and systems operator side-by-side in a McDonnell Douglas rocket-powered escape capsule

Armament (fixed): optional installation of one 20-mm General Electric M61A1 Vulcan rotary-barrel cannon and 2,028 rounds in the weapons bay

Armament (disposable): this is carried in a lower-fuselage weapons bay rated at 1,500 lb (680 kg) and on six hardpoints (three under each wing with each unit rated at 6,000 lb/2722 kg) up to a maximum weight of 31,500 lb (14228 kg); operational-level loads are up to three 1-megaton B43, or 10/20-kiloton B57 or 100/500-kiloton B61 nuclear weapons; tactical loads typically include 2,000-, 1,000-, 750- and 500-lb (907-, 454-, 340- and 227-kg) free-fall or retraded bombs, Paveway laser-guided bombs, GBU-15 EO-guided bombs, AGM-65 Maverick ASMs and CBU-series bomb dispensers

Electronics and operational equipment: communication and navigation equipment, plus General Electric APQ-144 attack and navigation radar, Texas Instruments APQ-146 terrain-following radar, Litton AJN-16 INS, GPL Doppler navigation, IBM ASQ-133 digital fire-control system, General Electric ASG-27 optical display sight, ALR-41 or Dalmo-Victor ALR-62 RWR, APS-109 RHAWS, Cincinnati Electronics AAR-44 IR warning receiver, Sanders ALQ-137 ECM receiver, ALE-28 chaff/flare launcher, Sanders ALQ-94 noise deception jammer, Ford AVQ-26 'Pave Tack' target-acquisition and designation pod, and optional ECM fits such as the Westinghouse ALQ-119 and ALQ-131 pods

Powerplant and fuel system: two 25,100-lb (11,385-kg) afterburning thrust Pratt & Whitney TF30-P-100 turbofans, and a total internal fuel capacity of 5,025 US gal (19,021 litres) plus provision for four 600-US gal (2271-litre) drop tanks; provision for inflight refuelling

Performance: maximum speed 1,650 mph (2655 km/h) or Mach 2·5 at 36,000 ft (10,970 m) and 915 mph (1473 km/h) or Mach 1·2 at sea level; cruising speed 571 mph (919 km/h); service ceiling 60,000 ft (18,290 m); range 2,925 miles (4707 km) with maximum internal fuel

Weights: empty 47,481 lb (21,537 kg); maximum take-off 100,000 lb (45,360 kg)

Dimensions: span spread 63 ft 0 in (19·20 m) and swept 31 ft 11·4 in (9·74 m); length 75 ft 6·5 in (23·03 m); height 17 ft 0·5 in (5·19 m); wing area spread 525·0 sq ft (48·77 m²) and swept 657·3 sq ft (61·07 m²)

Variants

F-111A: popularly known as the 'Aardvark', the F-111 was the world's first operational variable-geometry combat aircraft, the type having been schemed as a politically inspired single-design solution to the needs of the USAF for a strike fighter and of the US Navy for a fleet defence fighter (the latter being the vastly overweight F-111B that was cancelled after the building of five pre-production and two production aircraft); the F-111A prototype first flew in December 1964 and after a protracted development programme began to enter service in October 1967 though there were still many problems with the advanced airframe and its complex avionics centred on the APQ-113 main and APQ-110 terrain-following radars as part of its Mk 1 avionics suite;

this initial model is powered by two 18,500-lb (8392-kg) afterburning thrust Pratt & Whitney TF30-P-3 turbofans and has the original Triple Plow 1 inlets; such is the importance of the F-111 in US service that an extremely costly AMP (Avionics Modernization Program) is being undertaken to upgrade 120 F-111A/E, 57 FB-111A, 166 F-111D/F and 38 EF-111A aircraft with more capable General Electric attack radar, Texas Instruments terrain-following radar, and a host of navigation and control systems; production amounted to 159 aircraft each able to carry a maximum warload of 30,000 lb (13,608 kg) at a maximum take-off weight of 91,300 lb (41,414 kg)

EF-111A Raven: 42 electronic warfare aircraft produced by Grumman as F-111A conversions; the type has the Tactical Jamming System of the Grumman EA-6B Prowler computer-assisted and repackaged as the ALQ-99E for one-man operation, and developing sufficient power to overwhelm the world's most intense radar defences; the type has a canoe fairing over the bomb bay (housing the TJS and its six digitally tuned receivers, five exciters and 10 jamming transmitters) and a pod at the top of the fin (housing the forward-, side- and aft-facing receiver antennae of the TJS), and other systems are the ALQ-137(V)4 deception jammer, the ALR-62(V)4 terminal threat-warning receiver, the ALE-28 chaff dispenser, the ALR-23 countermeasures receiver system and (for possible retrofit) the ALQ-131 jammer system in pods under the wings; the Raven can thus support tactical aircraft as an escort, in the penetration role or as a stand-off jammer; the EF-111A has empty and maximum take-off weights of 55,275 lb (25,072 kg) and 88,948 lb (40,346 kg) respectively, and the type may be retrofitted to carry the AGM-88 HARM radar-homing missile on its four underwing hardpoints; the ALQ-99E electronic system is being upgraded in concert with the ALQ-99 system of the EA-6B; other electronic features of this variant include APQ-160 main radar and APQ-110 terrain-following radar, and fuel capacity is limited to the 5,010 US gal (18,965 litres) carried internally

FB-111A: medium strategic bomber version of the basic design for the USAF's Strategic Air Command; powered by two 20,350-lb (9231-kg) afterburning thrust TF30-P-7 turbofans, this variant has strengthened landing gear, longer-span wings (70 ft 0 in/21·34 m spread and 33 ft 11 in/10·34 m swept with a spread area of 550·0 sq ft/51·10 m²), empty and maximum take-off weights of 47,980 lb (21,764 kg) and 119,243 lb (54,089 kg) respectively, and a combination of APQ-114 attack radar and APQ-134 terrain-following radar for the delivery of 37,500 lb (17,010 kg) of weapons (six free-fall nuclear weapons, or six AGM-69A SRAMs or 50 (normally 42) 750-lb/340-kg bombs) over the considerable range made possible by 5,610 US gal

(21,236 litres) of internal fuel, including bomb-bay tankage, and up to six 600-US gal (2271-litre) drop tanks; this version has eight underwing hardpoints for maximum external payload when limited sweep is used, and further upgrading includes ALQ-137 ECM equipment; production amounted to 76 aircraft; in a programme due to start in 1990 and finish in 1994, this and all other F-111 variants are to be retrofitted with a new digital flight-control system using General Dynamics software running in a Lear Astronics computer

F-111C: 24 hybrid aircraft for Australia, combining the wings and drop-tank capability of the FB-111A with the fuselage, empennage, powerplant and avionics of the F-111A and the strengthened landing gear, wheels and brakes developed for the RAF's abortive F-111K variant; the type has empty and maximum take-off weights of 47,303 lb (21,457 kg) and 110,000 lb (49,896 kg respectively; four aircraft have been modified to **RF-111C** reconnaissance configuration with a mission pallet accommodating high/low-level cameras, TV and IR linescan equipment; the pallet is installed in the weapon bay instead of the 'Pack Tack' pod of the interdiction variant

F-111D: improved version of the F-111A with 19,600-lb (8890-kg) afterburning thrust TF30-P-9 turbofans, improved Triple Plow 2 inlets, Mk 2 avionics including HUDs, APQ-130 attack radar and APQ-128 terrain-following radar; the variant has empty and maximum take-off weights of 46,631 lb (21,152 kg) and 100,000 lb (45,360 kg) respectively; production amounted to 96 aircraft in total

F-111E: improved F-111A with Triple Plow 2 inlets, the AJQ-20A INS and improved attack radar; production amounted to 94 aircraft

F-111F: definitive production model of the tactical variant based on the F-111D with a revised wing structure with six underwing hardpoints, strengthened landing gear and considerably uprated powerplant, but also incorporating the best avionics features of the F-111E and FB-111A; aircraft fitted with the 'Pave Tack' target-acquisition/targeting package have General Electric APQ-116 radar; production amounted to 106 aircraft

F-111G: under this designation SAC's FB-111 medium-range strategic bombers will be reconfigured for European operations to plug the operational gap left by the withdrawal of BGM-109 Tomahawk and MGM-31 Pershing ground-launched missiles in the aftermath of the 1988 Intermediate Nuclear Forces Treaty; the reconfiguration of the FB-111As will possibly add capability for carriage and launch of the AGM-86B air-launched cruise missile, the new Convair AGM-129A Advanced Cruise missile and, in succession to the AGM-69A SRAM-As currently operated, the new AGM-131A SRAM-II

Grumman A-6E/TRAM Intruder

(USA)

Type: carrierborne all-weather strike and attack aeroplane

Accommodation: pilot and systems operator side-by-side on Martin-Baker GRU7 zero/zero ejector seats

Armament (fixed): none

Armament (disposable): this is carried on five hardpoints (one under the fuselage and two under each wing, with each unit rated at 3,600 lb/1633 kg) up to a maximum weight of 18,000 lb (8165 kg); typical strategic/operational-level loads are up to three B28, B43, B57 or B61 thermonuclear free-fall bombs, and typical tactical-level loads include five 2,000-lb (907-kg) or 15 1,000-lb (454-kg) free-fall or retarded bombs, or 30 500-lb (227-kg) free-fall or retarded bombs, or four AGM-45 Shrike or AGM-88 HARM radar-homing missiles, or two AGM-84 Harpoon anti-ship missiles, or four AGM-65 Maverick ASMs

Electronics and operational equipment: communication and navigation equipment, plus Norden APQ-148/156 attack, navigation and terrain-following/avoidance radar, IBM ASQ-133 digital nav/attack computer system, Kaiser AVA-1 HDD, Litton ASN-92 Carrier Airborne INS, APN-153 Doppler navigation, chin-mounted Hughes AAS-33 Target Recognition and Attack Multi-sensor (TRAM) package with FLIR and laser sensors, Sanders ALQ-41 or ALQ-100 deception jammer, Sanders ALQ-126B deception jammer, Itek ALR-45 RWR, Magnavox ALR-50 SAM-warning receiver, Tracor ALE-29 chaff or ALE-40 chaff/flare dispenser, and also provision for ECM pods

Powerplant and fuel system: two 9,300-lb (4218-kg) thrust Pratt & Whitney J52-P-8B non-afterburning turbojets, and a total internal fuel capacity of 2,385 US gal (9028 litres) plus provision for four 300-US gal (1136-litre) drop tanks; provision for inflight refuelling

Performance: maximum speed 644 mph (1037 km/h) or Mach 0·85 at sea level; cruising speed 474 mph (763 km/h); initial climb rate 8,600 ft (2621 m) per minute; service ceiling 44,600 ft (13,595 m); range 1,077 miles (1733 km) with maximum warload; ferry range 3,100 miles (4989 km)

Weights: empty 25,630 lb (11,626 kg); maximum take-off 60,400 lb (27,397 kg)

Dimensions: span 53 ft 0 in (16·15 m); length 54 ft 9 in (16·69 m); height 16 ft 2 in (4·93 m); wing area 528·9 sq ft (49·1 m²)

Variants

EA-6A Intruder: strike support version of the A-6A Intruder, the initial production version of this important carrierborne medium attack aircraft series whose prototype first flew in April 1960; the A-6A entered service in February 1963 with two 8,500-lb (3856-kg) thrust Pratt & Whitney J52-P-6 turbojets and the original Digital Integrated Attack Navigation Equipment comprising a Litton ASQ-61 digital computer to integrate the inputs of the Norden APQ-92 search radar, NAF APQ-88 track radar, APN-153 Doppler navigation and Litton ASN-31 inertial platform; of the 484

A-6As built, the only variant left in service is the EA-6A, which is powered by 9,300-lb (4218-kg) thrust J52-P-8A/Bs; this variant retains a partial attack capability, but is used solely for the support role as a tactical jamming aircraft with 30 antennae (the ALH-6 and ALQ-86 systems) to detect, locate and classify enemy radars which can then be jammed by the onboard ALQ-31 noise, ALQ-53 track-breaking and ALQ-76 noise jammers

KA-6D Intruder: 'buddy' refuelling version produced by converting A-6A aircraft with TACAN navigation equipment and a hose-and-drogue refuelling kit in the rear fuselage; the type first flew in May 1966, and its capabilities include the transfer of 3,150 US gal (11,924 litres) of fuel immediately after take-off or 2,250 US gal (8517 litres) at a radius of 288 miles (463 km); later aircraft were converted from A-6E standard and can carry five 480-US gal (1817-litre) drop tanks rather than the five 360-US gal (1363-litre) tanks of the earlier aircraft; 54 KA-6Ds were produced by converting surplus A-6As

A-6E Intruder: definitive mid-life attack model which entered service in 1972 with a more advanced version of the DIANE system (with an IBM ASQ-133 computer and Norden APQ-148 multi-mode radar, later replaced by the same company's APQ-156 set), a Conrac stores-management system and more powerful engines; surviving A-6As were brought up to this standard, numbers being increased by new construction; further enhancement of capabilities has been ensured by the evolution of the highly capable **A-6E/TRAM** upgraded version with a stabilized Hughes AAS-33 TRAM (Target Recognition and Attack Multi-sensor) optronic chin turret with a FLIR sensor and a laser system for rangefinding, designating and marked-target seeking; the variant first flew in March 1974 to enter service in 1979, and this is now the production standard, to which surviving aircraft are being upgraded; other features are the addition of the ASN-92 Carrier Airborne Inertial Navigation System, a

Sperry automatic carrier landing system, and provision for fire-and-forget and/or laser-homing weapons; 50 A-6E aircraft were additionally modified to carry up to six AGM-84 Harpoon anti-ship missiles, and this capability is being added to conversions and new-build aircraft; the last 20 production aircraft will be fitted with a Boeing-developed composite wing, and this will also be retrofitted to 163 older aircraft

A-6F Intruder: version due to have entered production in 1989 for service in the 1990s, but cancelled by the US Congress in 1988; the variant was to have had the Boeing-developed composite wing and two 10,700-lb (4854-kg) thrust General Electric F404-GE-400D non-afterburning turbofans (for greater fuel economy and range) with a self-contained APU for self-start capability; the avionics suite was to have been considerably enhanced into an all-digital type (featuring considerable commonality with those of the Grumman F-14D Tomcat and McDonnell Douglas F/A-18 Hornet) with a HUD, five coloured HDDs and Norden APQ-177 high-resolution synthetic-aperture radar; the weapons capability was to have included stand-off ASMs and, on one extra hardpoint under each wing, AIM-9 Sidewinder and/or AIM-120 AMRAAM AAMs

A-6G Intruder: under this designation Grumman developed an upgrade package to provide remanufactured A-6Es with much of the cancelled A-6F's capabilities through the use of the new digital avionics suite including Norden APQ-173 synthetic-aperture radar, the AYK-14 mission computer, and ASN-130/139 INS; other avionic features were to have been a HUD with FLIR imaging, night vision goggles and an Integrated Defense Avionics Program installation; it was planned to use the Boeing-developed composite wing with an extra pair of hardpoints for AAMs, and wing-root fillets to improve low-speed handling; the powerplant remained a pair of J52 turbojets, though of the J52-P-408/409 improved version offering some 25% additional thrust, but this programme too was cancelled in 1989

Left: An F-111A of the 474th Tactical Fighter Wing based at Nellis AFB, Nevada.

Right: An A-6E Intruder of Attack Squadron 34 refuels from a KA-6D Intruder 'buddy' tanker with two Vought A-7E Corsair IIs escorting.

Grumman EA-6B Prowler

(USA)
Type: carrierborne electronic warfare aeroplane
Accommodation: pilot, navigator/systems operator and two systems operators in two side-by-side pairs on Martin-Baker GRUEA7 zero/zero ejector seats
Armament (fixed): none
Armament (disposable): two AGM-88 HARM radar-homing missiles can be carried under the wings
Electronics and operational equipment: communication and navigation equipment, plus APQ-92 search radar and the Raytheon ALQ-99 tactical jamming system, in which receivers in the fintop fairing pick up electromagnetic emissions and pass the data to the central digital computer for display and recording before the emissions' identities, bearings and jamming set-on frequencies are analyzed (automatically or manually) and any one of the five external and self-powered jamming pods activated; each pod covers one of seven frequency bands and contains two powerful jammers
Powerplant and fuel system: two 11,200-lb (5080-kg) thrust Pratt & Whitney J52-P-408 non-afterburning turbojets, and a total internal fuel capacity of 2,268 US gal (8585 litres) plus provision for 300-US gal (2271-litre) drop tanks at the expense of jammer pods; provision for inflight refuelling
Performance: maximum speed 623 mph (1002 km/h) at sea level; cruising speed 481 mph (774 km/h); initial climb rate 10,030 ft (3057 m) per minute; service ceiling 38,000 ft (11,580 m); radius 332 miles (535 km) with a patrol endurance of 1 hour; ferry range 2,022 miles (3254 km)

Weights: empty 32,162 lb (14,588 kg); normal take-off 54,461 lb (24,703 kg); maximum take-off 65,000 lb (29,483 kg)
Dimensions: span 53 ft 0 in (16·15 m); length 59 ft 10 in (18·24 m); height 16 ft 3 in (4·95 m); wing area 528·9 sq ft (49·1 m²)

Variant
EA-6B Prowler: developed from the EA-6A Intruder, the EA-6B first flew in May 1968 as the prototype of a powerful stand-off EW aeroplane for the US Navy; the airframe is based on that of the A-6A but stretched by 4·5 ft (1·37 m) and strengthened for operations at higher weights as a result of extra fuel capacity and the addition of the ALQ-99 radar detection, location, classification and jamming system, whose two operators are located in a side-by-side cockpit aft of the standard cockpit for the pilot and navigator; production aircraft were delivered from January 1971, and this type remains a key component of the US Navy's attack capability thanks to a succession of improvement programmes which have enhanced the original capability (based on the AYA-6 computer) to deal only with single emitters in four frequency bands, to the EXCAP (Expanded Capability) standard of 1973 for the jamming of radars in eight frequency bands, the ICAP (Improved CAPability) standard of 1977 with digitally tuned receivers and computer-controlled systems for the jamming of several emitters forming a weapon system, the ICAP-2 standard of 1983 with the AYA-14 computer (four times the memory and three times the speed of the AYA-6) for the jamming in nine frequency bands of several weapon systems forming a defence complex, the DECM (Defensive Electronic Counter-Measures) standard and the

ACAP (Advanced CAPability) standard for service from 1992 with an Amecom (Litton) receiver/processor group operating in 10 frequency bands for improved jamming of communications, a more capable signal processor, a better chaff/flare dispenser, and two underwing hardpoints for the carriage of AGM-88 HARM radar-homing missiles; APS-130 advanced navigation radar is to be installed, and other improvements may include the Airborne Self-Protection Jammer, Joint Tactical Information Distribution System and Global Positioning System; the US Navy is also planning to fit the Pratt & Whitney PW1212 (to be designated J52-P-409) turbojet into the Prowler; this engine is an improved version of the basic J52 with features of the JT8D offering faster response to throttle movements, greater fuel economy and stall-free operation, and will help to offset the greater drag of the EA-6B Prowler ACAP's larger fintop and new underfuselage antennae groups; other improvements will be centred on aerodynamic enhancement such as drooped leading-edge slats, wing root leading-edge strakes, a taller vertical fin and modified wingtip speed brakes/ailerons; in the 1990s the aircraft is to be retrofitted with the Sanders ALQ-149 TCCS (Tactical Communications Countermeasures System), and automatic system carried internally for the detection, identification, evaluation and jamming of hostile communications and long-range early warning radars

Flightdeck crew of the USS *Dwight D. Eisenhower* perform final pre-launch checks on an EA-6B Prowler carrying an external load of three jammers and two drop tanks.

Grumman E-2C Hawkeye

(USA)

Type: land-based and carrierborne airborne early warning aeroplane

Accommodation: flightcrew of two, and a mission crew of three in the cabin

Armament (fixed): none

Armament (disposable): none

Electronics and operational equipment: communication and navigation equipment, plus General Electric APS-125 or (from 1983 production) APS-138 or (from 1988 production and for retrofit in older aircraft) APS-139 surveillance radar with its antenna in the Randtron APA-171 rotodome, Litton ALR-59 or Litton ALR-73 passive detection system, Hazeltine APA-172 control indicator group, Litton ASN-92 INS, APN-153(V) Doppler navigation, Conrac air-data computer and Litton L-304 central computer system

Powerplant and fuel system: two 4,910-shp (3663-kW) Allison T56-A-425 or (from 1988 production) 5,250-shp (3915-kW) T56-A-427 turboprops, and a total internal fuel capacity of 1,862 US gal (7050 litres); no provision for drop tanks but provision for inflight refuelling

Performance: maximum speed 374 mph (602 km/h) at optimum altitude; cruising speed 310 mph (499 km/h) for maximum endurance; initial climb rate not revealed; service ceiling 30,800 ft (9390 m); radius 200 miles (322 km) with a patrol endurance of 4 hours; ferry range 1,605 miles (2583 km)

Weights: empty 38,063 lb (17,265 kg); maximum take-off 51,933 lb (23,556 kg)

Dimensions: span 80 ft 7 in (24·56 m); length 57 ft 6·75 in (17·54 m); height 18 ft 3·75 in (5·58 m); wing area 700·0 sq ft (65·03 m²)

Variants

C-2A Greyhound: COD (Carrier Onboard Delivery) version of the E-2A without the radar and rotodome and provided with a portly fuselage accessed by a ventral ramp; the type first flew in November 1964 and 19 aircraft were delivered in the 1960s, while another 39 were delivered from 1983 into the second half of the 1980s; the type has two 5,250-shp (3915-kW) T56-A-427 turboprops, a maximum take-off weight of 57,500 lb (26,082 kg) and has a payload of 39 troops, or 28 passengers, or 20 litters plus four attendants, or 15,000 lb (6804 kg) of freight; this variant has Bendix APN-215 radar, and can carry a 10,000-lb (4536-kg) payload over a range of 1,200 miles (1931 km)

E-2B Hawkeye: improved version of the E-2A Hawkeye initial production model, which first flew in W2F-1 prototype form during October 1960 and entered service in January 1964 to provide the US Navy with an exceptional airborne early warning capability through the use of General Electric APS-96 radar with its antenna in a revolving rotodome above the fuselage; the E-2B was introduced in 1969 by converting E-2As first with the Litton L-304 digital computer and then with the more capable APS-120 radar which added an overland capacity to the APS-96's basic overwater capability; the type also added provision for inflight refuelling and introduced enlarged vertical tail surfaces

E-2C Hawkeye: definitive version of the Hawkeye, which began to enter service in November 1973 after the first flight of a prototype in January 1970; this variant entered service with the General Electric/Grumman APS-125 radar able to detect aircraft at ranges of 230 miles (370 km) even in ground clutter and able to perform the simultaneous detection and tracking of more than 250 ship and aircraft targets while controlling 30 or more interceptions at the same time; the radar incorporates ECCM capability, but later E-2Cs have the more advanced APS-138 radar with low sidelobes and active-element arrays to permit automatic and simultaneous tracking of up to 600 targets out to a range of 300 miles (483 km); these aircraft also feature a passive detection system (initially the Litton ALR-59 ESM system and from 1980 the improved ALR-73 ESM system) for the automatic detection, plotting and identification of electronic emitters in a high-density environment at ranges up to 500 miles (805 km); the provision of data-link equipment allows the secure transmission/receipt of information between E-2Cs and other aircraft or surface vessels; from 1988 the standard radar has been an improved version of the APS-138, namely the APS-139 with enhanced capability to detect slow-moving and indeed stationary targets such as warships; and from the early 1990s new-production aircraft will be delivered with the new APS-145 radar, while older aircraft will be retrofitted with this system; the APS-145 is under current development as a system able to operate effectively over normal rather than comparatively featureless terrain

TE-2C Hawkeye: training version of the E-2C

An E-2C Hawkeye of Airborne Early Warning Squadron 127 is seen during an engine test on board the carrier USS *Coral Sea* in the Mediterranean during 1986.

Grumman F-14A Tomcat

(USA)

Type: carrierborne variable-geometry fleet defence fighter

Accommodation: pilot and systems operator in tandem on Martin-Baker GRU7A zero/zero ejector seats

Armament (fixed): one 20-mm General Electric M61A1 Vulcan rotary-barrel cannon with 675 rounds

Armament (disposable): this is carried on six hardpoints (four under the fuselage and two under each wing root) up to a maximum weight of 14,500 lb (6577 kg); the four underfuselage hardpoints can each carry one AIM-54 Phoenix, AIM-7 Sparrow or AIM-120 AMRAAM AAM, and the two underwing hardpoints can each carry two AIM-9 Sidewinder AAMs, or one AIM-54, AIM-7 or AIM-120 plus one AIM-9; the originally specified attack load is never carried

Electronics and operational equipment: communication and navigation equipment, plus Hughes AWG-9 pulse-Doppler fire-control radar, Northrop AXX-1 TCS (Television Camera Set), Kaiser AVG-12 HUD, ALR-25/45 RWR, Sanders ALQ-100/226 deception jammer, Goodyear ALE-29 and ALE-39 chaff/flare dispensers, and provision for TARPS (Tactical Air Reconnaissance Pod System) with optical cameras and IR linescanner, ALQ-100 deception ECM and other electronic countermeasures

Powerplant and fuel system: two 20,900-lb (9480-kg) afterburning thrust Pratt & Whitney TF30-P-412A or (from 1984 production onward) TF30-P-414A turbofans, and a total internal fuel capacity of 2,385 US gal (9093 litres) plus provision for two 267-US gal (1011-litre) drop tanks; provision for inflight refuelling

Performance: maximum speed 1,564 mph (2517 km/h) or Mach 2·37 at 36,000 ft (10,970 m) and 910 mph (1464 km/h) or Mach 1·2 at sea level; cruising speed 633 mph (1019 km/h); initial climb rate 30,000+ ft (9145+ m) per minute; service ceiling 56,000+ ft (17,070 m); range 2,000 miles (3220 km) as an interceptor with drop tanks

Weights: empty 40,104 lb (18,191 kg); normal take-off 58,539 lb (26,553 kg); maximum take-off 74,349 lb (33,724 kg)

Dimensions: span 64 ft 1·5 in (19·55 m) spread and 38 ft 2·5 in (11·65 m) swept; length 62 ft 8 in (19·10 m); height 16 ft 0 in (4·88 m); wing area 565·0 sq ft (52·49 m²)

Variants

F-14A Tomcat: first flown in December 1970, the Tomcat is without doubt the world's most powerful fighter, offering an unrivalled combination of performance (in terms principally of speed and range) with dogfighting, short-, medium- and long-range armament used with the appropriate avionics and sensors; the type owes its career to the failure of the General Dynamics F-111B naval version of the F-111 strike fighter, a programme in which Grumman had been heavily involved; Grumman's proposal for an F-111B replacement drew heavily on this experience, and used the same primary weapon system (the AIM-54A Phoenix long-range AAM and the Hughes AWG-9 radar) in a sophisticated airframe with

The Tomcat configurations are shown by these F-14As (left) and the F-14A upgraded to F-14D standard (below) with undernose tracker.

Grumman OV-1D Mohawk

automatically-programmed variable-geometry wings, small moving foreplanes, a two-seat cockpit, considerable fuel and two afterburning turbofans; the type began to enter service in October 1972, and the principal service problem has been that of reliability in the engines

F-14A/TARPS Tomcat: interim reconnaissance version of the F-14A necessitated by the retirement of the North American RA-5C Vigilante; this version is fitted under the fuselage with the Tactical Air Reconnaissance Pod System containing optical and IR sensors

F-14A(Plus) Tomcat: perhaps to be redesignated **F-14C Tomcat**, this version began to enter service in the later 1980s as an interim type between the F-14A and now-cancelled production version of the definitive F-14D; the type's main modification is the adoption of a new powerplant in the form of two 23,100-lb (10,478-kg) afterburning thrust General Electric F110-GE-400 turbofans for greater thrust and, perhaps more importantly, greater operational reliability; detail improvements include a fatigue-monitoring system, a new radio system, a new RWR, and modification of the direct lift-control system to ensure compatibility with the F110 engines; it is possible that F-14D electronic improvements may be retrofitted to provide the US Navy's Tomcat force with a single operational type

F-14D Tomcat: considerably revised and upgraded model planned for service in the 1990s with two F110 afterburning turbofans and a completely revised digital rather than analog avionics suite based on two AYK-14 central computers matched to the long-range AIM-54C and medium-range AIM-120 AMRAAM AAMs with target data provided by the new Hughes APG-71 pulse-Doppler radar incorporating programmable digital signal processing; the type will also have a new cockpit with four multi-function HDDs and Martin-Baker NACES ejector seats, while other significant improvements will be an IR search and tracking system, the Hughes/ITT Joint Tactical Information Distribution System for secure voice and data transmission, the Westinghouse ALQ-165 Airborne Self-Protection Jammer system linked with the Litton ALR-67 threat-warning system, and an ASN-130 laser-gyro INS; the US Department of Defense's 1989 review of financial commitments in the face of the USA's enormous budget deficit included amongst its provisional proposals that no production of the F-14D should be undertaken, though more than 400 F-14As are to be remanufactured to this standard by 1998

Tomcat 21: company designation for a Grumman proposal design to produce a much improved version of the Tomcat as a low-cost/low-risk alternative to the Navalized Advanced Tactical Fighter; the proposal is centred on an upgraded version of the F-14D's avionics package plus additional items to give the aeroplane a full air-to-air and air-to-ground combat capability, a navalized version of the USAF's F110 Improved Performance Engine to provide supersonic performance at dry thrust without modification of the F-14's inlets, a high-lift flap system to increase lift at approach angles of attack by more than 30%, new leading edges on the gloves to accommodate an additional 2,500 lb (1134 kg) of fuel, and accommodation for undernose and underfuselage pods housing FLIR, laser and TV nav/attack systems

(USA)

Type: tactical reconnaissance aeroplane

Accommodation: pilot and systems operator side-by-side on Martin-Baker J5 ejector seats

Armament (fixed): none

Armament (disposable): this can be carried on two hardpoints (one under each wing) up to a maximum weight of 2,700 lb (1225 kg)

Electronics and operational equipment: communication and navigation equipment including ASN-86 INS, plus APQ-94F SLAR or AAS-4 IR reconnaissance sensor, one ADR-6 radiation-monitoring system, one KA-76 and two KA-60C cameras, one APR-25/26 RWR, one ALQ-147 'Hot Brick' IR countermeasures system and various ECM pods on the underwing hardpoints

Powerplant and fuel system: two 1,400-shp (1044-kW) Avco Lycoming T53-L-701 turboprops, and a total internal fuel capacity of 297 US gal (1125 litres) plus provision for two 150-US gal (568-litre) drop tanks; no provision for inflight refuelling

Performance: maximum speed 305 mph (409 km/h) with IR sensor or 289 mph (465 km/h) with SLAR sensor at 10,000 ft (3050 m); cruising speed 242 mph (389 km/h); initial climb rate 3,618 ft (1103 m) per minute with SLAR sensor; service ceiling 25,000 ft (7620 m); range 1,080 miles (1738 km) with IR sensor or 1,027 miles (1653 km) with SLAR sensor

Weights: empty 11,757 lb (5333 kg) with IR sensor or 12,054 lb (5468 kg) with SLAR sensor; maxi-

The OV-1 Mohawk's bulged cockpit glazing provides excellent fields of vision.

mum take-off 17,826 lb (8085 kg) with IR 18,000 lb (8164 kg) with SLAR sensor

Dimensions: span 48 ft 0 in (14·83 m); length 44 ft 11 in (13·69 m) with SLAR pod; height 12 ft 8 in (3·86 m); wing area 360·0 sq ft (33·45 m²)

Variants

OV-1D Mohawk: all earlier variants of the Mohawk in service with the US Army for battlefield reconnaissance have now been upgraded to this standard with strengthened structure and more powerful engines, and offering the reconnaissance capabilities of the OV-1B (APS-94 SLAR) and OV-1C (AAS-4 IR surveillance system) in a single airframe; the original OV-1A had a span of 42·00 ft (12·80 m) and first flew in April 1959, but the current type offers considerably improved capabilities, the choice between SLAR or IR primary sensors being complemented by an updated vertical panoramic camera for photographic reconnaissance, improved INS, radiological monitoring and ECM; a block upgrade programme is revising the entire Mohawk force with a MIL 1553B databus, entirely new avionics systems, and a new cockpit with CRT displays for reduced crew workloads

RV-1D Mohawk: 12 OV-1Bs converted for the tactical reconnaissance and Elint roles with the ALQ-133 'Quick Look II' target locator radar system

EV-1E Mohawk: 16 OV-1Bs converted for the electronic surveillance role with the ALQ-133 'Quick Look II' target locator radar system packaged in underfuselage and wingtip fairings; the type also has other advanced electronic systems

rumman S-2E Tracker

(USA)

Type: land-based and carrierborne anti-submarine and maritime patrol aeroplane

Accommodation: flightcrew of two, and a mission crew of two in the cabin

Armament (fixed): none

Armament (disposable): this is carried in a lower-fuselage weapons bay and on six hardpoints (three under each wing) up to a maximum weight of 4,810 lb (2182 kg); a typical load is two Mk 44/46 torpedoes or four 385-lb (175 depth bombs in the weapons bay, and 250-lb (113-kg) bombs or 5-in (127-mm) rockets on the underwing hardpoints

Electronics and operational equipment: communication and navigation equipment, plus APS-38 search radar (being replaced by the Eaton AIL APS-128 Digital Tactical Radar System), APN-122 Doppler navigation, ASQ-10 MAD in the tail 'sting', 'Julie' active acoustic ranging equipment with 60 echo-sounding charges, and AQA-3 'Jezebel' passive acoustic search equipment with 32 sonobuoys carried in nacelle compartments

Powerplant and fuel system: two 1,525-hp (1137-kW) Wright R-1820-82WA Cyclone piston engines, and a total internal fuel capacity of 728 US gal (2755 litres); no provision for drop tanks or inflight refuelling

Performance: maximum speed 265 mph (426 km/h) at sea level; patrol speed 150 mph (241 km/h) at 1,500 ft (460 m); initial climb rate 1,390 ft (425 m) per minute; service ceiling 21,000 ft (6400 m); patrol endurance 9 hours; ferry range 1,300 miles (2092 km)

Weights: empty 18,750 lb (8505 kg); maximum take-off 29,150 lb (13,222 kg)

Dimensions: span 72 ft 7 in (22·12 m); length 43 ft 6 in (13·26 m); height 16 ft 7 in (5·05 m); wing area 496·0 sq ft (46·08 m²)

Variants

C-1A Trader: COD (Carrier Onboard Delivery) variant of the Tracker series with a wider fuselage for the carriage of nine passengers or 3,500 lb (1588 kg) of freight; the variant spans 69 ft 8 in (21·23 m) and has a maximum take-off weight

of 24,649 lb (11,181 kg)

S-2A Tracker: this was the US Navy's first dedicated carrierborne aeroplane able to undertake the ASW hunter/killer role in a single airframe, and flew in XS2F-1 prototype form during December 1952; the type has a narrower fuselage than later variants, the dimensions of the aircraft including a length of 42 ft 0 in (12·80 m) and a span of 69 ft 8 in (21·25 m); maximum take-off weight is 26,300 lb (11,929 kg); there is also a trainer version designated **TS-2A Tracker**, and the basic model serves in Canada with the designation **CP-141**, of which many have been updated with Litton Canada APS-504(V) radar and other modifications to suit the type for patrol of Canada's maritime economic zone; the S-2A is at best obsolescent, and many surviving aircraft have been converted into liaison or training aircraft

S-2E Tracker: definitive ASW version produced by conversion of S-2Ds with yet more modern sensors and processing equipment; the S-2D was itself a much developed version of the S-2B (which introduced 'Julie' active acoustic ranging and 'Jezebel' passive long-range search systems) with a wider fuselage, greater span, increased fuel capacity and accommodation for 32 rather than 16 sonobuoys in the engine nacelles; Brazil is to improve its S-2E aircraft with an electronic package from Thomson-CSF, which will include Varan radar and the Tactical Radar Electronic Support System upgraded with MAD and a FLIR sensor

S-2F Tracker: S-2Bs converted to S-2E standard

S-2G Tracker: S-2Es modified by Martin Marietta with enhanced electronics suiting the type for service on the US Navy's carriers of the 1960s and 1970s pending deliveries of Lockheed S-3 Vikings

S-2T Turbo-Tracker: updated version of the S-2E with two 1,645-shp (1227-kW) Garrett TPE331-1-5AW turboprops for a maximum speed of 311 km/h (500 km/h), a 1,100-lb (499-kg) increase in payload and a maximum take-off weight of 27,962 lb (12,683 kg); the type is being produced by conversion of older aircraft, and features much-improved ASW capability

Gulfstream Aerospace

(USA)

Type: long-range multi-role light transport aeroplane

Accommodation: flightcrew of two or three, and 19 passengers or freight in the cabin

Armament (fixed): none

Armament (disposable): none

Electronics and operational equipment: communication and navigation equipment

Powerplant and fuel system: two 11,400-lb (5171-kg) thrust Rolls-Royce Spey Mk 511-8 non-afterburning turbofans, and a total internal fuel capacity of 4,192 US gal (15868 litres); no provision for drop tanks or inflight refuelling

Performance: maximum cruising speed 576 mph (928 km/h) or Mach 0·85 at 30,000 ft (9145 m); normal cruising speed 508 mph (818 km/h) or Mach 0·77 at 30,000 ft (9145 m); initial climb rate 3,800 ft (1158 m) per minute; service ceiling 45,000 ft (13,715 m); range 4,721 miles (7598 km)

Weights: empty 32,000 lb (14,515 kg); maximum take-off 69,700 lb (31,615 kg)

Dimensions: span 77 ft 10 in (23·72 m); length 83 ft 1 in (25·32 m); height 24 ft 4·5 in (7·43 m); wing area 934·6 sq ft (8683 m²)

Variants

Gulfstream III: developed as a high-performance corporate transport on the basis of the preceding Gulfstream II with a longer fuselage and greater-span wing of supercritical section fitted with winglets, the Gulfstream III first flew in December 1979 and offers excellent range as well as good payload; the type has thus been

Below left: The Brazilian air force flies 14 S-2A/E Trackers for the navy's sole carrier.

Below: The SRA-1 offers great endurance, and is seen here with SLAMMR underfuselage radar.

Gulfstream III

HAL (Hindustan Aeronautics Ltd) Ajeet

bought by some air arms as a VIP transport (the US designation for its services' 18 aircraft being **C-20A**), and Denmark took three such aircraft modified for offshore patrol with Texas Instruments APS-127 surveillance radar and other specialized avionics under the company designation **SMA-3**

Gulfstream IV: further improved model with the fuselage lengthened by 4 ft 6 in (1·37 m) to seat a maximum of 19 passengers, or by 18 ft 6 in (5·64 m) for the accommodation of 24 passengers in the **Gulfstream IV-B**; these two variants are powered by two 12,420-lb (5634-kg) thrust Rolls-Royce Tay Mk Mk 610-8 non-afterburning turbofans, and the US Navy has three aircraft of this basic type in service under the **EC-20F** for the tactical ECM role

SRA-1: surveillance and reconnaissance platform derivative of the Gulfstream IV with Goodyear UPD-8 synthetic-aperture radar or Motorola SLAMMR (Side-Looking Airborne Multi-Mode Radar) in an underfuselage pod, a Rank/Optical KS-146 mirror-lens camera, optional ECM and ESM equipment, and underwing hardpoints for advanced weapons such as the AGM-65 Maverick and AGM-84 Harpoon missiles, and the Paveway laser-guided bomb

SRA-4: proposed military special-missions variant of the Gulfstream IV with an Israeli radar system, the Elta Phalcon with six phased-array sets of conformal antennae on the fuselage sides to provide 360° coverage in the AEW role, plus the Elta EL/K-7036 tactical Comint system carried internally

Right: The Ajeet Trainer is a simple evolution of the Ajeet (shown) but with a longer fuselage.

Below right: The Gulfstream III is operated by the USAF as the C-20A in the VIP role.

(India)
Type: lightweight interceptor and attack aeroplane
Accommodation: pilot on a Martin-Baker GF4 zero/167-km/h (104-mph) ejector seat
Armament (fixed): two 30-mm Aden Mk 4 cannon with 90 rounds per gun
Armament (disposable): this is carried on four hardpoints (two under each wing) up to a maximum weight of 850 kg (1,874 lb); typical weapons are 500-lb (227-kg) bombs, cluster bombs, and pods for 55- or 68-mm (2·17- or 2·68-in) rockets
Electronics and operational equipment: communication and navigation equipment, plus a Ferranti F195R/3 ISIS sight
Powerplant and fuel system: one 4,500-lb (2041-kg) thrust Rolls-Royce (Bristol) Orpheus Mk 701-01 non-afterburning turbojet, and a total internal fuel capacity of 1350 litres (297 Imp gal) plus provision for two 273-litre (60-Imp gal) drop tanks; no provision for inflight refuelling
Performance: maximum speed 1022 km/h (635 mph) or Mach 0·96 at 12,000 m (39,370 ft) and 1102 km/h (685 mph) or Mach 0·90 at sea level; climb to 12,000 m (39,370 ft) in 6 minutes from brakes-off; service ceiling 13,700 m (44,950 ft); radius 172 km (107 miles) on a lo-lo-lo mission

with two 500-lb (227-kg) bombs
Weights: empty 2307 kg (5,085 lb); normal take-off 3538 kg (7,800 lb); maximum take-off 4173 kg (9200 lb)
Dimensions: span 6·73 m (22 ft 1 in); length 9·04 m (29 ft 8 in); height 2·46 m (8 ft 1 in); wing area 12·69 m² (136·6 sq ft)

Variants

Ajeet: developed on the basis of the Hawker Siddeley (Folland) Gnat lightweight fighter, the Ajeet (invincible) is a 'Gnat Mk 2' with features such as integral wing tanks (freeing the underwing hardpoints for armament) and greater longitudinal stability; the first aircraft flew in March 1975 and the type was built in small numbers

Ajeet Trainer: simple advanced and operational conversion trainer derivative of the Ajeet, the fuselage being stretched by 1·4 m (4 ft 7·1 in) to an overall figure of 10·45 m (34 ft 3·5 in) as the means of accommodating the second cockpit; there is provision for the cannon to be removed, allowing internal fuel capacity to be increased by 273 litres (60 Imp gal); the first Ajeet Trainer flew in September 1982, and the type has empty and maximum take-off weights of 2940 and 4536 kg (6,482 and 10,000 lb) respectively

HAL (Hindustan Aeronautics Ltd) HJT-16 Kiran Mk II

(India)
Type: flying and weapon trainer with secondary light attack capability

Accommodation: pupil and instructor side-by-side on Martin-Baker H4HA zero/167-km/h (104-mph) ejector seats

Armament (fixed): two 7·62-mm (0·3-in) FN MAG machine-guns with 150 rounds per gun

Armament (disposable): this is carried on four hardpoints (two under each wing, with each unit rated at 500 kg/1,102 lb) up to a maximum weight of 1000 kg (2,205 lb); typical loads are four 250-kg (551-lb) or 500-lb (227-kg) bombs, or two HAL pods each with two 7·62-mm (0·3-in) machine-guns, or four launchers each with 18 68-mm (2·68-in) rockets

Electronics and operational equipment: communication and navigation equipment, plus two Mk IIIB reflector sights

Powerplant and fuel system: one 4,200-lb (1905-kg) thrust Rolls-Royce (Bristol) Orpheus 711-01 non-afterburning turbojet, and a total internal fuel capacity of 1145 litres (295·5 Imp gal) plus provision for two 227-litre (50-Imp gal) drop tanks; no provision for inflight refuelling

Performance: maximum speed 672 km/h (418 mph) at sea level; cruising speed 621 km/h (386 mph) at 4575 m (15,000 ft); initial climb rate 1600 m (5,250 ft) per minute; service ceiling 12,000 m (39,375 ft); range 735 km (457 miles)

Weights: empty 2995 kg (6,303 lb); normal take-off 4250 kg (9,369 lb); maximum take-off 5000 kg (11,023 lb)

Dimensions: span 10·70 m (35 ft 1·25 in); length 10·60 m (34 ft 9 in); height 3·635 m (11 ft 11 in); wing area 19·00 m² (204·5 sq ft)

Variants
Kiran Mk I: this unarmed basic trainer first flew in September 1964 and began to enter service in 1968; the type is a basic flying trainer powered by the 2,500-lb (1134-kg) thrust Rolls-Royce Viper Mk 11 non-afterburning turbojet, and at empty and maximum take-off weights of 2561 and 4234 kg (5,645 and 9,335 lb) respectively the type has a maximum speed of 695 km/h (432 mph) at sea level, a time of 20 minutes to 9145 m (30,000 ft), a service ceiling of 9145 m (30,000 ft) and a range of 1630 km (1,013 miles)

Kiran Mk IA: late-production Kiran Mk I with provision for 450 kg (992 lb) of weapons on two underwing hardpoints for the weapons training and light attack roles

Kiran Mk II: developed version available from 1983 (after a first flight during July 1976) in the weapons training, light attack and COIN roles with considerably more power, inbuilt machine-gun armament and four rather than two underwing hardpoints

Right: The Kiran Mk I is an unarmed basic trainer that has been developed into Mk IA and Mk II armed versions.

Opposite: The Israeli air force operates four IAI 201 Aravas mainly for the Elint role with a secondary transport tasking.

Harbin Aircraft Manufacturing Corporation SH-5

(China)
Type: anti-submarine, maritime patrol, SAR and transport amphibian aeroplane

Accommodation: flightcrew of five, and a basic mission crew of three supplemented as required by 10,000 kg (22,046 lb) of freight

Armament (fixed): none

Armament (disposable): this is carried in a rear-fuselage bay and on four underwing hardpoints up to a maximum weight of 6000 kg (13,228 lb) and comprises two C-101 or similar anti-ship missiles on the inner hardpoints and six lightweight homing torpedoes, depth charges or other disposable weapons on the outer hardpoints

Electronics and operational equipment: communication and navigation equipment, plus Doppler search radar in a nose 'thimble', MAD in a tail 'sting', sonobuoys in a rear-fuselage dispenser, INS and other (as yet unspecified) items

Powerplant and fuel system: four 3170-kW (4,252-shp) Harbin Wojiang-6 turboprops, and a total internal fuel weight of 16,500 kg (36,376 lb); no provision for drop tanks or inflight refuelling

Performance: maximum speed 555 km/h (345 mph) at optimum altitude; cruising speed 450 km/h (280 mph); initial climb rate not revealed; service ceiling 7000 m (22,965 ft); radius 2375 km (1,475 miles); endurance 12-15 hours

Weights: empty 26,500 kg (58,422 lb); normal take-off 36,000 kg (79,366 lb); maximum take-off 45,000 kg (99,208 lb)

Dimensions: span 36·00 m (118 ft 1·25 in); length 38·90 m (127 ft 7·5 in); height 9·79 m (32 ft 1·5 in); wing area 144·00 m² (1,550·05 sq ft)

Variant
Harbin SH-5: developed in China on the basis of the wings and powerplant of the Y-8 (Chinese-built Antonov An-12) combined with the empennage of the Beriev Be-12 and a new fuselage/hull clearly owing much to that of the Japanese Shin Meiwa US-1A, the SH-5 (otherwise known as the **PS-5**) first flew in April 1976 and entered service in 1986 as the Chinese navy's dedicated maritime patrol/anti-submarine amphibian; the few details of this machine are still largely speculative

IAI (Israel Aircraft Industries) 201 Arava

(Israel)

Type: short-range STOL utility transport aeroplane

Accommodation: flightcrew of two, and 24 troops, or 16 paratroops and two despatchers, or 2350 kg (5,181 lb) of freight in the hold

Armament (fixed): optional installation of two 0·5-in (12·7-mm) Browning M2 machine-guns (one on each side of the forward fuselage) and flexible rear-firing machine-guns

Armament (disposable): this is carried on two hardpoints (one on each side of the fuselage) and comprises two pods each with six 81-mm (3·2-in) rockets

Electronics and operational equipment: communication and navigation equipment

Powerplant and fuel system: two 750-shp (559-kW) Pratt & Whitney Canada PT6A-34 turboprops, and a total internal fuel capacity of 1663 litres (366 Imp gal) plus provision for two

1022-litre (225-Imp gal) auxiliary tanks in the hold; no provision for drop tanks or inflight refuelling

Performance: maximum speed 326 km/h (203 mph) at 3050 m (10,000 ft); cruising speed 319 km/h (198 mph) at 3050 m (10,000 ft); initial climb rate 393 m (1,290 ft) per minute; service ceiling 7620 m (25,000 ft); range 280 km (174 miles) with maximum payload or 1056 km (656 miles) with maximum standard fuel

Weights: empty 4000 kg (8,818 lb); maximum take-off 6805 kg (15,002 lb)

Dimensions: span 20·96 m (68 ft 9 in); length 13·03 m (42 ft 9 in); height 5·21 m (17 ft 1 in); wing area 43·68 m² (470·2 sq ft)

Variants

IAI 201 Arava: this is the military transport version of the IAI 101B civil commuter (18 passengers or some 1815 kg/4,000 lb of freight) and IAI 102

civil utility (20 passengers, freight, VIP transport etc) aircraft; the type is slow and short-ranged, but is also rugged and possesses good short-field performance thanks to its STOL design; the IAI 201 can carry 24 troops, or 16 paratroops or freight, but is generally used for maritime patrol or EW, in the latter role fitted with a palletized suite comprising Elta EL/K-1250 and L-8310 Comint receivers, one Elta L-8312 computer and Elta L-8200 series spot and barrage noise jammers; production was completed early in 1988

IAI 202 Arava: version with the fuselage pod lengthened from 9·33 m to 10·23 m (30 ft 7·3 in to 33 ft 6·75 in), tip winglets (which can also be retrofitted to the IAI 201) and extra fuel in a 'wet' wing for the carriage of 30 troops, or 20 paratroops, or 12 litters and five attendants, or 2500 kg (5,511 lb) of freight over a range of 630 km (392 miles) on the power of two 750-shp (559-kW) PT6A-36 turboprops

IAI (Israel Aircraft Industries) 1124N Sea Scan

(Israel)
Type: medium/long-range maritime patrol aeroplane
Accommodation: flightcrew of two, and a mission crew of two or three in the cabin
Armament (fixed): none
Armament (disposable): this can be carried on two hardpoints (one on each side of the fuselage), but is generally not fitted
Electronics and operational equipment: communication and navigation equipment, plus Litton APS-504(V)2 search radar, Omega navigation and other items
Powerplant and fuel system: two 3,700-lb (1678-kg) thrust Garrett TFE731-3-1G non-afterburning turbofans, and a total internal fuel capacity of 4920 litres (1,082 Imp gal); no pro-

vision for drop tanks or inflight refuelling
Performance: maximum speed 870 km/h (541 mph) at 5900 m (19,355 ft); cruising speed 740 km/h (460 mph) at 12,500 m (41,010 ft); initial climb rate 1525 m (5,000 ft) per minute; service ceiling 13,725 m (45,030 m); range 4445 km (2,762 miles)
Weights: empty 5760 kg (12,698 lb); maximum take-off 10,660 kg (23,500 lb)
Dimensions: span 13·65 m (44 ft 9·5 in) over tiptanks; length 15·93 m (52 ft 3 in); height 4·81 m (15 ft 9·5 in); wing area 28·64 m² (308·26 sq ft)

Variant

IAI 112N Seascan: this is the coastal patrol version of the IAI 1124 Westwind executive transport; the type has a low-altitude range of 2555 km

(1588 miles), allowing the Seascan to cover a 268,056-km² (103,496-sq mile) search area in the course of a 6·5-hour patrol at an altitude of 915 m (3,000 ft); at an altitude of 13,720 m (45,000 ft) the patrol endurance is 8 hours and range 4633 km (2,878 miles); IAI is currently planning an armed version for the anti-ship and anti-submarine roles with the appropriate sensors and weapons such as the Gabriel Mk III missile and acoustic-homing torpedoes

The IAI 1124N Seascan has very considerable endurance, and its main sensor is the APS-504(V)2 nose radar. The type has two lateral hardpoints, but these are seldom used for the carriage of weapons.

IAI (Israel Aircraft Industries) Kfir-C7

(Israel)

Type: multi-role fighter and attack aeroplane

Accommodation: pilot on a Martin-Baker IL10P zero/zero ejector seat

Armament (fixed): two 30-mm DEFA 552 cannon with 140 rounds per gun

Armament (disposable): this is carried on nine hardpoints (one on the centreline rated at 1000 kg/2,205 lb, two underfuselage tandem pairs with each unit rated at 500 kg/1,1012 lb, and two under each wing with the inner two units each rated at 1000 kg/2,205 lb and the outer two units each at 150 kg/331 lb) up to a maximum weight of 6085 kg (13,415 lb); a wide assortment of weapons can be carried, including the Shafrir 2, Python 3 and AIM-9 Sidewinder AAMs, the Luz-1 and AGM-65 Maverick ASMs, the AGM-45 Shrike and AGM-78 Standard radar-homing missiles, Paveway laser-guided bombs, HOBOS EO-guided bombs, 3,000-, 2,000-, 1,000-, 750-, 500- and 250-lb (1361-, 907-, 454-, 340-, 227- and 113-kg) free-fall or retarded bombs, cluster bombs, napalm bombs and rocket pods

Electronics and operational equipment: communication and navigation equipment, plus Elta EL/M-2001B ranging radar or Elta EL/M-2021 fire-control, mapping and terrain-avoidance radar, Israel Electro-Optics HUD, Elbit HDDs, Elbit-Kearfott S-8600 INS, IAI WDNS-341 weapon-delivery and navigation system, Elbit system 82 stores-management system, Tamam central computer, Elta RWR, chaff/flare dispenser and provision for ECM pods such as the Elta L-8202

Powerplant and fuel system: one 18,750-lb (8505-kg) afterburning thrust General Electric J79-J1E turbojet, and a total internal fuel capacity of 3243 litres (713 Imp gal) plus provision for a maximum of five drop tanks carrying a maximum of 4700 litres (1,034 Imp gal) in 1700-, 1300-, 825-, 600- and 500-litre (374-, 286-, 181·5-, 132- and 110-Imp gal) sizes; provision for inflight refuelling

Performance: maximum speed 2440 + km/h (1,516 + mph) or Mach 2·3 + at 11,000 m (36,090 ft) and 1389 km/h (863 mph) or Mach 1·13 at sea level; initial climb rate 14,000 m (45,930 ft) per minute; service ceiling 17,700 m (58,070 ft); radius 776 km (482 miles) on an hi-hi-hi interception mission with two Shafrir AAMs and one 825-litre (181·5-Imp gal) and two 1300-litre (286-Imp gal) drop tanks, or 1186 km (737 miles) on a hi-lo-hi mission with two AAMs, four bombs, and one 1300-litre (286-Imp gal) and two 1700-litre (374-Imp gal) drop tanks; ferry range 3232 km (2,008 miles)

Weights: empty 7285 kg (16,060 lb); normal take-off 9390 kg (20701 lb) for an interception mission or 14,670 kg (32,341 lb) for a ground-attack mission; maximum take-off 16,500 kg (36,376 lb)

Dimensions: span 8·22 m (26 ft 11·5 in); length including probe 15·65 m (51 ft 4·5 in); height 4·55 m (14 ft 11·25 in); wing area 34·80 m² (374·6 sq ft) plus 1·66 m² (17·87 sq ft) for the canard foreplane

Variants

Kfir-C1: first flown in June 1973, this initial model of the Kfir (lion cub) was in essence the airframe of the Dassault-Mirage III/5 series mated to the General Electric J79 afterburning turbojet and fitted with a suite of Israeli electronics; the type was designed after the manufacturer had gained experience with the **Nesher** (eagle), itself merely an unlicensed copy of the Dassault Mirage IIICJ with an equally unlicensed Atar turbojet, produced mainly for Israeli service but later exported as the **Dagger**; the Kfir-C1 entered only limited production (27 aircraft), a mere two squadrons being equipped with the type from 1974 pending the introduction of more advanced derivatives with much improved combat capability

Kfir-C2: introduced in 1976 after a first flight in 1974, this is a much developed version of the Kfir-C2 designed to keep the type viable against all possible threats well into the 1990s; the type is distinguishable from the Kfir-C1 by its dogtoothed outer wing panels, small undernose strakes and, most importantly of all, swept delta canard foreplanes; the result is a warplane with formidable combat capabilities plus short-field performance thanks to the sustained manoeuvrability and control effectiveness resulting from the aerodynamic developments; the type is fitted with Elta EL/M-2001 ranging radar or, in later examples, the improved EL/M-2001B and a 17,900-lb (8118-kg) afterburning thrust version of the General Electric J79 turbojet; the maximum weapon load is 5775 kg (12,731 lb) of disposable weapons controlled with the aid of a Rafael Mahat or IAI WDNS-141 weapon-delivery system; the empty and maximum take-off weights of the variant are 7285 and 16,200 kg (16,060 and 35,714 lb) respectively, and the performance is slightly inferior to that of the Kfir-C7; Kfir-C1 fighters with small canards but no armament were delivered to the US Navy and Marine Corps with the designation **F-21A** for use as 'aggressor' aircraft in dissimilar air combat training

Kfir-TC2: designation of the combat-capable two-seat conversion trainer variant of the Kfir-C2; the type was first flown in February 1981, and the main distinguishing feature of the type is the visibility-improving droop of its nose section, which is lengthened by 0·84 m (2 ft 9 in) to accommodate the second cockpit

Kfir-C7: definitive single-seat version introduced in 1983; this is based on the Kfir-C2, but uses a specially adapted version of the J79-GE-J1E with some 1,000-lb (454-kg) more afterburning thrust in combat situations; the type has two extra hardpoints and a number of advanced features including capability for the carriage and use of 'smart' weapons, Elta EL/M-2021B pulse-Doppler radar, a revised cockpit with more sophisticated electronics and HOTAS (Hands On Throttle And Stick) controls, and provision for inflight-refuelling; maximum take-off weight is increased by 1540 kg (3,395 lb), but combat radius and (more importantly) thrust-to-weight ratio are improved to a marked degree

Kfir-TC7: tandem two-seat operational conversion trainer variant of the Kfir-C7, developed along lines similar to those that led to the Kfir-TC2; however, it is likely that the Kfir-TC7 is more than a mere conversion trainer, for the provision of the full electronic suite may mean that the type is designed to undertake the two-seat EW role in addition to its more mundane tasks

Nammer: under the name Nammer (tiger), Israel Aircraft Industries is proposing a hybrid fighter with the airframe of the Kfir and a turbofan powerplant (8228-kg/18,140-lb afterburning thrust General Electric F404, Pratt & Whitney PW1120 or SNECMA M53) as the so-called Nammer Option 1, which can also use reworked Mirage III airframes, or as the Nammer Option 2 with the above plus key features of the electronic suite developed for the cancelled Lavi multi-role fighter including the Elta EL/M-2032 radar or EL/M-2011 lightweight radar, a HUD and other systems; the primary powerplant option is the F404 in the RM12 version developed for the Swedish Saab-Scania JAS 39 Gripen and rated at 8228-kg (18,140-lb) afterburning thrust; with this engine the Nammer has a length of 16·00 m (52 ft 5·76 in), a payload of 6260 kg (13,801 lb) on nine hardpoints, and normal and maximum take-off weights of 10,250 and 16,500 kg (22,597 and 36,376 lb) respectively; performance includes a maximum sustained speed of Mach 2·2 at altitude (up Mach 0·2 from that of the Kfir), a service ceiling of 17,675 m (57,990 ft) and a typical lo-lo-lo attack mission radius of 1060 km (659 miles) with two AAMs, four CBU-58 cluster bombs and three drop tanks

Super Mirage: designation of a Kfir export version for Chile

The Kfir-C2 was the first version of this Israeli Mirage development with foreplanes.

Ilyushin Il-14M 'Crate'

(USSR)

Type: short/medium-range utility light transport aeroplane

Accommodation: flightcrew of two, and 36 passengers or 3300 kg (7,275 lb) of freight in the cabin

Armament (fixed): none

Armament (disposable): none

Electronics and operational equipment: communication and navigation equipment

Powerplant and fuel system: two 1417-kW (1,900-hp) Shvetsov ASh-82T piston engines, and a total internal fuel capacity of 6500 litres (1,330 Imp gal); no provision for drop tanks or inflight refuelling

Performance: maximum speed 430 km/h (267 mph) at 2400 m (7,875 ft); cruising speed 350 km/h (217 mph) at 3000 m (9,845 ft); service ceiling 7400 m (24,280 ft); range 400 km (249 miles) with maximum payload or 1500 km (932 miles) with 26 passengers

Weights: empty 12,700 kg (27,998 lb); maximum take-off 17,500 kg (38,581 lb)

Dimensions: span 31·70 m (104 ft 0 in); length 22·31 m (73 ft 2·25 in); height 7·90 m (25 ft 11 in); wing area 100·00 m² (1,076·4 sq ft)

Variants

Il-14 'Crate': designed as an improved Ilyushin Il-12 to succeed the Lisunov Li-2 (the Soviet version of the Douglas DC-3/C-47 series) as the nation's standard feederliner and tactical transport, the Il-14 flew in prototype form during 1952 and began to enter service in 1954; several variants were built for civil and military use, typical being the **Il-14P** for 18/26 passengers, the **Il-14M** lengthened by 1·0 m (3 ft 3·4 in) for 24/28 passengers, the **Il-14T** freight version of the Il-14P and the **Il-14G** freight version of the Il-14M

Il-14 'Crate-C': Comint version first seen in 1979 and fitted with a number of unspecified equipment items for service with the Polish air force

Right: The Il-14 is a venerable design still in service for a number of secondary tasks.

Below: Il-18s have been used by civil and military operators for long-range transport.

Ilyushin Il-18D 'Coot'

(USSR)

Type: medium/long-range medium transport aeroplane

Accommodation: flightcrew of five, and 120 passengers or 13500 kg (29,762 lb) of freight in the cabin

Armament (fixed): none

Armament (disposable): none

Electronics and operational equipment: communication and navigation equipment

Powerplant and fuel system: four 3170-kW (4,252-shp) Ivchyenko AI-20M turboprops, and a total internal fuel capacity of 23,700 litres (5,213 Imp gal); no provision for drop tanks or inflight refuelling

Performance: maximum cruising speed 675 km/h (419 mph) at 8500 m (27,890 ft); cruising speed 625 km/h (388 mph) at 8000 m (26,245 ft); service ceiling 10,000 m (32,810 ft); range 3700 km (2,299 miles) with maximum payload or 6500 km (4,040 miles) with maximum fuel

Weights: empty 35,000 kg (77,162 lb); maximum take-off 64,000 kg (141,093 lb)

Dimensions: span 37·40 m (122 ft 8·5 in); length 35·90 m (117 ft 9 in); height 10·17 m (33 ft 4 in); wing area 140·00 m² (1,507·0 sq ft)

Variants

Il-18 'Coot': first flown in July 1957, the Il-18 was designed as a medium-capacity turboprop airliner for the USSR's internal and European routes, and was produced in a number of variants with revised seating arrangements and powerplants; the basic Il-18 accommodated 75 passengers and had four 2983-ekW (4,000-ehp) Kuznetsov NK-4 turboprops, the **Il-18B** was similar but seated 84 passengers, the **Il-18V** appeared in 1961 with accommodation for between 90 and 100 passengers, the **Il-18D** had AI-20M turboprops and seating for 122 passengers in a lengthened fuselage, the **Il-18E** was similar to the Il-18D with reduced fuel capacity, and the **Il-18T** was a pure freighter model; many example of this series passed into military service as transports, freighters and VIP aircraft

Il-20 'Coot-A': taken into Soviet service during the mid-1970s, this is a dedicated Elint derivative of the Il-18; the airframe is substantially unaltered, but under the forward fuselage is a canoe fairing approximately 10·25 m (33 ft 7 in) long and 1·15 m (3 ft 9 in) deep, probably housing a SLAR; other modifications include a pair of box fairings on the sides of the fuselage just aft of the flight deck, 10 blade antennae (eight under and two over the fuselage), and blister fairings on the underside of the fuselage

Il-22 'Coot-B': no details have been made public about this conversion of surplus Il-18 transports as airborne command post aircraft, presumably with a number of antennae to reflect the large quantity of command and communication equipment carried in the cabin

Ilyushin Il-28 'Beagle'

(USSR)
Type: light bomber
Accommodation: pilot, bomb-aimer/navigator and gunner in separate positions
Armament (fixed): two 23-mm NR-23 cannon with 100 rounds per gun in the lower nose, and two 23-mm NR-23 cannon with 225 rounds per gun in the rear turret
Armament (disposable): this is carried in a lower-fuselage weapons bay up to a maximum weight of 3000 kg (6,614 lb); the normal loads are four 500-kg (1,102-lb) or eight 250-kg (551-lb) free-fall bombs
Electronics and operational equipment: communication and navigation equipment, plus all-weather bombing radar and a tail-warning radar
Powerplant and fuel system: two 2700-kg (5,952-lb) thrust Klimov VK-1A non-afterburning turbojets, and a total internal fuel capacity of 7908 litres (1,740 Imp gal) plus provision for wingtip auxiliary tanks; no provision for drop tanks or inflight refuelling
Performance: maximum speed 900 km/h (559 mph) at 4500 m (14,765 ft) and 800 km/h (497 mph) at sea level; cruising speed 770 km/h (478 mph) at 10,000 m (32,810 ft); climb to 10,000 m (32,810 ft) in 18 minutes; service ceiling 12,300 m (40,355 ft); range 2180 km (1,350 miles) with a 1000-kg (2,205-lb) warload, or 2400 km (1,490 miles) with maximum fuel
Weights: empty 13,000 kg (26,455 lb); normal take-off 18,400 kg (40,565 lb); maximum take-off 21,200 kg (46,737 lb)
Dimensions: span 21·45 m (70 ft 4·5 in); length 17·65 m (57 ft 11 in); height 6·70 m (22 ft 0 in); wing area 60·80 m² (654·4 sq ft)

Variants

Il-28 'Beagle': though obsolete (the prototype having flown in 1948) in its basic light bomber role, the Il-28 remains in fairly widespread service with Soviet allies
Il-28R 'Beagle': three-seat tactical reconnaissance variant of the Il-28 series, the erstwhile bomb bay being used to accommodate three or five cameras plus some 12 to 18 photo-flash bombs; some aircraft have an electronic reconnaissance package with a radome under the rear fuselage
Il-28T 'Beagle': designation of the torpedo bomber version, the bomb bay being able to accommodate one large or two small torpedoes, or (in an alternative role) a few mines
Il-28U 'Mascot': two-seat operational conversion trainer with a solid nose and two stepped cockpits
Harbin Aircraft Manufacturing Corporation H-5: Chinese-built copy of the Il-28, versions of the basic bomber being the **HZ-5** tactical reconnaissance aircraft and the **HJ-5** operational conversion trainer

Below: The Il-38 is a derivative of the Il-18 for long range maritime patrol, and in addition to obvious features such as reduced cabin glazing, a MAD 'stinger' and an underfuselage 'guppy' radome, differs from the airliner model in having its wing set considerably farther forward on the fuselage.

Bottom: The Il-28 is an obsolete bomber still in limited service with some Soviet clients.

Ilyushin Il-38 'May-A'

(USSR)
Type: long-range maritime patrol and anti-submarine aeroplane
Acccommodation: flightcrew of three or four, and a mission crew of eight or nine in the cabin
Armament (fixed): none
Armament (disposable): this is carried in a lower-fuselage weapons bay up to an unknown weight of torpedoes and other anti-submarine weapons
Electronics and operational equipment: communication and navigation equipment, plus 'Wet Eye' search radar with its antenna in an under-nose radome, MAD in the tail 'sting', sonobuoys and onboard analysis and computing equipment
Powerplant and fuel system: four 3170-kW (4,252-shp) Ivchyenko AI-20M turboprops, and a total internal fuel capacity of about 30,000 litres (6,599 Imp gal); no provision for drop tanks or inflight refuelling
Performance: maximum speed 722 km/h (448 mph) at 6400 m (20,995 ft); cruising speed 611 km/h (380 mph) at 8250 m (27,065 ft); initial climb rate not revealed; service ceiling not revealed; range 7200 km (4,474 miles); endurance 12 hours
Weights: empty 36,000 kg (79,366 lb); maximum take-off 63,500 kg (139,994 lb)
Dimensions: span 37·40 m (122 ft 8·5 in); length 39·60 m (129 ft 11·1 in); height 10·16 m (33 ft 4 in); wing area 140·00 m² (1,507·0 sq ft)

Variants

Il-38 'May-A': this is a fairly radical development of the Il-18 as a dedicated ASW aircraft; the type was first flown in 1966 or 1967 and features a longer fuselage with the wing set relatively farther forward than on the Il-18, presumably to maintain the centre of gravity position with the installation of heavy mission equipment in the forward fuselage; the design philosophy is exactly the same as that used by the Americans to develop the Lockheed P-3 Orion from the Electra airliner, but there is little doubt that the Soviet aircraft is inferior in terms of electronic capability in the maritime reconnaissance and ASW roles
Il-38 'May-B': variant identified in 1984 and notable for a second large radome (under the weapon bay); it is likely that this version is intended for mid-course missile guidance, and thus lacks anti-submarine capability

Ilyushin Il-76M 'Candid-B'

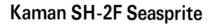

(USSR)

Type: long-range strategic freight transport aeroplane

Accommodation: flightcrew of seven, and 140 troops, or 125 paratroops, or an unknown number of litters plus attendants, or 40,000 kg (88,183 lb) of freight in the hold

Armament (fixed): two 23-mm NR-23 cannon in the rear turret

Armament (disposable): none

Electronics and operational equipment: communication and navigation equipment

Powerplant and fuel system: four 12,000-kg (26,455-lb) thrust Soloviev D-30KP non-afterburning turbofans, and a total internal fuel capacity of about 81,830 litres (18,000 Imp gal); no provision for drop tanks or inflight refuelling

Performance: maximum speed 850 km/h (528 mph) at 11,000 m (36,090 ft); cruising speed 800 km/h (497 mph) at 12,000 m (39,370 ft); initial climb rate not revealed; service ceiling 12,000 m (39,370 ft); range 5000 km (3,107 miles) with a 40,000-kg (88,183-lb) payload; ferry range 6700 km (4,163 miles)

Weights: empty 75,000 kg (165,347 lb); maximum take-off 170,000 kg (374,786 lb)

Dimensions: span 50·50 m (165 ft 8·2 in); length 46·59 m (152 ft 10·25 in); height 14·76 m (48 ft 5·1 in); wing area 300·00 m² (3,229·28 sq ft)

Variants

Il-76 'Candid-A': first flown in March 1971, this is the Soviet replacement for the Antonov An-12 series in both the civil freighting and military transport roles with Soloviev D-30KP turbofans; the upswept rear fuselage has a ramp and rear doors for ease of access to the unobstructed hold, which measures 20·0 m (65 ft 7 in) in length (24·5 m/80 ft 5 in including the ramp), 3·46 m (11 ft 4 in) in width and 3·4 m (11 ft 2 in) in height and can handle freight with the aid of roller panels in the floor and two overhead winches; the **Il-76T** version has additional fuel (in a centre-section tank above the hold) and higher operating weights for the carriage of greater payload; the **Il-76TD** has improved D-30KP-1 turbofans to maintain performance at higher ambient temperatures plus a 10,000-kg (22,046-lb) increase in fuel weight for a 1200-km (745-mile) stretch of maximum-fuel range; the model can also carry a payload of 48,000 kg (105,820 lb), and its maximum take-off weight is 190,000 kg (418,871 lb)

Il-76M 'Candid-B': specifically military version of the Il-76T with a rear turret (often seen without its cannon armament), ECM blisters on the fuselage sides in line with the navigator's compartment, and provision for chaff/flare dispenser packs; the **Il-76MD** is the military version equivalent to the Il-76TD; both variants are extremely capable, their design, landing gear, high-lift devices and powerful engines bestowing good field performance even under adverse conditions; the Indian air force uses the type under the name **Gajaraj**

Il-76 'Mainstay': entering service in the mid-1980s, this is the Soviets' AEW version of the Il-76 freighter, with a lengthened forward fuselage and tactical compartment for a mission crew deriving data from the large surveillance radar with its antenna in a rotodome above the fuselage; full production is allowing the phasing-out (or relegation to secondary areas) of obsolescent Tupolev Tu-126 'Moss' AEW aircraft; the 'Mainstay' has no provision for tail guns, but is fitted with active/passive EW systems, and carries as standard an inflight-refuelling probe

Il-78 'Midas': inflight-refuelling tanker version of the series with three hose-and-drogue units (one under each wing and one on the port side of the rear fuselage) and considerable extra fuel filling tanks located in the erstwhile cargo hold and providing Soviet tactical and long-range aircraft with significantly improved refuelling capabilities; it is thought that Iraq has also developed its own inflight-refuelling tanker version of the Il-76 with comparable capabilities

Adnan 1: in 1989 Iraq revealed that it had undertaken initial development of the **Baghdad 1** AEW platform based on the Il-76MD with its rear ramp/door of the basic freighter replaced by a glassfibre-reinforced plastics radome over the antenna of the Thomson-CSF Tiger G surveillance radar supplied by France in a system providing less than 360° (but more than 180°) coverage; developed in parallel was a more orthodox AEW platform based on the same airframe, and this Adnan 1 has now replaced the Baghdad 1 in Iraqi plans; the Adnan 1 has its radar antenna located in an over-fuselage rotodome to provide 360° coverage; radar developments have been introduced to reduce the problem of ground clutter, and it is claimed that the system can detect, track and identify targets to a maximum range of 350 km (217·5 miles) and the data are passed by the four-man mission crew to a ground station by voice or a data-link; the Adnan 1 also possesses ESM systems and a Cossor IFF system

Adnan 2: under this designation Iraq is upgrading the Adnan 1 concept with a control function to allow the direct vectoring of fighter aircraft

Kaman SH-2F Seasprite

(USA)

Type: shipborne anti-submarine, missile defence, SAR and utility helicopter

Accommodation: pilot, co-pilot and sensor operator

Armament (fixed): none

Armament (disposable): this is carried on two hardpoints (one on each side of the fuselage) and comprises one or two Mk 46 torpedoes

Electronics and operational equipment: communication and navigation equipment, plus Canadian Marconi LN-66HP surveillance radar with its antenna in an underfuselage radome, Texas Instruments ASQ-81(V)2 MAD with a towed 'bird', General Instruments ALR-66 RWR, Teledyne ASN-123 tactical navigation system, APN-182 Doppler navigation, and a bank of 15 launch tubes for SSQ-41 passive and SSQ-47 active sonobuoys (being replaced by DIFAR and DICASS sonobuoys respectively)

Powerplant and fuel system: two 1,350-shp (1007-kW) General Electric T58-GE-8F turboshafts, and a total internal fuel capacity of 276 US gal (1046 litres) plus provision for 120 US gal (454 litres) of auxiliary fuel; no provision for drop tanks or inflight refuelling

Performance: maximum speed 150 mph (241 km/h) at sea level; cruising speed 138 mph (222 km/h); initial climb rate 2,440 ft (774 m) per minute; service ceiling 22,500 ft (6860 m); hovering ceiling in ground effect 18,600 ft (5670 m) and out of ground effect 15,400 ft (4695 m); range 431 miles (695 km) on standard fuel

Weights: empty 7,040 lb (3193 kg); normal take-off 12,800 lb (5806 kg); maximum take-off 13,500 lb (6123 kg)

Dimensions: main rotor diameter 44 ft 0 in (13·41 m); length overall, rotors turning 52 ft 7 in (16·03 m) and with nose and rotors folded 38 ft 4 in (11·68 m); height 15 ft 6 in (4·72 m); main rotor disc area 1,520·23 sq ft (141·26 m²)

Variants

SH-2F Seasprite: first flown in July 1959 as the single-engined HU2K-1, the Seasprite was redesignated UH-2 in 1962, and the sole versions now

Kamov Ka-25 'Hormone-A'

in service are the SH-2F and SH-2G; the SH-2F variant was introduced in 1972 and began to enter service in May 1973 as the LAMPS (Light Airborne Multi-Purpose System) helicopter for anti-submarine, anti-ship missile defence, SAR, and utility transport service on the US Navy's smaller surface combatants; the two-engine configuration had been pioneered by the UH-2C variant, and the SH-2F still offers capabilities unmatched in any helicopter of comparable size; 85 UH-2A, UH-2B and UH-2C helicopters were upgraded to SH-2F standard, as were most surviving SH-2Ds; the variant can carry a slung load of 4,000 lb (1814 kg), and current helicopters are being upgraded with improved avionics and General Electric T700-GE-401 turboshafts for better performance (in terms of range and reliability) and to promote commonality with the Sikorsky SH-60B Seahawk; helicopters delivered before October 1985 have a maximum take-off weight of 12,800 lb (5806 kg)

SH-2G Super Sprite: improved SH-2F with two 1,690-shp (1260-kW) General Electric T700-GE-401 turboshafts driving a new main rotor with composite-structure rotor blades, MIL-1553 databus and much enhanced acoustic/tactical system including a Global Positioning System receiver, an acoustic system data-link, AAQ-16 FLIR, an improved ESM and dunking sonar; the type entered service in the late 1980s as six new-build and 42 converted SH-2F helicopters; Kaman is offering the type in the anti-shipping role with stub wings for the carriage of AGM-65D Maverick ASMs; the SH-2G has empty and maximum take-off weights of 7,680 and 13,500 lb (3483 and 6123 kg) respectively, and its performance figures include a maximum speed of 150 mph (241 km/h) at sea level and a patrol endurance of 1 hour 30 minutes with two torpedoes at a 40-mile (64-km) radius

Below: The SH-2F Seasprite is the LAMPS MK I helicopter for frigates and some destroyers.

Below left: The 'Mainstay' is the AEW version of the Il-76.

(USSR)
Type: shipborne anti-submarine and utility helicopter

Accommodation: flightcrew of two, and a mission crew of three, or 12 passengers or 1300 kg (2,866 lb) of freight in the cabin

Armament (fixed): none

Armament (disposable): this is carried in a lower-fuselage weapons bay up to an unknown maximum weight, and generally comprises two torpedoes or depth charges

Electronics and operational equipment: communication and navigation equipment, plus 'Big Bulge' search radar with its antenna in an under-nose radome, 'Tie Rod' optronic sensor, either dunking sonar or MAD with a towed 'bird', two externally mounted boxes of sonobuoys (optional), 'Odd Rods' IFF, RWR, and IR counter-measures; the existence of other blisters and fairings on the airframe indicates that other sensors and/or equipment are carried

Powerplant and fuel system: (early aircraft) two 670-kW (898-shp) Glushenkov GTD-3F or (late aircraft) two 740-kW (992·5-shp) Glushenkov GTD-3BM turboshafts, and a total internal fuel capacity of unrevealed quantity plus provision for auxiliary fuel in two tanks carried on the sides of the fuselage; no provision for drop tanks or inflight refuelling

Performance: maximum speed 290 km/h (130 mph) at optimum altitude; cruising speed 193 km/h (120 mph); initial climb rate not revealed; service ceiling 3350 m (10,990 ft); hovering ceiling out of ground effect 2100 m (6,890 ft); range 400 km (249 miles) with standard fuel and 650 km (404 miles) with auxiliary fuel

Weights: empty 4765 kg (10,404 lb); maximum take-off 7500 kg (16,535 lb)

Dimensions: rotor diameter, each 15·74 m (51 ft 7·7 in); length, fuselage 9·75 m (31 ft 11·9 in); height 5·37 m (17 ft 7·4 in); rotor disc area, total 194·58 m² (2,094·5 sq ft)

Variants
Ka-25 'Hormone-A': introduced to service in 1965, the Ka-25 was clearly derived from the Ka-20 prototype revealed in 1961 and itself developed on the conceptual basis of the Ka-15/Ka-18 series; the 'Hormone-A' is the dedicated ASW version of the series

Ka-25 'Hormone-B': missile support version of the Ka-25 family fitted with A-346Z data-link equipment for the provision of targeting data and the mid-course updating of long-range anti-ship missiles such as the SS-N-3, SS-N-12, SS-N-19 and SS-N-22 missiles launched by major surface ships varying in size from destroyers to battle-cruisers; the variant is distinguishable from the 'Hormone-A' by the domed undersurface of its 'Short Horn' nose radome and the provision of a different radar with a cylindrical radome under the rear of the cabin

Ka-25 'Hormone-C': utility and SAR variant of the family without the offensive avionics and armament of the 'Hormone-A', but often carrying a winch and other specialist equipment

Below: The 'Hormone-A' with its flat-bottomed radome is the specialist ASW version of the Ka-25 helicopter, whose co-axial rotors produce a compact design for shipborne use.

115

Kamov Ka-27 'Helix-A'

(USSR)
Type: shipborne anti-submarine and utility helicopter
Accommodation: flightcrew of two or three, and a mission crew of three, or 4000 kg (8,818 lb) of freight in the cabin, or a slung load of 5000 kg (11,023 lb)
Armament (fixed): none
Armament (disposable): this is carried in a lower-fuselage weapons bay up to an unknown maximum weight, and can comprise two torpedoes or depth charges
Electronics and operational equipment: communication and navigation equipment, plus surveillance radar with its antenna in an undernose radome, optronic sensor, either dunking sonar or MAD with a towed 'bird', two externally mounted boxes of sonobuoys (optional) and a sophisticated ECM/ESM suite; the existence of other blisters and fairings on the airframe indicates that other sensors and/or equipment are carried
Powerplant and fuel system: two 1660-kW (2,226-shp) Isotov TV3-117V turboshafts, and a total internal fuel capacity of unrevealed quantity plus provision for auxiliary fuel in two external tanks; no provision for drop tanks or inflight refueling
Performance: maximum speed 250 km/h (155 mph) at optimum altitude; cruising speed 230 km/h (143 mph); initial climb rate not revealed; service ceiling 6000 m (19,685 ft); hovering ceiling out of ground effect 3500 m (11,485 ft); range 800 km (497 miles) with maximum fuel; endurance 4 hours 30 minutes
Weights: empty 6100 kg (13,448 lb); normal take-off 11,000 kg (24,251 lb); maximum take-off 12,600 kg (27,778 lb)
Dimensions: rotor diameter, each 15·90 m (52 ft 2 in); length, fuselage 11·30 m (37 ft 0·9 in); height 5·40 m (17 ft 8·6 in); rotor disc area, total 198·56 m² (2,137·35 sq ft)

Variants

Ka-27 'Helix-A': successor to the Ka-25 series, this important type was introduced to service in 1982; it has considerably greater power and slightly greater dimensions for much enhanced performance and payload within an airframe still able to fit into the same hangar as the Ka-25; the 'Helix-A' is the dedicated ASW variant of the series
Ka-28 'Helix-A': export version of the 'Helix-A', presumably delivered with a different (probably lower) standard of avionics fit
Ka-27 'Helix-B': dedicated Naval Infantry assault transport, with accommodation for 16 fully equipped troops and the ability to deliver precision-guided weapons in support of amphibious landings; the NATO reporting designation 'Helix-C' has been given to the Ka-32 civil helicopter which can carry a 5000-kg (11,023-lb) payload over a range of 180 km (112 miles)
Ka-27 'Helix-D': general-purpose member of the Ka-27 series, and can be used in roles as diverse as SAR and under-way replenishment of warships at sea
Ka-29 'Helix-E': revealed in 1989, this is an updated version of the 'Helix-B' intended for the Naval Infantry assault role with armament that can comprise rockets and air-to-surface missiles, the former including four launchers for 80-mm (3·15-in) rockets and the latter AT-6 'Spiral' anti-tank missiles; the type carries a dorsal EW pod, and the powerplant of two 1640-kW (2,200-shp) TV3-117BK turboshafts provides for a maximum take-off weight of 12,000 kg (26,455 lb), a maximum speed of 265 km/h (165 mph) at sea level, a service ceiling of 3500 m (11,485 ft), and a range of 500 km (311 miles)

Below: Kamov Ka-27 'Helix-A' anti-submarine helicopter hovers above the guided missile destroyer *Udaloy*.

Opposite, bottom: The Ka-41 is the Naval Infantry's counterpart of the land-based Mi-28, and is designed for the support of amphibious operations with specialist sensors and weapons.

Kamov Ka-41 'Hokum'

(USSR)
Type: battlefield air-combat and close-air support helicopter
Accommodation: pilot and weapons officer
Armament (fixed): probably one 23- or 30-mm cannon
Armament (disposable): this is carried on six hardpoints (two under each stub wing and one at each wingtip) up to an unrevealed maximum weight of rocket launchers, anti-tank missiles, ASMs and AAMs
Electronics and operational equipment: communication and navigation equipment, plus a wide assortment of sensors such as low-light-level TV, FLIR, LRMTS etc
Powerplant and fuel system: two turboshafts of unrevealed rating and type, and a total internal fuel capacity of unrevealed quantity; no provision for inflight refuelling
Performance: maximum speed 350 km/h (217 mph); initial climb rate not revealed; service ceiling not revealed; radius 250 km (155 miles)
Weights: empty not revealed; maximum take-off about 7500 kg (16,534 lb)
Dimensions: rotor diameter, each 14·00 m (45 ft 11·2 in); length 13·50 m (44 ft 3·5 in); height 5·40 m (17 ft 8·6 in); rotor disc area, total 307·88 m² (3,314·06 sq ft)

Variant

Ka-41 'Hokum': designed with the co-axial twin main rotors typical of Kamov practice, the 'Hokum' is generally thought to be an advanced battlefield helicopter although few details of the type are available; in combination with a slim fuselage and retractable landing gear, the rotor design offers a high degree of agility and speed, while the elimination of the tail rotor offers the possibility of a shorter fuselage for reduced battlefield visibility and vulnerability; it is likely that the type is given the task of acting in the anti-helicopter escort role in conjunction with offensive operations by Mil Mi-24s and Mi-28s, and since it entered service in the later 1980s the 'Hokum' has provided the Soviets with a genuine combat helicopter type possessing advanced capabilities

Kawasaki C-1

(Japan)

Type: short-range STOL tactical transport aeroplane

Accommodation: flightcrew of five, and 60 troops, or 45 paratroops, 36 litters plus attendants, or 11900 kg (26,235 lb) of freight in the hold

Armament (fixed): none

Armament (disposable): none

Electronics and operational equipment: communication and navigation equipment

Powerplant and fuel system: two 14,500-lb (6577-kg) thrust Mitsubishi-built Pratt & Whitney JT8D-M-9 non-afterburning turbofans, and a total internal fuel capacity of 15,200 litres (3,344 Imp gal); no provision for drop tanks or inflight refuelling

Performance: maximum speed 805 km/h (500 mph) at 7620 m (25,000 ft); cruising speed 655 km/h (407 mph) at 10,670 m (35,000 ft); initial climb rate 1065 m (3,600 ft) per minute; service ceiling 11,580 m (38,000 ft); range 1300 km (808 miles) with maximum payload or 3355 km (2,085 miles) with maximum fuel

Weights: empty 23,320 kg (51,412 lb); normal take-off 38,700 kg (85,317 lb); maximum take-off 45,000 kg (99,206 lb)

Dimensions: span 30·60 m (100 ft 4·7 in); length 29·00 m (95 ft 1·7 in); height 10·00 m (32 ft 9·3 in); wing area 120·50 m² (1,297·1 sq ft)

Variants

C-1: developed as a medium-capacity STOL transport to replace Japan's ageing Curtiss C-46 Commando transports, the C-1 was a co-operative effort co-ordinated by Kawasaki, and the first prototype flew in November 1970, with deliveries of 24 aircraft made between 1974 and 1978, plus that of another three in 1981; five **C-1A** aircraft have 4732 litres (1,041 Imp gal) of additional tankage in the centre section for greater range

C-1 Kai: EW trainer version of the basic C-1A tactical transport, fitted with the TRDI/Mitsubishi Electrics ALQ-5 suite with eight nose/tail antennae, three underfuselage antennae and two lateral nose antennae

Below: The C-1 is a useful tactical airlifter operated in comparatively modest numbers by the Japanese air force.

117

Kawasaki (Boeing Vertol) KV 107/IIA-4

(Japan/USA)

Type: short-range transport medium helicopter

Accommodation: flightcrew of two, and 26 troops, or 15 litters or freight in the hold

Armament (fixed): none

Armament (disposable): none

Electronics and operational equipment: communication and navigation equipment

Powerplant and fuel system: two 1044-kW (1,400-shp) Ishikawajima-Harima-built General Electric CT58-IHI-140-1 turboshafts, and a total internal fuel capacity of 1324 litres (291 Imp gal) plus provision for 2551 litres (561 Imp gal) of auxiliary fuel in two extended-range fuel tanks on the fuselage sides; no provision for drop tanks or inflight refuelling

Performance: maximum speed 254 km/h (158 mph) at sea level; cruising speed 241 km/h (150 mph) at 1525 m (5,000 ft); initial climb rate 625 m (2,025 ft) per minute; service ceiling 5200 m (17,060 ft); hovering ceiling out of ground effect 2680 m (8,795 ft); range 1097 km (682 miles) with maximum fuel

Weights: empty 5251 kg (11,576 lb); normal take-off 8618 kg (19,000 lb); maximum take-off 9707 kg (21,400 lb)

Dimensions: rotor diameter, each 15·24 m (50 ft 0 in); length overall, rotors turning 25·40 m (83 ft 4 in) and fuselage 13·59 m (44 ft 7 in); height 5·13 m (16 ft 10 in); rotor disc area, total 182·41 m² (1,963·5 sq ft)

Variants

KV 107/II-3: the Japanese manufacturer of the Boeing Vertol Model 107 bought first a licence manufacturing agreement and then world rights in the late 1950s and early 1960s, and has since developed the Model 107 basic design for a number of specific applications; this is the mine countermeasures version with long-range tanks, an external hook and provision for the sweeping and (occasionally) the retrieval of mines

KV 107/II-4: tactical version of the series with a strengthened floor for the carriage of light vehicles and other loads of comparable weight

KV 107/II-5: long-range SAR variant, with tankage for 3785 litres (833 Imp gal) of fuel and specialized rescue equipment; the version delivered to Sweden is the **HKP 4C**, which has two Rolls-Royce Gnome H.1400-1 turboshafts for use in the anti-submarine role with different avionics (including Bendix ASQ-13B dunking sonar) and an armament of one FFV Tp 427 torpedo

KV 107/IIA-3: uprated version of the KV 107/II-3 with 1044-kW (1,400-shp) CT58-IHI-140-1 turboshafts

KV 107/IIA-4: uprated version of the KV 107/II-4 with 1044-kW (1,400-shp) CT58-IHI-140-1 turboshafts

KV 107/IIA-5: uprated version of the KV 107/II-5 with 1044-kW (1,400-shp) CT58-IHI-140-1 turboshafts

KV 107/IIA-SM-1: fire-fighting and crash rescue variant for Saudi Arabia with 606 litres (1033 Imp gal) of additional standard tankage and provision for a 1893-litre (416-Imp gal) internal ferry tank

KV 107/IIA-SM-2: casevac variant for Saudi Arabia; this has the same fuel provisions as the KV 107/IIA-SM-1

KV 107/IIA-SM-3: variant for Saudi Arabia

KV 107/IIA-SM-4: variant for Saudi Arabia

Kawasaki (Lockheed) P-2J

(Japan)

Type: maritime patrol and anti-submarine aeroplane

Accommodation: flightcrew of two, and a mission crew of 10 in the fuselage

Armament (fixed): none

Armament (disposable): this is carried in a lower-fuselage weapons bay up to an unrevealed maximum weight, and can include torpedoes and depth charges

Electronics and operational equipment: communication and navigation equipment, plus APS-80-N search radar with its antenna in an underfuselage radome, HSQ-101 MAD with its sensor in the tail 'sting', 'Julie' active acoustic ranging equipment with echo-sounding charges, AQA-3 'Jezebel' passive acoustic search equipment with sonobuoys, HSA-116 data processing and display system, APN-178B-N Doppler navigation, and HLR-101 ESM system

Powerplant and fuel system: two 3,060-shp (2282-kW) Ishikawajima-Harima-built General Electric T64-IHI-10E turboprops and two 1550-kg (3,417-lb) thrust Ishikawajima-Harima J3-IHI-7C non-afterburning turbojets, and a total internal fuel capacity of 12,947 litres (2,848 Imp gal): no provision for drop tanks or inflight refuelling

Performance: maximum speed 402 km/h (250 mph) at optimum altitude; cruising speed 370 km/h (230 mph) at 3050 m (10,000 ft); initial climb rate 550 m (1,804 ft) per minute; service ceiling 9145 m (30,000 ft); range 4450 km (2,765 miles) with maximum fuel

Weights: empty 19,278 kg (42,500 lb); maximum take-off 34,019 kg (75,000 lb)

Dimensions: span 30·87 m (101 ft 3·5 in) over tiptanks; length 29·23 m (95 ft 10·75 in); height 8·93 m (29 ft 3·5 in); wing area 92·90 m² (1,000·0 sq ft)

Variants

P-2J: Japanese development of the Lockheed P-2H Neptune with a stretched fuselage, additional power (in the form of two underwing turbojet engines) and a high percentage of Japanese electronics; first flown in July 1966 for service from late 1969, the type is now being phased out in favour of the Lockheed P-3C Orion, the type whose niche in the Japanese inventory the P-2J was designed to fill as a cheaper alternative

EP-2J: P-2Js converted to the Elint role with the HLR-105 and HLR-106 systems

UP-2J: P-2Js converted for the ECM and the drone launching and control roles

Below: The KV 107–II is the Japanese version of the American Boeing Vertol Model 107, and is produced in many specialized variants.

Kawasaki T-4

(Japan)
Type: basic and advanced flying and weapon trainer with secondary light attack capability
Accommodation: pupil and instructor in tandem on Stencel S-IIIS-3ER ejector seats
Armament (fixed): none
Armament (disposable): this is carried on five hardpoints (one under the fuselage and four under the wings) up to a maximum weight of about 2000 kg (4,409 lb) of bombs, rocket pods, gun pods and (later) AAMs and ASMs
Electronics and operational equipment: communication and navigation equipment, plus a Shimadze/Kaiser J/AVQ-1 HUD, a laser-gyro attitude and heading reference system, and (possibly as a retrofit) search radar
Powerplant and fuel system: two 1665-kg (3,671-lb) thrust Ishikawajima-Harima F3-IHI-30 non-afterburning turbofans, and a total internal fuel capacity of 2241 litres (493 Imp gal) plus provision for two 450-litre (99-Imp gal) drop tanks; no provision for inflight refuelling
Performance: maximum speed 955 km/h (593 mph) or Mach 0·9 at 11,000 m (36,090 ft) and 1038 km/h (645 mph) or Mach 0·85 at sea level; initial climb rate 3050 m (10,000 ft) per minute; service ceiling 15,240 m (50,000 ft); range 1297 km (806 miles) on internal fuel or 1668 km (1,036 miles) with two drop tanks
Weights: empty 3700 kg (8157 lb); normal take-off 5500 kg (12,125 lb); maximum take-off 7500 kg (16,534 lb)
Dimensions: span 9·94 m (32 ft 7·5 ft); length 13·00 m (42 ft 7·8 in); height 4·60 m (15 ft 1 in); wing area 21·00 m ^{2} (226·05 sq ft)

Variant

T-4: designed indigenously by Fuji, Kawasaki and Mitsubishi, and first flown in July 1985 with indigenously developed turbofan engines, the T-4 is developed as a basic and advanced trainer, but its five external hardpoints clearly mark it as capable of the light attack as well as weapon training role

Below: Illustrated here is the Kawasaki XT-4, first prototype of the twin-turbofan intermediate trainer. Rolled out on 17 April 1985, it made its first flight on 29 July and the first delivery was in December of the following year.

Above left: Though in the process of replacement by the P-3 Orion, the P-2J still serves the Japanese naval air force to the extent of 30 or more aircraft.

Lockheed C-5A Galaxy

(USA)
Type: long-range strategic freight transport aeroplane

Accommodation: flightcrew of five, 15 relief personnel and 75 troops on the upper deck, and 270 troops or 275,000 lb (124,740 kg) of freight in the hold

Armament (fixed): none

Armament (disposable): none

Electronics and operational equipment: communication and navigation equipment

Powerplant and fuel system: four 43,000-lb (19,504-kg) thrust General Electric TF39-GE-1C non-afterburning turbofans, and a total internal fuel capacity of 49,000 US gal (185,485 litres); no provision for drop tanks but provision for inflight refuelling

Performance: maximum cruising speed 564 mph (908 km/h) at 25,000 ft (7620 m); initial climb rate 1,725 ft (526 m) per minute; service ceiling 35,750 ft (10,895 m); range 3,434 miles (5526 km) with maximum payload

Weights: empty 374,000 lb (169,644 kg); maximum take-off 837,000 lb (379,663 kg)

Dimensions: span 222 ft 8·5 in (67·88 m); length 247 ft 10 in (75·54 m); height 65 ft 1·5 in (19·85 m); wing area 6,200·0 sq ft (575·98 m²)

Variants

C-5A Galaxy: designed as a strategic airlifter able to operate into and out of tactical airstrips, the Galaxy first flew in June 1968 and, though it never achieved the payload/range figures of the over-ambitious specification, it soon acquired an enviable reputation as a heavy-lift transport for items of outsize equipment such as artillery, armoured fighting vehicles and complete missile systems; the type features a multiple-wheel landing gear for low ground loadings, and a fuselage with rear ramp and lifting nose for the through-loading/unloading of freight, which is handled by powered cargo systems; in an effort to meet the US Air Force's payload/range requirements the manufacturer designed the wings to reduced fatigue limits, resulting in service problems, so the survivors of the 81-strong fleet of C-5As have been re-engined (with TF39-GE-1C turbofans in place of the original 41,000-lb/18,598-kg thrust TF39-GE-1s) and rewinged to a higher standard by July 1987, resulting in an increase in maximum take-off weight from 768,980 lb (348,809 kg) to 837,000 lb (379,663 kg), and in 2-g payload to 275,000 lb (124,740 kg)

C-5B Galaxy: 50 new aircraft built up to February 1989 to supplement the 77 upgraded C-5As; these aircraft are to the same basic standard as the remanufactured C-5As but with such refinements as more fuel-economical TF39-GE-1C turbofans, triple INSs, colour weather radar, and improved fatigue and corrosion resistance

The C-5B Galaxy is in essence a version of the upgraded C-5A with an improved airframe, more economical engines and updated systems.

Lockheed C-130H Hercules

(USA)
Type: short/medium-range medium tactical transport aeroplane

Accommodation: flightcrew of four or five, and 92 troops, or 64 paratroops, or 74 litters and two attendants, or 42,645 lb (19,344 kg) of freight in the hold

Armament (fixed): none

Armament (disposable): none

Electronics and operational equipment: communication and navigation equipment

Powerplant and fuel system: four 4,508-ehp (2796-kW) Allison T56-L-15 turboprops, and a total internal fuel capacity of 6,960 US gal (26,346 litres) plus provision for two 1,360-US gal (5146-litre) underwing tanks; no provision for drop tanks but provision for inflight refuelling

Performance: maximum speed 384 mph (618 km/h) at 30,000 ft (9145 m); cruising speed 375 mph (603 km/h); initial climb rate 1,900 ft (579 m) per minute; service ceiling 42,900 ft (13,075 m); range 2,487 miles (4002 km) with maximum payload or 4,721 miles (7600 km) with maximum fuel

Weights: empty 76,470 lb (34,687 kg); normal take-off 155,000 lb (70,310 kg); maximum take-off 175,000 lb (79,380 kg)

Dimensions: span 132 ft 7 in (40·41 m); length 97 ft 9 in (29·79 m); height 38 ft 3 in (11·66 m); wing area 1,745·0 sq ft (162·12 m²)

Variants

C-130A Hercules: first flown in YC-130 prototype form during August 1954 with 3,250-ehp (2423-kW) T56-A-1 turboprops driving three-blade propellers, the Hercules tactical transport is the mainstay of Western air arms' transport capabilities, and was responsible for what is now the standard configuration for military airlifters, namely a portly fuselage with an unobstructed hold of regular rectangular section accessed at truckbed height by an air-openable rear ramp/door under an upswept tail unit, and supported on the ground by multi-wheel landing gear with main units retracting into fuselage blisters and in the air by a high-mounted wing; the C-130A was the first production version, and entered service in December 1956 with 3,750-ehp (2796-kW) T56-A-1A or -9 turboprops driving three-blade propellers for a maximum take-off weight of 116,000 lb (52,616 kg); production amounted to 216, and machines of this basic type were converted into **C-130A-II** electronic reconnaissance aircraft, **AC-130A Spectre** gunships (with a side-firing armament of four 20-mm M61A1 cannon and four 7·62-mm/0·3-in Miniguns), **DC-130A** drone launch and control aircraft, **JC-130A** missile-tracking aircraft for use over the Atlantic test range, **NC-130A** special test aircraft, and **RC-130A** photo-survey aircraft

C-130B Hercules: improved production model with increased fuel capacity and 4,050-ehp (3021-kW) T56-A-7/7A turboprops driving four-blade propellers for a maximum take-off weight of 135,000 lb (61,235 kg); production amounted to 145 aircraft, and variants of this model were the **C-130B-II** (later **RC-130B**) electronic reconnaissance aircraft, the **HC-130B** SAR aircraft, the **JC-130B** recovery aircraft for satellite data capsules, the **KC-130B** inflight-refuelling tankers, and the **WC-130B** weather reconnaissance aircraft

C-130D Hercules: ski-equipped version for arctic and antarctic service; 13 were produced as conversions of C-130As

C-130E Hercules: third production version of the transport series, in essence a long-range version of the C-130B with two permanent underwing tanks as well as increased internal capacity; production for the US air Force amounted to 428, and variants of the transport version were the **AC-130E Spectre** gunships (redesignated AC-130H after the retrofitting of T56-A-15 turboprops and the addition of inflight-refuelling capability), the **DC-130E** drone launch and control aircraft, the **EC-130E ABCCC** special forces command and control aircraft fitted with the USC-15 battlefield command capsule in the hold (redesignated **EC-130H** after the retrofitting of T56-A-15 turboprops), the **EC-130E 'Coronet Solo II'** electronic surveillance aircraft for the Air National Guard, the **HC-130E** crew recovery aircraft, the **MC-130E 'Combat Talon I'** special forces insertion and extraction aircraft (redesignated **MC-130H(CT)** after the retrofitting of T56-A-15 turboprops and more advanced avionics), and the **WC-130E** weather reconnaissance aircraft; the MC-130E/MC-130H(CT) type has a crew of nine including the winch operation for the Fulton equipment for the inflight recovery of a 500-lb (227-kg) load from the ground, APQ-122(V) dual-mode terrain-following and/or terrain-avoidance radar, an EW suite based on that of the B-52G/H and including the ALR-69 RWR, 'Have Quick' secure voice communications, and satellite navigation capability

C-130F Hercules: US Navy equivalent of the C-130B with T56-A-16 engines, extra fuselage fuel tankage, provision for RATO gear, and wheel/ski landing gear; production amounted to four aircraft; the **KC-130F** is a US Marine Corps inflight-refuelling tanker based on the C-130F but featuring 4,910-ehp (3661-kW) T56-A-16 turboprops plus underwing refuelling pods of the hose-and-drogue variety, and another variant is the ski-equipped **LC-130F** for antarctic use

C-130G Hercules: US Navy equivalent of the C-130E but powered by T56-A-16 turboprops; the four aircraft were revised as VLF aircraft with the TACAMO II package (for relay of communications with submerged submarines) under the designation **EC-130G**

C-130H Hercules: uprated version of the C-130E with airframe/avionics modifications and T56-A-15 turboprops flat-rated to 4,508 ehp (3362 kW); variants of this major production model were the **AC-130H Spectre** gunships with heavy side-firing armament (two 20-mm cannon, one 40-mm Bofors gun and one 105-mm/4·13-in howitzer) plus an advanced avionics/sensor fit (including AAD-7 FLIR, ASQ-115 low-light-level TV, AVQ-19 laser ranger and designator, ASD-5 'Black Crow' vehicle ignition system detector, ALQ-119 podded ECM, SUU-42 IR countermeasures, APQ-150 beacon tracking radar, and ALR-69 RWR), the **DC-130H** drone launch and control aircraft, the **EC-130H 'Compass Call II'** communication jamming aircraft with the special 'Compass Call' equipment package, the **HC-130H** rescue and recovery aircraft with spacecraft re-entry tracking radar and Fulton recovery gear (redesignated **JHC-130H** after conversion for the aerial recovery of satellite data capsules), the **KC-130H** inflight-refuelling tankers, the **LC-130H** aircraft similar to the LC-130R, the **MC-130H 'Combat Talon II'** 9/11-crew special forces aircraft (based on the MC-130E but with a higher level of automation and Emerson APQ-170 digital terrain-following/terrain-avoidance radar, Texas

Instruments AAQ-15 IR detector, FLIR in a retractable pod, dual INSs, a Global Positioning System receiver, and highly complex ECM and ESM equipment based on those of the Boeing B-52G/H and including the ITT ALQ-172 'Pave Mint' EW suite and the ALQ-8 ECM pod), the **PC-130H** maritime patrol aircraft (originally designated **C-130H-MP** and fitted with search radar, SLAR, FLIR, low-light level TV, IR linescan and imaging IR sensors), the **VC-130H** VIP transport and the **WC-130H** weather reconnaissance aircraft

C-130H-30 Hercules: C-130H derivative with the fuselage of the L-100-30 civil model, which features a stretch in overall length to 112ft 9 in (34·37 m) at an empty weight of 80,242 lb (36,397 kg) to make possible the carriage of 128 troops, or 98 paratroops, or 97 litters plus attendants, or an equivalent freight load

C-130K Hercules: C-130H derivative with T56-A-15 turboprops and other detail modifications for British service, in which the type is known as the **Hercules C.Mk 1**; some aircraft have been converted for inflight-refuelling as six **Hercules C.Mk 1K** tankers and 16 **Hercules C.Mk 1P** probe-equipped receiver types; one has been converted for weather reconnaissance as the **Hercules W.Mk 2**, and 20 have been revised with the stretched fuselage of the L-100-30 as the **Hercules C.Mk 3** or, with inflight-refuelling capability, **Hercules C.Mk 3P**; all other Hercules C.Mk1 and Hercules C.Mk3 aircraft are to be fitted with inflight-refuelling probes; these British aircraft carry a variety of countermeasures, most commonly the Racal Orange Blossom (repackaged MIR-2) ESM system and the General Instrument ALR-66(V)7 RWR

HC-130N Hercules: advanced spacecraft and satellite data capsule recovery aircraft based on the C-130H

HC-130P Hercules: tanker derivative of the HC-130H for the inflight-refuelling of helicopters and the aerial recovery of aircrew

EC-130Q Hercules: advanced version of the EC-130G for the TACAMO (TAke Charge And Move Out) role associated with communications relay between the national command authority and submerged SSBNs; the aircraft have the TACAMO III, IV or IVB equipment suites

KC-130R Hercules: version of the KC-130H for the US Marine Corps with 6,320 US gal (23,924 litres) of fuel in addition to the normal internal capacity

LC-130R Hercules: ski-equipped derivative of the C-130H for the US Navy

RC-130S Hercules: redesignation of JC-130A aircraft retrofitted with high-intensity lighting for nocturnal SAR missions

KC-130T Hercules: advanced version of the KC-130R for the US Marine Corps with the capability to refuel helicopters and/or high-performance combat aircraft

AC-130U Spectre: updated AC-130H gunship produced as new-build aircraft; this variant has a modified version of the Hughes APG-70 radar for genuine all-weather capability; the armament fit includes one 105-mm (4·13-in) howitzer, one 40-mm Bofors gun, and one trainable GAU-12 25-mm cannon

C-130 AEW: Lockheed proposal for an AEW aircraft based on the airframe/powerplant combination of the current military Hercules fitted with a palletized tactical compartment fed with data from the two antennae (mounted in bulbous nose and tail fairings) of the GEC APY-920 radar developed for the BAe Nimrod AEW.Mk 3; for a cost considerably more modest than those of current AEW aircraft, this proposal offers 360° surveillance to a radius of 230 miles (370 km) from 27,000 ft (8230 m); on-station patrol time is planned as 12 hours

L-100: civil transport version of the basic C-130 with 4,050-shp (3020-kW) Allison 501-D22 turboprops; several of these and later aircraft have been sold to smaller air arms

L-100-20: version of the L-100 with the fuselage stretched by 8·33ft (2·54m) and powered by 4,508-shp (3362-kW) 501-D22A turboprops

L-100-30: derivative of the L-100-20 with the fuselage stretched 6·67 ft (2·03 m)

The C-130 Hercules is operated in many variants by a large number of air forces. This is an aeroplane of the Italian air force, which operates 12 C-130Hs in the basic transport role.

Lockheed C-141B StarLifter

(USA)
Type: long-range logistic transport aeroplane
Accommodation: flightcrew of four, and 154 troops or 90,880 lb (41,222 kg) of freight in the hold
Armament (fixed): none
Armament (disposable): none
Electronics and operational equipment: communication and navigation equipment
Powerplant and fuel system: four 21,000-lb (9526-kg) thrust Pratt & Whitney TF33-P-7 non-afterburning turbofans, and a total internal fuel capacity of 23,600 US gal (89,335 litres); no provision for drop tanks but provision for inflight refuelling
Performance: maximum cruising speed 566 mph (910 km/h) at optimum altitude; initial climb rate 2,920 ft (890 m) per minute; service ceiling 41,600 ft (12,680 m); range 2,935 miles (4725 km) with maximum payload; ferry range 6,390 miles (10280 km)
Weights: empty 148,120 lb (67,186 kg); maximum take-off 343,000 lb (155,580 kg)
Dimensions: span 159 ft 11 in (48·74 m); length 168 ft 3·5 in (51·29 m); height 39 ft 3 in (11·96 m); wing area 3,228·0 sq ft (299·88 m²)

Variant
C-141B StarLifter: first flown in 1963, the StarLifter was the USAF's first turbofan-powered airlifter, and designed in reponse to a requirement for a long-range strategic partner to the short/medium-range C-130 series; production of the initial C-141A series amounted to 284 aircraft, and these began to enter service in April 1965, soon building a good reputation for reliability and structural strength; however, the principal limitation of the type was soon discovered to be its volume-limited freight capacity, meaning that the hold in the 145-ft (44·20-m) fuselage was generally full long before the designed payload weight of 70,847 lb (32,136 kg) had been reached; in March 1977, therefore, Lockheed flew the prototype of a version with the fuselage stretched 13 ft 4 in (4·06 m) in front of the wing and 10 ft 0 in (3·05 m) aft of the wing; this allowed the carriage of 13 rather than 10 standard pallets; it was thus decided to revise all 270 surviving aircraft to this much superior C-141B standard, an inflight-refuelling capacity being added at the same time; the last conversion was redelivered in June 1982, the programme having added the equivalent of 87 new C-141As to the fleet without additional crew requirements or anything like the purchase cost of the new aircraft

(USA)
Type: multi-role attack, strike and reconnaissance fighter
Accommodation: pilot on a Martin-Baker GQ7F zero/zero ejector seat
Armament (fixed): one 20-mm General Electric M61A1 Vulcan rotary-barrel cannon with 750 rounds
Armament (disposable): this is carried on seven hardpoints (one under the fuselage rated at 2,000 lb/907 kg, two under each wing with the inner two units each rated at 1,000 lb/454 kg and the outer two units each at 500 lb/227 kg, and one at each wingtip rated at 1,000 lb/454 kg) up to a maximum weight of 4,310 lb (1955 kg); the wingtip rails carry AIM-9 Sidewinder AAMs, and the weapons accommodated on the other hardpoints include the 10/20-kiloton B57 or 100/500-kiloton B61 free-fall nuclear weapons, Kormoran and Penguin anti-ship missiles, AGM-65 Maverick ASM, 2,000-, 1,000-, 750-, 500- and 250-lb (907-, 454-, 340-, 227- and 113-kg) free-fall or retarded bombs, cluster bombs, and LAU-series pods for 2·75- and 5-in (70- and 127-mm) rockets
Electronics and operational equipment: communication and navigation equipment, plus Autonetics F15A NASARR (North American Search And Ranging Radar) fire-control radar, General Electric ASG-14 optical sight, Litton LN-3 INS, and provision for options such as ECM pods and the Oldelft Orpheus reconnaissance pod
Powerplant and fuel system: one 15,800-lb (7167-kg) afterburning thrust General Electric J79-GE-11A turbojet, and a total internal fuel capacity of 896 US gal (3392 litres) plus provision for one 225-US gal (852-litre), two 195-US gal (740-litre) and two 170-US gal (645-litre) drop tanks; no provision for inflight refuelling
Performance: maximum speed 1,450 mph (2333 km/h) or Mach 2·2 at 36,000 ft (10,970 m); cruising speed 610 mph (981 km/h); initial climb rate 55,000 ft (15,765 m) per minute; service ceiling 58,000 ft (17,680 m); range 300 miles (483 km) with maximum warload or 1,815 miles (2920 km) with four drop tanks
Weights: empty 14,900 lb (6758 kg); normal take-off 21,690 lb (9838 kg); maximum take-off 28,779 lb (13,054 kg)
Dimensions: span 21 ft 11 in (6·68 m) without tip stores; length 54 ft 9 in (16·69 m); height 13 ft 6 in (4·11 m); wing area 196·1 sq ft (18·22 m²)

Variants
F-104A Starfighter: evolved in response to a Korean War US Air Force requirement for a fast-

climbing interceptor, the Starfighter was designed with a barrel-like fuselage containing the avionics, pilot, afterburning turbojet and fuel, and with unswept but diminutive flying surfaces of exceptionally low thickness/chord ratio; the XF-104 prototype first flew in March 1954 on the power of a 10,200-lb (4627-kg) thrust Wright XJ65-W-6, but four years of testing and evaluation followed before the F-104A entered service with a fuselage lengthened by 5 ft 6 in (1·68 m) and power provided by the 14,800-lb (6713-kg) afterburning thrust General Electric J79-GE-3A turbojet; production amounted to 153 aircraft, and a

few of these elderly fighters (armed with a single 20-mm M61A1 cannon and two AIM-9 Sidewinder AAMs) remain in service as interceptors with the Taiwanese air force

F-104D Starfighter: two-seat conversion trainer variant of the F-104C tactical strike version, and powered by the 15,800-lb (7167-kg) afterburning thrust J79-GE-7 turbojet; the **F-104DJ** was the version for Japan; production amounted to 21 US and 20 Japanese aircraft

F-104G Starfighter: the earlier Starfighter variants had not been very successful in US service, but with the development of the F-104G variant the type became a major commercial and military success, for this multi-role fighter was accepted for widespread European service; features of the design were a strengthened structure, an enlarged empennage and other aerodynamic improvements, advanced avionics, superior weapons capability (in terms of quantity and type), and a more powerful engine; 1,127 of this model were built, mostly in Europe, the number being swelled by 200 basically similar **CF-104** aircraft (J79-OEL-7 turbojet and inflight-refuelling capability) built under licence in Canada by Canadair and 210 **F-104J** aircraft mostly built under licence in Japan by Mitsubishi

RF-104G Starfighter: tactical reconnaissance variant of the F-104G with three cameras

TF-104G Starfighter: two-seat operational conversion trainer of the F-104G but retaining full combat capability; the **CF-104D** was the Canadian equivalent powered by the J79-OEL-7 turbojet

Below: F-104G Starfighters.

Below left: A C-141A StarLifter of the 63rd Military Airlift Wing.

Lockheed F-117A

Lockheed P-3C Orion

(USA)

Type: 'stealth' reconnaissance and attack aeroplane

Accommodation: pilot on an ejector seat

Armament (fixed): none

Armament (disposable): this is carried in a paired lower-fuselage weapons bay up to a maximum weight of about 4,000 lb (1814 kg) of specialized anti-radiation and comparable 'smart' weapons

Electronics and operational equipment: communication and navigation equipment, plus one INS and a number of passive sensors and target-acquisition systems including a fixed FLIR under the forward fuselage, and a FLIR and laser designator in a trainable turret forward of the cockpit

Powerplant and fuel system: probably two 12,000-lb (5443-kg) thrust General Electric F404 non-afterburning turbofans, and an internal fuel capacity of unrevealed quantity; provision for inflight refuelling

Performance: highly classified, but probably including subsonic speed at altitude and a combat radius of about 500 miles (805 km)

Weights: ('guesstimated') empty 15,000 lb (6804 kg); maximum take-off 30,000 lb (13,608 kg); maximum take-off 45,250 lb (20,525 kg)

Dimensions: ('guesstimated') span 42 ft 0 in (12·80 m); length 67 ft 3 in (20·50 m); height between 12 ft 0 in (3·66 m); and 16 ft 0 in (4·88 m); wing area not revealed

Variant

F-117A: virtually nothing is known of this important machine, the world's first 'stealth' aircraft to reach operational status after development from 1978 via the XST (Experimental Stealth Technology) aeroplane, of which six were built in the 1970s; the first F-117A flew in June 1981 and the type entered service in October 1983, but until November 1988 the US Air Force denied the very existence of the design, which was planned after a number of Israeli setbacks with US aircraft pitted against Soviet surface-to-air weapon systems in the 1973 'Yom Kippur' War; but though it was first imagined that development was undertaken on the conceptual basis of the Lockheed A-12/SR-71 series with highly curvaceous surfaces and a large proportion of radar-absorbent materials to create an aeroplane designated F-19A, the release of a poor photograph in 1988 and better photographs in 1989 revealed that the real F-117A type is a highly angular type of flying-wing basic design with a butterfly tail and elements of lifting-body vehicle design, the whole concept being schemed to reflect incoming electromagnetic radiation from the emitter and to penetrate enemy airspace to detect and then destroy high-value SAM systems and their radar systems, relying on low visual, electromagnetic and IR signatures to achieve this without detection; the weapon bays each appear to measure some 14 ft 9 in (4·50 m) in length and 5 ft 0 in (1·52 m) in width, suggesting a single weapon of the AGM-65 Maverick or AGM-88 HARM type or a larger laser-guided bomb; all data are designed to indicate probabilities rather than actualities; production is to total 59 aircraft up to 1990 (100 are planned) and three were lost in accidents up to mid-1989

(USA)

Type: maritime patrol and anti-submarine aeroplane

Accommodation: flightcrew of five, and a mission crew of five in the cabin

Armament (fixed): none

Armament (disposable): this is carried in a lower-fuselage weapon bay to a maximum of 7,250 lb (3289 kg) and on 10 hardpoints (five under each wing, with the units of the pairs from inboard each rated at 2,000 lb/907 lb, 2,000 lb/907 kg, 2,000 lb/907 kg, 1,000 lb/454 kg and 500 lb/227 kg) up to an overall maximum weight of 20,000 lb (9072 kg); the weapon bay can accommodate two 10/20-kiloton B57 nuclear weapons, or one 2,000-lb (907-kg) mine, or three 1,000-lb (454-kg) mines, or between three and eight depth bombs, or between four and eight torpedoes; the underwing hardpoints can carry six 2,000-lb (907-kg) mines, or 10 1,000- or 500-lb (454- or 227-kg) mines, or rockets, or four AGM-84 Harpoon anti-ship missiles

Electronics and operational equipment: communication and navigation equipment, plus Texas Instruments APS-115 search radar with nose and tail antennae, Texas Instruments ASQ-81(V)1 MAD with its sensor in the tail 'sting', ASA-64 sub-

Below: The F-117A 'stealth' aeroplane marks a technical revolution in warplane history.

Below right: The P-3C Orion (here in Australian markings) is the Western world's most important land-based maritime patroller.

marine anomaly detector, AAS-36 FLIR, AXR-13 low-light-level TV, 84 sonobuoys plus associated ARR-72 receivers and AQA-7 indicator sets, ASQ-114 digital computer, AYA-8 data processor, ASA-66 tactical consoles, two Litton LTN-72 INSs, APN-227 Doppler navigation, ALQ-78 ECM pods (being replaced by ALQ-77 wingtip ESM) and cameras

Powerplant and fuel system: four 4,910-ehp (3661-kW) Allison T56-A-14 turboprops, and a total internal fuel capacity of 9,200 US gal (34,826 litres); no provision for drop tanks or inflight refuelling

Performance: maximum speed 473 mph (761 km/h) at 15,000 ft (4570 m); cruising speed 378 mph (608 km/h) at 25,000 ft (7620 m); initial climb rate 1,950 ft (594 m) per minute; service ceiling 28,300 ft (8625 m); radius 1,550 miles (2494 km) for a 3-hour patrol

Weights: empty 61,490 lb (27,892 kg); normal take-off 135,000 lb (61,235 kg); maximum take-off 142,000 lb (64,410 kg)

Dimensions: span 99 ft 8 in (30·37 m); length 116 ft 10 in (35·61 m); height 33 ft 8·5 in (10·27 m); wing area 1,300·0 sq ft (120·77 m²)

Variants

P-3A Orion: first flown in prototype form in November 1959 as a development of the airframe/powerplant combination of the L-188 Electra turboprop airliner (though with the fuselage shortened by 7 ft 4 in/2·24 m), the P-3A entered service in August 1962 with 4,500-ehp (3356-kW) T56-A-10W turboprops, 10 underwing hardpoints for a variety of stores up to a weight of 3,000 lb (1361 kg), and a substantial weapons bay built into a bulged lower fuselage for an additional 6,000 lb (2722 kg) of stores; the type could also be used as an emergency transport with seating for 50 troops; production amounted to 157 aircraft, some of them retrofitted with T56-A-14 turboprops, and though the type no longer serves in its maritime patrol and anti-submarine roles, in-service derivatives (all produced by conversion) are the **CP-3A** transport, the **RP-3** oceanographic reconnaissance, and the **VP-3A** staff transport models

P-3B Orion: this second production series is powered by the 4,910-ehp (3661-kW) T56-A-14 without the water/alcohol injection of the P-3A's powerplant; the type was fitted with the Deltic tactical processing system rather than the suite derived from that of the P-2 Neptune used in the initial P-3A aircraft; in-service modification to the survivors of the US Navy's original 125-strong fleet has kept the anti-submarine capability of the type up to high standards, and export models have customer-dictated variations on the basic theme (the Australian aircraft using the Marconi AQS-901 acoustic processing system and the New Zealand aircraft having the Boeing UDACS display and control consoles) plus Texas Instruments APS-134(V) search radar

P-3C Orion: current model, of which 233 were built with the same basic airframe and powerplant as the P-3B but incorporating the A-NEW avionics suite with new sensors and controls, and based on the Univac ASQ-114 computer system; from 1975 the designation **P-3C Update I** was used for new-production aircraft with increased computer memory, more sensitive acoustic processing equipment and upgraded navigation equipment; a year later the **P-3C Update II** was introduced with an IR detection system and provision for AGM-84 Harpoon anti-ship missiles;

the **P-3C Update III** was introduced in 1985 with an IBM Proteus acoustic processing system and a new ARS-3 sonobuoy signal receiver allowing the aeroplane to plot the position of any buoy without flying over it; for service in the late 1980s Boeing is developing an Update IV mission avionics package with further enhanced processing capability and more sensitive acoustic sensors plus the Litton ALR-77 tactical ESM suite; some existing aircraft have been improved to a partial Update IV standard with the semi-official designation **P-3C Update 3·5**; the Update IV suite is to retrofitted in 80 P-3C Upate II aircraft to produce a type to which the designation **P-3D Orion** will probably be allocated; it is also possible that the aircraft will be retrofitted with General Electric turboprops

RP-3D Orion: one P-3C reconfigured as a special research aircraft

WP-3D Orion: two P-3Cs reconfigured for weather reconnaissance

EP-3E Orion: 12 aircraft (10 P-3As and two EP-3Bs) reworked as electronic surveillance/countermeasures aircraft; this variant has canoe fairing above and below the fuselage, and a ventral radome forward of the wing; in the electronic fit are the ALQ-110 radar signal-gathering system, the ALD-8 radio direction finder, the ARGO Systems ALR-52 frequency-measuring receiver, the Magnavox ALQ-108 IFF jammer, the Loral ALQ-78 ESM system, the ALQ-171 Elint system, GTE-Sylvania ALR-60 radio communications interception, recording and analysis system, the Sander ALR-132 IR jammer, and the Raytheon ALQ-76 noise jamming pod; the type's maximum take-off weight is 142,000 lb (64411 kg)

P-3F Orion: six Iranian aircraft, basically similar to the P-3C

P-3K Orion: six New Zealand aircraft to basic P-3B standard when delivered; in the early 1980s the aircraft were modernized by Boeing to a standard approximating the P-3C in the 'Rigel I' programme with new control consoles, the Litton LTN-72 inertial and LTN-211 Omega navigation systems, Texas Instruments APS-134(V) radar and AAS-36 IR detection system; the RNZAF is planning a 'Rigel II' upgrade for a new ESM system and a better acoustic processing system able to handle inputs from a mix of sonobuoy types

P-3P Orion: six ex-Australian P-3Bs reworked to

approximately P-3C standard for the air force; the P-3P has a combined rad and navigation suite featuring n updated sensors linked by MIL-1553B digital databus

P-3 AEW&C: development of surplus P-3B airframes as AWACS aircraft with a tactical compartment in the fuselage fed with data from an overhead rotodome for the antenna of the APS-138 radar; the concept offers potential customers with a comparatively cheap AEW aircraft, while the attractions for current Orion operators are reduced spares holdings, reduced crew and maintenance training requirements, and a considerable background of operating experience with the basic airframe/powerplant combination; the first 'production' aircraft are US Coast Guard machines with APS-125 (possibly APS-145) radar and the name **Blue Sentinel**

CP-140 Aurora: Canadian equivalent of the P-3C series, but fitted with an electronic suite based on that of the Lockheed S-3A Viking carrierborne anti-submarine aircraft; the type first flew in March 1979, and has a maximum range of 5,180 miles (8336 km), which translates to an 8·2-hour patrol endurance at a radius of 1,150 miles (1850 km); the type also has an important resources exploration and SAR responsibility

CP-140A Arcturus: arctic and maritime surveillance derivative of the CP-140 with less sophisticated equipment and Texas Instruments APS-137 radar as its only sensor; the type has a crew of six, can carry but not release torpedoes, and has provision for aerial release of two search and rescue packs each containing a multi-seat liferaft

Kawasaki (Lockheed) P-3C: P-3C Orion Update II manufactured under licence in Japan with engines produced under licence by Ishikawajima-Harima; the **EP-3C** is an Elint version of the P-3C being developed by Kawasaki for the Japanese Maritime Self-Defense Force, and the first of nine aircraft is due for delivery in 1991

L-188 Electra: airliner from which the Orion series was developed, but not a great commercial success after a series of three crashes broke public confidence in the type; the type is still in service, often as a freighter, and several have been acquired by smaller air arms

ckheed P-7A

(USA)

Type: maritime patrol and anti-submarine aeroplane

Accommodation: flightcrew of five, and a mission crew of five in the cabin

Armament (fixed): none

Armament (disposable): this is carried in a lower-fuselage weapon bay and on 12 hardpoints (six under each wing) up to a maximum weight of 38,400 lb (17,418 kg) of nuclear weapons, mines, depth bombs, torpedoes and anti-ship missiles

Electronics and operational equipment: communication and navigation equipment, plus Texas Instruments APS-137(V) search radar with nose and tail antennae, Texas Instruments ASQ-81(V)1 MAD with its sensor in the tail 'sting', FLIR, low-light-level TV, sonobuoys with a new acoustic data-processing system, digital computer, tactical consoles, two INSs, Doppler navigation, Litton ALR-77 ESM and cameras

Powerplant and fuel system: four 5,000-shp (3728-kW) General Electric T407-GE-400 turboprops, and a total internal fuel weight of 66,350 lb (30,096 kg); no provision for drop tanks or inflight refuelling

Performance: maximum speed 473+ mph (761+ km/h) at 15,000 ft (4570 m); initial climb rate 2,890+ ft (881+ m) per minute; service ceiling 28,000 ft (8535 m); radius 1,840 miles (2961 km) for a patrol of 5 hours 54 minutes

Weights: empty 73,750 lb (33,453 kg); maximum take-off 171,000 lb (77,566 kg)

Dimensions: span 106 ft 8 in (32·51 m); length 123 ft 0 in (37·49 m); height not revealed; wing area not revealed

Variant

P-7A: initial designation of 125 new-build Orions to meet the US Navy's LRAACA (Long-Range Air Anti-submarine Capable Aircraft) requirement, with General Electric turboprops and the Boeing-integrated Update IV mission avionics package; the type was first proposed with the designation P-3G Orion, but in recognition of the 78 major revisions incorporated in the new type it was redesignated P-7 during 1989; externally, the P-7A will be virtually indistinguishable from the P-3 apart from its slightly larger dimensions and lack of a MAD 'sting', but will in reality be almost completely a new design retaining only the fuselage barrel of the older variants, in this instance mated to new engines, a new flightdeck with 'glass' instruments and a fly-by-wire control system, new mission avionics, and even new structural materials; whereas the P-3C can carry a maximum of 84 sonobuoys, the P-7A will carry 120 pre-loaded sonobuoys in pre-loaded packs fore and aft of the wing, 38 inside the aeroplane for loading into pressurized chutes during flight, and up to 150 in dense packs on up to 10 underwing hardpoints; the first of two prototypes should fly late in 1991 for a service entry in 1994, and it is likely that more than 125+ will be produced for the US Navy, plus 12 for West Germany and possibly more for other Western nations

Right: The S-3A Viking is a truly remarkable achievement that combines the operational capabilities of the P-3 with a long-ranged airframe small enough for carrierborne use.

Opposite: The SR-71A is disappearing from US Air Force first-line service, but is still the world's fastest operational aeroplane.

Lockheed S-3A Viking

(USA)

Type: carrierborne anti-submarine aeroplane

Accommodation: flightcrew of two, and a mission crew of two in the fuselage, all on Douglas Escapac 1-E ejector seats

Armament (fixed): none

Armament (disposable): this is carried in a lower-fuselage weapons bay to a maximum weight of 4,000 lb (1814 kg) and on two hardpoints (one under each wing) up to a maximum weight of 3,000 lb (1361 kg); the weapons bay can carry one 10/20-kiloton B57 nuclear weapon, or four 1,000-lb (454-kg) bombs or mines, or two or four depth bombs, or four torpedoes, and the underwing hardpoints can carry six 500-lb (227-kg) bombs, rocket pods and Rockeye II cluster bombs

Electronics and operational equipment: communication and navigation equipment, with, in addition, Texas Instruments APS-116 search radar, Texas Instruments ASQ-81(V)1 MAD with its sensor in the tail 'sting', OR-89 FLIR, 60 sonobuoys and associated OL-82 processing system and separate sonobuoy reference system, plus an AYK-10 digital central computer, ALR-87 ESM system, ASN-92(V) INS and APN-200 Doppler navigation

Powerplant and fuel system: two 9,275-lb (4207-kg) thrust General Electric TF34-GE-2 non-afterburning turbofans, and a total internal fuel capacity of 1,900 US gal (7192 litres) plus provision for two 300-US gal (1136-litre) drop tanks. In addition, there is also provision for inflight refuelling

Performance: maximum speed 518 mph (834 km/h) at optimum altitude; cruising speed 426 mph (686 km/h); initial climb rate 4,200+ ft (1280+ m) per minute; service ceiling 35,000+ ft (10,670+ m); range 2,300+ miles (3700+ km)

Weights: empty 26,650 lb (12,088 kg); normal take-off 42,500 lb (19,277 kg); maximum take-off 52,540 lb (23,832 kg)

Dimensions: span 68 ft 8 in (20·93 m); length 53 ft 4 in (16·26 m); height 22 ft 9 in (6·93 m); wing area 598·0 sq ft (55·56 m²)

Variants

S-3A Viking: delivered from October 1973 after a first flight in January 1973, the S-3A is the US Navy's mainstay carrierborne anti-submarine aircraft, and a classic example of how to pour a quart into a pint pot; the capacious fuselage holds the flight and tactical crews in considerable comfort, together with the mass of computerized mission avionics, while the wings hold the substantial fuel load and support the two fuel-economical turbofans

ES-3A Viking: under this designation Lockheed is developing an electronic reconnaissance variant of the Viking to succeed the Douglas EA-3B Skywarrior; the type will carry some 63 Elint-dedicated antennae for an electronic suite based on that of the land-based EP-3E Orion; current plans call for nine such aircraft, whose most important distinguishing features are a dorsal hump to accommodate the omni-directional receiver antenna, and bulged 'cheek' fairings in place of the S-3's bomb bay doors; the automation of this suite allows the ES-3A to have a crew of only four (all carried on ejector seats) by comparison with the EA-3B's crew of seven (of whom only two are carried on ejector seats)

KS-3A Viking: sole inflight-refuelling variant

US-3A Viking: six COD (Carrier Onboard Delivery) aircraft

S-3B Viking: upgraded S-3A variant produced by conversion of existing aircraft in the Viking's Weapon System Improvement Program (WSIP); the modification programme includes a Sanders OL-82A acoustic signal-processing system, improved ESM system for greater cover, a Hazeltine ARR-78 sonobuoy receiver system with enhanced reference capabilities, a Texas Instruments APS-116 radar upgraded to APS-137(V) standard with inverted synthetic-aperture techniques and other improvements, and provision for AGM-84 Harpoon anti-ship missiles; the first of 40 aircraft was converted with a Lockheed-produced kit for redelivery in December 1987, and the total number of conversions may reach 160 aircraft

Lockheed SR-71A

(USA)
Type: strategic reconnaissance aeroplane
Accommodation: pilot and systems operator in tandem on ejector seats
Armament (fixed): none
Armament (disposable): none
Electronics and operational equipment: communication and navigation equipment, plus a

speed 1,980 mph (3186 km/h) or Mach 3·0 at high altitude; service ceiling 100,000 ft (30,480 m); range 2,980 miles (4800 km) on internal fuel
Weights: empty 60,000 lb (27,216 kg); maximum take-off 170,000 lb (77,111 kg)
Dimensions: span 55 ft 7 in (16·94 m); length 107 ft 5 in (32·74 m); height 18 ft 6 in (5·64 m); wing area 1,800·0 sq ft (167·3 m²)

turbojets burning special JP-7 fuel carried by dedicated Boeing KC-135Q inflight-refuelling tankers for maximization of the type's prodigious range; at Mach 3 the engines produce only 18% of the powerplant's total thrust, the remainder being generated by inlet suction (54%) and the special nozzles at the rear of the multiple-flow nacelles (28%); the reconnaissance systems car-

number of classified optical, thermal and electronic reconnaissance systems
Powerplant and fuel system: two 32,500-lb (14,742-kg) afterburning thrust Pratt & Whitney JT11D-20B bleed turbojets, and a total internal fuel capacity of 12,000+ US gal (45,425+ litres); no provision for drop tanks but provision for inflight refuelling
Performance: maximum speed 2,250 mph (3620 km/h) or Mach 3·4 at high altitude; cruising

Variants
SR-71A: this is the world's highest-performance aircraft, and began to enter service in 1966 after a evolutionary design process from the A-11 drone-carrying reconnaissance aircraft and YF-12 interceptor; the aircraft is built largely of titanium to withstand the extreme heat generated by air friction at Mach 3 even at high altitude, and the type's advanced aerodynamics are matched by a potent powerplant centred on the two bleed-

ried by the 'Blackbird' (so-called for its heat-radiating black finish) are highly classified, but it is known that optical, IR and electronic sensors are carried in special bays in the wing/fuselage chine fairings, and can survey more than 100,000 sq miles (259,000 km²) per hour
SR-71B: two-seat operational conversion trainer variant
SR-71C: one SR-71A converted to SR-71B standard

Lockheed TR-1A

(USA)

Type: tactical/operational reconnaissance aeroplane

Accommodation: pilot on an ejector seat

Armament (fixed): none

Armament (disposable): none

Electronics and operational equipment: communication and navigation equipment, plus classified optical, thermal and electronic (including Hughes ASARS-2 side-looking airborne radar) reconnaissance systems in fuselage bays and two wing-mounted pods

Powerplant and fuel system: one 17,000-lb (7711-kg) thrust Pratt & Whitney J75-P-13B non-afterburning turbojet, and a total internal fuel capacity of about 1,175 US gal (4448 litres); no provision for drop tanks or inflight refuelling

Performance: cruising speed 430+ mph (692+ km/h) at 70,000+ ft (21,650+ m); initial climb rate not revealed; service ceiling 90,000 ft (27430 m); radius 1,500+ miles (2414+ km); ferry range 3,000+ miles (4828+ km); endurance 12 hours

Weights: empty 15,100 lb (6849 kg); maximum take-off 40,000 lb (18,143 kg)

Dimensions: span 103 ft 0 in (31·39 m); length 63 ft 0 in (19·20 m); height 16 ft 0 in (4·88 m); wing area about 1,000·0 sq ft (92·9 m²)

Variants

U-2CT: two-seat operational conversion trainer variant (with stepped separate cockpits) of the U-2C Elint version of the initial U-2 series

U-2R: final production model of the U-2 high-altitude reconnaissance aircraft series, which first flew as a prototype in August 1955 as the realization of the concept of marrying a sailplane-type airframe to a highly reliable turbojet for long-range cruise at very high altitudes; the U-2 series entered service in the second half of the 1950s and went through a number of variants before the U-2R was developed in the mid-1960s to overcome the basic U-2 series' mismatch of engine and airframe; thus the U-2R resembles its predecessors externally, but internally is a virtually new and completely restressed design carefully matched to the J75 engine introduced in the U-2B as replacement for the U-2A's Pratt & Whitney J57-P-7 or J57-P-57A of 10,500- or 11,200-lb (4763- or 5080-kg) thrust respectively; produced in 1969 and 1970, the U-2R has greater structural strength, an increased-span wing and much increased fuel capacity, and carries five 70-mm cameras for high-resolution photo-reconnaissance; large pods can be mounted on the wings for additional reconnaissance equipment, and this feature is carried over to the TR-1A

series; there are also at least two U-2Rs configured for the Comint role with a large dorsal radome containing the equipment for real-time transmission for data for analysis via a satellite

TR-1A: introduced in the early 1980s as an advanced development of the U-2R, the TR-1A carries more advanced avionics, and though designated as a tactical reconnaissance type it serves mainly in the strategic role (14 of the 24 aircraft), only 10 being configured for the tactical role with a synthetic-aperture SLAR able to look 34·2 miles (55 km) into hostile territory; the tactical aircraft were also to be fitted with the Lockheed Precision Location Strike System for the stand-off detection, classification and localization of hostile radar systems, whose position would then be relayed by data-link to friendly forces for immediate attack, but development of this system was cancelled in 1986; the US Air Force is considering a programme to re-engine all its U-2Rs and TR-1s with the General Electric F101-GE-F29 turbofan, a non-afterburning relation of the F101-GE-102 used in the Rockwell B-2 strategic bomber; the engine is lighter and more powerful than the current J75 turbojet, and in addition to easing logistic problems would provide better climb rate, higher ceiling and greater range

TR-1B: two-seat conversion trainer variant

Lockheed TriStar K.Mk 1

(USA & UK)

Type: long-range strategic transport and inflight-refuelling tanker aeroplane

Accommodation: flightcrew of three, and 204 passengers or 98,110 lb (44,500 kg) of palletized freight in the cabin

Armament (fixed): none

Armament (disposable): none

Electronics and operational equipment: communication and navigation equipment, and a twin Mk 17T hose-and-drogue unit under the rear fuselage

Powerplant and fuel system: three 50,000-lb (22,680-kg) thrust Rolls-Royce RB.211-524B4 non-afterburning turbofans, and a total internal fuel weight of 213,240 lb (96,724 kg) plus 100,060 lb (45,387 kg) in two fuselage tanks; no provision for drop tanks but provision for inflight refuelling

Performance: maximum cruising speed 600 mph (964 km/h) at 35,000 ft (10,670 m); long-range cruising speed 552 mph (889 km/h) at 33,000 ft (10,060 m); initial climb rate not revealed; service ceiling 43,000 ft (13,105 m); range 4,835 miles (7780 km) with maximum payload

Weights: empty 242,864 lb (110,163 kg); maximum take-off 540,000 lb (245,000 kg)

Dimensions: span 164 ft 4 in (50.09 m); length excluding probe 164 ft 2.5 in (50.05 m); height 55 ft 4 in (16.87 m); wing area 3,541.0 sq ft (329.0 m²)

Variants

TriStar K.Mk 1: this most capable heavy airlifter/inflight-refuelling tanker has been developed to meet the Royal Air Force's strategic needs, the type being converted from four ex-British Airways L-1011-500 TriStars with under-floor tanks for transfer fuel, and above-floor accommodation for passengers or freight; the type has a 38,710-Imp gal (175,974-litre) maximum fuel load, and can offload some 15,321 Imp gal (69,650 litres) of fuel, weighing 124,000 lb (56,246 kg), at a radius of 2,647 miles (4260 km) through either of the twin Mk 17T hose-and-drogue units fitted in the ventral position; the type first flew in July 1985 for service in 1986, and future developments include provision of full freighting/refuelling capabilities with a pair of Mk 32 hose-and-drogue units under the wings

TriStar KC.Mk 1: two ex-British Airways aircraft converted for the tanker/freight role with additional tankage and HDU arrangement as on the TriStar K.Mk 1, and provision for the installation of 194 seats

TriStar K.Mk 2: three ex-Pan Am aircraft converted to a standard similar to that of the TriStar K.Mk 1 but with about 10,000 lb (4536 kg) less fuel

McDonnell Douglas EA-3B Skywarrior

(USA)

Type: land-based and carrierborne electronic reconnaissance aeroplane

Accommodation: flightcrew of three, and a mission crew of four in the fuselage

Armament (fixed): none

Armament (disposable): none

Electronics and operational equipment: communication and navigation equipment, plus ESM gear (ALR-40 surveillance recording equipment and ALR-63 frequency-measuring receiver), forward-looking radar, SLAR, IR sensors, and chaff dispensers

Powerplant and fuel system: two 12,400-lb (5625-kg) thrust Pratt & Whitney J57-P-10 non-afterburning turbojets, and a total internal fuel capacity (KA-3B) of 5,025 US gal (19,022 litres); no provision for drop tanks but provision for inflight refuelling

Performance: maximum speed 610 mph (982 km/h) or Mach 0.83 at 10,000 ft (3050 m); cruising speed 520 mph (837 km/h); initial climb rate not revealed; service ceiling 41,000 ft (12,495 m); range 2,900 miles (4665 km)

Weights: empty 39,409 lb (17,856 kg); maximum take-off 73,000 lb (33,112 kg)

Dimensions: span 72 ft 6 in (22.10 m); length 76 ft 4 in (23.27 m); height 22 ft 9.5 in (6.95 m); wing area 812.0 sq ft (75.44 m²)

Variants

EA-3B Skywarrior: the most important of three Skywarrior versions left in US Navy service, the EA-3B is the electronic reconnaissance and ECM aircraft derived from the A-3B carrierborne attack aircraft, and first flew in December 1958 as the A3D-2Q with a pressurized fuselage compartment for electronic receiving, analysing and countermeasures equipment and four operators; production amounted to 25 aircraft

EKA-3B Skywarrior: US Navy Reserve TACOS (Tanker Aircraft, Countermeasures Or Strike) version that combines ECM training and inflight-refuelling roles with a limited attack capability; the first role uses the ALQ-76 noise jammer, and about 40 EKA-3Bs were produced by converting A-3Bs

ERA-3B Skywarrior: electronic 'aggressor' version to test US Navy ECCM, and also to evaluate new ECM equipment; an unrevealed number were produced by converting A-3Bs

KA-3B Skywarrior: US Navy Reserve inflight-refuelling tanker model, produced by converting A-3Bs with the US Navy's standard hose-and-drogue refuelling system

Top: Flight deck crew manhandling an EA-3B.

Opposite: The TR-1A's wing pods carry a mass of reconnaissance equipment.

Bottom: The TriStar K.Mk 1 has twin ventral HDUs, though only one is being streamed here.

McDonnell Douglas A-4M Skyhawk II

(USA)
Type: land-based and carrierborne light attack aeroplane
Accommodation: pilot on a Douglas Escapac 1-3C ejector seat
Armament (fixed): two 20-mm Mk 12 cannon with 200 rounds per gun
Armament (disposable): this is carried on five hardpoints (one under the fuselage rated at 3,500 lb/1588 kg, and two under each wing with the inner two units each rated at 2,250 lb/1021 kg and the outer two units each at 1,000 lb/454 kg) up to a maximum of weight 9,155 lb (4153 kg); a very wide assortment of ordnance can be carried, typical weapons being the AGM-12 Bullpup and AGM-65 Maverick ASMs, AIM-9 Sidewinder AAMs, AGM-45 Shrike radar-homing missile, AGM-62 Walleye TV-guided glide bomb, 2,000-, 1,000-, 750-, 500- and 250-lb (907-, 454-, 340-, 227- and 113-kg) free-fall or retarded bombs, BLU-series napalm bombs, CBU-series cluster bombs, LAU-series pods for 2·75- and 5-in (69·85- and 127-mm) rockets, and gun pods of various types
Electronics and operational equipment: communication and navigation equipment, plus Marconi AVQ-24 HUD, Hughes ASB-19 Angle-Rate Bombing Set, Texas Instruments AJB-3 loft-bombing system, APN-153(V)7 ground-mapping and terrain-avoidance radar, ASN-41 INS, Itek ALR-45 RWR, Magnavox ALR-50 SAM-warning system, Tracor ALE-39 chaff/flare dispenser, and optional ECM such as the Sanders ALQ-100 deception ECM and Sanders ALQ-130 tactical communications jammer
Powerplant and fuel system: one 11,200-lb (5080-kg) thrust Pratt & Whitney J52-P-408 non-afterburning turbojet, and a total internal fuel capacity of 800 US gal (3028 litres) plus provision for three 400-, 300- or 150-US gal (1514-, 1136- or 568-litre) drop tanks; provision for one Douglas D-704 'buddy' refuelling pack with 300 US gal (1136 litres) of transfer fuel, and for inflight refuelling
Performance: maximum speed 685 mph (1102 km/h) or Mach 0·9 at sea level, and 646 mph (1040 km/h) with 4,000-lb (1814-kg) bombload; initial climb rate 10,300 ft (3140 m) per minute; service ceiling not revealed; radius 340 miles (547 km) on a hi-lo-hi mission with 4,000-lb (1814-kg) warload; range 2,000 miles (3222 km) with maximum fuel
Weights: empty 10,465 lb (4747 kg); normal take-off 24,500 lb (11,113 kg); maximum take-off 27,420 lb (12,437 kg)
Dimensions: span 27 ft 6 in (8·38 m); length excluding probe 40 ft 4 in (12·29 m); height 15 ft 10 in (4·57 m); wing area 260·0 sq ft (24·16 m²)

Variants
A-4F Skyhawk: developed in the early 1950s, the XA4D-1 prototype of the Skyhawk first flew during June 1954 and soon displayed outstanding speed and manoeuvrability even with a substantial warload; the design team had achieved the near miraculous of combining all the US Navy's design requirements and payload into a diminutive airframe powered by a 7,200-lb (3266-kg) thrust Wright J65 non-afterburning turbojet and possessing only half the maximum take-off weight originally specified; the production A4D-1 (later A-4A) entered service in October 1956 with the 7,700-kg (3493-kg) thrust J65-W-4 turbojet and could carry 5,000 lb (2268 kg) of disposable ordnance in addition to its two inbuilt 20-mm cannon; the oldest variant still in service is the A-4F

powered by the 9,300-lb (4218-kg) thrust Pratt & Whitney J52-P-8A turbojet (the engine type introduced on the A4D-5/A-4E variant) and featuring additional avionics in a humped dorsal fairing
TA-4F Skyhawk: two-seat trainer version of the A-4F; there are also a few examples of the **ETA-4F Skyhawk** in service as EW trainers with the ALE-41 chaff dispenser
A-4H Skyhawk: version of the A-4E for Israel with a square-topped vertical tail, revised avionics, an inbuilt armament of two 30-mm DEFA cannon with 150 rounds per gun, a braking parachute and the J52-P-8A turbojet; in Israeli service the type has been considerably upgraded with a lengthened jetpipe to lessen the effectiveness of IR-homing SAMs, a modern stores-management system, more modern but lighter avionics, optional chaff/flare dispensers, an extra hardpoint under each wing, and a braking parachute
TA-4H Skyhawk: two-seat operational conversion trainer variant of the A-4H for Israel, which has modified a small number for the EW role with Elta chaff and jammer pods
TA-4J Skyhawk: two-seat training version for the US Navy, similar to the TA-4F but with reduced operational capability (only one 20-mm cannon, often omitted) and powered by the 8,500-lb (3856-kg) thrust J52-P-6 turbojet
A-4K Skyhawk: version of the A-4F for New Zealand but fitted with the braking parachute of the A-4H; these aircraft are being radically upgraded electronically by SLI Avionics Systems to produce capability roughly equivalent to that of the General Dynamics F-16; the nose is revised to accommodate Westinghouse APG-66(NZ) radar, the cockpit is modified to a Hands On Throttle and Stick (HOTAS) configuration with a Ferranti HUD and two multi-function HDDs, and a Litton LN-93 INS is fitted; armament provisions include AGM-65 Maverick ASMs and AIM-9L Sidewinder AAMs
TA-4K Skyhawk: two-seat operational conversion trainer variant of the A-4K
A-4KU Skyhawk II: version for Kuwait, generally similar to the A-4M
TA-4KU Skyhawk II: two-seat operational conversion trainer variant of the A-4KU
A-4M Skyhawk II: much improved version of the basic series for the US Marine Corps, featuring the square-top tail of the A-4H, a relocated braking parachute, much enhanced avionics, and the considerably more powerful J52-P-408A turbojet
OA-4M Skyhawk II: TA-4F aircraft converted (for the US Marine Corps' FAC role) to the basic standard of the A-4M and, though fitted for armament, generally carrying none as fuel capacity and loiter time are more important; the type also carries special communications equipment
A-4N Skyhawk II: version of the A-4M for Israel, but featuring the 30-mm cannon armament of the A-4H, upgraded electronics and an Elliott HUD; the A-4M has received the same updating as the A-4H
A-4P Skyhawk: ex-US Navy A-4B and A-4C aircraft refurbished and upgraded for the Argentine air force
A-4PTM Skyhawk: ex-US Marine Corps aircraft refurbished and updated by Grumman for Malaysia with enhanced avionics, two additional underwing hardpoints, a braking parachute, provision for two AIM-9 Sidewinder AAMs (and later for AGM-65 Maverick ASMs), and the Hughes Angle-Rate Bombing Set; some aircraft are being modified to a two-seat operational conversion trainer standard similar to the TA-4F by the inser-

tion of a lengthened cockpit section
A-4Q Skyhawk: ex-US Navy A-4B aircraft refurbished and upgraded for the Argentine navy
A-4S Skyhawk: ex-US Navy A-4B aircraft refurbished and much improved for Singapore with items such as APQ-145 mapping and ranging radar, 30-mm Aden cannon, more advanced electronics and the 8,100-lb (3674-kg) thrust Wright J65-W-20 turbojet; local development has produced the **A-4S-1 Super Skyhawk** derivative of the A-4S with more advanced avionics, uprated hardpoints and a completely new powerplant in the form of the 11,000-lb (4990-kg) thrust General Electric F404-GE-100D non-afterburning turbofan for a revitalized aircraft whose 30% more power provides 35% better climb rate, 40% greater acceleration and 15% greater dash speed; another powerplant option, this time offered by Pratt & Whitney, is the PW1212 modernization of the J52 turbojet with a thrust rating of 12,000 lb (5443 kg) and 20% more rapid acceleration than the basic J52; the manufacturer claims considerably improved range and loiter time for the Skyhawk with this powerplant, which is stall-free throughout the flight envelope
TA-4S Skyhawk: two-seat operational conversion trainer variant of the A-4S with two separate cockpits

Below: The A-4N is the Skyhawk II variant for Israel generally similar to the A-4M.

Right: A KC-10A Extender passes fuel to an F-16A via the latter's dorsal receptacle.

McDonnell Douglas KC-10A Extender

(USA)
Type: inflight-refuelling tanker aeroplane with a secondary airlift capability
Accommodation: flightcrew of three and a mission crew of three, and various seating options or 169,410 lb (76,843 kg) of freight
Armament (fixed): none
Armament (disposable): none
Electronics and operational equipment: communication and navigation equipment, plus a McDonnell Douglas flying boom/hose-and-drogue refuelling system
Powerplant and fuel system: three 52,500-lb (23,814-kg) thrust General Electric CF6-50C2 non-afterburning turbofans, and a total internal fuel capacity of 54,780 US gal (207,364 litres) for self-use and transfer; no provision for drop tanks but provision for inflight refuelling
Performance: maximum speed 610 mph (982 km/h) at 25,000 ft (7620 m); cruising speed 564 mph (908 km/h); initial climb rate 2,900 ft (884 m) per minute; service ceiling 33,400 ft (10,180 m); range 4,370 miles (7032 km) with maximum payload or 11,500 miles (18507 km) with maximum fuel

Weights: empty 241,025 lb (196,329 kg) in tanker configuration; maximum take-off 590,000 lb (267,620 kg)
Dimensions: span 165 ft 4·4 in (50·41 m); length 181 ft 7 in (55·35 m); height 58 ft 1 in (17·70 m); wing area 3,958·0 sq ft (367·7 m²)

Variant

KC-10A Extender: this is an advanced tanker and cargo aircraft derivative of the McDonnell Douglas DC-10-30CF convertible freighter in fairly widespread service use; the procurement of the type was desired by the US Air Force to provide a more capable aircraft than the Boeing KC-135 for the support of long-range deployments of tactical aircraft; the Extender suffered from severe political problems, but after a first flight in July 1980 and service deliveries from March 1981 the type has fully proved itself; the main advantages of the Extender over the Stratotanker are its considerably greater volume of transfer fuel, its own considerable range, its ability to serve as navigational mothership to smaller aircraft, the high-capacity refuelling boom that can pass fuel at the rate of 1,500 US gal (5678 litres) per minute,

the independent hose-and-drogue system that can pass fuel at the rate of 600 US gal (2271 litres) per minute, and the ability of the hold to carry a substantial load of spares, equipment and groundcrew for the support of overseas deployments; seven tanks in the lower hold accommodate 18,075 US gal (88,421 litres) of transfer fuel, which can be supplemented from the Extender's standard tankage to make possible the transfer of 30,000 US gal (113,562 litres) of fuel at a radius of 2,200 miles (3540 km); out to a range of 5,150 miles (8288 km) the KC-10A has cargo capacity comparable to that of the Lockheed C-5 Galaxy, but between that range and 11,500 miles (18507 km) the payload/range figures are better than those of the Galaxy; the last Extender, which rolled off the production line in November 1988, was fitted with Flight Refuelling Mk 32B hose-and-drogue units under each wing to allow the type to refuel US Navy, US Marine Corps and NATO tactical aircraft at the rate of 600 US gal (2271 litres) of fuel per minute; all earlier aircraft are then to be retrofitted for the underwing HDUs, though only 39 shipsets of HDUs have been ordered

McDonnell Douglas C-17A

McDonnell Douglas F-4E Phantom II

(USA/UK)

Type: long-range strategic transport aeroplane
Accommodation: flightcrew of three or four, and 144 troops, or 102 paratroops or 172,200 lb (78,110 kg) of freight in the cabin
Armament (fixed): none
Armament (disposable): none
Electronics and operational equipment: communication and navigation equipment
Powerplant and fuel system: four 37,000-lb (16,873-kg) thrust Pratt & Whitney F117-P-100 non-afterburning turbofans, and a total internal fuel weight of 175,835 lb (79,759 kg); no provision for drop tanks but provision for inflight refuelling
Performance: maximum cruising speed 515 mph (829 km/h) or Mach 0·77 at 35,000 ft (10,670 m); initial climb rate not revealed; service ceiling 45,000 ft (13,715 m); radius 575 miles (975 km) with an 86,100-lb (39,055-kg) payload; range 2,750 miles (4425 km) with maximum payload; ferry range 5,755 miles (9262 km)
Weights: empty 265,000 lb (120,204 kg); maximum take-off 580,000 lb (263,088 kg)
Dimensions: span 165 ft 0 in (50·29 m); length 175 ft 2 in (53·39 m); height 58 ft 0 in (17·68 m); wing area 3,800·0 sq ft (353·02 m²)

Variant

C-17A: the C-17 was chosen as winner of the US Air Force's CX long-range transport aeroplane competition, but development was then deferred in favour of C-5B procurement; the first example is due to fly at the end of 1990, and the type can be classified as a transport with the overall size of the Lockheed C-141 StarLifter but with the fuselage diameter of the Lockheed C-5 Galaxy to permit the loading of large freight items (main battle tanks etc) through the inbuilt rear ramp/door; the type is designed for use in the tactical and operational roles after approach flights from the USA, and therefore possesses long range as well as STOL and rough-field capability

(USA)

Type: all-weather multi-role fighter and attack aeroplane
Accommodation: pilot and systems operator in tandem on Martin-Baker H7 zero/zero ejector seats
Armament (fixed): one 20-mm General Electric M61A1 Vulcan rotary-barrel cannon with 640 rounds
Armament (disposable): this is carried in four semi-recessed lower-fuselage missile positions (each able to carry one AIM-7 Sparrow AAM) and on five hardpoints (one under the fuselage rated at 3,500 lb/1588 kg, and two under each wing with the inner two units each rated at 3,500 lb/1588 kg and the outer two units each at 2,240 lb (1016 kg) up to a maximum weight of 16,000 lb (7257 kg); the centreline hardpoint can carry one 70/35-kiloton B28RG, or 1-megaton B43, or 10/20-kiloton B57 or 100/500-kiloton B61 free-fall nuclear weapon, or alternatively 3,020 lb (1371 kg) of conventional weapons such as free-fall or retarded bombs or an SUU-16 or SUU-23 20-mm cannon pod; the underwing hardpoints can lift four AGM-65 Maverick ASMs, or four AGM-45 Shrike radar-homing missiles, or two Paveway laser-guided bombs, or four AGM-62 Walleye TV-guided bombs, or four AIM-9 Sidewinder AAMs or two AIM-7 Sparrow AAMs, or alternatively combine with the outer underwing hardpoints for a total of 12,980 lb (5888 kg) of free-fall or retarded bombs, cluster bombs, bomb dispensers and rocket pods
Electronics and operational equipment: communication and navigation equipment, plus Hughes APQ-120 fire-control radar, AJB-7 bombing system, ASQ-91 weapon-release system, Elbit SCS (Sidewinder Control System to slave the missile seeker to the radar or helmet-mounted sight for off-boresight engagements), General Electric ASG-26A computing sight, Northrop ASX-1 TISEO (Target Identification System Electro-Optical), ASN-63 INS, CKP-92A central

computer and Itek APR-36 RWR, plus provision for podded ECM such as the ALQ-101, ALQ-119, ALQ-130 and ALQ-131 systems and for the Sanders ALQ-140 IR countermeasures system
Powerplant and fuel system: two 17,900-lb (8119-kg) afterburning thrust General Electric J79-GE-17A turbojets, and a total internal fuel capacity of 1,855 US gal (7022 litres) plus provision for one 600-US gal (2271-litre) and two 370-US gal (1401-litre) drop tanks; provision for inflight refuelling
Performance: maximum speed 1,430 mph (2301 km/h) or Mach 2·17 clean at 36,000 ft (10,970 m); cruising speed 570 mph (917 km/h) with stores; initial climb rate 49,800 ft (15,180 m) per minute; service ceiling 58,750 ft (17,905 m); radius 712 miles (1145 km) on a hi-lo-hi mission; ferry range 1,978 miles (3184 km)
Weights: empty 30,328 lb (13,757 kg); normal take-off 41,487 lb (18,818 kg); maximum take-off 61,795 lb (28,030 kg)
Dimensions: span 38 ft 7·5 in (11·77 m); length 63 ft 0 in (19·20 m); height 16 ft 5·5 in (5·02 m); wing area 530·0 sq ft (49·24 m²)

Variants

RF-4B Phantom II: oldest surviving operational variant of the legendary Phantom II series, the RF-4B first flew in March 1965 as a tactical day/night photo-reconnaissance aircraft (derived from the F-4B fighter) for the US Marine Corps; the type is unarmed and provided with a lengthened nose for forward and oblique cameras (radar and IR reconnaissance equipment also being carried); in the second half of the 1970s the SURE programme updated surviving RF-4Bs with ASN-92 INS, APD-10 SLAR, AAD-5 IR reconnaissance and ALQ-26 ECM systems; the Phantom II was conceived in the early 1950s as the McDonnell AH-1 strike and attack aircraft, but finally built as a dual-role fleet defence and attack fighter for the US Navy, first flying as the XF4H-1 in May 1958 with two 14,800-lb (6713-kg) afterburning thrust General Electric J79-GE-3A turbojets; the type was planned round a missile (fighter) or missile/free-fall bomb (attack) armament, a radar fire-control system removing the need (for the first time in a naval fighter) for surface radar assistance; performance was thus optimized for climb rate, speed and range; the pre-production and interim-production F4H-1F (later F-4A) began to enter service in 1958 with two J79-GE-2 turbojets (pending delivery of the proposed J79-GE-8 turbojets), four semi-active radar-homing Sparrow III missiles and APQ-50 or improved APQ-72 radar; the following F4H-1 (later F-4B) was the first definitive production variant from 1961 with J79-GE-8 turbojets, APQ-72 radar, provision for 16,000 lb (7257 kg) of disposable stores, a missile armament of four Sparrow IIIs plus four IR-homing Sidewinders and a bulged cockpit canopy
F-4C Phantom II: limited-change equivalent of the F-4B for the US Air Force with larger wheels, inflight-refuelling capability, APQ-100 radar, several system changes and 17,000-lb (7711-kg) afterburning thrust J79-GE-15 turbojets; the type first flew in May 1963, and several of the aircraft were later passed on to Spain with the revised designation **F-4C(S)** after the aircraft had been refurbished
RF-4C Phantom II: US Air Force tactical reconnaissance version of the F-4C, first flown in production form during May 1964 and generally

equivalent to the RF-4B with APQ-99 forward-looking radar (upgraded to APQ-172 standard), APQ-102 SLAR, AAS-18A IR linescanner and a combination of forward and oblique cameras; some aircraft have been updated with the ALQ-125 TEREC (Tactical Electronic REConnaissance) package for determination of the enemy's electronic order of battle

F-4D Phantom II: improved variant of the F-4C for the US Air Force, with avionics tailored to USAF needs and fitted with APQ-109 radar; the type first flew in December 1965

F-4E Phantom II: major production version for the US Air Force and incorporating features found wanting in early models during operations over Vietnam; the type flew in prototype form during August 1965 and in production form during June 1967; notable features are an inbuilt cannon (the 20-mm M61A1 Vulcan six-barrel 'Gatling' type), leading-edge slots on the tailplane and (added retrospectively in place of blown leading-edge flaps) slatted outer wing panels for increased combat manoeuvrability, a remodelled nose with reduced-diameter APQ-120 radar, additional fuel capacity bestowed by the introduction of a seventh fuel cell in the rear fuselage, and J79-GE-17 turbojets; the type was also produced for Japan under the designation **Mitsubishi (McDonnell Douglas) F-4EJ**, and 100 of these 140 aircraft are being updated as close-support aircraft under the designation **F-4EJ Kai** with another 17 transformed into **RF-4EJ** tactical reconnaissance platforms each carrying a Thomson-CSF reconnaissance pod; the F-4EJ Kai modification involves the installation of Westinghouse APG-66J pulse-Doppler radar, a Kaiser/Shimadzu HUD, a Litton LN-39 INS, and an APR-4 Kai RWR; the type's radar has a look-down capability against targets to be engaged with AIM-9L Sidewinder and AIM-7F Sparrow AAMs, and the fighter can also be used in the anti-ship role with two ASM-1 missiles; Israel operates a substantial fleet of F-4E aircraft, most in the ground-attack role but the survivors of 24 others in the 'Wild Weasel' defence-suppression role with J79-GE-17B engines, APQ-120(V)4 radar, the TISEO long-range visual identification sensor, and provision for AGM-65 Maverick missiles as an alternative to the standard complement of four AGM-78 Standard ARMs; 140 of the ground-attack aircraft are being upgraded locally to **Phantom 2000** standard for redelivery from 1989 to meet the threat of advanced Soviet AA weapons supplied to the Arab nations by the USSR; it has been decided not to re-engine the aircraft with Pratt & Whitney PW1120 afterburning turbofans that would have created the true **Super Phantom** variant, but each is being structurally strengthened and refurbished, and additionally fitted with fixed strakes above the inlet trunks to increase agility (the original notion of fitting small canards having been dropped), stronger landing gear, a 600-US gal (2728-litre) external belly tank and an improved cockpit featuring HOTAS (Hands-On-Throttle-And-Stick) controls and advanced avionics, the last being an Elbit responsibility that includes a new Norden/UTC multi-mode radar with Elbit ACE-3 data processor, an Electro Optical Industries licence-built Kaiser wide-angle HUD, multi-function HDDs, trebling of the mission computer capacity by the addition of an Elbit digital avionic interface computer, replacement of the original 500-harness wiring loom with a 300-harness loom to reduce its weight by some 30%,

integration of all avionics by dual MIL 1553B digital databuses, and a new nav/attack system; Israel also operates a small number of **F-4E(S)** special reconnaissance aircraft of the type modified by General Electric with the HIAC-1 photo-reconnaissance system in a drastically revised nose; the converted aircraft have been further revised in the powerplant for high-altitude high-speed flight for long-range strategic and operational reconnaissance

RF-4E Phantom II: tactical reconnaissance version of the F-4E with the same basic characteristics as the RF-4C, and first flown in September 1970

F-4F Phantom II: variant of the F-4E optimized for the air-superiority role in the hands of the West German air force; the type lacks the seventh fuselage fuel cell, slotted tailplane and air-to-surface weapons capability, but has APQ-100 radar, outer wing slats and Sparrow armament; the type is about to be modernized with Hughes APG-65 look-down/shoot-down fire-control radar with AEG displays, Applied Technology ALR-68A(V)2 RWR, AIM-120A AMRAAM AAMs, MIL 1553 databus and Honeywell ring laser INS for continued air-defence viability into the late 1990s

F-4G 'Advanced Wild Weasel': this is currently the most important Phantom II variant, the EF-4E prototype first flying in December 1976 on the basis of an F-4E aircraft converted for the defence-suppression role; the concept was pioneered in Vietnam with North American F-100 Super Sabre, Republic F-105 Thunderchief and EF-4C/D 'Wild Weasel' aircraft and proved itself to be both feasible and tactically important; the F-4G conversions thus have no internal cannon, which is replaced by the APR-38 system, which has a multitude of aerials for the detection, classification, identification and localization of enemy radars which are then engaged with AGM-45 Shrike and AGM-88 HARM radar-homing missiles; other elements of the 'Advanced Wild Weasel' suite are the APR-36 or APR-37 radar-homing and warning systems, and the ALQ-119-12, ALQ-119-14 or ALQ-131 defensive jammer pods

F-4J Phantom II: this was the US Navy's and US Marine Corps' second-generation Phantom, fitted with 17,900-lb (8119-kg) afterburning thrust J79-GE-8 or J79-GE-10 turbojets and first flown in prototype form during June 1965 for service from mid-1966; the type has APG-59 pulse-Doppler radar with the AWG-10 fire-control system, the AJB-7 bombing system, seven fuselage fuel tanks, the slotted tailplane, drooping ailerons, and provision for automatic carrier landings; a small number were later transferred to the UK with minimum modifications under the designation **F-4J(UK)**, known in the RAF as the **Phantom**

F.Mk 3, and carrying the General Instruments ALR-66 RWR

F-4K Phantom II: under this designation the manufacturer developed a version of the F-4J for British carrierborne requirements; extensive redesign of the fuselage was required for the installation of two 20,515-lb (9305-kg) afterburning thrust Rolls-Royce Spey RB.168-25R Mk 202/203 turbofans, and other modifications were an extending nosewheel leg for increased wing incidence at take-off, a folding radome for the AWG-11 fire-control radar system, and reduced anhedral on the tailplane; the type entered service at the beginning of 1967 as the **Phantom FG.Mk 1**, and the aircraft were subsequently transferred to the RAF; the aircraft carry the Marconi ARI.18228 RWR

F-4M Phantom II: F-4K variant for the Royal Air Force, with which the type entered service early in 1968 as the **Phantom FGR.Mk 2**; the type lacks the extending nosewheel leg and folding nose of the F-4K, while other modifications are the AWG-12 radar fire-control system, Sky Flash AAM and flush-fitting ventral EMI reconnaissance pod capability, a Ferranti INS, an unslotted tailplane and, as a retrofit, the Marconi ARI.18228 RWR

F-4N Phantom II: F-4B aircraft upgraded structurally and in terms of avionics to F-4J standard; the first such conversion flew in May 1972

F-4S Phantom II: F-4J aircraft converted from 1977 to an improved standard with a strengthened structure, the AWG-10A radar fire-control system, leading-edge slats on the outer panels of the wings and J79-GE-10B turbojets; systems improvements include the installation of the APR-43 RWR in place of the original APR-32 system

Modernized F-4 Phantom II: Boeing has suggested a programme for maintaining the military viability of the F-4E (in particular) with a radical update centred on the use of two 20,600-lb (9344-kg) afterburning thrust Pratt & Whitney PW1120 turbofans, an underfuselage conformal tank with an additional 1,100 US gal (4164 litres) of fuel plus an ALE-40 chaff/flare dispenser in its rear, and modern avionics based on the MIL 1553 databus to include (to customer requirement) Hughes APG-65 multi-mode radar, GEC wide-angle HUD, Sperry HDDs, GEC air-data computer, and Honeywell laser ring-gyro INS

Opposite: Artist's impression of the C-17A, which will combine heavyweight payload/range capability with the field performance of the C-130 tactical airlifter.

Below: F-4G 'Advanced Wild Weasel' fighters of the 3rd Tactical Fighter Wing, based at Clark AB in the Philippines.

McDonnell Douglas F-15C Eagle

(USA)

Type: air-superiority fighter with a secondary attack capability

Accommodation: pilot on a Douglas ACES II zero/zero ejector seat

Armament (fixed): one 20-mm General Electric M61A1 Vulcan rotary-barrel cannon with 940 rounds

Armament (disposable): this is carried on four tangential positions (each accommodating one AIM-7 Sparrow AAM to be replaced later by one AIM-120 AMRAAM AAM) and on five hardpoints (one under the fuselage rated at 4,500 lb/2041 kg and two under each wing with the inner two units each rated at 5,100 lb/2313 kg and the outer two units each at 1,000 lb/454 kg) up to a maximum weight of 16,000 lb (7257 kg) or 23,600 lb (10,705 kg) if the FAST packs and their four tangential hardpoints are used; in the air-superiority role the four Sparrows are generally matched by four AIM-9 Sidewinder AAMs, and in the attack role the warload comprises a wide variety of weapons such as the AGM-65 Maverick ASM, GBU-15 TV-guided bomb, Paveway laser-guided bombs, 2,000-, 1,000-, 750-, 500- and 250-lb (907-, 454-, 340-, 227- and 113-kg) free-fall or retarded bombs, Rockeye II cluster bombs, BLU-series napalm bombs, CBU-series cluster bombs and LAU-series pods for 2·75-in (70-mm) rockets

Electronics and operational equipment: communication and navigation equipment, plus Hughes APG-63 (or from 1985 APG-70) pulse-Doppler fire-control radar, McDonnell Douglas AVQ-20 HUD, Sperry Rand HDDs, IBM digital central computer, Sperry Rand air-data computer, Litton ASN-109 INS, Dynamic controls Corporation stores-management system, Northrop ALQ-135(V) internal ECM system, Loral ALR-56C RWR, ALQ-128 EW warning set, Magnavox ALR-50 SAM-warning receiver, Tracor ALE-45 chaff dispenser, and provision for podded items such as the Westinghouse ALQ-119(V) and ALQ-131 ECM systems and the Ford AVQ-26 'Pave Tack' targeting system

Powerplant and fuel system: two 23,450-lb (10,637-kg) afterburning thrust Pratt & Whitney F100-P-220 turbofans, and a total internal fuel capacity of 2,070 US gal (7836 litres) plus provision for 1,500 US gal (5678 litres) in two conformal FAST packs and for three 610-US gal (2309-litre) drop tanks; provision for inflight refuelling

Performance: maximum speed 1,650 + mph (2655 + km/h) or Mach 2·5 + at 36,000 ft (10,970 m) and 915 mph (1473 km/h) or Mach 1·21 at 1,000 ft (305 m); cruising speed 570 mph (917 km/h); initial climb rate 50,000 + ft (15,240 + m) per minute; service ceiling 60,000 ft (18,290 m); radius 1,222 miles (1967 km) on a hi-hi-hi mission with AAMs; ferry range 2,880 miles (4635 km) without FAST packs and 3,450 + miles (5562 + km) with FAST packs

Weights: empty 28,600 lb (12,973 kg); normal take-off 44,630 lb (20,244 kg) for interception role; maximum take-off 68,000 lb (30,844 kg) with FAST packs

Dimensions: span 42 ft 9·75 in (13·05 m); length 63 ft 9 in (19·43 m); height 18 ft 5·5 in (5·63 m); wing area 608·0 sq ft (56·48 m²)

Variants

F-15A Eagle: designed during the late 1960s to reflect the air combat lessons of the Vietnam War, the F-15 series is intended primarily for the air-superiority role, but has an excellent secondary capability in the attack role; the type flew in prototype form during July 1972, and amongst its key features are a high thrust-to-weight ratio for exceptional climb rate and altitude performance, advanced avionics including the APG-63 radar and a HUD, and superb aerodynamic design for low drag and sustained manoeuvrability; the type began to enter service in November 1974 with 23,830-lb (10809-kg) afterburning thrust F100-P-100 turbofans

F-15B Eagle: combat-capable two-seat operational conversion trainer derivative of the F-15A, at first designated TF-15A and flown in July 1973

F-15C Eagle: upgraded single-seat model delivered from June 1979 with increased internal fuel capacity, a programmable signal processor for the APG-63 radar (replaced in production machines from 1985 by the APG-70 radar with inbuilt programmable signal processor, synthetic-aperture ground mapping, and track-while-scan air-to-air capability), other avionic and EW improvements, slightly less powerful but more flexible F100-P-220 turbofans with digital control, and provision for FAST (Fuel And Sensor Tactical) packs; these last are conformal pallets that can be attached to the outside of the inlets to carry additional fuel, sensors such as low-light-level TV and ECM; these low-drag pallets degrade performance by no appreciable degree, and are stressed for the tangential carriage of missiles and free-fall ordnance; the Japanese version of this model is the **Mitsubishi (McDonnell Douglas) F-15J**; from the early 1990s the F-15C will enjoy the fruits of the US Air Force's Increased Performance Engine programme when the the newest aircraft are fitted with the 29,000-lb (13,154-kg) afterburning thrust Pratt & Whitney F100-P-229 turbofan, which is not only more reliable and rated at slightly higher thrust than the standard F100-P-220, but offers 30% thrust improvement in the critical areas of the fighter's operational envelope

F-15D Eagle: combat-capable two-seat operational conversion trainer derivative of the F-15C, and delivered from mid-1979; the Japanese version of this model is the **Mitsubishi (McDonnell Douglas) F-15DJ**

F-15E Eagle: based on the F-15D, this is an advanced all-weather interdictor and strike aircraft, the adoption of the two-seat formula marking a radical shift in US Air Force thinking, which has hitherto opted for single-seat aircraft in this role even for areas with such problematical weather as Europe; the manufacturer paved the way for the change with the development of the private-venture F-15 Enhanced Eagle optimized for the European theatre, and the F-15E was selected in preference to the proposed F-16E variant of the General Dynamics Fighting Falcon in March 1984 for delivery from 1988, the first example having flown in December 1986; the type is designed to carry the LANTIRN (Low-Altitude Navigation and Targeting Infra-Red for Night) podded nav/attack system; the front cockpit is equipped with a wide-angle HUD for the presentation of navigation/combat information, and the rear cockpit has head-down CRT displays for radar, FLIR, digital map and threat-warning systems; FAST tanks will be standard for the carriage of an additional 9,000 lb (4082 kg) or more of fuel and of tangentially mounted weapons; the

total external weapons load will be 24,250 lb (11000 kg) of the weapons al lified for the F-15 series, plus the AIM-120 AMRAAM AAM, AGM-65 Maverick ASM, and AGM-88 HARM radar-homing missile; the type's radar capability is considerably better than that of the basic F-15 series (though the Multi-Stage Improvement Program began to add features of these developments to the F-15C from June 1985) through installation of the APG-70 radar (see F-15C above) and AWG-27 armament control system; other avionics improvements are an upgraded central computer system, an advanced programmable stores-management system and more modern ECM; further development of the series could include canard foreplanes and 2D vectoring nozzles for enhanced combat manoeuvrability and to allow operations from damaged runways, the last with the aid of strengthened landing gear; first flown in 1989 was an F-15B modified in such a fashion to allow operations from runways as short as 500 yards (457 m)

This F-15E reveals the variant's two-seat accommodation, tangential bomb carriage on its FAST packs, underwing AIM-9 Sidewinder AAMs, and the twin pods of the LANTIRN night and adverse-weather nav/attack system.

cDonnell Douglas F/A-18C Hornet

(USA)

Type: land-based and carrierborne multi-role fighter and attack aeroplane

Accommodation: pilot on a Martin-Baker SJU-5/6 zero/zero ejector seat

Armament (fixed): one 20-mm General Electric M61A1 Vulcan rotary-barrel cannon with 570 rounds

Armament (disposable): this is carried on nine hardpoints (one under the fuselage rated at 3,300 lb/1497 kg, two under the inlets with each unit rated at 1,300 lb/590 kg, two under each wing with the inner two units each rated at 2,500 lb/1134 kg and the outer two units each rated at 2,350 lb/1066 kg, and one at each wingtip rated at 600 lb/272 kg) up to a maximum weight of 17,000 lb (7711 kg); amongst the varied weapons that can be carried are the 10/20-kiloton B57 and 100/500-kiloton B61 nuclear weapons, AIM-7 Sparrow and AIM-9 Sidewinder AAMs, AGM-88 HARM radar-homing missile, AGM-65 Maverick ASM, AGM-84 Harpoon anti-ship missile, AGM-62 Walleye TV-guided bomb, Paveway laser-guided bombs, 2,000-, 1,000-, 750-, 500- and 250-lb (907-, 454-, 340-, 227- and 113-kg) free-fall or retarded bombs, Rockeye II cluster bomb, CBU-series cluster bomb, BLU-series napalm bomb and LAU-series pods for 2·75-in (70-mm) rockets

Electronics and operational equipment: communication and navigation equipment, plus Hughes APG-65 pulse-Doppler multi-mode radar, Kaiser AVQ-28 HUD, three Smiths/Kaiser HDDs, two AYK-14 central computers, Litton ASN-130A INS, Honeywell digital moving map display, Magnavox ALR-50 RWR, Itek ALR-67 RWR, Ferranti Type 107 laser designator, ITT/Westinghouse ALQ-165 Airborne Self-Protection Jammer or Sanders ALQ-126B ECM system, Goodyear ALE-39 chaff dispenser, and provision for inlet-mounted sensors (Martin-Marietta ASQ-173 laser spot tracker to starboard and Ford AAS-38 FLIR to port) plus a number of podded ECM options

Powerplant and fuel system: two 16,000-lb (7257-kg) afterburning thrust General Electric F404-GE-400 turbofans, and a total internal fuel capacity of 1,700 US gal (6435 litres) plus provision for three 330-US gal (1250-litre) drop tanks; provision for inflight refuelling

Performance: maximum speed 1,189 + mph (1913 + km/h) or Mach 1·8 + at high altitude; initial climb rate 45,000 ft (13,715 m) per minute; service ceiling about 50,000 ft (15,240 m); radius 460 + miles (740 + km) on a hi-hi-hi interception mission without drop tanks, and 662 miles (1065 km) on a hi-lo-hi attack mission with drop tanks; ferry range 2,300 + miles (3702 + km)

Weights: empty 23,050 lb (10,455 kg); normal take-off 36,710 lb (16,652 kg) on a fighter mission; maximum take-off 49,224 lb (22,328 kg) on an attack mission

Dimensions: span 37 ft 6 in (11·43 m) without tip stores; length 56 ft 0 in (17·07 m); height 15 ft 3·5 in (4·66 m); wing area 400·0 sq ft (37·16 m²)

Variants

F/A-18A Hornet: first flown in November 1979 for service from late 1983, the F/A-18A is a dual-role fighter and attack aircraft designed to replace both the McDonnell Douglas F-4 Phantom II multi-role fighter and Vought A-7 Corsair II attack aircraft in service with the US Navy and US Marine Corps; the origins of the type lie with the Northrop YF-17, unsuccessful contender with the General Dynamics YF-16 in the US Air Force's Light-Weight Fighter competition; the type has been considerably reworked by the McDonnell Douglas/Northrop partnership to produce the multi-role carrierborne F/A-18A, which has significant capabilities in the apparently incompatible fighter and attack roles; further improvement in range may result from a McDonnell Douglas-funded programme to develop a conformal external fuel tank carried in the dorsal position, and adding only 300 lb (136 kg) to empty weight yet adding capacity for an additional 3,000 lb (1361 kg) of fuel for a total of 13,865 lb (6289 kg)

F/A-18B Hornet: combat-capable two-seat operational conversion trainer variant of the F/A-18A, originally designated **TF/A-18A** and possessing 6% less internal fuel capacity though otherwise similar to the F/A-18A

F/A-18C Hornet: improved tactical version first flown in 1986 with internal ASPJ (Airborne Self-Protection Jammer), a Martin-Baker SJU-5/6 rather than US10S zero/zero ejector seat, databus-linked small computers rather than one large mission computer, and provision for reconnaissance equipment as well as the AIM-120 AMRAAM AAM and AGM-65F IIR Maverick ASM

F/A-18D Hornet: two-seat version of the F/A-18C in many ways equivalent to the F/A-18B but optimized for night attack with a front-seat pilot and rear-seat weapons officer (with three colour HDDs) in a development programme paralleling that for the Night Attack AV-8B Harrier II; this version has the Hughes AAR-50 TINS (Thermal Imaging Navigation Set), a FLIR based on the AAQ-16 turret used mainly be helicopters; the TINS is located in a pod attached to the starboard inlet hardpoint and projects a thermal image of the area ahead of the aircraft on an improved HUD that is used in conjunction with a Honeywell digital colour moving-map generator working from a laser-scanned optical disc for access to navigational and intelligence data; the pilot has GEC Cats Eyes indirect-view image-intensification night vision goggles; the first F/A-18D flew in May 1988; though pioneered on the F/A-18D, the night attack capability is common to single- and two-seaters delivered from October 1989

RF-18D Hornet: designation of the dedicated tactical and operational reconnaissance variant of the F/A-18D to replace the McDonnell Douglas RF-4B Phantom II in US Marine Corps squadrons from 1990; production of 83 such aircraft is planned, each carrying a centreline ATARS (Advanced Tactical Airborne Reconnaissance System) pod under development by Loral with the UPD-4 synthetic-aperture SLAR; data from this pod, as well as the carrying aeroplane's standard optical and IR sensors, will be transmitted to a ground station via a real-time data-link; the reconnaissance variant originally planned for the Hornet was the **F/A-18(RC)** based on the F/A-18A modified with a pallet for cameras (including the KA-99) and an AAD-5 IR linescanner in a bulged nose no longer fitted with the 20-mm cannon

AF-18A Hornet: F/A-18A version for Australia

ATF-18A Hornet: F/A-18B version for Australia

CF-18A Hornet: F/A-18A version for Canada with a different instrument landing system and intended for land-based operations; a basically similar aircraft is being bought by Australia

CF-18B Hornet: F/A-18B version for Canada with a different instrument landing system and intended for land-based operations; a basically similar aircraft is being bought by Australia

EF-18A: F/A-18A for Spain

EF-18B: F/A-18B for Spain

Hornet 2000: under this overall designation McDonnell Douglas has proposed a number of updates for US Navy and US Marine Corps F/A-18C/D aircraft; the Hornet 2000 Configuration I is a comparatively simple electronic upgrade; the Hornet 2000 Configuration II adds a measure of wing strengthening, uprated engines and a dorsal tank for an extra 5,950 lb (2699 kg) of fuel; the Hornet 2000 Configuration III combines the Configuration I and II improvements with yet more fuel, a revised tailplane and a wider-chord wing; the Hornet 2000 Configurations IIIA, B and C offer varying combinations of dorsal tankage, new wings and a lengthened fuselage based on Configuration III; and Hornet 2000 Configuration IV provides for a radical modification with cranked delta wings, a canard foreplane and larger vertical tail surfaces in a CCV (Control-Configured Vehicle) system providing unparalleled manoeuvrability

Super Hornet Plus: McDonnell Douglas has proposed a number of less and more radical updates of the Hornet to suit a number of export requirements, the most advanced being the Super Hornet Plus proposed as an alternative to the European Fighter Aircraft; this has an updated APG-65 multi-mode radar, revised F404-GE-400 afterburning turbofans behind enlarged air inlets, a new cranked-arrow wing, dihedral canards instead of the slab tailplane halves, enlarged fins and new flight-control hardware

McDonnell Douglas Helicopters (Hughes) AH-64A Apache

(USA)

Type: battlefield close air support and anti-tank helicopter

Accommodation: co-pilot/weapons operator and pilot in tandem

Armament (fixed): one 30-mm Hughes M230 Chain Gun cannon with 1,200 rounds

Armament (disposable): this is carried on four hardpoints (two under each stub wing) up to a maximum weight of 3,880 lb (1760 kg); typical loads are 16 AGM-114 Hellfire anti-tank missiles, or four launchers each with 19 2·75-in (70-mm) rockets, or a combination of these weapons and four AIM-92A Stinger lightweight AAMs

Electronics and operational equipment: communication and navigation equipment, plus the Martin Marietta sensor suite (Target Acquisition and Designation Sight in parallel with the AAQ-11 Pilot's Night-Vision Sensor) and the Honeywell Integrated Helmet And Display Sighting System using the CPG stabilized sight with FLIR sensor, laser rangefinder and laser designator, Teledyne fire-control system, Singer-Kearfott ASN-128 Doppler navigation, Aerospace APR-39 RWR, AVR-2 laser warning receiver, ALQ-136 radar jammer, Sanders ALQ-144 IR countermeasures, M130 chaff/flare dispenser, and Hughes 'Black Hole' IR suppression system

Powerplant and fuel system: two 1,696-shp (1265-kW) General Electric T700-GE-701 turboshafts, and a total internal fuel capacity of 376 US gal (1422 litres) plus provision for external tanks; no provision for inflight refuelling

Performance: maximum speed 184 mph (296 km/h) a optimum altitude; cruising speed 182 mph (293 km/h); initial climb rate 2,880 ft (878 m) per minute; service ceiling 21,000 ft (6400 m); hovering ceiling in ground effect 15,000 (4570 m) and out of ground effect 11,500 ft (3505 m); range 380 miles (611 km) on internal fuel; ferry range 1,057 miles (1701 km)

Weights: empty 10,670 lb (4881 kg); normal take-off 14,445 lb (6552 kg); maximum take-off 21,000 lb (9525 kg)

Dimensions: main rotor diameter 48 ft 0 in (14·63 m); length overall, rotors turning 48 ft 2 in (14·68 m) and fuselage 49 ft 1·5 in (14·97 m); height 15 ft 3·5 in (4·66 m); main rotor disc area 1,809·5 sq ft (168·11 m²)

Variants

AH-64A Apache: first flown in September 1975, the Apache has become the US Army's most important battlefield helicopter; though large, complex and costly, the Apache is a highly capable machine offering advanced sensors and useful performance for the accurate delivery of a heavy ordnance load; particular features of the design are high survivability, good protection of the crew and primary systems, and avionics such as the TADS (for the optical, thermal or TV acquisition of targets that can then be laser-ranged and laser-designated) and PNVS for nap-of-the-earth flight profiles under all weather conditions by day and night; some 227 Apache helicopters are to be retrofitted with a mast-mounted radar, the Longbow system first designated Airborne Adverse-Weather Weapon System and carrying millimetric-wavelength radar for use with a version of the Hellfire missile with a radio-frequency seeker; the manufacturer is also proposing that the type be retrofitted under a three-stage programme with the Global Positioning System, Doppler navigation and improved versions of the TADS and PNVS; current improvements are centred (100th helicopter onward) on composite-construction main rotor blades; since the late 1980s all Apaches have had upgraded self-protection capability in the form of four FIM-92A Stinger lightweight AAMs attached (two on each side) to the outboard underwing pylons

AH-64B Apache: improved version for delivery

in the 1990s with voice controls a fibre-optical control system us side-arm control stick; the ty improved armament, including Sidewinder AAMs, a Global Positioning System receiver, Doppler radar, improved night vision equipment, an advanced composite rotor hub, and a reinforced thermoplastic secondary structure

AH-64 Sea Apache: under this basic designation the company is proposing a version for the US Navy with the avionics bay moved to an under-fuselage position to allow a fuel capacity of 853 US gal (3229 litres) as the means of providing a mission endurance of six or more hours in defence of surface battle groups operating without an aircraft-carrier; a retractable inflight-refuelling probe would also be fitted; the type would have an IR search and tracking system, the APG-65 radar and much of the avionics of the F/A-18 Hornet in a considerably modified cockpit under a larger canopy for greater levels of crew visibility; the helicopter could carry AIM-7 Sparrow, AIM-9 Sidewinder, AIM-120 AMRAAM and AIM-132 ASRAAM AAMs for its primary air-defence role, but would have provision for a quartet of AGM-84 Harpoon and/or AGM-119 Penguin anti-ship missiles; the Sea Apache would lack the underfuselage cannon of the land-based variant, and so too would the proposed version for the US Marine Corps, which would otherwise be similar to the land-based model in avionics and weapon capability

Opposite: An F/A-18A Hornet of Fighter Attack Squadron 125 in flight with underwing bombs near Fallon NAS, Nevada.

Below: This AH-64A Apache sports underwing rocket-launcher pods and quartets of Hellfire anti-tank missiles.

Donnell Douglas Helicopters (Hughes) Model 300C

(USA)

Type: utility light helicopter

Accommodation: pilot and two passengers in the cabin

Armament (fixed): none

Armament (disposable): none

Electronics and operational equipment: communication and navigation equipment

Powerplant and fuel system: one 190-hp (142-kW) Avco Lycoming HIO-360-D1A piston engine, and a total internal fuel capacity of 27 US gal (103 litres) plus provision for 19 US gal (72 litres) of auxiliary fuel; no provision for drop tanks or inflight refuelling

Performance: cruising speed 94 mph (151 km/h) at sea level; initial climb rate 750 ft (229 m) per minute; service ceiling 10,200 ft (3110 m); range 230 miles (370 km)

Weights: empty 1,050 lb (476 kg); maximum take-off 2,050 lb (930 kg)

Dimensions: main rotor diameter 26 ft 10 in (8·18 m); length overall, rotors turning 30 ft 10 in (9·40 m); height 8 ft 9 in (2·67 m) to rotor head; main rotor disc area 565·5 sq ft (52·5 m²)

Variants

Model 200 Utility: a light utility helicopter intended for communications, training and observation, the two-seat Model 200 series first flew in October 1956 as the **Model 269** initial version and secured considerable sales success in the civil market before being revised as the Model 200 Utility refined variant and as the **Model 200 Deluxe** up-market variant; the Model 269C variant was procured as a trainer by the US Army under the designation **TH-55A Osage**, of which

792 were built with the 180-hp (134-kW) Avco Lycoming HIO-360 B1A engine, and a similar version was produced under licence in Japan as the **Kawasaki (Hughes) TH-55J** trainer

Model 300: three-seat production version of the Model 269B development variant, and available from 1967 with a quieter tail rotor

Model 300C: improved model with 45% better payload and available from 1969; the type was also produced under licence in Italy as the **BredaNardi NH-300C**

Model 300QC: version of the Model 300C with noise emission reduced by 75%; this variant has a maximum take-off weight of 1,925 lb (873 kg)

TH300C: dual-control trainer version of the Model 300C produced by Schweizer

McDonnell Douglas Helicopters (Hughes) OH-6A Cayuse

(USA)
Type: light observation and utility helicopter

Accommodation: flightcrew of two, and four passengers or freight in the cabin rear

Armament (fixed): provision for an armament package on the port side of the fuselage containing one 7·62-mm (0·3-in) M134 Minigun or one 40-mm M75 grenade-launcher

Armament (disposable): none

Electronics and operational equipment: communication and navigation equipment

Powerplant and fuel system: one 317-shp (236-kW) Allison T63-A-5A turboshaft derated to 215 shp (160 kW), and a total internal fuel capacity of 63 US gal (240 litres) plus a number of combinations for auxiliary fuel; no provision for drop tanks or inflight refuelling

Performance: cruising speed 150 mph (241 km/h) at sea level; initial climb rate 1,840 ft (561 m) per minute; service ceiling 15,800 ft (4815 m); range 413 miles (665 km) with standard fuel; ferry range 1,560 miles (2511 km)

Weights: empty 1,156 lb (524 kg); normal take-off 2,400 lb (1089 kg); maximum take-off 2,700 lb (1225 kg)

Dimensions: main rotor diameter 26 ft 4 in (8·03 m); length overall, rotors turning 30 ft 3·8 in (9·24 m) and fuselage 23 ft 0 in (7·01 m); height 8 ft 1·5 in (2·48 m); main rotor disc area 544·63 sq ft (50·6 m²)

Variants

OH-6A Cayuse: first airborne in February 1963 as the Model 369 and flown in the US Army's Light Observation Helicopter competition as the HO-6, this type was ordered into production against requirements for some 4,000 aircraft and began to enter service in September 1966; service reports were highly enthusiastic, but production was cancelled after the delivery of 1,434 helicopters because of a declining production rate and increasing procurement costs; the reopened LOH competition was then won by the Bell Model 205, which entered service as the OH-58A Kiowa

OH-6C Cayuse: US Army experimental model based on 'The Quiet One' development version with the 400-shp (298-kW) Allison 250-C20, a five-blade main rotor and an acoustic blanket round the engine

OH-6D Aeroscout: development of the OH-6A to meet the US Army's Advanced Scout Helicopter programme

MH-6 Cayuse: version of the OH-6 for the US Army's Special Forces, essentially the Model 530MG Defender with features such as IR suppression of the engine exhaust, noise-reducing items, a mast-mounted sight, comprehensive vision equipment (including FLIR and pilot's night vision goggles), and in the **AH-6** variant provision for light armament (including 7·62-mm/0·3-in machine-gun and 2·75-in/70-mm rocket pods); there is also an **EH-6** variant thought to be fitted with specialist electronic reconnaissance equipment associated with special forces' operations

Model 500: commercial derivative of the original Model 369 with the 278-shp (207-kW) Allison 250-C18A turboshaft, and in the export version, limited military applications such as medevac

Model 500C: hot-and-high version of the Model 500 with the 400-shp (298-kW) Allison 250-C20 turboshaft and a main rotor 26 ft 4 in (8·03 m) in diameter; the type is built under licence by Kawasaki in Japan as the **Kawasaki (Hughes) Model 500C**, and by RACA in Argentina as the **RACA (Hughes) Model 500C**

Model 500D: export version of the OH-6C test helicopter with a number of quietening features such as a slow-turning five-blade main rotor and four-blade tail rotor driven by a 420-shp (313-kW) Allison 250-C20B turboshaft; the main rotor has a diameter of 26 ft 5 in (8·05 m), and the rotor hub has a low-drag 'coolie hat' fairing; the type is built under licence in Japan as the **Kawasaki (Hughes) Model 500D** for use by the Japan Ground Self-Defense Force

Model 500E: developed version of the Model 500D with a more pointed nose for better streamlining and increased cabin volume

Model 500M: dedicated military export variant based on the OH-6A but fitted with the Allison 250-C18A turboshaft derated to 275 shp (207 kW); examples in Spanish service are used in the light anti-submarine role with Texas Instruments ASQ-81 MAD and an armament of two Mk 46 light anti-submarine torpedoes; the type is also built under licence in Argentina as the **RACA (Hughes) 500M**, in Italy as the **BredaNardi NH-500M** (and **NH-500MC** with hot-and-high features) and in Japan as the **Kawasaki (Hughes) 500M**, which serves with the Japanese forces as the **OH-6J**

Model 500MD Defender: uprated military variant based on the Model 500D with the 420-shp (313-kW) Allison 250-C20B turboshaft, five-blade main rotor, T-tail and other improvements; the type has also been built under licence in Italy as the **BredaNardi (Hughes) NH-500MD** and in South Korea as the **KAL (Hughes) 500MD**; the Defender can be used in a number of forms for virtually the whole gamut of battlefield and naval tasks, and has been developed in a number of subvariants such as the **Model 500MD Scout Defender** (battlefield reconnaissance and light attack with Black Hole Ocarina IR suppression, a nose-mounted stabilized sight and a wide assort-

ment of light armament provision including rockets and a gun up to 30-mm calibre), the **Model 500MD Quiet Advanced Scout Defender** (similar to the Scout Defender but with noise reduction features and a mast-mounted sight for 'nap-of-the-earth' flight profiles), the **Model 500MD/TOW Defender** (a dedicated anti-tank version with four BGM-71 TOW missiles and appropriate sight), the **Model 500MD/MMS-TOW Defender** (as the Model 500MD/TOW but with a mast-mounted sight on a pylon 2 ft/0·61 m above the rotor head), the **Model 500MD/ASW Defender** (a dedicated ASW variant with search radar, ASQ-81 MAD and two Mk 46 torpedoes), and the **Model 500MD Defender II** (an upgraded model with Stinger lightweight AAMs for self-defence, and fitted for items such as a mast-mounted sight, FLIR and the APR-39 RWR)

Model 500MG Defender: improved multi-role military export version with a revised and sharper nose profile, advanced avionics and the 420-shp (313-kW) Allison 250-C20B turboshaft

Model 530F Lifter: hot-and-high version of the Model 500D with the fuselage of the Model 500E and a 650-shp (485-kW) Allison 250-C30 turboshaft derated to 430 shp (317 kW)

Model 530MG Defender: military version of the Model 530F with an advanced cockpit incorporating the Racal RAMS 3000 integrated display and control system (based on a MIL 1553B digital databus to allow the use of the latest weapons), mast-mounted sight and a removable beam with provision for a wide assortment of weapons; this version has a main rotor diameter of 27 ft 6 in (8·38 m), a maximum take-off weight of 3,550 lb (1610 kg), a maximum speed of 150 mph (241 km/h) and a range of 275 miles (443 km); the accommodation is a pilot and up to five passengers or an equivalent weight of cargo; the US Army special operations version is the **MH-6A** with night vision gear

Nightfox: low-cost nocturnal surveillance helicopter available in Model 500MG and Model 530MG versions and fitted with FLIR

Paramilitary MG Defender: low-cost patrol and rescue helicopter available in Model 500MG and Model 530MG versions

Left: TH-55A Osages are used by the US Army for helicopter pilot training.

Right: This OH-6A Cayuse has an M129 40-mm grenade launcher in its port cabin door.

McDonnell Douglas/British Aerospace AV-8B Harrier II

(USA & UK)

Type: land-based and shipborne STOVL close-support aeroplane

Accommodation: pilot on a Stencel SJU-13 zero/zero ejector seat

Armament (fixed): one 25-mm General Electric GAU-12/A Equaliser rotary-barrel cannon with 300 rounds in two underfuselage pods

Armament (disposable): this is carried on seven hardpoints (one under the fuselage rated at 1,240 lb/562 kg, and three under each wing with the inner two units each rated at 2,310 lb/1048 kg, the intermediate two units each at 1,400 lb/635 kg and the outboard two units each at 630 lb/286 lb) up to a maximum weight of 6,750 lb (3062 kg) for VTO or 17,000+ lb (7711+ kg) for STO; typical loads are four AIM-9 Sidewinder AAMs, or four AGM-65 Maverick ASMs, or 16 500-lb (227-kg) bombs, or 12 Rockeye II or CBU-series cluster bombs, or 10 Paveway laser-guided bombs, or 10 LAU-series pods for 2·75-in (70-mm) rockets, or two 30-mm GPU-5/A cannon pods; other weapon types that can be carried are the AGM-62 Walleye TV-guided bomb, GBU-15 EO-guided bomb, AGM-84 Harpoon anti-ship missile, and 2,000-, 1,000- and 250-lb (907-, 454- and 113 kg) free-fall or retarded bombs

Electronics and operational equipment: communication and navigation equipment, plus Hughes ASB-19(V)2 or 3 Angle-Rate Bombing Set, Smiths SU-128/A HUD, HDD, IBM weapon-delivery system, Litton ASN-130A INS, Litton ALR-67(V)2 RWR, Goodyear ALE-39 chaff/flare dispenser, and provision for the ALQ-164 and Westinghouse/ITT ALQ-165 Airborne Self-Protection Jammer (in a converted ALQ-131 pod) jammer pods

Powerplant and fuel system: one 21,450-lb (9730-kg) thrust Rolls-Royce F402-RR-406 or digitally controlled F402-RR-406A vectored-thrust non-afterburning turbofan, and a total internal fuel capacity of 1,100 US gal (4163 litres) plus provision for four 300-US gal (1136-litre) drop tanks; provision for inflight refuelling

Performance: maximum speed 601 mph (967 km/h) or Mach 0·91 at 36,000 ft (10,970 m) and 661 mph (1065 km/h) or Mach 0·87 at sea level; initial climb rate 14,715 ft (4485 m) per minute; service ceiling 50,000+ ft (15,240+ m); radius 103 miles (167 km) on a lo-lo-lo mission after STO with 12 500-lb (227-kg) bombs and 1-hour loiter; ferry range 2,418 miles (3891 km)

Weights: empty 13,086 lb (5936 kg); normal take-off 22,950 lb (10,410 kg); maximum take-off for VTO 18,950 lb (9596 kg) or for STO 31,000 lb (14,061 kg)

Dimensions: span 30 ft 4 in (9·25 m); length 46 ft 4 in (14·12 m); height 11 ft 7·75 in (3·55 m); wing area 238·7 sq ft (22·18 m²)

Variants

AV-8B Harrier II: US development of the British Harrier V/STOL aeroplane with significant improvements for enhanced capability, developed largely by BAe's US licensee, McDonnell Douglas, after US Marine Corps experience with the AV-8A Harrier; among these improvements are a wing (and portions of the fuselage and tail unit) of graphite epoxy composite construction, a wing of larger area and supercritical section (fitted with bigger flaps, drooping ailerons and leading-edge root extensions for additional manoeuvrability), extra hardpoints for greater offensive load, underfuselage lift improvement devices (large-area gun pod/strake units and a retractable barrier forward of the pods to boost trapped-gas lift for vertical take-off), strengthened landing gear, larger inlets for greater power, and a redesigned forward fuse-

McDonnell Douglas/British Aerospace T-45A Goshawk

lage to provide the pilot with better fields of vision; the type flew in YAV-8B prototype form in November 1978, and service deliveries began in 1983; from 1990 production aircraft have been powered by the 25,000-lb (11,340-kg) thrust Rolls-Royce F402-RR-408 (Pegasus 11-61) vectored-thrust turbofan; the AV-8B is also being provided with a night-attack capability by the installation of equipment similar to that of the McDonnell Douglas F/A-18A Hornet (a GEC Sensors fixed-position FLIR, GEC Avionics Cat's Eye pilot's night vision goggles, a digital moving map display and a HUD able to accommodate FLIR imaging); the first such night attack Harrier II flew in June 1987 with service deliveries following from September 1989

AV-8B Harrier II Plus: due to fly early in 1991, this is to have additional capability through the use of a nose-mounted Hughes APG-65 radar; if trials are successful, the US Marine Corps expects to take 76 such aircraft within its overall procurement plan for 328 AV-8Bs

TAV-8B: combat-capable two-seat operational conversion trainer variant of the AV-8B with a fuselage stretch of 4 ft (1·22 m) to allow the incorporation of a longer cockpit section for a weight penalty of 1,325 lb (601 kg)

EAV-8B Matador II: version of the AV-8B for the Spanish navy

Harrier GR.Mk 5: British equivalent to the AV-8B assembled in the UK and featuring a Martin-Baker Mk 12 ejector seat, a Marconi Zeus RWR/jammer system, a Plessey missile-approach warner, a Tracor ALE-40 chaff/flare dispenser (possibly to be augmented by two Philips dispensers located in the Sidewinder pylons), a Ferranti FIN1075 INS, a Ferranti moving map display, a panoramic camera in the nose, a BAe IR linescanner in the nose, provision for different weapons (including two AIM-9 Sidewinder AAMs on small pylons added just forward of the wing-mounted outrigger wheels, and two 25-mm Aden 25 cannon) and one 21,750-lb (9866-kg) thrust Rolls-Royce Pegasus 11-21 Mk 105 turbofan; the Harrier GR.Mk 5 has empty and maximum take-off weights of 13,798 lb (6258 kg) and 31,000 lb (14,061 kg) respectively; the first 40 are being built to the standard described above, and the 41st to 62nd will have provision for the retrofitting of the night-attack package developed for the USMC's Harrier II

Harrier GR.Mk 7: designation of the night-attack Harrier variant (34 aircraft) scheduled for service debut in the early 1990s; the electronics for this model are currently under development in the **Nightbird Harrier T.Mk 4**, a converted T.Mk 4 two-seat trainer with a Ferranti HUD in each cockpit, and a GEC thermal imager in the nose feeding an HDD in each cockpit, the latter also serving the aircraft's projected map display system; further upgrade of the GR.Mk 7 may be provided by the retrofit of radar, probably of the Ferranti Blue Vixen type; when the Harrier GR.Mk 7 begins to enter service, some Harrier T.Mk 4s will be converted into appropriate trainers under the designation Harrier T.Mk 6

Harrier T.Mk 10: proposed combat-capable two-seat development of the Harrier GR.Mk 5

Above left: The Av-8B Harrier II can operate from small dispersed sites.

Left: The AV-8B's much improved LIDs allow VTO with larger loads of disposable ordnance.

Right: The T-45A Goshawk is the navalized version of the British Aerospace Hawk

(UK)

Type: carrierborne and land-based basic and advanced flying and weapon trainer

Accommodation: pupil and instructor in tandem on Martin-Baker Mk 14 NACES zero/zero ejector seats

Armament (fixed): none

Armament (disposable): this is carried on three hardpoints (one permanent unit under each wing and one optional unit under the fuselage) for the carriage of multiple racks for light and practice bombs

Electronics and operational equipment: communication and navigation equipment, plus a CAI Industries sight in the rear cockpit

Powerplant and fuel system: one 5,845-lb (2651-kg) thrust Rolls-Royce/Turboméca F405-RR-401 (Adour Mk 871) non-afterburning turbofan, and a total internal fuel capacity of 450 US gal (1703 litres) plus provision for two 156-US gal (591-litre) drop tanks; no provision for inflight refuelling

Performance: maximum speed 620 mph (997 km/h) at 8,000 ft (2440 m) or Mach 0·84; initial climb rate 6,980 ft (3166 m) per minute; service ceiling 42,250 ft (12,880 m); range 1,150 miles (1850 km)

Weights: empty 9,394 lb (4261 kg); maximum take-off 12,798 lb (5787 kg)

Dimensions: span 30 ft 9·75 in (9·39 m); length including probe 39 ft 3 in (10·89 m); height 13 ft 5 in (4·09 m); wing area 179·6 sq ft (16·69 m²)

Variant

T-45A Goshawk: navalized trainer being produced jointly by BAe and McDonnell Douglas for the US Navy as replacement for the Rockwell T-2 Buckeye and McDonnell Douglas TA-4 Skyhawk; the type is based on the Hawk T.Mk 1 but has full carrier capability with strengthened landing gear (including long-stroke main units and a twin-wheel nose unit stressed for catapult take-offs), a fin increased in height by 6 in (0·152 m) and ventral finlets, a revised wing leading edge, a US Navy cockpit and the new ejector seats; the type was to have been powered by the 5,700-lb (2586-kg) thrust Rolls-Royce F405-RR-400A (Adour Mk 861-49) turbofan derated to 5,450-lb (2472-kg) thrust for economy and longevity, though pilot demands and higher drag levels than expected have led to the decision to use the F405-RR-401

Messerschmitt- Bölkow-Blohm (MBB) PAH-1

(West Germany)
Type: anti-tank helicopter
Accommodation: pilot and weapons operator side-by-side
Armament (fixed): generally none, but provision for one HBS 202 underfuselage system with a Rheinmetall MK 20 Rh 202 cannon, or one side-mounted Emerson Flexible Turret System with a 7·62-mm (0·3-in) General Electric GAU-2/A Minigun
Armament (disposable): this is carried on two hardpoints (one on each side of the fuselage rated at 500 kg/1,102 lb) and comprises six HOT or eight BGM-71 TOW anti-tank missiles
Electronics and operational equipment: communication and navigation equipment, plus (HOT installation) APX-Bézu 397 or (TOW installation) Hughes M65 roof-mounted gyro-stabilized sight
Powerplant and fuel system: two 420-shp (313-kW) Allison 250-C20B turboshafts, and a total internal fuel capacity of 580 litres (128 Imp gal); no provision for drop tanks or inflight refuelling
Performance: maximum speed 240 km/h (149 mph) at sea level; cruising speed 220 km/h (137 mph) at sea level; initial climb rate 540 m (1,770 ft) per minute; service ceiling 4250 m (13,950 ft); range 318 km (198 miles)
Weights: empty 1673 kg (3,688 lb); maximum take-off 2400 kg (5,291 lb)
Dimensions: main rotor diameter 9·84 m (32 ft 3·4 in); length, rotors turning 11·86 m (38 ft 11 in) and fuselage 8·56 m (28 ft 11 in); height 3·00 m (9 ft 10·1 in) to rotor head; main rotor disc area 76·05 m² (818·62 sq ft)

Variants

BO 105C: initial production version of MBB's highly capable five-seat utility helicopter, powered by 400-shp (298-kW) Allison 250-C20 turboshafts and bought by many military operators; the type first flew in February 1967; this and other basically civil variants have been assembled under licence in Indonesia, the Philippines and Spain, many going to military customers in roles such as maritime patrol and SAR
BO 105CB: standard version since 1975 with 420-shp (313-kW) Allison 250-C20B turboshafts, which are also used on the **BO 105CBS** subvariant with the cabin lengthened by 0·25 m (9·8 in) for greater passenger and freight capacity; Sweden uses a version of the BO 105CB in the anti-tank role with an outfit of eight TOW missiles and a Heli-TOW stabilized roof sight
BO 105LS: uprated version for hot-and-high operations with 550-shp (410-kW) Allison 250-C28C turboshafts and the cabin of the BO 105CBS; this type has a maximum take-off weight of 2600 kg (5,732 lb) with a slung load, and a cruising speed of 244 km/h (152 mph)
BO 105M: liaison and observation version for the West German army, by which the type is designated **VBH**; the primary differences between this military model and the civilian series are the uprated dynamic system, crash-resistant fuel tanks and seats, and high-impact landing gear
BO 105P: anti-tank version for the West German army, by which the type is designated **Panzerab-wehrhubschrauber-1** (**PAH-1**); the basic BO 105P type is also used by Spain with the underfuselage cannon installation; because of delays in deciding on the Franco-German successor to the PAH-1, the current model is to be given a mid-life update in two phases; the first phase will be centred on a more powerful engine installation using a pair of Allison 250-C20R-3 turboshafts driving a more efficient rotor to allow a maximum take-off weight of 2400 kg (5,291 lb) without any loss of performance; this will also permit the carriage of six HOT-2 anti-tank missiles (on a revised angled-down outrigger arrangement) and their associated digital (and thus lighter) fire-control system; the second phase is designed to incorporate a Leitz/Eltro/MBB night-vision system (based on a roof-mounted stabilized optical package) and enhanced self-defence measures; MBB is also considering an escort derivative of the PAH-1 under the designation **Begleitschutzhub-schrauber-1** (**BSH-1**) with taller landing gear to allow the underfuselage carriage of a Lucas gun turret adapted for the carriage of four AIM-92A Stinger lightweight AAMs together with associated electronic and sight equipment

Mikoyan-Gurevich MiG-17F

(USSR)
Type: fighter and ground-attack aeroplane
Accommodation: pilot on an ejector seat
Armament (fixed): one 37-mm N-37D cannon with 40 rounds, and two 23-mm NR-23 cannon with 80 rounds per gun
Armament (disposable): this is carried on two hardpoints (one under each wing rated at 500 kg/1,102 lb) up to a maximum weight of 500 kg (1,102 lb) of weapons such as two 250- or 125-kg (551- or 276-lb) bombs, or two 240-mm (9·45-in) S-240 rockets, or two launchers for eight or 16 55-mm (2·17-in) rockets
Electronics and operational equipment: communication and navigation equipment, plus a gyro sight

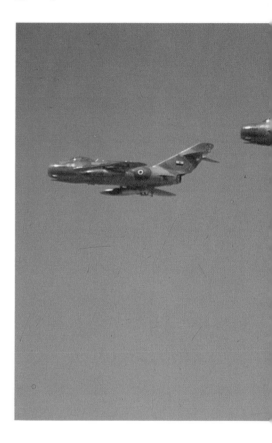

Left: When fitted with the Bezu 397 sight and six HOT anti-tank missiles, the BO 105P helicopter is designated PAH-1 by its sole operator, the West German army.

Powerplant and fuel system: one 3170-kg (6,989-lb) afterburning thrust Klimov VK-1F turbojet, and a total internal fuel capacity of 1565 litres (344 Imp gal) plus provision for two 240- or 400-litre (53- or 88-Imp gal) drop tanks; no provision for inflight refuelling
Performance: maximum speed 1145 km/h (711 mph) or Mach 0·97 at 3000 m (9,845 ft); initial climb rate 3900 m (12,795 ft) per minute; service ceiling 16,600 m (54,460 ft); range 1470 km (913 miles)
Weights: empty 4100 kg (9,040 lb); normal take-off 5340 kg (11,773 lb); maximum take-off 6700 kg (14,770 lb)
Dimensions: span 9·63 m (31 ft 7 in); length 11·26 m (36 ft 11·25 in); height 3·35 m (11 ft 0 in); wing area 22·60 m² (243·3 sq ft)

'Fresco-C'

Mikoyan-Gurevich MiG-19SF 'Farmer-C'

Variants

MiG-17F 'Fresco-C': the MiG-17 was developed in the 1950s as a much improved version of the MiG-15, and was authorized for full-scale production in June 1951, deliveries beginning in 1952; the MiG-17 retained the VK-1 non-afterburning turbojet of the MiG-15bis and has now disappeared from service, but was followed by the MiG-17F with the VK-1F afterburning turbojet, wider airbrakes and an exposed jetpipe; the type was also built in Poland as the **LIM-5P**; Poland also developed a special variant, the **LIM-5M** STOL tactical aircraft with a braking parachute, provision for RATO units and additional hardpoints

MiG-17PF 'Fresco-D': all-weather version of the

(USSR)

Type: fighter and ground-attack aeroplane
Accommodation: pilot on an ejector seat
Armament (fixed): three 30-mm NR-30 cannon with 80 rounds per gun
Armament (disposable): this is carried on two hardpoints (one under each wing and rated at 250 kg/551 lb) up to a maximum weight of 500 kg (1,102 lb) of weapons such as two 250- or 125-kg (551- or 276-lb) bombs, or two 137-mm (5·4-in) M-100, 160-mm (6·3-in) S-16, 190-mm (7·5-in) TRS-190 or 212-mm (8·35-in) ARS-212 rockets, or two launchers for eight or 16 55-mm (2·17-in) rockets
Electronics and operational equipment: communication and navigation equipment, plus a

reflector sight
Powerplant and fuel system: two 3250-kg (7,165-lb) afterburning thrust Tumanskii RD-9BF turbojets, and a total internal fuel capacity of 2170 litres (477 Imp gal) plus provision for two 1520-, 800-, 400- 300- or 200-litre (344-, 176-, 88-, 66- or 44-Imp gal) drop tanks; no provision for inflight refuelling
Performance: maximum speed 1450 km/h (901 mph) or Mach 1·35 at 10,000 m (32,810 ft); cruising speed 950 km/h (590 mph) at 10,000 m (32,810 ft); initial climb rate 6900 m (22,635 ft) per minute; service ceiling 17,900 m (58,725 ft); range 1390 km (863 miles) on internal fuel
Weights: empty 5170 kg (11,397 lb); normal take-off 7400 kg (16,314 lb); maximum take-off 8900 kg (19,621 lb)
Dimensions: span 9·20 m (30 ft 2·25 in); length 12·60 m (41 ft 4 in) excluding probe; height 3·90 m (12 ft 9·5 in); wing area 25·00 m² (269·1 sq ft)

Variants

MiG-19SF 'Farmer-C': vying with the North American F-100 Super Sabre for the historical niche as the world's first operational aeroplane with supersonic performance, the MiG-19 resulted from a Soviet appreciation that the MiG-17 was little more than an upgraded MiG-15, and that a new design was required for truly supersonic performance; the result was the conceptually advanced MiG-19, which flew in definitive prototype form during September 1953 on the power of two Mikulin AM-5 turbojets, earlier prototypes having experimented with a single Lyul'ka AL-5, or twin Klimov VK-7Fs or twin AM-5s; the type began to enter service in 1954 as the MiG-19F 'Farmer-A' with AM-5F afterburning turbojets and as the MiG-19PF 'Farmer-B' with radar, but these types were withdrawn because of high accident rates; the first major production version was thus the MiG-19S (later redesignated MiG-19SF) with an all-moving slab tailplane, Tumanskii RD-9B turbojets, a revised control system and a gun armament of three long-barrel 30-mm cannon in place of the mixed 23- and 37-mm battery carried by the earlier aircraft

MiG-19PF 'Farmer-D': limited all-weather development of the MiG-19SF with RP-5 Izumrud radar (in the inlet centrebody and a 'bullet' on the inlet lip) and an armament of two 30-mm cannon; the MiG-19PM was similar but carried 'Scan Odd' radar, four AA-1 'Alkali' beam-riding AAMs and no cannon

Above: The MiG-17F is obsolete as a fighter, but is still employed by some Arab and third-world countries as a ground-attack and advanced training aeroplane.

Below: Early MiG-19s from an aerobatic display team.

MiG-17F day fighter with RP-5 Izumrud radar and an armament of three 23-mm cannon (supplemented in the out-of-service MiG-17PFU 'Fresco-E' derivative by four AA-1 'Alkali' beam-riding AAMs)

Shenyang Aircraft Factory J-5: MiG-17F built in China, and exported with the designation **F-5**
Shenyang Aircraft Factory J-5A: MiG-17PF built in China, and exported with the designation **F-5A**
Shenyang Aircraft Factory JJ-5: Chinese-developed operational trainer version, combining the forward fuselage of the MiG-15UTI with the rest of the airframe of the J-5A; the type has ranging radar in the upper portion of the inlet lip, armament of one 23-mm cannon, powerplant of one 2700-kg (5,952-lb) thrust Wopen-5D (VK-1A) turbojet, a maximum take-off weight of 6215 kg (13,700 lb) and a length of 11·50 m (37 ft 8·75 in); the type has been exported as the **FT-5** and **F-5T**

Mikoyan-Gurevich MiG-21MF 'Fishbed-J'

(USSR)
Type: fighter and ground-attack aeroplane
Accommodation: pilot on a KM-1 zero/zero ejector seat
Armament (fixed): one 23-mm GSh-23L twin-barrel cannon with 200 rounds in a detachable belly pack
Armament (disposable): this is carried on four hardpoints (two under each wing with each rated at 500 kg/2,205 lb) up to a maximum weight of 2000 kg (4,409 lb); typical loads are two AA-2 'Atoll' AAMs plus two AA-2-2 'Advanced Atoll' AAMs or two launchers each with 16 55-mm (2·17-in) rockets, or four launchers each with 16 55-mm (2·17-in) rockets, or two 500-kg (1,102-lb) and two 250-kg (551-lb) bombs, or four 240-mm (9·45-in) S-24 rockets
Electronics and operational equipment: communication and navigation equipment, plus 'Jay Bird' fire-control radar, HUD, OR-69 Sirena 3 RWR, ARL-S data-link and provision for an under-fuselage reconnaissance pod (generally with three cameras, one IR linescanner and one chaff dispenser), ECM jammer pods and wingtip ECM pods
Powerplant and fuel system: one 6600-kg (14,550-lb) afterburning thrust Tumanskii R-13-300 turbojet, and a total internal fuel capacity of 2600 litres (572 Imp gal) plus provision for one 800- or 490-litre (176- or 108-Imp gal) and two 490-litre (108-Imp gal) drop tanks; no provision for inflight refuelling
Performance: maximum speed 2230 km/h (1,385 mph) or Mach 2·1 at 11,000 m (36,090 ft) and 1300 km/h (807 mph) or Mach 1·06 at sea level; initial climb rate 6400 m (20,995 ft) per minute; service ceiling about 15,250 m (50,030 ft); radius 370 km (230 miles) on a hi-lo-hi mission with four 250-kg (551-lb) bombs; ferry range 1800 km (1,118 miles) with three drop tanks
Weights: empty 5845 kg (12,886 lb); normal take-off 8200 kg (18,077 lb) with four AA-2 missiles; maximum take-off 9800 kg (21,605 lb)
Dimensions: span 7·15 m (23 ft 5·5 in); length including probe 15·76 m (51 ft 8·5 in); height 4·00 m (13 ft 1·5 in); wing area 23·00 m² (247·58 sq ft)

Variants

MiG-21F 'Fishbed-C': this was the first large-scale production variant of the MiG-21, a type of great military importance in its day, and still serving in large numbers after development into a capable though limited multi-role fighter; the type was designed in response to a 1953 requirement for a short-range clear-weather interceptor, and developed through a series of prototypes with different wing planforms and sweeps but all powered by the Tumanskii RD-9E or R-11 turbojet; the tailed delta configuration was adopted in 1956 as offering the best combination of desired attributes, and the pre-production E-6 flew in 1957; full production began in 1958 with the MiG-21 'Fishbed-B' powered by the 5100-kg (11,243-lb) afterburning thrust R-11 fed by 2340 litres (515 Imp gal) of fuel, and possessing an armament of two 30-mm cannon; from 1959 this type was supplanted by the MiG-21F with 5750-kg (12,676-lb) afterburning thrust R-11, provision for a centreline tank of 490-litre (108-Imp gal) capacity and an armament of one 30-mm cannon plus either two AA-2 'Atoll' AAMs or two UV-16-57 rocket pods; the type was also built in Czechoslovakia without significant modification, and in China as the somewhat modified J-7

MiG-21PF 'Fishbed-D': 1960 model with an inlet of increased diameter (to allow the incorporation of a larger centrebody with R1L 'Spin Scan-A' interception radar for limited all-weather capability), greater power from the 5950-kg (13,117-lb) afterburning thrust R-11F and 2850 litres (627 Imp gal) of internal fuel to overcome in part the problems of chronically short range; late-production variants on this basic model were the **MiG-21PFS** with blown flaps and RATO capability, the NATO-designated **'Fishbed-E'** with broader-chord vertical tail surfaces and provision for a GP-9 under-fuselage gun pod carrying the twin-barrel GSh-23L 23-mm cannon, and the **MiG-21FL** export model with R2L 'Spin Scan-B' radar and the 6200-kg (13,668-lb) afterburning thrust R-11-300, but without blown flaps; this last model was built under licence in India

MiG-21PFM 'Fishbed-F': full-production model incorporating the various improvements of earlier models, and thus having blown flaps, the R-11-300 turbojet, broader-chord vertical tail and R2L radar; the type also introduced a conventional cockpit enclosure, with fixed windscreen plus side-opening canopy in place of the earlier models' single-piece front-hinged unit

MiG-21PFMA 'Fishbed-J': straightforward development of the MiG-21PFM in most respects, this marked the start of the MiG-21 series' second generation as a multi-role fighter; the type introduced a radical enlargement of the dorsal fairing for reduced drag plus extra avionics and revised tankage for 2600 litres (572 Imp gal) of internal fuel, this reduction being offset by provision for three drop tanks with a total capacity of 1470 litres (323 Imp gal); other improvements were the KM-1 zero/zero ejector seat, more powerful 'Jay Bird' radar, and four rather than two underwing hardpoints for the carriage of AA-2-2 'Advanced Atoll' as well as AA-2 'Atoll' AAMs; early MiG-21PFMAs had provision for an external GP-9 gun pod, but later aircraft were fitted with an internal GSh-23L cannon installation; the export version was the **MiG-21M**, which was built under licence in India

MiG-21R 'Fishbed-H': tactical reconnaissance version of the MiG-21PFMA with three cameras (instead of the cannon pack) in the bay just aft of the nosewheel, and also able to carry an under-fuselage pod (for optical or IR equipment) and tip-mounted ECM equipment comparable to that

of the 'Fishbed-K'; a derivative of this type was the **MiG-21RF** derived from the MiG-21MF but otherwise similar to the MiG-21R

MiG-21MF 'Fishbed-J': much improved version of the MiG-21PFMA with the 6600-kg (14,550-lb) afterburning thrust R-13-300 turbojet offering greater power for lower installed weight; another modification was the addition of a small rear-view mirror in a neat fairing above the windscreen; an improved version of the MiG-21MF, designated **'Fishbed-K'** by NATO and at one time thought to be designated MiG-21SMT by the Soviets, introduced a still larger dorsal fairing for greater fuel capacity and yet further enhanced aerodynamics; the subvariant also has provision for detachable ECM pods at the wing and fin tips; the export version is the **MiG-21M** with the R-11F2S-300 engine

MiG-21SMB 'Fishbed-K': variant of the MiG-21MF with the dorsal fairing extended aft as far as the braking parachute housing to provide maximum fuel capacity consonant with minimum wetted area

MiG-21bis 'Fishbed-L': initial third-generation development of the MiG-21 series with a re-engineered airframe for greater stength but reduced weight, updated avionics and a further enlarged dorsal fairing to allow an increase to 2900 litres (638 Imp gal) of internal fuel

MiG-21Mbis 'Fishbed-N': definitive third-generation model with the 7500-kg (16,535-lb) afterburning thrust Tumanskii R-25-300 and further improvements to the avionics, in this instance characterized by the 'bow-and-arrow' probe on the nose for air-data sensors necessary for the accurate delivery of air-to-surface ordnance; the model has empty and normal take-off weights of 6000 and 8500 kg (13,228 and 18,739 lb) respectively, initial climb rate at a weight of 6800 kg (14,991 lb) being 17,700 m (58,070 ft) per minute; the type can carry AA-8 'Aphid' as well as AA-2 'Atoll' AAMs, and licence production was undertaken in India; it is believed that all production of the MiG-21 series ended with this variant in 1987

MiG-21U 'Mongol-A': two-seat conversion trainer based on the MiG-21F but with the larger mainwheels and tyres introduced on the MiG-21PF

MiG-21US 'Mongol-B': two-seat conversion trainer with broader-chord vertical tail and flap blowing; the instructor also has a retractable periscope for improved vision during take-offs and landings

MiG-21UM 'Mongol-B': two-seat conversion trainer derived from the MiG-21MF with R-13 engine, but otherwise similar to the MiG-21US

Late-production MiG-21s were considerably more effective aircraft than their earlier counterparts, but were still optimized for clear-weather operations.

Mikoyan-Gurevich MiG-23ML 'Flogger-G'

(USSR)

Type: variable-geometry air-combat fighter with a secondary ground-attack capability

Accommodation: pilot on a KM-1 zero/zero ejector seat

Armament (fixed): one 23-mm GSh-23L two-barrel cannon with about 400 rounds in a belly pack

Armament (disposable): this is carried on five hardpoints (one under the fuselage, one under each engine inlet duct and one under each fixed inner wing panel) up to a maximum weight of 3000+ kg (6,614+ lb) of disposable stores including 500- and 250-kg (1,102- and 551-lb) bombs, launchers for 55-mm (2·24-in) rockets, and AAMs such as the AA-2 'Atoll', AA-2-2 'Advanced Atoll', AA-7 'Apex' and AA-8 'Aphid'; a typical load in the air-combat role is six AA-7 missiles (four on twin launchers under the inlet ducts and two under the inner wings)

Electronics and operational equipment: communication and navigation equipment, plus 'High Lark' radar (with a search range of 85 km/53 miles and a tracking range of 55 km/34 miles), undernose IR sensor, SO-69 Sirena 3 RWR, SRO-2 IFF, Doppler navigation, 'Swift Rod' instrument landing system, and unspecified ECM

Powerplant and fuel system: one 12,475-kg (27,502-lb) afterburning thrust Tumanskii R-29B turbojet, and a total internal fuel capacity of 5750 litres (1,265 Imp gal) plus provision for three 800-litre (176-Imp gal) drop tanks; no provision for inflight refuelling

Performance: maximum speed 2500 km/h (1,553 mph) or Mach 2·35 at high altitude and 1470 km/h (913 mph) or Mach 1·2 at sea level; initial climb rate 9145+ m (30,000+ ft) per minute; service ceiling 18,300 m (60,040 ft); radius 950 km (590 miles) on a hi-lo-hi mission with one drop tank; ferry range 2500 km (1,553 miles) with three drop tanks

Weights: empty 10,200 kg (22,487 lb); normal take-off 16,100 kg (35,494 lb); maximum take-off 18,900 kg (41,667 lb)

Dimensions: span 13·95 m (45 ft 9 in) spread and 7·77 m (25 ft 6 in) swept; length including probe 16·71 m (54 ft 10 in); height 4·82 m (15 ft 9·75 in); wing area 31·3 m² (336·9 sq ft) spread and 34·6 m² (372·4 sq ft)

Variants

MiG-23M 'Flogger-B': first production variant of the MiG-23 air-combat fighter, one of the USSR's most important tactical aircraft; the type was schemed in the late 1950s and early 1960s as a variable-geometry successor to the MiG-21 with modest field requirements but considerably better payload/range figures plus higher-performance radar and advanced weapons; the type flew in two basic prototype forms (the E-230 tailed delta with a Lyul'ka AL-7F-1 main engine and a battery of Koliesov lift engines for V/STOL capability, and the E-231 variable-geometry type with an AL-7F-1 for STOL capability) during the first half of the 1960s, the E-231 proving superior in all important respects; the new Tumanskii R-27/R-29 series of afterburning turbojets was planned for the production model, but pending deliveries of these powerful engines the pre-production aircraft were completed with the AL-5F-1 turbojet for operational evaluation, resulting in the MiG-23S and MiG-23SM with two and four hardpoints respectively, and both designated 'Flogger-A' by NATO; the first large-scale production model was thus the MiG-23M which appeared in 1971 with the 10,200-kg (22,485-lb) afterburning thrust R-27 turbojet; because this engine is lighter and shorter than the AL-5 series, the airframe had to be revised quite considerably, the wings being located 0·61 m (2 ft) farther forward with greater sweep on the inner portions, the chord of the outer wings being extended to create a large dogtooth, and the rear fuselage being shortened; the radar of this model was initially a less capable 'High Lark' set, though the full-performance equipment has since been retrofitted

MiG-23MF 'Flogger-B': upgraded production model delivered from 1975 with the R-29 afterburning turbofan and the full-capability version of the 'High Lark' radar; this type has limited lookdown/shoot down capability

MiG-23UM 'Flogger-C': tandem two-seat operational conversion trainer version of the MiG-23M and developed on the basis of the pre-production **MiG-21U** based on the MiG-23S; the type has full weapons capability but reduced fuel and the smaller 'Jay Bird' radar

MiG-23MS 'Flogger-E': export version of the MiG-23M with lower standards of equipment (including the 'Jay Bird' radar with a search range of 29 km/18 miles and a tracking range of 19 km/12 miles), lacking the IR sensor and Doppler navigation, and fitted only for the AA-2 'Atoll' AAM

MiG-23BN 'Flogger-F': derivative of the MiG-23MF, introduced in 1974 and originally believed to be only for export but since adopted in large numbers by the USSR and its Warsaw Pact allies in the fighter-bomber role; the type is a hybrid with MiG-23 and MiG-27 features, and thus capable of the air combat and attack roles; the model is fitted with the MiG-27's nose without search radar but offering the better-protected pilot (external armour is added to the sides of the forward fuselage) a considerably enhanced view forward and downward, and fitted with an LRMTS, terrain-avoidance radar, and Doppler navigation; the type also has the R-29B turbojet, larger tyres for operations from semi-prepared airstrips, additional ECM, and an IR seeker; the type can carry 4500 kg (9,921 lb) of ordnance on five hardpoints (one under the fuselage, two under the inlet trunks and two under the fixed inner wings) each fitted with tandem racks

MiG-23ML 'Flogger-G': dedicated air-combat fighter version of the MiG-23MF delivered from 1978 with simpler avionics (including a lighter radar and a revised undernose sensor blister), a smaller dorsal fin and a revised nosewheel leg

MiG-23BN 'Flogger-H': version of the 'Flogger-F' with small RWR blisters on each side of the lower fuselage just forward of the nosewheel doors, and intended for the USSR's Warsaw Pact allies

MiG-23 'Flogger-K': aerodynamically improved version of the 'Flogger-G' with a smaller ventral fin, dogtoothed inboard leading edges on the wing gloves and provision for AA-11 'Archer' AAMs; it is thought that all Soviet production of the MiG-23 and MiG-27 series ended in the mid- to late 1980s

In common with other Soviet tactical fighters, this MiG-23ML has guards on its wheels to prevent damage from the earth and gravel of semi-prepared airstrips.

Mikoyan-Gurevich MiG-25 'Foxbat-A'

(USSR)
Type: interceptor fighter
Accommodation: pilot on a KM-1 zero/zero ejector seat
Armament (fixed): none
Armament (disposable): this is carried on four hardpoints (two under each wing, with each unit rated at 1000 kg/2,205 lb) up to a maximum weight of 4000 kg (8,818 lb); the disposable load generally comprises four AA-6 'Acrid' AAMs, or two AA-7 'Apex' and four AA-8 'Aphid' or AA-11 'Archer' AAMs
Electronics and operational equipment: communication and navigation equipment, plus 'Fox Fire' radar (with a lock-on range of 90 km/56 miles), SO-69 Sirena 3 RWR, unspecified ECM and continuous-wave illuminators for the radar-homing AAMs
Powerplant and fuel system: two 12,250-kg (27,005-lb) afterburning thrust Tumanskii R-31 turbojets, and a total internal fuel capacity of about 17,410 litres (3,838 Imp gal); no provision drop tanks or for inflight refuelling
Performance: maximum speed 3400 km/h (2,113 mph) or Mach 3·2 clean at high altitude or 2975 km/h (1,849 mph) or Mach 2·8 at altitude with 50% fuel and four AA-6 'Acrid' AAMs; initial climb rate 12,480 m (40,945 ft) per minute; service ceiling 24,500 m (80,380 ft); radius 1130 km (702 miles) on a typical hi-hi-hi mission
Weights: empty 20,000 + kg (44,092 + lb); maximum take-off 37,425 kg (82,507 lb)
Dimensions: span 13·95 m (45 ft 9·2 in); length including probe 23·82 m (78 ft 1·8 in); height 6·10 m (20 ft 0·2 in); wing area 56·83 m² (611·7 sq ft)

Variants

MiG-25 'Foxbat-A': developed to deal with the North American B-70 Valkyie Mach 3 strategic bomber, which was then cancelled, the MiG-25 is the world's fastest interceptor though limited in this performance to non-manoeuvring flight; the

type's avionics are also of somewhat elderly vintage; first flown in April 1965 as the E-266 prototype and research aircraft, the MiG-25 began to enter service in 1970
MiG-25R 'Foxbat-B': basic operational reconnaissance version of the MiG-25 with a maximum take-off weight of 33,400 kg (73,633 lb) and unkinked wings reduced in span to 13·40 m (44 ft 0 in); this version has a combat radius of 1100 km (694 miles), and carries a small SLAR and five cameras in the nose (one vertical and four oblique), a small 'Jay Bird' radar in the nose forward of the SLAR installation, Doppler and ground-mapping radar in ventral radomes, and ECCM equipment
MiG-25U 'Foxbat-C': two-seat operational conversion trainer using a new nose section with a separate trainee cockpit; overall length is 23·82 m (78 ft 1·8 in)
MiG-25R 'Foxbat-D': variant of the 'Foxbat-B' with a larger SLAR but no nose cameras, and probably fitted for the strategic role with Elint equipment
MiG-25MP 'Foxbat-E': 'Foxbat-A' converted to an updated standard for limited look-down/shoot-down capability at a lower-altitude cruise; the type has a new pulse-Doppler search-and-track radar and a new undernose IR sensor blister, and the engines are uprated R-31F units each with an afterburning thrust of 14,000 kg (30,864 lb); the type has an internal gun, and the radar is matched to six of the new AA-9 AAMs as well as the AA-11 AAMs
MiG-25 'Foxbat-F': dedicated defence-suppression variant carrying AS-11 'Kilter' radar-homing missiles launched on the basis of data provided by a specialized radar-warning suite

The 'Foxbat-E' has new radar and an undernose infra-red search and track unit.

Mikoyan-Gurevich MiG-27

(USSR)
Type: variable-geometry ground-attack aeroplane
Accommodation: pilot on a KM-1 zero/zero ejector seat
Armament (fixed): one 30-mm rotary-barrel cannon with about 700 rounds
Armament (disposable): this is carried on seven hardpoints (one on the centreline rated at 1000 kg/2,205 lb, two under the rear fuselage each rated at 500 kg/1,102 lb, one under each inlet rated at 1000 kg/2,205 lb, and one under each wing glove rated at 500 kg/1,102 lb) up to a maximum weight of 4000 + kg (8,818 + lb); typical weapons are AA-2 'Atoll' and AA-8 'Aphid' AAMs, AS-7 'Kerry', AS-10 'Karen', AS-12 'Kegler' and AS-14 'Kedge' ASMs, AS-9 'Kyle' radar-homing missile, 500- and 250-kg (1,102- and 551-lb) bombs, and launchers for 16 and 32 55-mm (2·17-in) rockets; the type can also carry two free-fall nuclear weapons
Electronics and operational equipment: communication and navigation equipment, plus HUD, LRMTS, terrain-avoidance radar, Doppler navigation, 'Odd Rods' IFF, OR-69 Sirena 3 RWR, and internal/external ECM
Powerplant and fuel system: one 11,500-kg (25,352-lb) afterburning thrust Tumanskii R-29-300 turbojet, and a total internal fuel capacity of 5750 litres (1,265 Imp gal) plus provision for three 800-litre (176-Imp gal) drop tanks; no provision for inflight refuelling
Performance: maximum speed 1807 km/h (1,123 mph) or Mach 1·7 at high altitude and 1345 km/h (836 mph) or Mach 1·1 at sea level; initial climb rate not revealed; service ceiling 16,000 m (52,495 ft); radius 390 km (240 miles) on a lo-lo-lo mission with two AA-2 AAMs, four 500-kg (1,102-lb) bombs and one 800-litre (176-Imp gal) drop tank; ferry range 2500 km (1,553 miles)
Weights: empty 10,790 kg (23,788 lb); normal take-off 15,500 kg (34,172 lb); maximum take-off

'Flogger-D'

20,100 kg (44,313 lb)
Dimensions: span 13·95 m (45 ft 9 in) spread and 7·77 m (25 ft 6 in) swept; length including probe 16·00 m (52 ft 6 in); height 4·82 m (15 ft 9·75 in); wing area 31·3 m² (336·9 sq ft) spread and 34·6 m² (372·4 sq ft)

Variants

MiG-27 'Flogger-D': derived from the MiG-23 as a dedicated ground-attack aircraft, the MiG-27 has a new forward fuselage with fixed rather than variable-geometry air inlets (and two-position nozzles) plus a radarless 'duck' nose; this nose section has a fair degree of armour protection and seats the pilot relatively higher than in the MiG-23, offering him far better fields of vision to the front, sides and below over the flattened nose; the nose itself its fitted with an LRMTS, and with terrain-avoidance radar; the weapon capability is similar to that of the MiG-23BN in terms of weapons carried, but somewhat greater in terms of weight, and the type has a new six-barrel cannon optimized for the ground-attack role

MiG-27M 'Flogger-J': revised version produced from 1981 with small leading-edge root extensions (probably accommodating ECM equipment), sensors that differ in detail from the earlier model's fit, and provision for two gun pods each with one 23-mm GSh-23L twin-barrel cannon angled to fire obliquely downward; this variant is also built in India with very slight modifications as the **MiG-27M Bahadur**

These Egyptian aircraft reveal the 'duck' nose of the 'Flogger-D'.

Mikoyan-Gurevich MiG-29 'Fulcrum-A'

(USSR)
Type: air-superiority fighter with secondary attack capability
Accommodation: pilot on a K-36D zero/zero ejector seat
Armament (fixed): one 30-mm rotary-barrel cannon with an unrevealed number of rounds
Armament (disposable): this is carried on six hardpoints (three under each wing) up to an unrevealed maximum weight, and can comprise six AA-10 'Alamo' medium-range AAMs or two AA-10 'Alamo' and four AA-11 'Archer' short-range AAMs, bombs, rockets pods and other stores including ECM pods and drop tanks
Electronics and operational equipment: communication and navigation equipment, plus NO-93 'Slot Back' (or 'Flash Dance') coherent pulse-Doppler nose radar, HUD, IR sensor (with search and tracking functions) collimated with a laser rangefinder, helmet-mounted sight, OR-69 Sirena 3 RWR, 'Odd Rods' IFF, upward-firing chaff dispensers on the fin extensions, and other systems
Powerplant and fuel system: two 8300-kg (18,298-lb) afterburning thrust Tumanskii R-33D turbofans, and a total internal fuel weight of 4000 kg (8,818 lb); provision for one external tank under the fuselage but no provision for drop tanks or inflight refuelling
Performance: maximum speed 2445+ km/h (1,519+ mph) or Mach 2·3+ at high altitude and 1300 km/h (805 mph) or Mach 1·06 at sea level; initial climb rate 19·800 m (64,960 ft) per minute; service ceiling 17,000 m (55,775 ft); radius 1150 km (715 miles) on a typical mission; ferry range 2100 km (1,305 miles)
Weights: empty 7825 kg (17,251 lb); normal take-off 15,000 kg (33,069 lb); maximum take-off 18,000 kg (39,683 lb)
Dimensions: span 11·36 m (37 ft 3·25 in); length including probe 17·32 m (56 ft 9·85 in); height 4·73 m (15 ft 6·2 in); wing area 35·5 m² (382·1 sq ft)

Variants

MiG-29 'Fulcrum-A': entering service in 1985, the MiG-29 is a dual-role fighter resembling the McDonnell Douglas F-15 Eagle in configuration but sized like the McDonnell Douglas F/A-18 Hornet and, like that latter fighter, optimized for the air combat role with attack as a powerful secondary capability; despite its lack of a conventional control system, the type possesses great agility; a genuine look-down/shoot-down capability is offered by the combination of a 40-km (25-mile) range pulse-Doppler radar and the new AA-10 snap-down AAM; the 'Fulcrum-A' has undergone a number of changes since it was first seen, the consensus being that these indicate a number of fixes to bring the design up to its present fully operational standard; the first variant was probably a pre-production model and carried small ventral fins reminiscent of those carried by the Su-27 'Flanker'; the first service model was that shown off at Kuopio Risalla in Finland during July 1986; the third variant has wider-chord rudders; and the standard type seen in 1988 has an enlarged dorsal spine housing either more fuel or revised electronics (possibly for the attack role); the type is operated by India with the name **Baaz**
MiG-29U 'Fulcrum-B': two-seat combat-capable operational conversion trainer derivative of the 'Fulcrum-A' with a ranging radar in place of the pulse-Doppler unit of the 'Fulcrum-A', and with an overall length of 17·42 m (57 ft 1·8 in)
MiG-29 'Fulcrum-C': NATO designation for an electronically upgraded version of the 'Fulcrum-A' with additional equipment most notably in a dorsal hump fairing

With the 'Fulcrum-A' the Soviets have all but eliminated the technical inferiority of their warplanes to Western types.

Mikoyan-Gurevich MiG-31 'Foxhound'

(USSR)

Type: all-weather interceptor and electronic warfare aeroplane

Accommodation: pilot and systems operator in tandem on zero/zero ejector seats

Armament (fixed): none

Armament (disposable): this is carried on four tangential positions (two on the lower corner of each inlet) and on four hardpoints (two under each wing) up to an unrevealed maximum weight, and comprises eight AAMs, generally four AA-9 'Amos' and four AA-8 'Aphid' weapons

Electronics and operational equipment: communication and navigation equipment, plus pulse-Doppler fire-control radar, HUD, HDDs, INS, Doppler navigation, Sirena 3 IFF, RWR and other systems

Powerplant and fuel system: two 14,000-kg (30,864-lb) afterburning thrust Tumanskii R-31F turbojets, and a total internal fuel capacity of 17,410 litres (3,830 Imp gal) plus provision for two drop tanks; no provision for inflight refuelling

Performance: maximum speed 2553 km/h (1,586 mph) or Mach 2·4 at high altitude; initial climb rate not revealed; service ceiling not revealed; radius 1500 km (932 miles)

Weights: empty 21,825 kg (48,115 lb); maximum take-off 41,150 kg (90,725 lb)

Dimensions: span 14·00 m (45 ft 11·2 in); length 25·00 m (82 ft 0·25 in); height 6·10 m (20 ft 0·2 in);

wing area 58·00 m² (624·33 sq ft)

Variant

MiG-31 'Foxhound': entering service by mid-1985, the MiG-31 is a fairly radical development of the MiG-25 for reduced outright flight performance but considerably enhanced electronic and weapon capability, the latter being derived from the installation of a pulse-Doppler radar for genuine look-down/shoot-down capability with the AA-9 AAM, of which four are carried in two tandem pairs under the fuselage; the MiG-31 also has revised leading-edge root extensions, a different powerplant with longer jetpipes, and much improved ECM capability, the last being handled by the systems operator in the rear seat

Below: Like the Sikorsky S-55, the 'Hound-A' has a large piston engine low in the nose and an oblique transmission shaft.

Mil Mi-4 'Hound-A'

(USSR)
Type: tactical and utility medium helicopter
Accommodation: flightcrew of two, and 11 passengers or 1600 kg (3,525 lb) of freight in the hold
Armament (fixed): optional installation of one 7·62- or 12·7-mm (0·3- or 0·5-in) machine-gun under the fuselage
Armament (disposable): this is carried on the fuselage sides, where optional hardpoints allow the carriage of two UV-8-57 or UV-16-57 launchers for eight or 16 55-mm (2·17-in) rockets
Electronics and operational equipment: communication and navigation equipment
Powerplant and fuel system: one 1268-kW (1,700-hp) Shvetsov ASh-82V piston engine, and a total internal fuel capacity of 1000 litres (220 Imp gal) plus provision for one 500-litre (110-Imp gal) auxiliary tank in the cabin; no provision for drop tanks or inflight refuelling
Performance: maximum speed 210 km/h (130 mph) at 1500 m (4,920 ft); cruising speed 160 km/h (99 mph); service ceiling 6000 m (19,685 ft); hovering ceiling out of ground effect 700 m (2,295 ft); range 400 km (249 miles) with 10 passengers
Weights: empty 5270 kg (11,618 lb); normal take-off 7350 kg (16,204 lb); maximum take-off 7800 kg (17,196 lb)
Dimensions: main rotor diameter 21·00 m (68 ft 11 in); length overall, rotors turning 25·02 m (82 ft 1 in) and fuselage 16·80 m (55 ft 1 in); height 4·40 m (14 ft 5·25 in); main rotor disc area 346·36 m² (3,728·3 sq ft)

Variants

Mi-4 'Hound-A': first flown in May 1952, the Mi-4 is a conventional but still useful general-purpose helicopter of the piston-engined variety; the type can carry 14 troops or a light vehicle loaded through the clamshell rear doors; in recent years many 'Hound-A' tactical helicopters have been upgraded electronically with features such as TACAN, a Sirena 3 RWR and other items
Mi-4 'Hound-B': ASW version with undernose search radar, MAD (using a towed 'bird'), and sonobuoys
Mi-4 'Hound-C': ECM version equipped to jam enemy battlefield air-defence radars
Harbin Aircraft Manufacturing Corporation Zhi-5: Chinese-built version with the Pratt & Whitney Canada PT6T coupled turboshaft

Below: The MiG-31 is the MiG-25 reworked for the interception of low-level intruders.

Mil Mi-6A 'Hook'

(USSR)
Type: transport and assault heavy helicopter
Accommodation: flightcrew of five, and 90 troops, or 41 litters and two attendants, or 12,000 kg (26,455 lb) of freight in the hold, or 8000 kg (17,637 lb) of freight as a slung load
Armament (fixed): provision for one 12·7-mm (0·5-in) machine-gun in the nose
Armament (disposable): none
Electronics and operational equipment: communication and navigation equipment
Powerplant and fuel system: two 4100-kW (5,499-shp) Soloviev D-25V (TV-2BM) turboshafts, and a total internal fuel capacity of 7910 litres (1,740 Imp gal) plus provision for 8750 litres (1,925 Imp gal) of ferry fuel in two internal and two external tanks; no provision for drop tanks or inflight refuelling
Performance: maximum speed 300 km/h (186 mph) at optimum altitude; cruising speed 250 km/h (155 mph); initial climb rate not revealed: service ceiling 4500 m (14,765 ft); hovering ceiling in ground effect 2500 m (8,200 ft); range 620 km (385 miles) with an 8000-kg (17,637-lb) payload; ferry range 1450 km (900 miles)
Weights: empty 27,240 kg (60,055 lb); normal take-off 40,500 kg (82,285 lb); maximum take-off 42,500 kg (93,700 lb)
Dimensions: main rotor diameter 35·00 m (114 ft 10 in); length overall, rotors turning 41·739 m (136 ft 11·3 in) and fuselage 33·18 m (108 ft 10·5 in); height 9·86 m (32 ft 4 in); main rotor disc area 962·1 m² (10,356·4 sq ft)

Variants

Mi-6 'Hook': first flown in September 1957, the Mi-6 was for its time the world's largest helicopter, and is still a prodigious machine capable of lifting a substantial slung load as an alternative to the internal payload of troops, freight and light vehicles in a hold accessed by clamshell rear doors
Mi-6A 'Hook': late-production model with a number of detail improvements

The Mi-6 is a large and potentially vulnerable type, but provides a massive troop or freight payload capability.

Mil Mi-8 'Hip-C'

(USSR)
Type: assault and transport medium helicopter
Accommodation: flightcrew of two or three, and 24 troops or 4000 kg (8,818 lb) of freight in the hold, or 3000 kg (6,614 lb) of freight as a slung load
Armament (fixed): none
Armament (disposable): this is carried on two outriggers (one on each side of the fuselage) up to an unrevealed maximum weight, and comprises four UV-32-57 launchers each containing 32 55-mm (2·17-in) rockets
Electronics and operational equipment: communication and navigation equipment
Powerplant and fuel system: two 1270-kW (1,703-shp) Isotov TV2-117A turboshafts, and a total fuel capacity (internal and external) of 1870 litres (411 Imp gal) plus provision for 1830 litres (403 litres) of ferry fuel in two cabin tanks; no provision for drop tanks or inflight refuelling
Performance: maximum speed 260 km/h (161 mph) at 1000 m (3,280 ft); cruising speed 180 km/h (112 mph); initial climb rate not revealed: service ceiling 4500 m (14,760 ft); hovering ceiling in ground effect 1900 m (6,235 ft) and out of ground effect 800 m (2,625 ft); range 445 km (276 miles) with maximum payload; ferry range 1200 km (745 miles)
Weights: empty 7260 kg (16,799 lb); normal take-off 11,100 kg (24,470 lb); maximum take-off 12,000 kg (26,455 lb)
Dimensions: main rotor diameter 21·29 m (69 ft 10·5 in); length overall, rotors turning 25·24 m (82 ft 9·7 in) and fuselage 18·17 m (59 ft 7·5 in); height 5·65 m (18 ft 6·5 in); main rotor disc area 356·00 m² (3,832·0 sq ft)

Variants
Mi-8 'Hip-C': basically a turbine-engined development of the Mi-4 for civil and military applications, and first flown in 1961 as the 'Hip-A' with a four-blade main rotor driven by a single Soloviev turboshaft transmission-limited to 2013 kW (2,700 shp), the Mi-8 was clearly a highly capable machine, and the second prototype (first flown in September 1962) pioneered the twin-turboshaft powerplant, the definitive five-blade main rotor being evaluated in the 'Hip-B' prototype; the

Above: The round windows reveal this civil-marked Mi-8 as a utility model with strengthened floor and clamshell rear doors.

'Hip-C' was thus the first production model, and has proved itself in every way an excellent machine; features found only on the military version are Doppler navigation and provision for a considerable weight and diversity of armament
Mi-8 'Hip-D': battlefield communications relay helicopter distinguishable by its additional antennae and external box fairings
Mi-8 'Hip-E': advanced battlefield version of the 'Hip' series, and generally reckoned to be the world's most heavily armed helicopter, with provision for six UV-32-57 launchers containing a total of 192 55-mm (2·17-in) rockets plus four AT-2 'Swatter' anti-tank missiles (to a maximum weight of 1500 kg/3,307 lb), complemented by a 12·7-mm (0·5-in) flexible machine-gun in the nose
Mi-8 'Hip-F': export version of the 'Hip-E' with six AT-3 'Sagger' missiles in place of the 'Swatters' of the Soviet type
Mi-8 'Hip-G': battlefield communications relay helicopter with detail differences from the 'Hip-D'
Mi-8 'Hip-J': EW derivative of the basic series with a number of unspecified systems characterized by external aerials for the jamming of battlefield air-defence radars
Mi-8 'Hip-K': advanced ECM and communications-jamming variant with antennae on the sides of the rear fuselage and box fairings on the cabin sides; the type has no Doppler navigation
Mi-8MT 'Hip-?': no NATO reporting name has yet been revealed for this latest version of the Mi-8 series, which was revealed in 1989 and appears to be the long-awaited battlefield support version of the Mi-17 with that type's dynamic system matched to a pair of TV3-117MT turboshafts each downrated to 1455 kW (1,951 shp) for a cruising speed of 240 km/h (149 mph), a service ceiling of 3980 m (13,060 ft) and a range of 495 km (308 miles) with the normal load of 2000 kg (4,409 lb); the maximum load is 4000 kg (8,818 lb)
Mi-14PL 'Haze-A': land-based ASW variant with retractable landing gear, a boat hull and stabi-

Mil Mi-24 'Hind-D'

lizing sponsons for ditching capability; in prototype and initial production forms the helicopter was powered by a pair of 1270-kW (1,703-shp) TV2-117A turboshafts, but in later production form the type switched to a pair of 1415-kW (1,898-shp) TV3-117M turboshafts and in current form to two 1640-kW (2,200-shp) Isotov TV3-117MT turboshafts for an estimated maximum take-off weight of 13,000 kg (28,660 lb); operational equipment includes search radar in an undernose radome, two sonobuoy-launching chutes, and MAD (using a towed 'bird') plus a weapons load of torpedoes and/or depth charges; the type can also be used in the SAR role with armament replaced by a rescue winch and other mission equipment

Mi-14BT 'Haze-B': mine countermeasures version of the 'Haze-A', identifiable by the strake and pod on the lower starboard side of the fuselage

Mi-14PS 'Haze-C': dedicated SAR variant of the 'Haze-A' with the starboard-side stake and pod of the 'Haze-B' but a larger door on the port side

Mi-17 'Hip-H': much uprated and updated version of the Mi-8 with the dynamic system of the Mi-14 and the tail rotor relocated to the port side of the fin for improved hot-and-high performance; the cabin is enlarged slightly to allow carriage of the greater payload made possible by the improved powerplant; the type began to enter service in 1981 as a utility and assault helicopter well-suited to hot-and-high operations; the parameters in which the Mi-17 differs from the Mi-8 are principally an overall length of 25·352 m (83 ft 2 in), a maximum take-off weight of 13,000 kg (28,660 lb), a maximum speed of 250 km/h (155 mph) at maximum take-off weight, a service ceiling of 5000 m (16,405 ft), and a range of 495 km (307 miles) on internal fuel; these performance improvements are maintained even under hot-and-high conditions, and the Mi-17 can also carry additional weapons such as UPK-23 gun pods containing the 23-mm GSh-23L twin-barrel cannon

Right: This Hungarian helicopter reveals features of the 'Hind-D' such as nose-mounted sensors, chin gun and underwing hardpoints.

(USSR)

Type: gunship helicopter

Accommodation: flightcrew of two in tandem, and one weapon specialist plus reload weapons in the hold

Armament (fixed): one 12·7-mm (0·5-in) four-barrel rotary machine-gun in the turret

Armament (disposable): this is carried on six hardpoints (two under and one at the tip of each stub wing) up to a maximum weight of 1500 kg (3,307 lb); a typical load is four UV-32-57 launchers each with 32 55-mm (2·17-in) rockets or two launchers for 80-mm (3·15-in) rockets under the wings, and four AT-2 'Swatter' anti-tank missiles on a double installation at each tip; other weapons are AAMs, UPK-23 cannon pods each with a 23-mm GSh-23L twin-barrel cannon, bombs, cluster bombs, napalm tanks, chemical tanks and drop tanks

Electronics and operational equipment: communication and navigation equipment, plus undernose pods for EO and RF missile guidance, RWR, 'Hot Brick' IR jammer, and missile-decoy launcher

Powerplant and fuel system: two 1640-kW (2,200-shp) Isotov TV3-117 turboshafts, and a total internal fuel weight of 1500 kg (3,307 lb) plus provision for 1000 kg (2,205 lb) more fuel in an auxiliary tank carried in the cabin, or four 300-kg (661-lb) drop tanks; no provision for inflight refuelling

Performance: maximum speed about 310 km/h (193 mph) at optimum altitude; initial climb rate 750 m (2,460 ft) per minute; service ceiling 4500 m (14,765 ft); hovering ceiling out of ground effect 2200 m (7,220 ft); radius 160 km (99 miles) with maximum warload; ferry range 750 km (466 miles)

Weights: empty 8400 kg (18,519 lb); normal take-off 11,000 kg (24,250 lb); maximum take-off 12,500 kg (27,557 lb)

Dimensions: main rotor diameter 17·00 m (55 ft 9 in); length overall, rotors turning 21·50 m (70 ft 6·5 in) and fuselage 17·50 m (57 ft 5 in); height 6·50 m (21 ft 3·9 in); main rotor disc area 226·98 m² (2,443·3 sq ft)

Variants

Mi-24 'Hind-A': developed in the mid-1960s as a high-performance multi-role helicopter, the Mi-24 has been the subject of contested evaluations in the West, in relation largely to the tactical capability of the gunship models; the type is based on the dynamic system of the Mi-14 using two TV2-117 (later TV3-117) turboshafts, in this application married to a new fuselage of slender lines to enhance performance and battlefield survivability; the type has a crew of three or four, and can carry an eight-man infantry squad in the hold at a maximum take-off weight of 11,000 + kg (24,250 + lb); the 'Hind-A' was the second pro-

duction model, the initial **'Hind-B'** having been produced in only small numbers, probably as a pre-production batch, for service from 1973; this 'Hind-B' is distinguishable by its straight wings with only four hardpoints, and by the location of the tail rotor on the starboard side of the fin; it is unlikely that the survivors of these two variants are still used for the infantry assault role, a more likely task being the battlefield movement of anti-tank missile teams

Mi-24 'Hind-C': version of the 'Hind-A' without the nose gun and wingtip missile launcher rails, and used mainly as a trainer with dual controls

Mi-24 'Hind-D': much altered version used in the dedicated gunship role with a new forward fuselage featuring stepped cockpits for the gunner (nose) and pilot (behind and slightly above the gunner); the gunner controls a four-barrel 12·7-mm (0·5-in) heavy machine-gun in a turret under the nose, while the wing-mounted armament is similar to that of the 'Hind-A', though more extensive; the sensor fit for the accurate firing of air-to-surface ordnance includes an air-data probe, low-light-level TV, radar and a laser tracker; though the cabin can carry an eight-man infantry squad it is likely that only one man and reload weapons are carried for battlefield replenishment of the underwing hardpoints; the type clearly possesses considerable speed and offensive capability, but Western analysts point out that the type is large and relatively unmanoeuvrable for the gunship role; Soviet experience with the type in Afghanistan has led to the adoption of a dispenser under the tail boom loaded with 128 IR decoys for heat-seeking missiles, an IR jammer and an RWR

Mi-24 'Hind-E': improved version of the 'Hind-D' with upgraded systems, improved defensive features and provision for AT-6 'Spiral' instead of AT-2 'Swatter' anti-tank missiles

Mi-24 'Hind-F': version of the 'Hind-E' with a revised nose armament of one 30-mm twin-barrel cannon (originally thought to be a 23-mm GSh-23L) in a pack fixed on the starboard side of the nose; the type carries AT-6 'Spiral' anti-tank missiles and, as a result of Soviet experience in Afghanistan, is fitted with a number of measures to defeat heat-seeking SAMs; these measures include inlet and exhaust shrouds, a dorsally mounted 'Hot Brick' IR jammer and stub wing-mounted dispensers for IR decoy flares

Mi-24 'Hind-G': specialized radiation-sampling variant

Mi-25 'Hind-D': export version of the Mi-24 'Hind-D' with avionics of a reduced standard

Mi-35P 'Hind-?': export version of the 'Hind' with additional armour for the crew and vital dynamic system components, a heavier weapon load carried on six hardpoints, different avionics, and inbuilt chaff/flare launchers rather than the boom-mounted IR jammer of Soviet models

Mil Mi-26 'Halo-A'

(USSR)

Type: transport heavy helicopter
Accommodation: flightcrew of five, and 85 troops or 20,000 kg (44,092 lb) of freight in the hold, or 20,000 kg (44,092 lb) of freight carried as a slung load
Armament (fixed): none
Armament (disposable): none
Electronics and operational equipment: communication and navigation equipment
Powerplant and fuel system: two 8500-kW (11,400-shp) Lotarev D-136 turboshafts, and a total internal fuel capacity of 12,000 litres (2,640 Imp gal); no provision for drop tanks or inflight refuelling
Performance: maximum speed 295 km/h (183 mph) at optimum altitude; cruising speed 265 km/h (158 mph); initial climb rate not revealed; service ceiling 4600 m (15,090 ft); hovering ceiling out of ground effect 1800 m (5,905 ft); range 800 km (497 miles) with maximum fuel
Weights: empty 28,200 kg (62,170 lb); normal take-off 49,500 kg (109,127 lb); maximum take-off 56,000 kg (123,457 lb)
Dimensions: main rotor diameter 32·00 m (105 ft 9 in); length overall, rotors turning 40·025 m (131 ft 3·8 in) and fuselage 33·73 m (110 ft 8 in); height 8·055 m (26 ft 5·25 in) to rotor head; main rotor disc area 804·25 m² (8,657·2 sq ft)

Variant

Mi-26 'Halo-A': first flown in December 1977, the 'Halo' is the world's largest production helicopter, a highly capable heavy-lift type scaled up from the Mi-6 but with proportionally more power to drive an eight-blade main rotor; as with other such Soviet helicopters the large hold is accessed by clamshell rear doors and a ramp for the loading of vehicles and items of artillery; the hold is 12·00 m (39 ft 4·25 in) long increased to 15·00 m (49 ft 2·5 in) if the ramp is kept open, the width is 3·25 m (10 ft 8 in), and the height varies between 2·95 m (9 ft 8 in) and 3·17 m (10 ft 4·75 in)

Mil Mi-28 'Havoc-A'

(USSR)

Type: air-combat and gunship helicopter
Accommodation: weapons operator and pilot in tandem in separate stepped cockpits, plus provision for two in the fuselage
Armament (fixed): one 30-mm 2A42 cannon in an underfuselage turret with 300 rounds
Armament (disposable): this is carried on four hardpoints (two under each stub wing) up to an unrevealed maximum weight, and is believed to include 16 modified AT-6 'Spiral' anti-tank missiles in four four-tube boxes, UV-20-57 rocket launchers each with 20 55-mm (2·17-in) S-8 unguided rockets, and four AAMs in two twin launchers
Electronics and operational equipment: communication and navigation equipment, plus nose-mounted sensors (including radar for the guidance of beam-riding anti-tank missiles, and in the trainable undernose turret TV, FLIR and a laser rangefinder/marked-target seeker), pilot's HUD, RWR, ECM system, IR countermeasures system, and IR decoy launcher
Powerplant and fuel system: two 1640-kW (2,200-shp) Isotov TV3 turboshafts, and a total internal fuel capacity of unrevealed quantity; no provision for inflight refuelling
Performance: maximum speed 300 km/h (186 mph); cruising speed 265 km/h (165 mph); initial climb rate not revealed; service ceiling not revealed; hovering ceiling in ground effect 3600 m (11,810 ft); service ceiling 6000 m (19,685 ft); radius 240 km (149 miles)
Weights: empty 7000 kg (15,432 lb); normal take-off 10,400 kg (22,928 lb); maximum take-off 11,400 kg (25,132 lb)
Dimensions: main rotor diameter 17·00 m (55 ft 9·3 in); length overall, rotors turning 19·05 m (62 ft 6 in) and fuselage 16·00 m (52 ft 5·9 in); height not revealed; main rotor disc area 226·98 m² (2,443·3 sq ft)

Below: The Mi-26 provides a very large payload capability in civil and military use.

Variant

Mi-28 'Havoc-A': first flown in November 1982 for service from 1990, the 'Havoc' seems to have confirmed Western doubts about the battlefield viability of the Mi-24 gunship models, for while this new machine is clearly derived from earlier Mil helicopters (the dynamic system of the Mi-24 driving a new five-blade articulated main rotor), it has adopted the US practice of a much slimmer

Mitsubishi F-1

and smaller fuselage for increased manoeuvrability and reduced vulnerability over the modern high-technology battlefield; the 'Havoc' thus bears a passing resemblance to the Hughes AH-64A Apache in US Army service, and amongst its features are IR suppression of exhausts of the podded engines, IR decoys, upgraded armour, optronic sighting and targeting systems for use in conjunction with the undernose 30-mm cannon

and disposable weapons (including AAMs) carried on the stub wing hardpoints, and millimetre-wavelength radar; the type clearly possesses an air-combat capability against other battlefield helicopters, and other notable features are a far higher level of survivability and the provision of a small compartment on the left-hand side of the fuselage, probably for the rescue of downed aircrew

(Japan)
Type: close air support fighter and attack aeroplane
Accommodation: pilot on a Weber ES-7J zero/zero ejector seat
Armament (fixed): one 20-mm JM61A1 rotary-barrel cannon with 750 rounds
Armament (disposable): this is carried on seven hardpoints (one under the fuselage rated at 1000 kg/2,205 lb, two under each wing with each unit rated at 500 kg/1,102 lb, and one at each wingtip rated at 275 kg/606 lb) up to a maximum weight of 2780 kg (6,129 lb); typical loads are four AIM-9 Sidewinder or AAM-1 AAMs, or two ASM-1 (Type 80) anti-ship missiles, or four pods each with seven or 19 2·75-in (70-mm) rockets, or four pods each with four 5-in (127-mm) rockets, or eight 750-lb (340-kg) bombs, or 12 500- or 250-lb (227- or 113-kg) free-fall or retarded bombs
Electronics and operational equipment: communication and navigation equipment, plus Mitsubishi Electric J/AWG-11 air-to-air and air-to-surface radar, Mitsubishi Electric (Thomson-CSF) HUD, Mitsubishi Electric J/AWG-1 fire-control system and bombing computer, Ferranti 6TNJ-F INS, Lear Siegler 5010BL attitude and heading reference system, Tokyo Keiki APR-4 RWR, and provision for ECM pods
Powerplant and fuel system: two 3315-kg (7,308-lb) afterburning thrust Ishikawajima-Harima TF40-IHI-801A (licence-built Rolls-Royce/Turboméca Adour Mk 801A) turbofans, and a total internal fuel capacity of 3823 litres (841 Imp gal) plus provision for three 821-litre (180-Imp gal) drop tanks; no provision for inflight refuelling
Performance: maximum speed 1700 km/h (1,056 mph) or Mach 1·7 at 11,000 m (36,090 ft); initial climb rate 6000 m (19,685 ft) per minute; service ceiling 15,240 m (50,000 ft); radius 350 km (218 miles) on a hi-lo-hi mission with eight 500-lb (227-kg) bombs, or 555 km (345 miles) with two ASM-1 missiles and one drop tank; ferry range 2600 km (1,616 miles)
Weights: empty 6358 kg (14,017 lb); normal take-off 9860 kg (21,737 lb); maximum take-off 13,700 kg (30,203 lb)
Dimensions: span 7·88 m (25 ft 10·25 in); length including probe 17·86 m (58 ft 7 in); height 4·39 m (14 ft 5 in); wing area 21·17 m² (227·9 sq ft)

Variants
F-1: this trim close-support and anti-shipping attack fighter was derived from the T-2 supersonic trainer, and bears more than a passing resemblance to the SEPECAT Jaguar, with which it shares a twin Adour powerplant; the type first flew as a T-2 conversion in June 1975, the primary modification being the plating over of the rear cockpit to provide volume for an INS, bombing computer and radar-warning/ECM system
T-2: designed as Japan's first supersonic aircraft, the T-2 first flew in prototype form during July 1971 and entered service as an unarmed flying trainer; the **T-2A** is the weapons training and light attack equivalent, this having the armament potential of the F-1 but with the less capable J/AWG-11 search and ranging radar and without the INS, bombing and ECM system

Above left: The Mi-28 battlefield helicopter.

Below: The Mitsubishi F-1

Myasishchyev M-4 'Bison-C'

(USSR)

Type: maritime reconnaissance aeroplane

Accommodation: flightcrew of four or five, and a mission crew of variable size in the cabin

Armament (fixed): six 23-mm NR-23 cannon in twin-gun tail turret and twin-gun ventral and dorsal barbettes

Armament (disposable): this is carried in a lower-fuselage weapons bay up to a maximum weight of 4500 kg (9,921 lb) of free-fall stores

Electronics and operational equipment: communication and navigation equipment, plus 'Puff Ball' search radar with its antenna in a nose radome, 'Bee Hind' tail-warning and gunlaying radar, and a wide diversity of mission electronics with their antennae in the nose, along the fuselage and in the wingtips

Powerplant and fuel system: four 13,000-kg (28,660-lb) thrust Soloviev D-15 or 9500-kg (20,943-lb) thrust Mikulin AM-3D non-afterburning turbojets, and a total internal fuel capacity of unrevealed quantity; no provision for drop tanks but provision for inflight refuelling

Performance: maximum speed 900 km/h (559 mph) or Mach 0·85 at high altitude; initial climb rate not revealed; service ceiling 15,000 m (49,215 ft); range 10,000 km (6,835 miles) with maximum warload

Weights: empty 90,000 kg (198,413 lb); normal take-off 170,000 kg (374,780 lb); maximum take-off 210,000 kg (462,963 lb)

Dimensions: span 50·48 m (165 ft 7·5 in); length 47·20 m (154 ft 10 in); height 14·10 m (46 ft 3 in); wing area 320·00 m² (3,444·0 sq ft)

Variants

M-4 'Bison-A': conceived as a long-range strategic bomber, the M-4 first flew in late 1953 and entered service in 'Bison-A' form with four 8700-kg (19,180-lb) thrust Mikulin AM-3D turbojets during 1955; the type has a defensive armament of six 23-mm cannon in three positions (one manned in the tail and two remotely controlled above and below the fuselage) plus at least 15,000 kg (33,060 lb) of free-fall weapons; most of the bombers have been revised since the early 1960s as inflight-refuelling tankers with extra fuel and a hose reel unit in the erstwhile bomb bay, and additional tankage in the front and rear portions of the fuselage; all 'Bison' variants are being phased out of service during the late 1980s

M-4 'Bison-B': maritime version with an observation nose and ventral blister, and equipped for multi-sensor reconnaissance; the type also has an inflight-refuelling capability, and by the 1980s the type was known to have at least 12 Elint receivers and (possibly) the capability for mid-course updating of anti-ship missiles

M-4 'Bison-C': updated version of the 'Bison-B' with large radar (believed to be 'Puff Ball' for AS-2 missile guidance) in a lengthened nose, as well as reconnaissance equipment

Above right: The alteration of the inlet arrangement effectively disguises the derivation of the Q-5 attack aeroplane from the J-6 (and thus MiG-19) fighter series.

Right: A 1967 photograph of the Myasishchyev M4 'Bison-A' being exhibited at the Moscow Air Show in July. This was the first Soviet Air Show for six years.

Nanchang Aircraft Manufacturing Company Q-5 III 'Fantan-C'

(China)

Type: close air support and attack aeroplane with a secondary air-to-air capability

Accommodation: pilot on a zero/250-km/h (155-mph) or (Pakistani aircraft) Martin-Baker PKD10 zero/zero ejector seat

Armament (fixed): two 23-mm Type 23-2 cannon with 100 rounds per gun

Armament (disposable): this is carried in a lower-fuselage weapons bay (rated at 1000 kg/2,205 lb but rarely used as it is generally used for additional fuel) and on 10 hardpoints (two tandem pairs under the fuselage with each unit rated at 250 kg/551 lb and three under each wing with each unit rated at 500 kg/1,102 lb) up to a maximum weight of 2000 kg (4,409 lb); the weapon bay can accommodate one 20-kiloton nuclear weapon or four 250-kg (551-lb) bombs, but more common loads are externally carried 250- and 100-kg (551- and 220-lb) bombs, cluster bombs, PL-2 or PL-7 AAMs, or pods for 55- and 90-mm (2·17- and 3·54-in) rockets

Electronics and operational equipment: communication and navigation equipment, plus an optical sight and (on air-defence model) 'High Fix' ranging radar

Powerplant and fuel system: two 3250-kg (7,165-lb) afterburning thrust Shenyang Wopen-6 turbojets, and a total internal fuel capacity of 3720 litres (818·5 Imp gal) plus provision for an unrevealed quantity of auxiliary fuel in a weapon-bay tank and for two 400- or 760-litre (88- or 167-Imp gal) drop tanks; no provision for inflight refuelling

Performance: maximum speed 1190 km/h (739 mph) or Mach 1·12 at 11,000 m (36,090 ft) and 1210 km/h (752 mph) or Mach 0·99 at sea level; initial climb rate 6000 m (19,685 ft) per minute; service ceiling 15,850 m (52,000 ft); radius 400 km (248 miles) on a lo-lo-lo mission with maximum external load or 600 km (373 miles) on a hi-lo-hi mission with maximum external load; ferry range 1850 km (1,150 miles)

Weights: empty 6495 kg (14,319 lb); normal take-off 9530 kg (21,010 lb); maximum take-off 12,000 kg (26,455 lb)

Dimensions: span 9·70 m (31 ft 10 in); length with nose probe 16·255 m (53 ft 4 in); height 4·516 m (13 ft 9·75 in); wing area 29·75 m² (300·85 sq ft)

Variants

Q-5 I 'Fantan-A': first flown in June 1965, this is a drastic but basically conventional Chinese development of the Mikoyan-Gurevich MiG-19/Shenyang J-6 series with slightly larger overall dimensions, a comparable powerplant and a completely redesigned forward fuselage (to make possible the installation of a small bomb bay) with the previous single nose inlet replaced by two lateral inlets; the original Chinese scheme was apparently to fit turbofan engines and nose radar when these became available, making the Q-5 I an able medium-range tactical strike aircraft with free-fall nuclear weapons; the type has now been kept as a conventional attack aircraft and fighter-bomber with turbojets, the erstwhile bomb bay being used for the accommodation of some 70% extra fuel; the **A-5B** (**Q-5 II 'Fantan-B'**) is apparently the export version for North Korea, but how this variant differs from the Q-5 I is not known

Q-5 III 'Fantan-C': current production version with revised avionics and (on later aircraft) an additional pair of hardpoints for self-defence AAMs; the **A-5C** export aircraft in Pakistani service have been considerably upgraded by the addition of Western avionics and provision for Sidewinder AAMs

Q-5K 'Fantan': starting prototype trials in 1988, this is an upgraded version produced under a joint Chinese and French agreement signed in 1987 to provide an alternative to the Q-5M; the electronics are the responsibility of Thomson-CSF, and include a HUD, laser rangefinder, INS, radar altimeter, new instrumentation and a video camera; the export version will be designated **A-5K**

Q-5M 'Fantan': improved and upengined version under test in the late 1980s after development with the aid of Aeritalia, which is responsible for advanced avionics (based on those of the Aeritalia/Aermacchi/EMBRAER AMX) including ranging radar, HUD, INS and air-data computer; the export version will be designated **A-5M**, and deliveries are scheduled to begin in 1990; the type is powered by two 3750-kg (8,267-lb) afterburning thrust Wopen-6A turbojets, and its performance data include maximum speeds of 1275 km/h (792 mph) or Mach 1·2 at high altitude and 1225 km/h (761 mph) or Mach 1 at sea level, a service ceiling of 16,000 m (52,500 ft), and combat radii with maximum external load of 300+ km (186+ miles) on a lo-lo-lo mission and 400+ km (248+ miles) on a hi-lo-hi mission

North American T-28B Trojan

(USA)

Type: flying trainer

Accommodation: pupil and instructor in tandem

Armament (fixed): none

Armament (disposable): none

Electronics and operational equipment: communication and navigation equipment

Powerplant and fuel system: one 1,425-hp (1062·5-kW) Wright R-1820-26 Cyclone piston engine; no provision for drop tanks or inflight refuelling

Performance: maximum speed 343 mph (522 km/h); cruising speed 310 mph (499 km/h) at 30,000 ft (9145 m); initial climb rate 3,540 ft (1079 m) per minute; service ceiling 35,500 ft (10,820 m); range 1,060 miles (1706 km)

Weights: empty 6,424 lb (2914 kg); maximum take-off 8,486 lb (3849 kg)

Dimensions: span 40 ft 1 in (12·22 m); length 33 ft 0 in (10·06 m); height 12 ft 8 in (3·86 m); wing area 268·0 sq ft (24·9 m²)

Variants

T-28A: designed as successor to the same company's T-6 Texan/Harvard series of basic trainers, the T-28 featured more advanced lines, a considerably upgraded powerplant (the 800-hp/597-kW Wright R-1300-1 radial piston engine in this US Air Force model), a frameless canopy and retractable tricycle landing gear; the prototype first flew in September 1949 and proved an immediate success

T-28B Trojan: version for the US Navy with considerably more power and revised avionics

T-28C Trojan: version for the T-28B with an arrester hook

T-28D: ground-attack and COIN aeroplane developed from the T-28A but fitted with the 1,425-hp (1062·5-kW) R-1820-56S radial and six underwing hardpoints for gun pods, napalm tanks, bombs and rocket-launchers; the type was also developed as the **AT-28D** attack trainer; and in France many T-28As were modified to T-28D standard under the name **Fennec**, these aircraft having two 0·5-in (12·7-mm) machine-guns pods and four 136-kg (300-lb) bombs for use in the close-support role

Below: The most important trainer version of the T-28 series is the T-28B that was developed for the US Navy.

Northrop B-2

(USA)

Type: strategic bomber and missile-carrying aeroplane

Accommodation: flightcrew of two on ejector seats, with provision for a third man

Armament (fixed): none

Armament (disposable): this is carried in two side-by-side weapons bays to a maximum weight of 80,500 lb (36,515 kg) of disposable stores; each bay is thought to accommodate one eight-round rotary strategic launchers for a total of 16 AGM-131 SRAM-II missiles or 1·1-megaton B83 thermonuclear free-fall bombs; alternative loads are 20 megaton-range B61 thermonuclear free-fall bombs, or 22 1,500-lb (680-kg) free-fall bombs, or a large number of smaller bombs

Electronics and operational equipment: communication and navigation equipment, plus Hughes Aircraft covert strike radar with conformal phased-array antennae in the leading edge, and an integrated passive EW suite

Powerplant and fuel system: four 19,000-lb (8618-kg) thrust General Electric F118-GE-100 non-afterburning turbofans, and a total internal fuel capacity of unrevealed quantity; no provision for drop tanks but provision for inflight refuelling

Performance: maximum speed 475 mph (764 km/h) or Mach 0·76 at high altitude; initial climb rate not revealed; service ceiling not revealed; radius 3,800 miles (6115 km) with eight SRAMs and eight B61s

Weights: empty not revealed; maximum take-off 371,000 lb (168,286 kg)

Dimensions: span 172 ft 0 in (54·43 m); length 69 ft 0 in (21·03 m); height 17 ft 0 in (5·18 m); wing area not revealed

Below: The startling B-2 built in the belief that it can fly undetected into enemy territory.

Variant

B-2: developed at enormous cost during the late 1970s and 1980s, and first revealed in November 1988 for an initial flight in July 1989, the B-2 is designed as successor to the B-1B in the penetration bomber role; unlike the low-altitude B-1B, however, the type is designed for medium and high altitude penetration of hostile airspace, relying on its stealth design and composite structure to evade detection by enemy air defence systems until it has closed to within a few miles of its target; the relaxed-stability design is a flying wing with 40° swept leading edges and W-shaped trailing edges featuring simple flight-control surfaces (elevons for pitch and roll control, and 'differential drag' surfaces for yaw control) operated by a fly-by-wire control system, the emphasis being placed on completely smooth surfaces with blended flightdeck and nacelle bulges; radar reflectivity is very low because of the use of radiation-absorbent materials and a carefully optimized shape (including shielded upper-surface inlets), and a head-on radar cross section of 10·76 sq ft (1 m²) has been quoted for the B-2 in comparison with 107·64 sq ft (10 m²) for the B-1B and 1,076·37 sq ft (100 m²) for the B-52; additionally, the careful mixing of hot exhaust gases with cold freestream air before release through the type's 2D nozzles reduces thermal and acoustic signatures to a very significant degree in this firmly subsonic design; production is planned of 132 B-2s, these being the carriers for 2,000 of the 4,845 strategic nuclear weapons in the US Air Force's inventory; the US Department of Defense's 1989 review of financial commitments in the face of the USA's enormous budget deficit includes amongst its provisional proposals that the service debut of the B-2 be postponed for at least one year to save on financial outlay and also allow additional time for development of this extremely ambitious and complex aeroplane

Northrop F-5A Freedom Fighter

(USA)
Type: lightweight tactical fighter
Accommodation: pilot on an ejector seat
Armament (fixed): two 20-mm Philco-Ford (Pontiac) M39E cannon with 280 rounds per gun
Armament (disposable): this is carried on seven hardpoints (one under the fuselage rated at 2,000 lb/907 kg, two under each wing with the inner two units each rated at 1,000 lb/454 kg and the outer two units each at 500 lb/227 kg, and two at the wingtips each rated at 600 lb/272 kg) up to a maximum weight of 4,400 lb (1996 kg); typical loads are four AIM-9 Sidewinder AAMs, or one 2,000-lb (907-kg) bomb and two AIM-9 AAMs, or two AGM-12 Bullpup ASMs, or two 1,000-lb (454-kg) and two 500-lb (227-kg) bombs, or four pods each for 19 2·75-in (70-mm) rockets
Electronics and operational equipment: communication and navigation equipment, plus a Norsight optical sight and Bullpup missile-control gear
Powerplant and fuel system: two 4,080-lb (1850-kg) afterburning thrust General Electric J85-GE-13 turbojets, and a total internal fuel capacity of 583 US gal (2207 litres) plus provision for 150- and 50-US gal (568- and 189-litre) drop tanks; provision for inflight refuelling
Performance: maximum speed 925 mph (1489 km/h) or Mach 1·4 at 36,000 ft (10,970 m); cruising speed 640 mph (1031 km/h) or Mach 0·97 at 36,000 ft (10,970 m); initial climb rate 28,700 ft (8750 m) per minute; service ceiling 50,500 ft (15,390 m); radius 215 miles (346 km) on a hi-lo-hi mission with maximum warload; ferry range 1,612 miles (2594 km)

Weights: empty 8,085 lb (3667 kg); maximum take-off 20,677 lb (9379 kg)
Dimensions: span 25 ft 3 in (7·70 m); length 47 ft 2 in (14·38 m); height 13 ft 2 in (4·01 m); wing area 170·0 sq ft (15·79 m²)

Variants
F-5A Freedom Fighter: designed as the N-156F private venture, the F-5A was adopted as part of the USA's military support programme for important allies and thus supplied in considerable numbers to NATO countries and other allies; keys to the design were useful weapons capability plus small size and limited (though supersonic) performance for low unit cost and easily achieved servicing and airfield requirements; the type first flew in July 1959 and the first production machine followed in October 1963
RF-5A Freedom Fighter: reconnaissance version of the F-5A with with four KS-92 cameras in a modified nose
F-5B Freedom Fighter: tandem two-seat operational conversion trainer version of the F-5A, which entered service in April 1964; the type is similar to the F-5A apart from the lengthened cockpit and lack of nose guns
T-38A Talon: US Air Force supersonic basic and advanced flying trainer based on the N-156T version of the Northrop N-156 basic design; the type first flew in April 1959 and began to enter service in March 1961; fitted with two 3,850-lb (1746-kg) afterburning thrust J85-GE-5 turbojets, the Talon has a maximum take-off weight of 12,093 lb (5485 kg) and a maximum speed of Mach 1·3 at 36,000 ft (10,975 m); the length is 46 ft 4·5 in

(14·14 m)
AT-38B Talon: weapon training ᴏ the T-38A with two underwing har in the fighter lead-in and weapons training roles
Canadair CF-5A: F-5A version for the Canadian Armed Forces with 4,300-lb (1950-kg) afterburning thrust Orenda J85-CAN-15 turbojets and a number of detail modifications including manoeuvring flaps; in common with Canada's CF-5D trainers, these aircraft are being extensively modernized and upgraded in a programme run for the Canadian Armed Forces by Bristol Aerospace; within the context of the programme the airframe of each aircraft is being extensively refurbished and fitted with new components (including wings, flying controls, fin and landing gear), an upgraded Litton INS, a GEC Avionics digital air-data computer and a Ferranti HUD and weapon-aiming computer
Canadair CF-5D: version of the F-5B for the Canadian Armed Forces
Canadair NF-5A: CF-5A version for the Netherlands with manoeuvring flaps and other more advanced features
Canadair NF-5B: version of the F-5B for the Netherlands
CASA SF-5A: F-5A version for Spain
CASA SRF-5A: RF-5A version for Spain
CASA SF-5B: F-5B version for Spain

Seen in the USAF markings in which it was evaluated, the RF-5E Tigereye is the reconnaissance variant of the Tiger II series with interchangeable equipment packages.

157

rthrop F-5E Tiger II

Type: lightweight tactical fighter

Accommodation: pilot on an ejector seat

Armament (fixed): two 20-mm Philco-Ford M39A2 cannon with 280 rounds per gun

Armament (disposable): this is carried on seven hardpoints (one under the fuselage rated at 2,000 lb/907 kg, two under each wing with the inner two units each rated at 1,500 lb/680 kg and the outer two units each rated at 1,000 lb/454 kg, and two at the wingtips each rated at 600 lb/272 kg) up to a maximum weight of 7,000 lb/3175 kg); weapons that can be carried are the AIM-9 Sidewinder AAM, AGM-65 Maverick ASM, 2,000-, 1,000-, 750-, 500- and 250-lb (907-, 454-, 340-, 227- and 113-kg) free-fall or retarded bombs, cluster bombs, bomb dispensers, napalm bombs and pods for 2·75- and 5-in (70- and 127-mm) rockets

Electronics and operational equipment: communication and navigation equipment, plus Emerson APQ-153 or APQ-159(V) multi-mode radar, General Electric ASG-29 optical sight, and options such as a Litton INS, Itek ALR-46 RWR, Northrop ALQ-171 conformal ECM, and Tracor ALE-40 chaff/flare dispenser

Powerplant and fuel system: two 5,000-lb (2268-kg) afterburning thrust General Electric J85-GE-21 turbojets, and a total internal fuel capacity of 670 US gal (2538 litres) plus provision for 275-, 150- and 50-US gal (1041-, 568- and 189-litre) drop tanks; provision for inflight refuelling

Performance: maximum speed 1,083 mph (1743 km/h) or Mach 1·64 at 36,000 ft (10,970 m) and 708 mph (1139 km/h) or Mach 0·93 at sea level; initial climb rate 34,500 ft (10,515 m) per minute; service ceiling 51,800 ft (15,790 m); radius 138 miles (222 km) on a lo-lo-lo mission with 5,200-lb (2358-kg) warload and two AIM-9 missiles; ferry range 2,314 miles (3720 km)

Weights: empty 9,723 lb (4410 kg); maximum take-off 24,722 lb (11,214 kg)

Dimensions: span 26 ft 8 in (8·13 m); length 47 ft 4·75 in (14·45 m); height 13 ft 4 in (4·06 m); wing area 186·0 sq ft (17·28 m²)

Variants

F-5E Tiger II: this is essentially an upgraded version of the F-5A series with better performance and weapon capability derived from the installation of more powerful engines; other enhancements are improved manoeuvrability (derived from better aerodynamics and a greater thrust-to-weight ratio), increased fuel capacity, reduced field requirements and an integrated fire-control system (though still without radar); the type flew in prototype form in March 1969 and began to enter service in April 1973; apart from overseas sales success, the type has found favour with the US forces as a dissimilar air combat training aircraft as its performance and agility are comparable to those of the MiG-21 series; considerable aerodynamic, powerplant and electronic development then led to the F-20A Tigershark with genuine Mach 2+ performance and extremely good radar, but the project was cancelled late in 1986 when no orders were forthcoming; production of the F-5 series ended in 1986 with the delivery of the last two of a total 2,610 aircraft (including more than 1,400 F-5Es) built over a 24-year period

RF-5E Tigereye: reconnaissance derivative of the F-5E with the forward fuselage modified and lengthened by 8 in (0·203 m) to accept a wide variety of tactical reconnaissance equipment including Lorop cameras, oblique cameras and an IR linescanner

F-5F Tiger II: this is the tandem two-seat operational conversion derivative of the F-5E, with the fuselage lengthened by 42·5 in (1·08 m) to allow the insertion of the second seat; the type has Emerson APQ-157 radar and only one inbuilt 20-mm cannon, but otherwise retains the full combat capability of the F-5E

Right: F-5E Tiger IIs in the special finish used by USAF 'aggressor' training squadrons.

Below: The F-5E achieves supersonic performance on relatively little power.

PAC/AMF (Pakistan Aeronautical Complex/Aircraft Manufacturing Factory) Mushshak

(Pakistan)

Type: primary and basic flying trainer with a secondary counter-insurgency capability

Accommodation: pupil and pilot side-by-side

Armament (fixed): none

Armament (disposable): this is carried on six hardpoints (three under each wing, with the inner two units each rated at 150 kg/330 lb and the outer four units each at 100 kg/220 lb) up to an unrevealed maximum weight; typical loads include two pods each containing one 7·62-mm (0·3-in) machine-gun, six wire-guided anti-tank missiles, and two or four rocket launchers

Electronics and operational equipment: communication and navigation equipment, plus optical sight

Powerplant and fuel system: one 200-hp (149-kW) Avco Lycoming IO-360-A1B6 piston engine, and a total internal fuel capacity of 190 litres (41·8 Imp gal); no provision for drop tanks or inflight refuelling

Performance: maximum speed 236 km/h (146 mph) at sea level; cruising speed 208 km/h (129 mph); initial climb rate 246 m (807 ft) per minute; service ceiling 4100 m (13,450 ft); endurance 5 hours 10 minutes

Weights: empty 646 kg (1,424 lb); normal take-off 900 kg (1,984 lb); maximum take-off 1200 kg (2,645 lb)

Dimensions: span 8·85 m (29 ft 0·5 in); length 7·00 m (22 ft 11·5 in); height 2·60 m (8 ft 6·5 in); wing area 11·90 m² (128·1 sq ft)

Variant

Mushshak: Pakistani licence-built version of the Saab Safari/Supporter, the Mushshak (proficient) is a simple light plane well suited to the training role and for counter-insurgency in Pakistan's more inhospitable regions; from 1986 aircraft have been re-engined with the 210-hp (156·6 kW) Teledyne Continental TIO-360-MB for much improved performance and control responsiveness

PAC/AMF Mushshak primary trainer.

Panavia Tornado IDS

(West Germany, Italy & UK)
Type: variable-geometry STOL multi-role all-weather attack and strike aeroplane
Accommodation: pilot and systems operator in tandem on Martin-Baker Mk 10A zero/zero ejector seats
Armament (fixed): two 27-mm Mauser BK27 cannon with 180 rounds per gun
Armament (disposable): this is carried on seven hardpoints (one on the centreline and two triple units on the shoulders with each unit rated at 1000 kg/2,205 lb, and two under each wing with the inner units each rated at 1500 kg/3,307 lb and the outer units each at 500 kg/1,102 lb) up to a maximum weight of 9000 kg (19,840 lb); among the wide variety of weapons that can be carried are the WE-177 nuclear free-fall bomb, AIM-9 Sidewinder AAM, ALARM and AGM-88 HARM radar-homing missiles, AGM-65 Maverick, AS.30 and AS.30L ASMs, GBU-15 TV-guided bomb, Paveway laser-guided bombs, Kormoran and Sea Eagle anti-ship missiles, 1,000-, 750-, 500- and 250-lb (454-, 340-, 227- and 113-kg) free-fall or retarded bombs, cluster bombs, napalm bombs and bomblet dispensers including specialist weapons such as the JP233 airfield attack and MW-1 battlefield attack dispensers
Electronics and operational equipment: communication and navigation equipment, plus Texas Instruments pulse-Doppler multi-mode radar with a ground-mapping function and terrain-following sub-unit, Smiths/Teldix/OMI HUD and HDDs, Ferranti FIN1010 INS, Decca Type 72 Doppler navigation, Litef Spirit 3 digital central computer, Microtecnica air-data system, Ferranti LRMTS, Marconi/Selenia stores-management system, RWR (Elettronica in Italian aircraft, Marconi ARI.18241/1 in British aircraft, and Itek/AEG-Telefunken in West German aircraft), and options such as Westinghouse ASQ-153(V) 'Pave Spike' laser pod, data-link pod, MBB reconnaissance pod, BAe reconnaissance pod, ECM pods such as the British Marconi ARI.23246/1 Sky Shadow, Italian/West German Elettronica/AEG-Telefunken EL/73, and Italian Elettronica ELT/553, and chaff dispenser pods such as the Philips BOZ 107
Powerplant and fuel system: two 16,800-lb (7620-kg) afterburning thrust Turbo-Union RB 199-34R Mk 103 turbofans, and a total internal fuel capacity of 6090 litres (1,340 Imp gal) and in RAF aircraft 551 litres (121 Imp gal) in a fin tank, plus provision for one or two 1500-litre (330-Imp gal) drop tanks under the fuselage and up to four 1500- or 2250-litre (330- or 495-Imp gal) drop tanks on the shoulder and inner underwing hard-points; provision for inflight refuelling
Performance: maximum speed 2337+ km/h (1,453+ mph) or Mach 2·2+ at 11,000 m (36,090 ft) and 1480+ km/h (980+ mph) or Mach 1·2+ at sea level; climb to 9000 m (29,530 ft) in less than 2 minutes from brakes-off; service ceiling 15,240+ m (50,000+ ft); radius 1390 km (863 miles on a hi-lo-hi mission with heavy warload; ferry range 3890 km (2,420 miles)
Weights: empty 14,090 kg (31,063 lb); normal take-off 20,410 kg (44,996 lb); maximum take-off about 27,215 kg (60,000 lb)
Dimensions: span 13·91 m (45 ft 7·5 in) spread and 8·60 m (28 ft 2·5 in) swept; length 16·72 m (54 ft 10·25 in); height 5·95 m (28 ft 2·5 in); wing area about 25·0 m² (269·1 sq ft)

Variants

Tornado IDS: this is one of the most important combat aircraft to have been developed in recent years, and forms the main interdiction and strike strength available to the British, West German and Italian air forces; the type has also secured useful Middle Eastern export orders; the type was designed as a high-performance type with fly-by-wire control system and advanced avionics for extremely accurate navigation and safe flight at supersonic speeds and very low levels in all weathers for pinpoint day/night first-pass attacks on a variety of targets; the type also possesses good STOL characteristics through its variable-geometry wings, powerful afterburning turbofan engines and extensive high-lift devices; the use of a Texas Instruments radar with terrain-following capability allows the Tornado to fly at Mach 1·2+ at an altitude of only 200 ft (60 m), so reducing the warning time available to the defences to organize themselves; the design was originated in the 1960s as the Multi-Role Combat Aircraft (able to undertake the close air support, battlefield interdiction, long-range interdiction, counter-air attack, air-superiority, interception and air defence, reconnaissance and naval strike roles), and the first prototype flew in April 1974 for service delivery from 1980; the type is known to the Royal Air Force as the **Tornado GR.Mk 1**, an operational conversion trainer derivative being the **Tornado GR.Mk 1(T)**; recent developments in British aircraft have been the adoption of the ALARM radar-homing missile, and this requires the upgrading of the Tornado's avionics system with a MIL 1553B databus, improved computer and revised missile-control system; some 30 of the RAF's Tornado GR.Mk 1s are configured as reconnaissance aircraft with the two cannon removed to provide accommodation for the electronics associated with the reconnaissance suite, which includes a BAe IR linescanner for horizon-to-horizon coverage, plus two BAe side-looking IR systems to provide additional resolution at the edges of the main scanner's spectrum; all three main operating countries are moving independently towards a mid-life upgrade in features such as improved navigation, increased range and superior target-acquisition capability, and to this end late-production aircraft are being completed with MIL 1553B digital databuses and upgraded computers; from 1991 British Tornadoes will carry the Ferranti Airborne Laser Designator Pod, which was selected in 1988 in preference to two American podded systems (the Ford Aerospace Nite Owl and Martin Marietta LANTIRN) to provide all-weather targeting for laser-guided weapons through the use of a thermal imager, an automatic video tracker and a boresighted laser designator; from 1992 all surviving Tornado GR.Mk 1 and GR.Mk 1A aircraft are to be rebuilt to the improved **Tornado GR.Mk 4** standard suggested above with greater computer power, a digital databus system for compatibility with a greater range of weapons and sensors, a new integrated defensive suite with the Marconi ARI.18241/1 RWR, Plessey missile-approach warner and Marconi ARI.123246/1 ECM, and a totally new all-weather passive terrain reference navigation system; this last will be backed by a FLIR system, and allow Tornado GR.Mk 4s to penetrate enemy airspace at low level in all weathers without use of the terrain-following radar and its giveaway emissions; Tornado GR.Mk 4 crews will be able to use night vision goggles

Tornado ECR: electronic combat and reconnaissance variant under development for the West German and Italian air forces with the Mk 105 version of the RB.199 engine for improved performance at low level; this model will have an emitter location system (possibly the APR-38 system) in place of the internal cannon, a low- and medium-altitude reconnaissance system, a data-link system and MBB-developed Elint and jammer pods; the use of a MIL 1553 databus and other avionics improvements also provide capability for the carriage and launch of the AGM-88 HARM radar-homing missile as the Tornado ECR's primary 'hard-kill' EW weapon

This Tornado GR.Mk 1 carries two 1500-litre tanks and (under the starboard wing) a BOZ 107 chaff and flare dispenser; the latter is generally paired with a Sky Shadow ECM pod.

Panavia Tornado ADV

(UK, West Germany & Italy)

Type: variable-geometry STOL all-weather air-defence interceptor fighter

Accommodation: pilot and systems operator in tandem on Martin-Baker Mk 10A zero/zero ejector seats

Armament (fixed): one 27-mm Mauser BK27 cannon with 180 rounds per gun

Armament (disposable): this is carried on four semi-recessed missile stations under the fuselage for Sky Flash medium-range AAMs and on two underwing hardpoints for two (Tornado F.Mk 2 and F.Mk 2A) or four (Tornado F.Mk 3) AIM-9L Sidewinder short-range AAMs

Electronics and operational equipment: communication and navigation equipment, plus GEC Avionics AI-24 Foxhunter pulse-Doppler multi-mode track-while scan radar, Smiths/Teldix/OMI HUD and HDDs, two Ferranti FIN1010 INSs, Litef Spirit 3 digital central computer, Microtecnica air-data system, Marconi ARI.18241 Hermes RWR, Tracor ALE-40 chaff/flare dispenser, ECM, ECCM, and Singer-Kearfott ECM-resistant data link

Powerplant and fuel system: two 16,290-lb (7675-kg) afterburning thrust Turbo-Union RB.199-34R Mk 103 turbofans or (Tornado F.Mk 3) 17,430-lb (7906-kg) afterburning thrust RB.199-34R Mk 104 afterburning turbofans, and a total internal fuel capacity of about 7250 litres (1,595 Imp gal) plus provision for two 330- or 495-Imp gal (1500- or 2250-litre) drop tanks; provision for inflight refuelling

Performance: maximum speed 2337 km/h (1,453 mph) or Mach 2·2 at 11,000 m (36,090 ft); initial climb rate not revealed; service ceiling about 21,335 m (70,000 ft); radius 1850 km (1,150 miles); endurance 2-hour combat air patrol at 740-km (460-mile) radius

Weights: empty 14,500 kg (31,996 lb); maximum take-off 27,986 kg (61,700 lb)

Dimensions: span 13·91 m (45 ft 7·5 in) spread and 8·60 m (28 ft 2·5 in) swept; length 18·082 m (59 ft 4 in); height 5·95 m (28 ft 2·5 in); wing area about 25·0 m² (269·1 sq ft)

Variant

Tornado ADV: dedicated air-defence variant of the Tornado developed in the UK for the Royal Air Force and designed for the long-range interception of intruders detected by Boeing Sentry AEW.Mk 1 AEW aircraft; to allow the semi-recessed carriage of four Sky Flash AAMs under the fuselage the aeroplane's fuselage has been stretched, this having the useful by-products of 909 litres (200 Imp gal) more internal fuel and finer aerodynamic lines for reduced transonic drag and hence superior acceleration; the rest of the armament comprises two or four AIM-9L Sidewinder short-range AAMs, and a single 27-mm cannon; the primary equipment changes are the adoption of twin INSs, the updating of the main computer, the installation of advanced cockpit displays, the provision of automatic wing sweep and flap/slat scheduling, the use of a Marconi ARI.18241 radar-warning receiver and ALE-40 chaff/flare dispenser, and the replacement of the Texas Instruments multi-mode radar by Foxhunter pulse-Doppler interception radar; this has considerable ECCM capability and possesses a track-while-scan capability to a range of 115 miles (185 km); there have been considerable development problems with the Foxhunter radar, and great efforts are being made towards an improvement in close-combat capability, the enhancement of ECM and ECCM, and the processing of target data in a new and larger-memory automatic data processor; power is provided by two analog-controlled 16,290-lb (7675-kg) RB.199 Mk 103 turbofans for an additional 7% afterburning thrust; the Tornado ADV is known in the RAF as the **Tornado F.Mk 2** (pre-production version with Mk 103 engines and Spin-Prevention and Incidence Limitation System), **Tornado F.Mk 2A** (pre-production version brought up to basic F.Mk 3 standard with Automatic Wing Sweep and the Automatic Manoeuvre Defence System, but without the Mk 104 engines) or **Tornado F.Mk 3** (full production version with digitally controlled Mk 104 afterburning turbofans and lengthened jetpipes for greater afterburning thrust, AWS, AMDS, dual INSs and revised pylons for an additional pair of Sidewinder AAMs); the type first flew in October 1979 and began to enter service in 1986

A Saudi Tornado ADV carries four Sky Flash and (under the wings) four Sidewinder AAMs.

Pilatus PC-7 Turbo-Trainer

Pilatus PC-9

Pilatus PC-7 Turbo-Trainer

(Switzerland)

Type: basic/intermediate flying and weapon training aeroplane

Accommodation: pupil and instructor in tandem on fixed seats or (optional) **Martin-Baker MK 15** lightweight ejector seats

Armament (fixed): none

Armament (disposable): this is carried on six hardpoints (three under each wing, with the inner two units each rated at 250 kg/551 lb, the intermediate two units each at 160 kg/353 lb and the outer two units each at 110 kg/243 lb) up to a maximum weight of 1040 kg (2,293 lb) of bombs, rocket pods and gun pods

Electronics and operational equipment: communication and navigation equipment, plus optical sight and provision for a reconnaissance pod

Powerplant and fuel system: one 650-shp (485-kW) Pratt & Whitney Canada PT6A-25A turboprop flat-rated to 550 shp (410 kW), and a total internal fuel capacity of 474 litres (104 Imp gal) plus provision for two 152- or 240-litre (33·5- or 53-Imp gal) drop tanks; no provision for inflight refuelling

Performance: maximum speed 500 km/h (311 mph); cruising speed 410 km/h (255 mph) at 6100 m (20,025 ft); initial climb rate 610 m (2,000 ft) per minute; service ceiling 9750 m (31,990 ft); range 1200 km (745 miles); ferry range 2630 km (1,634 miles)

Weights: empty 1330 kg (2,932 lb); normal take-off 1900 kg (4,188 lb); maximum take-off 2700 kg (5,952 lb)

Dimensions: span 10·40 m (34 ft 1·5 in); length 9·775 m (32 ft 0·75 in); height 3·21 m (10 ft 6·5 in); wing area 16·60 m² (179·7 sq ft)

Variant

PC-7 Turbo-Trainer: first flown in P-3-06 (later P-3B) prototype form during April 1966 with a 550-shp (410-kW) Pratt & Whitney Canada PT6A turboprop as a derivative of the piston-engined P-3 trainer, this is a useful multi-role trainer with secondary attack capability; the type began to enter service in 1978 and substantial sales have been made to third-world air forces

Below: In the PC-7 Pilatus took a well-proved basic airframe and combined it with a fuel-efficient turboprop to produce a new and commercially successful trainer.

Pilatus PC-9

(Switzerland)

Type: basic/intermediate flying and weapon trainer with a secondary counter-insurgency capability

Accommodation: pupil and instructor in tandem on Martin-Baker CH11A ejector seats

Armament (fixed): none

Armament (disposable): this is carried on six hardpoints (three under each wing, with the inner two units each rated at 250 kg/551 lb, the intermediate two units each at 160 kg/353 lb and the outer two units each at 110 kg/243 lb) up to a maximum weight of 1040 kg (2,293 lb) of bombs, rocket pods and gun pods

Electronics and operational equipment: communication and navigation equipment, plus optical sight and provision for a reconnaissance pod

Powerplant and fuel system: one 1,150-shp (857-kW) Pratt & Whitney Canada PT6A-62 turboprop flat-rated to 950 shp (708 kW), and a total internal fuel capacity of 535 litres (118 Imp gal) plus provision for two 154- or 248-litre (34- or 54·5-Imp gal) drop tanks; no provision for inflight refuelling

Performance: maximum speed 556 km/h (345 mph) at 6100 m (20,015 ft) and 500 km/h

PZL Mielec PZL-130 Orlik

(311 mph) at sea level; initial climb rate 1250 m (4,100 ft) per minute; service ceiling 12,200 m (40,025 ft); range 1642 km (1,020 miles)
Weights: empty 1685 kg (3,715 lb); normal take-off 2250 kg (4,960 lb); maximum take-off 3200 kg (7,055 lb)
Dimensions: span 10·124 m (33 ft 2·5 in); length 10·175 m (33 ft 4·75 in); height 3·26 m (10 ft 8·3 in); wing area 16·29 m² (175·3 sq ft)

Variant

PC-9: developed in 1983 and 1984 as an unsuccessful contender in the competition to find a replacement for the BAe Jet Provost trainer in British service, the PC-9 is a much improved derivative of the PC-7 with a more powerful engine and a number of aerodynamic improvements (notably a reduced-span wing with larger ailerons) to offer much improved performance and handling; other modifications are a stepped cockpit with zero/zero ejector seats, structural strengthening, a four-blade propeller, a longer dorsal fin, revised airbrakes, and the addition of landing gear doors; the type is being produced in Australia as the **PC-9/A**

Below: The PZL-130 Orlik.

Bottom: The PC-9 is a considerable improvement over the baseline PC-7.

(Poland)

Type: primary and basic flying and weapon trainer with a secondary counter-insurgency capability
Accommodation: pupil and pilot in tandem
Armament (fixed): none
Armament (disposable): this is carried on four hardpoints (two under each wing) up to an unrevealed maximum weight of light stores including 100-kg (220-lb) bombs, UV-8-57 launchers each with eight 55-mm (2·17-in) rockets, and 7·62-mm (0·3-in) machine-gun pods
Electronics and operational equipment: communication and navigation equipment, plus optical sight
Powerplant and fuel system: one 245-kW (329-hp) Vedeneyev M-14Pm piston engine, and a total internal fuel capacity of 420 litres (92·4 Imp gal); no provision for drop tanks or inflight refuelling
Performance: maximum speed 340 km/h (211 mph) at optimum altitude; cruising speed 290 km/h (180 mph); initial climb rate 420 m (1,378 ft) per minute; service ceiling 4250 m (13,945 ft); range 1416 km (880 miles)
Weights: empty 1147 kg (2,529 lb); maximum take-off 1600 kg (3,527 lb)
Dimensions: span 8·00 m (26 ft 3 in); length 8·45 m (27 ft 8·75 in); height 3·53 m (11 ft 7 in); wing area 12·28 m² (132·2 sq ft)

Variants

PZL-130 Orlik: first flown in October 1984, the Orlik (spotted eaglet) is an attractive flying and weapon trainer that can also undertake the reconnaissance, target towing and counter-insurgency roles
PZL-130T Turbo-Orlik: developed under the team leadership of AirTech of Canada and first flown in July 1986, this is an upgraded version of the Orlik offering much superior offensive capability through the use of a 550-shp (410-kW) Pratt & Whitney Canada PT6A-25A turboprop for greater performance and agility with an increased weapon load carried on hardpoints rated at 200 kg (441 lb) for each unit of the inner pair and 160 kg (353 lb) for each unit of the outer pair; internal fuel capacity is the same as that for the Orlik, but the type can also carry two 150-litre (33-Imp gal) drop tanks; the type has a length of 8·68 m (28 ft 5·75 in), empty and maximum take-off weights of 1150 and 2155 kg (2,535 and 4,751 lb) respectively, and performance data that include a maximum speed of 500 km/h (311 mph) at 4575 m (15,000 ft), a cruising speed of 438 km/h (272 mph) at sea level, an initial climb rate of 954 m (3,130 ft) per minute, a service ceiling of 10,060 m (33,000 ft) and a range of 1287 km (800 miles) on internal fuel; PZL also envisages a version with a Czech turboprop, the Walter M 601D

PZL Mielec I-22 Iryd

(Poland)

Type: advanced training, reconnaissance and light close-support aeroplane

Accommodation: pupil and pilot in tandem on VS-1 zero/150-km/h (93-mph) ejector seat

Armament (fixed): one 23-mm GSh-23L twin-barrel cannon in an underfuselage pack with 200 rounds

Armament (disposable): this is carried on four hardpoints (two under each wing, with each unit rated at 500 kg/1,102 lb) up to a maximum weight of 1200 kg (2,646 lb) of light stores including 100-, 250- or 500-kg (220-, 551 or 1,102-lb) bombs, UV-8-57 or UV-16-57 launchers each with eight or 16 55-mm (2·17-in) rockets, 7·62-mm (0·3-in) machine-gun pods and other stores

Electronics and operational equipment: communication and navigation equipment, plus a gyro sight, RWR and reconnaissance equipment

Powerplant and fuel system: two 1100-kg (2,425-lb) thrust PZL-Rzeszow SO-3W22 non-afterburning turbojets, and a total internal fuel capacity of 2540 litres (558·5 Imp gal) plus provision for two 400-litre (88-Imp gal) drop tanks; no provision for inflight refuelling

Performance: maximum speed 915 km/h (569 mph) at sea level; cruising speed 924 km (574 mph) at high altitude; initial climb rate 2220 m (7,285 ft) per minute; service ceiling 12,600 m (41,340 ft); range 1670 km (1,037 miles)

Weights: empty 3962 kg (8,735 lb); normal take-off 6275 kg (13,834 lb); maximum take-off 7493 kg (16,519 lb)

Dimensions: span 9·60 m (31 ft 6 in); length 13·22 m (43 ft 4·5 in); height 4·30 m (14 ft 1·3 in); wing area 19·92 m² (214·42 sq ft)

Variant

I-22 Iryd: first flown in March 1985, the Iryd (iridium) is planned as successor to the TS-11 Iskra, and is a trim aeroplane resembling the Dassault-Breguet/Dornier Alpha Jet though it is slightly smaller and somewhat lighter; the I-22 is unusual amongst modern trainer/light attack aircraft in being powered by a pair of turbojets rather than turbofans, but possesses sprightly performance

PZL Mielec TS-11 Iskra-bis DF

(Poland)

Type: light close-support and reconnaissance aeroplane

Accommodation: pilot on an ejector seat

Armament (fixed): one 23-mm NR-23 cannon with an unrevealed number of rounds

Armament (disposable): this is carried on four hardpoints (two under each wing with each unit rated at 100 kg/220 lb) up to a maximum weight of 400 kg (882 lb) of light stores including 100-kg (220-lb) bombs, UV-8-57 launchers each with eight 55-mm (2·17-in) rockets, and 7·62-mm (0·3-in) machine-gun pods

Electronics and operational equipment: communication and navigation equipment, plus an optical sight and reconnaissance equipment

Powerplant and fuel system: one 1100-kg (2,425-lb) thrust IL SO-3W non-afterburning turbojet, and a total internal fuel capacity of 1400 litres (308 Imp gal); no provision for drop tanks or inflight refuelling

Performance: maximum speed 770 km/h (478 mph) at 5000 m (16,405 ft); cruising speed 600 km/h (373 mph); initial climb rate 1164 m (3,820 ft) per minute; service ceiling 11,000 m (36,090 ft); range 1260 km (783 miles)

Weights: empty 2560 kg (5,644 lb); normal take-off 3243 kg (7,150 lb); maximum take-off 3840 kg (8,465 lb)

Dimensions: span 10·06 m (33 ft 0 in); length 11·15 m (36 ft 7 in); height 3·50 m (11 ft 5·5 in); wing area 17·50 m² (188·4 sq ft)

Variants

Iskra-bis A: initial production version of the Iskra (spark) two-seat primary and advanced trainer; the type first flew in February 1960 and began to enter service in March 1963 with the 780-kg (1,720-lb) HO-10 turbojet and two underwing hardpoints for weapons training; aircraft delivered from 1964 have the more powerful SO-1 or improved SO-3 turbojet

Iskra-bis B: derivative of the Iskra-bis A with four underwing hardpoints and originally designated **Iskra 100**

Iskra-bis C: single-seat reconnaissance deriva-

tive of the Iskra-bis B and originally called the **Iskra 200**, with the rear cockpit replaced by additional fuel tankage, and reconnaissance equipment carried in the lower fuselage aft of the cockpit

Iskra-bis D: final production version of the original Iskra series before production ceased in 1979, and is in essence an improved Iskra-bis B with greater weapons versatility

Iskra-bis DF: version for resumption of production in 1982, a combination of Iskra-bis C and D features in the reconnaissance and close air support role with four hardpoints and three cameras (in the lower fuselage and the bottom of the two inlets)

Below: The two-seater PZL Mielec TS-11 Iskra-bis DF entered production in 1982 as a replacement for the piston-engined TS-8 Bies and will itself be replaced by the I-22 Iryd.

Rockwell B-1B

(USA)

Type: long-range variable-geometry strategic bomber and missile-carrying aeroplane

Accommodation: flightcrew of four all on McDonnell Douglas ACES II ejector seats

Armament (fixed): none

Armament (disposable): this is carried in three lower-fuselage weapons bays rated at 75,000 lb (34,020 kg) and on six underfuselage hardpoints rated at 59,000 lb (26,762 kg) up to a typical maximum weight of 64,000 lb (29,030 kg); in the strategic nuclear role the weapon bays can accommodate 24 megaton-range B61 or 1·1-megaton B83 thermonuclear bombs, or 12 1·45-megaton B28 or 1-megaton B43 thermonuclear bombs, or eight 200-kiloton AGM-86B air-launched cruise missiles, or 24 170-kiloton AGM-69A SRAM defence-suppression missiles, while the underfuselage hardpoints can carry 14 B43, B61 or B83 bombs, or eight B28 bombs, or 14 AGM-86B or AGM-69A missiles; in the conventional role the weapons bays can accommodate 24 2,000-lb (907-kg) or 128 500-lb (227-kg) free-fall or retarded bombs, while the underfuselage hardpoints can carry 14 2,000-lb (907-kg) or 44 500-lb (227-kg) bombs

Electronics and operational equipment: communication and navigation equipment, plus extremely advanced offensive and defensive avionics suites; the Offensive Avionics System is co-ordinated by Boeing on the basis of the same company's OAS for the B-52 bomber and comprises Westinghouse APQ-164 multi-mode attack, ground-mapping and terrain-following radar, Singer-Kearfott INS, Teledyne Ryan APN-218 Doppler navigation, Northrop NAS-26 astro-inertial navigation, IBM avionic control units and computers and Sperry offensive display sets; the Defensive Avionics System is co-ordinated by Eaton-AIL as the ALQ-161A with quickly reprogrammable digital computers and Sanders display units with Raytheon phased-array antennae and Northrop jammers for the near-instantaneous detection, location, analysis and jamming of hostile emissions

Powerplant and fuel system: four 30,780-lb (13,962-kg) afterburning thrust General Electric F101-GE-102 turbofans, and a total internal fuel capacity of 24,000 US gal (90,850 litres) plus provision for an unrevealed quantity of auxiliary fuel in weapon-bay tanks; no provision for drop tanks but provision for inflight refuelling

Performance: maximum speed 825 mph (1330 km/h) or Mach 1·25 at high altitude and 600 mph (966 km/h) or Mach 0·79 at sea level; initial climb rate not revealed; service ceiling not revealed; radius 3,225 miles (5190 km) with eight SRAMs and eight B61s on a hi-hi-hi mission

Weights: empty 192,000 lb (87,091 kg); normal take-off 431,600 lb (195,774 kg); maximum take-off 477,000 lb (216,367 kg)

Dimensions: span 136 ft 8·5 in (41·67 m) spread and 78 ft 2·5 in (23·84 m) swept; length 147 ft 0 in (44·81 m); height 34 ft 0 in (10·36 m); wing area 1,950·0 sq ft (181·2 m²)

Variant

B-1B: entering service from 1986 to replace the Boeing B-52 in the penetration role, the B-1B resulted from a protracted development history from the time the US Air Force issued its 1969 requirement for a high-level bomber with dash capability of Mach 2·2+ for delivery of free-fall and stand-off weapons; the Rockwell submission was accepted as the B-1 in 1970, and the full-scale development of the initial production version was soon under way, this B-1A being a complex variable-geometry type with General Electric F101 turbofans and variable inlets; the prototype first flew in December 1974 and the flight test programme moved ahead without undue delay; in June 1977 President Carter decided to scrap the programme in favour of cruise missiles, and it was only with the inauguration of President Reagan that the new administration decided in October 1981 to procure 100 B-1B bombers in the low-level high-subsonic penetration role with fixed inlets and revised nacelles (reducing maximum speed to Mach 1·25) but a strengthened airframe and landing gear for operation at higher weights with nuclear and conventional weapons over very long ranges; other changes were concerned with reduction of the type's already low radar signature, S-shaped ducts with streamwise baffles shielding the face of the engine compressors, and radar absorbent materials being used in sensitive areas to reduce reflectivity; the second and fourth B-1As were used from March 1983 to flight-test features of the B-1B, which first flew in September 1984 with the advanced offensive and defensive electronic systems; from the ninth aircraft the type was built with revised weapons bays, the forward bay having a movable bulkhead allowing the carriage of 12 AGM-86B ALCMs internally, as well as additional fuel tanks and SRAMs; the initial fit is eight ALCMs carried internally plus another 14 externally; when the Northrop B-2 enters service in the 1990s as the USAF's penetration 'stealth' bomber, the B-1B will be relegated increasingly to the stand-off and conventional bombing roles

Below: The B-1B shows off its contours in the fully swept high-speed configuration.

Rockwell OV-10A Bronco

(USA)

Type: multi-role counter-insurgency aeroplane

Accommodation: system operator and pilot in tandem on LW-3B ejector seats

Armament (fixed): four 7·62-mm (0·3-in) M60C machine-guns with 500 rounds per gun

Armament (disposable): this is carried on seven hardpoints (one under the fuselage rated at 1,200 lb/544 kg, two under each sponson with each unit rated at 600 lb/272 kg, and one under each wing rated at 600 lb/272 kg) up to a maximum weight of 4,000 lb (1814 kg); the underwing hardpoints can carry only AIM-9 Sidewinder AAMs, but the others can carry a wide diversity of stores such as 1,000-, 750-, 500- and 250-lb (454-, 340-, 227- and 113-kg) free-fall or retarded bombs, cluster bombs, napalm bombs, LAU-series pods for 2·75-in (70-mm) rockets, and 7·62-mm (0·3-in) or 20-mm gun pods

Electronics and operational equipment: communication and navigation equipment, plus an optical sight and Doppler navigation

Powerplant and fuel system: two 715-shp (533-kW) Garrett T76-G-416/417 turboprops, and a total internal fuel capacity of 252 US gal (954 litres) plus provision for one 150-US gal (568-litre) drop tank; no provision for inflight refuelling

Performance: maximum speed 281 mph (452 km/h) at sea level; initial climb rate 2,600 ft (790 m) per minute; service ceiling 24,000 ft (7315 m); radius 228 miles (367 km) with maximum warload; ferry range 1,382 miles (2224 km)

Weights: empty 6,893 lb (3127 kg); normal take-off 9,908 lb (4494 kg); maximum take-off 14,444 lb (6552 kg)

Dimensions: span 40 ft 0 in (12·19 m); length 41 ft 7 in (12·67 m); height 15 ft 2 in (4·64 m); wing area 291·0 sq ft (27·03 m²)

Variants

OV-10A Bronco: a much-underestimated type designed for the battlefield reconnaissance and counter-insurgency roles, the Bronco first flew during July 1965 in response to the US Marine Corps' Light Armed Reconnaissance Aircraft requirement, and this YOV-10A prototype was powered by two 600-shp (447-kW) Garrett T76-G-6/8 turboprops; the type was generally satisfactory and entered production as the OV-10A with a 10-ft (3·05-m) increase in span and

more powerful T76-G-10/12 (later T76-G-416/417) turboprops; the first production aeroplane flew in August 1976, and since that time the Bronco has performed admirably in the battlefield reconnaissance, FAC and helicopter escort roles

OV-10B Bronco: target-towing version of the OV-10A for West Germany, later supplemented by **OV-10B(Z)** aircraft with a 2,950-lb (1330-kg) thrust General Electric J85-GE-4 turbojet pod-mounted above the centre section for better performance

OV-10C Bronco: version of the OV-10A for Thailand

OV-10D Bronco: USMC OV-10As revised for the night surveillance and observation roles with 1,040-shp (776-kW) T76-G-420/421 turboprops (with IR suppression kits) and uprated armament provision (up to a maximum weight of 3,600 lb/1633 kg, and including laser-guided weapons) used in conjunction with the chin-mounted AAS-37 FLIR and a laser designator; this AAS-37 system can also be used with the M97 20-mm cannon turret that can be fitted in place of the standard weapon fit; other modifications in this important type are the APR-38 RWR and the ALE-39 chaff dispenser

OV-10E Bronco: version of the OV-10A for Venezuela

OV-10F Bronco: version of the OV-10A for Indonesia

Rockwell T-2C Buckeye

T-2B Buckeye: designed as the North American NA-264 to meet a 1956 US Navy requirement for a multi-role trainer, the Buckeye used proved components and features of other North American (later Rockwell) aircraft to speed the development of the T2J-1 (from 1962 the T-2A) initial model powered by a single 3,400-lb (1542-kg) thrust Westinghouse J34-W-36 non-afterburning turbojet; though the type proved successful, it was clear that greater power and a twin-engine layout would offer better performance and greater reliability, and there thus appeared in August 1962 the T-2B with two 3,000-lb (1361-kg) thrust Pratt & Whitney J60-P-6 turbojets

T-2C Buckeye: definitive twin-engine model with General Electric J85 turbojets for the first flight of a production aircraft in December 1968

T-2D Buckeye: T-2C variant for Venezuela

T-2E Buckeye: T-2C variant for Greece with a secondary attack capability though the provision of six underwing hardpoints for a maximum load of 3,500 lb (1587 kg) of disposable stores

Left: A Greek-operated T-2E.

Opposite, bottom: An OV-10E Bronco of the Venezuelan air force.

Below: A Saab 105 shows its plan view.

Bottom: Saab 105, note the side-by-side seats.

(USA)

Type: basic and advanced flying and weapon trainer

Accommodation: pupil and instructor in tandem on LS-1 ejector seats

Armament (fixed): none

Armament (disposable): this is carried on two hardpoints (one under each wing) up to a maximum weight of 640 lb (290 kg) of light bombs and rocket pods

Electronics and operational equipment: communication and navigation equipment, and an optical sight

Powerplant and fuel system: two 2,950-lb (1339-kg) thrust General Electric J85-GE-4 non-afterburning turbojets, and a total internal fuel capacity of 691 US gal (2616 litres); no provision for drop tanks or inflight refuelling

Performance: maximum speed 522 mph (840 km/h) at 25,000 ft (7620 m); initial climb rate 6,200 ft (1890 m) per minute; service ceiling 40,400 ft (12,315 m); range 1,047 miles (1685 km)

Weights: empty 8,115 lb (3680 kg); maximum take-off 13,179 lb (5977 kg)

Dimensions: span 38 ft 1·5 in (11·62 m) over tiptanks; length 38 ft 3·5 in (11·67 m); height 14 ft 9·5 in (4·51 m); wing area 255·0 sq ft (23·69 m²)

(Sweden)

Type: flying and weapon trainer, and light attack aeroplane

Accommodation: pupil and instructor side-by-side on ejector seats

Armament (fixed): none

Armament (disposable): this is carried on six hardpoints (three under each wing, with the inner two units each rated at 275 kg/610 lb, the intermediate two units each at 500 kg/1,102 lb and the outer two units each at 275 kg/610 lb) up to a maximum weight of 2000 kg (4,409 lb); typical loads are two 1,000-lb (454-kg) and four 500-lb (227-kg) bombs, or four 500-lb (227-kg) bombs and two 30-mm cannon pods, or four 500-lb (227-lb) napalm bombs and two 7·62-mm (0·3-in) Minigun pods, or six pods each with four 5-in (127-mm) or 19 75-mm (2·95-in) rockets, or two Rb05 ASMs and two Rb24 Sidewinder AAMs

Electronics and operational equipment: communication and navigation equipment, plus optical sights

Powerplant and fuel system: two 2,850-lb (1293-kg) thrust General Electric J85-GE-17B non-afterburning turbojets, and a total internal fuel capacity of 1400 litres (310 Imp gal) plus provision for drop tanks; no provision for inflight refuelling

Performance: maximum speed 970 km/h (603 mph) or Mach 0·79 at sea level; climb to 10,000 ft (32,810 ft) in 4 minutes 30 seconds; service ceiling 13,000 m (42,650 ft); range 2400 km (1,491 miles)

Weights: empty 2550 kg (5,534 lb); maximum take-off 6500 kg (14,330 lb)

Dimensions: span 9·50 m (31 ft 2 in); length 10·50 m (34 ft 5 in); height 2·70 m (8 ft 10 in); wing area 16·30 m² (175·46 sq ft)

Saab 105: this private-venture development first flew in June 1963 with two 745-kg (1,642-lb) thrust Turboméca Aubisque non-afterburning turbofans; the type was soon ordered for the Swedish air force in three variants, namely the **Sk 60A** trainer and liaison aircraft with conventional seating for four, the **Sk 60B** light attack aircraft with accommodation for two on ejector seats, and the **Sk 60C** dual-role light attack and reconnaissance aircraft with ejector seats for two and a camera installation in the nose

Saab 105O: improved trainer and light attack version for Austria with a new and more potent powerplant, and a strengthened wing for greater underwing stores capability

Saab J 35F Draken

(Sweden)

Type: all-weather fighter and attack aeroplane

Accommodation: pilot on a Saab 73SE-F ejector seat

Armament (fixed): one 30-mm Aden M/55 cannon with 100 rounds

Armament (disposable): this is carried on nine hardpoints (three under the fuselage and three under each wing, with the underfuselage and inner two underwing unit each rated at 500 kg/1,102 lb and the outer four underwing units each at 100 kg/220 lb) up to a maximum weight of 2900 kg (6,393 lb); weapons that can be carried are the Rb24 and Rb74 Sidewinder AAMs, Rb27 and Rb28 Falcon AAMs, 500- and 250-kg (1,102- and 551-lb) free-fall bombs, 500-kg (1,102-lb) napalm bomb, 120-kg (265-lb) fragmentation bomb, 135-mm (5·3-in) rockets, and pods for 19 75-mm (2·95-in) rockets

Electronics and operational equipment: communication and navigation equipment, plus Ericsson UAP 13102 (PS-01/A) or UAP 13103 (PS-011/A) fire-control radar, Hughes S71N IR system, Hughes/Saab-Scania S7B fire-control system, Saab BT9 bombing system, data-link system (associated with the STRIL-60 national air-defence network), integrated nav/attack system, RWR and provision for external ECM such as the Pod KA and Pod 70 systems

Powerplant and fuel system: one 8000-kg (17,637-lb) afterburning thrust Svenska Flygmotor RM6B turbojet (licence-built Rolls-Royce Avon with SFA-designed afterburner), and a total internal fuel capacity of 4000 litres (880 Imp gal) plus provision for 1275- and 500-litre (280- and 110-Imp gal) drop tanks; no provision for inflight refuelling

Performance: maximum speed 2125 km/h (1,320 mph) or Mach 2·0 at high altitude; initial climb rate 10,500 m (34,450 ft) per minute; service ceiling 20,000 m (65,615 ft); radius 635 km (395 miles) on a hi-lo-hi mission with external warload; ferry range 3250 km (2,020 miles)

Weights: empty 8250 kg (18,188 lb); maximum take-off 12,270 kg (27,050 lb) on an air defence mission or 15,000 kg (33,069 lb) on an attack mission

Dimensions: span 9·40 m (30 ft 10 in); length 15·35 m (50 ft 4 in); height 3·89 m (12 ft 9 in); wing area 49·20 m² (529·6 sq ft)

Variants

Sk 35C Draken: the Draken (dragon) was Europe's first genuinely supersonic fighter and designed in the first half of the 1950s; the type was a very great achievement in aerodynamic and propulsion terms, the double-delta wing provid-

ing good area and considerable fuel volume with comparatively little drag so that a single Avon turbojet with locally designed afterburner provided sufficient thrust for high performance; the type first flew in prototype form during October 1955, and production J 35A aircraft with the 7000-kg (15,432-lb) thrust Svenska Flygmotor RM6B engine (licence-built Avon 200) began to enter service in March 1960, being followed by the J 35B with data-link equipment (for use in association with the Swedish STRIL-60 integrated air-defence network), collision-course radar and greater armament; the oldest version left is service is the Sk 35C, a tandem two-seat operational conversion trainer derived from J 35A airframes but without armament

J 35D Draken: much improved interceptor with the more powerful RM6C (Avon 300) afterburning turbojet, enlarged air inlets, more advanced avionics (PS-03 radar and S7A fire-control system), two Aden M/55 cannon and a zero/zero ejector seat

J 35F Draken: definitive interceptor with Hughes pulse-Doppler radar for use with semi-active radar-homing Hughes Falcon AAMs and generally upgraded avionics

J 35J Draken: J 35F Drakens reworked to a more modern standard with improvements to the radar, IR scanner, IFF and navigation systems, plus strengthened wings for greater warloads with an additional hardpoint under each inner wing

J 35Oe Draken: 24 ex-Swedish J 35D aircraft refurbished for Austria without provision for missile armament

Saab 35X: export version of the Draken with 30% greater internal fuel capacity, two 30-mm Aden M/55 cannon, and strengthening for operation at higher weights to a maximum of 16,000 kg (32,275 lb) including a warload of up to 4500 kg (9,921 lb); the version for Denmark is the **Saab 35XD** with 11 hardpoints, produced in **F-35** radarless ground-attack, **RF-35** tactical reconnaissance and **TF-35** two-seat trainer subvariants, recently upgraded to a more modern standard with a Marconi HUD, Ferranti 105D laser ranger, Lear-Siegler nav/attack system and Singer-Kearfott INS; the version for Finland is the **Saab 35XS**, delivered with the designation **J 35XS** and generally similar to the J 35F but with two cannon; Finland has also bought ex-Swedish aircraft, namely the **J 35BS** radarless operational trainer (ex-J 35B), the **J 35FS** interceptor (ex-J 35F) and the **J 35CS** two-seat trainer (ex-Sk 35C)

This J 35F Draken carries two examples each of the Rb27 and Rb28 variants of the Falcon.

Saab-Scania AJ 37 Viggen

(Sweden)
Type: all-weather attack aeroplane
Accommodation: pilot on a Saab-Scania ejector seat
Armament (fixed): none
Armament (disposable): this is carried on seven hardpoints (three under the fuselage with the centreline unit rated at some 2000 kg/4,409 lb and the two flanking units each at some 500 kg/1,102 lb, and two under each wing with the inner two units each rated at some 1000 kg/2,205 lb and the outer two units each at some 500 kg/1,102 lb) up to a maximum weight of 6000 kg (13,228 lb); the centreline hardpoint generally carries a 30-mm Aden cannon pod, the two flanking underfuselage hardpoints normally accommodate two launchers each with six 135-mm (5·3-in) rockets, or two Rb24 or Rb74 Sidewinder or Rb28 Falcon AAMs, the inner underwing hardpoints are usually associated with two launchers each with six 135-mm (5·3-in) rockets, or two Rb04E or Rbs15 anti-ship missiles, or two Rb05 or Rb75 ASMs, or two Rb24 or Rb74 Sidewinder AAMs, and the outer underwing hardpoints most commonly lift two Rb24 or Rb74 Sidewinder AAMs; an alternative load is 16 free-fall or fragmentation bombs of various sizes
Electronics and operational equipment: communication and navigation equipment, plus Ericsson PS-37/A multi-mode radar, Marconi HUD, Saab-Scania CK-37 central computer, Philips air-data computer, Decca 72 Doppler navigation,, SATT RWR, and options for various ECM and reconnaissance pods
Powerplant and fuel system: one 11,800-kg (26,015-lb) afterburning thrust Volvo Flygmotor RM8A turbofan (licence-built Pratt & Whitney JT8D-22 with Swedish-designed afterburner), and internal fuel capacity of about 5700 litres (1,254 Imp gal) plus provision for one drop tank; no provision for inflight refuelling
Performance: maximum speed 2125 km/h (1,320 mph) or Mach 2·0 at 12,000 m (39,370 ft) and 1335+ km/h (830+ mph) or Mach 1·1+ at sea level; climb to 10,000 m (32,810 ft) in less than 1 minute 40 seconds; service ceiling about 18,300 m (60,040 ft); radius 1000+ km (621+ miles) on a hi-lo-hi mission with external warload, and 500 km (311 miles) on a lo-lo-lo mission with external warload
Weights: empty about 11,800 kg (26,015 lb); normal take-off 15,000 kg (33,069 lb); maximum take-off 20,500 kg (45,194 lb)
Dimensions: span 10·60 m (34 ft 9·25 in); length including probe 16·30 m (53 ft 7·75 in); height 5·80 m (19 ft 0·25 in); wing area 46·00 m² (495·1 sq ft) and canard area 6·20 m² (66·74 sq ft)

Variants

AJ 37 Viggen: the Viggen (thunderbolt) is one of the most advanced warplanes in the world, custom-designed by Saab-Scania to a Swedish requirement for an integrated weapon system with high performance, great versatility and STOL capability from dispersed sites using lengths of road for runways; extensive research confirmed that the canard configuration offered the best possibilities in conjunction with advanced high-lift devices, an integral thrust reverser (the first such installation on an afterburning turbofan) actuated by compression of the nosewheel leg after a no-flare landing; the comprehensive avionics are vital to effective operation in conjunction with the national air-defence network, and also provide ECM and an instru-

ment landing system; the first prototype flew in February 1967, and the initial production aircraft was an AJ 37 attack fighter that flew in February 1971 for service in the middle of the year
SF 37 Viggen: all-weather overland reconnaissance version of the AJ 37, with a revised nose for one IR and six optical cameras plus an IR sensor, an ECM registration system and an air-data camera (to record altitude, position, course etc);

underwing loads can include two Rb24 or Rb74 Sidewinder AAMs and two ECM pods (one active and one passive), while drop tanks can be carried on the underfuselage hardpoints; the first SF 37 flew in May 1973 and the type entered service in April 1977
SH 37 Viggen: maritime reconnaissance version of the AJ 37 with a revised nose for a surveillance radar and ECM registration system, together with

the same type of data camera as carried by the SF 37; under the wings the type can carry two Rb24 or Rb74 AAMs and two ECM pods (one active and one passive), while the underfuselage hardpoints can accommodate a drop tank on the centreline, a night reconnaissance pod on the port hardpoint, and a long-range camera pod or FFV Red Baron IR reconnaissance pod on the starboard hardpoint; the first SH 37 flew in December 1973 and

the type entered service in the second half of 1975
Sk 37 Viggen: tandem two-seat operational conversion trainer variant of the AJ 37 with reduced fuel capacity and a revised forward fuselage for the accommodation of the separate instructor's cockpit behind and above that of the pupil; the type also has a slightly taller vertical tail, increasing height by 10 cm (3·94 in); the Sk 37 is fully combat-capable, with the same armament pro-

vision as the AJ 37, and began to enter service in the second half of 1972 after the type's first flight in July 1970

The SH 37 is the Viggen model optimized for maritime reconnaissance with specialized mission equipment and provision for two Rb24 or Rb74 Sidewinder self-defence missiles.

Saab-Scania JA 37 Viggen

(Sweden)

Type: all-weather interceptor and attack aeroplane

Accommodation: pilot on a Saab-Scania zero/zero ejector seat

Armament (fixed): one 30-mm Oerlikon KCA cannon with 150 rounds in an underfuselage pack

Armament (disposable): this is carried on seven hardpoints (three under the fuselage, with the centreline unit rated at some 2000 kg/4,409 lb and the two flanking units each at some 500 kg/1,102 lb, and two under each wing with the inner two units each rated at some 1000 kg/2,205 lb and the outer two units each at some 500 kg/1,102 lb) up to a maximum weight of 6000 kg (13,228 lb); in the dedicated interceptor role the JA 37 usually carries six AAMs (Rb71 Sky Flash and/or Rb24 or Rb74 Sidewinder types) and the centreline hardpoint always carries the 30-mm Oerlikon cannon pack; for the attack role the two flanking underfuselage hardpoints normally accommodate two launchers each with six 135-mm (5·3-in) rockets, or two Rb24 or Rb74 Sidewinder or Rb28 Falcon AAMs, the inner underwing hardpoints are usually associated with two launchers each with six 135-mm (5·3-in) rockets, or two Rb04E or Rbs15 anti-ship missiles, or two Rb05 or Rb75 ASMs, or two Rb24 Sidewinder AAMs, and the outer underwing hardpoints most commonly lift two Rb24 Sidewinder AAMs; an alternative load is 16 free-fall or fragmentation bombs of various sizes

Electronics and operational equipment: communication and navigation equipment, plus Ericsson UAP-1023 (PS-46/A) multi-mode pulse-Doppler radar, Smiths HUD, HDDs, Saab-Scania/Singer-Kearfott SKC-2037 central computer, Saab-Scania/Garrett LD-5 air-data computer, Singer-Kearfott KT-70L INS, Decca 72 Doppler navigation,, SATT RWR, and options for various ECM pods such as the BOZ-100 chaff dispenser and SATT AQ31 ECM system

Powerplant and fuel system: one 12,750-kg (28,108-lb) afterburning thrust Volvo Flygmotor RM8B (licence-built Pratt & Whitney JT8D-22 with Swedish-designed afterburner) turbofan, and internal fuel capacity of about 5700 litres (1,254 Imp gal) plus provision for drop tanks; no provision for inflight refuelling

Performance: maximum speed 2125 km/h (1,320 mph) or Mach 2·0 at 12,000 m (39,370 ft) and 1335+ km/h (830+ mph) or Mach 1·1+ at sea level; climb to 10,000 m (32,810 ft) in less than 1 minute 40 seconds; service ceiling about 18,300 m (60,040 ft); radius 1000+ km (621+ miles) on a hi-lo-hi with external warload, and 500 km (311 miles) on a lo-lo-lo mission with external warload

Weights: empty not revealed; normal take-off 15,000 kg (33,069 lb); maximum take-off 17,000 kg (37,478 lb) in the interceptor role or 20,500 kg (45,194 lb) in the attack role

Dimensions: span 10·60 m (34 ft 9·25 in); length including probe 16·30 m (53 ft 7·75 in); height 5·90 m (19 ft 4·25 in); wing area 46·00 m² (495·1 sq ft) and canard area 6·20 m² (66·74 sq ft)

Variant

JA 37 Viggen: this is the dedicated interceptor version (with secondary attack capability) of the Viggen family, but is sufficiently different from its predecessors to be treated separately; the airframe has been revised (combining the fuselage and wings of the AJ 37 with the tail of the Sk 37) and fitted with the considerably more powerful RM8B afterburning turbofan for enhanced performance in the interception role under command of the national air-defence network; the JA 37 is fitted with a new generation of electronics and with a revised armament configuration, including a fixed gun in the form of the potent 30-mm Oerlikon KCA; this fires 0·36-kg (0·79-lb) shells at the rate of 1,350 rounds per minute with a muzzle velocity of 1050 m (3,445 ft) per second, producing after a flat trajectory of 1500 m (4,920 ft) as much penetrative power as the British Aden and French DEFA cannon (of the same calibre) develop at the muzzle; the first JA 37 flew in November 1977, the type entered service in 1979 and the last aeroplane was delivered early in 1990

Below: The JA 37 is the dedicated air-defence variant of the multi-role Viggen family.

Saab-Scania JAS 39A Gripen

(Sweden)
Type: all-weather fighter, attack and reconnaissance aeroplane

Accommodation: pilot on a Martin-Baker S10LS zero/zero ejector seat

Armament (fixed): one 27-mm Mauser BK27 cannon with an unrevealed number of rounds

Armament (disposable): this is carried on six hardpoints (two under each wing and two at the wingtips) up to a maximum weight of about 6500 kg (14,330 lb); weapons that can be carried include the Rb24 or Rb74 Sidewinder, Rb71 Sky Flash and other advanced AAMs, Rb75 Maverick ASM, Rbs15F anti-ship missile, MBB VBW or other anti-armour dispenser weapon, bombs of various 'smart' and 'dumb' types, and rocket pods

Electronics and operational equipment: communication and navigation equipment, plus Ericsson PS-05/A pulse-Doppler search and acquisition radar, podded FLIR, Hughes HUD, three SRA HDDs (one for flight data, one for ground mapping and one for radar/FLIR data), digital central computer used in conjunction with the Lear Siegler fly-by-wire flight-control system, Honeywell laser INS, and several ECM and ESM systems (such as the BOZ-100 chaff pod and Lake 200 jammer pod) as well as reconnaissance pods

Powerplant and fuel system: one 8200-kg (18,080-lb) afterburning thrust Volvo Flygmotor RM12 (licence-built General Electric F404J) turbofan, and a total internal fuel capacity of unrevealed quantity plus provision for drop tanks; no provision for inflight refuelling

Performance: (estimated) maximum speed 2125 km/h (1,320 mph) or Mach 2·0 at high altitude; initial climb rate not revealed; service ceiling not revealed; range not revealed

Weights: empty not revealed; normal take-off 8000 kg (17,637 lb); maximum take-off 11,350 kg (25,022 lb)

Dimensions: span 8·00 m (26 ft 3 in); length 14·10 m (46 ft 3 in); height 4·70 m (15 ft 5 in); wing area not revealed

Variants

JAS 39A Gripen: designed from 1980 as a successor to the Viggen in the fighter, attack and reconnaissance roles, the Gripen (griffin) is further proof of the Swedish aerospace industry's ability to design advanced combat aircraft tailored to Sweden's peculiar requirements; the basic design (a canard delta configuration) is developed from that of the Viggen, but the adoption of composite materials for some 30% of the airframe increases strength while reducing weight and making possible the effective use of the RM12 afterburning turbofan developed jointly by Flygmotor and General Electric on the basis of the latter's F404J; other features are the triplex fire-by-wire flight-control system for enhanced manoeuvrability, one wide-angle HUD and three HDDs (flight information, computer-generated terrain map with tactical overlay, and computer-controlled radar/IR sensor information); these and other features offer performance and capabilities (including STOL and dispersed-site operations) comparable or superior to those of the 15,000-kg (33,068-lb) Viggen in an 8000-kg (17,637-lb) aircraft; the first prototype was scheduled to fly in 1987 for a planned in-service date of 1992, but in fact flew only in December 1988 because of difficulties with the fly-by-wire control system; further problems with the control system led to the loss of the first prototype in February 1989

JAS 39B Gripen: two-seat version being designed with company funding in expectation of a Swedish air force requirement

Above: The JAS 39 offers similar capabilities to the Viggen in a much smaller airframe.

SEPECAT (Société Européenne de Production de l'avion ECAT) Jaguar S

(France & UK)

Type: all-weather tactical support and attack aeroplane

Accommodation: pilot on a Martin-Baker Mk 9B II zero/zero ejector seat

Armament (fixed): two 30-mm Aden Mk 4 cannon with 150 rounds per gun

Armament (disposable): this is carried on five hardpoints (one under the fuselage rated at 2,500 lb/1134 kg, and two under each wing with the inner two units each rated at 2,500 lb/1134 kg and the outer two units each at 1,250 lb/567 kg) up to a maximum weight of 10,500 lb (4763 kg); typical loads are eight 1,000-lb (454-kg) free-fall or retarded bombs, 11 500-lb (227-kg) free-fall or retarded bombs, six BL755 cluster bombs, six JP233 anti-airfield bombs and pods for 19 2·75-in (70-mm) or 36 68-mm (2·68-in) rockets; the Mk 13/18 Paveway laser-guided bomb, AJ.168 Martel ASM and AIM-9 Sidewinder AAM can also be carried

Electronics and operational equipment: communication and navigation equipment, plus Smiths HUD, Ferranti FIN1064 digital inertial and weapon-aiming system, Marconi-Elliott MCS 920 digital central computer, Ferranti Type 105/106 LRMTS, Marconi ARI.18223 RWR, and options such as the Philips/Matra Phimat chaff dispenser, Westinghouse ALQ-101(V)10 ECM pod and BAe reconnaissance pod with five cameras and an IR linescanner

Powerplant and fuel system: two 8,040-lb (3647-kg) afterburning thrust Rolls-Royce/Turboméca Adour Mk 104 turbofans, and a total internal fuel capacity of 924 Imp gal (4200 litres) plus provision for three 264-Imp gal (1200-litre) drop tanks; provision for inflight refuelling

Performance: maximum speed 1,056 mph (1700 km/h) or Mach 1·6 at 36,000 ft (10,970 m) and 840 mph (1350 km/h) or Mach 1·1 at sea level; climb to 30,000 ft (9145 m) in 1 minute 30 seconds; service ceiling 46,000 ft (14,020 m); radius 334 miles (537 km) on a lo-lo-lo mission with typical warload but no drop tanks; ferry range 2,190 miles (3525 km)

Weights: empty 15,430 lb (7000 kg); normal take-off 24,150 lb (10,955 kg); maximum take-off 34,610 lb (15,700 kg)

Dimensions: span 28 ft 6 in (8·69 m); length 55 ft 2·5 in (16·83 m) including probe; height 16 ft 0·5 in (4·89 m); wing area 260·27 sq ft (24·18 m²)

Variants

Jaguar A: the Jaguar resulted from separate British and French efforts in the early 1960s to develop a two-seat advanced/operational trainer and a single-seat close-support and attack aircraft; the countries decided to work on a collaborative basis, and from the Breguet Br·121 project developed the Jaguar, which first flew in two-seat prototype form in September 1968; the Jaguar A is the French single-seat attack version, first flying in March 1969 for delivery up to the end of 1981; this type is powered by 3315-kg (7,305-lb) afterburning thrust Adour Mk 102 turbofans, has different avionics (including a SFIM 250-1 twin-gyro platform, Decca Type 72 Doppler navigation, Crouzet 90 navigation computer, CSF 31 weapon-aiming computer and control gear for the AS.37 Martel ASM), and carries French weapons such as the AS.30 ASM, Durandal runway-cratering bomb, Belouga cluster bomb,

BAP 100 anti-runway bomb, BAT 120 anti-vehicle bomb and 15-kiloton AN-52 free-fall nuclear weapon; the last 30 of France's 160 aircraft were completed with provision for the AS.30L laser-homing ASM and associated ATLIS II designator pod; the standard EW suite of the Jaguar A is the Thomson-CSF Thomson-CSF Barracuda or Barem jammer pod and a Matra chaff/flare dispenser, though some aircraft have the more capable combination of a Thomson-CSF Type BF RWR, an Alkan 5020/5021 conformal chaff dispenser and an 18-shot IR flare launcher; some aircraft are configured for the EW escort role with the Caiman and Basilisk jamming pods

Jaguar B: Royal Air Force **Jaguar T.Mk 2** operational conversion trainer version; only 38 examples were built, the first flying in August 1971, and the main change is the lengthening of the fuselage to 17·53 m (57·51 ft) to accommodate the second cockpit; the type has the complete weapons capability of the Jaguar S (Jaguar GR.Mk 1), and like that aircraft has been upgraded with the Ferranti FIN1064 INS, resulting in the revised designation **Jaguar T.Mk 2A**

Jaguar E: French air force two-seat trainer, first flown in September 1968 and built to the extent of 40 aircraft with Adour Mk 102 turbofans for delivery from May 1972

Jaguar S: British **Jaguar GR.Mk 1** single-seat close support aircraft first flown in October 1969 and built to the extent of 165 aircraft; delivered with Adour Mk 102 turbofans, from 1978 the survivors were upgraded with Adour Mk 104s; from 1983 surviving aircraft were modified with the Ferranti FIN1064 INS in place of the original HUDWAS (Head-Up Display and Weapon-Aiming System), resulting in the revised designation **Jaguar GR.Mk 1A**

Jaguar International: first flown in August 1976, this is an improved multi-role type based on the Jaguar A/S single-seater but fitted with 3900-kg (8,598-lb) afterburning thrust Adour Mk 804s or (in later aircraft) 4205-kg (9,270-lb) afterburning thrust Adour Mk 811s plus revised avionics and weapons; aircraft of this type have been sold to Ecuador, India, Nigeria and Oman, India also building the type under licence with the name **Shamsher** (assault sword); the Jaguar International has two overwing hardpoints for AAMs such as the Matra 550 Magic or AIM-9 Sidewinder, and the underwing hardpoints can accept anti-ship missiles such as the AGM-84 Harpoon, AM.39 Exocet and Kormoran; late-production Indian aircraft have the most advanced avionics, the DARIN system including Thomson-CSF Agave multi-mode radar (in some aircraft) with target indication for anti-ship missiles (probably the Sea Eagle) on the Smiths HUD and weapon-aiming system, Smiths Darin nav/attack system, Sagem INS and Ferranti COMED 2045 combined map and electronic display; the Jaguar International has empty, normal and maximum take-off weights of 15,432, 24,149 and 34,612 lb (7000, 10,954 and 15,700 kg) respectively

A Jaguar International of the Omani air force reveals the salient features of this much underestimated warplane: compact overall design, and a combination of high-set wing and stalky landing gear legs to permit the carriage of large loads on five hardpoints.

Shenyang Aircraft Company J-6C

(China)
Type: fighter, ground-attack and reconnaissance aeroplane
Accommodation: pilot on an ejector seat (Martin-Baker PKD10 zero/zero seat in most export aircraft)
Armament (fixed): three 30-mm NR-30 cannon with an unrevealed number of rounds per gun
Armament (disposable): this is carried on four hardpoints (two under each wing) up to a maximum weight of 500 kg (1,102 lb); typical loads are two PL-2 or PL-7 AAMs, or two 250-kg (551-lb) bombs, or two pods for 55-mm (2·17-in) rockets, or eight 212-mm (8·35-in) rockets
Electronics and operational equipment: communication and navigation equipment, plus a gyro sight
Powerplant and fuel system: two 3250-kg (7,175-lb) afterburning thrust Shenyang Wopen-6 (Tumanskii R-9BF-811) turbojets, and a total internal fuel capacity of 2170 litres (477 Imp gal) plus provision for two 760-litre (167-Imp gal) drop tanks; no provision for inflight refuelling
Performance: maximum speed 1540 km/h (957 mph) or Mach 1·45 at 11,000 m (36,090 ft) and 1340 km/h (832 mph) or Mach 1·09 at sea level; cruising speed 950 km/h (590 mph); initial climb rate 9145+ m (30,000+ ft) per minute; service ceiling 17,900 m (58,725 ft); radius 685 km (426 miles) on a hi-lo-hi mission with two AAMs and two drop tanks; ferry range 2200 km (1,366 miles)
Weights: empty 5670 kg (12,700 lb); normal take-off 7545 kg (16,634 lb); maximum take-off 8965 kg (19,764 lb)
Dimensions: span 9·20 m (30 ft 2·25 in); length 12·60 m (41 ft 4 in) with probe; height 3·88 m (12 ft 8·75 in); wing area 25·00 m² (269·1 sq ft)

Variants

J-6: Chinese-built version of the Mikoyan-Gurevich MiG-19SF 'Farmer-C', produced after the signature of a licence agreement in January 1958 with deliveries beginning in December 1961; since that time the type has been built in large numbers and also exported with the designation **F-6**, impressing customers with the excellence of the finish and the great attention to detail; the aircraft is technically obsolete, but still a formidable close-range air-combat adversary as a result of its great agility and powerful close-range gun armament
J-6A: Chinese equivalent of the MiG-19PF with two 30-mm cannon (in the wing roots) and limited interception radar
J-6B: Chinese equivalent of the MiG-19PM 'Farmer-D' with two 30-mm cannon, interception radar and radar-homing AAMs
J-6C: Chinese development of the J-6 with the brake parachute relocated to a bullet fairing at the base of the rudder
J-6Xin: Chinese development of the J-6A with Chinese radar in a sharp-tipped radome on the splitter plate rather than Soviet radar in the inlet centrebody
JJ-6: Chinese trainer development equivalent to (but not identical with) the MiG-19UTI; the forward fuselage is lengthened by 0·84 m (33·1 in) forward of the wing to provide volume for the insertion of a tandem-seat cockpit; armament comprises a single 30-mm cannon, and the type is exported with the designation **FT-6**
JZ-6: Chinese version of the MiG-19R reconnaissance aircraft with the fuselage cannon replaced by a camera installation

Below: A Pakistan air force Shenyang-built Jian 6C version of the MiG-19SF 'Farmer-C'.

Shenyang Aircraft Company

(China)
Type: air-superiority fighter and with secondary close air support capability
Accommodation: pilot on an ejector seat
Armament (fixed): one 23-mm Type 23-3 twin-barrel cannon with 200 rounds in a ventral installation
Armament (disposable): this is carried on seven hardpoints (one under the fuselage and three under each wing) up to an unrevealed maximum weight of AAMs, bombs, rocket pods and drop tanks
Electronics and operational equipment: communication and navigation equipment, plus monopulse search radar, gyro sight, 'Odd Rods' IFF, RWR, ECM and other items
Powerplant and fuel system: two 6720-kg (14,815-lb) afterburning thrust Liyang Wopen-13A turbojets, and a total internal fuel capacity of about 5400 litres (1,188 Imp gal) plus provision for three 1140-litre (251-Imp gal) drop tanks; no provision for inflight refuelling
Performance: maximum speed about 2300 km/h (1,429 mph) or Mach 2·16 at high altitude; initial climb rate 12,000 m (39,370 ft) per minute: service ceiling 20,000 m (65,615 ft); radius 800 km (497 miles) on a hi-hi-hi mission; maximum range 2200 km (1,367 miles)
Weights: empty 9820 kg (21,649 lb); normal take-off 14,300 kg (31,526 lb); maximum take-off 17,800 kg (39,242 lb)
Dimensions: span 9·344 m (30 ft 8 in); length including probe 21·59 m (70 ft 10 in); height 5·41 m (17 ft 9 in); wing area 42·2 m² (454·2 sq ft)

Variants

J-8 I 'Finback': revealed in September 1984 after entering limited service in the late 1960s in its initial **J-8 0** day fighter form, the long-expected J-8 I all-weather fighter is a radical Chinese development of the Chengu J-7 (Mikoyan-Gurevich MiG-21) along the lines of the Mikoyan-Gurevich E-152A experimental aircraft about which the

J-8 II 'Finback'

Chinese received limited data in the late 1950s; compared with the J-7 the airframe has been scaled up for a twin-engine powerplant of two 6200-kg (13,668-lb) afterburning thrust Wopen WP-7B turbojets; the programme was long in development, work having started in the early 1960s and accelerated once the success of the Nanchang Q-5 had proved the basic soundness of such changes; the type uses two Chinese-built versions of the Tumanskii R-11 afterburning turbojet to secure Mach 2 performance, the engines being fed through a single large nose inlet with a translating centrebody; the armament comprises a pair of 30-mm Type 30 cannon with an unrevealed number of rounds per gun and well as an unrevealed weight of disposable stores carried on four underwing hardpoints

J-8 II 'Finback': upgraded version first flown in May 1984 but revealed only in 1986, with a revised powerplant (derived from the Tumanskii R-13-300) and a heavily modified nose in which the central inlet with small radar bullet is replaced by a large nose radome and lateral inlets just forward of the wing leading edges; the type also has a ventral fin that folds to starboard for landing and take-off; the type is offered for export as the **F-8 II**, and China is seeking the participation of Western companies in the provision of avionics and medium-range semi-active radar-homing AAMs; in 1986 the US government approved the export to China of 55 J-8 II shipsets of equipment, each set including interception radar, INS, HUD, and flight and mission computers; the first two J-8 II fighters were delivered to Grumman in the first half of 1989 for the integration of this electronic package, but the programme was suspended by the US government after the Chinese suppression of a democracy movement later in the year

Below: The J-8 II is exported as the F-8 II but is still a derivative of the MiG-21.

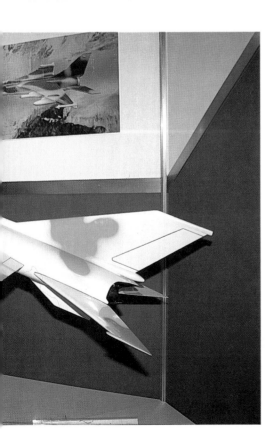

Shin Meiwa PS-1

(Japan)
Type: STOL anti-submarine flying boat
Accommodation: flightcrew of five, and a mission crew of five in the cabin
Armament (fixed): none
Armament (disposable): this is carried in a lower-fuselage weapons bay rated at 600 kg (1,323 lb) and on four hardpoints (one under each wing rated at 500 kg/1,102 lb and two at the wingtips with each rated at 200 kg/441 lb) up to a maximum weight of 2000 kg (4,409 lb); the weapons bay can carry four 150-kg (331-lb) depth bombs, the pods carried on the two underwing hardpoints can each accommodate two Mk 46 torpedoes, and the wingtip hardpoints can each accept three 5-in (127-mm) rockets
Electronics and operational equipment: communication and navigation equipment, plus APS-80N search radar with its antenna in the thimble radome on the nose, AQS-101B dunking sonar, ASQ-10A MAD with its sensor in the tail 'sting', 'Julie' active ranging system with 12 charges, AQA-3 'Jezebel' passive detection system with 20 sonobuoys, APN-153 Doppler navigation and N-OA-35/HSA plotting group
Powerplant and fuel system: four 2285-kW (3,064-shp) Ishikawajima-Harima T64-IHI-10 (licence-built General Electric T64) turboprops, and a total internal fuel capacity of 17,900 litres (2,387 Imp gal); no provision for drop tanks or inflight refuelling
Performance: maximum speed 547 km/h (340 mph) at 1525 m (5,000 ft); cruising speed 315 km/h (196 mph) at 1525 m (5,000 ft); initial climb rate 690 m (2,264 ft) per minute; service ceiling 9000 m (29,530 ft); range 2170 km (1,348 miles) on a normal mission; ferry range 4745 km (2,948 miles)
Weights: empty 26,300 kg (58,000 lb); normal take-off 36,000 kg (79,365 lb); maximum take-off 43,000 kg (94,797 lb)
Dimensions: span 33·14 m (108 ft 8·75 in); length 33·50 m (109 ft 11 in); height 9·715 m (31 ft 10·5 in); wing area 135·8 m² (1,461·8 sq ft)

Variants

PS-1: one of the few modern flying boats in service anywhere in the world, the PS-1 is a thoroughly capable machine with excellent anti-submarine sensors capable of deployment with the aircraft floating or in the air; the type has good STOL performance and can operate in rough water; the first example flew in October 1967, and production was completed in 1979 with the 23rd aeroplane; the type was phased out of first-line service by March 1

US-1: SAR variant of the PS-1 with retractable wheeled landing gear to turn the type into an amphibian; the type has a crew of nine, and can carry 20 passengers or 12 litters

US-1A: version of the US-1 with uprated 2600-kW (3,487-shp) General Electric T64-IHI-10J turboprops built by Ishikawajima-Harima to give the type better performance; this powerplant is being retrofitted to the US-1 aircraft

Below: A US-1 SAR amphibian flies ahead of the prototype PS-1 ASW flying boat.

Shorts 330-UTT

(UK)

Type: short-range tactical transport aeroplane

Accommodation: flightcrew of two, and 33 troops, or 30 paratroops, or 15 litters plus attendants, or 8,000 lb (3629 kg) of freight in the cabin

Armament (fixed): none

Armament (disposable): none

Electronics and operational equipment: communication and navigation equipment

Powerplant and fuel system: two 1,198-shp (893-kW) Pratt & Whitney Canada PT6A-45R) turboprops, and a total internal fuel capacity of 560 Imp gal (2546 litres); no provision for drop tanks or inflight refuelling

Performance: maximum speed 231 mph (372 km/h); cruising speed 219 mph (352 km/h) at 10,000 ft (3050 m); initial climb rate 1,180 ft (360 m) per minute; service ceiling 20,000 ft (6095 m); range 865 miles (1392 km) with a 5,135-lb (2329-kg) payload

Weights: empty 14,210 lb (6446 kg); maximum take-off 24,600 lb (11,159 kg)

Dimensions: span 74 ft 8 in (22·76 m; length 58 ft 0·5 in (17·69 m); height 16 ft 3 in (4·95 m); wing area 453·0 sq ft (43·1 m²)

Variants

Shorts 330-UTT: this is the Utility Tactical Transport version of the successful Shorts 330 feederliner, which first flew in August 1974 after development as the SD3-30; the UTT is essentially a stripped-out Model 330-200 with a strengthened floor and two inward-opening doors for the use of paratroops; six standard Model 330 aircraft are used by the US Army for range-support duties

C-23A Sherpa: logistic support version of the Model 330-UTT with the standard port-side forward freight door supplemented by a full-width hydraulically operated rear ramp/door to allow the straight in/out loading/unloading of bulky items such as packaged aero engines; the first C-23A flew in August 1984, and its rectangular-section cargo hold (fitted with a roller conveyor system in the reinforced floor) can accommodate two half-ton light vehicles, or seven C08 or four LD3 cargo containers, or passengers

Below: A C-23A Sherpa of the US Army.

Below right: A Tucano T.Mk 1 of the RAF.

Shorts Tucano T.Mk 1

(Brazil & UK)

Type: basic flying and weapon trainer

Accommodation: pupil and instructor in tandem on Martin-Baker Mk 8LCP lightweight ejector seats

Armament (fixed): none

Armament (disposable): this is carried on four hardpoints (two under each wing) up to a maximum weight of 1,000 lb (454 kg); typical weapons are 0·5-in (12·7-mm) machine-guns pods each with 350 rounds, 250-lb (113-kg) bombs, and launchers for seven 2·75-in (70-mm) rockets

Electronics and operational equipment: communication and navigation equipment

Powerplant and fuel system: one 1,100-shp (820-kW) Garrett TPE331-12B turboprop, and a total internal fuel capacity of 159 Imp gal (724 litres) plus provision for two 73-Imp gal (330-litre) ferry tanks; no provision for inflight refuelling

Performance: maximum speed 315 mph (507 km/h) at 10,000 ft (3050 m); initial climb rate 3,510 ft (1070 m) per minute; service ceiling 34,000 ft (10,365 m); radius 495 miles (797 km) with maximum warload; range 1,035 miles (1665 km)

Weights: empty 4,447 lb (2017 kg); normal take-off 5,952 lb (2700 kg); maximum take-off 7,220 lb (3275 kg)

Dimensions: span 37 ft 0 in (11·28 m); length 9·86 m (32 ft 4·25 in); height 3·40 m (11 ft 2 in); wing area 19·40 m² (208·82 sq ft)

Variant

Tucano T.Mk 1: to meet British requirements, Shorts has developed this S.312 version of the EMBRAER EMB-312 Tucano; the type required considerable modification from the Brazilian baseline version, and the first British-built aeroplane flew in December 1986 with a Garrett TPE331 turboprop for enhanced performance; other modifications include a ventral airbrake, a revised cockpit layout and a large number of structural revisions for a longer airframe life; developments of the British version have been ordered by Kenya and Kuwait, these aircraft having an ML Aviation stores-management system and four underwing hardpoints for the carriage of weapons such a light bombs, rocket pods, gun pods and, on the inner pair, drop tanks

SIAI-Marchetti S.211

SIAI-Marchetti SF.260TP

(Italy)

Type: flying and weapon trainer with a secondary light attack capability

Accommodation: pupil and instructor in tandem on Martin-Baker Mk 10 zero/zero ejector seats

Armament (fixed): none

Armament (disposable): this is carried on four hardpoints (two under each wing, with the inner two units each rated at 330 kg/727·5 lb and the outer two units each at 165 kg/364 lb) up to a maximum weight of 660 kg (1,455 lb); typical loads include four pods each containing one or two 7·62-mm (0·3-in) machine-guns, four pods each containing one 0·5-in (12·7-mm) Browning M2HB machine-gun, pods containing 18 50-mm (1·98-in), six or 18 68-mm (2·68-in), seven 2·75-in (70-mm), or six or 12 81-mm (3·2-in) rockets, bombs up to 150 kg (330 lb) in weight, cartridge dispensers and other stores

Electronics and operational equipment: communication and navigation equipment, plus provision for optional items such as radar, HUD, RWR, Doppler navigation, ECM, a reconnaissance pod with four cameras and an IR linescanner, and two underwing photographic reconnaissance pods

Powerplant and fuel system: one 2,500-lb (1134-kg) thrust Pratt & Whitney Canada JT15D-4D non-afterburning turbofan, and a total internal fuel capacity of 800 litres (176 Imp gal) plus provision for two 270-litre (59-Imp gal) drop tanks; no provision for inflight refuelling

Performance: maximum cruising speed 667 km/h (414 mph) at 7620 m (25,000 ft); initial climb rate 1280 m (4,200 ft) per minute; service ceiling 12,200 m (40,025 ft); radius 555 km (345 miles) on a hi-lo-hi mission with four rocket pods; ferry range 2485 km (1,544 miles)

Weights: empty 1850 kg (4,078 lb); normal take-off 2750 kg (6,063 lb) as a trainer; maximum take-off 3150 kg (6,944 lb) as an attack aircraft

Dimensions: span 8·43 m (27 ft 4·75 in); length 9·31 m (30 ft 6·5 in); height 3·80 m (12 ft 5·5 in); wing area 12·60 m² (135·63 sq ft)

Variant

S.211: first flown in April 1981, the S.211 is a lightweight trainer with good secondary attack capability; the main operator of the type is Singapore, where the type is being assembled largely from knock-down kits supplied from Italy; Singapore Aircraft Industries is also co-operating with SIAI-Marchetti in the development of a single-seat dedicated light attack variant with a navigation computer and HUD, and it is believed that the two companies are pressing forward with the evolution of an S.211 variant with a longer fuselage

(Italy)

Type: flying and weapon trainer with a secondary tactical support capability

Accommodation: pupil and instructor side-by-side, and provision for one passenger in the cockpit rear

Armament (fixed): none

Armament (disposable): this is carried on four hardpoints (two under each wing each rated at 150 kg/331 lb) up to a maximum weight of 300 kg (661 lb) of light bombs, gun pods and rocket pods

Electronics and operational equipment: communication and navigation equipment, plus an optical sight and provision for a reconnaissance pod

Powerplant and fuel system: one 350-shp (261-kW) Allison 250-B17C turboprop, and a total internal fuel capacity of 243 litres (53·5 Imp gal) plus provision for two 80-litre (17·6-Imp gal) drop tanks; no provision for inflight refuelling

Performance: maximum speed 422 km/h (262 mph) at 3050 m (10,000 ft); cruising speed 400 km/h (248 mph) at 2440 m (8,000 ft); initial climb rate 661 m (2,170 ft) per minute; service ceiling 7500 m (24,605 ft); range 950 km (590 miles)

Weights: empty 750 kg (1,654 lb); normal take-off 1140 kg (2,513 lb) as a trainer; maximum take-off 1300 kg (2,886 lb) as an attack aeroplane

Dimensions: span 8·35 m (27 ft 4·75 in) over tip-tanks; length 7·40 m (24 ft 3·25 in); height 2·41 m (7 ft 11 in); wing area 10·10 m² (108·7 sq ft)

Variants

SF.260M: first flown in October 1970 as the military trainer derived from the F.250 prototype of 1964, the SF.260M has proved successful as a primary and basic trainer in Italian and third-world service

SF.260W Warrior: armed weapons trainer and tactical support derivative of the SF.260M; the type is powered by a 260-hp (194-kW) Avco Lycoming O-540-E4A5 piston engine, and first flew in May 1972; the Warrior is similar in all basic ways to the SF.260TP apart from the engine installation, which results in a length of 7·10 m (23 ft 3·5 in); the type has a maximum take-off weight of 1300 kg (2,866 lb) and a maximum speed of 305 km/h (190 mph) at sea level

SF.260TP: turboprop-powered derivative of the SF.260W and first flew in July 1980, deliveries beginning in 1982; SF.260M and SF.260W aircraft can be upgraded to this standard with a company-developed conversion kit

Below: An S.211 trainer in flight.

Bottom: An SF.260TP under evaluation.

Sikorsky S-58A (CH-34A Choctaw)

(USA)
Type: general-purpose medium helicopter
Accommodation: flightcrew of two, and 18 passengers, or eight litters or freight in the cabin
Armament (fixed): none
Armament (disposable): none
Electronics and operational equipment: communication and navigation equipment
Powerplant and fuel system: one 1,525-hp (1137-kW) Wright R-1820-84 Cyclone piston engine, and a total internal fuel capacity of 306 US gal (1159 litres); no provision for drop tanks or inflight refuelling
Performance: maximum speed 122 mph (196 km/h) at sea level; cruising speed 97 mph (156 km/h); initial climb rate 1,100 ft (335 m) per minute; service ceiling 9,500 ft (2895 m); range

182 miles (293 km) with maximum payload or 247 miles (400 km) with maximum fuel
Weights: empty 7,750 lb (3515 kg); normal take-off 13,000 lb (5900 kg); maximum take-off 14,000 lb (6350 kg)
Dimensions: main rotor diameter 56 ft 0 in (17·07 m); length, fuselage 46 ft 9 in (14·25 m); height 15 ft 11 in (4·85 m); main rotor disc area 2,463·0 sq ft (228·8 m²)

Variants

S-58A: basic designation of a civil and military general-purpose helicopter that first flew in prototype form during March 1954 as a far more capable machine than the preceding S-55 series thanks to the use of a considerably more powerful engine and a rethought fuselage with larger

cabin; the type was produced for the American services as the US Army's CH-34 Choctaw, the US Marine Corps' UH-34 Seahorse and US Navy's SH-34 Seabat, and the type was also widely exported; most survivors conform generally to the standard described above
S-58T: under this designation many S-58s have been revised with a turboshaft powerplant, namely the 1,875-shp (1398-kW) Pratt & Whitney Canada PT6TB Turbo Twin Pac with consequent improvements in reliability and payload, the latter deriving from the turboshaft's considerably lighter weight

Below: The Westland Wessex is a British turbine-powered version of the S-58 series.

Sikorsky S-61B (SH-3D Sea King)

(USA)

Type: anti-submarine helicopter

Accommodation: flightcrew of two, and a mission crew of two in the cabin

Armament (fixed): none

Armament (disposable): this is carried on two hardpoints (one on each sponson strut) up to a maximum weight of 840+ lb (381+ kg) of depth bombs or two Mk 46 torpedoes

Electronics and operational equipment: communication and navigation equipment, plus Bendix ASQ-13 dunking sonar and APN-130 Doppler navigation

Powerplant and fuel system: two 1,400-shp (1044-kW) General Electric T58-GE-10 turboshafts, and a total internal fuel capacity of 840 US gal (3180 litres); no provision for drop tanks or inflight refuelling

Performance: maximum speed 166 mph (267 km/h) at optimum altitude; cruising speed 136 mph (219 km/h); initial climb rate 2,200 ft (667 m) per minute; service ceiling 14,700 ft (3200 m); range 625 miles (1005 km/h)

Weights: empty 11,685 lb (5382 kg); normal take-off 18,626 lb (8449 kg); maximum take-off 20,500 lb (9300 kg)

Dimensions: main rotor diameter 62 ft 0 in (18·90 m); length overall, rotors turning 72 ft 8 in (22·15 m) and fuselage 54 ft 9 in (16·69 m); height 15 ft 6 in (4·72 m) to rotor head; main rotor disc area 3,019·0 sq ft (280·5 m²)

Variants

SH-3A Sea King: the S-61 was designed in the later 1950s to a US Navy requirement for an ASW helicopter combining, for the first time in such a machine, the hunter and the killer roles previously requiring two helicopters; Sikorsky's design featured a boat hull with outrigger sponsons for emergency waterborne stability and to provide accommodation for the retracted main landing gear units, far greater payload and reliability being ensured by the use of a powerful twin-turboshaft powerplant; the prototype of the **S-61B** naval helicopter first flew in March 1959,

and the HSS-2 Sea King (from 1962 the SH-3A Sea King) began to enter service in September 1961 with 1,250-shp (932-kW) General Electric T58-GE-8B turboshafts, ASQ-13 dunking sonar and up to 840 lb (381 kg) of weapons; subvariants of the SH-3A are the **HH-3A** VIP transport and the **CH-124** for Canada

SH-3D Sea King: improved ASW version with more powerful engines; the warload figure quoted above is the officially quoted figure, but as the type has the ability to carry an 8,000-lb (3629-kg) slung load the warload can clearly be considerably higher than the quoted figure; the type is also built under licence in Italy as the Agusta (Sikorsky) ASH-3D; the only current variant of the basic model is the **VH-3D** VIP transport

HH-3E Jolly Green Giant: US Air Force combat SAR variant evolved during the Vietnam War for the recovery of aircrew downed in combat areas or behind enemy lines; the variant was developed from the CH-3C and CH-3E transport helicopters (now both out of service) produced as the **S-61R** variant with retractable tricycle landing gear, a completely revised fuselage and a rear ramp for the straight-in loading of freight; the HH-3E was produced with two 1,500-shp (1119-kW) T58-GE-5 turboshafts, armour, an armament of two 7·62-mm (0·3-in) Miniguns, external fuel for greater range, an inflight-refuelling probe and specialist rescue equipment

HH-3F Pelican: US Coast Guard SAR version of the HH-3E without armour or armament, but with advanced search radar

SH-3G Sea King: SH-3As converted into utility helicopter with removable ASW equipment

SH-3H Sea King: multi-role version of the SH-3G with upgraded ASW equipment (including Bendix ASQ-13B dunking sonar, active/passive sonobuoys and Texas Instruments ASQ-81(V)2 MAD with a towed 'bird') plus specialist equipment (including Canadian Marconi LN-66 high-performance radar and General Intruments ALQ-166(V)1 RWR) for the fleet missile defence role, primarily the detection and localization of incoming anti-ship missiles

S-61A: amphibious transport version able to carry 26 troops, or 15 litters, or 12 VIPs, or a comparatively substantial freight load

S-61A-4 Nuri: version of the S-61 for Malaysia with additional fuel and able to carry 31 passengers

S-61D-4: SH-3D equivalent for Argentina

Agusta (Sikorsky) ASH-3D: Italian licence-built version of the Sikorsky SH-3D Sea King anti-submarine helicopter, differing only slightly from the original in items such as airframe strengthening, a revised tailplane and an uprated powerplant; the ASH-3D also has modified armament and avionics, the former including up to four 515-lb (234-kg) Mk 46 torpedoes or two large anti-ship missiles, and the latter including SMA APS 707 surveillance radar with a chin-mounted antenna

Agusta (Sikorsky) ASH-3H: licence-built version of the SH-3H Sea King with role optimization for anti-submarine and anti-ship warfare; the type can also carry a freight load of 2720 kg (5,996 lb) carried internally or 3630 kg (8,003 lb) carried externally as a slung load; other tasks undertaken by the ASH-3H are anti-ship missile defence, EW and tactical trooping; the type is powered by a pair of 1,500-shp (1119-kW) General Electric T58-GE-100 turboshafts with 3180 litres (699 Imp gal) of fuel excluding ferry fuel carried in an optional auxiliary tank, its maximum take-off weight is 9525 kg (20,999 lb), and its performance data include a maximum cruising speed of 222 km/h (138 mph), an initial climb rate of 670 m (2,200 ft) per minute, a service ceiling of 3720 m (12,200 ft), and a range of 1166 km (725 miles) declining to 582 km (362 miles) in the alternative transport role with 31 troops; there is also an **AS-61R** SAR version of this helicopter basically equivalent to the American HH-3F Pelican

Mitsubishi (Sikorsky) HSS-2: Japanese licence-built version of SH-3A

Mitsubishi (Sikorsky) HSS-2A: Japanese licence-built version of the SH-3D

Mitsubishi (Sikorsky) HSS-2B: Japanese licence-built version of the SH-3H

Sikorsky S-65 (CH-53D Sea Stallion)

(USA)

Type: assault and transport heavy helicopter

Accommodation: flightcrew of three, and 55 troops, or 24 litters plus four attendants, or freight carried in the hold or slung externally

Armament (fixed): none

Armament (disposable): none

Electronics and operational equipment: communication and navigation equipment

Powerplant and fuel system: two 3,925-shp (2927-kW) General Electric T64-GE-413 turboshafts, and a total internal fuel capacity of 630 US gal (2384 litres); no provision for drop tanks or inflight refuelling

Performance: maximum speed 196 mph (315 km/h) at sea level; cruising speed 173 mph (278 km/h); initial climb rate 2,180 ft (664 m) per minute; service ceiling 21,000 ft (6400 m); range 257 miles (413 km)

Weights: empty 23,485 lb (10,653 kg); maximum take-off 36,400 lb (16,510 kg)

Dimensions: main rotor diameter 72 ft 3 in (22·02 m); length overall, rotors turning 88 ft 3 in (26·90 m) and fuselage excluding probe 67 ft 2 in (20·47 m); height 17 ft 1·5 in (5·22 m) to rotor head; main rotor disc area 4,070·0 sq ft (378·1 m²)

Variants

CH-53A Sea Stallion: developed as the **S-65** under a US Navy requirement for an assault transport helicopter for the US Marine Corps, the Sea Stallion first flew in prototype form during October 1964, and deliveries to the US Marine Corps began in 1966; the type is powered by two 2,850-shp (2125-kW) General Electric T64-GE-6 turboshafts, and the load can include one 105-mm (4·13-in) howitzer and ammunition, or 38 troops; all but 32 were built with provision to tow a minesweeping sled

RH-53A: 15 CH-53As converted into dedicated minesweepers for the US Navy with 3,925-shp (2927-kW) T64-GE-413 turboshafts

HH-53B Super Jolly: US Air Force combat SAR variant, fitted out with the same provisions as the HH-3E Jolly Green Giant (including a retractable inflight-refuelling probe and all-weather flight instrumentation) and powered by two 3,080-shp (2297-kW) T64-GE-3 turboshafts

HH-53C Super Jolly: upgraded version of the HH-53B for the US Air Force, fitted with 3,925-shp (2927-kW) T64-GE-7 turboshafts for greater performance and payload; the type has Texas Instruments APQ-158 terrain-following and terrain-avoidance radar

CH-53D Sea Stallion: improved version of the CH-53A for the US Marine Corps with greater power for higher performance and increased payload (55 troops) over short ranges; most of the type have provision to tow a minesweeping sled

RH-53D: first flown in October 1972, this is a dedicated minesweeping version of the CH-53D for the US Navy; the type is powered by two 4,380-shp (3266-kW) T64-GE-415 turboshafts, has a 500-US gal (1893-litre) fuel tank in each sponson, and can tow the Mk 103 mechanical, Mk 104 acoustic, Mk 105 magnetic and Mk 106 magnetic/acoustic sweeps as well as the SPU-1 Magnetic Orange Pipe for dealing with shallow-water magnetic mines; two 0·5-in (12·7-mm) machine-guns are carried for the detonation of any mines brought to the surface, and the type can carry AQS-14 minehunting sonar

CH-53E Super Stallion: radical development of the basic type, developed as the **S-80E** series and first flown in prototype form during March 1974 for service in 1981; the type has a seven- rather than six-blade main rotor with a diameter of 79 ft 0 in (24·08 m) and driven by three rather than two engines, in this instance 4,380-shp (3266-kW) T64-GE-416 turboshafts; this much improved dynamic system allows an increase in maximum take-off weight to 73,500 lb (33,339 kg) with a freight load of 36,000 lb (16,329 kg) slung externally, or alternatively of 55 fully-equipped troops or 30,000 lb (13,608 kg) of freight in a fuselage lengthened to 73 ft 4 in (22·35 m); the variant has an empty weight of 33,228 lb (15,072 kg), and is to be fitted with the Helicopter Night Vision System kit once development has been completed, providing the CH-53E with full capability at night or in adverse weather conditions

MH-53E Sea Dragon: US Navy mine-countermea- sures version of the CH-53E with 1,000-US gal (3785-litre) greater fuel capacity in larger sponsons, and provision for inflight-refuelling; the type was developed as the **S-80M**, and is available for export as the **S-80M-1**; further improvements are planned for the series, including composite-structure rotor blades and main rotor hub, night vision equipment, IR suppressors for uprated engines, and other operational improvements; the variant has empty and maximum take-off weights of 36,336 and 73,500 lb (16,482 and 33,339 kg)

CH-53G: version of the Sea Stallion series for West Germany with T64-GE-7 turboshafts

MH-53H Super Jolly: improved version of the HH-53C for nocturnal SAR and special forces insertion/extraction capability with an AAQ-10 IR sensor, APQ-158 terrain-following radar, and much improved navigational capability including an INS working in concert with a colour moving-map display; the maximum take-off weight is 42,000 lb (19,051 kg)

MH-53J 'Pave Low III Enhanced': HH-53H helicopters adapted and improved for use by the US Special Forces in clandestine and anti-insurgency missions; the type has a maximum take-off weight of 50,000 lb (22,680 kg) to allow the addition of 1,000 lb (454 kg) of titanium armour around vital points, the improvement of the terrain-avoidance/terrain-following radar and IR countermeasures, the installation of a missile-warning receiver, the retrofit of the original naval folding tail, and addition of a Texas Instruments AAQ-10 FLIR in a stabilized turret under the inflight-refuelling probe, precision navigation equipment, secure voice communications and a satellite communication system; the type has provision for two 650-US gal (2461-litre) drop tanks, and an armament of three 7·62-mm (0·3-in) Miniguns or three 0·5-in (12·7-mm) machine-guns

Opposite: An SH-3 with the 'bird' of its ASQ-81(V) MAD tucked into the starboard float.

Below: An HH-53C Super Jolly combat SAR helicopter of the 67th ARRS.

Sikorsky S-70 (UH-60A Black Hawk)

(USA)

Type: light combat assault helicopter

Accommodation: flightcrew of two or three, and between 11 and 14 troops, or four litters, or 8,000 lb (3629 kg) of freight carried in the cabin or as a slung load

Armament (fixed): optional installation of one or two 7·62-mm (0·3-in) M60 flexible machine-guns in the cabin doors

Armament (disposable): from the 431st helicopter the type is fitted for (but not necessarily with) the External Stores Support System whose stub wings are fitted with four hardpoints able to lift 5,000 + lb (2268 + kg) of disposable stores including gun pods, rocket launchers, M56 mine dispensers, or up to 16 AGM-114 Hellfire anti-tank missiles

Electronics and operational equipment: communication and navigation equipment, plus Singer-Kearfott ASN-128 Doppler navigation, E-Systems/Loral APR-39(V)1 RWR, M130 chaff dispenser and Sanders ALQ-144 IR countermeasures

Powerplant and fuel system: two 1,560-shp (1151-kW) General Electric T700-GE-700 turboshafts transmission-limited to a combined maximum of 2,828 shp (2109 kW), and a total internal fuel capacity 360 US gal (1361 litres) plus provision for two 230-US gal (871-litre) and two 450-US gal (1703-litre) external tanks; no provision for inflight refuelling

Performance: maximum speed 184 mph (296 km/h) at sea level; cruising speed 167 mph (269 km/h); initial climb rate 450 ft (137 m) per minute; service ceiling 19,000 ft (5790 m); hovering ceiling in ground effect at a temperature of +35 > C (+95 > F) 9,500 ft (2895 m) and out of ground effect 10,400 ft (3170 m); range 373 miles (600 km) on internal fuel; ferry range 1,380 miles (2220 km/h)

Weights: empty 11,284 lb (5118 kg); normal take-off 16,994 lb (7708 kg); maximum take-off 22,000 lb (9979 kg)

Dimensions: main rotor diameter 53 ft 8 in (16·36 m); length overall, rotors turning 64 ft 10 in (19·76 m) and fuselage 50 ft 0·75 in (15·26 m); height 12 ft 4 in (3·76 m) to rotor head; main rotor disc area 2,261·0 sq ft (210·05 m²)

Variants

UH-60A Black Hawk: designed as the **S-70** to meet a Utility Tactical Transport Aircraft System requirement by the US Army for a Bell UH-1 replacement able to carry an 11-man infantry squad, the Black Hawk first flew in October 1974 and beat a Boeing Vertol competitor for selection as the production model in late 1976; the type began to enter service in 1979, and is a versatile helicopter able to carry a slung load of 8,000 lb (3631 kg); there have been in-service problems with the transmission, but a new gearbox has been developed to improve reliability and increase maximum take-off weight to 26,450 lb (11,997 kg), which allows the carriage of a greater assortment of external loads as well as improved armament; the UH-60A is also qualified for the carriage of AGM-114 Hellfire anti-tank missiles (four on each of the ESSS's four hardpoints, plus another 16 in the cabin as reloads) and the Honeywell Volcano mine-dispensing system

HH-60A Night Hawk: US Air Force combat SAR variant of the UH-60A with the dynamic system and rescue winch of the SH-60B; the avionics of this important type include advanced radar, FLIR, Litton INS, and multi-function cockpit and helmet

displays; other equipment includes stub wings for two 230-US gal (871-litre) external tanks, a retractable inflight-refuelling probe, two side-mounted machine-guns and other items; the type was cancelled in 1989, placing emphasis on interim versions such as the **UH-60A Credible Hawk** with 117 US gal (443 litres) more fuel and inflight-refuelling capability but without terrain-following radar or FLIR, and the **MH-60G Pave Hawk** development of the Credible Hawk retrofitted with the 'Pave Low III' system's FLIR, Doppler radar, Litton INS and various self-protection systems integrated via a MIL 1553B digital databus

VH-60A Seahawk: VIP transport version of the UH-60A procured by the US Marine Corps; the airframe is that of the UH-60A, but the powerplant and some of the avionics are those of the SH-60B and the rotor is fitted with the brake of the HH-60A; other modifications are additional fuel, hardening against electro-magnetic pulse, secure communications, and countermeasures such as exhaust suppression, IR jamming and an optional chaff/flare dispenser

SH-60B Seahawk: maritime **S-70L** version produced to meet the US Navy's requirement for a Light Airborne Multi-Purpose System Mk III to replace the Sikorsky SH-3 Sea King series on destroyers and larger frigates as complement to the lighter Kaman SH-2F Seasprite LAMPS Mk I

helicopter carried by smaller surface vessels; first flown in December 1979 for service in 1983, the SH-60B has a folding main rotor, a relocated twin-wheel rear landing gear unit and a deck-recovery system, is powered by two 1,690-shp (1261-kW) T700-GE-401 turboshafts or, from 1988, two 1,900-shp (1417-kW) T700-GE-401C turboshafts, and has empty and maximum take-off weights of 13,648 and 21,884 lb (6191 and 9926 kg), the latter with an armament of two Mk 46 (to be replaced by Mk 50 Barracuda) anti-submarine torpedoes and an electronics fit comprising Texas Instruments APS-124 search radar in a chin radome, Texas Instruments ASQ-81(V)2 MAD on a starboard-side pylon, Raytheon ALQ-142 ESM equipment (with four antennae, two in two lateral chin fairings and the other two in lateral fairings just forward of the tail boom), an ARQ-44 data-link system for real-time control from the parent ship and for mid-course updating of RGM-84 Harpoon anti-ship missiles, and a port-side 25-round pneumatic launcher for 125 sonobuoys used with an advanced acoustic data-processing system; the Seahawk can also carry two AGM-119 Penguin Mk 2 (Mod) IR-homing anti-ship missiles

EH-60C Black Hawk: EW version of the UH-60A designed for the jamming of battlefield communications with the 1,800-lb (817-kg) ALQ-151 'Quick Fix IIB' package, a development of the system

originally fitted on the Bell EH-1H and comprising an intercept receiver and a jammer; the 66 helicopters were originally designated EH-60A, and the type also possesses an ASN-32 INS and the Aircraft Survivability Equipment defensive suite comprising an APR-39(V)2 RWR and two M130 chaff/flare dispensers

SH-60F Ocean Hawk: SH-60B version designed as the inner-zone anti-submarine helicopter carried by aircraft-carriers, and fitted with Bendix ASQ-13F dunking sonar for this important task in association with an armament of Mk 50 Barracuda advanced anti-submarine torpedoes; the type is planned for service in 1988, and also possesses a MIL 1553B digital databus (to make possible the integration of yet more advanced weapons and electronics) and a Teledyne ASN-123 tactical navigation system

HH-60H Rescue Hawk: under development in the late 1980s for service from 1989, this is the US Navy's helicopter combat support (combat SAR) variant of the SH-60F Seahawk with T700-GE-401C turboshafts, and can also be configured for the support of special warfare forces; the type has a crew of four and a combat radius of 290 miles (467 km)

HH-60J Rescue Hawk: under development in the late 1980s for service from 1990, this is the US Coast Guard's medium-range recovery helicopter, a counterpart to the HH-60J and also derived from the SH-60F; the type has a crew of four and has a radius of at least 345 miles (555 km), with a loiter capability of 45 minutes at extreme range where at least six persons can be recovered from the surface

MH-60K Black Hawk: under this designation Sikorsky is developing for the US Army a special-operations version for the insertion and extraction of special forces' teams under adverse terrain and climatic conditions; based on the UH-60M, this is to have inflight-refuelling capability whose retracted probe increases overall length to 57 ft 0·25 in (17·38 m), provision for external fuel in an installation increasing overall width to 17 ft 11 in (5·46 m) and boosting endurance from the UH-60A's 2 hours 18 minutes to 4 hours 51 minutes, weapons capability, survivability features, a four-screen 'glass cockpit' and an advanced avionics package; this latter is a Boeing responsibility and based on that for the Boeing Vertol MH-47E with features such as night vision equipment, Hughes AAQ-16 FLIR, Texas Instruments APQ-168 terrain-following, and secure communications gear

UH-60L Black Hawk: delivered from October 1989, this is the standard production model based on the UH-60A but fitted with 1,900-shp (1417-kW) T700-GE-701C turboshafts to restore the performance lost in the UH-60A by addition of 2,000 lb (907 kg) more payload

UH-60M Black Hawk: due to enter service in 1992, this is the second-generation land-based version with T700-GE-701C turboshafts, the fuselage stretched by 12 in (30·5 cm), new Sikorsky/Boeing composite-structure main rotor blades and revised section to provide 11% more lift, digital avionics based on a MIL 1553B databus, an integrated navigation/communications system, a new automatic flight-control system, and a 15% increase in fuel capacity for a 10% increase in range

S-70A: export version of the UH-60A

S-70B: export version of the SH-60; the **S-70B-2** is operated by the Royal Australian Navy for its RAWS (Role-Adaptable Weapon System) requirement with MEL Super Searcher radar and an integrated suite of Collins avionics, and Spain is procuring a version

S-70C: utility version available in civil and military forms, and optimized for hot-and-high operations

Mitsubishi (Sikorsky) SH-60J Seahawk: licence-built Japanese version of the SH-60B basically similar to the US helicopter but featuring items of specifically Japanese nature such as a ring-laser gyro and equipment compatible with Japanese destroyers

An SH-60B Seahawk LAMPS Mk III on patrol.

Sikorsky S-76B (H-76 Eagle)

(USA)

Type: multi-role utility light helicopter

Accommodation: flightcrew of two, and between 12 and 16 troops, or four litters plus attendants, or 5,100 lb (2313 kg) of freight carried internally or 3,300 lb (1497 kg) of freight carried as a slung load

Armament (fixed): optional installation of one or two 7·62-mm (0·3-in) flexible machine-guns in the cabin doors

Armament (disposable): this is carried on four hardpoints (two under each of the stub wings of the optional Multi-Purpose Pylon System or Pitch-Compensated Armament Pylon) up to an unrevealed maximum weight

Electronics and operational equipment: communication and navigation equipment, IR suppression equipment, plus options such as the Hughes Aircraft Mast-Mounted Sight, M65 TOW stabilized roof-mounted sight, FLIR, or Saab-Scania reticle sight

Powerplant and fuel system: two 980-shp (731-kW) Pratt & Whitney Canada PT6B-36 turboshafts, and a total internal fuel capacity 262 US gal (993 litres) plus provision for 110 US gal (416 litres) of auxiliary fuel; no provision for drop tanks or inflight refuelling

Performance: maximum cruising speed 167 mph (269 km/h) at optimum altitude; initial climb rate 1,500 ft (457 m) per minute; service ceiling 13,900 ft (4235 m); hovering ceiling in ground effect 8,700 ft (2650 m) and out of ground effect 5,900 ft (1800 m); range 335 miles (539 km) on internal fuel

Weights: empty 5,610 lb (2545 kg); normal take-off 10,300 lb (4672 kg); maximum take-off 11,400 lb (5171 kg)

Dimensions: main rotor diameter 44 ft 0 in (13·41 m); length overall, rotors turning 52 ft 6 in (16·00 m) and fuselage 43 ft 4·5 in (13·22 m); height 14 ft 9·7 in (4·52 m); main rotor disc area 1,520·53 sq ft (141·26 m²)

Variants

H-76B Eagle: military variant of the S-76 that first flew in March 1977 as a civil utility helicopter; the rotors are essentially scaled-down versions of those of the S-70 series with the same type of advanced aerodynamics and structure; the type can be fitted with a wide diversity of armament fits, the PCAP system being an integrated type offering reduced crew workload while adding to weapon-delivery accuracy, especially when used with the Integrated Armament Management System that allows control from the collective-pitch lever via a switch that activates the PCAP and the pilot's HUD; over a period of some 10 years some 270 H-76 helicopters are being produced in South Korea as a joint venture by Daewoo Sikorsky Aerospace

H-76N Eagle: maritime version with specialized naval equipment plus provision for Ferranti Seaspray 3 or MEL Super Searcher radar used with Sea Skua lightweight anti-ship missiles; other sensors and weapons can be fitted

The S-76 was developed as a civil helicopter in the utility role, but has been marketed aggressively in its H-76B military version, which can accept a wide assortment of armament options as an alternative load to freight or troops carried in the cabin.

SOKO G-4 Super Galeb

(Yugoslavia)
Type: basic and advanced flying and weapon trainer with a secondary attack capability
Accommodation: pupil and instructor in tandem on Martin-Baker J8 (zero/104-mph/167-km/h) or J10 (zero/zero) ejector seats
Armament (fixed): one 23-mm GSh-23L two-barrel cannon with 200 rounds in a 750-kg (1,653-lb) removable ventral pack
Armament (disposable): this is carried on four hardpoints (two under each wing, with the inner two units each rated at 500 kg/1,102 lb and the outer two units each at 350 kg/772 lb) up to a maximum weight of 1950 kg (4,299 lb) including the centreline cannon pack; the disposable load can include bombs, cluster bombs, anti-personnel/anti-tank bomblet dispensers, napalm tanks and rocket launchers
Electronics and operational equipment: communication and navigation equipment, plus a Ferranti D282 gyro sight
Powerplant and fuel system: one 4,000-lb (1814-kg) thrust Rolls-Royce Viper Mk 632 non-afterburning turbojet, and an internal fuel capacity of 1720 litres (378 Imp gal) plus provision for two 312·5-litre (68·7-Imp gal) drop tanks; no provision for inflight refuelling
Performance: maximum speed 910 km/h (565 mph) at 6000 m (19,685 ft); initial climb rate 2330 m (7,645 ft) per minute; absolute ceiling 15,000 m (49,215 ft); radius 300 km (186 miles) on a lo-lo-lo mission with ventral gun pod and 32 55-mm (2·17-in) rockets; ferry range 2630 km (1,635 miles)
Weights: empty 3250 kg (7,165 lb); normal take-off 4760 kg (10,494 lb) on a training mission; maximum take-off 6330 kg (13,955 lb) on an attack mission
Dimensions: span 9·88 m (32 ft 5 in); length 11·86 m (38 ft 11 in); height 4·28 m (14 ft 0·5 in); wing area 19·50 m² (209·9 sq ft)

Variant

G-4 Super Galeb: first flown in July 1978, the Super Galeb bears no more relationship to the G-2 Galeb than an identity of role, being an altogether more advanced aircraft with marked similarities to the BAe Hawk; the prototypes and pre-production aircraft had a conventional, flat tailplane with elevators but the production variant that began to enter service in 1983 has a slab tailplane of distinct anhedral; the type offers a capable light attack facility to the standard training role; a reconnaissance pod (fitted with cameras and an IR linescanner) is under development to give the type a useful tactical reconnaissance capability

SOKO J-1 Jastreb

(Yugoslavia)
Type: light attack aeroplane
Accommodation: pilot on an HSA (Folland) Type 1-B ejector seat
Armament (fixed): three 0·5-in (12·7-mm) Colt-Browning M3 machine-guns with 135 rounds per gun
Armament (disposable): this is carried on eight hardpoints (four under each wing, with the inner four units each rated at 250 kg/551 lb and the outer four units each at 50 kg/110 lb) up to a maximum weight of 800 kg (1,764 lb); the inner hardpoints can lift two 250-kg (551-lb) bombs, or two clusters of smaller bombs, or two 150-litre (33-Imp gal) napalm tanks, or two pods each with 12 55-mm (2·17-in) rockets, and the outer six hardpoints can carry six 5-in (127-mm) rockets
Electronics and operational equipment: communication and navigation equipment, plus an optical sight
Powerplant and fuel system: one 3,000-lb (1361-kg) thrust Rolls-Royce Viper Mk 531 non-afterburning turbojet, and a total internal fuel capacity of 975 litres (214 Imp gal) plus provision for two 275-litre (60·5-Imp gal) drop tanks; no provision for inflight refuelling
Performance: maximum speed 820 km/h (510 mph) at 6000 m (19,685 ft); cruising speed 740 km/h (450 mph) at 5000 m (16,405 ft); initial climb rate 1260 m (4,135 ft) per minute; service ceiling 12,000 m (39,370 ft); range 1520 km (945 miles) with maximum fuel
Weights: empty 2820 kg (6,217 lb); maximum take-off 5100 kg (11,243 lb)
Dimensions: span 11·68 m (38 ft 4 in) over tiptanks; length 10·88 m (35 ft 8·5 in); height 3·64 m (11 ft 11·5 in); wing area 19·43 m² (209·14 sq ft)

Variants

G-2A Galeb: this was SOKO's first design, the programme being launched in 1957 to provide the Yugoslav air force with a capable yet simple turbojet-powered trainer; the Galeb first flew in May 1961 and immediately impressed Western analysts with its similarity to the Aermacchi M.B.326 series; production started in 1963 and the type entered service with the Yugoslav air force powered by the 2,500-lb (1134-kg) thrust Viper Mk 22-6 non-afterburning turbojet; the pupil and instructor are seated in tandem but unstepped Folland Type 1-B lightweight ejector seats, and the Galeb has a maximum speed of 812 km/h (505 mph) at 6200 m (20,350 ft)
G-2AE Galeb: export model delivered from 1974 to Libya and Zambia with a number of detail modifications and improvements, especially in the navigation system
J-1 Jastreb: single-seat light attack derivative of the G-2, with a strengthened airframe and uprated powerplant for higher performance and greater payload
J-1-E Jastreb: export version of the J-1 with updated equipment and other improvements
RJ-1 Jastreb: tactical reconnaissance version of the J-1 with cameras in the forward fuselage and in the forward portion of the tiptanks
RJ-1-E Jastreb: export version of the RJ-1 with various combinations of Vinten cameras and flash equipment for day and night photo-reconnaissance
TJ-1 Jastreb: operational conversion trainer version of the J-1

Below: The SOKO G-4 Super Galeb trainer. Bottom: The Yugoslav Jastreb ground attack version of the Galeb.

SOKO J-22B Orao 2/CNIAR (Centrul Nacional al Industriei Aeronautice Romane) IAR-93B

(Yugoslavia & Romania)

Type: close air support, ground-attack and tactical reconnaissance aeroplane

Accommodation: pilot on a Martin-Baker U10J zero/zero ejector seat

Armament (fixed): two 23-mm GSh-23L twin-barrel cannon with 200 rounds per gun in the undersides of the inlets

Armament (disposable): this is carried on five hardpoints (one under the fuselage and two under each wing, with the centreline unit rated at 800 kg/1,763 lb and each of the underwing units at 500 kg/1,102 lb) up to a maximum weight of 2800 kg (6,173 lb); typical loads are five 500-, 250- or 100-kg (1,102-, 551- or 220-lb), or 12 100-kg (220-lb) bombs, or eight 250-kg (551-lb) fragmentation bombs, or clusters of smaller fragmentation or incendiary bombs; other stores that can be carried are 150-litre (33-Imp gal) napalm tanks, and launchers for 127- and 55-mm (5- and 2·17-in) rockets

Electronics and operational equipment: communication and navigation equipment, plus a Thomson-CSF VE-120T HUD, Iskra SO-1 RWR and provision for a reconnaissance pod

Powerplant and fuel system: two 5,000-lb (2268-kg) afterburning thrust ORAO/Turbo-mécanica-built Rolls-Royce Viper Mk 633-41 turbojets, and a total internal fuel capacity of 3100 litres (682 Imp gal) plus provision for three 540-litre (119-Imp gal) drop tanks; no provision for inflight refuelling

Performance: maximum speed 1160 km/h (721 mph) or Mach 0·95 at sea level; cruising speed 730 km/h (453 mph) at 7000 m (22,965 ft); initial climb rate 4200 m (13,780 ft) per minute; service ceiling 13,500 m (44,290 ft); radius 450 km (280 miles) on a lo-lo-hi mission with six 250-kg (551-lb) bombs and two rocket launchers

Weights: empty 5750 kg (12,676 lb); normal take-off 8400 kg (18,519 lb); maximum take-off 11,250 kg (24,802 lb)

Dimensions: span 9·62 m (31 ft 6·75 in); length including probe 14·90 m (48 ft 10·6 in); height 4·45 m (14 ft 7·25 in); wing area 26·00 m² (279·86 sq ft)

Variants

J-22A Orao 1/IAR-93A: a simple yet effective light attack and tactical reconnaissance aircraft well suited to the operational requirements and capabilities of the two sponsor nations, this type was designed from 1970 under the Yugoslav designation/name J-22A Orao 1 and the Romanian designation IAR-93A; two prototypes were flown on 31 October 1974 (one in each country), and the type entered service in the late 1970s with 4,000-lb (1814-kg) thrust Viper Mk 632-41R non-afterburning turbojets and a fuel capacity of 2950 litres (649 Imp gal) in wing bag tanks; the type has provision for a disposable load of only 1500 kg (3,307 lb) on five hardpoints rated at 500 kg (1,102 lb) each for the centreline and two inner underwing units and 300 kg (662 lb) each for the two outer underwing units; the model has empty and maximum take-off weights of 6150 and 10,326 kg (13,558 and 22,765 lb) respectively, and its performance figures include a maximum speed of 1070 km/h (665 mph) at sea level, an initial climb rate of 2040 m (6,693 ft) per minute, and a service ceiling of 10,500 m (34,450 ft) there is also a two-seat operational conversion trainer version of this initial model with a length of 14·44 m (47 ft 4·5 in) and fuel capacity reduced to 2700 litres (594 Imp gal); most Orao 1/IAR-93A aircraft are being refitted to Orao 2/IAR-93B standard

IAR-93B: upgraded Romanian version retaining the armament and fuel capacity of the IAR-93A but fitted with Viper Mk 633-41 afterburning turbojets for performance comparable with that of the Orao 2; the variant has empty and maximum take-off weights of 5700 and 11,200 kg (12,566 and 24,692 lb) respectively

J-22B Orao 2: upgraded Yugoslav version with greater armament capability, Viper Mk 633-41 afterburning turbojets and integral fuel tankage, as well as a HUD and provision for an optical or IR reconnaissance pod carried on the centreline hardpoint; this variant has also been developed as a two-seater for operational conversion

Below: A single-seat SOKO J-22B Orao 2 of the Yugoslav air force.

Sukhoi Su-7BMK 'Fitter-A'

(USSR)
Type: close air support and ground-attack aeroplane

Accommodation: pilot on a KM-1 zero/zero ejector seat

Armament (fixed): two 30-mm NR-30 cannon with 70 rounds per gun

Armament (disposable): this is carried on six hardpoints (two under the fuselage each rated at 500 kg/1,102 lb, and two under each wing with the inner two units each rated at 500 kg/1,102 lb and the outer two units each at 250 kg/551 lb) up to a nominal maximum weight of 2500 kg (5,511 lb) limited in practice to 1000 kg (2,205 lb) by the tactical necessity of carrying 600-litre (132-Imp gal) drop tanks on the underfuselage hardpoints; free-fall nuclear weapons can be carried, but more typical loads are two 500- or 250-kg (1,102- or 551-lb) bombs of various types, or two or four pods each with 16 or 32 55-mm (2·17-in) rockets, or two UPK-23 pods each containing one 23-mm GSh-23L twin-barrel cannon

Electronics and operational equipment: communication and navigation equipment, plus SRD-5M 'High Fix' ranging radar, ASP-5F gyro sight, 'Odd Rods' IFF, OR-69 Sirena 3 RWR, chaff dispenser and provision for ECM pods

Powerplant and fuel system: one 10,000-kg (22,046-lb) afterburning thrust Lyul'ka AL-7F-1 turbojet, and a total internal fuel capacity of 2940 litres (647 Imp gal) plus provision for two 600-litre (132-Imp gal) and two 900- or 1800-litre (198- or 396-Imp gal) drop tanks; no provision for inflight refuelling

Performance: maximum speed 1700 km/h (1,055 mph) or Mach 1·6 at 11,000 m (36,090 ft) and 1350 km/h (840 mph) or Mach 1·1 at sea level; initial climb rate about 9120 m (29,920 ft) per minute; service ceiling 15,150 m (49,700 ft); radius 345 km (215 miles) on a hi-lo-hi mission with weapons and two drop tanks; ferry range 1450 km (901 miles)

Weights: empty 8620 kg (19,004 lb); normal take-off 12,000 kg (26,455 lb); maximum take-off 13,500 kg (29,762 lb)

Dimensions: span 8·93 m (29 ft 3·5 in); length 17·37 m (57 ft 0 in) including probe; height 4·57 m (15 ft 0 in); wing area 31·50 m² (339·1 sq ft)

Variants

Su-7B 'Fitter-A': the Su-7 was designed in the early 1950s as the Soviet counter to the North American F-100 Super Sabre and McDonnell F-101 Voodoo, and first flew in 1955 after development through a number of prototype aircraft; the type was ordered into production in 1958 and entered service in 1959 as the Su-7B tactical fighter with the 9000-kg (19,841-lb) afterburning thrust Lyul'ka AL-7F turbojet, a powerful but very thirsty engine that requires the use of drop tanks on at least two of the four hardpoints (two under the fuselage and one under each wing) to secure even the minimum acceptable combat radius

Su-7BKL 'Fitter-A': version optimized for operation from poor airfields and featuring redesigned landing gear with low-pressure tyres (requiring bulged doors over the nose unit) and a steel skid outboard of each main wheel, as well as twin braking parachutes, and more efficient brakes

Su-7BM 'Fitter-A': uprated Su-7B with the 10,000-kg (22,046-lb) afterburning thrust AL-7F-1 turbojet and detail modifications such as a relocated pitot boom, twin ducts above the central fuselage, a Sirena 3 RWR, a KM-1 zero/zero ejector seat, improved air data sensors to provide input for a fire-control system based on a ballistic computer, and higher-velocity cannon

Su-7BMK 'Fitter-A': version combining features of the Su-7BKL and Su-7BM, and possessing improved avionics and an additional pair of hardpoints behind the main landing gear units

Su-7U 'Moujik': two-seat operational conversion trainer variant of the Su-7B

Su-7UM 'Moujik': two-seat operational conversion trainer variant of the Su-7BM

Su-7UMK 'Moujik': two-seat operational conversion trainer variant of the Su-7BMK

The Su-7 'Fitter-A' is a notably rugged ground-attack platform able to deliver its weapon load with great accuracy.

Sukhoi Su-17M 'Fitter-C'

(USSR)
Type: variable-geometry ground-attack aeroplane

Accommodation: pilot on a KM-1 zero/zero ejector seat

Armament (fixed): two 30-mm NR-30 cannon with 70 rounds per gun

Armament (disposable): this is carried on eight hardpoints (two tandem pairs under the fuselage and four under the wings, with each underfuselage unit rated at 500 kg/1,102 lb, the inner two underwing units each at 500 kg/1,102 lb and the outer two underwing units each at 750 kg/1,653 lb) up to a maximum weight of 4000 kg (8,818 lb); various types of tactical nuclear weapons can be carried, but more common loads are two or four AS-7 'Kerry' ASMs, or six 500-kg (1,102-lb) and two 250-kg (551-lb) bombs, or eight 240-mm (9·45-in) anti-runway rockets, or eight pods each with 16 or 32 55-mm (2·17-in) rockets

Electronics and operational equipment: communication and navigation equipment, plus SRD-5M 'High Fix' ranging radar, terrain-avoidance radar, HUD, 'Odd Rods' IFF, OR-69 Sirena 3 RWR and Doppler navigation

Powerplant and fuel system: one 11,200-kg (24,690-lb) afterburning thrust Lyul'ka AL-21F-3 turbojet, and a total internal fuel capacity of 4550 litres (1,000 Imp gal) plus provision for four 800-litre (176-Imp gal) drop tanks; no provision for inflight refuelling

Performance: maximum speed 2220 km/h (1,379 mph) or Mach 2·09 at 11,000 m (36,090 ft) and 1285 km/h (798 mph) or Mach 1·05 at sea level; initial climb rate 14,950 m (49,050 ft) per minute; service ceiling 18,000 m (59,055 ft); radius 685 km (426 miles) on a hi-lo-hi mission with 2000-kg (4,409-lb) warload or 445 km (277 miles) on a lo-lo-lo mission with 2000-kg (4,409-lb) warload

Weights: empty 10,000 kg (22,046 lb); normal take-off 14,000 kg (30,864 lb); maximum take-off 17,700 kg (39,021 lb)

Dimensions: span 13·80 m (45 ft 3 in) spread and 10·00 m (32 ft 10 in) swept; length including probes 18·75 m (61 ft 6·25 in); height 5·00 m (16 ft 5 in); wing area 40·00 m² (430·0 sq ft) spread and 37·00 m² (398·0 sq ft) swept

Variants

Su-17 'Fitter-C': first flown in 1966 as the Su-7IG 'Fitter-B' prototype derived from the fixed-wing Su-7, the Su-17 is a radical development of the 'Fitter' family with variable-geometry outer wing panels to provide improved field performance and better range with a useful weapon load; the solution offered a significant bettering of capabilities without the cost and potential technical problems of a new design with variable geometry applied to the entire wing planform, but the 'Fitter-C' with manual wing-sweep control entered service only in modest numbers with the 10,000-kg (22,046-lb) afterburning thrust Lyul'ka AL-21F-1 turbojet and additional fuel; other features that differentiate this and later variants from the 'Fitter-A' are an extra fence on each wing, a long dorsal fairing between the cockpit and the fin, larger pylons, revised braking parachute accommodation, and the addition of an RWR

Su-17M and Su-20 'Fitter-C': definitive early version of the variable-geometry 'Fitter' series derived from the Su-17 but fitted with the 11,200-kg (24,691-lb) afterburning thrust AL-21F-3 turbojet and improved avionics; the type is used by the USSR (Su-17MK) and by Warsaw Pact countries and favoured export customers (Su-20) with reduced avionics standards

Su-17MK 'Fitter-D': important derivative of the 'Fitter-C' with the nose drooped slightly and lengthened by 0·25 m (9·85 in); this variant features a small blister radome under the inlet for terrain-avoidance radar (or possibly for Doppler navigation), an LRMTS in the inlet centrebody, a HUD, an RWR, an internal chaff/flare dispenser and (most significantly) the ability to deliver tactical nuclear weapons

Su-17UM 'Fitter-E': tandem two-seat operational conversion trainer variant, based on the Su-17MK but with a lengthened and drooped nose for improved visibility and a widened dorsal fairing for additional fuel; the type has only the starboard wing-root cannon and no undernose electronics blister

Su-22 'Fitter-F': export derivative of the Su-20MK for third-world clients, and distinguishable by its larger dorsal fin, enlarged dorsal spine and modified undernose electronics blister; the type is powered by the 11,500-kg (25,353-kg) afterburning thrust Tumanskii R-29BS-300 turbojet, but has generally inferior avionics in comparison with Soviet and Warsaw Pact variants

Su-17UM 'Fitter-G': two-seat operational conversion trainer based on the 'Fitter-E' but distinguishable by its taller tail, small ventral fin, an enlarged dorsal spine and the provision of a laser ranger and marked-target seeker in the inlet centrebody

Su-17BM 'Fitter-H': Lyul'ka-powered single-seater based on the 'Fitter-D' but incorporating the refinements of the 'Fitter-E' (including the down-tilted forward fuselage), updated avionics including Doppler navigation in a deepened nose, an additional hardpoint under the inner portion of each wing for the carriage of two ASMs, and a deeper dorsal fairing aft of the cockpit presumably for enlarged fuel capacity

Su-22BKL 'Fitter-J': third-world export version of the Su-17BM with the rear fuselage and powerplant of the 'Fitter-F', a total internal fuel capacity of 6270 litres (1,379 Imp gal) but less advanced avionics and weapons (the AAM fit being limited to AA-2 'Atoll' and AA-2-2 'Advanced Atoll' weapons); the type is also distinguishable by a small ventral fin and its more angular dorsal fin; there is also a two-seat operational conversion trainer development of the 'Fitter-J', but as yet no designation or NATO reporting name has been revealed

Su-17 'Fitter-K': latest Lyul'ka-powered version based on the 'Fitter-H' and intended for service with the USSR and Warsaw Pact, with additional avionics and ECM to permit effective operation in areas of intense air and ground defences; this variant is based on the 'Fitter-H' but distinguishable by the enlargement of the cooling air inlet at the base of the fin

Below: The Su-20 'Fitter-C' is the downgraded export version of the Su-17M.

Bottom: Sukhoi's formidable Su-21 'Flagon-F'.

Sukhoi Su-21 'Flagon-F'

(USSR)

Type: all-weather interceptor fighter

Accommodation: pilot on a KM-1 zero/zero ejector seat

Armament (fixed): none

Armament (disposable): this is carried on six hardpoints (two under the fuselage each rated at 500 kg/1,102 lb, and two under each wing each rated at 350 kg/772 lb) to a maximum weight of 1500 kg (3,307 lb); typical weapons are the AA-2 'Atoll', AA-2-2 'Advanced Atoll', AA-3 'Anab', AA-3-2 'Advanced Anab' and AA-8 'Aphid' AAMs, and two pods each with a 23-mm GSh-23L twin-barrel cannon

Electronics and operational equipment: communication and navigation equipment, plus 'Improved Skip Spin' or 'Twin Scan' fire-control radar, visual search system, 'Odd Rods' IFF, OR-69 Sirena 3 RWR and several ECM systems

Powerplant and fuel system: two 11,200-kg (24,691-lb) afterburning thrust Lyul'ka AL-21F-3 turbojets, and a total internal fuel capacity of about 8000 litres (1,760 Imp gal) plus provision for two 800- or 600-litre (176- or 132-Imp gal) drop tanks; no provision for inflight refuelling

Performance: maximum speed 2655 km/h (1,650 mph) or Mach 2·5 at 11,000 m (36,090 ft); initial climb rate 13,700 m (44,950 ft) per minute; service ceiling 20,000 m (65,615 ft); radius 725 km (450 miles) on a hi-hi-hi mission; ferry range 2250 km (1,398 miles)

Weights: empty 12,250 kg (27,006 lb); normal take-off 18,000 kg (39,683 lb); maximum take-off 20,000 kg (44,092 lb)

Dimensions: span 10·50 m (34 ft 5·4 in); length 22·00 m (72 ft 2·1 in); height 5·00 m (16 ft 5 in); wing area 35·70 m² (384·3 sq ft)

Variants

Su-15U 'Flagon-C': this is the combat-capable operational conversion trainer variant of the 'Flagon' family derived from the 'Flagon-D' initial-production single-seater but fitted with two separate cockpits, though these are on the same level and require that the instructor be provided with a periscope for forward vision; the Su-15 series was derived from the Su-11 after a 1962 requirement for genuine Mach 2·5 interceptors, with two afterburning turbojets drawing air through lateral inlets (instead of one afterburning turbojet with a single nose inlet), nose-mounted radar and updated avionics; the prototype probably flew in 1964, and the pre-production 'Flagon-A' of the late 1960s had Su-11 wings spanning 9·30 m (30 ft 6·1 in) and a powerplant of two 10,000-kg (22,046-lb) afterburning thrust Lyul'ka AL-21F-1 turbojets

Su-15F or Su-15MF 'Flagon-D': first true production model, based on the 'Flagon-A' but having greater-span wings with compound sweep and deeper inlets, probably signifying the adoption of AL-21F-3 afterburning turbojets

Su-21 'Flagon-E': improved model introduced in 1973 with AL-21F-3 turbojets, twin nosewheels and 'Twin Scan' air-interception radar

Su-21 'Flagon-F': definitive single-seat model introduced from 1975 with a low-drag ogival rather than conical radome for a larger radar providing limited look-down/shoot-down capability; as with earlier models of the series, the facts about this highly effective fighter are uncertain

Su-21U 'Flagon-G': two-seat operational conversion trainer based on the 'Flagon-F' with a periscope-fitted rear cockpit behind the standard cockpit

Sukhoi Su-24 'Fencer-C'

(USSR)

Type: variable-geometry all-weather strike and attack aeroplane

Accommodation: pilot and systems operator side-by-side on KM-1 zero/zero ejector seats

Armament (fixed): one 30-mm rotary-barrel cannon with an unrevealed number of rounds (starboard underfuselage fairing) and possibly one 30-mm single-barrel cannon with an unrevealed number of rounds (port underfuselage fairing)

Armament (disposable): this is carried on eight hardpoints (four under the fuselage as one tandem pair and two flanking units, one under each wing glove and one under each wing, with each unit rated at 1500 kg/3,307 lb except the underwing hardpoints which are each rated at 1000 kg/2,205 lb) up to a maximum weight of 11,000 kg (24,250 lb); the type can carry tactical nuclear weapons, but more common weapons are AA-2 'Atoll', AA-7 'Apex' and AA-8 'Aphid' AAMs, AS-7 'Kerry', AS-9 'Kyle', AS-10 'Karen', AS-11 'Kilter', AS-12 'Kegler' and AS-14 'Kedge' ASMs, and 1000-, 750- and 500-kg (2,205-, 1,653- and 1,102-lb) bombs of various types

Electronics and operational equipment: communication and navigation equipment, plus pulse-Doppler multi-mode radar, twin terrain-following radars, HUD, HDDs, RWR, IR warning receivers, INS, Doppler navigation, LRMTS, and a variety of ECM and target acquisition/designation systems

Powerplant and fuel system: two 11,200-kg (24,691-lb) afterburning thrust Lyul'ka AL-21F-3 turbojets, and a total internal fuel capacity of about 13,000 litres (2,860 Imp gal) plus provision for two 3000-litre (660-Imp gal) drop tanks; provision for inflight refuelling

Performance: maximum speed 2320 km/h (1,441 mph) or Mach 2·18 at 11,000 m (36,090 ft) and 1470 km/h (913 mph) or Mach 1·2 at sea level; initial climb rate not revealed; service ceiling 16,500 m (54,135 ft); radius 320 km (199 miles) on a lo-lo-lo mission with 8000-kg (17,637-lb) warload and 1300 km (805 miles) on a hi-lo-hi mission with 3000-kg (6,614-lb) warload and two drop tanks; ferry range 6450 km (4,008 miles)

Weights: empty 19,000 kg (41,887 lb); normal take-off 29,000 kg (63,933 lb); maximum take-off 41,000 kg (90,388 lb)

Dimensions: span 17·50 m (57 ft 5 in) spread and 10·50 m (34 ft 5·5 in) swept; length excluding probe 21·29 m (69 ft 10 in); height 6·00 m (19 ft 8 in); wing area 47·0 m² (505·9 sq ft) spread and 42·5 m² (457·5 sq ft) swept

Variants

Su-24 'Fencer-A': the Su-24 was the USSR's first true variable-geometry combat aircraft, initially flying in prototype form during the late 1960s and entering service during 1974 as the 'Fencer-A' initial production model with two 10,000-kg (22,046-lb) afterburning thrust Lyul'ka AL-21F-1 turbojets with their jetpipes enclosed in a rear-fuselage box fairing; since that time the aircraft has displayed range and weapon capabilities that make it likely that its wartime role would be unrefuelled interdiction raids launched from Eastern European bases against targets of operational importance in Western Europe; the type has the latest in Soviet avionics, allowing blind first-pass attacks in all weathers by day and night

Su-24 'Fencer-B': revised version of the 'Fencer-A' with a bullet fairing at the base of the fin for a larger braking parachute, possibly indicating higher operational weights, and a dished bottom to the box enclosing the jetpipes

Su-24 'Fencer-C': 1981 variant based on the 'Fencer-B' but has an RWR with antennae on the fin and on the inlet lips, a revised air-data probe, an underfuselage aerial (possibly for mid-course missile-update purposes) and modified tailpipes, the last suggesting that the variant is possibly powered by two uprated AL-21F-3 turbojets

Su-24MK 'Fencer-D': 1983 variant similar to the 'Fencer-C' but with a retractable inflight-refuelling probe, a broader-chord lower portion to the fin, the nose section forward of the cockpit lengthened by 0·75 m (29·5 in) possibly indicating a new radar type, glove pylons integral with the large overwing fences, and an undernose blister window/fairing

Su-24 'Fencer-E': EW variant designed to supplant the Yak-28 'Brewer-E' in the escort and stand-off roles

Su-24 'Fencer-F': reconnaissance variant with internal SLAR, IR linescanner and cameras

The Su-24 'Fencer' series provides the USSR with its best operational-level interdictor for nuclear strike and conventional attack.

Sukhoi Su-25K 'Frogfoot-C'

(USSR)

Type: close air support aeroplane

Accommodation: pilot on an ejector seat

Armament (fixed): one 30-mm twin-barrel cannon with 250 rounds in port side of lower nose

Armament (disposable): this is carried on 10 hardpoints (five under each wing with each unit rated at 500 kg/1,102 lb) up to a maximum weight of 4500 lb (9,921 lb) of bombs, rocket launchers, AAMs, ASMs, ECM pods, and UPK-23 cannon pods each containing one 23-mm GSh-23L cannon and 260 rounds

Electronics and operation equipment: communication and navigation equipment, plus an LRMTS, optical sight, ECM system, IR countermeasures system, OR-69 Sirena 3 RWR, 'Odd Rods' IFF, and other items

Powerplant and fuel system: two 4500-kg (9,921-lb) thrust Tumanskii R-195 non-afterburning turbojets, and a total internal fuel weight of about 5000 kg (11,023 lb) plus provision for at least two drop tanks; no provision for inflight refuelling

Performance: maximum speed 850 km/h (528 mph) at optimum altitude; initial climb rate not revealed; service ceiling 7000 m (22,965 ft); radius 550 km (342 miles) with a 4000-kg (8,818-lb) warload

Weights: empty 9500 kg (20,944 lb); normal take-off 14,600 kg (32,187 lb); maximum take-off 17,600 kg (38,801 lb)

Dimensions: span 14·36 m (47 ft 1·4 in); length 15·55 m (51 ft 0·2 in); height not revealed; wing area 37·60 m² (404·74 sq ft)

Variant

Su-25 'Frogfoot-A': following the path pioneered by the US Air Force with its AX programme that led to the adoption of the Fairchild Republic A-10A Thunderbolt II battlefield attack and close-support aircraft, the USSR moved more slowly during the definition and design phases during the early and mid-1970s, the resulting Su-25 being comparable in many respects to the A-10A but slightly smaller, lighter, considerably higher powered and possessing markedly better performance; the type was developed with great care after the first flight of the prototype in February 1975 on the power of two Tumanskii RD-9 turbojets, the out-of-production engine type of the Mikoyan-Gurevich MiG-19 being replaced by a non-afterburning version of the MiG-21's Tumanskii R-13; pre-production types seen in Afghanistan from 1982 had a 23-mm GSh-23L twin-barrel cannon installation (with 260 rounds) and a less refined avionics/weapon fit; the 'Frogfoot' accommodates its pilot in a 'bath' of titanium and armoured glass, whilst the engines are each located in a stainless steel protective box and the fuel tanks/lines are cased in protective foam

Su-25K 'Frogfoot-B': introduced from 1984, this is the full-production development of the pre-production 'Frogfoot-A' with a better cannon installation, more capable flight and mission elec-tronics, and probably two AAMs on the outermost pair of underwing hardpoints for self defence; the type has rough-field capability with rugged landing gear and an autonomous-operating kit (deployed in four pods carried under the wings and containing toolkits, a test kit, spares, covers, fuel lines, a pump for self-refuelling, a generator and APU)

Su-25UBK 'Frogfoot-C': two-seat operational conversion trainer derivative of the 'Frogfoot-B' with a longer forward fuselage with a second cockpit inserted behind the original enclosure and its vertical tail heightened by 0·40 m (1 ft 3·75 in); the variant is also used for the training of naval pilots in deck operations, and in this form is fitted with an arrester hook

Su-28 'Frogfoot-D': introduced in 1986, and initially designated **Su-25UT**, this is a flying trainer powered by two 4100-kg (9,039-kg) thrust R-95Sh non-afterburning turbojets and lacking the nose cannon, armoured cockpit and (normally) the underwing hardpoints of the operational models; it is thought that the type is to replace older basic and advanced flying trainers in Soviet service, most notably the Mikoyan-Gurevich MiG-17UTI and the Aero L-29

With straight wings and multiple hardpoints, the Su-25 can carry a substantial warload of conventional weapons including bombs, rocket pods and a variety of 'smart' weapons.

Sukhoi Su-27 'Flanker-B'

(USSR)

Type: air-superiority fighter with a secondary attack capability

Accommodation: pilot on a KM-1 zero/zero ejector seat

Armament (fixed): one 30-mm six-barrel rotary cannon with an unrevealed number of rounds in a starboard wing root installation

Armament (disposable): this is carried on 10 hardpoints (one tandem pair under the fuselage, one under each inlet duct, two under each wing and one at each wingtip) up to a maximum weight of about 6000 kg (13,228 lb) of missiles and free-fall ordnance; a typical load can include 10 AAMs in the form of six AA-10 'Alamo' weapons (four radar-homers under the fuselage and inlet ducts plus two IR-homers on the inner pair of under-wing hardpoints), and four AA-8 'Aphid' or AA-11 'Archer' IR-homing short-range weapons on the outer pair of underwing hardpoints and on the wingtip missile rails; in the secondary attack role the Su-27 can carry 12 500-kg (1,102-lb) bombs

Electronics and operational equipment: communication and navigation equipment, plus 'Flash Dance' pulse-Doppler nose radar (with a search range of 240 km/149 miles and a tracking range of 185 km/115 miles), HUD, HDDs, IR search and tracking system, helmet-mounted sight system, digital data-link system, ECM systems, OR-69 Sirena 3 RWR and other items

Powerplant and fuel system: two 13,600-kg (29,982-lb) afterburning thrust Lyul'ka AL-31F turbofans, and a total internal fuel weight of about 7000 kg (15,432 lb) plus provision for drop tanks; no provision for inflight refuelling

Performance: maximum speed 2495 km/h (1,550 mph) or Mach 2·35 at high altitude and 1350 km/h (839 mph) or Mach 1·1 at sea level; initial climb rate 18,300 m (60,040 ft) per minute; service ceiling 15,000 + m (49,215 + ft); radius 1500 km (932 miles) with four AAMs; ferry range 4000 + km (2,486 + miles)

Weights: empty 17,700 kg (39,021 lb); normal take-off 22,000 kg (45,801 lb); maximum take-off 30,000 kg (66,138 lb)

Dimensions: span 14·70 m (48 ft 2·75 in); length excluding probe 21·90 m (71 ft 10·2 in); height 5·50 m (18 ft 0·5 in); wing area 46·5 m² (500·5 sq ft)

Variant

Su-27 'Flanker-A': developed during the 1970s as a direct counterpart to the US Air Force's McDonnell Douglas F-15 Eagle air-superiority fighter, the Su-27 is a high-performance type with a fly-by-wire control system, and almost certainly the USSR's first genuine look-down/shoot-down fighter with its pulse-Doppler radar and an offensive complement of 10 AAMs including six AA-10 weapons of two major variants; the type began to enter service in 1985 in its initial 'Flanker-A' form, though current thinking now suggests that these early aircraft were of the pre-production type with the vertical tails located centrally above the engine installations and with rounded wingtips lacking the missile launch rails of the 'Flanker-B'

Su-27 'Flanker-B': full-production version of the 'Flanker' with squared-off wingtips carrying missile launch rails, plus a number of aerodynamic refinements such as vertical tail surfaces located farther outboard and leading-edge flaps; this type began to enter service early in 1986, and the fly-by-wire control system automatically limits manoeuvres to a maximum 30° angle of attack and the load factor to 9 g, the leading- and trailing-edge flaps being scheduled automatically to maximize lift and minimize drag during combat manoeuvres

Su-27UB 'Flanker-C': tandem two-seat variant first revealed in 1989 with a normal take-off weight of 22,500 kg (49,603 lb); this model has 'Improved Flash Dance' radar in a slightly longer nose, and for this reason is probably as much a combat type as an operational conversion trainer, with the rear-seat officer seated 0·7 m (27·6 in) higher than the pilot and tasked with management of the aeroplane's electronic and weapon systems, which are in all probability more advanced than those of the basic 'Flanker-B'; a possible role is that of the McDonnell Douglas F-15E, namely long-range interdiction under all weather conditions; an alternative and more likely role could be interception under ECM conditions with the rear-seater managing the more advanced electronic systems of this variant to allow the pilot to concentrate on closing high-value targets that would then be engaged with a mix of AA-9 'Amos' long-range missiles (used against types such as the Boeing E-3 Sentry) and AA-8 'Aphid' and/or 'AA-11 'Archer' short-range missiles for close-range engagements; the installation of the second crew member's position has resulted in a reduction of internal fuel capacity, and hence a reduction in range to just over 3000 km (1,864 miles)

Transall (Transporter Allianz)

(France & West Germany)

Type: medium-range tactical transport aeroplane

Accommodation: flightcrew of three, and 93 troops, or 88 paratroops, or 62 litters plus four attendants, or 16,000 kg (35,273 lb) of freight in the hold

Armament (fixed): none

Armament (disposable): none

Electronics and operational equipment: communication and navigation equipment

Powerplant and fuel system: two 6,100-shp (4549-kW) Rolls-Royce Tyne RTy·20 Mk 22 turboprops, and a total internal fuel capacity of 28,050 litres (6170 Imp gal) plus provision for 9000 litres (1,980 Imp gal) of auxiliary fuel in a centre-section tank; no provision for drop tanks but provision for inflight refuelling

Performance: maximum speed 513 km/h (319 mph) at 5000 m (16,405 ft); initial climb rate 396 m (1,300 ft) per minute; service ceiling 8230 m (27,000 ft); range 1853 km (1,150 miles) with maximum payload; ferry range 8858 km (5,504 miles)

Weights: empty 29,000 kg (63,935 lb); maximum take-off 51,000 kg (112,435 lb)

Dimensions: span 40·00 m (131 ft 3 in); length 32·40 m (106 ft 3·5 in); height 11·65 m (38 ft 2·75 in); wing area 160·00 m² (1,722·3 sq ft)

Variants

C.160: this Franco-German venture was conceived in the late 1950s as a twin-turboprop tactical transport to replace the Nord Noratlas and Douglas C-47; the design was of the standard transport configuration pioneered by the Lockheed C-130 (large-volume hold accessed by a rear ramp/door under an upswept tail, high wing with turboprop engines, and multi-wheel main

C.160   Tupolev Tu-16 'Badger-A'

landing gear retracting into fuselage blister fairings); the prototype first flew during March 1963, and from 1967 to 1972 production aircraft were built for France (**C.160F**), West Germany (**C.160D**), Turkey (**C.160T**) and South Africa (**C.160Z**); by the mid-1970s the French decided that additional aircraft would be useful and the production line was reopened for 25 more aircraft to an updated standard with new-generation avionics and (to meet the requirements of France's overseas commitments) additional tankage in the centre section plus an inflight-refuelling probe; the revised model first flew in 1981, deliveries beginning in the same year; 10 of the aircraft are outfitted an inflight-refuelling tankers with a hose-and-drogue unit in the starboard main landing gear blister, and another five can be so converted at short notice with the aid of kits; there exist plans for the development of other variants such as the C.160S maritime surveillance aircraft (with search radar and other role equipment), the C.160SE electronic surveillance and intelligence aircraft (Thomson-CSF Varan radar, FLIR, SLAR, and Elint and Sigint systems), and the C.160AAA AEW aeroplane (with the radar and electronics of the now-abandoned BAe Nimrod AEW.Mk 3 as well as ESM pods at the wingtips)

C.160 ASTARTE: four C.160s specially outfitted with a Collins package of hardened electronics to serve in the ASTARTE (Avion Station de Relais de Transmission Exceptionelle) airborne communication-relay role between the French nuclear deterrent forces and the national command authorities

C.160 GABRIEL: two C.160s specially outfitted with a Thomson-CSF Sigint suite for the operational/tactical surveillance role

Tupolev Tu-16 'Badger-A'

(USSR)

Type: medium bomber and maritime reconnaissance aeroplane

Accommodation: flightcrew of six

Armament (fixed): seven 23-mm NR-23 cannon (one fixed in the nose and six in two-gun tail turret and in ventral and dorsal barbettes)

Armament (disposable): this is carried in a lower-fuselage weapons bay up to a maximum of 9000 kg (19,841 lb) of free-fall ordnance

Electronics and operational equipment: communication and navigation equipment, plus bombing radar

Powerplant and fuel system: two 9500-kg (20,944-lb) thrust Mikulin AM-3M non-afterburning turbojets, and a total internal fuel capacity of about 44,900 litres (9,877 Imp gal) plus provision for an unrevealed quantity of auxiliary fuel in underwing tanks; no provision for drop tanks but provision for inflight refuelling

Performance: maximum speed 990 km/h (615 mph) or Mach 0·87 at 6000 m (19,685 ft); cruising speed 850 km/h (530 mph); initial climb rate 1250 m (4,100 ft) per minute; service ceiling 12,300 m (40,335 ft); radius 2900 km (1802 miles) with 3790-kg (8,355-lb) warload

Weights: empty 37,200 kg (82,010 lb); normal take-off 75,800 kg (167,708 lb); maximum take-off not revealed

Dimensions: span 32·93 m (108 ft 0·5 in); length 36·25 m (118 ft 11·25 in); height 14·00 m (45 ft 11·25 in); wing area 164·65 m² (1,772·3 sq ft)

Variants

Tu-16 'Badger-A': for its period a remarkable type that still serves in large numbers with great utility in a number of roles, the Tu-16 was designed in the late 1940s and first flew early in 1952 as the Tu-88 prototype; the type began to enter service in late 1953 or early 1954 as a strategic bomber with free-fall nuclear weapons; some of the surviving aircraft in Soviet service have been converted for other roles, the same designation being retained for two inflight-refuelling tanker derivatives (one with additional tanks in the erstwhile bomb bay and a hose trailed from the starboard wingtip to meet a receptacle on the port wingtip of the receiving aircraft, and the other with an underfuselage hose-and-drogue unit)`

Tu-16 'Badger-B': 'Badger-A' variant for the carriage, aerial launch and guidance of two AS-1 'Kennel' anti-ship missiles on underwing hardpoints; the type carried Komet III guidance radar in a retractable bin under the fuselage, and most aircraft have now been rebuilt to 'Badger-G' standard

Tu-16 'Badger-C': anti-shipping variant first seen in 1961 with one AS-2 'Kipper' missile carried semi-recessed under the fuselage; the nose is revised to eliminate the bombardier's position and nose gun in favour of 'Puff Ball' acquisition radar and A-39Z missile-guidance equipment; in recent years the type has been reworked to carry an alternative load of two AS-6 'Kingfish' missiles under the wings; overall length is 36·60 m (120 ft 1 in)

Opposite: The Su-27 'Flanker-B' has revised aerodynamics and wingtip missile rails.

Above left: A C.160D of the West German air force, which still operates 84 of the type.

Left: Tu-16 'Badger-As' demonstrate the type's unusual inflight-refuelling system.

Tu-16 'Badger-C (Modified)': 'Badger-C' subvariant designed to carry two AS-6 'Kingfish' anti-ship missiles on underwing pylons; AS-2 capability is retained by this variant

Tu-16 'Badger-D': maritime reconnaissance and Elint variant with a row of three ventral blisters for receiver antennae and a comprehensive suite of multi-sensor reconnaissance equipment; the type has the same nose as the 'Badger-C' but without the missile-guidance equipment; overall length is 36·60 m (120 ft 1 in)

Tu-16 'Badger-E': 'Badger-A' bombers rebuilt for multi-sensor (photographic and electronic) reconnaissance with a revised bomb bay to accommodate additional fuel and a pallet-mounted photographic reconnaissance system, and two Elint receivers under the rear fuselage

Tu-16 'Badger-F': 'Badger-E' subvariant with two Elint pods (probably broad-band receivers) mounted under the wings and no radomes under the central part of the fuselage

Tu-16 'Badger-G': advanced anti-ship missile variant of the 'Badger-A' with two AS-5 'Kelt' anti-ship or stand-off missiles under the wings; the nose is similar to that of the 'Badger-A' but reworked to accommodate 'Short Horn' navigation and bombing radar

Tu-16 'Badger-G (Modified)': subvariant of the 'Badger-G' designed to carry AS-6 'Kingfish' rather than AS-5 missiles; the variant has chin radar replaced by a large target-acquisition and missile-guidance radar in a ventral installation

Tu-16 'Badger-H': dedicated EW variant based on the 'Badger-A' but intended for the escort or stand-off role with the bomb bay revised to accommodate broad-band receiver/analysis and jammer equipment; the type also dispenses up to 9000 kg (19,841 lb) of chaff, flares and electronic decoys from a ventral tube and other ejectors; the type is distinguishable by two teardrop radomes (one forward and one aft of the payload bay), two blade antennae and a hatch aft of the payload bay

Tu-16 'Badger-J': dedicated EW variant comparable to the 'Badger-H' but with improved receiver/analysis and jammer capability (spot and barrage types, resulting in a large ventral canoe fairing) at the expense of dispensing capability

Tu-16 'Badger-K': long-range Elint variant with additional fuel and receiving antennae in two teardrop radomes (one in the weapons bay and the other just ahead of it) and four small strut-mounted pods on the underside of the fuselage just ahead of the rear radome

Tu-16 'Badger-L': apparently a variant based on the 'Badger-A' but fitted with a thimble radome on the nose and a new chin radar characterized by a rotary strip antenna in a flat dish radome

Xian Aircraft Company H-6: 'Badger-A' model produced in China for the strategic bomber role; the USSR began to transfer an assembly capability in 1958, but this move was halted in 1960 with the break-off of Sino-Soviet relations; in 1962 the Chinese began the laborious task of reverse-engineering the Tu-16, and deliveries of H-6s began in about 1968; the type is powered by two 9500-kg (20,944-lb) thrust Xian Wopen-8 turbojets, and has performance comparable with that of the 'Badger-A'; China is currently investigating the conversion of some aircraft as inflight-refuelling tankers

Xian Aircraft Company H-6D: maritime patrol/anti-ship variant equivalent to the 'Badger-C/G' with two underwing C-601 anti-ship missiles; the type is also known as the **H-6 IV**

Tupolev Tu-22 'Blinder-A'

(USSR)
Type: medium bomber and maritime reconnaissance aeroplane
Accommodation: flightcrew of three in tandem on ejector seats
Armament (fixed): one 23-mm NR-23 cannon in the tail barbette
Armament (disposable): this is carried in a lower-fuselage weapons bay up to a maximum weight of 10,000 kg (22,046 lb) of free-fall ordnance
Electronics and operational equipment: communication and navigation equipment, plus 'Short Horn' nav/attack radar, 'Fan Tail' gunlaying radar, OR-69 Sirena 3 RWR, 'Odd Rods' IFF and several ECM systems
Powerplant and fuel system: two 14,000-kg (30,864-lb) afterburning thrust Koliesov VD-7F turbojets, and a total internal fuel capacity of about 45,450 litres (10,000 Imp gal); no provision for drop tanks or inflight refuelling
Performance: maximum speed 1480 km/h (920 mph) or Mach 1·4 at 12,000 m (39,370 ft); initial climb rate not revealed; service ceiling 18,300 m (60,040 ft); radius 3100 km (1,926 miles)
Weights: empty 40,000 kg (88,183 lb); maximum take-off 83,900 kg (184,965 lb)
Dimensions: span 23·75 m (78 ft 10 in); length 40·53 m (132 ft 11·5 in); height 10·67 m (35 ft 0 in); wing area not revealed

Variants

Tu-22 'Blinder-A': this supersonic bomber and maritime patrol aircraft began development in 1955 as the Tu-105, the prototype first flying during 1959; the type was seen initially as replacement for the Tu-16 in the role of high-altitude penetration against increasingly sophisticated Western defences; entering service in 1961, the initial 'Blinder-A' variant is a reconnaissance bomber with cameras in the rear of the main landing gear fairings (protruding aft of the wing trailing edges and a 'trademark' of large Tupolev aircraft) and SLAR or IR linescan equipment between the nose radar and the crew compartment
Tu-22 'Blinder-B': basic missile-carrying variant with one AS-4 'Kitchen' weapon semi-recessed under the fuselage for use with the 'Down Beat' radar that replaces the 'Short Horn' type of the 'Blinder-A'; this variant also introduced an inflight-refuelling capability by means of a semi-retractable probe above the nose
Tu-22 'Blinder-C': dedicated maritime reconnaissance variant in which the weapons bay is occupied by a substantial reconnaissance package with six or seven cameras, SLAR, IR linescan equipment, Elint and ECM equipment
Tu-22 'Blinder-D': operational conversion trainer variant with a cockpit for the instructor added behind and above the standard cockpit; this model appeared in 1968, at about the time modifications to the inlet design indicated that a new engine type had been introduced; although not confirmed, it is believed that initial models were powered by Mikulin AM-3 afterburning turbojets, these giving way to Koliesov VD-7 or VD-7F engines later in the production run, which was comparatively short as the type was not deemed a great success because of its limited performance (especially in speed and range)

Right: The Tu-22 has the Tupolev 'trademark' of rear-projecting pods for the landing gear.

Tupolev Tu-26 'Backfire-B'

(USSR)
Type: variable-geometry strategic medium bomber and maritime reconnaissance aeroplane
Accommodation: flightcrew of four on ejector seats
Armament (fixed): two 23-mm GSh-23L twin-barrel cannon in a rear barbette
Armament (disposable): this is carried in a lower-fuselage weapons bay and on four hardpoints (one under each wing glove and one under each inlet duct for tandem triple ejector racks) up to a maximum weight of 12,000 kg (26,455 lb) of free-fall ordnance, or one semi-recessed AS-4 'Kitchen' ASM, or two AS-6 'Kingfish' ASMs
Electronics and operational equipment: communication and navigation equipment, plus 'Down Beat' nav/attack radar, 'Bee Hind' gunlaying radar, OR-69 Sirena 3 RWR, 'Odd Rods' IFF and a number of ECM systems
Powerplant and fuel system: two 20,000-kg (44,092-lb) afterburning thrust Kuznetsov NK-144 turbofans, and a total internal fuel capacity of about 60,000 litres (13,200 Imp gal); no provision for drop tanks but provision for inflight refuelling
Performance: maximum speed 2125 km/h (1,320 mph) or Mach 2·0 at 11,000 m (36,090 ft) and 1100 km/h (684 mph) or Mach 0·9 at sea level; initial climb rate not revealed; service ceiling 16,000 + m (52,495 + ft); radius 5500 km (3,420 miles) on a hi-lo-hi mission; ferry range 12,000 km (7,457 miles)
Weights: empty 54,000 kg (119,048 lb); normal take-off 122,000 kg (268,959 lb); maximum take-off 130,000 kg (286,596 lb)
Dimensions: span 34·30 m (112 ft 6·5 in) spread and 23·40 m (76 ft 9·25 in) swept; length including probe 42·00 m (137 ft 10 in); height 10·80 m (35 ft 5·25 in); wing area 170·00 m² (1,829·9 sq ft) spread

Variants

Tu-22M 'Backfire-A': this powerful bombing, missile-carrying and reconnaissance aeroplane was clearly derived from the Tu-22 in the same way as the Sukhoi Su-17 was developed from the Su-7, with pivoting outer wings for improved field performance and better range in the cruising regime without detriment to dash performance with the wings fully swept; in the case of the Tu-22M the revision was extended further, the engine installation being modified from two afterburning turbojets pod-mounted on each side of the vertical tail surfaces to two afterburning turbofans in a conventional lateral installation with variable-geometry inlets; the revised type fea-

Below: The Tu-26 'Backfire-B' is a highly capable strategic medium bomber.

Tupolev Tu-28P 'Fiddler-B'

tured a number of other differences, and the Tu-136 prototype first flew in 1969, allowing a small number of Tu-22M 'Backfire-A' aircraft to enter service by 1973; like the Tu-22, the type proved disappointing in range, largely because of the drag of the main landing gear pod fairings, and only a few pre-production aircraft (possibly Tu-22 conversions rather than new-build machines) were built

Tu-26 'Backfire-B': definitive version of the basic design, considerably revised and re-engineered for better performance and offensive capability; the only parts of the Tu-22M retained were the vertical tail, fuselage shell and inner wing structure, the rest of the aircraft being new and featuring main landing gear units retracting inwards into centre section bays rather than rearwards into trailing-edge pods

Tu-26 'Backfire-C': revised version introduced in 1983 with ramp inlets; this offers higher dash performance, and may mark the introduction of a new engine type; the Tu-26 is used by the strategic bonber force for offensive operations with free-fall weapons and cruise missiles, and by the naval air force for electronic reconnaissance and anti-shipping attack with ASMs; the type has only a single 23-mm GSh-23L twin-barrel cannon in a tail barbette of improved aerodynamic contours

(USSR)
Type: long-range interceptor
Accommodation: pilot and systems operator in tandem on ejector seats
Armament (fixed): none
Armament (disposable): this is carried on four hardpoints (two under each wing each rated at 500 kg/1,102 lb) up to a maximum weight of 2000 kg (4,409 lb) and comprises four AA-5 'Ash' AAMs
Electronics and operational equipment: communication and navigation equipment, plus 'Big Nose' fire-control radar, Doppler navigation and several ECM systems
Powerplant and fuel system: two 11,000-kg (24,250-lb) afterburning thrust Lyul'ka AL-21F-3 turbojets, and a total internal fuel capacity of 13000 kg (28,660 lb); no provision for drop tanks or inflight refuelling
Performance: maximum speed 1850 km/h (1,150 mph) or Mach 1·75 at 11,000 m (36,090 ft); initial climb rate 7500 m (24,605 ft) per minute; service ceiling 18,300 m (60,040 ft); radius 1250 km (777 miles); ferry range 3200 km (1,988 miles)
Weights: empty 24,500 kg (54,012 lb); normal take-off 40,000 kg (88,183 lb); maximum take-off 45,000 kg (99,206 lb)

Dimensions: span 18·00 m (59 ft 0·7 in); length 27·20 m (89 ft 2·9 in); height 7·00 m (22 ft 11·6 in); wing area 80·00 m² (861·1 sq ft)

Variant
Tu-28P 'Fiddler-B': this is the world's largest fighter, a truly enormous aeroplane for its role and designed for the unusual long-range patrol requirements of the USSR's great northern reaches, which lack any abundance of airfields; the type originated as the Tu-102 prototype for a planned series of multi-role fighter and reconnaissance aircraft that did not in the event enter production; the prototype flew in 1960 or 1961, and was followed by a small number of Tu-128 'Fiddler-A' pre-production aircraft which, like the Tu-102, had canted ventral fins; the type was then developed as the Tu-28P 'Fiddler-B' pure interceptor with high performance, considerable range and a powerful missile armament allied to the 100-km (62-mile) range 'Big Nose' search and target-illumination radar

Below: The Tu-28 'Fiddler' provides a useful air-defence capability in the vast northern and western regions of the USSR where there are few major air bases.

Tupolev Tu-95 'Bear-A'

(USSR)
Type: long-range strategic heavy bomber
Accommodation: flightcrew of 10
Armament (fixed): six 23-mm NR-23 cannon (two each in tail turret and in dorsal and ventral barbettes)
Armament (disposable): this is carried in two lower-fuselage weapons bays up to a maximum weight of 20,000 kg (44,092 lb) of free-fall ordnance
Electronics and operational equipment: communication and navigation equipment, plus 'Short Horn' nav/attack radar, 'Bee Hind' (later 'Box Tail') tail-warning and gunlaying radar, A-322Z Doppler navigation and several ECM systems
Powerplant and fuel system: four 11,035-kW (14,800-shp) Kuznetsov NK-12MV turboprops, and a total internal fuel capacity of 72,980 litres (16,540 Imp gal); no provision for drop tanks or inflight refuelling
Performance: maximum speed 925 km/h (575 mph) or Mach 0·83 at 7600 m (24,935 ft); cruising speed 708 km/h (440 mph); climb to 5000 m (16,405 ft) in 13 minutes; service ceiling 13,500 m (44,290 ft); radius 7400 km (4,598 miles) with 11340-kg (25,000-lb) warload
Weights: empty 86,000 kg (189,594 lb); maximum take-off 154,200 kg (339,947 lb)
Dimensions: span 51·10 m (167 ft 7·75 in); length excluding probe 47·50 m (155 ft 10 in); height 12·12 m (39 ft 9·2 in); wing area 310·50 m² (3,342·3 sq ft)

Variants

Tu-95 'Bear-A': the Tu-95 series of bombers, reconnaissance aircraft and (eventually) missile-carriers first flew in prototype form during the summer of 1954 and began to enter service in 1955; the type was developed as a long-range strategic bomber able to carry two thermonuclear bombs or 20,000 kg (44,092 lb) of conventional bombs over intercontinental ranges, and was conceived as a technically less-demanding fallback for the conceptually more advanced Myasishchev M-4 'Bison'; in the event the Tupolev aircraft has proved far superior to the M-4 in terms of versatility and range, and despite its propeller propulsion it achieves jet speeds; the 'Bear-A' was the original bomber version and is still in limited service

Tu-95 'Bear-B': missile-carrying variant first seen in 1961 with the AS-3 'Kangaroo' in a semi-recessed position under the fuselage and the nose revised to accommodate the 'Crown Drum' high-definition search radar and A-336Z missile-guidance system; from 1962 the type was revised with an inflight-refuelling probe, and some aircraft have been modified subsequently for the strategic reconnaissance role with a blister fairing on the starboard side of the rear fuselage

Tu-95 'Bear-C': introduced in about 1963, this is a dedicated maritime reconnaissance and Elint derivative of the 'Bear-B'; the type has the search radar and inflight-refuelling nose of the 'Bear-B', and can carry the 'AS-3 'Kangaroo' missile; the weapon bays are reworked for an additional 19,000 litres (4,179 Imp gal) of fuel and EW equipment characterized by two lateral blister fairings on the rear fuselage and a number of ventral radomes

Tu-95 'Bear-D': introduced in about 1966, this is a maritime multi-sensor reconnaissance and missile-support version produced by converting 'Bear-A' aircraft; there are a number of detail differences between aircraft, but most have 'Short Horn' radar in a chin radome, 'Big Bulge' surface-search radar in a ventral radome, blister fairings on both sides of the rear fuselage, pods at the tip of each tailplane half, anti-flutter masses (probably containing the antennae for a Sirena 3 radar-warning system), a longer inflight-refuelling probe, and 'Box Tail' rear-warning and tail-turret fire-control radar; for the missile-support part of its task the 'Bear-D' carries A-346Z digital data-link equipment used in association with the 'Short Horn' undernose navigation and weapon-delivery radar; in the mid-1970s some 'Bear-Ds' were revised with a long fairing (with four aerials) in place of the tail turret

Tu-95 'Bear-E': introduced in the later 1960s, this is a multi-sensor maritime reconnaissance aircraft produced by converting 'Bear-As' with inflight-refuelling capability plus (in the rear weapons bay) additional fuel tankage and a conformal pallet for six or seven cameras and other sensors (probably SLAR and IR linescan equipment) and (in the forward weapons bay) electronic equipment characterized by two external blister fairings; the type also has the lateral rear-fuselage blister strakes of the 'Bear-C' and 'Bear-D'

Tu-142 'Bear-F': the Tu-142 designation is believed to apply to new-build aircraft produced from the late 1960s in response to the continued demand for this highly versatile long-range type; the Tu-142 has a number of design, engineering and equipment improvements compared with the original series (including more highly cambered wings and a longer fuselage forward of the wings), allowing take-off at a maximum weight of some 188,000 kg (414,462 lb) attributable in part to considerably greater fuel capacity of 95,000 litres (20,897·5 Imp gal); fuselage length is increased to 49·50 m (162 ft 5 in) and the protruding flaps of the earlier variants are replaced by narrower-chord units in a completely restressed wing with stronger landing gear units and larger tyres; the 'Bear-F' was designed for the long-range anti-submarine role and began to enter service in 1972; the rear fuselage accommodates a crew rest area (with galley and toilet) as well as stowage and launchers for sonobuoys, MAD is housed in a pod at the top of the fin (only on later aircraft), the gun armament is reduced to the two-gun rear turret, a smaller ventral radar is fitted, and there is provision for a smaller chin radar; in addition to the initial 'Bear-F', this important anti-submarine type has been produced in a number of subvariants identified as the **'Bear-F Model 1'** with the original type of small engine nacelle, no chin radar and fewer fuselage protuberances, the **'Bear-F Model 2'** with the nose lengthened by 0·23 m (9 in), the angle of the inflight-refuelling probe lowered, and the height of the flightdeck roof increased, the **'Bear-F Model 3'** with a MAD sensor projecting rearwards from the top of the fin, the fairing at the tips of the tailplane removed, and the rear weapon bay made longer and narrower, and the **'Bear-F Model 4'** with chin radar restored and ECM added in a nose-mounted 'thimble' radome; the designation **Tu-142M** has been applied to the model operated by the Indian air force in the long-range maritime reconnaissance role (with a secondary heavy bombing capability), and though details of this model are uncertain it is thought to be the export subvariant of the 'Bear-F Model 2' with a range of 8300 km (5,158 miles)

Tu-95 'Bear-G': 'Bear-B' and 'Bear-C' aircraft reworked as Elint aircraft and launch platforms for two AS-4 'Kitchen' missiles carried under the wings; the type also has an ECM 'thimble' under the inflight-refuelling probe, ECM fairings on each side of the centre and rear fuselage, and a solid tailcone resembling that of the 'Bear-D'

Tu-142 'Bear-H': new-build variant based on the 'Bear-F' but with a shorter fuselage for use as a launch platform for the AS-15 'Kent cruise missile (six carried internally in the weapon bay and another four or eight as twins or quadruplets on two pylons under the wing roots); these missiles will in due course be supplemented and then replaced by the more advanced AS-19, a supersonic type under final development in the late 1980s; the fuselage has been considerably refined, the ventral barbette being eliminated to leave only the tail turret (sometimes fitted with a twin-barrel cannon rather than two cannon), and external ECM and ESM equipment being replaced by internal units; the type has a maximum take-off weight of 154,000 kg (339,512 lb) and an unrefuelled radius of 8285 km (5,148 miles)

Tu-95 'Bear-J': older aircraft reworked as VLF communications relay aircraft, with a long trailing antenna to allow the Soviet national command authority to communicate with submerged nuclear submarines

Tupolev Tu-126 'Moss'

(USSR)

Type: airborne warning and control system aeroplane

Accommodation: flightcrew of four or five, and a mission crew of seven or eight in the cabin

Armament (fixed): none

Armament (disposable): none

Electronics and operational equipment: communication and navigation equipment, plus 'Flap Jack' surveillance radar with its antenna in a rotodome above the fuselage, IFF and data-processing, tactical plotting and other systems including ECM and ESM systems

Powerplant and fuel system: four 11,185-kW (15,000-shp) Kuznetsov NK-12MK turboprops, and a total internal fuel capacity of about 75,000 litres (16,498 Imp gal); no provision for drop tanks but provision for inflight refuelling

Performance: maximum speed 850 km/h (528 km/h) or Mach 0·78 at 9000 m (29,530 ft); operating speed 520 km/h (323 mph); initial climb rate not revealed; service ceiling 11,000 m (36,090 ft); range 12,550 km (7,798 miles); endurance 25 hours

Weights: empty 105,000 kg (231,481 lb); maximum take-off 175,000 kg (385,802 lb)

Dimensions: span 51·20 m (168 ft 0 in); length without probe 55·20 m (181 ft 1 in); height 16·05 m (52 ft 7·9 in); wing area 311·10 m² (3,348·8 sq ft)

Variant

Tu-126 'Moss': adapted from the airframe of the obsolete Tu-114 airliner (itself developed from the Tu-95 bomber), the 'Moss' was the USSR's first AWACS aeroplane; the type first flew in 1967 or 1968 to enter service in 1971, and the 'Flap Jack' surveillance radar (with its antenna in an 11-m/36-ft) rotodome above the rear fuselage, is believed to be of only limited capability, effective performance being secured only over water; the type has inbuilt IFF capability, and the tactical compartment in the fuselage is data-linked to ground stations and supporting fighters

Below left: A Tu-95 'Bear-D' maritime aeroplane is escorted by an F-14A Tomcat.

Right: The Tu-160 'Blackjack' is the Soviet counterpart to the B-1B penetration bomber.

Below: The Tu-126 'Moss' was the USSR's first AEW platform, a limited but useful type.

Tupolev Tu-160 'Blackjack'

(USSR)

Type: variable-geometry supersonic penetration bomber and missile-carrying aeroplane

Accommodation: flightcrew probably of four on ejector seats

Armament (fixed): none

Armament (disposable): this is carried in two lower-fuselage weapons bays and on hardpoints under the wing gloves up to a maximum weight generally quoted in the West at about 16,500 kg (36,376 lb) of bombs and/or missiles (including up to eight AS-15 'Kent' air-launched cruise missiles)

Electronics and operational equipment: communication and navigation equipment, plus attack radar, ECM and ESM systems and other items

Powerplant and fuel system: four 23,000-kg (50,705-lb) afterburning thrust turbofans of unknown designation, and a total internal fuel capacity of unrevealed quantity; no provision for drop tanks but provision for inflight refuelling

Performance: maximum speed 2230 km/h (1,386 mph) or Mach 2·1 at high altitude; long-range cruising speed 955 km/h (594 mph) at 13,500 m (44,290 ft); initial climb rate not revealed; service ceiling not revealed; radius 7300 km (4,536 miles) on a hi-lo-hi penetration mission

Weights: empty 118,000 kg (260,140 lb); normal take-off 267,600 kg (589,947 lb); maximum take-off 275,000 kg (606,261 lb)

Dimensions: span 55·50 m (182 ft 10·4 in) spread and 33·75 m (110 ft 9 in) swept; length 53·90 m (176 ft 10 in); height 13·75 m (45 ft 1·3 in); wing area 360·0 m² (3,875·1 sq ft)

Variant

Tu-160 'Blackjack': conceptually akin to the Rockwell B-1B in being a variable-geometry supersonic penetration bomber designed for the strategic role, the 'Blackjack' is thought to have entered service in 1988 after a first flight in 1982; the Soviet type is somewhat larger than the B-1B, and the unrefuelled combat radius (estimated at 7300 km/4,536 miles) is posited on the assumption of high-level subsonic cruise, low-level transonic penetration and high-level supersonic attack; all data are highly speculative, and it seems likely that the type probably possesses far greater payload than that with which it has generally been credited; the warload is generally of the cruise missile type, the current subsonic AS-15 to be supplemented and then replaced in the 1990s by the supersonic AS-19

199

Vought A-7E Corsair II

Type: carrierborne attack and strike aeroplane
Accommodation: pilot on a McDonnell Douglas Escapac ejector seat
Armament (fixed): one 20-mm General Electric M61A1 Vulcan rotary-barrel cannon with 1,000 rounds
Armament (disposable): this is carried on eight hardpoints (two on the fuselage sides each rated at 500 lb/227 kg, and three under each wing with the inner two units each rated at 2,500 lb/1134 kg, the intermediate two units each at 3,500 lb/1588 kg and the outer two units each at 3,500 lb/1588 kg) up to a maximum weight of 15,000 lb (6804 kg); among the weapons that can be carried are the 70/350-kiloton B28, 1-megaton B43, 10/20-kiloton B57 and 100/500-kiloton B61 free-fall nuclear weapons, AIM-9 Sidewinder AAMs, AGM-65 Maverick ASM, AGM-45 Shrike and AGM-88 HARM radar-homing missiles, GBU-15 and AGM-62 Walleye TV-guided bombs, Paveway laser-guided bombs, 2,000-, 1,000-, 750-, 500- and 250-lb (907-, 454-, 340-, 227- and 113-kg) free-fall and retarded bombs, BLU-series napalm bombs, CBU-series bomb dispensers, LAU-series pods for 2·75- and 5-in (70- and 127-mm) rockets, and 30- or 20-mm cannon pods
Electronics and operational equipment: communication and navigation equipment, plus Texas Instruments APQ-126(V) multi-mode nav/attack radar, AVQ-7(V) or Marconi raster HUD, Texas Instruments AAR-42 FLIR pod, ASN-91 INS, ASN-190 Doppler navigation, ASU-99 projected-map display, Itek ALR-45 RWR, Magnavox ALR-50 SAM-warning system, Sanders ALQ-126 ECM, Loral APR-43 tactical radar-warning system, Tracor ALE-39 chaff/flare dispenser and provision for podded items such as Westinghouse ALQ-119 and ALQ-131 ECM, Xerox ALQ-123 IR countermeasures, Sanders ALQ-126 DECM, Eaton AIL ALQ-130 tactical communications jammer and Northrop ALQ-162 radar jammer
Powerplant and fuel system: one 15,000-lb (6804-lb) thrust Allison TF41-A-2 (Rolls-Royce Spey) non-afterburning turbofan, and a total internal fuel capacity of 1,500 US gal (5678 litres) plus provision for four 300-US gal (1136-litre) drop tanks; provision for inflight refuelling
Performance: maximum speed 690 mph (1110 km/h) or Mach 0·9 at sea level and 645 mph (1038 mph) or Mach 0·86 at 5,000 ft (1525 m) with 12 500-lb (227-kg) bombs; initial climb rate 15,000 ft (4572 m) per minute; service ceiling 42,000 ft (12,800 m); radius 715 miles (1151 km) on a hi-lo-hi mission; ferry range 2,860 miles (4603 km)
Weights: empty 18,800 lb (8528 kg); normal take-off 29,000 lb (13,154 kg); maximum take-off 42,000 lb (19,050 kg)
Dimensions: span 38 ft 9 in (11·80 m); length 46 ft 1·5 in (14·06 m); height 16 ft 0·75 in (4·90 m); wing area 375·0 sq ft (34·83 m²)

Variants
TA-7C Corsair II: this is the oldest variant of the Corsair family still in service, a tandem-two seat operational conversion trainer based on the A-7B and A-7C single-seaters and powered by the 13,400-lb (6078-kg) thrust Pratt & Whitney TF30-P-408 non-afterburning turbofan; the type has the operational capabilities of the A-7E; the Corsair II is the US Navy's standard medium attack aircraft, and was derived aerodynamically from the supersonic Vought F-8 Crusader to save time when the US Navy issued an urgent requirement

for a carrierborne medium attack aircraft in the early 1960s; the prototype first flew during September 1965 and the Corsair II entered service during October 1966 in the A-7A initial production form with the 11,350-lb (5148-kg) thrust TF30-P-6 turbofan for great range with a substantial load of disposable ordnance; following the A-7A were the A-7B with the 12,200-lb (5534-kg) thrust TF30-P-8 or TF40-P-408 turbofan and A-7C with the latter engine and the avionics of the A-7E; a version in very limited service is the **ETA-7C Corsair II**, an EW training subvariant with the ALE-41 chaff dispenser system
A-7D: tactical fighter for the US Air Force with the 14,500-lb (6577-kg) thrust Allison TF41-A-1 turbofan (derived from the Rolls-Royce Spey), M61A1 internal cannon, inflight-refuelling capability, and an advanced all-weather nav/attack system; the type was later retrofitted with automatic manoeuvring flaps and the 'Pave Penny' laser tracker; many A-7Ds are also being upgraded with the LANA (Low-Altitude Night Attack) package comprising a Texas Instruments AAR-49 FLIR (under the starboard wing) with input to the Singer-Kearfott nav/attack computer in conjunction with the APQ-126 radar for the generation of information on the GEC Avionics wide-angle HUD
A-7E Corsair II: definitive attack, close support and interdiction variant for the US Navy, based on the A-7D but using the TF41-A-2 engine; later aircraft were equipped with a FLIR pod under the starboard wing for enhanced adverse-weather and nocturnal attack capability
A-7H: land-based A-7E for Greece, denavalized but retaining wing-folding capability
TA-7H: two-seat operational conversion trainer derivative of the A-7H for the Greek air force
A-7K: two-seat operational conversion trainer derivative of the A-7D for the Air National Guard; some A-7Ks are also being fitted with the same LANA package as the A-7D
EA-7L Corsair II: EW conversions of TA-7C two-seaters
A-7P: A-7As refurbished for the Portuguese air force with TF40-P-408 engines and the avionics of the A-7E
A-7 Plus: under this company designation (known to the USAF as the **YA-7F**), Vought is modifying two A-7D aircraft to a revised configuration for evaluation by the USAF for their 1985 Close Air Support/Battlefield Air Interdiction specification, having already offered the highly capable A-7 Strikefighter upgrade; the A-7 Plus is re-engined with a 26,000-lb (11,794-kg) afterburning thrust Pratt & Whitney F100-PW-220, (or possibly a 27,850-lb/12,633-kg afterburning thrust General Electric F110-GE-100) turbofan for supersonic performance (also aided by aerodynamic developments such as leading-edge root extensions, a fuselage lengthened by two plugs (that forward of the wing 18 in/0·457 m long and that aft of the wing 29·5 in/0·749 m long), a revised nose radome, augmented flaps, and modifications to the wing leading and trailing edges); the avionics are also to be modernized, and the envisaged payload is 17,380 lb (7886 kg) with a maximum take-off weight of 46,000 lb (20,866 kg) for a 7-g turning limit; if successful, some 337 A-7D and A-7K aircraft might be converted to this considerably higher standard; with the F100 a maximum speed of Mach 1·1 is anticipated, rising to Mach 1·4 with the F110; hi-lo-hi and lo-lo-lo combat radii of 772 and 334 miles (1242 and 537 km) are expected with the F100, or of 789 and 334 miles (1270 and 537 km) with the F110

Vought F-8E(FN) Crusader

Type: carrierborne interceptor fighter and attack aeroplane
Accommodation: pilot on an ejector seat
Armament (fixed): four 20-mm Philco-Ford M39 cannon with 144 rounds per gun
Armament (disposable): this is carried on four hardpoints (two on the fuselage sides each rated at 1,200 lb/544 kg, and one under each wing rated at 2,500 lb/1134 kg) up to a maximum weight of 5,000 lb (2268 kg); the fuselage hardpoints can carry two Matra R.530 AAMs or eight 5-in (127-mm) rockets, and the underwing hardpoints can lift two 2,000- or 1,000-lb (907- or 454-kg) bombs, or four 500-lb (227-kg) bombs, or 12 250-lb (113-kg) bombs, or pods for 68-mm (2·68-in) rockets
Electronics and operational equipment: communication and navigation equipment, plus Magnavox APQ-94 fire-control radar and other systems
Powerplant and fuel system: one 18,000-lb (8165-kg) afterburning thrust Pratt & Whitney J57-P-20 turbojet, and a total internal fuel capacity of 1,400 US gal (5300 litres); no provision for drop tanks but provision for inflight refuelling
Performance: maximum speed 1,135 mph (1827 km/h) or Mach 1·72 at 36,000 ft (10,970 m); cruising speed 560 mph (901 km/h) at 40,000 ft (12,190 m); initial climb rate about 21,000 ft (6400 m) per minute; service ceiling 58,000 ft (17,680 m); radius 600 miles (966 km)
Weights: empty not revealed; normal take-off 28,000 lb (12,701 kg); maximum take-off 34,000 lb (15,420 kg)
Dimensions: span 35 ft 8 in (10·87 m); length 54 ft 6 in (16·61 m); height 15 ft 9 in (4·80 m); wing area 350·0 sq ft (32·52 m²)

Variant
F-8E(FN) Crusader: resulting from a 1952 US Navy requirement for a carrierborne supersonic air-superiority fighter, this type first flew in March 1955 as the XF8U-1 with the 14,800-lb (6713-kg) afterburning thrust Pratt & Whitney J57-P-11 turbojet; it entered service in March 1957 as the F8U-1 (later F-8A) with an armament of four 20-mm cannon plus a retractable rocket pack (Sidewinder AAMs being added later) and powered by the 16,200-lb (7348-kg) thrust J57-P-4A; the type underwent considerable development, the F-8E(FN) being the last production model, derived from the F-8E with blown flaps and other high-lift improvements for operation from French aircraft-carriers after delivery in January 1965

Below: A UH-14A (Lynx Mk 25) helicopter of the Dutch navy.

Westland Lynx HAS.Mk 2

(UK)

Type: anti-submarine and anti-ship light helicopter

Accommodation: flightcrew of two, and a mission crew of two in the cabin

Armament (fixed): none

Armament (disposable): this is carried on two hardpoints (one on each side of the fuselage) and comprises two Mk 46 or Sting Ray torpedoes, or two Mk 11 depth charges, or four Sea Skua or AS.12 anti-ship missiles

Electronics and operational equipment: communication and navigation equipment, plus Ferranti ARI.5979 Seaspray search radar, Texas Instruments ASQ-81 MAD with a towed 'bird', Racal MIR-2 Orange Crop ESM equipment, ARI.23363 or ARI.23379 noise jammer (in place of one Sea Skua anti-ship missile), Decca Type 71 Doppler navigation and (in AS.12-fitted helicopters) SFIM APX Bézu M334 gyro-stabilized sight

Powerplant and fuel system: two 900-shp (671-kW) Rolls-Royce Gem 2 turboshafts, and a total internal fuel capacity of 202 Imp gal (918 litres) plus provision for 180 Imp gal (818 litres) of auxiliary fuel in two fuselage tanks; no provision for drop tanks or inflight refuelling

Performance: maximum speed 144 mph (232 km/h) at sea level; initial climb rate 2,170 ft (661 m) per minute; hovering ceiling out of ground effect 8,450 ft (2575 m); radius 58 miles (98 km) for a 2·5-hour patrol; ferry range 650 miles (1048 km)

Weights: empty 7,370 lb (3343 kg); maximum take-off 10,500 lb (4763 kg)

Dimensions: main rotor diameter 42 ft 0 in (12·80 m); length overall, rotors turning 49 ft 9 in (15·16 m) and fuselage 39 ft 1·3 in (11·92 m); height 11 ft 5 in (3·48 m); main rotor disc area 1,385·0 sq ft (128·7 m²)

Variants

Lynx AH.Mk 1: baseline land-based variant of the Lynx helicopter, which first flew in prototype form during March 1971 and began to enter service in 1977, and possesses better performance than the naval Lynx as it has the same basic powerplant but a reduced maximum take-off weight of 10,000 lb (4536 kg); other major divergences from the naval Lynx are skid landing gear, a slightly longer fuselage (39 ft 6·75 in/12·06 m), and a different combination of avionics and weapons; the Lynx has been qualified for a wide assortment of weapons, but in its basic anti-tank role with the British army the type is fitted with launchers for eight BGM-71 TOW heavyweight anti-tank missiles guided with the

Below right; An F-8E(FN) bolts after missing the arrester wire on USS *Dwight D. Eisenhower*.

aid of a stabilized roof-mounted M65 sight; the cabin can accommodate reload TOW missiles, or eight troops, or a Milan ground-launched anti-tank missile crew with launcher and other equipment, or casualties, or freight; the increasing threat posed by battlefield SAMs, especially of the shoulder-launched variety, is attested by the retrofit on most helicopters of the Sanders ALQ-144(VE) IR countermeasures system; in 1989 it was decided to retrofit all battlefield Lynx helicopters with the Ferranti AWARE-3 RWR

Lynx HAS.Mk 2: baseline naval Lynx model, an advanced anti-submarine and anti-ship helicopter suitable for deployment on small surface vessels; the type has non-retractable but castoring tricycle landing gear, a folding tail and a naval avionics/weapons fit; as an alternative to the primary roles, the Lynx HAS.Mk 2 can be used for the carriage of 10 troops, or of 2,000 lb (907 kg) of freight carried internally or 3,000 lb (1361 kg) carried externally; Lynx helicopters used in high-threat areas such as the Persian Gulf are fitted with an upgraded EW suite including Tracor chaff/flare dispenser, and the Yellow Veil jammer pod; the type also carries a revised Sea Skua anti-ship missile with a lower minimum-height setting

Lynx Mk 2(FN): French navy version of the Lynx HAS.Mk 2 with Thomson DUAV 4 or Thomson HS 12 dunking sonar and Omera-Segid ORB 31-W search radar

Lynx HAS.Mk 3: improved British naval model with 1,120-shp (835-kW) Gem 41-1 turboshafts; all HAS.Mk 2s are being upgraded to this standard

Lynx Mk 4(FN): French navy equivalent of the Lynx HAS.Mk 3

Lynx AH.Mk 5: improved version of the Lynx AH.Mk 1 with 1,120-shp (835-kW) Gem 41-1 turboshafts

Lynx AH.Mk 7: improved model for the British army with improved systems, Gem 42-1 turboshafts, swept-tip BERP main rotor blades of composite construction (retrofitted as the original metal blades are withdrawn) and a tail rotor rotating in the opposite direction to that of the Lynx AH.Mk 1; all AH.Mk 1s are being upgraded to this standard, which also includes the TITOW (Thermal Imaging TOW) anti-tank missile sight system; the complete package offers better low-level hovering and manoeuvring capabilities, facilitating nap-of-the-earth anti-tank operations, and protection from IR-homing missiles is improved by the use of large hot gas/cool freestream air mixers suppressors fitted over the turboshaft exhausts; Westland is considering an export version of this helicopter with a pair of LHTEC (Allison/Garrett) T800 turboshafts for improved hot-and-high performance

Lynx HAS.Mk 8: latest anti-ship and anti-submarine variant of the naval Lynx series, a standard to which all HAS.Mk 3s are to be upgraded; it had originally been planned to fit the type with 360° scan radar (the Ferranti Seaspray Mk 3 and MEL Super Searcher had been shortlisted with the antenna in a chin radome), but the installation of such a radar has been foregone for financial reasons and the final electronic fit includes the

Racal CTS (Control Tactical System, with all tactical data processed for display at multi-function consoles) and a GEC Sea Owl thermal imaging system; Westland is offering a Lynx HAS.Mk 8 variant for export as the **Super Lynx** with 360 > scan radar and 1,120-shp (835-kW) Gem 42 turboshafts as standard plus customer options such as dunking sonar, Sea Skua or Penguin anti-ship missiles, Sting Ray torpedoes and the main and tail rotor developments of the AH.Mk 7

Lynx AH.Mk 9: unarmed mobile command post and tactical transport version of the Lynx AH.Mk 7 with upgraded avionics, BERP rotor blades, 1,120-shp (835-kW) Gem 42 turboshafts, tricycle landing gear and 11,300-lb (5126-kg) maximum take-off weight; as a private venture Westland has also developed an armed version as the **Battlefield Lynx** with a roof-mounted sight and provision for eight BGM-91 TOW anti-tank missiles

Lynx Mk 21: Brazilian navy version of the Lynx HAS.Mk 2

Lynx Mk 23: Argentine navy version of the Lynx HAS.Mk 2

Lynx Mk 25: Dutch navy version of the Lynx HAS.Mk 2 used mainly for SAR, and designated **UH-14A** in that service

Lynx Mk 27: Dutch navy version of the Lynx HAS.Mk 3 used for the ASW role with Alcatel dunking sonar, and designated **SH-14B** in that service

Lynx Mk 28: version of the Lynx AH.Mk 1 for the Qatari police with Gem 41-1 turboshafts and special equipment, including emergency flotation gear

Lynx Mk 80: Danish navy version of the Lynx HAS.Mk 3 used for ASW and maritime patrol work; in the late 1980s and early 1990s the original Gem 2 and Gem 4 turboshafts were upgraded to Gem 28 standard

Lynx Mk 81: Dutch navy version of the Lynx HAS.Mk 3 with MAD equipment for the ASW role, and designated **SH-14C** in that service

Lynx Mk 86: Norwegian air force version of the Lynx HAS.Mk 3 with Gem 41-2 turboshafts, non-folding tail and specialist equipment for the coastal SAR role

Lynx Mk 87: Argentine navy version of the Lynx HAS.Mk 3 with Gem 41-2 turboshafts

Lynx Mk 88: West German navy version of the Lynx HAS.Mk 3 with Gem 41-2 turboshafts and Bendix ASQ-18 dunking sonar and designed for the ASW role

Lynx Mk 89: Nigerian navy version of the Lynx HAS.Mk 3 with Gem 43-1 turboshafts and RCA Primus radar for use in the SAR role

Lynx Mk 90: Danish navy improved version of the Mk 80 with Orange Crop ESM and tactical data system; the Mk 80s are being upgraded to this standard to complement three new-build helicopters

Lynx-3: much improved dedicated anti-tank development with 1,346-shp (1004-kW) Gem 60 turboshafts, an advanced-technology main rotor, and a slightly lengthened fuselage housing two pilots and a deployable anti-tank missile team, the missile team's reloads, and pylon-mounted weapons such as Hellfire, HOT or TOW anti-tank missiles, and Stinger lightweight AAMs

Westland Sea King HAS.Mk 5

(UK)
Type: anti-submarine and general-purpose medium helicopter
Accommodation: flightcrew of two, and a mission crew of two in the cabin
Armament (fixed): none
Armament (disposable): this is carried on two hardpoints (one on each sponson strut) up to a maximum weight of 2,500 lb (1134 kg); typical loads are four Mk 46 or Sting Ray torpedoes, or four Mk 11 depth charges
Electronics and operational equipment: communication and navigation equipment, plus Marconi ARI.5991 Sea Searcher surveillance radar, Plessey 195 dunking sonar, Ultra Electronic minisonobuoys, Marconi/GEC AQS-902C LAPADS acoustic data-processing and tactical display system (to be upgraded to ASQ-902G-DS standard), Racal MIR-2 Orange Crop ESM equipment, ARI.23363 or ARI.23379 noise jammer, Tactical Air Navigation System-G and Decca Type 71 Doppler navigation
Powerplant and fuel system: two 1,660-shp (1238-kW) Rolls-Royce Gnome H.1400-1 turboshafts, and a total internal fuel capacity of 800 Imp gal (3636 litres); no provision for drop tanks or inflight refuelling
Performance: cruising speed 129 mph (208 km/h) at sea level; initial climb rate 2,020 ft (616 m) per minute; service ceiling 4,000 ft (1220 m) on one engine; range 764 miles (1230 km)
Weights: empty 13,672 lb (6201 kg); maximum take-off 21,000 lb (9525 kg)
Dimensions: main rotor diameter 62 ft 0 in (18·90 m); length overall, rotors turning 72 ft 8 in (22·15 m) and fuselage 55 ft 9·75 in (17·01 m); height 15 ft 6 in (4·72 m) to rotor head; main rotor disc area 3,019·1 sq ft (280·47 m²)

Variants

Sea King AEW.Mk 2A: derived from the Sikorsky S-61B (SH-3) series for the US Navy, the licence-built Westland Sea King is a better-equipped helicopter designed for autonomous rather than ship-controlled ASW operations by virtue of its onboard tactical compartment fed, in early variants, with data from the Plessey Type 195 dunking sonar, the Ekco AW391 radar (with its antenna in a dorsal radome) and the Marconi AD580 Doppler navigation system; the type first flew in British form during May 1969, and entered service during the same year as the Sea King HAS.Mk 1 with two Rolls-Royce Gnome H.1400 turboshafts; the Sea King HAS.Mk 2 was basically similar, but was powered by 1,660-shp (1238-kW) Gnome H.1400-1 turboshafts and incorporated features developed for Australia's Sea King Mk 50; the designation Sea King AEW.Mk 2A is used for Sea King HAS.Mk 2s converted into AEW helicopters with the Thorn EMI Searchwater LAST (Low-Altitude Surveillance Task) radar, its 360° scan antenna in a pressurized radome on a swivelling arm on the starboard side of the fuselage; the arm and radome are turned to the rear for carrier operations and cruising flight, then swivelled down to the vertical position below the fuselage for patrol operations; the type also has Cossor Jubilee Guardsman IFF, Racal MIR-2 Orange Crop ESM equipment and Ferranti FIN 1110 INS, and may be retrofitted with the Orange Reaper (Racal Kestrel) ESM equipment
Sea King HAR.Mk 3: dedicated SAR derivative of the Sea King HAS.Mk 2 for the Royal Air Force; the type entered service in 1977 and has no ASW

equipment to allow additional avionics (including MEL ARI.5955 search radar), Gnome H.1400-1 engines and an additional 113 Imp gal (514 litres) of fuel, and a cabin outfitted for the carriage (in addition to the two rescue crew) of 19 survivors, or six litters, or two litters and 11 survivors
Sea King HC.Mk 4: assault transport version of the Commando Mk 2 for the Royal Marines with the folding tail and main rotor of the Sea King series, and able to carry 28 troops or 6,000 lb (2272 kg) of freight internally, or an 8,000-lb (3629-kg) slung load
Sea King HAS.Mk 5: much upgraded ASW and SAR variant for the Royal Navy with advanced sensors and data-processing capability in a cabin enlarged by the rearward movement of the rear bulkhead by 6 ft 6 in (1·98 m); the Sea Searcher radar has twice the range of the AW391 type as well as better discrimination against ECM, and the LAPADS allows faster and more accurate processing of data from the dunking sonar and sonobuoys; the current AQS-902C version of the LAPADS is being updated in the late 1980s to AQS-902G-DS standard for improved operational capability; other developments for the Sea King include provision for the Whittaker ALQ-167(V) jammer pod
Sea King HAS.Mk 6: improved version of the Sea King HAS.Mk 5 based on the Advanced Sea King concept and under development for service with the Royal Navy from 1989; the variant has an integrated ASW acoustic-processing system (with inputs from sonobuoys and dipping sonar to CRT displays), improved radar, provision for two Sea Eagle anti-ship missiles, a strengthened fuselage, two 1,660-shp (1238-kW) Gnome H.1400-1T turboshafts transmission-limited to a combined maximum of 2,950 shp (2200 kW), and an uprated dynamic system including composite-structure blades on both the main and tail rotors
Sea King Mk 41: SAR variant for the West German navy with Gnome H.1400 turboshafts; surviving aircraft are being revised as combat helicopters with provision for two or four Kormoran 2 anti-ship missiles, Ferranti Seaspray radar, an RWR receiver and chaff/flare dispenser
Sea King Mk 42: ASW variant of the Sea King HAS.Mk 1 for the Indian navy with Gnome H.1400 turboshafts
Sea King Mk 42A: ASW variant of the Sea King HAS.Mk 2 for the Indian navy with Gnome H.1400-1 turboshafts and haul-down gear
Sea King Mk 42B: Advanced Sea King anti-submarine and anti-ship variant for the Indian

navy with features such as composite-structure rotor blades, an uprated transmission, a strengthened airframe, Super Searcher surveillance radar, a Marconi AQS-902B acoustic processing system used with the Thomson SINTRA HS 12 active dunking sonar and passive sonobuoys, a Marconi Hermes ESM system, and provision for Sea Eagle anti-ship missiles
Sea King Mk 42C: utility version of the Sea King Mk 42B with Bendix RDR-1400C search radar in the nose
Sea King Mk 43: SAR variant for the Norwegian air force with Gnome H.1400 turboshafts
Sea King Mk 43A: improved SAR variant for the Norwegian air force with Gnome H.1400-1 turboshafts
Sea King Mk 45: anti-submarine and anti-ship variant for the Pakistani navy with Gnome H.1400 turboshafts and provision for AM.39 Exocet missiles
Sea King Mk 47: ASW variant for the Egyptian navy with Gnome H.1400-1 turboshafts
Sea King Mk 48: dual-role VIP transport/SAR variant for the Belgian air force with Gnome H.1400-1 turboshafts
Sea King Mk 50: ASW variant of the Sea King HAS.Mk 1 for the Australian navy with Gnome H.1400-1 turboshafts and Bendix ASQ-13B dunking sonar
Sea King Mk 50A: improved ASW variant of the Sea King Mk 50 for the Australian navy
Commando Mk 1: land-based derivative of the Sea King series that first flew in September 1973 and which has Gnome H.1400 turboshafts, non-retractable wheeled landing gear, no sponsons, and provision for a wide variety of armament; the type is operated by the Egyptian air force in the trooping role with accommodation for 21 men in the cabin
Commando Mk 2: uprated version of the Commando Mk 1 with Gnome H.1400-1 turboshafts and able to carry 27 men or 3,000 lb (2722 kg) of freight
Commando Mk 2A: version of the Commando Mk 2 for the Qatari air force
Commando Mk 2B: VIP derivative of the Commando Mk 2 for the Egyptian air force
Commando Mk 2C: VIP derivative of the Commando Mk 2A for the Qatari air force
Commando Mk 2E: Elint intelligence and jamming version for the Egyptian air force, fitted with the Selenia IHS-6 Elint and jamming system
Commando Mk 3: armed multi-role version with sponsons; eight built for Qatar

Westland Wasp HAS.Mk 1

WSK-PZL Swidnik (Mil) Mi-2 'Hoplite'

(UK)

Type: anti-submarine and anti-ship light helicopter

Accommodation: flightcrew of two, and four passengers or freight in the cabin rear

Armament (fixed): none

Armament (disposable): this is carried on two hardpoints (one on each side of the fuselage) and comprises two Mk 46 or StingRay torpedoes, or two Mk 11 depth charges, or two AS.11 ASMs

Electronics and operational equipment: communication and navigation equipment, plus APX-Bézu 260 gyro-stabilized sight

Powerplant and fuel system: one 710-shp (530-kW) Rolls-Royce Nimbus Mk 503 turboshaft, and a total internal fuel capacity of 155 Imp gal (755 litres); no drop tanks or inflight refuelling

Performance: maximum speed 120 mph (193 km/h) at sea level; initial climb rate 1,440 ft (439 m) per minute; service ceiling 12,200 ft (3720 m); range 270 miles (435 km) with four passengers

Weights: empty 3,452 lb (1566 kg); maximum take-off 5,500 lb (2495 kg)

Dimensions: main rotor diameter 32 ft 3 in (9·83 m); length overall, rotors turning 40 ft 4 in (12·29 m) and fuselage 30 ft 4 in (9·24 m); height 8 ft 11 in (2·72 m) to rotor head; main rotor disc area 816·9 sq ft (75·89 m²)

Variants

Scout AH.Mk 1: the British army's version of the Wasp, with a Nimbus Mk 102 turboshaft derated from 1,050 shp (783 kW) to 685 shp (511 kW) and skid landing gear; it has better performance than the Wasp as it is lighter; can be armed with a flexible cannon or machine-gun, rocket pods or wire-guided missiles such as the AS.11 or AS.12, but is generally used as a five-seat utility helicopter; first flew as the Saunders-Roe P.531 in July 1958, and began service in 1963

Wasp HAS.Mk 1: naval version with the 1,050-shp (783-kW) Nimbus Mk 103 or Mk 104 turboshaft derated to 710 shp (529 kW), castoring quadricycle landing gear, a folding tail and main rotor blades, and naval avionics and armament

Below left: A Sea King Mk 48 SAR and VIP helicopter of the Belgian air force.

Right: A Wasp HAS.Mk 1 from one of the Royal New Zealand Navy's 'Leander' class frigates.

Below: Designed in the USSR but built in Poland, the Mi-2 is a utility helicopter.

(Poland & USSR)

Type: general-purpose light helicopter

Accommodation: pilot, and 10 passengers, or four litters plus one attendant, or 700 kg (1,543 lb) of freight in the cabin

Armament (fixed): none

Armament (disposable): this is carried on two hardpoints (one on each side of the fuselage) and comprises two pods for 55-mm (2·17-in) rockets, or four anti-tank missiles

Electronics and operational equipment: communication and navigation equipment

Powerplant and fuel system: two 335-kW (449-shp) Polish-built Isotov GTD-350P turboshafts, and a total internal fuel capacity of 600 litres (131 Imp gal) plus provision for two 238-litre (52-Imp gal) auxiliary tanks on the fuselage sides; no provision for drop tanks or inflight refuelling

Performance: cruising speed 200 km/h (124 mph) at 500 m (1,640 ft); initial climb rate 270 m (885 ft) per minute; service ceiling 4000 m (13,125 ft); hovering ceiling in ground effect about 2000 m (6,560 ft) and out of ground effect about 1000 m (3,280 ft); range 170 km (105 miles) with maximum payload or 440 km (273 miles) with maximum internal fuel; ferry range 797 km (495 miles)

Weights: empty 2365 kg (5,213 lb); normal take-off 3550 kg (7,286 lb); maximum take-off 3700 kg (8,157 lb)

Dimensions: main rotor diameter 14·50 m (47 ft 6·9 in); length overall, rotors turning 17·42 m (57 ft 2 in) and fuselage 11·40 m (37 ft 4·75 in); height 3·75 m (12 ft 3·5 in) to rotor head; main rotor disc area 165·13 m² (1,777·5 sq ft)

Variants

Mi-2 'Hoplite': this is basically a turboshaft-powered derivative of the Mil Mi-1, two small turboshafts replacing the single piston engine of the earlier machine for enhanced reliability and greater power at reduced weight; the develop-

ment was undertaken by the parent design bureau in the USSR, the prototype first flying in September 1961; thereafter final development and production was switched to Poland, where the first series machine was flown in 1965; early aircraft had two 300-kW (402-shp) GTD-350 turboshafts, but in 1974 the 335-kW (449-shp) turboshafts became the production norm; the type can undertake the whole range of military tasks, and an 800-kg (1,764-lb) slung load can be lifted

Mi-2M 'Hoplite': advanced battlefield version of the Mi-2 with a capable EW warfare system, smokelaying equipment and an armament of SA-7 'Grail' missiles in the short-range air-to-air role

Mi-2US: gunship version of the Mi-2, with an assembly on the port side of the fuselage for one 14·5-mm (0·57-in) and two 12·7-mm (0·5-in) heavy machine-guns belt-fed from magazines in the cabin

Yakovlev Yak-28P 'Firebar'

Yakovlev Yak-38 'Forger-A'

(USSR)
Type: all-weather fighter
Accommodation: pilot and systems operator in tandem on ejector seats
Armament (fixed): none
Armament (disposable): this is carried on four hardpoints (two under each wing, with the inner units each rated at 300 kg/661 lb and the outer units each at 100 kg/220 lb) up to a maximum weight of 800 kg (1,653 lb) comprising two AA-3 'Anab' and two AA-2 'Atoll' AAMs
Electronics and operational equipment: communication and navigation equipment, plus 'Skip Spin' fire-control radar, optical sight and possibly an RWR
Powerplant and fuel system: two 6000-kg (13,288-lb) afterburning thrust Tumanskii R-11 turbojets, and a total internal fuel capacity of unrevealed quantity plus provision for two slipper tanks of unrevealed quantity on the wing leading edges outboard of the engines; no provision for inflight refuelling
Performance: maximum speed 2000 km/h (1,241 mph) or Mach 1·88 at 11,000 m (36,090 ft); cruising speed 920 km/h (571 mph); initial climb rate 8500 m (27,885 ft) per minute; service ceiling 16,750 m (55,000 ft); radius 925 km (575 miles) with maximum warload; range 2575 km (1,600 miles)
Weights: empty 13,600 kg (29,982 lb); normal take-off 15,875 kg (34,998 lb); maximum take-off 20,000 kg (44,092 lb)
Dimensions: span 12·95 m (42 ft 6 in); length 23·00 m (75 ft 5·5 in); height 3·95 m (12 ft 11·5 in); wing area 37·60 m² (404·7 sq ft)

Variants

Yak-28R 'Brewer-D': the Yak-28 series has served the Soviet air forces well over a long period, the basic type having proved itself capable of considerable development and versatility; the type was evolved from the twin-engined Yak-25 all-weather interceptor with more sharply swept flying surfaces and twin wheels on each unit of the bicycle landing gear, whose main unit was moved aft to allow the incorporation of a weapon bay in the lower fuselage; the type first flew in 1960, and the series was developed for a number of tactical roles, those now in service being the Yak-28 'Brewer-A' light bomber prototype, the Yak-28I 'Brewer-B' strike bomber, and the Yak-28I 'Brewer-C' strike bomber with features of the Yak-28P such as a lengthened fuselage and longer engine inlets; the 'Brewer-D' is a multi-sensor reconnaissance aircraft introduced in the late 1960s for the carriage of optical, SLAR or IR linescan equipment on interchangeable pallets in the erstwhile weapons bay; the type also has a large blister radome under the fuselage behind the nosewheel bay
Yak-28E 'Brewer-E': electronic escort version of the series, introduced in the late 1960s and crewed by a pilot plus a mission officer, the latter operating the electronic systems and associated countermeasures jammers (both spot and barrage) and dispensers of the ECM system built into the weapon bay and protruding from it as a cylindrical fairing
Yak-28P 'Firebar': original production model, introduced in 1962 and featuring 'Skip Spin' radar in a solid nose; this radar provides tracking to a range of 60 km (37·3 miles) and tracking to shorter ranges; from 1967 the original short nose and short air inlets were replaced by longer units with lower drag, increasing overall length from 21·70 m (71 ft 2·3 in) to 23·00 m (75 ft 5·5 in) and boosting transonic performance
Yak-28U 'Maestro': two-seat operational conversion trainer variant with two separate cockpits

(USSR)
Type: carrierborne STOVL combat aeroplane
Accommodation: pilot on a zero/zero ejector seat
Armament (fixed): none
Armament (disposable): this is carried on four hardpoints (two under each wing, each rated at 1000 kg/2,205 lb) up to a maximum weight of 3600 kg (7,937 lb); typical loads are two AA-2 'Atoll' or four AA-8 'Aphid' AAMs, or two AS-7 'Kerry' ASMs, or two AA-8 AAMs and two 500-kg (1,102-lb) bombs, or two UV-16-57 pods each with 16 55-mm (2·17-in) rockets and two 250-kg (551-lb) bombs, or two AA-2 AAMs and two UPK-23 pods each with one 23-mm GSh-23L two-barrel cannon
Electronics and operational equipment: communication and navigation equipment, plus ranging radar, HUD, 'Odd Rods' IFF, OR-69 Sirena 3 RWR, and various ECM systems
Powerplant and fuel system: one 8160-kg (17,989-lb) thrust Lyul'ka AL-21F vectored-thrust non-afterburning turbojet and two 3750-kg (7,870-lb) thrust Koliesov ZM non-afterburning lift turbojets, and a total internal fuel capacity of about 2900 litres (638 Imp gal) plus provision for two 600-litre (132-Imp gal) drop tanks; no provision for inflight refuelling
Performance: maximum speed 1110 km/h (627 mph) or Mach 0·95 at 11,000 m (36,090 ft) and 980 km/h (610 mph) or Mach 0·8 at sea level; initial climb rate 4500 m (14,765 ft) per minute; service ceiling 12,000 m (39,370 ft); radius 240 km (150 miles) on a lo-lo-lo mission with maximum warload, or 370 km (229 miles) on a hi-lo-hi mission with maximum warload
Weights: empty 7385 kg (16,281 lb); maximum take-off 11,700 kg (25,794 lb) for VTO or 13,000 kg (28,660 lb) for STO
Dimensions: span 7·32 m (24 ft 0·2 in); length 15·50 m (50 ft 10·3 in); height 4·37 m (14 ft 4 in); wing area 18·50 m² (199·14 sq ft)

Variants

Yak-38 'Forger-A': developed from the Yak-36 VTOL prototype and initially thought to be designated Yak-36MP, the Yak-38 is a carrierborne tactical aircraft with STOVL capability although up to 1984 Western analysts thought the type capable only of VTOL performance; the type first flew in the early 1970s and entered service in 1976, and though a limited type designed to provide operational experience with such aircraft, it provides Soviet helicopter carriers and aircraft-carriers with useful interception and attack capabilities when out of reach of land-based air defences
Yak-38UV 'Forger-B': tandem two-seat conversion trainer variant with the fuselage lengthened to 17·68 m (58 ft 0 in) to accommodate the pupil's cockpit
Yak-41: it is thought that the Soviets are developing a variant of the Yak-38 under this designation with search radar in a revised nose, and possibly with vectored-thrust of the four-poster type to remove the need for the two direct-lift engines which are so much dead weight except for take-off and landing; the resulting aeroplane was evaluated from 1989, and probably possesses supersonic performance

Above left: The Yak-28 'Firebar' is now obsolete in the all-weather fighter role.

Left: Yak-38 'Forger-As' of the Soviet navy on board their aircraft carrier.

Dong Feng-2 (CSS-1)

(China)
Type: single-stage medium-range ballistic missile
Dimensions: diameter 1·60 m (5·25 ft); length 22·80 m (74·80 ft)
Weight: total round 26,000 kg (57,319 lb)
Payload vehicle: not revealed
Propulsion: one liquid-propellant rocket
Range: 1200 km (745 miles)
CEP: 2780 m (3,040 yards)
Warhead: one 15/20-kiloton nuclear or conventional RV in early examples (perhaps first 50), or 1/3-megaton thermonuclear RV in later examples (perhaps last 50)
Launch: hot type from pad
Guidance: radio-updated inertial

Variant
Dong Feng-2: designated **CSS-1** in the US terminology for Chinese weapons, the DF-2 (East Wind-2) is a simple weapon that was China's first strategic missile and was introduced in 1970; it is based on the technology of the Soviet SS-3 'Shyster', itself based generally on the German Peenemunde A-4 (V-2) of World War II; the type remains in limited Chinese service (some 50 such weapons), but has only very limited value

Dong Feng-3 (CSS-2)

(China)
Type: single-stage intermediate-range ballistic missile
Dimensions: diameter 2·46 m (8·07 ft); length 20·60 m (67·59 ft)
Weight: total round 27,000 kg (59,524 lb)
Post-boost vehicle: not revealed
Propulsion: one storable liquid-propellant rocket
Range: 3200 km (1,988 miles)
CEP: 1390 m (1,520 yards)
Warhead: one 1/3-megaton thermonuclear RV in early examples, or three 100-kiloton nuclear MIRVs in later examples
Launch: hot type from pad
Guidance: radio-updated inertial

Variants
Dong Feng-3: designated **CSS-2** in the US terminology for Chinese weapons, the DF-3 (East Wind-3) missile began to enter service in 1971, and is based on Soviet technology using storable

hypergolic propellants; some 60 such missiles are in service, and an alternative estimate puts range at 2700 km (1,680 miles) with the megaton-class single warhead; the improved variant with MIRVed warhead was first tested in 1986, and is a two-stage weapon
Dong Feng-3A: in 1988 China supplied some 60 modified DF-3s to Saudi Arabia, and these are of a variant trading range for increased payload in the form of a large conventional warhead; maximum payload is thought to be 2045 kg (4,510 lb) of HE carried over a range of 2700 km (1,680 miles)

Dong Feng-4 (CSS-3)

(China)
Type: two-stage limited-range intercontinental ballistic missile
Dimensions: diameter 2·43 m (7·97 ft); length 26·80 m (87·93 ft)
Weight: total round 50,000 kg (110,229 lb)
Payload vehicle: not revealed
Propulsion: (first stage) one storable liquid-propellant rocket and (second stage) one storable liquid-propellant rocket
Range: 7000 km (4,350 miles)
CEP: 930 m (1,017 yards)
Warhead: one 2-megaton thermonuclear RV
Launch: hot type from silo
Guidance: inertial

Variant
Dong Feng-4: designated **CSS-3** in the US terminology for Chinese weapons, the DF-4 (East Wind-4) began to enter service in 1978; only a very few such missiles (perhaps 30) are in service, but the type also forms the basis for the CZ-1 (Long March-1) series of satellite-launch vehicles

Dong Feng-5 (CSS-4)

(China)
Type: two-stage intercontinental ballistic missile
Dimensions: diameter 3·35 m (10·99 ft); length 43·25 m (141·90 ft)
Weight: total round 202,000 kg (445,326 lb)
Payload vehicle: 1400 kg (3,086 lb)
Propulsion: (first stage) four storable liquid-propellant rockets each delivering 70,000-kg (154,321-lb) thrust and (second stage) one storable liquid-propellant rocket
Range: 10,000 km (6,214 miles)

CEP: 930 m (1,017 yards)
Warhead: one 4-megaton thermonuclear RV
Launch: hot type from silo
Guidance: inertial

Variants
Dong Feng-5: designated **CSS-4** in the US terminology for Chinese weapons, the DF-5 (East Wind-5) began to enter very limited service in 1981, and has also been developed as the CZ-2 (Long March-2) two-stage and CZ-3 (Long March-3) three-stage satellite launchers, the former having a length of 32·57 m (106·86 ft)
Dong Feng-6: improved version (also designated CSS-4 by the USA) of the DF-5 but able to carry a 5-megaton thermonuclear warhead over a range of 13,000 km (8,078 miles), and believed to be the genuine production version of the type

Dong Feng-7 (CSS-5)

(China)
Type: three-stage intercontinental ballistic missile
Dimensions: not revealed
Weight: not revealed
Payload vehicle: not revealed
Propulsion: not revealed
Range: not revealed
CEP: not revealed
Warhead: up to 10 MIRVs each with an unrevealed yield
Launch: hot type from a silo
Guidance: inertial

Variant
Dong Feng-7: known in US terminology as the **CSS-5**, the DF-7 (East Wind-7) is China's latest and most capable ICBM with an advanced type of warhead; the whole launch system is based on that of the CZ-3 (Long March-3) satellite launcher, itself derived from the DF-4 ICBM

Aérospatiale SSBS S-3D

(France)
Type: two-stage intermediate-range ballistic missile
Dimensions: diameter 1·50 m (4·92 ft); length 13·80 m (45·28 ft)
Weight: total round 25,800 kg (56,878 lb)
Payload vehicle: not revealed
Propulsion: (first stage) one SEP 902 Herisson (P16) solid-propellant rocket delivering 55,000-kg (121,252-lb) thrust for 76 seconds and (second stage) one SEP Rita II (P6) solid-propellant rocket delivering 32,000-kg (70,547-kg) thrust for 52 seconds
Range: 3000 km (1,864 miles)
CEP: 830 m (908 yards)
Warhead: one 1·2-megaton thermonuclear RV with penetration aids
Launch: hot type from silo
Guidance: Sagem/EMD inertial

Variant
SSBS S-3D: designed as a successor to the SSBS S-2 during the mid- and late 1970s, the S-3D mounts a higher-performance second stage on the first stage of the S-2, and began to enter ser-

vice in 1980 in France's 18 IRBM silos; the improved TN-61 warhead is hardened against high-altitude nuclear explosions, and carries a new generation of penetration aids; some estimates put the range as high as 3500 km (2,175 miles)

Jericho II

(Israel)

Israel is extremely reluctant to divulge any details of the country's ballistic missile development programme, and indeed the first overt public information about such developments came in July 1986, when the USSR warned Israel against the continued development of such weapons; it is thought that the programme began in the early 1960s, resulting in the **Jericho I** development weapon, produced with considerable technical aid from the French and capable of a range of between 450 and 650 km (280 and 404 miles) with a 500-kg (1,102-lb) warhead, probably of the HE type though suggestions of a nuclear type should not be discounted; but after the Franco-Israeli split of 1967, the programme was pushed ahead by Israel and, from 1977, with financial support from Iran when still ruled by Shah Reza Pahlavi, resulting in the **Jericho IIA** which is now operational, probably at a base or bases in the Negev desert close to the Dimona facility at which Israel's nuclear weapons are manufactured; the Jericho II is reported to possess a range of 1500 km (932 miles) and to carry a nuclear warhead, though test flights have revealed a possible alternative of 820-km (510-mile) range with a larger 750-kg (1,653-lb) conventional warhead; it is thought that in the late 1980s the Israelis had an improved **Jericho IIB** version under development, probably to carry a heavier warload over the same basic range; the Jericho IIB may have been test launched for the first time in September 1989

Boeing LGM-30F Minuteman II

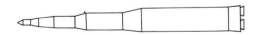

(USA)
Type: three-stage lightweight intercontinental ballistic missile
Dimensions: diameter: 6·00 ft (1·83 m); length 59·71 ft (18·20 m)
Weight: total round 70,000 lb (31,752 kg) with TU-120 motor or 72,810 lb (33,027 kg) with TU-122 motor
Post-boost vehicle: 1,610 lb (730 kg)
Propulsion: (first stage) one Thiokol M55 (TU-120) or M55A1 (TU-122) solid-propellant rocket delivering 200,600- or 202,600-lb (90,992- or 91,900-kg) thrust respectively, (second stage) one Aerojet SR18-AJ-1 solid-propellant rocket delivering 60,000-lb (27,216-kg) thrust, and (third

stage) one Hercules M57A1 solid-propellant rocket delivering 35,000-lb (15,876-kg) thrust
Range: 7,775 miles (12,510 km)
CEP: 400 yards (365 m)
Warhead: one 1·2-megaton W56 thermonuclear warhead (with plutonium for fission, lithium-6 deuteride for fusion and an explosive for the implosion leading to the fission/fusion reaction) carried in an Avco Mk 11C Model 4 RV with Tracor Mk 1A penetration aids
Launch: hot type from a hardened silo
Guidance: Rockwell Autonetics inertial

Variant
LGM-30F Minuteman II: this second-generation lightweight ICBM entered service in 1966, swiftly replacing the LGM-30A and LGM-30B variants of the original Minuteman I type; the Minuteman II is a simple upgrading of the LGM-30B with more advanced guidance (including an eight-target selection capability and chaff-dispensing penetration aids) and greater range; eight of the 450 current rounds are fitted as launch vehicles for the Emergency Rocket Communications System to provide a short-term pre-launch link between the US National Command Authorities and the US strategic forces should the USA's satellite communications system be knocked out; the W56 warhead was developed from December 1960 by the Livermore National Laboratory, and began to enter service in 1965; the warhead dimensions have not been revealed, and weight estimates vary from 1,600 to 2,200 lb (726 to 998 kg); the original W56 Mod 1 warhead has been fully upgraded in current missiles to the W 56 Mod 4 standard with additional safety features and electronic hardening

Boeing LGM-30G Minuteman III

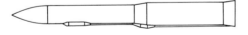

(USA)
Type: three-stage lightweight intercontinental ballistic missile
Dimensions: diameter 6·07 ft (1·85 m); length 59·71 ft (18·20 m)
Weight: total round 78,000 lb (35,381 kg)
Post-boost vehicle: (Mk 12) 2,400 lb (1087 kg) or (Mk 12A) 2,535 lb (1150 kg)
Propulsion: (first stage) one Thiokol M55A1 (TU-122) solid-propellant rocket delivering 202,600-lb (91,900-kg) thrust, (second stage) one Aerojet SR18-AJ-1 solid-propellant rocket delivering 60,625-lb (27,500-kg) thrust, (third stage) one Aerojet/Thiokol SR73-AJ/AG-1 solid-propellant rocket delivering 33,800-lb (15,332-kg) thrust, and (post-boost vehicle) one Bell Aerospace bi-propellant rocket delivering 315-lb (143-kg) thrust
Range: 8,700 miles (14,000 km)
CEP: 300 yards (275 m) with Mk 12 RV or 240 yards (220 m) with Mk 12A RV
Warhead: three 170-kiloton W62 nuclear warheads in three General Electric Mk 12 RVs, or three 335-kiloton W78 nuclear warheads in three Mk 12A MIRVs, both types with penetration aids
Launch: hot type from a hardened silo
Guidance: Rockwell Autonetics inertial

Variant
LGM-30G Minuteman III Model 1: this lightweight ICBM was introduced in 1970 as the third-generation companion to the second-generation Minuteman II, with an improved third stage and MIRVed payload, whose Mk 12 bus contains both chaff- and decoy-dispensing penetration aids
LGM-30G Minuteman III Model 2: introduced in 1979, this upgraded model has an improved Mk 12A RV with higher-yield warheads and more advanced penetration aids, made possible by miniaturization of the warheads and RV components

Martin Marietta LGM-118A Peacekeeper

Left: A dramatic launch view of Minuteman.

Above: An early Peacekeeper launch.

(USA)
Type: four-stage heavyweight intercontinental ballistic missile
Dimensions: diameter 7·67 ft (2·337 m); length 70·87 ft (21·60 m)
Weight: total round 195,000 lb (88,452 kg)
Post-boost vehicle: 7,935 lb (3600 kg)
Propulsion: (first stage) one Thiokol solid-propellant rocket delivering 570,000-lb (258,552-kg) thrust, (second stage) one Aerojet solid-propellant rocket delivering 335,000-lb (151,956-kg) thrust, (third stage) one Hercules solid-propellant rocket delivering 77,000-lb (34,927-kg) thrust, and (fourth stage) one Rockwell hypergolic liquid-propellant rocket delivering unrevealed thrust
Range: 8,700 miles (14,000 km)
CEP: 65/100 yards (60/90 m)
Warhead: 10 335-kiloton W78 thermonuclear warheads carried in 10 Avco Mk 21 (Mk 12 Modified) MIRVs in a Rockwell RS-34 bus
Launch: cold type from a hardened silo, offering a reload capability
Guidance: Rockwell Autonetics/Honeywell/Northrop inertial

Variant
LGM-118A Peacekeeper: conceived as a replacement for the LGM-25 and LGM-30 series, the Peacekeeper is a fourth-generation heavyweight ICBM, and was greatly troubled by political opposition during its relatively smooth development life; the Peacekeeper, previously known as the **Advanced ICBM** or **MX**, began to enter service during 1986 in upgraded Minuteman silos because political pressure prevented any of the proposed mobile basing methods; the type's accuracy makes it a potent counterforce weapon

SS-4 'Sandal'

(USSR)
Type: single-stage medium-range ballistic missile
Dimensions: diameter 1·65 m (5·41 ft); length 22·77 m (74·70 ft)
Weight: total round 27,000 kg (59,524 lb)
Payload vehicle: 1350 kg (2,976 lb)
Propulsion: one liquid-propellant rocket
Range: 2000 km (1,243 miles)
CEP: 2400 m (2,625 yards)
Warhead: one 1-megaton thermonuclear RV or one HE RV of unrevealed weight
Launch: hot type from pad with reload capability when fired from unhardened sites
Guidance: inertial

Variant
SS-4 'Sandal': a development of the SS-3 'Shyster', the SS-4 entered service in 1958 and is now being phased out in favour of the SS-20; another estimate of CEP puts the figure at 2000 m (2,187 yards); the type has the Soviet service designation **R-12** and the production designation **8K63**

SS-11 'Sego'

(USSR)
Type: two-stage lightweight intercontinental ballistic missile
Dimensions: diameter 2·50 m (8·20 ft); length 20·00 m (65·62 ft)
Weight: total round between 45,000 and 48,000 kg (99,205 and 105,820 lb) depending on variant
Payload vehicle: (Models 1 and 2) 1000 kg (2,205 lb) or (Model 3) 1135 kg (2,502 lb)
Propulsion: (first stage) one storable liquid-propellant rocket and (second stage) one storable liquid-propellant rocket
Range: (Model 1) 10,000 km (6,215 miles), (Model 2) 13,000 km (8,080 miles), or (Model 3) 10,600 km (6,585 miles)
CEP: (Model 1) 1400 m (1,530 yards) or (Models 2 and 3) 1110 m (1,215 yards)
Warhead: (Model 1) one 950-kiloton thermonuclear RV, (Model 2) one 950-kiloton thermonuclear RV with penetration aids, or (Model 3) three 100/250-kiloton thermonuclear MRVs
Launch: hot type from hardened silo, with limited reload capability
Guidance: inertial

Variants
SS-11 'Sego' Model 1: this highly capable missile was introduced in 1966 and is a third-generation light ICBM built in very substantial numbers, the Model 1 being distinguished by its single RV and medium range; the missile has the Soviet service designation **UR-100** and the production designation **8K84**; some estimates put the diameter at 2·40 m (7·87 ft) and the length at 19·00 m (62·34 ft)
SS-11 'Sego' Model 2: model of the late 1960s with a single RV and advanced penetration aids
SS-11 'Sego' Model 3: improved operational variant, with longer range and three MRVs; deployed from 1973
SS-11 'Sego' Model 4: development model of the late 1970s with three or six low-yield MIRVs

SS-13 'Savage'

(USSR)
Type: three-stage lightweight intercontinental ballistic missile
Dimensions: diameter 1·70 m (5·58 ft); length 20·00 m (65·62 ft)
Weight: total round 34,000 kg (74,955 lb)
Payload vehicle: 680 kg (1,499 lb)
Propulsion: (first stage) liquid-propellant rocket, (second stage) liquid-propellant rocket and (third stage) liquid-propellant rocket

Range: 8000 km (4,970 miles)
CEP: 1850 m (2,025 yards)
Warhead: one 600-kiloton nuclear RV
Launch: hot type from silo
Guidance: inertial

Variant
SS-13 'Savage': deployed from 1969 onwards, the SS-12 is a third-generation light ICBM comparable to the US Minuteman but built and deployed only in small numbers; other estimates of the type suggest a 750-kiloton warhead carried in a 450-kg (992-lb) payload vehicle over a range of 10,000 km (6,214 miles); the missile has the Soviet military designation **RS-12**

SS-17 'Spanker'

(USSR)
Type: two-stage lightweight intercontinental ballistic missile
Dimensions: diameter 2·50 m (8·20 ft); length 24·00 m (78·74 ft)
Weight: total round 65,000 kg (143,298 lb)
Post-boost vehicle: (Models 1 and 3) 2740 kg (6,041 lb) or (Model 2) 2730 kg (6,019 lb)
Propulsion: (first stage) storable liquid-propellant rocket and (second stage) storable liquid-propellant rocket
Range: (Models 1 and 3) 10,000 km (6,214 miles) or (Model 2) 11,000 km (6,835 miles)
CEP: (Model 1) 440 m (480 yards), (Model 2) 425 m (465 yards) or (Model 3) 350 m (385 yards)
Warhead: (Models 1 and 3) four 750-kiloton nuclear MIRVs or (Model 2) one 6-megaton thermonuclear RV
Launch: cold type from a hardened silo, offering a reload capability
Guidance: inertial

Variants
SS-17 'Spanker' Model 1: this fourth-generation lightweight ICBM was introduced in 1975 and has the Soviet military designation **RS-16**; the type is comparable in many performance regards to the SS-11, but offers the decided strategic advantage of cold launch and thus the practical possibility of the silo being reloaded rapidly
SS-17 'Spanker' Model 2: introduced in 1977, this variant differs from the Model 1 in having a single medium-yield RV and slightly longer range
SS-17 'Spanker' Model 3: introduced in the early 1980s, this variant differs from the Model 1 in having an improved guidance system for reduced CEP; the accuracy of the type enhances the SS-17 family's capability against US missile silos and thus makes it a powerful aspect of the counterforce balance between the USA and USSR

SS-18 'Satan'

(USSR)
Type: two-stage heavyweight intercontinental ballistic missile
Dimensions: diameter 3·00 m (9·84 ft); length 35·00 m (114·83 ft)
Weight: total round 225,000 kg (496,032 lb)
Post-boost vehicle: (Model 1) 7560 kg (16,667 lb), (Models 2 and 4) 7590 kg (16,733 lb) or (Model 3) 7500 kg (16,534 lb)
Propulsion: (first stage) storable liquid-

Above: The latest SS-18 embodies ten warheads.

propellant rocket and (second stage) storable liquid-propellant rocket
Range: (Model 1) 12,000 km (7,455 miles), (Models 2 and 4) 11,000 km (6,835 miles) or (Model 3) 16,000 km (9,940 miles)
CEP: (Models 1 and 2) 425 m (465 yards), (Model 3) 350 m (385 yards), (Model 4) 260 m (285 yards), or (Model 5) less than 260 m (285 yards)
Warhead: (Model 1) one 27-megaton thermonuclear RV, (Model 2) eight to 10 900-kiloton thermonuclear MIRVs, (Model 3) one 20-megaton thermonuclear RV, (Model 4) 10 500-kiloton thermonuclear MIRVs, or (Model 5) 10 1-megaton thermonuclear MIRVs
Launch: cold type from a hardened silo, offering a reload capability
Guidance: inertial

Variants
SS-18 'Satan' Model 1: introduced in 1974 with the Soviet military designation **RS-20**, this fourth-generation heavyweight ICBM is the largest missile so far deployed, and a truly prodigious weapon with range, accuracy and warhead making it primarily effective as a counterforce weapon against missile silos and buried command/communications centres
SS-18 'Satan' Model 2: following the Model 1 in 1976, this variant has a computer-controlled post-boost bus with eight or 10 MIRVs
SS-18 'Satan' Model 3: introduced in 1977, this variant offers greater range and accuracy than the Model 1 with a slightly smaller but still enormously formidable warhead
SS-18 'Satan' Model 4: introduced in 1979, this variant is derived from the Model 2 but has greater accuracy and an improved post-boost bus carrying up to 14 MIRVs (usually 10 real weapons and four decoys, plus penetration aids)
SS-18 'Satan' Model 5: introduced in the mid-1980s, this new variant is still relatively unknown, but is believed to have a range of 9000 km (5,592 miles) with a post-boost bus carrying 10 750-kiloton or 1-megaton thermonuclear MIRVs, probably with greater accuracy than the Model 4; there has been some dispute about this model, which was thought by some to be the SS-18's successor, the SS-26

SS-19 'Stiletto'

(USSR)
Type: two-stage lightweight intercontinental ballistic missile
Dimensions: diameter 2·75 m (9·02 ft); length 22·50 m (73·82 ft)
Weight: total round 78,000 kg (171,958 lb)
Post-boost vehicle: (Model 1) 3420 kg (7,540 lb), (Model 2) 3180 kg (7,011 lb) or (Model 3) 3410 kg (7,518 lb)
Propulsion: (first stage) storable liquid-propellant rocket and (second stage) storable liquid-propellant rocket
Range: (Model 1) 9600 km (5,965 miles) or (Models 2 and 3) 10,000 km (6,215 miles)
CEP: (Model 1) 390 m (425 yards), (Model 2) 260 m (285 yards) or (Model 3) 280 m (305 yards)
Warhead: (Models 1 and 3) six 550-kiloton nuclear MIRVs, or (Model 2) one 10-megaton thermonuclear RV
Launch: hot type from a hardened silo, with limited reload capability
Guidance: inertial

Variants
SS-19 'Stiletto' Model 1: introduced in 1975 as a lightweight ICBM successor (together with the SS-17) to the SS-11, this fourth-generation missile is designated **RS-18** in Soviet military terminology; the type features the same type of advanced guidance as the SS-17 and SS-18, the onboard computer being used either to correct the course (by removing any deviations from the planned norm), or alternatively to generate a new course if this is more efficient; like the SS-17 and SS-18, the SS-19 has the range, accuracy and warhead to make it primarily a counterforce weapon against US missile silos and against buried command and communications centres
SS-19 'Stiletto' Model 2: introduced in 1978, this variant has a single medium-yield RV and much improved accuracy
SS-19 'Stiletto' Model 3: introduced in 1980, this variant reverts to a MIRVed payload, but with better accuracy and range than the Model 1; it is believed that surviving Model 1 and 2 weapons have been retrofitted to this standard, which could have taskings at the operational as well as strategic levels

SS-20 'Saber'

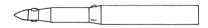

(USSR)
Type: land-mobile intermediate-range ballistic missile
Dimensions: diameter 1·79 m (5·87 ft); length 16·49 m (54·10 ft)
Weight: total round 36,000 kg (79,365 lb)
Post-boost vehicle: not revealed
Propulsion: (first stage) solid-propellant rocket thrust and (second stage) solid-propellant rocket
Range: (Models 1 and 2) 4000 km (2,485 miles) or (Model 3) 7400 km (4,600 miles)
CEP: 425 m (465 yards)
Warhead: (Model 1) one 650-kiloton nuclear or 1·5-megaton thermonuclear RV, (Model 2) three 150-kiloton nuclear MIRVs, or (Model 3) one 50-kiloton nuclear RV
Launch: cold type from wheeled transporter/erector/launcher, with reload capability
Guidance: inertial

Variants
SS-20 'Saber' Model 1: based on the upper two stages of the SS-16 lightweight ICBM, and designed to replace the SS-4 and SS-5 missile systems in the intermediate role, the SS-20 began to enter service in 1977 and is a formidable system offering the advantages of good accuracy with tactical land mobility; the warhead is believed to be a 650-kiloton type, though many reports indicate a 1·5-megaton type; this more powerful variant may have entered only limited service; the type has the production designation **OTR-22** and the Soviet service designation and name **RSD-10 Pioner**
SS-20 'Saber' Model 2: also introduced in 1977, this model offers comparable performance but increased tactical capability through the use of a MIRVed warhead
SS-20 'Saber' Model 3: increased-range variant with a single low-yield warhead and greater range; possibly not operational

SS-24 'Scalpel'

(USSR)
Type: three-stage intercontinental ballistic missile
Dimensions: diameter 2·00 m (6·56 ft); length 21·25 m (69·72 ft)
Weight: total round 100,000 kg (220,459 lb)
Post-boost vehicle: 3625 kg (7,992 lb)
Propulsion: (first stage) solid-propellant rocket, (second stage) solid-propellant rocket and (third stage) solid-propellant rocket
Range: 12,000 + km (7,455 miles)
CEP: 185 m (202 yards)
Warhead: up to 10 100-kiloton nuclear MIRVs
Launch: cold type from superhardened silos or special rail cars, offering a reload capability
Guidance: stellar-inertial

Variant
SS-24 'Scalpel': entering service in the mid-1980s, the SS-24 is the Soviet fifth-generation counterpart to the US Peacekeeper, and has also been developed for a mobile basing system using special rail cars hidden in the tunnels of those parts of the Soviet rail network without

overhead wires; the type entered development in about 1974, and suffered a comparatively high number of failures in test launches that began in 1982; the type has been operational since 1985 in its silo-based form and since 1987 in its rail-based form, mainly in northern Russia around Archangel, so it must be assumed that the failings (mainly in the first stage) have been overcome in the production weapon, which offers a formidable combination of range, accuracy and warhead; the missile has the Soviet designation **RS-22**, and it is an indication of how accurate the West believes this missile to be that yield estimates for each of the warheads has been reduced from 350 kilotons to 100 kilotons

SS-25 'Sickle'

(USSR)
Type: three-stage lightweight intercontinental ballistic missile
Dimensions: diameter 1·79 m (5·87 ft); length 18·00 m (59·06 ft)
Weight: total round 37,000 kg (81,570 lb)
Post-boost vehicle: between 680 and 1000 kg (1,500 and 2,205 lb)
Propulsion: (first stage) solid-propellant rocket, (second stage) solid-propellant rocket and (third stage) solid-propellant rocket
Range: 9000+ km (5,590+ miles)
CEP: between 190 and 600 m (208 and 656 yards)
Warhead: one 550-kiloton nuclear RV or three/four 150-kiloton nuclear MIRVs
Launch: cold type from hardened silo or wheeled transporter/erector/launcher vehicle, offering a reload capability
Guidance: stellar-inertial

Variant
SS-25 'Sickle': according to the Soviets this is an upgraded version of the SS-13 rather than a new design (hence the Soviet designation **RS-12M**), but the result is a fifth-generation road-mobile

weapon with great accuracy, considerably greater throw-weight, and the offensive capability of the US Minuteman lightweight ICBM; the type is replacing the SS-11, and is an outgrowth of the SS-13 and SS-16 programmes, the failure of the latter adding impetus to the development of the SS-25 from the early 1970s

SS-X-26

(USSR)
Type: three-stage intercontinental ballistic missile
Dimensions: not revealed
Weight: not revealed
Post-boost vehicle: not revealed
Propulsion: (first stage) solid-propellant rocket, (second stage) solid-propellant rocket and (third stage) solid-propellant rocket
Range: not revealed
CEP: not revealed
Warhead: up to 10 MIRVs of unrevealed kiloton yield
Launch: cold-launch from a hardened silo, offering reload capability
Guidance: inertial

Variant
SS-X-26: beginning flight trials in 1986, this is believed to be the prospective replacement for the SS-18, and is thus a massive solid-propellant weapon offering greater throw-weight (a post-boost bus with 10 warheads) and accuracy than its predecessor

SS-X-27

(USSR)
Type: three-stage intercontinental ballistic missile
Dimensions: not revealed

Weight: not revealed
Post-boost vehicle: not revealed
Propulsion: (first stage) solid-propellant rocket, (second stage) solid-propellant rocket and (third stage) solid-propellant rocket
Range: not revealed
CEP: not revealed
Warhead: not revealed
Launch: cold type from a hardened silo, offering reload capability
Guidance: inertial

Variant
SS-X-27: apparently designated **RS-20M** by the Soviets in an attempt to convince the world that it is an SS-18 derivative, this truly enormous prototype solid-propellant weapon entered flight test in 1986 and is clearly designed as successor to the SS-18

SS-X-28

(USSR)
Type: two-stage intermediate-range ballistic missile
Dimensions: not revealed
Weight: not revealed
Post-boost vehicle: not revealed
Propulsion: not revealed
Range: not revealed
CEP: not revealed
Warhead: one nuclear RV of unrevealed kiloton yield
Launch: cold type from wheeled transporter/erector/launcher, with reload capability
Guidance: inertial

Variant
SS-X-28: currently in flight test, this is believed to be a high-mobility IRBM that may possibly be the missile once thought to be designated **SS-20 Model 5**

Aérospatiale ASMP

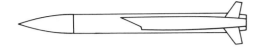

(France)
Type: air-launched theatre/strategic cruise missile
Dimensions: diameter about 0·38 m (1,25 ft) and width across inlets about 0·82 m (2·69 m); length 5·38 m (17·65 ft); span 0·956 m (3·14 ft)
Weight: total round 900 kg (1,984 lb)
Warhead: CEA 100/150-kiloton nuclear, though estimates of 300-kiloton yield have also been quoted
Propulsion: one SNPE Alain integral solid-propellant booster rocket and one ramjet sustainer
Performance: speed Mach 3 at high altitude and Mach 2 at low altitude; range varies from 300 km (186 miles) at high altitude to 80 km (50 miles) at low altitude
CEP: not revealed
Guidance: Sagem inertial and terrain-following

Variant
ASMP: designed from 1978 after an abortive beginning from 1971, the Air-Sol Moyenne Portée (medium-range air-to-surface) is an air-launched cruise missile carried by the Dassault-Breguet Mirage IVP bomber (after conversion from Mirage IVA standard), the Dassault-Breguet Mirage 2000N low-altitude strike aeroplane and the Dassault-Breguet Super Etendard strike fighter. The ASMP entered service in 1986, and provides the French air forces with a stand-off nuclear capability against large targets such as railway yards and other communications hubs, major concentrations of reinforcements and/or materiel, and command centres; the type can fly a high-altitude profile ending with a steep supersonic dive, or a low-altitude terrain-following profile of shorter range

---

Boeing AGM-86B

(USA)
Type: air-launched strategic cruise missile
Dimensions: diameter 2·275 ft (0·69 m); length 20·75 ft (6·325 m); span 12·00 ft (3·66 m)
Weight: total round 3,200 lb (1452 kg)
Warhead: 270-lb (122·5-kg) 200-kiloton W80 Mod 1 nuclear (using oralloy for fission, tritium for fusion and PBX-9502 Improved HE for implosion leading to fission/fusion reaction)
Propulsion: one Williams Research F107-WR-101 turbofan delivering 600-lb (272-lb) thrust
Performance: speed 500 mph (805 km/h); range 1,550 miles (2495 km)
CEP: between 30 and 100 ft (9 and 30·5 m)
Guidance: Litton P-1000 inertial with McDonnell Douglas DPW-23 TERCOM (TERrain COntour Matching) update

Left: An AGM-86B with flight surfaces unfolded.

Variant
AGM-86B: entering service in 1981, this air-launched cruise missile is one of the US Air Force's most important weapons, some 170 Boeing B-52G bombers being configured to carry 12 such weapons apiece (six on each of two underwing stations) plus four AGM-69A SRAMs and four free-fall nuclear weapons in the bomb bay; work is under way on modifying 95 B-52H bombers to the same standard, with provision on both Stratofortress variants for the weapons-bay carriage of the Common Strategic Rotary Launcher to carry eight AGM-86B and/or AGM-69A SRAM missiles; it is estimated that 85% per cent of the strategic targets in the USSR can be reached by AGM-86Bs launched safely from areas more than 225 miles (360 km) from Soviet airspace, with the SRAMs available for defence suppression should the bombers have to penetrate Soviet airspace; the Rockwell B-1B supersonic penetration bomber can carry eight AGM-86Bs on a rotary launcher in the weapons bay, plus another 14 under the wings; though 4,348 AGM-86Bs were planned, only 1,715 have been built as newer cruise missiles (of the Convair ACM type) are planned with greater capabilities at a time when the Soviets are strengthening their defence against air-launched cruise missiles; from 1985 AGM-86Bs have been retrofitted with an ECM package to improve their capabilities against such Soviet defences

---

General Dynamics (Convair) AGM-129A Advanced Cruise Missile

(USA)
Type: air-launched long-range cruise missile
Dimensions: not revealed
Weight: total round probably in the order of 3,300 lb (1497 kg)
Warhead: 200-kiloton nuclear
Propulsion: one Williams International F112 turbofan delivering unrevealed
Performance: speed about 500 mph (805 km/h); range at least 1,700 miles (2735 km)
CEP: not revealed
Guidance: not revealed

Variant
AGM-129 Advanced Cruise Missile: very little is known of the development of this highly classified missile, which is scheduled to enter service in the early 1990s; the programme was launched in 1977 with the object of improving performance in crucial fields such as low observability ('stealth') and thus increased capability to penetrate into airspace protected by advanced air defences, improved propulsion for greater range through installation of greater power with reduced specific fuel consumption to allow the missile to detour round the most heavily defended Soviet airspace areas, greater survivability through the incorporation of the most advanced electronic and IR countermeasures, and enhanced operational flexibility through the use of the latest computer hardware and software; that development of the ACM had been awarded to General Dynamics was announced in 1983, and the type is intended for use on Boeing B-52, Rockwell B-1 and Northrop B-2 bombers;

the most significant features are longer range than the AGM-86B combined with a high measure of 'stealth' technology, especially in terms of IR emission and radar reflectivity, to reduce the missile's observability

---

AS-15 'Kent'

(USSR)
Type: air-launched theatre/strategic cruise missile
Dimensions: diameter 0·65 m (2·13 ft); length 6·90 m (22·64 ft); span 3·45 m (11·32 ft)
Weight: total round 1500 kg (3,310 lb)
Warhead: 150/250-kiloton thermonuclear or HE of unrevealed weight
Propulsion: one turbojet or turbofan delivering unrevealed thrust
Performance: speed about Mach 0·9; range 2750 or 3000 km (1,710 or 1,865 miles)
CEP: estimated at 45 m (150 ft)
Guidance: inertial with terrain-following update

Variant
AS-15 'Kent': this is the air-launched version of the USSR's standard cruise missile, and began to enter service during the mid-1980s in air-, ground-, ship- and submarine-launched forms; the AS-15 is currently operated by the Tupolev Tu-95 'Bear-H', and will initially equip the new Tupolev Tu-160 'Blackjack' supersonic variable-geometry bomber; the weapon is roughly comparable with the US AGM-86B; all data are highly speculative, other estimates putting the diameter at 0·50 m (1·64 ft), length at 7·00 m (22·97 ft) and span at 3·00 m (9·84 ft)

AS-19

(USSR)
Type: air-launched strategic cruise missile
Dimensions: diameter not revealed; length about 7·00 m (22·97 ft); span not revealed
Weight: total round about 2000 kg (4,409 lb)
Warhead: 200-kiloton thermonuclear
Propulsion: one ramjet or hybrid rocket/ramjet delivering unrevealed thrust
Performance: speed Mach 2+; range about 3250 km (2,020 miles)
CEP: not revealed
Guidance: not revealed

Variant
AS-19: virtually nothing is known of this advanced cruise missile, which is currently under development with the Western interim designation **BL-10** as the definitive armament of the Tupolev Tu-160 'Blackjack' strategic bomber; it is certain, however, that the Soviets have moved along the same basic design and development path as the Americans, and therefore emphasized 'stealth' (low observability) in an airframe of higher performance than the US Advanced Cruise Missile; this may mean that while the AS-19 has low electro-magnetic observability, its IR emission may be significantly higher than that of the Convair AGM-129A ACM

CPMIEC C-101

(China)

Type: air-launched short/medium-range tactical anti-ship missile

Dimensions: diameter 0·54 m (1·77 ft); length 5·60 m (18·37 ft); span not revealed

Weight: total round not revealed

Warhead: HE (blast fragmentation type)

Propulsion: two solid-propellant booster rockets each delivering an unrevealed thrust, and two sustainer ramjets each delivering an unrevealed thrust

Performance: speed supersonic; range 80 km (50 miles)

Guidance: strapdown inertial for midcourse phase, and monopulse active radar for terminal phase

Variants

C-101: more is known of other Chinese air-launched anti-ship weapons than of the C-101, due to enter service in 1990; it is launched with the aid of two solid-propellant boosters whose nozzles are angled obliquely downward, and cruises on two ramjets for a very high attack speed

Hai Ying-3: larger Sea Eagle-3 version of the C-101 for surface- and air-launch applications; the missile has a diameter of 0·76 m (2·49 ft) and a length of 9·00 m (29·53 ft), providing volume for a larger warhead and more fuel to avoid any loss of range; the increased diameter could also allow the installation of a wider-diameter radar antenna for greater lock-on range, and the missile is launched (possibly in its surface-launched form) by four strap-on solid-propellant boosters

CPMIEC C-601

(China)

Type: air-launched medium-range tactical anti-ship missile

Dimensions: diameter 0·90 m (2·95 ft); length 7·38 m (24·21 ft); span 2·40 m (8·87 ft)

Weight: total round 2440 kg (5,379 lb)

Warhead: 225-kg (496·0-lb) HE (blast fragmentation type)

Propulsion: one solid-propellant booster rocket delivering an unrevealed thrust, and one sustainer turbojet delivering an unrevealed thrust

Performance: speed 1100 km/h (684 mph); range 160 km (100 miles)

Guidance: strapdown inertial for midcourse phase, and monopulse active radar for terminal phase

Variant

C-601: few facts have been revealed about this useful anti-ship missile, which began to enter service in 1982 as the primary armament of the H-6D, the dedicated anti-shipping version of the Chinese-built version of the Soviet Tupolev Tu-16 'Badger' bomber, which can carry two of the type on underwing hardpoints for launch after a suitable target has been acquired by the aircraft's substantial undernose search radar; after launch the missile descends to low altitude for the approach to its target, probably descending to sea-skimming height for the attack, which is undertaken under control of the missile's active monopulse radar incorporating ECCM; the C-601 has large delta wings and triple tail surfaces set at an angle of 120° to each other, and some West-

ern analysts have suggested liquid-propellant rocket rather than turbojet propulsion; the weapon is clearly derived from the HY-2 ship-launched missile, and thus ultimately from the Soviet SS-N-2 'Styx' weapon with features of the AS-5 'Kelt', and in the US standard terminology is known as the **CAS-N-1**; the missile is possibly produced in different variants as the FL-2 and improved FL-7 ship-launched versions

CPMIEC C-801

(China)

Type: air-launched medium-range tactical anti-ship missile

Dimensions: diameter 0·36 m (1·18 ft); length 5·814 m (19·07 ft); span 1·11 m (3·64 ft)

Weight: total round 815 kg (1,797 lb)

Warhead: 165-kg (363·75-lb) HE (semi-armour-piercing type)

Propulsion: one solid-propellant booster rocket delivering an unrevealed thrust, and one solid-propellant sustainer rocket delivering an unrevealed thrust

Performance: speed 1100 km/h (684 mph); range 50 km (31·1 miles)

Guidance: strapdown inertial for midcourse phase, and monopulse active radar for terminal phase

Variants

C-801: introduced to Chinese service in 1983, the C-801 is an advanced anti-ship missile of which little is known; in its surface-launched versions the weapon is said to be compatible with the fire-control system used with the Chinese HY-2 and FL-1 derivatives of the Soviet SS-N-2 'Styx', and the missile can also be launched from aircraft, shore batteries, ships and surfaced submarines, thereafter cruising at a preset altitude of 20 or 30 m (66 or 98 ft) before descending to a height of between 5 and 7 m (16·4 and 23 ft) for the radar-homing approach and final diving attack; the weapon is known in Chinese service as the **Ying Ji-6** (Eagle Strike-6)

C-802: introduced in 1988, this is a version of the C-801 with a liquid-propellant turbojet rather than a solid-propellant rocket sustainer motor for greater range; the variant is externally identical with the C-801 in everything but its ventral inlet for the turbojet's air

CPMIEC Hai Ying-4

(China)

Type: air-launched medium-range tactical anti-ship missile

Dimensions: diameter 0·76 m (2·49 ft); length 7·36 m (24·15 ft); span 2·75 m (9·02 ft)

Weight: total round 3300 kg (7,275 lb)

Warhead: 500-kg (1,102-lb) HE (semi-armour-piercing type)

Propulsion: one solid-propellant booster rocket delivering an unrevealed thrust, and one turbojet delivering an unrevealed thrust

Performance: speed between 980 and 1040 km/h (609 and 646 mph); range 150 km (93 miles)

Guidance: strapdown inertial for midcourse phase, and monopulse active radar (or passive IR seeking) for terminal phase

Variant

Hai Ying-4: the Sea Eagle-4 is a development of the HY-2, the Chinese version of the Soviet SS-N-2 'Styx' surface-launched anti-ship missile, with a slightly longer fuselage and a small turbojet (aspirated through a ventral inlet) replacing the earlier missile's rocket propulsion for much-improved range; the HY-4 is designed for launch by the H-6D anti-ship variant of the H-6 bomber (Chinese-built version of the Soviet Tupolev Tu-16 'Badger'), which can carry two such missiles under its wings; after air launch the missile cruises at an altitude between 70 and 200 m (230 and 655 ft), and its effective range is from 35 to 135 km (22 to 84 miles); the type entered service in 1971, and there is also a shore-launched version with a jettisonable booster rocket

Aérospatiale AS.15TT

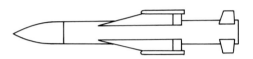

(France)

Type: helicopter-launched short-range tactical anti-ship missile

Dimensions: diameter 0·188 m (0·62 ft); length 2·30 m (7·55 ft); span 0·564 m (1·85 ft)

Weight: total round 103 kg (227 lb)

Warhead: 29·7-kg (65·5-lb) HE (blast fragmentation type)

Propulsion: one SNPE/Aérospatiale Anubis solid-propellant rocket delivering an unrevealed thrust for 45·2 seconds

Performance: speed 1000 km/h (621 mph); range 16 km (10 miles)

Guidance: (height) Thomson-CSF preprogrammed autopilot designed to produce a reducing cruise altitude to a height determined by TRT radar altimeter, and (bearing) radar command

Variant

AS.15TT: entering service in the mid-1980s, the AS.15TT (Air-Sol-15 Tous Temps, or all-weather air-to-surface type 15) missile was financed mainly by Saudi Arabia within the orbit of the 'Sawari' military equipment contract with France; the missile was designed as successor to the AS.12 as the primary weapon of ship- and shore-based light helicopters tasked with countering FACs and other small naval units, notably landing craft; the Aérospatiale SA 365 Dauphin 2 and Aérospatiale AS 332 Super Puma helicopters are the two helicopters qualified to operate the AS.15TT, which is controlled in bearing by the launch helicopter's Thomson-CSF Agrion-15 radar, and in height by a programme that lets the missile down to sea-skimming height for the approach and to wavetop height for the final 300 m (985 ft) of the attack

Aérospatiale AM.39 Exocet

(France)

Type: air-launched medium-range tactical anti-ship missile
Dimensions: diameter 0·35 m (1·15 ft); length 4·69 m (15·39 ft); span 1·10 m (3·61 ft)
Weight: total round 655 kg (1,444 lb)
Warhead: 165-kg (363·75-lb) HE (blast fragmentation type)
Propulsion: one SNPE Condor solid-propellant booster rocket delivering an unrevealed thrust for 2 seconds, and one SNPE Helios solid-propellant sustainer rocket delivering an unrevealed thrust for 150 seconds
Performance: speed 1140 km/h (708 mph) or Mach 0·93; range between 50 and 70 km (31 and 43·5 miles) depending on launch altitude
Guidance: inertial plus TRT RAM.01 radar altimeter for midcourse phase, and EMD ADAC monopulse active radar for terminal phase

Variants

AM.38 Exocet: most widely employed of Western anti-ship missiles so far as combat operations are concerned, the Exocet was designed in the late 1960s as the MM.38 ship-launched missile and began to enter service in 1974; since then the missile has been developed in several forms and seen extensive use in the Anglo-Argentine Falklands War of 1982 and in the Iraqi-Iranian Gulf War of 1979-1988; development of the Exocet's air-launched version began in 1975, and the first round was test fired in December 1976 with service deliveries following from July 1977; this initial AM.38 was a limited-production helicopter-launched version of the MM.38 using SNPE Epervier booster and SNPE Eole V sustainer rocket motors with concentric nozzles, and a 1-second ignition delay was built into the booster to avoid damage to the launch platform
AM.39 Exocet: full-production air-launched version of the MM.38 with revised propulsion in a shorter body, reducing weight but also increasing range; the missile is launched towards the target on range and bearing data provided by the launcher's sensors and fire-control system, and cruises at low altitude until some 10 km (6·21 miles) from the anticipated target position, when the active seeker head is turned on, the target acquired and the terminal phase initiated at the one of three heights preselected at launch on the basis of sea state; residual fuel adds considerably to the effects of the warhead detonation, which has in itself proved somewhat troublesome and at times unreliable; the French launch platforms most commonly associated with the Exocet are the Aérospatiale SA 321 Super Frelon helicopter and the Dassault-Breguet Super Etendard carrierborne attack fighter; late-production rounds have the Super ADAC homing radar, which offers the considerable tactical advantage of improved ECCM

Aérospatiale/MBB ANS

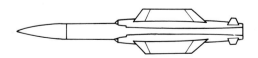

(France & West Germany)
Type: air-launched short/medium-range tactical anti-ship missile

Dimensions: diameter 0·35 m (1·15 ft); length 5·70 m (18·70 ft); span 1·10 m (3·61 ft)
Weight: total round 950 kg (2,094 lb)
Warhead: 180-kg (396·8-lb) HE (penetrating blast fragmentation type)
Propulsion: one MBB integral rocket-ramjet serving first as a solid-propellant booster rocket delivering an unrevealed thrust, and then as a rocket-ramjet sustainer delivering an unrevealed thrust
Performance: speed Mach 2 at sea level and Mach 3 at altitude; range 6/180+ km (3·7/112+ miles)
Guidance: strapdown inertial for midcourse phase, and ESD Super ADAC active radar for terminal phase

Variant

ANS: the Anti-Navire Supersonique (supersonic anti-ship) missile is currently under development by Aérospatiale and MBB for service in the early 1990s as successor to the Exocet and Kormoran air-launched missiles in French and West German service respectively, though selected export customers are likely to be offered the weapon; the new missile features an advanced propulsion system, with an integral rocket for acceleration to Mach 2 cruising speed, at which it becomes a hybrid rocket ramjet; this makes for very high attack speed thereby reducing the time available to the target for the target to implement any countermeasures, and the terminal guidance will probably incorporate a home-on-jam mode; the ANS is also planned with exceptional ECCM features

MBB Kormoran

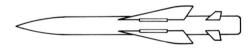

(West Germany)
Type: air-launched medium-range tactical anti-ship missile
Dimensions: diameter 0·344 m (1·13 ft); length 4·40 m (14·44 ft); span 1·00 m (3·28 ft)
Weight: total round 600 kg (1,323 lb)
Warhead: 165-kg (363·75-lb) HE (radial blast fragmentation type)
Propulsion: two SNPE Prades solid-propellant booster rockets each delivering 2750-kg (6,063-lb) thrust for 1 second, and one SNPE Eole IV solid-propellant sustainer rocket delivering 285-kg (628-lb) thrust for 100 seconds
Performance: speed 1160 km/h (721 mph); range 37 km (23 miles)
Guidance: SFENA-Bodenseewerk strap-down inertial plus TRT radar altimeter for midcourse phase, and Thomson-CSF RE576 active/passive radar for terminal phase

Variants

Kormoran: developed from the Nord AS.34 missile projected in France, the Kormoran entered West German naval service in 1977 as the primary anti-ship weapon of Lockheed F-104G Starfighters operated by the Marineflieger; the weapon is now used on the Panavia Tornados operated by the same service and by the Italian

air force; the missile cruises at a height of 30 m (100 ft) to the approximate location of the target, then descends to sea-skimming height for the preset passive or active radar attack; the warhead is particularly impressive, and is designed to penetrate up to 90 mm (3·54 in) of metal before the 16 radially-disposed charges detonate to pierce the ship's bottom, decks and internal bulkheads
Kormoran 2: improved 630-kg (1,389-lb) weapon with a new Thomson-CSF solid-state radar seeker (with digital signal processing for higher hit probability and enhanced ECCM), greater range, and a 220-kg (485-lb) warhead of greater penetration capability; the booster section of the rocket provides 6425-kg (14,164-lb) thrust, and the sustainer section 275-kg (606-lb) thrust

IMI Gabriel Mk IIIA/S

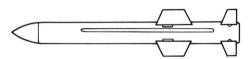

(Israel)
Type: air-launched short-range tactical anti-ship missile
Dimensions: diameter 0·34 m (1·12 ft); length 3·84 m (12·60 ft); span 1·10 m (3·61 ft)
Weight: total round 558 kg (1,230 lb)
Warhead: 150-kg (331-lb) HE (blast fragmentation type)
Propulsion: one solid-propellant rocket delivering 3600-kg (7,937-lb) thrust
Performance: speed transonic; range 40 km (25 miles)
Guidance: inertial plus radar altimeter for midcourse phase, and active radar for terminal phase

Variants

Gabriel Mk IIIA/S: air-launched version of the ship-launched Gabriel Mk III, itself derived from the earlier Gabriel Mk I and Gabriel Mk II anti-ship missiles; the Gabriel Mk I was developed in the 1960s as a 21-km (13-mile) range missile for use by FACs, while the Gabriel Mk II introduced a longer body for more fuel as a means of boosting range to 36 km (22 miles); the ship-launched Gabriel Mk III introduced a frequency-agile active radar seeker, though the optical and semi-active radar homing systems of the Gabriel Mks I and II can also be used to provide greater tactical flexibility and continued viability against ECM; the weapon therefore has three guidance modes (fire-and-forget, fire-and-update via a data-link from a targeting helicopter, and fire-and-command using the launch vessel's radar for better targeting data); the missile cruises at an altitude of 100 m (330 ft) and then descends to 20 m (66 ft) for the approach to the target, the attack phase being flown at a height pre-set height at 1·5, 2·5 or 4 m (4·9, 8·25 or 13·1 ft) depending on sea state; the Gabriel Mk IIIA/S is the air-launched version of this model with a slightly longer body, reduced-span wings and lighter weight in a weapon that is faster but shorter-ranged; the missile has three operating modes: range-and-bearing launch (using radar-derived data), range-and-bearing launch (using manually-entered data), and bearing-only launch

Gabriel Mk IIIA/S ER: extended-range version of the Gabriel Mk IIIA/S with a longer sustainer rocket that increases weight to 600 kg (1,323 lb) and range to 60 km (37 miles), which is about that of the ship-launched Gabriel Mk III; the Gabriel Mk IIIA/S ER has the same guidance options as the Gabriel Mk IIIA/S

Gabriel Mk IV: updated version planned for development in the late 1980s and early 1990s with a length of 4·70 m (15·42 ft) and powered by a small ventrally-aspirated turbojet for a range of 200 km (124 miles); there will no doubt be provision for mid-course update of the INS of this variant

Sistel Sea Killer Mk 2

(Italy)
Type: helicopter-launched short/medium-range tactical anti-ship missile
Dimensions: diameter 0·206 m (0·68 ft) for body and 0·316 m (1·04 ft) for warhead; length 4·832 m (15·85 ft); span 0·978 m (3·20 ft)
Weight: total round 340 kg (750 lb)
Warhead: 210-kg (463-lb) HE (semi-armour-piercing blast fragmentation type)
Propulsion: one SEP 299 double-base solid-propellant booster rocket delivering 4400-kg (9,700-lb) thrust for 1·6 seconds, and one SEP 300 composite solid-propellant sustainer rocket delivering 100-kg (220-lb) thrust for 73 seconds
Performance: speed 1080 km/h (671 mph); range 25 km (15·5 miles)
Guidance: combination of autopilot (azimuth) and radar altimeter (height) for midcourse phase to sea-skimming height, and SMA active radar for terminal phase

Variant
Sea Killer Mk 2: this is a light anti-ship weapon originally designed as the Sea Killer Mk 1 for use from fast attack craft and possessing a range of only 10 km (6·2 miles) with its 170-kg (375-lb) warhead as it had only single-stage propulsion; the Sea Killer Mk 2 introduced a tandem-propulsion system for greater range with a larger warhead; the specifically air-launched version of the Sea Killer Mk 2 is part of the Marte system, in which the missile is fired from a helicopter fitted with the SMA APQ-706 radar: smaller helicopters such as the Agusta (Bell) AB.212ASW can carry one missile and the appropriate guidance equipment, but larger machines such as the Agusta (Sikorsky) ASH-3 can carry two missiles; the original Marte Mk 1 system uses a simple development of the Sea Killer Mk 2 missile with the original parallel-section warhead weighing 70 kg (154 lb) within an overall missile weight of 300 kg (661 lb) and length of 4·70 m (15·42 ft) complete with the 1·06-m (3·48-ft) booster stage; guidance over the maximum range of 20 km (12·4 miles) is performed by an autopilot and radar altimeter for the midcourse phase and Sistel radar beam-riding and/or optical guidance for the terminal phase; the Marte Mk 2 system uses the improved Sea Killer Mk 2 described in the specification above, and possessing a revised warhead and guidance section based on that of the Otomat surface-launched anti-ship missile; the warhead weighs 210 kg (463 lb) with 60 kg (132 lb) of HE, and includes active radar homing to provide the missile with true 'fire-and-forget' capability; this improved Sea

Above: Italy's Sea Killer launched by an SH-3.

Killer Mk 2 is also planned for the Aeritalia/Aermacchi/EMBRAER AMX and Aermacchi M.B.339C fixed-wing light attack aircraft, though the higher speeds of these launch platforms allow the missile to be used without its 1·087-m (3·57-ft) booster

Mitsubishi Type 80 (ASM-1)

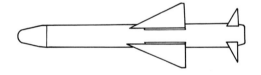

(Japan)
Type: air-launched medium-range tactical anti-ship missile
Dimensions: diameter 0·35 m (1·15 ft); length 4·00 m (13·12 ft); span 1·20 m (3·94 ft)
Weight: total round 610 kg (1,345 lb)
Warhead: 200-kg (440·9-lb) HE (blast fragmentation type)
Propulsion: one Nissan Motors single-stage solid-propellant rocket delivering an unrevealed thrust
Performance: speed 1100 km/h (684 mph); range 80 km (50 miles)
Guidance: Japan Aviation Electronics strapdown inertial plus TRT radar altimeter for midcourse phase, and Mitsubishi Electronics active radar for terminal phase

Variant
Type 80: developed between 1973 and 1980, and introduced in 1981 as the primary anti-ship armament of the Mitsubishi F-1 attack fighter, the **ASM-1** is a simple yet effective anti-ship missile of the fire-and-forget type; the missile is notable for its comparatively high speed; Mitsubishi is currently developing for the Japanese Self-Defense Air Force a long-range radar-homing missile optimized for the anti-ship role, and it is conceivable that this uses the Type 88 with a different seeker

Kongsberg Penguin Mk III

(Norway)
Type: air-launched medium-range tactical anti-ship missile
Dimensions: diameter 0·28 m (0·92 ft); length 3·17 m (10·40 ft); span 1·00 m (3·28 ft)
Weight: total round 372 kg (820 lb)
Warhead: 121-kg (267-lb) HE (semi-armour-piercing blast fragmentation type)
Propulsion: one Raufoss Ammunisjons/Atlantic Research Corporation solid-propellant rocket delivering an unrevealed thrust
Performance: speed 1100 km/h (684 mph); range 60 km (37 miles)
Guidance: Kongsberg Vapenfabrikk inertial for midcourse phase, and Kongsberg Vapenfabrikk IR homing for terminal phase

Variants
Penguin Mk II Mod 7: the Penguin was the Western world's first anti-ship missile, the original Penguin Mk I having been conceived in the early 1960s to enter service in 1972 as part of Norway's defence against maritime invasion; this initial model was optimized for good performance in the country's peculiar coastal waters after launch from FACs and other small naval platforms; the missile's launch weight is 340 kg (750 lb) including the powerful warhead, which is essentially identical with that of the US AGM-12B Bullpup ASM; the missiles still in service are being upgraded to Penguin Mk I Mod 7 standard with the seeker of the Penguin Mk II Mod 3; the Penguin Mk II is an improved Mk I with range boosted to 30 km (18·6 miles); the type entered service in the early 1980s, and surviving rounds are being upgraded to Penguin Mk II Mod 5 standard with enhanced seeker performance; the basic type has been further developed for helicopter launch as the Penguin Mk II Mod 7 (US designation **AGM-119B** for use with helicopters such as the Kaman SH-2F Seasprite and Sikorsky SH-60B Seahawk) with a weight of 385 kg (849 lb) and a length of 3·02 m (9·91 ft); this variant includes a number of Penguin Mk III improvements (notably in the seeker and signal processor), and has a new two-stage rocket and fully digital electronics, unlike

Above: Penguin slung beneath a Norwegian
F-104G.

Penguin Mk III: air-launched development
intended primarily for the Norwegian air force's
General Dynamics F-16 Fighting Falcon multi-
role fighters; the variant has the US designation
AGM-119A, and is characterized by its longer
body, shorter-span wings, single-stage rocket
and radar altimeter; the Penguin Mk III is a highly
capable weapon programmed to fly a circuitous
approach to the target via one or more waypoints
after launch on the basis of radar information from
the launch aircraft, or of visual sighting with data
entered into the missile via the pilot's HUD or
optical sight; as with the earlier versions of the
missile, the use of IR terminal homing (activated
only when the missile has reached the target's
anticipated position) gives the target vessel virtually no warning of the missile's imminent arrival,
so reducing the time which is available for
countermeasures

Saab Rbs15F

(Sweden)

Type: air-launched medium/long-range tactical anti-ship missile

Dimensions: diameter 0·50 m (1·64 ft); length 4·35 m (14·27 ft); span 1·40 m (4·59 ft)

Weight: total round 598 kg (1,318 lb)

Warhead: HE (blast fragmentation type)

Propulsion: one Microturbo TRI 60-2 Model 077 turbojet delivering 377-kg (831-lb) thrust

Performance: speed high subsonic; range 150 km (93 miles)

Guidance: preprogrammed autopilot plus radar altimeter for midcourse phase, and Philips Elektronikindustrier active radar for terminal phase

Variant

Rbs15F: this advanced weapon entered service in 1988 in its 780-kg (1,720-lb) Rbs15M ship-launched variant; after onboard programming using data derived from the ship's sensors and fire-control system, the missile is fired with the aid of two jettisonable boosters to fly at medium or low altitude (the former capability being essential in the Swedish archipelago) to the point at which the active seeker is turned on, whereupon the missile drops to sea-skimming height for the attack over a maximum range of 100 km (62 miles); development from 1982 has evolved the Rbs15F air-launched version, which has no requirement for the solid-propellant boosters, and is thus lighter as well as longer-ranged; the most notable feature of the Rbs15 is its advanced Philips seeker, which has digital signal processing for its frequency-agile operating method, a choice of search modes and patterns, variable ECCM, and target-choice logic to allow the missile to choose the most important of several possible targets

AS-2 'Kipper'

(USSR)

Type: air-launched long-range tactical/operational anti-ship missile

Dimensions: diameter 0·90 m (2·95 ft); length 10·00 m (32·81 ft); span 4·88 m (16·01 ft in)

Weight: total round 4200 kg (9,259 lb)

Warhead: 1000-kg (2,205-lb) HE (blast fragmentation type) or possibly nuclear with a medium-kiloton yield

Propulsion: one turbojet (possibly Lyul'ka AL-5) delivering 5500-kg (12,125-lb) thrust

Performance: speed Mach 1·2; range 185 km (115 miles) from a high-altitude launch

Guidance: autopilot with radio update capability for midcourse phase, and active radar for terminal phase

Variant

AS-2 'Kipper': introduced in 1960 as the main anti-ship weapon of the Tupolev Tu-16 'Badger-C', the AS-2 homes on targets with a large radar signature, and is obsolescent by modern standards because of its size and lack of electronic sophistication; the type flies to the anticipated target position under command of an autopilot, which can be overridden by data-linked commands from a midcourse guidance helicopter or aeroplane, and then homes on information provided by its onboard active radar seeker; the pri-

mary target for so massive a missile is a high-value type such as an aircraft-carrier; it should be noted that range estimates for the missile vary very considerably from a minimum of 185 km (115 miles) to a maximum of 560 km (348 miles), though it is likely that the comparative inaccuracy of the guidance system and the desire to maximize the warhead size probably dictated a small fuel capacity and thus only limited range

AS-3 'Kangaroo'

(USSR)

Type: air-launched long-range tactical/operational anti-ship and strategic area-attack missile

Dimensions: diameter 1·85 m (6·07 ft); length 14·90 m (48·88 ft); span 9·15 m (30·02 ft)

Weight: total round 11000 kg (24,250 lb)

Warhead: 800-kiloton/1-megaton thermonuclear or (possibly) 2300-kg (5,071-lb) HE (blast fragmentation type)

Propulsion: one turbojet (probably Tumanskii R-11 or R-13) delivering 5100- or 6800-kg (11,243- or 14,991-lb) thrust

Performance: speed Mach 1·8; range 650 km (405 miles) from a high-altitude launch

Guidance: autopilot and radio command, though the range of the missile suggests that inertial or preprogrammed guidance may have been retrofitted

Variant

AS-3 'Kangaroo': this very large weapon entered service in 1961 as a strategic weapon carried by the Tupolev Tu-95 'Bear-B', and was intended as an area-attack weapon without any form of terminal guidance; in the naval context the only realistic targets are battle groups centred on an aircraft-carrier or battleship; the size of the whole vehicle makes it feasible for some type of terminal guidance package to have been retrofitted for continued capability up to the present

AS-4 'Kitchen'

(USSR)

Type: air-launched long-range tactical/operational anti-ship and strategic area-attack missile

Dimensions: diameter 0·90 m (2·95 ft); length 11·30 m (37·07 ft); span 3·00 m (9·84 ft)

Weight: total round 5900 kg (13,007 lb)

Warhead: 200/350-kiloton thermonuclear or 1000-kg (2,205-lb) HE (blast fragmentation type)

Propulsion: one liquid-propellant rocket delivering an unrevealed thrust

Performance: speed Mach 3·5; range 460 km (286 miles) from a high-altitude launch reducing to 300 km (186 miles) from a low-altitude launch

Guidance: inertial for midcourse phase, and active radar or passive IR (see below) for terminal phase

Variant

AS-4 'Kitchen': introduced in 1965 and used by Tupolev Tu-22 'Blinder' and Tu-26 'Backfire' supersonic bombers, the AS-4 is a truly formidable weapon; the type was the USSR's first

genuine multi-role missile, being available with no terminal homing and a thermonuclear warhead as a strategic area attack weapon, or with a choice between active radar, passive IR and passive radar-homing terminal guidance as an anti-ship weapon with either a conventional or thermonuclear warhead; the missile's flight profile in the anti-ship role is a high altitude cruise followed by a devastating dive in which the combination of hypersonic speed and small frontal area would make the defence's task exceptionally difficult; the AS-4 is now tasked generally with operations against US surface battle groups, which are operationally and strategically important targets with the high electromagnetic and thermal signatures best suited to the AS-4's terminal guidance system

AS-5 'Kelt'

(USSR)

Type: air-launched long-range tactical anti-ship missile

Dimensions: diameter 0·90 m (2·95 ft); length 8·60 m (28·22 ft); span 4·60 m (15·09 ft)

Weight: total round 3400 kg (7,496 lb)

Warhead: 1000-kg (2,205-lb) HE (blast fragmentation type)

Propulsion: one liquid-propellant rocket delivering an unrevealed thrust

Performance: speed Mach 1·2; range 230 km (143 miles) from a high-altitude launch reducing to 180 km (112 miles) from a low-altitude launch

Guidance: autopilot for midcourse phase, and active or passive radar for terminal phase

Variant

AS-5 'Kelt': introduced in 1966 as replacement for the AS-1 'Kennel' in the air-launched role (and possibly using the same basic airframe), the AS-5 is used exclusively by the Tupolev Tu-16 'Badger-G' variant; the missile has the same basic aeroplane configuration as its predecessor, an HE warhead and more advanced avionics including two terminal homing options; these last are fitted in a nose resembling that of the SS-N-2 'Styx', and it has sensibly been suggested that, in addition to its active/passive radar homing system, the AS-5 also possesses a passive IR-homing system like that of the surface-launched SS-N-2

AS-6 'Kingfish'

(USSR)

Type: air-launched long-range tactical/operational anti-ship and strategic area-attack missile

Dimensions: diameter 0·80 m (2·62 ft); length 10·00 m (32·81 ft); span 2·50 m (8·20 ft)

Weight: total round 5000 kg (11,023 lb)

Warhead: 350-kiloton nuclear or 1000-kg (2,205-lb) HE (blast fragmentation type)

Propulsion: one storable liquid-propellant (or possibly solid-propellant) rocket delivering an unrevealed thrust

Performance: speed Mach 3; range 560 km (348 miles) from a high-altitude launch reducing to 250 km (155 miles) from a low-altitude launch

Guidance: inertial for midcourse phase, and active radar or passive radiation homing for terminal phase

Variant
AS-6 'Kingfish': introduced in the 1970s as a complement to the AS-4 'Kitchen', and generally carried in pairs by Tupolev Tu-16 'Badger-C (Mod)', Tu-16 'Badger-G (Mod)' and Tu-26 'Backfire-B' aircraft, the AS-6 has the same targeting and homing systems as the AS-4, and indeed was initially thought to be a development of the earlier weapon; but the AS-6 possesses greater range and cruises at an altitude of 18,000 m (59,055 ft) after launch at 11,000 m (36,090 ft) before the high-supersonic dive onto the target; it is believed that the AS-6 also has a low-level attack profile and, like the AS-4, is considered a potentially decisive weapon against US carrier and battleship battle groups

BAe Sea Eagle

(UK)
Type: air-launched medium/long-range tactical anti-ship missile
Dimensions: diameter 1·313 ft (0·40 m); length 13·58 ft (4·14 m); span 3·94 ft (1·201 m)
Weight: total round 1,325 lb (601 kg)
Warhead: 500-lb (227-kg) HE (penetrating blast fragmentation type)
Propulsion: one Microturbo TRI 60-1 Model 067 turbojet delivering 367-kg (787-lb) thrust
Performance: speed 685 + mph (1102 + km/h); range 80 miles (130 km) decreasing with lower launch altitude
Guidance: strapdown inertial plus Plessey radar altimeter for midcourse phase, and Marconi active radar for terminal phase

Variant
Sea Eagle: the Sea Eagle began to enter service in 1986 after development from 1976 as the P3T on the structural and aerodynamic basis of the Martel ASM, though in this longer-range application fitted with a turbojet (aspirated through a ventral inlet) rather than a solid-propellant rocket; the missile was designed mainly for aircraft (the BAe Sea Harrier being able to carry two and the BAe Buccaneer four), and is notable for its good speed and range; the Sea Eagle has a modern guidance system, the strapdown inertial portion having a microprocessor into which the launch platform loads data on the target's position, bearing, course and speed just before the missile is launched to cruise at low altitude as a means of reducing the chance of the target spotting it by electromagnetic or visual means; the active seeker is of an advanced type, and the large warhead is a potent Royal Ordnance type effective against most naval targets; the basic missile has also been developed as the Sea Eagle SL (P5T) surface-launched version for use by coastal batteries or warships, fitted with a pair of jettisonable solid-propellant booster rockets of the type developed to provide the missile with helicopter-launch capability for the Indian navy's Westland Sea King Mk 42s

Right: This Buccaneer S.Mk2 carries four Sea Eagles.

BAe Sea Skua

(UK)
Type: air-launched short-range tactical anti-ship missile
Dimensions: diameter 0·813 ft (0·248 m); length 8·21 ft (2·502 m); span 2·375 ft (0·724 m)
Weight: total round 325 lb (147 kg)
Warhead: 44-lb (20-kg) HE (blast fragmentation type)
Propulsion: one BAJ Vickers solid-propellant booster rocket delivering an unrevealed thrust, and one BAJ Vickers solid-propellant sustainer rocket delivering an unrevealed thrust
Performance: speed 685 + mph (1102 + km/h); range 12·5 miles (20 km)
Guidance: strapdown inertial plus BAe/TRT radar altimeter for midcourse phase, and Marconi semi-active radar for terminal phase

Variant
Sea Skua: the Sea Skua is a helicopter-launched missile that entered premature service in 1982 as a result of the demands of the Anglo-Argentine Falklands war; operational experience has com-

Above: Sea Skuas carried by Westland's Super Lynx.

bined with combat success to prove the missile an excellent weapon in its intended tasks of sinking small surface units and crippling medium-sized warships; its light weight and small size mean that the Sea Skua can be carried in useful numbers by helicopters such as the versatile Westland Lynx, which can lift four such missiles; after the cruise phase of the flight under control of the autopilot and altimeter at any one of the four pre-selected cruise altitudes, the missile climbs rapidly to the altitude at which the semi-active radar homing system can lock onto the reflections of the Ferranti Seaspray radar carried by the Lynx, though the adoption of other types as launch platforms will necessitate alterations to this system; the Sea Skua can also be launched on the basis of target and launcher information provided by ESM and the Decca Tactical Air Navigation System, with the Seaspray illuminating radar activated only at the last minute to provide the target with minimum reaction time

McDonnell Douglas AGM-84A Harpoon

(USA)

Type: air-launched medium-range tactical anti-ship missile

Dimensions: diameter 1·125 ft (0·343 m); length 12·58 ft (3·835 m); span 3·00 ft (0·914 m)

Propulsion: one Teledyne Continental J402-CA-400 turbojet delivering 680-lb (308-kg) thrust

Weight: total round 1,160 lb (526 kg)

Warhead: 488-lb (221-kg) HE (penetrating blast fragmentation type)

Performance: speed 645 mph (1038 km/h); range 68 miles (110 km)

Guidance: Lear-Siegler or Northrop strapdown inertial plus Honeywell APN-194 radar altimeter for midcourse phase, and Texas Instruments PR-53/DSQ-58 two-axis active radar for terminal phase

Variants

AGM-84A Harpoon: the Harpoon is the Western world's most important anti-ship missile, and was planned from the late 1960s as a capable but comparatively cheap weapon with emphasis on reliability rather than outright performance in all respects but electronic capability and range, where a turbojet rather than rocket sustainer pays dividends; the missile was first deployed during the mid-1970s in its RGM-84A ship-launched version with a jettisonable Aerojet booster rocket; this baseline missile can be fired in range and bearing mode, allowing the late switch-on of the active radar as a means of reducing the chances of the missile being detected through its own emissions, or in the bearing-only mode for earlier switch-on of the radar where the precise location of the target is not available at missile launch time; if no target is found after the low-level approach, the missile undertakes a pre-programmed search pattern, and acquisition of the target is followed in the 57-mile (92-km) range Block I missiles of the initial production batch by a steep pop-up climb and dive onto the target's more vulnerable upper surfaces; currently in production is the Block IC long-range type with range increased to more than 120 miles (193 km) by greater fuel capacity and a change from JP-5 to JP-10 fuel, plus an improved seeker and greater computer memory for variable flight profiles and increased ECCM; McDonnell Douglas has proposed a Block II version with all Block IC improvements as well as an advanced version of the current seeker; so far as the specifically air-launched version is concerned, this AGM-84A needs no booster and is thus shorter and lighter than the RGM-84A

AGM-84B Harpoon: air-launched version employing a wholly sea-skimming flight profile without the pop-up feature of the AGM-84A, thus reducing the target's chances of spotting and countering the weapon; the variant also possesses a larger 570-lb (259-kg) warhead

AGM-84C Harpoon: much improved air-launched model incorporating the flight profile capabilities of the AGM-84A (pop-up) and AGM-84B (sea-skimming) together with the latter's larger warhead, and entering service in the second half of the 1980s

AGM-84D Harpoon: longer-range version incorporating Block II range capability with improved ECCM and provision for the preprogramming of a dog-leg approach via three waypoints and for the selection of alternative terminal approaches

SLAM: starting trials in 1988, this Stand-off Land-Attack Missile is a company-funded derivative of the Harpoon for carriage by US Navy and US Marine Corps Grumman A-6 Intruder and McDonnell Douglas F/A-18 Hornet aircraft; the weapon combines the airframe, powerplant and warhead of the Harpoon with the imaging IR terminal guidance unit of the AGM-65D Maverick ASM, the data-link of the AGM-62 Walleye glide bomb, and a Global Positioning System receiver to create a missile 14·75 ft (4·50 m) long and 1,510 lb (685 kg) in weight; the SLAM is designed to provide a stand-off capability against high-value targets such as power stations, harbour equipment and bridges, using inertial guidance for the midcourse phase of the flight before the missile is aligned precisely at the target through the GPS link, allowing the operator to acquire the target visually at a maximum range of 5·7 miles (9·1 km), lock onto the image and depart the scene as the missile completes its attack

Texas Instruments Sea Ray

(USA)

Type: air-launched short-range tactical anti-ship missile

Dimensions: diameter 0·67 ft (0·203 m); length 9·75 ft (2·972 m); span not revealed

Weight: total round 400 lb (181 kg)

Warhead: 150-lb (68-kg) HE (blast fragmentation type)

Propulsion: one Aerojet Mk 78 solid-propellant rocket delivering an unrevealed thrust

Performance: speed supersonic; range 4·35 miles (7 km)

Guidance: semi-active laser homing

Variant

Sea Ray: an interesting weapon under development since 1981 as a private venture by Texas Instruments to the order of an undisclosed customer (possibly South Korea), the Sea Ray uses the powerplant of the AGM-45A Shrike radar-homing missile and the seeker system of the Paveway III series laser-homing bomb; the Sea Ray can be fired from ship, aircraft or land launch platforms, and flies a ballistic trajectory until some 10 seconds from anticipated impact, when the seeker is activated; the Sea Ray provides any operator with a comparatively light yet effective weapon that can be fitted to many launch platforms, the guidance system offering the possibility of third-party targeting for greater tactical flexibility

Below: Harpoon in sea-skimming cruise mode.

CITEFA ASM-2 Martin Pescador

(Argentina)
Type: air-to-surface tactical missile
Dimensions: diameter 0·219 m (0·717 ft); length 2·94 m (9·65 ft); span 0·73 m (2·40 ft)
Weight: total round 140 kg (308·6 lb)
Warhead: 40-kg (88-lb) HE (blast fragmentation type)
Propulsion: one solid-propellant rocket delivering an unrevealed thrust
Performance: speed Mach 2·3; range 2500/9000 m (2,735/9,845 yards) from an aircraft launch, or 2500/4300 m (2,735/4,705 yards) from a helicopter launch
Guidance: radio command

Variant

ASM-2 Martin Pescador: this is a simple radio command-guided missile which entered service in 1979 on aircraft such as the Fabrica Militar de Aviones IA 58 Pucara; the missile has an impact speed in the order of Mach 1·1 after a maximum flight time of 13 seconds, and CITEFA is currently working on an upgraded version with a heavier warhead and (presumably) a more advanced system of guidance

Avibras MAS-1 Carcara

(Brazil)
Type: air-to-surface light tactical missile
Dimensions: diameter 0·125 m (0·41 ft); length 1·20 m (3·94 ft); span 0·42 m (1·38 ft in)
Weight: total round 45 kg (99 lb)
Warhead: HE (blast fragmentation type)
Propulsion: one Avibras MFB 20 solid-propellant rocket delivering an unrevealed thrust
Performance: speed not revealed; range not revealed
Guidance: TV command

Variant

MAS-1 Carcara: though under active development since 1973, this light ASM is still not in service and little is known of current progress and scheduling; the small size and light weight of the weapon suggest that the type may be intended primarily for helicopter launch as an anti-tank missile, though it is possible that launch from light attack aircraft may be possible against targets such as bunkers or landing craft

Aérospatiale AS.11

(France)
Type: air-to-surface light tactical missile
Dimensions: diameter 0·164 m (0·54 ft); length 1·21 m (3·97 ft); span 0·50 m (1·64 ft)
Weight: total round 29·9 kg (66 lb)
Warhead: Type 140AC HE (hollow-charge anti-tank type), or Type 140AP02 HE (penetrating blast fragmentation type), or Type 140AP59 HE (blast fragmentation type) or Type 140CCN HE (anti-ship type)
Propulsion: one SNPE Simplet solid-propellant booster rocket delivering an unrevealed thrust for 1·2 seconds, and one SNPE Sophie solid-

Above: the wire-guided AS11

propellant sustainer rocket delivering an unrevealed thrust for 20 seconds
Performance: speed 580 km/h (360 mph); range 500/3000 m (545/3,280 yards)
Guidance: wire command to line of sight

Variants

AS.11: this is the helicopter-borne version of the SS.11 surface-launched anti-tank missile; the basic weapon was developed between 1953 and 1955, and was first developed for helicopter use in 1958; the type is obsolescent, but still useful against light armour and bunkers when used with a stabilized sight; the Type 140AC warhead can penetrate 140 mm (5·51 in) of armour, the Type 140AP02 detonates 2·6 kg (5·72 lb) of HE after penetrating 10 mm (0·4 in) of armour, the Type 140AP59 is an impact-fused fragmentation warhead, and the Type 140CCN can deal with landing craft and attack craft
AS.11B1: improved version with transistorized guidance and the option of TCA semi-automatic command to line of sight guidance

Aérospatiale AS.12

(France)
Type: air-to-surface light tactical misile
Dimensions: diameter 0·21 m (0·69 ft); length 1·87 m (6·14 ft); span 0·65 m (2·13 ft)
Weight: total round 76 kg (167·5 lb)
Warhead: OP.3C HE (penetrating blast fragmentation type)
Propulsion: one SNPE Achille solid-propellant booster rocket delivering an unrevealed thrust for 1·15 seconds, and one SNPE Hermioné solid-propellant sustainer rocket delivering an unrevealed thrust
Performance: speed 338 km/h (210 mph); range 8000 m (8,750 yards)
Guidance: wire command to line of sight

Variant

AS.12: this 1955 missile was designed as a scaled-

up version for the SS.10 for use against bunkers and warships, and is now of only limited use even in these two roles; the OP.3C warhead can detonate a 28·4-kg (63-lb) charge after penetrating 40 mm (1·57 in) of armour, and in its AS.11 helicopter-carried version is used with the APX 260 or SFIM 334 stabilized sights

Aérospatiale AS.30 Laser

(France)
Type: air-to-surface tactical missile
Dimensions: diameter 0·342 m (1·12); length 3·65 m (11·98 ft); span 1·00 m (3·28 ft)
Weight: total round 520 kg (1,146 lb)
Warhead: 240-kg (529-lb) HE (blast fragmentation or semi-armour-piercing types)
Propulsion: one SNPE/Aérospatiale two-stage solid-propellant rocket delivering an unrevealed thrust
Performance: speed Mach 1·5; range 3000 to 11250 m (3,280 to 12,305 yards); CEP 2 m (6·6 ft)
Guidance: strapdown inertial midcourse guidance, and Thomson-CSF Ariel semi-active laser terminal guidance

Variants

AS.30: introduced in 1960 to provide French Dassault Mirage IIIE fighter-bombers with a moderate stand-off capability, the AS.30 is essentially a scaled-up version of the AS.20 ASM, which is now out of service; use of this missile allowed the launch aircraft to come no closer than 3000 m (3,280 yards) to the target, the operator then radio-commanding the missile to the visual line of sight with a CEP of less than 10 m (33 ft); the weapon is 3·84 m (12·59 ft) long with the X12 warhead, or 3·89 m (12·75 ft) long with the X35 warhead
AS.30TCA: introduced in 1964, this is a semi-automatic command to line of sight development, obviating the need for the operator to track both the missile and the target, a severe tactical disadvantage for the AS.30 model
AS.30 Laser: introduced in 1983, this much-improved model is designed for use with the Thomson-CSF/Martin Marietta ATLIS II (Automa-

tic Tracking Laser Illuminator System II) pod, allowing the aircraft to launch and break away while the laser pod under the fuselage or wing continues to designate the locked-in target for the missile, whose maximum flight time is 21 seconds

the missile can be handled easily on the ground, and so that launch aircraft can carry useful multiples of the missile

Matra BGL 400

(France)

Type: air-to-surface guided tactical glide bomb
Dimensions: diameter 0·40 m (1·32 ft); length 3·40 m (11·16 ft); span 0·789 m (2·59 ft)
Weight: total round 475 kg (1,047 lb)
Warhead: 400-kg (882-lb) HE (basic free-fall bomb)
Propulsion: none
Performance: speed high subsonic; range 10000 m (10,935 yards)
Guidance: Thomson-CSF TMV 630 EBLIS semi-active laser homing

Variants

BGL 250: currently under development, this is a standard French 250-kg (551-lb) bomb with the same type of laser homing and flight-control system as that used on the in-service BGL 400 series; diameter is 0·23 m (0·75 ft), length 3·33 m (10·92 ft) and span 0·64 m (2·10 ft)
BGL 400: this is derived in concept from the US Paveway series, being a 400-kg (882-lb) HE bomb provided with cruciform wings/fins on a rearward extension of the body and fitted with a seeker/control section on the nose; the laser seeker is based on the Ariel seeker of the AS.30L missile, and the target can be designated from the ground or by an aircraft using the ATLIS II designator system, allowing a lock-on range of between 4000 and 10,000 m (4,375 and 10,935 yards); the weapon is designed for release at between 50 and 150 m (165 and 490 ft) by aircraft flying at speeds up to 1100 km/h (684 mph)
BGL 1000 Arcole: version based on the French standard 1000-kg (2,205-lb) HE bomb, with a diameter of 0·46 m (1·50 ft), a length of 4·21 m (13·82 ft) and a span of 0·90 m (2·95 ft); the type has a stand-off range of 8000 m (8,750 yards) and a specially strengthened nosecap for the penetration into high-value targets (such as the concrete piers of bridges) before detonation

Matra STAR

(France)

Type: air-to-surface anti-radar tactical missile
Dimensions: not revealed
Weight: total round 150 kg (330 lb)
Warhead: HE (blast fragmentation type)
Propulsion: one Matra-Onera Rustique ramjet delivering an unrevealed thrust
Performance: speed Mach 2+; range 100 km (62·1 miles)
Guidance: passive radiation homing

Variant

STAR: this Supersonique Tactique Anti-Radar missile is in the early stages of development as a weapon to open the way for attack aircraft operating against heavily defended targets; design emphasis is being placed on light weight so that

Matra/MBB Apache CWS

(France & West Germany)

Type: air-launched stand-off tactical dispenser missile
Dimensions: cross section of dispenser section includes a width of 0·63 m (2·07 ft) and a height of 0·48 m (1·58 ft); length 4·04 m (13·25 ft); span 2·53 m (8·30 ft)
Weight: total round (Apache CWS I) 1000 kg (2,205 lb), and (Apache CWS II and III) 1200 kg (2,645 lb)
Warhead: (all three versions) 750 kg (1,653 lb) of submunitions
Propulsion: (Apache CWS I) none, (Apache CWS II) one solid-propellant rocket delivering an unrevealed thrust, and (Apache CWS III) one small turbojet or turbofan delivering an unrevealed thrust
Performance: speed (all three versions) Mach 0·95; range (Apache CWS I) 12,000 m (13,125 yards), (Apache CWS II) 25/30 km (15·53/18·64 miles), and (Apache CWS III) 40/50 km (24·86/31·07 miles)
Guidance: inertial, or (Apache CWS III) inertial plus an unspecified terminal guidance system

Variants

Apache CWS I: this series of weapons based on a common airframe originated with separate studies for the Matra Apache and MBB Container Weapon System for successors to the Belouga and Durandal; the two design concepts were then combined into this important family with service entry planned for 1992; the rectangular-section fuselage has flip-out wings, a small tailplane and two ventral fins, and the 2·0-m (6·56-ft) boxlike central fuselage can be laid out for a number of modular payloads (initially of just two configurations) ejected laterally from transverse tubes to cover an area 350 m (385 yards) wide by 1000 m (1,095 yards) long; the submunitions are at first to be the same as those used in the MW-1 under-fuselage dispenser weapon, namely the 44-mm (1·73-in) KB 44 shaped-charge anti-tank bomblet, the MIFF anti-tank mine, the MUSA fragmentation mine for use against semi-hard targets, the MUSPA fragmentation mine for use against aircraft, the STABO runway-cratering munition and the ASW munition for attacks on hardened aircraft shelters
Apache CWS II: longer-range version with a solid-propellant rocket
Apache CWS III: longest-range version with a turbine engine

Dornier/Aérospatiale SR-SOM

(West Germany & France)

Type: air-launched short-range stand-off tactical missile
Dimensions: diameter not revealed; length (SOM 1) 3·40 m (11·15 ft) or (SOM 2) 4·30 m

(14·11 ft); span 2·60 m (8·53)
Weight: total round (SOM 1) 720 kg (1,587 lb), or (SOM 2) 1400 kg (3,086 lb)
Warhead: (SOM 1) 350 kg (772 lb) or (SOM 2) 900 kg (1,984 lb) of HE or submunitions
Propulsion: one solid-propellant rocket delivering an unrevealed thrust
Performance: speed Mach 0·8 at low altitude; range (SOM 1) 20 km (12·43 miles) or (SOM 2) 40 km (24·86 miles) at low altitude
Guidance: 'intelligent sensor' midcourse guidance and high-precision terminal guidance of types yet to be determined

Variants

SR-SOM 1: under the leadership of Dornier, a Franco-West German team is developing this Short-Range Stand-Off Missile as an all-weather fire-and-forget weapon in two basic forms; the SR-SOM 1 is planned for lighter tactical aircraft, and the core of the present configuration is the MoBiDic modular stand-off weapon schemed on the basis of Dornier's SR-SOM and Aérospatiale's Pegase II; development of the warhead and its associated submunitions has been entrusted to Diehl in West Germany and to Thomson Brandt in France, the proposed submunition types being designed to give the weapon autonomous capability against hardened aircraft shelters and moving armour; the basic MoBiDic vehicle is based on a longitudinal beam that supports the aircraft interface lugs, the rectangular wings and the tail section (the last incorporating the rocket motor and cruciform tail surfaces indexed at 45° to the wings); under the beam is the modular dispenser section with provision for sideways launching of submunitions, and at the nose is an aerodynamic fairing
SR-SOM 2: larger version of the basic SR-SOM, designed for higher-performance aircraft and possessing greater range

Israeli guided bombs

(Israel)

The **Elbit Opher** uses an IR guidance package comparable to that of the US Paveway laser-homing series in performance terms, but considerably cheaper to produce. The package can be added to many types of free-fall ordnance (typically the Mk 82 and Mk 82 'slick' bombs) to create 'semi-smart' weapons: the Opher-fitted bomb is launched either in a dive attack or using the standard continuously-computed impact point system, and homes of the IR radiation of fixed or moving targets; the core of the system is a simplified high-resolution FLIR with a 7° field of view that provides data to a high-speed digital computer which controls post-launch target lock-on and the actuation of the pneumatically powered control surfaces. The weapon has been developed primarily as a cost-effective counter to MBTs fitted with the ERA (explosive reactive armour) type of protection designed to 'snuff out' the gas/metal vapour jet of ground-launched hollow-charge projectiles, and a typical lock-on range is 1000 m (1,095 yards). The most common application of the Opher kit is on the Mk 82 500-lb (227-kg) bomb to produce a weapon 3·43 m (11·25 ft) long and 325 kg (716·5 lb) in weight. More precisely comparable to the Paveway series is the **Israel Aircraft Industries Guillo-**

tine; this is a laser-homing weapon, again based on the Mk 82 bomb, which experience has taught the Israelis to be the optimum size (balancing destructive effect with the ability to be carried in multiples by most tactical aircraft) for the engagement of the basic range of battlefield targets; the weapon has a cruciform of delta tail surfaces that spring-deploy after weapon release, and at the nose a hemispherically tipped cylindrical section that contains the seeker (with automatic search and lock onto reflected laser energy) and power-operated delta control surfaces; Israeli sources give the Guillotine a CEP of 2 m (6·56 ft) and a range of 30 km (18·64 miles) from a release altitude of 12,000 m (39,370 ft), the Guillotine hitting its target at an angle of 45°.

The **Rafael Pyramid** is a more advanced weapon, but again based on the warhead of the Mk 82 bomb; the Pyramid has a large cruciform of delta wings mounted at its rear, each wing being trailed at its inboard end by a small control surface, and the weapon is a comparatively cheap TV-guided bomb weighing 363 kg (800 lb); the weapon's principal dimensions include a diameter of 0·29 m (0·95 ft), a length of 2·77 m (9·09 ft) and a fin span of 1·18 m (3·86 ft); the weapon's operational concept is based on the need to provide Israeli aircraft with a point target-engagement capability, and the Pyramid has a CEP in the order of 1·0 m (3·3 ft) from a 30-km (18·64-mile) launch range; the Pyramid can be launched from any aeroplane able to carry it, for the weapon requires no electrical or electronic interface with the launch platform as it can be guided by any other aircraft carrying the associated receiver pod and onboard TV monitor/control system

Rafael Armament Development Authority Pop-Eye

(Israel)
Type: air-to-surface tactical missile
Dimensions: not revealed
Weight: total round 1360 kg (2,998 lb)
Warhead: 340-kg (750-lb) HE (blast fragmentation or semi-armour-piercing types)
Propulsion: one solid-propellant rocket delivering an unrevealed thrust
Performance: speed not revealed; range 93 km (57·8 miles)
Guidance: inertial for the midcourse phase and TV for the terminal phase

Variant
Pop-Eye: this missile was developed in Israel to meet indigenous as well as export requirements, and was in late 1987 tentatively adopted for the US Air Force under the 'Have Nap' programme for Boeing B-52 and General Dynamics F-111 aircraft; if a large-scale requirement follows, the US version will be licence-built by Martin Marietta; few details of this potentially important weapon have yet been revealed

Aeritalia/SNIA BPD CASMU

(Italy)
Type: air-launched stand-off tactical dispenser missile
Dimensions: body cross section 0·394 m² (4·24 sq ft); length 4·76 m (15·61 ft); span 1·50 m (4·92 ft)
Weight: total round (glider version) 1050 kg (2,315 lb) or (powered versions) 1170 kg (2,579 lb)
Warhead: 745 kg (1,642 lb) of submunitions
Propulsion: (powered versions) one solid-propellant rocket delivering an unrevealed thrust or (later) one turbofan delivering an unrevealed thrust
Performance: speed about 975 km/h (606 mph); range (glider version) 6 to 12 km (3·73/7·46 miles). or (rocket-powered version) 20/25 km (12·43/15·53 miles), or (turbofan-powered version) considerably greater than the rocket-powered version
Guidance: unrevealed guidance and fire-control system

Variant
Skyshark: this interesting vehicle is under development by the Consorzio Armamenti Spendibili Multi Uso (consortium for multi-role dispenser weapons), a joint venture by Aertialia and SNIA BPD; the vehicle is designed for stand-off attacks against high-value targets, and is intended for air-launch by most tactical aircraft; in its initial form the Skyshark is to be a glider, carrying as-yet unspecified submunition load to tackle the specific target envisaged, though the consortium is planning a rocket-powered medium-range successor and also has in mind a turbofan-powered long-range cruise version; the key to this Italian weapon concept is the combination of low radar cross section (resulting from the shape of the vehicle and its construction of radar-absorbent materials) and an extremely advanced onboard guidance and fire-control system

Mitsubishi XGCS-1

(Japan)
Under this designation Mitsubishi is developing for the Japanese Self-Defense Air Force an add-on guidance system for 500- and 750-lb (227- and 340-kg) free-fall bombs; unlike the French BGL and US Paveway series guided bombs, however, this Japanese development uses passive IR homing

Saab Rb04E

(Sweden)
Type: air-to-surface tactical missile
Dimensions: diameter 0·50 m (1·64 ft); length 4·45 m (14·60 ft); span 1·97 m (6·46 ft)
Weight: total round 616 kg (1,358 lb)
Warhead: 300-kg (661-lb) HE (blast fragmentation type)
Propulsion: one IMI Summerfield two-stage solid-propellant rocket delivering an unrevealed thrust
Performance: speed high subsonic; range varies with launch height to a maximum of 32 km (19·9 miles)
Guidance: Saab autopilot for midcourse phase, and Philips active radar for terminal phase

Variants
Rb04C: this was the first European ASM with active radar homing for a true all-weather fire-and-forget capability, and entered development in 1949 before the start of one of the world's longest running missile production programmes between 1958 and 1978; the Rb04C was the initial model, entering service in 1958, and spans 2·04 m (6·69 ft)
Rb04D: improved version of the later 1960s with upgraded rocket and guidance
Rb04E: final production version with smaller span and modernized guidance as well as an improved structure; despite the age of the basic concept, this final variant is believed to have very advanced technical features even by current standards

Saab-Bofors Rb05A

(Sweden)
Type: air-to-surface tactical missile
Dimensions: diameter 0·30 m (0·98 ft); length 3·60 m (11·81 ft); span 0·80 m (2·625 ft)
Weight: total round 305 kg (672 lb)
Warhead: HE (blast fragmentation type)
Propulsion: one Volvo Flygmotor VR-35 dual-thrust prepackaged liquid-propellant rocket delivering 2500-kg (5,511-lb) thrust in the boost phase and 510-kg (1,124-lb) thrust in the sustain phase
Performance: speed Mach 1+; range 9000 m (9,845 yards); CEP less than 10 m (33 ft)
Guidance: radio command

Variant
Rb05A: introduced in the early 1970s, the RB 05A is a moderately large but capable ASM designed for land and sea targets; the missile is launched at an altitude between 20 and 50 m (65 and 165 ft) and then climbs to some 400 m (1,315 ft) as the operator guides it to the target, where the blast fragmentation warhead is detonated by a proximity fuse

AS-7 'Kerry'

(USSR)
Type: air-to-surface tactical missile
Dimensions: diameter 0·30 m (0·98 ft); length 3·50 m (11·48 ft); span 0·95 m (3·12 ft)
Weight: total round 400 kg (882 lb)
Warhead: 100-kg (220·5-lb) HE (blast fragmentation type)
Propulsion: one solid-propellant rocket delivering an unrevealed thrust
Performance: speed Mach 1; range 11,100 m (12,140 yards)
Guidance: radio command, or (according to recent Western assessments) beam riding

Variant
AS-7 'Kerry': this was apparently the USSR's first combat-capable ASM even though it first appeared only in the late 1970s; earlier Soviet

types had been modified from AAMs or were even large-calibre rockets with primitive radio guidance, but the AS-7 is a more capable weapon roughly comparable to the AGM-12 Bullpup series; the recent thinking about the AS-7's guidance has not revealed whether this is of the radar or laser beam-riding type, either of which would make the AS-7 a far more capable weapon than at first thought, though radar beam-riding has clear disadvantages for the launch aeroplane over the battlefield; the missile has the Soviet service name **Grom**, but its service and production designations remain unknown

AS-9 'Kyle'

(USSR)
Type: air-to-surface anti-radar tactical missile
Dimensions: diameter 0·50 m (1·64 ft); length 6·00 m (19·685 ft in); span not revealed
Weight: total round about 650 kg (1,433 lb)
Warhead: HE (blast fragmentation type)
Propulsion: one solid-propellant rocket delivering an unrevealed thrust
Performance: speed Mach 0·8; range 80/90 km (49·7/55·9 miles)
Guidance: passive radar homing

Variants
AS-9 'Kyle': virtually nothing is known of this large and heavy, but long-ranged, anti-radar missile designed for use on Soviet tactical aircraft; some Western analysts believe that the type is powered by a small turbojet rather than by a rocket, and may therefore have supersonic performance to a range of 100+ km (62+ miles)
AS-11 'Kilter': the weapon originally thought in the West to have borne this designation (a US type allocated because of the West's virtually total ignorance of Soviet tactical missiles' real designations) is now known as the AS-14, and the AS-11 may thus be a variant of the AS-9 with a different homing system
AS-12 'Kegler': virtually nothing is known of this weapon, but some reports suggest that it may be another AS-9 variant with a different homing system, though another possibility is that the weapon is a tactical dispenser type

AS-10 'Karen'

(USSR)
Type: air-to-surface tactical missile
Dimensions: diameter 0·30 m (0·98 ft); length 3·50 m (11·48 ft); span not revealed
Weight: total round about 400 kg (882 lb)
Warhead: about 100-kg (220·5-lb) HE (blast fragmentation type)
Propulsion: one solid-propellant rocket delivering an unrevealed thrust
Performance: speed Mach 0·9; range 10,000 m (10,935 yards)
Guidance: EO or (possibly) semi-active laser homing

Variant
AS-10 'Karen': this weapon forms an important part of the inventory for the Mikoyan-Gurevich MiG-27 and Sukhoi Su-17 attack fighters, and also for the Sukhoi Su-24 interdictor; as with most Soviet ASMs, concrete information and even the real designation are woefully lacking, though there is reason to believe that the type may be an AS-7 derivative with precision guidance

AS-14 'Kedge'

(USSR)
Type: air-to-surface tactical missile
Dimensions: diameter 0·450 m (1·48 ft); length about 4·50 m (14·76 ft); span 1·30 m (4·63 ft)
Weight: total round about 600 kg (1,323 lb)
Warhead: about 300-kg (661-lb) HE (blast fragmentation type)
Propulsion: one solid-propellant rocket delivering an unrevealed thrust
Performance: speed transonic; range 40 km (25 miles)
Guidance: semi-active laser homing

Variant
AS-14 'Kedge': virtually nothing is known of this tactical ASM, which is a precision attack weapon associated with the Mikoyan-Gurevich MiG-27 and other tactical aircraft; it is believed that the illuminating laser is carried in an underwing or underfuselage pod; the missile may be a larger version of the AS-10, and there is evidence to suggest that the type may be able to use midcourse guidance update supplied via a data-link, and that there may be an EO terminal guidance alternative

BAe/Marconi ALARM

(UK)
Type: air-to-surface anti-radar tactical missile
Dimensions: diameter 0·72 ft (0·22 m); length 13·92 ft (4·24 m); span 2·36 ft (0·72 m)
Weight: total round 385 lb (175 kg)
Warhead: HE (blast fragmentation type)
Propulsion: one ROF Nuthatch solid-propellant two-stage rocket delivering unrevealed thrusts
Performance: not revealed
Guidance: Marconi passive radar seeking

Variant
ALARM: based aerodynamically on the Sky Flash AAM, the Air-Launched Anti-Radiation Missile was due to enter service in the late 1980s as the primary weapon of British tactical aircraft operating against hostile radars; the weapon has a Marconi seeker unit; after a low-level launch in the vicinity of likely targets, the missile is designed to zoom to 40,000 ft (12,190 m), thereupon descending nose down under a small drogue parachute as the seeker searches for hostile emissions; once a target has been selected, the drogue is discarded and the missile dives 'down the throat' of the hostile radar system

BAe/Matra Martel and ARMAT

(UK & France)
Type: (AJ.168) air-to-surface tactical missile or (AS.37 and ARMAT) anti-radar tactical missile
Dimensions: diameter 1·31 ft (0·40 m); length (AJ.168) 12·70 ft (3·871 m) or (AS.37) 4·12 m (13·52 ft); span 3·938 ft (1·20 m)
Weight: total round (AJ.168) 1,213 lb (550 kg) or (AS.37) 530 kg (1,168 lb)
Warhead: 330-lb (150-kg) HE (blast fragmentation type)
Propulsion: (AS.37) one Hotchkiss-Brandt/SNPE Basile solid-propellant booster rocket delivering an unrevealed thrust, and one Hotchkiss-Brandt/SNPE Cassandre solid-propellant sustainer rocket delivering an unrevealed thrust, or (AJ.168) one SNPE composite boost and cast double-base sustainer rocket delivering an unrevealed thrust
Performance: speed Mach 2; range 60 km (37·3 miles) from a high-altitude launch declining to 30 km (18·6 miles) from a low-altitude launch
Guidance: (AJ.168) Marconi TV command or (AS.37) EMD AD.37 passive radar seeker

Variants
AJ.168 Martel: the Martel (Missile Anti-Radar Television) grew from separate British and French ASM studies in the period 1960-3, and was then developed by France and the UK in one of the first European collaborative programmes for service introduction in the late 1960s; the British AJ.168 version of the Martel uses command guidance with a small TV camera in the nose of the missile for the accurate placement of the substantial warhead
AS.37 Martel: the French version of the Martel is designed for anti-radar use with a broadband passive seeker which is locked to the required frequency before the weapon is fired
ARMAT: developed by Matra on the basis of the Martel airframe, this is France's new anti-radar missile, differing from the AS.37 that it is replacing in having a length of 4·15 m (13·62 ft), a span of 1·20 m (3·94 ft), a weight of 550 kg (1,213 lb) including the 160-kg (357-lb) HE warhead, a range of between 15 and 120 km (9·3 and 74·6 miles) depending on launch altitude and flight profile, a higher-impulse rocket motor, and a more advanced ESD passive radar seeker

Martin Marietta AGM-12C Bullpup

(USA)
Type: air-to-surface tactical missile
Dimensions: diameter 1·50 ft (0·457 m); length 13·58 ft (4·14 m); span 4·00 ft (1·22 m)
Weight: total round 1,785 lb (810 kg)
Warhead: 1,000-lb (454-kg) HE (blast fragmentation type)
Propulsion: one Thiokol LR62-RM-2/4 prepackaged liquid-propellant rocket delivering an unrevealed thrust
Performance: speed Mach 1·75; range 17,600 yards (16,095 m)
Guidance: radio command

Variants
AGM-12B Bullpup: the Bullpup was developed to meet a US Navy requirement in the Korean War for a stand-off precision attack weapon for tactical

aircraft; the weapon was planned round the 250-lb (113-kg) general-purpose bomb with an Aerojet General solid-propellant rocket and pneumatically powered control surfaces on the nose for radio-control from the launch aircraft; the original ASM-N-7A was superseded in 1960 by the ASM-N-7B (in 1962 redesignated AGM-12B) with a Thiokol LR58 prepackaged liquid-propellant rocket, 12,000-yard (10,975-m) range and a revised warhead; this obsolete ASM has a weight of 571 lb (259 kg), a length of 10·50 ft (3·20 m) and span of 3·08 ft (0·94 m); the missile is still in limited service, and though restricted in terms of its guidance system, which requires that the aeroplane loiter in the vicinity of the target until impact of the weapon, the missile still packs a powerful punch in areas of reduced air-defence capability

AGM-12C Bullpup: improved version with 1,000-lb (454-kg) warhead, wider-chord wings and LR62 liquid-propellant rocket

---

Texas Instruments AGM-45A Shrike

(USA)
Type: air-to-surface anti-radar tactical missile
Dimensions: diameter 0·67 ft (0·203 m); length 10·00 ft (3·05 m); span 3·00 ft (0·91 m)
Weight: total round 390 lb (177 kg)
Warhead: 145-lb (66-kg) HE (blast fragmentation type)
Propulsion: one Rocketdyne Mk 39 or Aerojet Mk 53 solid-propellant rocket delivering an unrevealed thrust
Performance: speed Mach 2; range variable with launch altitude and speed from 18 to 25 miles (28·95 to 40·25 km)
Guidance: Texas Instruments passive radar seeking

Variants
AGM-45A Shrike: developed as the ASM-N-10 to meet a US Navy requirement and introduced in 1963, the Shrike was the USA's first tactical anti-radar missile; the weapon was produced in 10 blocks (AGM-45-1 to AGM-45-10), and there are at least 13 different seeker units matched with specific ground-based radars; this has proved a tactical disadvantage because it demands specific tuning before take-off and thus prevents attacks on targets of opportunity, as does the seeker's lack of inbuilt memory that results in a ballistic trajectory should the radar be closed down
AGM-45B Shrike: improved AGM-45A with the Aerojet Mk 78 solid-propellant rocket

---

Martin Marietta AGM-62A Walleye II

(USA)
Type: air-to-surface guided tactical glide bomb
Dimensions: diameter 1·50 ft (0·457 m); length 13·25 ft (4·039 m); span 4·25 ft (1·295 m)
Weight: total round 2,340 lb (1061 kg)
Warhead: 1,900-lb (862-kg) HE (shaped-charge blast type)

Propulsion: none
Performance: speed high subsonic; range 1,975/49,300 yards (1805/45,0802 m) depending on launch altitude
Guidance: optical imaging with nose-mounted TV

Variants
AGM-62A Walleye II: developed to overcome the limitations of the obsolete Walleye I against hard targets, the Walleye II Mk 5 Mod 4 was introduced in 1974 and has a considerably larger warhead (basically that of the Mk 84 free-fall bomb) and a revised seeker with a smaller optical gate for increased accuracy; built by Martin Marietta, the Walleye II requires a target with sharp visual contrasts for good lock-on before launch; the weapon's CEP is between 15 and 20 ft (4·6 and 6·1 m)
AGM-62A Walleye II ER/DL: introduced in 1976, this Extended-Range/Data-Link model was developed so that greater range can be ensured without any sacrifice of accuracy; the missile is dropped from high altitude (so extending range to 65,500 yards/59,895 m) and is locked onto the target late during the flight using the two-way data-link system to the launch aircraft, where the operator monitors the TV image in the weapon's guidance system

---

Hughes AGM-65 Maverick

(USA)
Type: air-to-surface tactical missile
Dimensions: diameter 1·00 ft (0·31 m); length 8·17 ft (2·49 m); span 2·36 ft (0·72 m)
Weight: total round (AGM-65A/D) 463 lb (210 kg) or (AGM-65E/F) 634 lb (287 kg)
Warhead: (AGM-65A/D) 125-lb (56·7-kg) HE (shaped-charge blast type) or (AGM-65E/F) 300-lb (136·1-kg) HE (penetrating blast fragmentation type)
Propulsion: one Thiokol TX-633 reduced-smoke solid-propellant rocket delivering an unrevealed thrust
Performance: speed supersonic; range 985/26,400 yards (900/24,140 m)
Guidance: (AGM-65A and AGM-65B) TV imaging, (AGM-65C and AGM-65E) semi-active laser homing, or (AGM-65D and AGM-65F) IR imaging

Variants
AGM-65A Maverick: developed from 1965 and introduced in 1972 as a US Air Force weapon, the Maverick is the smallest fully guided ASM in the US inventory, and one of the West's most important weapons of the type, largely because in all its versions it is a fire-and-forget type; the AGM-65A is the initial TV imaging version (often known as the **TV Maverick**), and suffers the tactical disadvantage that the low magnification of its nose-mounted camera forces the pilot of the launch aircraft to fly close to the target to secure seeker lock-on before missile launch and subsequent automatic attack; the shaped-charge warhead contains 83 lb (37·6 kg) of explosive
AGM-65B Maverick: improved TV imaging model introduced in 1980 with double the image magnification of the AGM-65A (based on a 2·5° field of view) to overcome the earlier version's tactical disadvantages; the type is often known as

the **Scene-Magnification Maverick**
AGM-65C Maverick: development using Rockwell laser homing compatible with the ground-based ILS-NT200 or aerial 'Pave Knife', 'Pave Penny', 'Pave Spike', 'Pave Tack' and several non-US designation systems; the weapon was known as the **Laser Maverick**, but was cancelled before reaching full service with the US Marine Corps in the close support role against targets generally designated by ground-based laser
AGM-65D Maverick: imaging IR version for the USAF with twice the lock-on range of the AGM-65A/B types, and capable of operation in adverse weather conditions and at night; the type is known as the **IIR Maverick** and uses a Hughes IR seeker designed for use in conjunction with FLIR systems; the CEP of all Maverick variants up to the AGM-65D is 5 ft (1·52 m)
AGM-65E Maverick: this **Laser Maverick** was introduced in 1985 as successor to the cancelled AGM-65C with a less costly laser seeker and digital processing, as well as a more powerful 300-lb (136-kg) warhead with impact or delay fuses; the CEP of this and later Maverick variants is less than 5 ft (1·52 m)
AGM-65F Maverick: version for the US Navy combining the airframe and guidance of the AGM-65D with the 250-lb (113-kg) Mk 19 blast fragmentation warhead and the fuse of the AGM-65E plus software changes to optimize the weapon's capabilities against warship targets
AGM-65G Maverick: USAF equivalent of the AGM-65F, and is designed for the destruction of 'hard' tactical targets

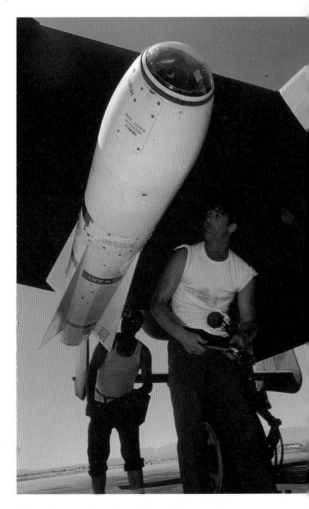

Above: the air-to-surface Maverick hangs from an A-10A.

Boeing AGM-69A SRAM

(USA)

Type: air-to-surface operational/strategic missile
Dimensions: diameter 1·46 ft (0·45 m); length for internal carriage 14·00 ft (4·27 m) or for external carriage 15·83 ft (4·83 m); fin diameter 2·50 ft (0·76 m)
Weight: total round 2,240 lb (1016 kg)
Warhead: 170/200-kiloton W69 nuclear with plutonium as the fissile material
Propulsion: one Lockheed SR75-LP-1 two-stage solid-propellant rocket delivering an unrevealed thrust
Performance: speed Mach 2·8 to 3·2 depending on altitude; range 100/137 miles (161/221 km) from a high-altitude launch declining to 35/50 miles (56/80 km) from a low-altitude launch
Guidance: Singer-Kearfott KT-76 inertial plus terrain-avoidance radar altimeter

Variant

AGM-69A SRAM: development of a Short-Range Attack Missile to be carried by fighters was initiated in the late 1950s, but the current weapon was designed from 1963 to give larger aircraft a genuine defence-suppression capability of a strategic nature; the type entered service in 1972 as part of the primary armament of heavy aircraft as replacement for the AGM-28 Hound Dog; the role at first envisaged for the weapon was stand-off attack against primary defensive installations, but it is now tasked with defence-suppression tasks in association with the launch of AGM-86B air-launched cruise missiles and the delivery of free-fall nuclear weapons; the SRAM has four basic attack profiles: semi-ballistic from launch to impact, altimeter-supervised terrain-following, ballistic pop-up from screening features followed by terrain-following, and combined terrain-following and inertial; any of these profiles can include preprogrammed 180° course changes, and the warhead can be set for ground- or air-burst; surviving missiles are being re-engined with a new Thiokol liquid-propellant rocket developed for the upgraded AGM-69B variant that was cancelled in 1977; since the proposed advent of the SRAM II, the original weapon has frequently been designated **SRAM-A** and its CEP is about 500 yards (457 m)

General Dynamics AGM-78B Standard ARM

(USA)

Type: air-to-surface anti-radar tactical missile
Dimensions: diameter 1·13 ft (0·34 mm); length 15·00 ft (4·57 m); span 3·58 ft (1·09 m)
Weight: total round 1,356 lb (615 kg)
Warhead: 214·7-lb (97-kg) HE (blast fragmentation type)
Propulsion: one Aerojet Mk 27 Mod 4 dual-thrust solid-propellant rocket delivering an unrevealed thrust
Performance: speed Mach 2·5; range varies with launch altitude and speed to a maximum of 56 miles (90 km)
Guidance: Maxson Electronics passive radar seeking

Variants

AGM-78A Standard ARM: derived from the RIM-66 Standard SAM, the US Navy's AGM-78A was introduced in 1968 as a longer-range complement to the AGM-45A Shrike, and uses the same no-memory Texas Instruments seeker with its attendant tactical limitations

AGM-78B Standard ARM: improved model with a gimballed broadband seeker plus memory; this requires no pre-launch tuning, thereby allowing targets of opportunity to be engaged, and keeps the missile on its committed course even if the emitter is closed down; the missile achieves its best results with naval aircraft carrying the TIAS (Target Identification and Acquisition System) and the US Air Force's McDonnell Douglas F-4G 'Wild Weasel' defence-suppression aircraft, whose APR-38 emitter-location system can fulfil the same role as the TIAS in supplying the seeker head with emitter information before launch

AGM-78C Standard ARM: upgraded version of the AGM-78B for the US Air Force and US Navy; many AGM-78A and B missiles have been upgraded to this standard with field modifications kits

AGM-78D Standard ARM: version (with the **AGM-78D2** subvariant) powered by the Mk 69 Model 0 solid-propellant rocket and marked by further-improved seeker capabilities; some AGM-78A and B missiles have been upgraded to this standard with field modification kits

Texas Instruments AGM-88A HARM

(USA)

Type: air-to-surface anti-radar tactical missile
Dimensions: diameter 0·83 ft (0·25 m); length 13·68 ft (4·17 m); span 3·67 ft (1·12 m)
Weight: total round 796 lb (361 kg)
Warhead: 145-lb (66-kg) HE (blast fragmentation type)
Propulsion: one Thiokol/Hercules YSR113-TC-1 solid-propellant rocket delivering an unrevealed thrust
Performance: speed Mach 3 + ; range 46 + miles (74 + km)
Guidance: Texas Instruments passive radar seeking

Variants

AGM-88A HARM: the High-speed Anti-Radiation Missile began to supersede the tactically limited AGM-45 Shrike and the costly (also heavy) AGM-78 Standard ARM during 1983; the type offers good passive radiation homing with detection from the launch aeroplane's sensor suite, in the form of the Itek ALR-45 or McDonnell Douglas APR-38 RWRs in US Air Force aircraft, and the AWG-25 equipment of the US Navy's Vought A-7 Corsair II; the missile's high speed provides the hostile radar only the shortest of close-down time;

the HARM can be used in any of three modes: self-protection when the launch aeroplane's RWR detects a hostile emitter and programmes the missile before launch, pre-briefed with the missile fired blind towards a possible target so that the the seeker can search in flight and command a self-destruct should no target be located, and target-of-opportunity when the seeker of the unfired missile detects and locks onto an emitter

AGM-88B HARM: improved Block III and Block IV missiles: Block III weapons have a reprogrammable memory allowing field modification of seeker parameters by changes to the software, and Block IV weapons have modifications improving their capability against advanced threats such as frequency-hopping or burst-mode emitters

AGM-88C HARM: a major upgrade of the standard weapon using either the Texas Instruments Block IV seeker or the Ford Aerospace 'Low-Cost Seeker' being developed as an alternative; the first seekers were delivered in November 1988, and this marks the first performance hardware change introduced during the HARM's production life

Below: Hellfire missiles mounted on an OV-10 Bronco

Rockwell AGM-114A Hellfire

(USA)

Type: air-to-surface tactical (anti-tank) missile
Dimensions: diameter 0·58 ft (0·178 m); length 5·33 ft (1·63 m); span 1·08 ft (0·33 m)
Weight: total round 98·86 lb (45 kg)
Warhead: 20-lb (9-kg) HE (hollow-charge anti-tank type)
Propulsion: one Thiokol TX-657 solid-propellant rocket delivering an unrevealed thrust
Performance: speed high subsonic; range 6,500 yards (5945 m)
Guidance: autopilot for midcourse, and Rockwell semi-active laser homing

Variants

AGM-114A Hellfire: this impressive weapon has made possible fire-and-forget helicopter attacks against armoured formations, the missile having proved itself able to home on the reflections of tanks laser-illuminated by aerial or ground-based designators; the target need only be illuminated once the missile has been launched, thereby reducing the time available for the target to undertake defensive measures and also reducing the launch platform's vulnerability to countermeasures; current development is centred on versions with millimetre-wavelength radar or RF guidance to provide all-weather capability even when the battlefield is obscured by laser-damping smoke

AGM-114B Hellfire: version of the AGM-114A for the US Navy and US Marine Corps with a different motor and homing guidance provided by three different seeker modules

AGM-114C Hellfire: US Army version of the AGM-114B without the safe arm feature

Motorola AGM-122A Sidearm

(USA)

Type: air-to-surface anti-radar tactical missile
Dimensions: diameter 0·42 ft (0·127 m); length 9·42 ft (2·87 m); span 2·07 ft (0·63 m)
Weight: total round 195 lb (88·5 kg)
Warhead: 10-lb (4·5-kg) HE (blast fragmentation type)
Propulsion: one Rocketdyne Mk 36 Mod 2 solid-propellant rocket delivering an unrevealed thrust
Performance: speed Mach 2·3; range 4,000 yards (3660 m)
Guidance: Motorola passive radar seeking

Variant

AGM-122A Sidearm: used on US Marine Corps Bell AH-1 SeaCobra attack helicopters and McDonnell Douglas/BAe AV-8 Harrier STOVL close-support aircraft, the Sidearm is a self-protection weapon of the radar-homing type produced at low cost and risk by the conversion of stored semi-active radar-homing AIM-9C Sidewinder AAMs; the type is light and moderately advanced, but the seeker unit needs pre-launch cue by parent-platform's RWR

Emerson Defense Systems AGM-123A Skipper 2

(USA)

Type: air-to-surface rocket-boosted guided tactical glide bomb
Dimensions: diameter 1·17 ft (0·36 m); length 14·08 ft (4·29 m); span 5·25 ft (1·60 m)
Weight: total round 1,283 lb (582 kg)
Warhead: 1,000-lb (454-kg) Mk 83 HE bomb
Propulsion: one Rocketdyne Mk 78 solid-propellant rocket delivering an unrevealed thrust
Performance: speed transonic; range 34 miles (55 km) but limited in practice to 10·25 miles (16·5 km)
Guidance: semi-active laser homing

Variant

AGM-123A Skipper 2: this simple yet potent tactical weapon uses off-the-shelf components (the Mk 83 1,000-lb/454-kg 'iron' bomb, the rocket motor of the AGM-45B Shrike and the guidance/control system of the Paveway II series guided bomb) to produce a stand-off weapon of great accuracy; the weapon entered production in 1986, initially for US Navy aircraft

Boeing AGM-131A SRAM II

(USA)

Type: air-to-surface operational/strategic missile
Dimensions: diameter 1·30 ft (0·40 m); length 13·98 ft (4·26 m); span about 2·63 ft (0·80 m)
Weight: total round 1,935 lb (878 kg)
Warhead: 585-lb (265·4-kg) 170/200-kiloton W80 or W90 nuclear with plutonium as the fissile material
Propulsion: one Hercules two-stage solid-propellant rocket delivering an unrevealed thrust in the boost phase and an unrevealed thrust in each of two sustainer burns
Performance: speed Mach 2·8 to 3·2; range ?/250 miles (?/402 km) from a high-altitude launch declining to an unrevealed range from a low-altitude launch
Guidance: Litton inertial plus terrain-avoidance radar altimeter

Variants

AGM-131A SRAM II: in December 1986 Boeing was selected to develop a new SRAM missile instead of the proposed Advanced Strategic Air-Launched Missile; the SRAM II is planned as a very small weapon (only about two-thirds the size of the SRAM-A) using an airframe of largely composite construction as well as an advanced laser ring-gyro INS based on the latest Very High Speed Integrated Circuit technology: the body has a squared-off hump section along its centre and rear to accommodate the electronics; the SRAM II will have an advanced solid-propellant rocket engine giving a boost and at least two sustain phases, and the thermonuclear warhead (either the AGM-86B's W80 or the purpose-designed W90) will have capability against hardened defence targets; the SRAM II is scheduled to enter service in 1993, rapidly replacing the SRAM-A

SRAM-T: version of the SRAM-II under development to arm tactical aircraft, most obviously the F-111G conversion of the General Dynamics FB-111A

Northrop AGM-136A 'Tacit Rainbow'

(USA)
Type: air-to-surface anti-radar tactical missile
Dimensions: diameter 1·17 ft (0·36 m); length 8·33 ft (2·54 m); span 5·78 ft (1·77 m)
Weight: total round about 440 lb (200 kg)
Warhead: HE (blast fragmentation type)
Propulsion: one Williams International J400-WR-404 turbojet delivering 240-lb (109-kg) thrust
Performance: speed 600 mph (966 km/h); endurance 30 minutes
Guidance: Texas Instruments passive radar seeking

Variant
AGM-136A 'Tacit Rainbow': resulting from a highly classified programme whose very existence was revealed only in early 1987, this potentially important missile has been developed on the basis of the BQM-74 Chukar target and reconnaissance drone; the use of a small turbojet indicates that this winged missile is planned for longer range and/or extended loiter time, the latter being used to search for ground-based emitters whose locations are then stored in the memory of the missile's advanced guidance and homing package even if they are switched off; the missile can thus select the most important emitter and institute its terminal dive attack with considerable accuracy

Rockwell GBU-8/KMU-353A/B

(USA)
Type: air-to-surface guided tactical glide bomb
Dimensions: see below
Weight: total round 2,100 lb (953 kg)
Warhead: 1,970-lb (894-kg) Mk 84 HE bomb (nominal weight 2,000 lb/907 kg)
Propulsion: none
Performance: speed transonic; range between 1,650 and 26,750 yards (1510 and 24,460 m) depending on launch altitude

Variants
GBU-8: the HOming BOmb System was developed by Rockwell during the 1960s in parallel with the Paveway I series, though this type uses EO rather than laser guidance, at first with a TV image-contrast tracker and then with more advanced TV and IR seekers for enhanced nocturnal and adverse-weather capability; the three kits for the GBU-8 initial production series are the KMU-353A/B and KMU-390/B image-contrast systems, and the KMU-359/B IR system, each comprising a nose-mounted guidance section and a tail-mounted finned control section; the packages

can be added to the 2,000-lb (907-kg) Mk 84 GP bomb (KMU-353A/B and KMU-359/B) and the 3,000-lb (1361-kg) M118E1 demolition bomb (KMU-390/B); CEP is in the order of 20 ft (6·1 m)
GBU-15: improved version of the HOBOS concept, developed by Rockwell on the basis of the Modular Guided Weapon System as a means of extending yet farther the range of the HOBOS concept; the core weapon is the 2,000-lb (907-kg) Mk 84 bomb to which is fitted guidance, control, two-way data-link and cruciform-wing aerodynamic packages; the guidance package of the **GBU-15(V)1/B** initial version is the daylight-only DSU-27A/B EO type using the AXQ-14 data-link system, while that of the later **GBU-15(V)2/B** model is the all-weather day/night WGU-10/B IIR guidance of the AGM-65D Maverick; the guidance system allows the missile to be locked onto its target before or after launch for automatic guidance, or alternatively for the weapon to be manually guided by the controller in the launch aeroplane; the GBU-15 weighs 2,450 lb (1111 kg), and has ranges between 1,650 yards (1,510 m) and 51 miles (82 km) depending on launch altitude; the weapon has a diameter of 1·50 ft (0·46 m), a length of 12·83 ft (3·91 m) and a span of 4·92 ft (1·50 m); a proposed development is the **GBU-15(V)N/B** carrying a payload of one SUU-54 dispenser with 1,800 BLU-63 and/or BLU-86 anti-tank bomblets, and guided by the EO or IIR nose packages for attacks against airfields and armour, with secondary capability against motor transport and air-defence installations
AGM-130A: longer-range version of the GBU-15 weighing 2,917 lb (1323 kg) with a Mk 84 bomb as payload and powered by a strap-on Hercules solid-propellant rocket for a range of 26,400 yards (24,140 m) from a low-altitude launch; the type has midcourse altitude and heading hold, and the terminal guidance system uses the same type of data-linked EO or IIR system as that used in the GBU-15; the weapon's principal dimensions include a diameter of 1·50 ft (0·46 m), a length of 12·875 ft (3·92 m) and a span of 4·92 ft (1·50 m); role of the missile is low-altitude stand-off attack against heavily-defended targets, and the weapon has the same launch qualifications and targeting options as the GBU-15
AGM-130B: proposed airfield-attack version comparable to the AGM-130A but carrying as its warhead an SUU-54 (15 BLU-106/B Boosted Kinetic-Energy Penetrator and 75 British-designed Hunting HB876 area-denial submunitions) and weighing 2,560 lb (1161 kg)

Texas Instruments Paveway I/KMU-351A/B

(USA)
Type: air-to-surface guided tactical glide bomb
Dimensions: see below
Weight: total round 2,100 lb (953 kg)
Warhead: 1,970-lb (894-kg) Mk 84 HE bomb (nominal weight 2,000 lb/907 kg)
Propulsion: none
Performance: range between 1,650 and 20,000 yards (1510 and 18,290 m) depending on launch altitude
Guidance: semi-active laser homing

Variants
Paveway I: introduced in 1967 after the first release of a laser-guided development weapon in 1965, Paveway I is a series of add-on laser-homing kits (marked-target seekers and associated control surfaces developed by Texas Instruments, and weighing about 30 lb/13·6 kg) that can be added to 'slick' bombs as a means of maximizing accuracy when used in conjunction with an air- or ground-based laser designator; the kits are the KMU-342/B used with the 750-lb (340-kg) M117 demolition bomb, the KMU-351A/B used with the 2,000-lb (907-kg) Mk 84 general-purpose bomb, the KMU-370B/B used with the 3,000-lb (1361-kg) M118E1 demolition bomb, the KMU-388A/B used with the 500-lb (227-kg) Mk 82 general-purpose bomb, the KMU-420/B used with the 500-lb (227-lb) Rockeye Mk 20 Mod 2 cluster bomb and the KMU-421/B used with the 2,000-lb (907-kg) SUU-54B or Pave Storm I cluster bomb; the advantage of the system is that the launch aeroplane needs no modification and can leave the target area (unless it is the laser-designator aircraft); the system works at night and in poor visibility, and the minimum cloud base for successful operation is 2,500 ft (760 m); the airborne designators most commonly associated with the series are two podded systems, the AVQ-26 'Pave Tack' and AVQ-23 'Pave Spike'
Paveway II: entering service in 1980, this is an improved series based on the same basic concept but with a simpler (thus cheaper) guidance package and the addition of a folding wing aerofoil group at the tail (for extra manoeuvrability and additional lateral range); the weapons within this important basic designation are the **GBU-10E/B** and **GBU-10F/B** both based on the 2,000-lb (907-kg) Mk 84 general-purpose bomb, the **GBU-12D/B** and **GBU-12F/B** both based on the 500-lb (227-kg) Mk 82 general-purpose bomb, the **GBU-16B/B** and **GBU-16C/B** both based on the 1,000-lb (454-kg) Mk 83 general-purpose bomb and the **Mk 13/18UK** based on the British 1,000-lb (454-kg) Mk 13/18 general-purpose bomb; the GBU-10 type has a diameter of 1·50 ft (0·457 m) and an overall length of 14·16 ft (4·32 m); the GBU-12 type has a diameter of 0·90 ft (0·27 m) and an overall length of 10·93 ft (3·33 m); in each case the weapon functions in a manner basically similar to that of the Paveway I series
Paveway III: entering service in 1987, this is an improved version of the Paveway II with microprocessor controls and a digital autopilot (with BAe Dart precision gyro) intended mainly for use in the degraded weather and high-threat scenario of European operations; the Paveway III is designed for release at low level (in either level flight or a zoom climb) and thus fitted with high-lift folding wings, but can also be released at higher altitudes in dives as steep as 60°; the result is a weapon of far greater operational flexibility than its predecessors; the type has the service designation **GBU-24/B** and also features an improved seeker and more advanced microprocessor technology, allowing low-level and off-axis stand-off delivery in conditions of low visibility, with the mid-course guidance providing the possibility of delayed laser-designating and trajectory shaping with all their tactical advantages

CITEFA Mathogo

(Argentina)

Type: helicopter-launched short/medium-range anti-tank missile
Dimensions: diameter 0·10 m (0·34 ft); length 1·00 m (3·27 ft); span not revealed
Weight: total round 11·3 kg (24·9 lb)
Warhead: 2·8-kg (6·17-lb) HE (hollow-charge anti-tank type)
Propulsion: one dual-thrust solid-propellant rocket delivering an unrevealed thrust
Performance: speed 325 km/h (202 mph); range 350/2100 m (385/2,295 yards)
Guidance: wire command to line of sight

Variant

Mathogo: this entered production in the late 1970s, and is by Western standards an obsolescent weapon resembling the Swedish Bantam; the type was developed as a surface-launched weapon, but has now been fully qualified as a helicopter-launched missile; the advantages offered by the Mathogo are light weight, compact dimensions and a warhead capable of penetrating 400 mm (15·75 in) of armour, while its disadvantages are low speed and a comparatively poor maximum range; these latter would force the launch helicopter to approach its target so closely that it would come under severe attack during the missile's flight time of 23 seconds to maximum range; in 1986 it was revealed that there are two subvariants of the Mathogo, one with the standard range quoted above, and the other with the usefully increased maximum range of 3000 m (3,280 yards)

NORINCO Hong Jian-8

(China)

Type: helicopter-launched medium/long-range anti-tank missile
Dimensions: diameter 0·12 m (0·39 ft); length 0·88 m (2·87 ft); span 0·32 m (1·05 ft)
Weight: total round 11·2 kg (24·7 lb)
Warhead: HE (hollow-charge anti-tank type)
Propulsion: one dual-thrust solid-propellant rocket delivering an unrevealed thrust
Performance: speed 865 km/h (537 mph); range 100/3000 m (110/3,280 yards)
Guidance: wire command to line of sight

Variant

Hong Jian-8: this Red Arrow-8 is China's most advanced anti-tank missile and, though the weapon has so far been seen only in the surface-launched role, it is likely that the type is used for helicopter applications. The weapon is an optically tracked wire-guided missile with semi-automatic command to line of sight guidance; the likely armour penetration of the warhead is 800 mm (31·5 in), and in many respects the missile bears a striking similarity to the Franco/West German Euromissile Milan

NORINCO Hong Jian-73

(China)

Type: helicopter-launched medium/long-range anti-tank missile
Dimensions: diameter 0·12 m (0·39 ft); length 0·87 m (2·85 ft); span 0·39 m (1·29 ft)
Weight: total round 11·3 kg (24·9 lb)
Warhead: 3-kg (6·6-lb) HE (hollow-charge anti-tank type)
Propulsion: one dual-thrust solid-propellant rocket delivering an unrevealed thrust
Performance: speed 430 km/h (267 mph); range 500/3000 m (545/3,280 yards)
Guidance: wire command to line of sight

Variant

Hong Jian-73: this Red Arrow-73 is essentially a Chinese development of the Soviet AT-3 'Sagger', to which it is basically similar in all respects other than its smaller wings; the warhead can penetrate 500 mm (19·7 in) of armour at 0° or 150 mm (5·9 in) at 65°

Aérospatiale Eryx

(France)

Type: helicopter-launched short-range light anti-tank missile
Dimensions: diameter 0·16 m (0·53 ft); length 0·93 m (3·03 ft); span not revealed
Weight: total round 14·4 kg (31·75 lb)
Warhead: 3·6-kg (7·9-lb) HE (hollow-charge anti-tank type)
Propulsion: one solid-propellant rocket delivering an unrevealed thrust
Performance: speed 72 km/h (44·7 mph) rising to 303 km/h (188 mph); range 25/600 m (27/655 yards)
Guidance: wire semi-automatic command to line of sight

Variant

Eryx: originally known as the Anti-Char Courte Portée (short-range anti-tank) missile, this is a lightweight anti-tank weapon selected for the French army in 1986; the type has an extremely small motor resulting in very low launch speed from the Kevlar launch tube, but this tactical limitation is offset by the type's minimal backblast and (in its ground-launched version) its ability to be fired from inside a building; the warhead can penetrate 900 mm (35·4 in) of armour, and after introduction as a ground-based weapon the Eryx is being developed as a helicopter-launched system for French and export orders; though the light weight of the missile is an obvious advantage, allowing even the lightest helicopters to carry a multiple installation, the short range of the missile is a tactical disadvantage as launch helicopters will have to approach very close to their prospective targets

Euromissile HOT 1

(France & West Germany)

Type: helicopter-launched long-range heavyweight anti-tank missile
Dimensions: diameter 0·17 m (0·54 ft); length 1·28 m (4·18 ft); span 0·31 m (1·02 ft)
Weight: total round 23·5 kg (51·8 lb)
Warhead: 6-kg (13·2-lb) HE (hollow-charge anti-tank type)
Propulsion: one SNPE Bugeat solid-propellant booster rocket delivering an unrevealed thrust for 0·9 second, and one SNPE Infra solid-propellant sustainer rocket delivering 24-kg (53-lb) thrust for 17·4 seconds
Performance: speed 865 km/h (537 mph); range 75/4250 m (82/4,650 yards)
Guidance: SAT/Eltro wire semi-automatic command to line of sight

Variants

HOT 1: entering service in the early 1970s, the Haute subsonique Optiquement téléguidé tire d'un Tube (high-subsonic optically-guided tube-launched) missile is a powerful anti-tank weapon designed for static ground use, or for installation in armoured fighting vehicles and helicopters; the missile can be used in single or multiple tube launchers, and its 136-mm (5·35-in) diameter warhead can penetrate more than 800 mm (31·5 in) of armour under optimum conditions, though a more realistic figure is 280 mm (11 in) at a 65° impact angle; the type's primary disadvantage is a modest speed, which means that the missile takes some 17 seconds to reach its maximum range even when launched from a helicopter, which thus has to remain exposed for this time; the stabilized sight generally associated with the HOT 1 is the SFIM APX M397 unit mounted in the roof of the launch helicopter
HOT 2: improved version of the basic weapon, introduced to service in 1985 and featuring the much-enhanced armour penetration of 1250 mm (49·2 in) as a result of its larger 150-mm (5·9-in) diameter warhead containing 4·1 kg (9·04 lb) rather than the 3 kg (6·61 lb) of HE carried in the HOT 1's warhead; the HOT 2 is also faster than its predecessor, with all the consequent tactical advantages of this fact; further improvement in capability will be provided by adoption of the stabilized Viviane day/night sight currently under development for a genuine night capability, and the West Germans are developing a similar capability with the integration of a licence-built Texas Instruments FLIR sight with the HOT system; further development of the HOT 2 continues towards the **HOT 2MP** and **HOT 2T**, the former being designed to penetrate 1250 mm (49·2 in) of armour and still have a potent behind-the-armour effect, and the latter being a tandem-warhead variant whose proximity-fused forward charge is designed to defeat explosive reactive armour before the main charge detonates to create the gas/metal vapour jet that can still pierce 1250 mm (49·2 in) of armour

Israel Military Industries Mapats

(Israel)

Type: helicopter-launched medium/long-range heavy anti-tank missile
Dimensions: diameter 0·15 m (0·486 ft); length 1·45 m (4·76 ft) with probe extended; span about 0·34 m (1·12 ft)
Weight: total round 18·5 kg (40·8 lb)
Warhead: 3·6-kg (7·94-lb) HE (hollow-charge anti-tank type)
Propulsion: one solid-propellant booster rocket delivering an unrevealed thrust, and one solid-propellant sustainer rocket delivering an unrevealed thrust
Performance: speed 1135 km/h (704 mph); range 65/4500 m (70/4,920 yards)

Guidance: laser beam-riding

Variant

Mapats: a highly capable weapon, with advanced unjammable guidance, capable of penetrating 800 mm (31·5 in) or, in its latest variant with a revised warhead, 1000 mm (39·37 in) of multi-layer armour; developed from the late 1970s, it was initially deployed in 1983 as a ground- and vehicle-launched missile; and is supplied as a certified round in a fibreglass container which serves as the launch tube, the complete missile/container assembly weighing 29 kg (63·9 lb) and measuring 1·50 m (4·92 ft) in length; after launch the booster drops away, and the sustainer ignites to power the missile to the maximum range, which is attained in 23·5 seconds; from 1987 the Mapats has been used in an air-launched role, the missile's agility giving it a secondary capability against helicopters; the laser guidance system has × 13 magnification optics for the operator

Kawasaki Type 64

(Japan)

Type: helicopter-launched short/medium-range anti-tank missile
Dimensions: diameter 0·12 m (0·39 ft); length 1·00 m (3·28 ft); span 0·60 m (1·97 ft)
Weight: total round 15·7 kg (34·6 lb)
Warhead: HE (hollow-charge anti-tank type)
Propulsion: one Daicel/Nippon Oil two-stage solid-propellant rocket delivering an unrevealed thrust
Performance: speed 305 km/h (190 mph); range 350/1800 m (385/1,970 yards)
Guidance: Nihon Electric wire command to line of sight

Variant

Type 64: introduced in 1965 and otherwise known as the **KAM-3D**, this is a simple and slow yet nonetheless effective missile now being replaced in the ground role by the Type 79 weapon

Bofors Rb53 Bantam

(Sweden)

Type: helicopter-launched short/medium-range tactical missile
Dimensions: diameter 0·11 m (0·36 ft); length 0·85 m (2·79 ft); span 0·40 m (1·31 ft)
Weight: total round 7·6 kg (16·75 lb)
Warhead: 1·9-kg (4·2-lb) HE (hollow-charge anti-tank type)
Propulsion: one Bofors dual-thrust solid-propellant rocket delivering an unrevealed thrust
Performance: speed 305 km/h (190 mph); range 300/2000 m (330/2,185 yards)
Guidance: wire command to line of sight

Variant

Rb53 Bantam: this is a first-generation anti-tank missile with simple guidance and low cruising speed; the weapon was adopted in 1963, and its warhead can penetrate 500 mm (19·68 in) of armour; the type was designed primarily for ground launch, but can also be fired from light helicopters, this application of the missile being aided by the Bantam's light weight and compact dimensions

Bofors Rbs56 Bill

(Sweden)

Type: helicopter-launched medium-range anti-tank missile
Dimensions: diameter 0·15 m (0·49 ft); length 0·90 m (2·95 ft); span 0·41 m (1·36 ft)
Weight: total round 10·7 kg (23·6 lb)
Warhead: HE (hollow-charge anti-tank type)
Propulsion: one Royal Ordnance dual-thrust solid-propellant rocket delivering an unrevealed thrust
Performance: speed 720 km/h (447 mph); range 150/2000 m (165/2,185 yards)
Guidance: wire semi-automatic command to line of sight

Variant

Rbs56 Bill: entering service in the later 1980s, the Bill (pick) is a highly advanced anti-tank missile fired (in its baseline ground-launched form) from a container tube fitted with a sight unit and mounted on a tripod; in the air-launched application the missile container (delivered complete with the missile as a certified round of ammunition and weighing 20·5 kg/45·19 lb) can be fitted to the outside of a helicopter in the standard fashion for such weapons; the keys to the Bill's capabilities are its guidance system, which causes the missile to fly 1 m (3·28 ft) above the operator's line of sight, and its combination of proximity fuse and shaped-charge warhead, which is angled to fire 30° downwards from the missile centreline as the weapon overflies the target's most vulnerable upper surfaces, allowing the vaporized metal/gas jet formed by the warhead's detonation to burn through the target tank's thinnest armour

AT-2 'Swatter-C'

(USSR)

Type: helicopter-launched medium/long-range heavyweight anti-tank missile
Dimensions: diameter 0·132 m (0·43 ft); length 1·16 m (3·81 ft); span 0·66 m (2·17 ft)
Weight: total round 29·4 kg (64·8 lb)
Warhead: HE (hollow-charge anti-tank type)
Propulsion: one solid-propellant rocket delivering an unrevealed thrust
Performance: speed 540 km/h (336 mph); range 500/4000 m (545/4,375 yards)
Guidance: radio semi-automatic command to line of sight and IR terminal homing

Variant

AT-2 'Swatter-C': this important series of anti-tank missiles was introduced in the mid-1960s with the 'Swatter-A' ground-launched weapon with the Soviet designation **PUR-62 Falanga**, simple radio-command guidance with all its vulnerability to countermeasures, and a warhead able to penetrate 480 mm (18·9 in) of armour under optimum conditions; the 'Swatter-C' is the dedicated helicopter-launched version of the improved 'Swatter-B', and possesses semi-automatic command to line of sight guidance and yet more range

AT-3 'Sagger'

(USSR)

Type: helicopter-launched medium/long-range anti-tank missile
Dimensions: diameter 0·12 m (0·39 ft); length 0·86 m (2·82 ft); span 0·46 m (1·51 ft)
Weight: total round 11·3 kg (24·9 lb)
Warhead: 3-kg (6·6-lb) HE (hollow-charge anti-tank type)
Propulsion: one solid-propellant booster rocket delivering an unrevealed thrust, and one solid-propellant rocket delivering an unrevealed thrust
Performance: speed 430 km/h (267 mph); range 300/3000 m (330/3,280 yards)
Guidance: wire command to line of sight

Variants

AT-3 'Sagger-A': introduced in about 1970, the AT-3 is a more capable and versatile weapon than the AT-2, with a countermeasures-proof wire guidance system and more powerful sustainer for greater (but still comparatively slow) speed; the type is designated **PUR-64 Malyutka** in the USSR, and its warhead can penetrate 410 mm (16·14 in) of armour
AT-3 'Sagger-B': introduced in 1973, this upgraded model has an improved motor for greater speed and reduced flight time
AT-3 'Sagger-C': introduced in the late 1970s, this is a much developed version with semi-automatic command to line of sight guidance

AT-5 'Spandrel'

(USSR)

Type: helicopter-launched long-range heavyweight anti-tank missile
Dimensions: diameter 0·17 m (0·56 ft); length 1·30 m (4·27 ft); span not revealed
Weight: total round 17 kg (37·5 lb)
Warhead: HE (hollow-charge anti-tank type)
Propulsion: one solid-propellant rocket delivering an unrevealed thrust
Performance: speed 720 km/h (447 mph); range 100/4000 m (110/4,375 yards)
Guidance: wire semi-automatic command to line of sight

Variant

AT-5 'Spandrel': introduced in about 1980, the AT-5 is a powerful second-generation vehicle-launched weapon using technology 'gleaned' from such Western types as the Euromissile HOT; the warhead can penetrate 750 mm (29·53 in) of armour and, though there is no concrete evidence of the fact, it is likely that this useful weapon can be launched from Soviet battlefield helicopters

AT-6 'Spiral'

(USSR)

Type: helicopter-launched long-range heavyweight anti-tank missile
Dimensions: diameter 0·14 m (0·46 ft); length 1·80 m (5·91 ft); span not revealed
Weight: total round about 32 kg (70·55 lb)
Warhead: HE (hollow-charge anti-tank type)
Propulsion: one dual-thrust solid-propellant rocket delivering an unrevealed thrust
Performance: speed 1000 km/h (621 mph); range 100/7000 m (110/7,655 yards)

Guidance: radio command to line of sight (or possibly laser beam-riding)

Variants

AT-6 'Spiral': so far seen only on the Mil Mi-24 'Hind' attack helicopter, the AT-6 is the first of the Soviets' third-generation anti-tank missiles, its good range being matched by the excellent armour penetration figure of about 800 mm (31·5 in)

AS-8: this is believed to be the aircraft-launched version of the 'Spiral', carried by tactical aircraft such as the Sukhoi Su-25 'Frogfoot'

Hughes BGM-71B Extended-Range TOW

(USA)

Type: helicopter-launched medium/long-range heavyweight anti-tank missile

Dimensions: diameter 0·50 ft (0·15 m); length 3·85 ft (1·17 m); span 1·13 ft (0·34 m)

Weight: total round 49·6 lb (22·5 kg)

Warhead: 8·6-lb (3·9-kg) HE (hollow-charge anti-tank type)

Propulsion: one Hercules K41 two-stage solid-propellant rocket delivering an unrevealed thrust

Performance: 700 mph (1127 km/h); range 70/4,100 yards (65/3750 m)

Guidance: Emerson Electric wire semi-automatic command to line of sight

Variants

BGM-71A TOW: entering service in 1970, the Tube-launched Optically-tracked Wire-guided missile is the West's most important anti-tank weapon; it is a heavyweight type designed for vehicle- or helicopter-borne launchers, and has proved its capabilities in several wars; the Picatinny Arsenal warhead contains 5·3 lb (2·4 kg) of explosive, and has shown itself able to penetrate 600 mm (23·62 in) of armour; the range of this initial model is limited to 3,280 yards (1000 m) by the length of its guidance wires

BGM-71B Extended-Range TOW: semi-official designation of the basic weapon produced from 1976 with greater range than the original model as the result of the lengthening of the guidance wires to 4,100 yards (3750 m)

BGM-71C Improved TOW: introduced in the early 1980s in response to the development of Soviet tanks with improved armour, this interim model features a larger-diameter 5-in (127-mm) warhead with LX-14 explosive and a telescoping 1·25-ft (0·38-m) nose probe that extends in flight to ensure a perfect stand-off distance for the detonation of the shaped-charge warhead. This model has a length of 5·83 ft (1·78 m) with the probe extended, and weighs 56·65 lb (25·7 kg); armour penetration with the new warhead increases to 700 mm (27·56 in); under the Further Improvements to the TOW programme, the British company Thorn-EMI is modifying BGM-71C missiles in British service to deal with the latest generation of Soviet tanks: the missile is modified for over-the-top attack with an active IR proximity fuse to trigger a new tandem warhead designed to fire obliquely forward and downward as the missile overflies the target tank's relatively poorly armoured upper surface

BGM-71D TOW 2: introduced in 1983 as the standard US weapon for tackling the latest Soviet tanks at long range, this model has an improved double-base motor (offering about 30% greater impulse) and a 13·2-lb (6-kg) warhead increased in diameter to 6 in (152 mm) and provided with a 1·77-ft (0·54-m) nose probe ensuring optimum stand-off distance for penetration of 800 mm (31·5 in) of armour; this variant weighs 61·95 lb (28·1 kg) and, though it can be fired from the original analog-electronics launcher, it is designed for use with an improved digital-electronics launcher fitted with thermal as well as optical sights, and with a more advanced guidance package; Hughes is also proposing four developments of this powerful weapon (and producing the first while developing the second for service in the early 1990s) with the designations **TOW 2A** for the model with an improved direct-attack warhead, the **TOW 2B** for the top-attack version with a millimetre-wave radar or EO fuse, the **TOW 2D** of which no details have been released, and the **TOW 2N** with wire-less command system of unspecified type, supersonic speed and a range of 10,000 yards (9145 m); entering service in 1988 was the TOW 2A variant, which has a small explosive charge on its nose probe to trigger detonation of the target's ERA (explosive reactive armour), so opening the way for the gas/metal vapour jet of the missile's main charge; the TOW 2B currently under development is similar in concept to the TOW 2A but is designed for 'pop up' top attack as the missile overflies the target tank: the tandem warheads are therefore arranged to fire obliquely forward and downward, the first triggering the target's ERA and the second thus having a clear path to penetrate the armour proper; the TOW 2B is designed to enter service by 1990; other improvements in the pipeline for the TOW series include a new motor to reduce the missile's time of flight, and hence the launch helicopter's window of vulnerability; the new motor will also extend range and prevent the 'pitch up' that occurs as current missiles reach their maximum range

Orbita MAA-1 Leo

(Brazil)

Type: short-range air-to-air missile
Dimensions: diameter 0·15 m (0·49 ft); length 2·72 m (8·92 ft); span 0·65 m (2·14 ft)
Weight: total round 86 kg (190 lb)
Warhead: 12-kg (26·5-lb) HE (blast fragmentation type)
Propulsion: one Vasconcelos-built Imbel Piquete solid-propellant rocket delivering an unrevealed thrust
Performance: speed Mach 2+; range 16 km (9·94 miles)
Guidance: IR homing

Variant

MAA-1 Leo: this simple yet capable AAM entered development in 1976, and was initially a joint-service project known as the Piranha, under the leadership of CTA and later of Vasconcelos; the weapon was twice cancelled for lack of a proper requirement, but with the imminent advent of the EMBRAER-produced version of the Brazilian/Italian AMX attack fighter was then revived as an air force responsibility with final design and manufacture entrusted to Orbita Sistemas Aeroespaciais; the weapon was scheduled to enter service in about 1990, but final development has been delayed or even halted by Brazil's financial problems

CATIC CAA-2

(China)

Type: short-range air-to-air missile
Dimensions: not revealed
Weight: total round not revealed
Warhead: HE (blast fragmentation type)
Propulsion: one solid-propellant rocket delivering an unrevealed thrust
Performance: not revealed
Guidance: IR or semi-active radar homing

Variant

CAA-2: US designation for an advanced weapon of which virtually nothing is known; the missile resembles the proposed NATO AIM-132A ASRAAM, and is known to have been produced in IR and semi-active radar homing versions for use on the Shenyang J-7 fighter

CATIC PL-2

(China)

Type: short-range air-to-air missile
Dimensions: diameter 0·12 m (0·39 ft); length 2·80 m (9·19 ft); span 0·53 m (1·74 ft)
Weight: total round 70 kg (154·3 lb)
Warhead: 11·3-kg (24·9-lb) HE (blast fragmentation type)
Propulsion: one solid-propellant rocket delivering an unrevealed thrust
Performance: speed Mach 2; range 5000/7800 m (5,470/8,530 yards)
Guidance: IR homing

Variants

PL-2: essentially the Chinese version of the Soviet AA-2 'Atoll', itself derived from early models of the AIM-9 Sidewinder; designated **CAA-1** in the standard US terminology for Chinese weapon systems, the PL-2 was developed in the late 1950s and early 1960s, has an uncooled seeker and is thus equivalent to the AIM-9B and restricted to pursuit interceptions at medium and high altitudes

PL-2A: improved pursuit-course missile introduced in the 1970s with greater discrimination against hot spots as a result of the thermo-electric cooling system for its seeker, allowing operation closer to the ground; the missile is basically similar to the AIM-9E conversion of the AIM-9B Sidewinder

CATIC PL-5B

(China)

Type: short-range air-to-air missile
Dimensions: diameter 0·13 m (0·42 ft); length 2·89 m (9·49 ft); span 0·53 m (1·74 ft)
Weight: total round 85 kg (187·4 lb)
Warhead: HE (continuous-rod blast fragmentation type)
Propulsion: one solid-propellant rocket delivering an unrevealed thrust
Performance: speed Mach 4·5; range 16 km (10 miles)
Guidance: IR homing

Variant

PL-5B: with double-delta control surfaces and off-boresight rather than all-aspect engagement capability (equivalent in some respects to the AIM-9L Sidewinder but with a lead-sulphide seeker cooled by compressed air), this is a useful AAM reflecting China's continued faith in the basic design, and has considerable agility for snap-up and snap-down engagements

CATIC PL-7

(China)

Type: short-range dogfighting air-to-air missile
Dimensions: diameter 0·16 m (0·52 ft); length 2·72 m (8·92 ft); span 0·66 m (2·17 ft)
Weight: total round 89 kg (196 lb)
Warhead: 13-kg (28·7-lb) HE (blast fragmentation type)
Propulsion: one solid-propellant rocket delivering an unrevealed thrust
Performance: speed supersonic; range 500/14,400 m (545/15,750 yards)
Guidance: IR homing

Variant

PL-7: limited 'all-aspect' development of the PL-2/5 series with a continuous-rod warhead and an indium-antimonide seeker cooled by liquid nitrogen; the missile is similar to the Matra R550 Magic in appearance, and was designed in the early 1980s probably as a short-range dogfighting missile with engagement capability from anywhere in the target's rear hemisphere

CATIC PL-9

(China)

Type: medium-range air-to-air missile
Dimensions: diameter 0·29 m (0·94 ft); length 3·99 m (13·09 ft); spam 1·17 m (3·84 ft)
Weight: total round 300 kg (661 lb)
Warhead: HE (blast fragmentation type)
Propulsion: one solid-propellant rocket delivering an unrevealed thrust
Performance: speed supersonic; range 10,000 m (10,935 yards)
Guidance: semi-active radar homing

Variant

PL-9: this is thought to be a a variant of the HQ-61 SAM, and as such is comparable in size and weight with the US AIM-7 Sparrow though with considerably inferior electronic and flight performance; the type is used by the J-8 II fighter with Doppler radar that provides the missile with modest ECM capability and also a useful capability against low-level targets

Matra R530

(France)

Type: medium-range air-to-air missile
Dimensions: diameter 0·26 m (0·86 ft); length (semi-active radar version) 3·28 m (10·77 ft) or (IR version) 3·20 m (10·49 ft); span 1·10 m (3·62 ft)
Weight: total round (semi-active radar version) 192 kg (423 lb) or (IR version) 193·5 kg (427 lb)
Warhead: 27-kg (59·5-lb) HE (pre-fragmented or continuous-rod blast fragmentation types)
Propulsion: one SNPE Madeleine dual-thrust solid-propellant rocket delivering an unrevealed thrust
Performance: speed Mach 2·7; range 18 km (11·2 miles)
Guidance: EMD AD26 semi-active radar homing or SAT AD3501 IR homing

Variant

R530: introduced in the early 1960s, the R530 was developed from 1957 as a substantial weapon with large fixed delta wings and small tail-mounted control surfaces indexed in line with the wings; the airframe/powerplant combination was produced with alternative semi-active radar and IR seekers (interchangeable at squadron level), but neither has proved particularly successful in combat; the standard operating practice with the R530 is similar to that used with most Soviet AAMs: fighters generally carry a pair of missiles with different homing heads to provide maximum capability under all electromagnetic and climatic conditions; the IR seeker is claimed to be of the all-aspect type, but such a facility is limited to engagements under unusually advantageous conditions

Matra Super 530F

(France)

Type: medium/long-range air-to-air missile
Dimensions: diameter 0·26 m (0·86 ft); length 3·54 m (11·61 ft); span 0·90 m (2·95 ft)
Weight: total round 250 kg (551 lb)
Warhead: 30-kg (66-lb) HE (blast fragmentation type)
Propulsion: one Thomson Brandt/SNPE Angele dual-thrust solid-propellant rocket delivering 3875-kg (8,543-lb) thrust for 2 seconds and 2550-kg (5,622-lb) thrust for 4 seconds

Performance: speed Mach 4·6; range 35 km (21·75 miles)
Guidance: EMD Super AD26 semi-active radar homing

Variants
Super 530F: developed from the early 1970s, this high-speed missile is based loosely on the aerodynamics of the R530 revised to resemble those of the American Standard series of SAMs with a cruciform of very low aspect ratio wings trailed by a cruciform of slightly greater-span control surfaces indexed in line with the wings and located at the very tail of the missile; internally the Super 530 is a completely new and advanced weapon matched to the Cyrano IV radar; the missile has twice the range and target-acquisition capabilities of the R530, as well as snap-up capability against aircraft 9000 m (29,530 ft) higher than the launch aircraft; the type also possesses a useful snap-down capability; the Super 530F began to enter service in 1979 after an eight-year development period, and has been produced in substantial numbers
Super 530D: improved version of the Super 530F matched to the RDI and RDM pulse-Doppler radars of the Dassault-Breguet Mirage 2000 series; the variant has a weight of about 265 kg (584 lb) and a length of 3·80 m (12·47 ft), uses an improved motor for a speed of Mach 4·6 + and a range of up to 60 km (37·3 miles), and has better snap-down capability than the Super 530F; the missile can deal with Mach 3 targets at a height of 24,000 m (78,740 ft) and, of considerable more importance, with targets flying fast and low in ground clutter conditions

Matra R550 Magic 1

(France)
Type: short-range dogfighting air-to-air missile
Dimensions: diameter 0·16 m (0·52); length 2·77 m (9·09 ft); span 0·66 m (2·17 ft)
Weight: total round 89·8 kg (198 lb)
Warhead: 12·5-kg (27·6-lb) HE (blast fragmentation type)
Propulsion: one SNPE Romeo single-stage double-base solid-propellant rocket delivering 2700-kg (5,952-lb) thrust for 1·9 seconds
Performance: speed about Mach 3; range 320/10,000 m (350/10,935 yards)
Guidance: SAT AD3601 IR homing

Variants
R550 Magic 1: developed from 1968, the Magic was designed for 140° rear hemisphere engagement at altitudes up to 18,000 m (59,055 ft), the engagement envelope being reduced above this altitude; the missile's lead sulphide seeker is cooled before launch by liquid nitrogen in a bottle carried inside the launch rail, and the missile can be fired by an aircraft manoeuvring at +6g at any speed between 0 and 1300 km/h (808 mph); especially significant features of the R550's design are the ability for snap-shot launch at ranges down to 300 m (985 ft), and the ability to cross safely only 50 m (165 ft) in front of the launch aircraft; the Magic's warhead is located in the centre of the body, and the triple set of cruciform aerodynamic surfaces includes freely-rotating fins at the rear, fixed delta canards near the nose and, just aft of the canards, angular control sur-

faces; the R550 series is generally associated with fighters of French design, but is installationally interchangable with the Sidewinder
R550 Magic 2: entering service in the mid-1980s, this improved version has a genuine all-aspect engagement capability through the adoption of a more sensitive multi-element IR seeker, an improved SNPE Richard motor, greater structural strength and better aerodynamic controls for enhanced dogfight manoeuvrability; just as importantly, the seeker can be slaved to the radar of Dassault-Breguet Mirage 2000 fighters to provide optimum firing conditions

Matra MICA

(France)
Type: short/medium-range air-to-air missile
Dimensions: diameter 0·15 m (0·50 ft); length 3·10 m (10·17 ft); span not revealed
Weight: total round 110 kg (242·5 lb)
Warhead: HE (blast fragmentation type)
Propulsion: one SNPE solid-propellant rocket delivering an unrevealed thrust
Performance: speed Mach 4; range ?/50 km (?/31 miles)
Guidance: strapdown inertial plus IR or semi-active radar homing

Variant
MICA: due to enter service in the 1990s as France's most important short- and medium-range AAM, the Missile d'Interception et de Combat Aérien (interception and air combat missile) was first trialled during 1982; the missile is similar in appearance to the US Standard series of SAMs, though of course much smaller; the type is slated to arm all current and projected French fighters, and combines the capabilities of other Western AAMs such as the AIM-120A AMRAAM and AIM-132A ASRAAM; the MICA is designed for great agility (more than the 50-g capability of the Magic, and allowing turns immediately after launch to engage targets on any bearing from the launch aircraft other than dead astern), and uses thrust-vector control until motor burn-out, after which the aerodynamic tail controls are used; the MICA is designed for launch on the basis of the parent aircraft's primary sensor, cruising under strapdown inertial guidance and receiving target-data updates before the seeker is turned on; the missile has a choice of two seekers (the IR type being used for shorter-range air combat and the semi-active radar type being used for longer-ranged interception), while its comparatively small size allows aircraft such as the Dassault-Breguet Mirage 2000 to carry as many as six missiles

Matra Mistral

(France)
Type: short-range air-to-air missile
Dimensions: diameter 0·09 m (0·30 ft); length 1·80 m (6·20 ft); span not revealed
Weight: total round 17 kg (37·5 lb)
Warhead: 3-kg (6·6-lb) HE (blast fragmentation type)
Propulsion: one SNPE dual-thrust solid-propellant rocket delivering an unrevealed thrust
Performance: speed Mach 2·6; range 300/6000 m

(330/6,560 yards)
Guidance: IR homing

Variant
Mistral: this is the Air-Air Tres Courte Portée (air-to-air very short range) air-launched derivative of the Sol-Air Tres Courte Portée (surface-to-air very short range) missile, and is an extremely capable tube-launched weapon designed for carriage mainly by helicopters, which can carry up to four twin-tube launchers with flick-open eyelid doors; the Mistral can be used for offensive as well as defensive purposes, and targets can be acquired with the helicopter's basic missile sight or, in advanced types, by a crew member's helmet-mounted sight; in both cases the target can be indicated to the missile before launch, as too can the seeker's scanning pattern

Rafael Python 3

(Israel)
Type: short-range dogfighting air-to-air missile
Dimensions: diameter 0·16 m (0·53 ft); length 3·00 m (9·84 ft); span 0·86 m (2·82 ft)
Weight: total round 120 kg (265 lb)
Warhead: 11-kg (24·25-lb) HE (blast fragmentation type)
Propulsion: one Rafael Armaments Developments Authority double-base solid-propellant rocket delivering an unrevealed thrust
Performance: speed Mach 3; range 500/15,000 m (545/16,405 yards)
Guidance: IR homing

Variant
Python 3: developed in the late 1970s and early 1980s as the Shafrir 3 evolution of the Shafrir 2, the Python is an advanced development of the basic Shafrir with an improved motor offering greater range, a revised seeker with radically improved sensitivity for all-aspect engagement capability, and aerodynamic improvements for enhanced manoeuvrability; the seeker/guidance system is claimed to offer the possibility of boresight, uncaged and radar-directed engagements; the Python 3 is claimed to offer engagement capabilities comparable to those of the AIM-9L variant of the Sidewinder

Rafael Shafrir 2

(Israel)
Type: short-range dogfighting air-to-air missile
Dimensions: diameter 0·16 m (0·53 ft); length 2·47 m (8·10 ft); span 0·52 m (1·71 ft)
Weight: total round 93 kg (205 lb)
Warhead: 11-kg (24·25-lb) HE (blast fragmentation type)
Propulsion: one Rafael Armaments Development Authority double-base solid-propellant rocket delivering an unrevealed thrust
Performance: speed Mach 2·5; range 500/5000 m (545/5,470 yards)
Guidance: IR homing

Variant
Shafrir 2: derived from a preproduction Shafrir 1, the Shafrir 2 began to enter Israeli service in 1969 and is a capable short-range AAM that has performed well in combat with a claimed 65/70%

'kill' rate; the weapon is based loosely on the AIM-9 Sidewinder, but from the start of development in 1961 it was decided to increase the diameter of the body in comparison with that of the Sidewinder, and so simplify the engineering of the weapon as well as making possible the use of a larger warhead containing 4 kg (8·82 lb) of explosive

Selenia Aspide

(Italy)
Type: medium/long-range air-to-air missile
Dimensions: diameter 0·20 m (0·67 ft); length 3·70 m (12·14 ft); span 1·00 m (3·28 ft)
Weight: total round 220 kg (485 lb)
Warhead: 33-kg (72·75-lb) HE (blast fragmentation type)
Propulsion: one SNIA-Viscosa single-stage solid-propellant rocket delivering an unrevealed thrust
Performance: speed Mach 4; range 100 km (62·1 miles) from a high-altitude launch dropping to 50 km (31·07 miles) from a low-altitude launch
Guidance: Selenia monopulse semi-active radar homing

Variants

Aspide 1: developed conceptually from the Raytheon AIM-7E Sparrow, the Aspide is like the American missile in being a multi-role type and entered service with the Italian air force in 1979; the type arms the Aeritalia F-104S and Panavia Tornado, and has greater low-altitude range and snap-down capability than the Sparrow, together with much improved accuracy and ECCM
Aspide 1A: upgraded version with a number of electronic and system improvements

Right: Aspide boosts away.

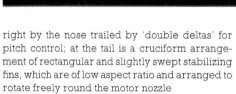

Armscor V3B

(South Africa)
Type: short-range dogfighting air-to-air missile
Dimensions: diameter 0·13 m (0·42 ft); length 2·94 m (9·66 ft); span 0·53 m (1·75 ft)
Weight: total round 73·4 kg (162 lb)
Warhead: 10-kg (225-lb) HE (blast fragmentation type)
Propulsion: one double-base solid-propellant rocket delivering an unrevealed thrust
Performance: speed Mach 3; range 300/5000 m (330/5,470 yards) at high altitude or 300/2000 m (330/2,185 yards) at low altitude
Guidance: IR homing

Variants

V3A: designed between 1971 and 1974, this dogfighting missile was introduced to service in 1975 on the French fighters operated by the South African air force, and was the world's first AAM used with a helmet-mounted sight for rapid designation of the target; the seeker is cooled by compressed air carried in the missile launcher, and the weapon has an unusual configuration for the 0·42-m (1·38-ft) span canard control fins, one pair being simple deltas for roll control and the other pair (indexed at 90° to the plain pair) being double surfaces with swept rectangular surfaces

right by the nose trailed by 'double deltas' for pitch control; at the tail is a cruciform arrangement of rectangular and slightly swept stabilizing fins, which are of low aspect ratio and arranged to rotate freely round the motor nozzle
V3B: improved model introduced in 1979 with greater seeker and helmet sight acquisition angles, and an upgraded motor; the export version introduced in 1982 is known as the **V3 Kukri**

Armscor V3C Darter

(South Africa)
Type: short-range dogfighting air-to-air missile
Dimensions: diameter 0·16 m (0·52 ft); length 2·75 m (19·02 ft); span 0·66 m (2·17 ft)
Weight: total round 89·0 kg (196 lb)
Warhead: 16-kg (35·3-lb) HE (blast fragmentation type)
Propulsion: one double-base solid-propellant rocket delivering an unrevealed thrust
Performance: speed Mach 3; range 300/10,000 m (330/10,935 yards) at high altitude or 300/5000 m (330/5,470 yards) at low altitude
Guidance: IR homing

Variant

V3C Darter: entering service in 1988, the V3C is a

completely upgraded development of the V3B to produce a weapon comparable in most respects to the Magic 2 and AIM-9L Sidewinder; in appearance the new missile is all but identical with the Magic 2, with electronics and surfaces for pitch-and-roll rather than twist-and-steer control; the motor burns for 2 seconds and provides higher acceleration than the motor of the V3B; the Darter's primary advantages over the V3B include considerably longer range, greater agility and a more discriminating seeker head (with a new level of IR filtering and signal processing to provide much-enhanced lock-on against difficult backgrounds) with a look angle, once fired, of 55° off missile flight path; the high level of discrimination gives an all-aspect attack capability to within 15° of the sun; the missile has the choice of three selectable acquisition modes: reduced-scan cage mode using the aircraft's standard sight for the acquisition of targets within a few degrees of the aircraft's flightpath (in this mode the pilot can authorize lock-on to allow the missile's seeker to continue tracking up to a maximum of 20° off the aircraft flight path), helmet mode in which an optional missile-aiming reticle is projected onto the helmet's visor and then placed over the selected target, which may be a maximum of 20° off the aircraft flight path (the particular advantages of this mode are claimed to be simple selection of the best target in a fleeting high-velocity engage-

ment involving the use of decoys) and conventional mode without the use of a helmet sight, with the missile's seeker scanning to a maximum of 14° off the aircraft flight path before receiving instruction to lock onto the strongest IR source; the missile then tracks this source until lock is broken (once the missile exceeds an angle of 20° from the aircraft flight path) or the pilot countermands the lock instruction

Saab Bofors Rbs70 Rayrider

(Sweden)
Type: short-range air-to-air missile
Dimensions: diameter 0·11 m (0·35 ft); length 1·32 m (4·33 ft); span 0·32 m (1·05 ft)
Weight: total round 15 kg (33 lb)
Warhead: 1-kg (2·2-lb) HE (blast fragmentation type)
Propulsion: one Bofors solid-propellant booster rocket delivering an unrevealed thrust, and one IMI solid-propellant sustainer rocket delivering an unrevealed thrust
Performance: speed supersonic; range 5000 m (5,470 yards)
Guidance: laser beam riding

Variant
Rbs70 Rayrider: this was developed in the mid-1970s as a man-portable short-range SAM using laser beam-riding guidance for unjammable homing; the type's performance, currently unjammable guidance system and light weight have made it a natural for helicopter use: in this application the launch aircraft can generally carry eight such missiles in two four-round containers, together with the associated Saab Helios roof-mounted sight allowing automatic hand-over of missile guidance to a laser system carried by another helicopter or, conceivably, in the hands of friendly ground forces

Chung Shan Institute Sky Sword 1

(Taiwan)
Type: short-range air-to-air missile
Dimensions: not revealed
Weight: total round not revealed
Warhead: HE (blast fragmentation type)
Propulsion: one solid-propellant rocket delivering an unrevealed thrust
Performance: speed supersonic; range between 10,000 and 15,000 m (10,935 and 16,405 yards)
Guidance: IR homing

Variants
Sky Sword 1: Taiwanese development of the Sidewinder concept, and bears a very strong similarity to the AIM-9G/H version of the American missile; the weapon was test-fired for the first time in 1985 or early 1986, but no details of the missile have been divulged: the missile is probably comparable in performance to the AIM-9L Sidewinder (a variant whose export to Taiwan the Americans have not allowed) but it is conceivable that elements of the Israeli technology developed for the Shafrir and Python have been used; the Sky Sword 1 has all-aspect engagement capability, and entered service in 1987
Sky Sword 2: due for initial test-firings in 1989, this is an advanced medium-range development of the Sky Sword 1, but no significant details have been released

AA-2-2C/D 'Advanced Atoll'

(USSR)
Type: short-range air-to-air missile
Dimensions: diameter 0·12 mm (0·39 ft); length (AA-2-2C) 2·80 m (9·19 ft) or (AA-2-2D) 3·10 m (10·17 ft); span 0·53 m (1·74 ft)
Weight: total round (AA-2-2C) 70 kg (154 lb) or (AA-2-2D) 75 kg (165 lb)
Warhead: 6-kg (13·2-lb) HE (blast fragmentation type)
Propulsion: one solid-propellant rocket delivering an unrevealed thrust
Performance: speed Mach 2·5; range 8000 m (8,750 yards)
Guidance: (AA-2-2C) IR homing or (AA-2-2D) semi-active radar homing

Variants
AA-2A 'Atoll': developed with the Soviet design designation **K-13** from the AIM-9B Sidewinder (using intelligence information and examples of the missile captured in 1958 and later years), the first-generation AA-2A IR homing missile began to enter Soviet service in the mid-1960s with the service designation **RS-3S** and production designation **5V06** in a variant with 5700-m (6,235-yard) range; the weapon has been produced in vast numbers for use on the whole range of Soviet tactical aircraft, and though the 'Atoll' is being replaced in Soviet service by the AA-8 'Aphid', it is likely to remain in the inventories of the USSR and its clients for many years to come despite its limitation to tailchase pursuit even in optimum conditions
AA-2B 'Atoll': produced in parallel with the AA-2A, this is the semi-active radar homing version of the first-generation series, and has an 8000-m (8,750-yard) range; 'Atolls' are generally carried in pairs (one or two AA-2As with one or two AA-2Bs) to give fighters the best chance of scoring a hit under all operational and climatic conditions, and this philosophy has been carried over into later Soviet AAMs
AA-2-2A 'Advanced Atoll': second-generation version of the IR homing missile with greater reliability and range, the latter resulting from a longer body containing more propellant
AA-2-2B 'Advanced Atoll': second-generation version of the semi-active radar homing missile with greater reliability and range, the latter resulting from a longer body containing more propellant

AA-3A/B 'Anab'

(USSR)
Type: short/medium-range air-to-air missile
Dimensions: diameter 0·28 m (0·92 ft); length (both versions) about 3·60 m (11·81 ft); span 1·30 m (4·63 ft)
Weight: total round 275 kg (606 lb)
Warhead: 30-kg (66-lb) HE (blast fragmentation type)
Propulsion: one solid-propellant rocket delivering an unrevealed thrust
Performance: speed Mach 2·5; range (AA-3A) 20 km (12·4 miles) or (AA-3B) 30 km (18·6 miles)
Guidance: (AA-3A) IR homing or (AA-3B) semi-active radar homing

Variants
AA-3A 'Anab': this was the USSR's second-generation AAM, and the first all-weather long-range weapon of this type in the Soviet inventory when it began to enter service in 1961; the type is generally associated with fighters fitted with the 'Skip Spin' radar for initial acquisition of the target beyond visual range
AA-3B 'Anab': following the Soviet practice of developing AAMs in IR and semi-active radar versions for maximum kill probability under all operational conditions, this is the semi-active radar homing version; as with the AA-3A, the type is being supplanted by the AA-7 'Apex'
AA-3-2 'Advanced Anab': this weapon was first revealed in the West during 1972, but how the weapon qualifies for the epithet 'Advanced' has not been released; if the NATO designation system used for the 'Atoll' has been followed, it can be assumed that this is a longer-ranged variant, and that there are also **AA-3-2A** and **AA-3-2B** variants with IR and semi-active radar terminal guidance respectively

AA-5A/B 'Ash'

(USSR)

Type: medium-range air-to-air missile
Dimensions: diameter 0·31 m (1·00 ft); length (AA-5A) 5·21 m (17·06 ft) or (AA-5B) 5·50 m (18·04 ft); span 1·30 m (4·27 ft)
Weight: total round 390 kg (860 lb)
Warhead: about 45-kg (99-lb) HE (blast fragmentation type)
Propulsion: one solid-propellant rocket delivering an unrevealed thrust
Performance: speed about Mach 3; range (AA-5A) 20 km (12·5 miles) or (AA-5B) 65 km (40·4 miles)
Guidance: (AA-5A) IR homing or (AA-5B) semi-active radar homing

Variants

AA-5A 'Ash': developed between 1954 and 1959 as the primary armament of the Tupolev Tu-28P 'Fiddler' long-range interceptor (and later of the Mikoyan-Gurevich MiG-25 'Foxbat-A' Mach 3 interceptor), the AA-5 remains in limited service despite its technical obsolescence; AA-5A is the Western designation for the IR-homing version, which first appeared in about 1965 and is generally carried in pairs with two of the AA-5B variant to optimize the launch aircraft's kill capabilities under all weather and electronic conditions
AA-5B 'Ash': initial production variant of the AA-5, its semi-active radar homing being associated with the 'Big Nose' radar of the Tu-28P; the model entered service in 1961 or 1962 at the same time as the Tu-28P, and Western estimates of the range possessed by the substantial missile may be far short of the real figure

AA-6A/B 'Acrid'

(USSR)

Type: long-range air-to-air missile
Dimensions: diameter 0·40 m (1·31 ft); length (AA-6A) 5·80 m (19·03 ft) or (AA-6B) 6·29 m (20·64 ft); span 2·25 m (7·38 ft)
Weight: total round (AA-6A) 750 kg (1,653 lb) or (AA-6B) 800 kg (1,764 lb)
Warhead: 90-kg (198-lb) HE (blast fragmentation type)
Propulsion: one dual-thrust solid-propellant rocket delivering an unrevealed thrust
Performance: speed Mach 4·5; range (AA-6A) 25 km (15·5 miles) or (AA-6B) 70 km (43·5 miles)
Guidance: (AA-6A) IR homing or (AA-6B) semi-active radar homing

Variants

AA-6A 'Acrid': developed in the period between 1959 and 1961 as a long-range bomber-destroying missile for use at medium and high altitudes (for which the missile was designed with large wings), the AA-6 is the world's largest AAM and entered service in the mid-1960s as the primary armament of the Mikoyan-Gurevich MiG-25 'Foxbat' and Sukhoi Su-21 'Flagon'; four missiles are generally carried as two pairs each of the IR- and radar-guided versions
AA-6B 'Acrid': semi-active radar homing version of the AA-6A matched to the 'Fox Fire' radar of the MiG-25; the Soviet practice is a ripple of two missiles (one of each homing type) to generate maximum kill probability; it is believed that the launch

aeroplane's extremely powerful radar can lock onto a target at a range of 160 km (100 miles) and then radar-illuminate the target at a range of about 100 km (62 miles), suggesting that Western estimates of the AA-6B's range are well short of reality

AA-7A/B 'Apex'

(USSR)

Type: medium-range air-to-air missile
Dimensions: diameter 0·22 m (0·73 ft); length (AA-7A) 4·20 m (13·78 ft) or (AA-7B) 4·60 m (15·09 ft); span 1·05 m (3·44 ft)
Weight: total round (AA-7A) 300 kg (661 lb) or (AA-7B) 320 kg (705·5 lb)
Warhead: 40-kg (88-lb) HE (blast fragmentation type)
Propulsion: one dual-thrust solid-propellant rocket delivering an unrevealed thrust
Performance: speed Mach 3·5; range (AA-7A) 20 km (12·5 miles) or (AA-7B) 55 km (34·2 miles)
Guidance: (AA-7A) IR homing or (AA-7B) semi-active radar homing

Variants

AA-7A 'Apex': developed in the period from 1971 to 1974, and introduced in the mid- to late 1970s, this third-generation Soviet AAM can be regarded as successor to the AA-3 'Anab' and comparable to the US AIM-7E Sparrow III but with greater manoeuvrability; the type is generally associated with the Mikoyan-Gurevich MiG-23MF 'Flogger' and MiG-25E 'Foxbat', and is believed to be optimized for the medium- and low-level roles; the Soviet service designation is **R-23T**
AA-7B 'Apex': semi-active radar homing version of the AA-7A; near the nose of the missile (in both versions) are four projecting surfaces, at first thought to be extra control surfaces but now considered to be the blister antennae for a semi-active radar homing system working on the interferometry principle; an odd feature of the design is the smaller diameter (0·195 m/7·68 in) of the body's forward section, for which no compelling reason has yet been revealed in the West: it perhaps confirms the lack of an internal dish antenna, the opportunity being taken to area-rule the nose in the region of the projections; the Soviet service designation is **R-23R**, and the variant is associated with the 'High Lark' radar system

AA-8A/B 'Aphid'

(USSR)

Type: short-range dogfighting air-to-air missile
Dimensions: diameter 0·12 m (0·39 ft); length (AA-8A) 2·15 m (7·05 ft) or (AA-8B) 2·35 m (7·71 ft); span 0·40 m (1·31 ft)
Weight: total round (AA-8A) 55 kg (121·25 lb) or (AA-8B) 60 kg (132·3 lb)
Warhead: 7- to 9-kg (15·4- to 19·8-lb) HE (blast fragmentation type)
Propulsion: one dual-thrust solid-propellant rocket delivering an unrevealed thrust
Performance: speed Mach 3; range (AA-8A) 10,000 m (10,935 yards) or (AA-8B) 15,000 m (16,405 yards)
Guidance: (AA-8A) IR homing or (AA-8B) semi-active radar homing

Variants

AA-8 'Aphid': introduced in the mid-1970s as the replacement for the AA-2 'Atoll' series and as the short-range companion to the medium-range AA-7 'Apex', the extremely capable AA-8 is one of the smallest air-launched guided missiles yet developed; the type is used by most modern Soviet fighters, and is notable for its high degree of manoeuvrability, resulting from its small size and advanced configuration with tail-mounted delta wings, canard delta control surfaces and, at the nose just in front of the control surfaces, four blade-like surfaces of rectangular form and very low aspect ratio; the Soviet service designation is **R-60T**
AA-8B 'Aphid': semi-active radar homing version of the AA-8A, which may not have entered production for service as the **R-60R**

AA-9 'Amos'

(USSR)

Type: medium/long-range air-to-air missile
Dimensions: diameter 0·40 m (1·31 ft); length 4·00 m (13·12 ft); span 1·23 m (4·02 ft)
Weight: total round about 450 kg (992 lb)
Warhead: 80-kg (176·4-lb) HE (blast fragmentation type) or possibly nuclear with a low-kiloton yield
Propulsion: one solid-propellant dual-thrust rocket delivering an unrevealed thrust in the boost phase and an unrevealed thrust in the sustain phase
Performance: speed Mach 3·5; range at least 130 km (81 miles)
Guidance: inertial or semi-active radar (midcourse phase) and active radar (terminal phase)

Variant

AA-9 'Amos': deployed on the Mikoyan-Gurevich MiG-29 'Fulcrum' and MiG-31 'Foxhound' fighters from the mid-1980s, the AA-9 was developed from the early 1970s as a weapon able to deal with low-altitude penetrations of Soviet airspace, particularly by US cruise missiles; trials have confirmed that the AA-9 can snap-down at least 6000 m (19,685 ft) to engage such targets flying at an altitude as low as 50 m (165 ft); US sources credit the missile with modest to good range performance, but these American figures almost certainly underestimate the weapon's capability by a great degree, because the most likely reason for the missile's unusually large diameter is the need to provide a cross section able to accommodate a large receiver antenna for the long-range semi-active radar homing system, which probably switches to active mode for the terminal phase of the attack; the diameter also suits the missile for the installation of a nuclear warhead of the type used against strategic targets; the arrangement of the AA-9's flying surfaces is also unusual, the cruciform wings having their swept leading edges aft of the midpoint, and these low-aspect-ratio surfaces being trailed by close-coupled control surfaces which are of greater span and higher aspect ratio than the wings

AA-10 'Alamo'

(USSR)

Type: medium-range air-to-air missile
Dimensions: diameter 0·185 m (0·61 ft); length ('Alamo-C' and 'Alamo-D') 4·00 m (13·12 ft) or ('Alamo-A' and 'Alamo-B') 3·20 m (10·50 ft); span 0·855 m (2·81 ft)
Weight: total round ('Alamo-C' and 'Alamo-D') about 200 kg (440 lb) or ('Alamo-A' and 'Alamo-B') about 155 kg (342 lb)
Warhead: HE (blast fragmentation type)
Propulsion: one solid-propellant booster rocket delivering an unrevealed thrust and one solid-propellant sustainer rocket delivering an unrevealed thrust
Performance: speed supersonic; range ('Alamo-C' and 'Alamo-D') about 30 km (18·64 miles) or ('Alamo-A' and 'Alamo-B') about 8 km (4·97 miles)
Guidance: IR or semi-active radar homing

Variants

AA-10 'Alamo': introduced in 1984 with the service designation **R-29**, this is an all-aspect snapdown missile matched to the radars of new-generation Soviet fighters capable of 'look-down/shoot-down' engagements; few details have been released, but American official artwork initially gave the impression that the type might be an advanced derivative of the AA-7 'Apex', indicating a similarity of dimensions and weights with those of the earlier weapon; the Mikoyan-Gurevich MiG-29 'Fulcrum' and Sukhoi Su-27 'Flanker' are each thought to be capable of carrying six examples of this missile; few details have been made public in the West, but photographs first released in 1987 show the AA-10 to be totally unlike the AA-7, possessing instead a faint similarity to the obsolescent AA-3 'Anab'; the most unusual feature of the AA-10 is the use of long-span canard control surfaces (with pronounced inverse taper) fitted to a control ring at the forward end of the very large motor section; the AA-10 is apparently available in four versions as a semi-active radar-homing **'Alamo-A'** model with a short body, an IR-homing **'Alamo-B'** model (presumably designated **R-23T**) with a short body, a semi-active radar-homing **'Alamo-C'** (**R-23R**) model with a long body (presumably to allow the incorporation of a longer-burning sustainer engine for the greater range appropriate to the launch platform's look-down/shoot-down fire-control system), and an **'Alamo-D'** IR-homing model with a long body; the IR-homing versions are usually carried on underwing hardpoints, and the radar-homing versions on underfuselage hardpoints; the latter types have to be launched with the aid of a powerful ejector mechanism to ensure clean separation from the launch aircraft, and this suggests that the missile has a strong airframe, a fact that would also support the suggestion that the AA-10 is highly manoeuvrable

AA-11 'Archer'

(USSR)

Type: short-range air-to-air missile
Dimensions: diameter 0·175 m (0·57 ft); length 3·05 m (10·01 ft); span 0·52 m (1·71 ft)
Weight: total round 125 kg (276 lb)

Warhead: 15-kg (33·1-lb) HE (blast fragmentation type)
Propulsion: one solid-propellant rocket delivering an unrevealed thrust
Performance: speed supersonic; range 8000 m (8,750 yards)
Guidance: IR homing

Variant

AA-11 'Archer': this latest Soviet short-range AAM entered service in 1987 as a key part of the inventory for aircraft such as the Mikoyan-Gurevich MiG-29 'Fulcrum' and Sukhoi Su-27 'Flanker'; the type is probably designed as partner to the AA-8 'Aphid', and has comparable flight performance (in terms of speed and range) coupled with considerably greater manoeuvrability and, through the use of a two-colour seeker with all-aspect engagement capability, superior operational characteristics; in configuration the missile has a cylindrical body (terminating at its forward end in a hemispherical seeker window) and four cruciform sets of flying surfaces indexed in line with each other: from nose to tail these are small swept guide vanes, low-aspect-ratio rectangular stabilizers, swept delta control fins and low-aspect-ratio cropped delta wings; manoeuvrability is provided mainly by the nose-mounted guide vanes and thrust-vectoring paddles around the exhaust section; the AA-11 is designed for use with a helmet-mounted sight and therefore clearly possesses a good off-boresight capability

SA-7 'Grail'

(USSR)

Type: short-range air-to-air missile
Dimensions: diameter 0·07 m (0·23 ft); length 1·35 m (4·43 ft); span 0·20 m (0·66 ft)
Weight: total round 9·2 kg (20·3 lb)-
Warhead: 2·5-kg (5·51-lb) HE (blast fragmentation type)
Propulsion: one dual-thrust solid-propellant rocket delivering an unrevealed thrust
Performance: speed Mach 1·5; range 800/5000 m (875/5,470 yards)
Guidance: IR homing

Variant

SA-7 'Grail': this somewhat limited weapon was introduced in the early 1960s as the Soviet army's standard shoulder-fired SAM for the protection of infantry formations; the basic missile has the Soviet production designation **9M32** and the service name **Strela 2**; since 1981 the weapon has been seen in two- and four-round helicopter installations (probably for defensive rather than offensive purposes), most notably on the Soviet Mil Mi-24 'Hind' and Aérospatiale SA 341 Gazelle in Yugoslav service; such an installation is greatly facilitated by the SA-7's uncooled seeker, which has the tactical disadvantage of restricting launch to tail-chase engagements; it is sensibly assumed that combat helicopters use their magnifying anti-tank missile sights for the acquisition of targets; it is also likely that a similar installation has been (or will shortly be) made of the SA-7's successors in Soviet service, the **SA-14 'Gremlin'** and **SA-16 'Griffon'**; these have considerably improved seekers, and could well be used for offensive as well as defensive purposes on the new genera-

tion of Soviet helicopters such as the Kamov Ka-41 'Hokum' battlefield combat helicopter and the Mil Mi-28 'Havoc' gunship and anti-tank helicopter

British Aerospace Sky Flash

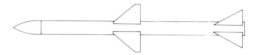

(UK)

Type: medium-range air-to-air missile
Dimensions: diameter 0·67 ft (0·20 m); length 12·08 ft (3·68 m); span 3·33 ft (1·02 m)
Weight: total round 425 lb (193 kg)
Warhead: 66-lb (30-kg) HE (blast fragmentation type)
Propulsion: one Aerojet or Rockwell Mk 52 solid-propellant rocket delivering an unrevealed thrust
Performance: speed Mach 4; range 31 miles (49·9 km) from a high-altitude launch
Guidance: Marconi XJ521 monopulse semi-active radar homing

Variants

Sky Flash: this is an advanced British development of the comparatively short-ranged AIM-7E2 Sparrow with a sophisticated homing system and improved fusing; the weapon entered development in 1969 and retains the classic aerodynamics of the Sparrow, with a cruciform of delta control wings mounted on the mid-point of the cylindrical body, and a comparable cruciform of delta stabilizing surfaces mounted at the tail; the weapon entered service in 1978, and is an extremely accurate missile with warm-up time reduced from the American original's 15 seconds to a mere 2 seconds; the Sky Flash has excellent capabilities against manoeuvring targets even in conditions of glint and heavy ECM, and the type is also used by Sweden with the designation **Rb71**; existing Swedish stocks are being modified as **Rb71A** missiles with improved motor and guidance systems

Sky Flash 90: manufacturer's designation for a proposed development based on the Sky Flash Mk 2 cancelled by the British government in 1981, even though its development was nearly complete, in favour of the AIM-120A AMRAAM; the missile is designed as a comparatively low-cost answer to the requirements of those countries needing a beyond-visual-horizon missile, and the design is based on a control package using a strapdown inertial platform for midcourse guidance and a Thomson-CSF active radar for terminal guidance, plus a Royal Ordnance Hoopoe solid-propellant rocket for greater speed and range; these latter factors are aided by thinner wings and a new low-drag rear end to the missile; Sweden has proposed a Mach 4 or 5 development of this active-homing type with a Volvo Flygmotor ramjet as the **Rb73**; whether using rocket or ramjet propulsion, the Sky Flash 90/Rb73 is likely to prove an important and popular weapon as its active radar guidance removes the need for the continuous-wave illumination of the target by an expensive radar carried by the basic Sky Flash's launch aircraft: this has to fly on towards the target until the missile impacts with the latter, and this course takes the vulnerable aircraft ever farther into airspace protected by surface-to-air as well as air-to-air weapon systems

British Aerospace/BGT/
Raufoss AIM-132A
ASRAAM

Above: The multi-national ASRAAM mounted beneath this Panavia Tornado F:3.

(UK, West Germany & Norway)
Type: short-range air-to-air missile
Dimensions: diameter 0·17 m (0·55 ft); length 2·73 m (8·96 ft); span not revealed
Weights: total round 100 kg (220·5 lb)
Warhead: 10-kg (225-lb) HE (blast fragmentation type)
Propulsion: one solid-propellant dual-thrust rocket delivering an unrevealed thrust
Performance: speed Mach 3+; range 300/15,000 m (330/16,405 yards)
Guidance: strapdown inertial plus IR homing

Variant
AIM-132A ASRAAM: this Advanced Short-Range Air-to-Air Missile is being developed initially by the BBG consortium (BAe and Bodenseewerk Geratetechnik) with BAe as prime contractor for the full-scale development phase and BGT and the Norwegian company Raufoss Ammunisjonsfa-brikker as subcontractors; ASRAAM was planned on the conceptual basis of BAe's Short-Range Air-to-Air Missile (originally called Tail-dog), a 1970s' development as a tube-launched weapon without aerodynamic surfaces and using a helmet-mounted sight system for pre-launch designation of the target; the missile's combination of thrust-vector control and a swivelling motor made for enormous agility, but the SRAAM and its fully-developed millimetre-wave active radar homing were abandoned; in its current form ASRAAM is later, less capable and more expensive than the SRAAM, and after an unfortunately protracted development phase is due to enter service in 1992 for use by all NATO countries; the ASRAAM uses lifting-body aerodynamics and has four tail fins for control

Hughes AIM-4F Falcon

(USA)
Type: short/medium-range air-to-air missile
Dimensions: diameter 0·55 ft (0·17 m); length 7·17 ft (2·18 m); span 2·00 ft (0·61 m)
Weight: total round 150 lb (68 kg)
Warhead: 28·65-lb (13-kg) HE (blast fragmentation type)
Propulsion: one Thiokol M46 two-stage solid-propellant rocket delivering 4,440-lb (2014-kg) thrust
Performance: speed Mach 4; range 12,350 yards (11,295 m)
Guidance: Hughes semi-active radar homing

Variant
AIM-4C Falcon: the Falcon was the world's first fully-guided AAM to enter service, initial opera-. tional capability being achieved with the semi-

active radar homing GAR-1 (later AIM-4) in 1956 after a development programme launched in 1947; all the early variants were powered by a Thiokol single-stage rocket giving acceleration in the order of 50 g, and the oldest variant still in service is the IR-guided AIM-4C (originally the GAR-2A, of which 4,000 were built), which is operational with the Swedish and Swiss air forces under the designations **Rb28** (3,000 built) and **HM-58** (1,000 built) respectively on Saab 35F Draken and Dassault-Breguet Mirage IIIS aircraft fitted with the Hughes TARAN radar associated with the Rb27 and HM-55 semi-active radar homing versions of the AIM-26 Super Falcon; the variant has a diameter of 0·53 ft (0·16 m), length of 6·63 ft (2·02 m), a span of 1·67 ft (0·51 m), a weight of 134 lb (61 kg), a speed of Mach 3 and a range of 10,560 yards (9655 m)

Raytheon/General Dynamics AIM-7M Sparrow

(USA)

Type: medium-range air-to-air missile
Dimensions: diameter 0·67 ft (0·203 m); length 12·08 ft (3·68 m); span 3·33 ft (1·02 m)
Weight: total round 503 lb (228 kg)
Warhead: 86-lb (39-kg) HE (blast fragmentation type)
Propulsion: one Hercules Mk 58 or Aerojet Mk 65 dual-thrust solid-propellant rocket delivering an unrevealed thrust
Performance: speed Mach 4; range 62 miles (100 km) from a high-altitude launch reducing to 27 miles (43·5 km) from a low-altitude launch
Guidance: Raytheon Advanced Monopulse Seeker semi-active radar homing

Variants

AIM-7E Sparrow: introduced in 1962 as the first version of the Sparrow III to enter large-scale production (the earlier radar beam-riding AIM-7A Sparrow I having totalled 2,000 rounds, the semi-active AIM-7C Sparrow III 2,000 rounds and the liquid-propelled AIM-7D Sparrow III 7,500 rounds), this variant remains in limited service with several important fighter types; the type is powered by a Rocketdyne Mk 38 Mod 2 or Aerojet Mk 52 single-stage motor for a burn-out speed of Mach 3·7, weighs 452 lb (205 kg), has a range of 28 miles (44 km) with a 66-lb (30-kg) warhead whose casing breaks into some 2,600 fragments on detonation, and is guided by Raytheon continuous-wave semi-active radar guidance matched to a number of radars; this variant was also built in Italy by Selenia and in Japan by Mitsubishi as the **AIM-7J Sparrow**, and a limited-production shorter-range and more manoeuvrable version was produced in the USA as the **AIM-7E2 Sparrow**; this last resulted from a need that became apparent in the Vietnam War, in which US fighters were seldom able to use long-range AIM-7E Sparrows because of the political ban on firing missiles against aircraft which had not been visually identified; the AIM-7E2 thus has a reduced minimum range, and the opportunity was taken to provide aerodynamic surfaces that could be plugged in rather than requiring attachment with the aid of special tools; the definitive version still in service is the **AIM-7E3 Sparrow**, which is a conversion of the AIM-7E2 with improved reliability and greater target-sensing capability

AIM-7F Sparrow: much redesigned version introduced in 1977 on the McDonnell Douglas F-15 Eagle and now carried also by the McDonnell Douglas F/A-18 Hornet; whereas the AIM-7E has its forward body (as far aft as the wings) filled with guidance equipment (homing head and autopilot), trailed aft of the wings by a comparatively small warhead and a short motor, the AIM-7F has more compact solid-state electronics that reduce guidance package volume by some 40%, allowing a larger warhead to be incorporated in the space vacated in front of the wings, and a longer motor to be used in the whole of the portion aft of the wings; the variant therefore possesses a much larger engagement envelope through the adoption of solid-state electronics and a Mk 58 or Mk 65 dual-thrust motor; like the AIM-7E it is 12·00 ft (3·66 m) long, but weighs 503 lb (228 kg) and has an 86-lb (39-kg) warhead; the use of continuous-wave and pulse-Doppler guidance considerably enhances look-down/shoot-down capability, even at the longer ranges possible with the variant; the variant also possesses superior resistance to ECM

AIM-7M Sparrow: introduced in 1982 pending availability of the AIM-120 AMRAAM, this interim variant has a new digital monopulse seeker offering performance comparable with that of the British Sky Flash derivative, especially in the longer-range look-down/shoot-down mode; the model also offers other electronic and engineering improvements to bring down production cost while enhancing reliability and performance at low altitude and in ECM environments

AIM-7P Sparrow: under development by Raytheon in the late 1980s, this is the latest Sparrow AAM; no details of the programme have been released, but it is likely that the development is centred on electronic rather than aerodynamic or powerplant features

Ford Aerospace/Raytheon/ Bodensee Geratetechnik AIM-9L Sidewinder

(USA)

Type: short-range dogfighting air-to-air missile
Dimensions: diameter 0·42 ft (0·13 m); length 9·35 ft (2·85 m); span 2·07 ft (0·63 m)
Weight: total round 188 lb (85 kg)
Warhead: 22·5-lb (10-kg) HE (blast fragmentation type)
Propulsion: one Thiokol or Bermite Mk 36 Model 7/8, or reduced-smoke TX-683 solid-propellant rocket delivering an unrevealed thrust
Performance: speed Mach 2·5; range 19,360 yards (17,700 m)
Guidance: Bodensee Geratetechnik ALASCA IR homing

Variants

AIM-9B Sidewinder: still in the operational inventory of a few nations (some 80,000 missiles of this variant having been built), this venerable version of the Sidewinder series is 9·82 ft (2·83 m) long and spans 1·83 ft (0·56 m); the model entered service in 1956 with a 10-lb (4·54-kg) blast fragmentation warhead plus IR proximity fuse. From 1982 this fuse has been replaced by an active laser fuse in all missiles carrying the same warhead (the AIM-9B, E, J, N and P variants); powered

by a Naval Propellant Plant-designed Aerojet Mk 17 single-stage motor, the 155-lb (70-kg) missile achieves a range of 3,500 yards (3200 m); the **AIM-9B/FWG.2** is an improved European-built model with greater seeker sensitivity, and this is used by Sweden with the designation **Rb24**; the **AIM-9E** is a US-built improvement with a Ford thermo-electrically cooled and thus more sensitive seeker plus 'revitalization' of the existing electronics; the AIM-9E began to enter service in 1967, and a version with a reduced-smoke motor is designated **AIM-9E2**; the Japanese **Mitsubishi AAM-1** is a virtual copy of the AIM-9E, though it is slightly smaller and lighter than the American weapon; some of the original weapons have been converted with reduced-smoke motors with the designation **AIM-9B2**, and are used for special missions or training
AIM-9G Sidewinder: introduced in 1967, this is an improved version of the US Navy's 1965 **AIM-9D Sidewinder** (the real precursor of the latest Sidewinder variants and fitted with the Raytheon Mk 18 Mod 1 IR seeker) with an IR/radar-proximity fused 22·4-lb (10·2-kg) continuous-rod HE warhead and the Thiokol Mk 36 solid-propellant rocket
AIM-9H Sidewinder: introduced in 1970, this 186-lb (84·4-kg) missile is a further improved AIM-9G with the same warhead, the Mk 36 Mod 6 motor, an improved solid-state seeker providing (in conjunction with cryogenic cooling) enhanced tracking speed and all-weather capability, and other modifications to improve manoeuvrability
AIM-9J Sidewinder: developed from the AIM-9E by converting obsolescent AIM-9Bs (**AIM-9J2**) and making new missiles (**AIM-9J1** and the product-improved **AIM-9J3**), this variant appeared in the mid-1970s and features a Mk 17 solid-propellant motor, a thermo-electrically cooled seeker, some solid-state electronics and revised double-delta control surfaces with more powerful actuators to generate greater manoeuvrability
AIM-9L Sidewinder: much improved version introduced in 1976; the variant combines the latest Sidewinder airframe (featuring an upgraded motor and pointed double-delta foreplanes of yet further refined shape for increased manoeuvrability) with an annular blast/fragmentation warhead. Hughes laser fusing and the AM/FM conical-scan seeker developed by Bodensee Geratetechnik for the abortive Viper AAM combined with a dogfighting airframe; the type is used by Sweden with the designation **Rb74**, and is also made under licence in Japan by a consortium headed by Mitsubishi

Below: AIM-9 Sidewinders carried by this F-16.

AIM-9M Sidewinder: exclusively US-made version of the AIM-9L with a weight of 190 lb (86 kg) as a result of using a closed-cycle cooler for improved seeker sensitivity (especially at low altitudes), greater resistance to IR countermeasures and a 'smokeless' Bermite/Hercules Mk 36 Mod 9 motor for reduced visual signature

AIM-9N Sidewinder: redesignation of AIM-9J1 missiles produced by converting AIM-9B and AIM-9E Sidewinders

AIM-9P Sidewinder: US-made model (either new-build or upgraded AIM-9B, E and J weapons) to AIM-9L standard with the canards of the AIM-9J series; the variant also offers greater reliability and a weight of 170 lb (77 kg); there are four subvariants in the form of the **AIM-9P1** with an active laser proximity fuse, the **AIM-9P2** with the 'smokeless' motor, the **AIM-9P3** combining AIM-9P1 and AIM-9P2 features with a new warhead of reduced thermal sensitivity and greater shelf life, and the **AIM-9P4** 'security assistance missile' for the US Air Force with increased target-acquisition and tracking capabilities combined with an advanced fuse

AIM-9R Sidewinder: 193-lb (87·5-kg) derivative of the AIM-9M (and originally designated **AIM-9M Improved**) produced from 1989 with a radically upgraded seeker (of the IIR variety that does away with the seeker cooling of all other recent Sidewinder variants) for greater acquisition range and better resistance to countermeasures. The type also has an active laser proximity fuse and a range of 21,125 yards (19,315 m)

Hughes AIM-26B Super Falcon

(USA)

Type: medium-range air-to-air missile
Dimensions: diameter 0·95 ft (0·29 m); length 6·79 ft (2·07 m); span 2·03 ft (0·62 m)
Weight: total round 262 lb (119 kg)
Warhead: 40-lb (18·1-kg) HE (blast fragmentation type)
Propulsion: one Thiokol M60 solid-propellant rocket delivering 5,625-lb (2552-kg) thrust
Performance: speed Mach 2; range 10,500 yards (9600 m)
Guidance: Hughes semi-active radar homing

Variant

AIM-26B Super Falcon: introduced in 1960 as the primary weapon of the Convair F-106 Delta Dart (to provide a very high kill probability in head-on engagements with Soviet strategic bombers), the AIM-26A Super Falcon was designed round semi-active radar homing as IR homing was thought impractical for collision-course engagements; but the comparative inaccuracy of semi-active radar homing dictated the use of a particularly powerful warhead, and the Super Falcon's initial variant was thus fitted with a 1·5-kiloton nuclear warhead based on the W25 of the AIR-2 Genie and detonated by a quartet of active radar proximity fuses; this initial variant is no longer in service, having been succeeded by the conventionally-armed AIM-26B, which still serves with Sweden and Switzerland under the designations **Rb27** and **HM-55** respectively, on the Saab 35F Draken and Dassault-Mirage IIIS fighters fitted with Hughes TARAN radar

Hughes AIM-54A Phoenix

(USA)

Type: long-range air-to-air missile
Dimensions: diameter 1·25 ft (0·38 m); length 13·15 ft (4·01 m); span 3·03 ft (0·93 m)
Weight: total round 985 lb (447 kg)
Warhead: 132-lb (59·9-kg) HE (blast fragmentation type)
Propulsion: one Aerojet Mk 60 or Rocketdyne Mk 47 Mk 0 single-stage solid-propellant rocket delivering an unrevealed thrust
Performance: speed Mach 4·3+; range 2·4/125+ miles (3·86/201·2+ km)
Guidance: Hughes DQS-26 system with Nortronics strapdown inertial for the cruise phase, semi-active radar homing for the approach phase and active radar for the terminal phase

Variants

AIM-54A Phoenix: designed together with the associated AWG-9 radar fire-control system for the abortive General Dynamics F-111B swing-wing naval fighter, the Phoenix was brought to fruition in the Grumman F-14 Tomcat fleet-defence fighter; the missile retains the classic aerodynamics of Hughes's earlier AAMs with a substantial body carrying a cruciform of low aspect ratio delta wings well aft and trailed by rectangular control surfaces indexed in line with the wings; the considerable body diameter allows the use of a wide planar-array radar antenna in the nose radome, and also provides volume for the missile's other primary components which are, from front to rear, the electronics (radar avionics, guidance package and radar proximity fuse system), warhead, solid-propellant rocket, and (round the nozzle) autopilot plus control-surface hydraulic actuators; after launch the missile climbs to a peak altitude of 81,400 ft (24,810 m), cruising under control of the onboard autopilot with guidance of the semi-active type using reflections of the radar in launch aircraft's AWG-9 system; this high-altitude cruise maximizes range by reducing drag and providing the rocket with optimum operating conditions, and as the missile dives down to the attack the energy potential of the cruise altitude is converted into kinetic energy for greater speed and manoeuvrability in the terminal phase of the flight; the missile's radar switches to the active mode for the final 20,000 yards (18,290 m) of the attack, the availability of three fusing modes offering maximum target-destruction capability; the Phoenix began to enter service in 1973

AIM-54B Phoenix: version that entered production in late 1977 as a product-improved AIM-54A with sheet metal rather than honeycomb aerodynamic surfaces, non-liquid hydraulic and thermal-conditioning systems, and a degree of simplified engineering to ease production

AIM-54C Phoenix: developed from 1977 and introduced in 1982, this is a considerably improved missile with digital rather than analog electronics, a new strapdown inertial reference unit, solid-state radar and very much more capable ECCM capability; the weight of this variant is 1,008 lb (457 kg), the speed Mach 5 and the ceiling 100,000+ ft (30,490+ m)

General Dynamics (Pomona) AIM-92A Air-Launched Stinger

(USA)

Type: short-range air-to-air missile
Dimensions: diameter 0·23 ft (0·07 m); length 5·00 ft (1·52 m); span 0·30 ft (0·09 m)
Weight: total round 30 lb (13·6 kg)
Warhead: 6·6-lb (3-kg) HE (blast fragmentation type)
Propulsion: tandem Atlantic Research solid-propellant rockets delivering an unrevealed thrust
Performance: speed Mach 2+; range 5,280 yards (4830 m)
Guidance: General Dynamics (Pomona) IR homing

Variant

AIM-92A Air-Launched Stinger: air-launched version of the FIM-92A Stinger shoulder-launched SAM, and has been developed as a self-protection weapon for helicopters and tactical aircraft in the form of the MLMS (Multi-purpose Lightweight Missile System), the initial application being on the Bell OH-58 Kiowa scout helicopter; this MLMS is a twin launcher complete with a coolant reservoir for the two missiles' seekers, and the units can be stacked up to four deep to give the helicopter a theoretical complement of 16 short-range missiles (eight on each side of the helicopter)

Hughes AIM-120A AMRAAM

(USA)

Type: medium-range air-to-air missile
Dimensions: diameter 0·58 ft (0·18 m); length 11·99 ft (3·66 m); span 2·06 ft (0·637 m)
Weight: total round 335·2 lb (152 kg)
Warhead: 45-lb (20·4-kg) HE (blast fragmentation type)
Propulsion: one solid-propellant rocket delivering an unrevealed thrust
Performance: speed about Mach 4; range 45 miles (72 km) from a high-altitude launch declining to 34 miles (55 km) from a low-altitude launch
Guidance: Nortronics strapdown inertial for mid-course phase, and Hughes active radar for terminal phase

Variant

AIM-120A AMRAAM: designed in the late 1970s and early 1980s for a service debut in the late 1980s as replacement for the AIM-7F/M variants of the Sparrow, the AMRAAM (Advanced Medium-Range Air-to-Air Missile) is a fire-and-forget weapon with size and weight little more than those of the AIM-9 Sidewinder but capabilities and performance better than those of the considerably larger Sparrow; the missile is launched from a standard rail, and cruises on a preprogrammed course (with the capability for mid-course update from the launch aircraft's radar) until it reaches the vicinity of the target, where it activates its active radar seeker, which also possesses a 'home-on-jam' mode; the whole programme has been bedevilled by technical problems, cost overruns and political antipathy, and service entry has been delayed to 1990